A Crisis of Tru

SPARE

A Crisis of Truth

Literature and Law in Ricardian England

Richard Firth Green

PENN

University of Pennsylvania Press

Philadelphia

THE MIDDLE AGES SERIES

A complete list of books in the series
is available from the publisher.

Publication of this volume was assisted by a grant from the University of Western Ontario.

First paperback printing 2002

Printed in the United States of America on acid-free paper

Published by
University of Pennsylvania Press
Philadelphia, Pennsylvania 19104-4011

Library of Congress Cataloging-in-Publication Data

Green, Richard Firth, 1943–
A crisis of truth : literature and law in Ricardian England / Richard Firth Green.
p. cm. — (Middle Ages series)
Includes bibliographical references (p.) and index.
ISBN 0-8122-3463-4 (hardcover : alk. paper)—ISBN 0-8122-1809-4 (pbk.)
1. English literature—Middle English, 1100–1500—History and criticism. 2. Law and literature—History—To 1500. 3. Great Britain—History—Richard II, 1377–1399. 4. Law, Medieval, in literature. 5. Truth in literature. 6. Law—Great Britain. I. Title. II. Series.
PR275.L35G74 1998
820.9'001—dc21 98-34383

For Beth, Colin, and Lucy

Chaque société a son régime de vérité, . . . les mécanismes et les instances qui permettent de distinguer les énoncés vrais ou faux.

— Michel Foucault, "Vérité et pouvoir"

Non igitur mireris, princeps, si lex qua in Anglia veritas inquiritur, alias non pervagetur naciones.

— Sir John Fortescue, *De laudibus legum Anglie*

Contents

Abbreviations

ANTS	Anglo-Norman Text Society
AWS	African Writers Series
BC	*Borough Customs* (SS)
BL	British Library
CA	*Confessio amantis* (Gower, *English Works*)
CFMA	Classiques françaises du moyen âge
CLR	*Chaucer Life Records*
CN	*Coutumiers de Normandie*
CPC	*Calendars of the Proceedings in Chancery*
CPR	*Calendar of Patent Rolls* (HMSO)
CS	Camden Society (n.s.: new series)
EETS	Early English Text Society (o.s.: original series; e.s.: extra series; s.s.: supplementary series)
EHD	*English Historical Documents*
HMC	Historical Manuscripts Commission
HMSO	His/Her Majesty's Stationery Office
HP	*Historical Poems of the Fourteenth and Fifteenth Centuries* (ed. R. H. Robbins)
I-E	Indo-European
K&D	Krapp and Dobbie
KJB	King James Bible
LHP	*Leges Henrici Primi*
ME	Middle English
MED	*Middle English Dictionary*
MGH	Monumenta Germaniae Historia
OE	Old English
OED	*Oxford English Dictionary*
OHG	Old High German
PJP	*Proceedings before the Justices of the Peace* (ed. Putnam)
PL	Patrilogia Latina
P&M	Pollock and Maitland
PPl	*Piers Plowman*
PRO	Public Record Office (London)

RL14C	*Religious Lyrics of the Fourteenth Century* (ed. C. Brown)
RL15C	*Religious Lyrics of the Fifteenth Century* (ed. C. Brown)
RP	*Rotuli parliamentorum* [1278–1503]
RS	Rolls Series (*Rerum Britannicarum Medii Aevii Scriptores*)
SCC	*Select Cases in Chancery* (SS)
SCD	*Select Cases on Defamation* (SS)
SCKB	*Select Cases in the Court of King's Bench* (SS)
SCKC	*Select Cases before the King's Council* (SS)
SCT	*Select Cases of Trespass* (SS)
SGGK	*Sir Gawain and the Green Knight*
SL	*Secular Lyrics of the Fourteenth and Fifteenth Centuries* (ed. R. H. Robbins)
SPC	*Select Pleas of the Crown* (SS)
SPM	*Select Pleas in Manorial and Other Seignorial Courts* (SS)
SR	*Statutes of the Realm*
SS	Selden Society (s.s.: supplementary series)
STC	*Short Title Catalogue*
STS	Scottish Text Society
VHCE	*Victoria History of the Counties of England*
YB	*Year Book(s)*

Translations (including modern scholarly works) are in most cases my own. Many legal texts (almost all the volumes in the Selden Society, for instance) have facing-page translations, and while I have inevitably relied on these much of the time, I have adapted them where necessary in the interests of clarifying legal technicalities for the general reader. Latin biblical quotations from the Vulgate are given in English translation from the Douay-Rheims Bible, unless otherwise noted. All Chaucer quotations are from *The Riverside Chaucer*, 3rd. ed., edited by Larry Benson (Boston: Houghton Mifflin, 1987).

Preface

In his preface to *The Cruise of the Nona* Hilaire Belloc suggested that a book should be written before it is named, but scholars nowadays must often devise working titles for books whose later chapters can still be little more than a distant dream. Two of the words of my title were chosen some time ago as deliberate acts of homage to books that first moved me to undertake this study: *crisis* was intended to evoke Charles Muscatine's *Poetry and Crisis in the Age of Chaucer* (1972), and *Ricardian*, John Burrow's *Ricardian Poetry*, published a year earlier. For this reason, I have been reluctant to modify my original title, but this preface allows me to make a few necessary qualifications to it.

While *crisis* can never be a wholly inappropriate term to use for a period as troubled by war, disease, economic decline, social unrest, political faction, and religious dissension as the late fourteenth century,[1] it no longer seems to me quite as unproblematic as it once did. Of course, people in the late fourteenth century undoubtedly felt that they were living through a critical period; the predominant mood of the time can be characterized as Saturnian (in both the main senses of that word). If Chaucer seeks in the malevolent influence of Saturn an explanation of the late-fourteenth-century crisis (Brown and Butcher 18), he also evinces a Saturnian nostalgia for a lost golden age (cf. McFarlane 1943/45, 179) with which his own stands in stark contrast:

> Allas, allas, now may men wepe and crye!
> For in oure dayes nis but covetyse,
> Doublenesse, and tresoun, and envye,
> Poysoun, manslawhtre, and mordre in sondry wyse.
> ("The Former Age" 60–63)

On the other hand, a Saturnian cast of mind is encountered in many periods, and, as Joel Hurstfield reminds us (16–17), similar allegations of universal corruption can be found at almost any time from the late Middle Ages to the eighteenth century. A disease that recurs over a period of three hundred years (and a case might be made for pushing back Hurstfield's terminus a quo at least to the end of the thirteenth century) might seem better characterized as chronic rather than critical.

The crisis I am here concerned with, however, is not simply the reflection of a general social malaise, but one that finds specific expression in the complex Middle English word *trouthe*. The idea for this book grew out of an attempt to explain two philological curiosities: why should a word that earlier meant something like 'integrity' or 'dependability' have begun to take on its modern sense of 'conformity to fact' in the late fourteenth century (see Chapter 1), while at the same time its antonym, *treason*, was shifting its semantic focus from personal betrayal to a crime against the state (see Chapter 6)? My investigation took me into what Michael Riffaterre has called "one of the most exciting controversies in today's literary theory . . . the shift from oral tradition to written literature" (29). The explanation I finally settled on was that the rapid spread of vernacular literacy in the Ricardian period, driven in large part by the bureaucratic and legal demands of an increasingly authoritarian central government, brought about a fundamental shift in popular attitudes to the nature of evidence and proof. The paradigmatic situation here, I suggest, is the shift (discussed in Chapters 2–4) from the communally authenticated trothplight to the judicially enforced written contract, from a truth that resides in people to one located in documents. Even in this narrower sense, of course, *crisis* may still seem a difficult word to use of a social phenomenon whose roots reach back to the earlier Middle Ages (cf. Starn 21).

This aspect of my study is deeply indebted to the pioneering work of Michael Clanchy, though, where Clanchy is chiefly interested in the process by which written record came to replace communal memory in the early Middle Ages, my own emphasis is on the continuing vitality of the older modes of social discourse well into the later period. An obvious methodological problem confronts anyone attempting to investigate the "residual orality" (for all its evolutionary overtones Walter Ong's term remains useful) of so remote a period: the nonliterate could not, and the fully literate had little reason to, leave us a clear picture of that huge body of social, commercial, and legal relationships that was routinely maintained without reference to writing in the late Middle Ages, and we quickly find ourselves wandering in unmapped regions with only the inarticulate and contradictory directions of taciturn local inhabitants to guide us. I find it ironic that the longer I have worked on the Middle Ages, the more alien and remote they have come to seem to me. One path I have found promising, though I cannot hope it will prove uncontroversial, is the analogous experience of twentieth-century societies similarly forced to negotiate between oral and literate modes of discourse; specifically (since I find novelists more congenial traveling companions than ethnognaphers), I have turned from time to time to such Nigerian writers as Achebe, Amadi, Echewa, and Soyinka. I fear that this may expose me to the charge of seeking to promote a Western ideology of technological determinism, of endorsing what Ruth Finnegan has called the "great divide theory," and Brian Street the "autonomous model," of orality/literacy studies. I can only insist that my motive in drawing such analogies is primarily heuristic, and that while I regard the phenomena they highlight as widespread, I would never have the temerity to claim that they are universal. Nor do I believe that literacy can ever be detached from its cultural context; Paul Zumthor's insistence that "the history of mentalities and of modes of reasoning (in fact, of almost everything we mean by the word *culture*) is determined by the evolution of methods and modes of communication" (50) is suspiciously easy to reverse ("the evolution of methods and modes of communication is determined by . . ."). On the other hand, it seems to me foolish to deny that the spread of literacy might be a cause as well as an effect of cultural change, or at the very least that it might help supply an answer to the question Jesse Gellrich has raised about the connection between language and social conflict in the closing decades of the fourteenth century (1988, 472).

This brings me to the second problematic word in my title, *Ricardian*. Though the philological evidence seems to locate the emergence of a new sense of the word *trouthe* firmly in the reign of Richard II (1377–1399), and though certain symptomatic events—the Peasants' Revolt (see Chapter 5), Arundel's treason trial (see Chapter 6), and the rise of Lollardy (see Chapter 7)—seem to support such a dating, I have found myself increasingly looking back to the beginning of the fourteenth century, and even to the end of the thirteenth, for the earliest signs of the shift. On the historical side, Edward I's legal reforms and the rise of indentured retaining seem to anticipate some of the themes I first detected in the Ricardian period, while on the literary side, the Saturnian tone of *The Simonie* or of some of the satirical poems in MS. Harley 2253 points in the same direction. In defense of the word Ricardian, however, I hope that the legal paradigm I seek to establish in this book can lead us to a deeper understanding of the major literary works of that remarkable period.

In one respect, at least, the title of this book should prove uncontroversial. Studies that investigate the interrelationship of literature and law are generally interested in one of two main topics (Weisberg and Barricelli 150): "the law *as* literature" (the formal question of legal writing as a species of literature—the adversarial trial as agonistic drama, for instance, or the witness's deposition as narrative), or "the law *in* literature" (the thematic question of the literary representation of law—the trials of Shylock or Billy Budd, for example, or the progress of Jarndyce v. Jarndyce, or the proceedings against Josef K). Except incidentally, neither of these approaches has been my main object in this book. Rather, I have sought to examine "the law *and* literature" of the late fourteenth century as parallel forms of discourse, each with its own conventions and traditions, and to ask how the lawyer's comparatively more formal analysis of mental or social processes can help us understand what the imaginative writer sometimes leaves unspoken or expresses only obliquely.[2] Thus, in the discussion of the literary treatment of promises and bargains that occupies Chapters 8 and 9 I have assumed that traditional legal concepts persist in some Foucauldian subterranean form even in the work of Chaucer, Langland, and the Pearl-poet. "It would be strange indeed," Owen Barfield has written, "if the study of jurisprudence were not well adapted to throw light on the mind and its workings" (126). I hope that one important by-product of this approach will be to provide nonspecialists with an entry into the arcane world of the medieval common law, and in particular into the history of evidence, where, to quote R. C. Van Caenegem, "the interaction of general culture and legal ideas can be followed most clearly" (62).

A final *captatio benevolentiae*: this study has taken me a long way from my home base in late medieval literary history; it has taken me not merely into the common law of the later Middle Ages, but into the folklaw of the Anglo-Saxons and other Germanic peoples; it has taken me into English philology, into social and political history, into medieval philosophy, theology, and political theory, into legal anthropology, and into the increasingly vexed area of literacy / orality studies; it has even taken me into the literature of modern West Africa. A lifetime would barely suffice to acquire expertise in any one of these fields, let alone all of them; I can only plead that if interdisciplinary work is to make any real contribution to scholarship it must hope for lenient treatment at the hands of the strict disciplinarian. At the very least, I trust there may be some places in this book where, to adapt a phrase from Tolkien, the traveling dwarf has seen things missed by the giant on the spot.

I

From Troth to Truth

Truth is that which a man *troweth*. Where there is no man there is no truth.
—Thomas Love Peacock, *Headlong Hall*

IN 1386 THE MEMBERS OF THE London guild of mercers submitted a petition to Parliament complaining of their treatment at the hands of a former mayor, Sir Nicholas Brembre. This petition (a skirmish in the war between Brembre's victualing guilds and Northampton's craft guilds that dominated city politics for much of Richard II's reign) turns at one point to the question of legal redress for a slander made by Brembre against the mercers at a civic meeting:

And we ben openlich disclaundred, holden vntrewe & traitours to owre Kyng, for the same Nichol [Brembre] sayd bifor Mair, Aldermen, & owre craft bifor hem gadred in place of recorde, that xx. or xxx. of vs were worthy to be drawen & hanged, the which thyng lyke to yowre worthy lordship by an euen Juge to be proued or disproued, the whether that trowthe may shewe, for trouthe amonges vs of fewe or elles no man many day dorst be shewed. And nought oonlich vnshewed or hidde it hath be by man now, but also of bifore tyme the moost profitable poyntes of trewe gouernaunce of the Citee, compiled togidre bi longe labour of discrete & wyse men, wyth-out conseille of trewe men, for thei shold nought be knowen ne contynued, in the tyme of Nichol Exton, Mair, outerliche were brent. (Chambers and Daunt 35)

The mercers' petition is of great value as a rare example of a Ricardian legal document written, not in the Latin or law French of Parliament and the courts, but in the vernacular of Chaucer's London, and the particular interest of this passage lies in the use it makes of the difficult word *trowthe*, a word of enormous importance for understanding the culture of late-fourteenth-century England.

Few Middle English scholars would feel very happy about being asked to provide a simple gloss for the word *trowthe* in this passage. Part of its difficulty lies in the tortuous syntax which seems to echo the mercers' own breathless incoherence in the face of so egregious a calumny, but part, too, must be laid at the door of the word's own semantic slipperiness. Of the several senses at work here, none quite conforms to modern expectations. Since the mercers are alleging that Brembre has falsely accused them of treason and are asking for a parliamentary commission to clear them of the charge, our immediate assumption is likely to be that the claim that *trowthe* will reveal their innocence implies that an investigation into the factual basis of the accusation will show it to be groundless. Some such sense may indeed be lurking in the background, but in general it is very much subordinate to another which makes truth the direct antonym of treason ("vntrewe & traitours") and denotes something much more like 'loyalty' or 'good faith' than 'the facts of the case'. In other words, it is not the truth of the charges against them that the mercers want exposed to view, but the truth of their own allegiance—not a truth that resides in exterior circumstances, but one to be found within their own hearts.

Editors have taken the phrase "the whether that trowthe may shewe" to mean that truth will reveal whether the charges may be proved or not (in which case *trowthe* is more likely to mean something like 'fairness' or 'impartiality'—the quality "an euen Juge" might be expected to bring to the proceedings—than 'the facts'), but this reading does not fit well with the causal clause that immediately follows, "for trouthe amonges vs of fewe or elles no man many day dorst be shewed." Rather than taking *whether* here as a disjunctive pronoun, it is perhaps better read as a conjunction—as in the later claim that Brembre's political scheming "sheweth hym self now open whether it hath be a cause . . . of dyuysion . . . or no" (37)—which would then mean understanding *trowthe* as either 'loyalty' (if it refers to the mercers) or 'honesty' (if to the judge). Finally, where the mercers charge that the truth "of bifore tyme" has also been compromised, they associate it with a specific book containing ordinances for the "trewe gouernaunce of the Citee" that Brembre's faction has had burned.[1] Truth in this last sentence seems to imply something like 'wise rule', or even 'just law'.

Despite its syntactical clumsiness this passage is deeply rooted in vernacular speech. The complaint that "trouthe amonges vs of fewe or elles no man many day dorst be shewed"—like the petitioners' later prediction that were parliament to enforce judicial impartiality, "wronges sholle more openlich be knowe & trouth dor apere" (36)—contains unmistakable echoes of the aphoristic rhymes on the evils of the times with which contemporary pulpit moralists peppered their sermons: "Treuth may no man fynde" (*RL15C* 268), "Manie ȝeres ben iwent / Siþen treuthe outȝ of londe is lent" (Grimestone 14), and so on.[2] *Trouthe* in such proverbial sayings is clearly not our factual truth (the second is paraphrasing "Multis annis iam transactis, nulla *fides* est in pactis"), even though their context is often legal abuse:

falsenes, I vnderstande,
haues dreuen trwvte of lande,
and tort and fort as sworen þar owth
þat law sal lose is ouer-cloþe.
(*RL14C* 54)

Or, as another contemporary sermon verse puts it, "treuþe is toned to tresoun and law is vnderlout" (quoted by Erb 77). When we try to reconstruct the nexus of associations that lies behind this passage from the mercers' petition, then, we will arrive at something like the following: "Brembre has accused us of being traitors, but, if you were to appoint impartial judges to look into the matter, they would find that we are men of our word, even though there are few who dare speak up for good faith in court nowadays; not content with attacking the reputation of the living, Brembre's cronies are even threatening the ancient loyalties, for they have thrown the written constitution of the city onto the fire." The mercers' outburst, in other words, is a thinly veiled protest against judicial corruption and the threat it poses to the traditional order.

I have discussed this passage at such length because it offers some of the best evidence for the claim that in late-fourteenth-century England *trowthe* was, in Raymond Williams's sense of the term, a keyword. On the continent the study of *Schlüsselwörter* or *mots-clés* has been particularly associated with the history of ideas (Veit-Brause), but Williams is careful to distinguish his notion of keywords from "the specialized vocabulary of a specialized discipline"; his own definition extends to "strong, difficult and persuasive words in everyday usage . . . the vocabulary we share with others, often imperfectly, when we wish to discuss many of the central processes of our common life" (12). Williams himself was no medievalist and though he will sometimes glance back at the medieval origins of words that were to become "strong, difficult and persuasive" at a later stage of their development (words such as *family, native,* and *tradition*), he only rarely touches on the cultural significance of one of his keywords for the Middle Ages themselves (*rational* and *society*, for instance); for the most part he is content to explore the far more familiar territory of post-Enlightenment Western culture. Had he chosen to extend the scope of his study backward, however, he could hardly have failed to recognize fourteenth-century *truth* as a keyword, for it fits both his major criteria: "significant, binding words in certain activities and their interpretation" and "significant, indicative words in certain forms of thought" (13). If, moreover, he had been seeking to illustrate one of the typical properties of the keyword—that "the problems of its meanings" tend to become "inextricably bound up with the problems it [is] being used to discuss" (13)—he could hardly have asked for a clearer example than *truth*. Arguably, *trouthe*, as it was used, not merely by Chaucer, Langland, and the poet of *Sir Gawain and the Green Knight*, but by a host of anonymous writers like the notary who drafted the mercers' petition in 1386, is the archetypal keyword in English.

Chaucer uses the word, not only frequently (over two hundred entries in the concordance) but in significant contexts. It heads the catalog of admirable qualities exemplified by his knight in the "General Prologue"—"Trouthe and honour, fredom and curteisie" (46); Troilus's "moral vertu, grounded upon trouthe" (*Troilus and Criseyde* 4:1672) is what first wins over Criseyde, even though she herself is finally found wanting in this same quality: "Allas, youre name of trouthe / Is now fordon" (5:1686–87); it is invoked at the climactic moment of "The Franklin's Tale"—"Trouthe is the hyeste thyng that man may kepe" (1479); and it provides the refrain for one of Chaucer's most enigmatic short poems, the "Balade de Bon Conseyl"—"And trouthe thee shal delivere, it is no drede." Numerous other examples might be adduced to show how truth and its imperfect realization in human terms became, in George Kane's words, "the principal formative concern of Chaucer's mature writing" (12). As with Chaucer, so with Langland and the Gawain-poet. The "tour on a toft trieliche ymaked" that dominates the "fair feeld ful of folk" in the opening scene of *Piers Plowman* (B-text, Prologue:13–19) is, as we soon learn from Holy Church, the residence of "truþe" (B.1:12), and her subsequent sermon on the theme, "Whan alle tresors arn tried treuþe is þe beste" (B.1:85), sets on foot a pilgrimage to *Seynt Truþe* that, as Elizabeth Salter points out, is to become "the great imaginative motif of the whole work" (8). So too the fact that the hero of *Sir Gawain and the Green Knight* sets off on his quest bearing the image of a pentangle on his shield "in bytoknyng of trawþe" (626) and returns wearing a green girdle as "a tokyn of vntrawþe" (2509) supports John Burrow's claim that *Sir Gawain* "is a poem about *truth*, in the medieval sense of the word" (1965, vii).

Kane, Salter, and Burrow are not the only critics to have been struck by the significance of the word *trouthe* for the major poets of late-fourteenth-century England—indeed, a substantial bibliography could be compiled of those who discuss its significance in Chaucer's "Franklin's Tale" alone (see Wurtele)—and many would agree with John Alford that "truth as a social ideal is the dominant, one might almost say the characterizing, concern of late fourteenth-century poetry" (1988b, 33). This is not to imply that such critics have been in complete agreement about what the word means in this period. Chaucerians have tended to regard it as the supreme virtue of an aristocratic honor society (Brewer), and Chaucer's particular concern with it as symptomatic of a crisis of late medieval chivalry (Patterson 196–97) or of the debasement of sworn relationships in a postfeudal society (Strohm 1989, 102–9).

Those who work primarily with other Ricardian poets, in contrast, will often tend to interpret it as a theological virtue: T. P. Dunning, for instance, argues that Langland uses it to express various aspects of "the entire Christian moral law as made known to man through right reason" (46), while Gerald Morgan calls it "the native word [in *Sir Gawain*] that most fully expresses the perfection of Christian chivalry" (790).

The critical appraisal of literary themes is a notoriously subjective undertaking, however, and we shall need more than a consensus among modern critics, no matter how distinguished, to prove that *trouthe* was a keyword in Ricardian England. Chaucer, Langland, and the Gawain-poet appear to have been wrestling with the meanings of a word that also preoccupied many of their less prominent contemporaries. We have already seen that the mercers' phrase "trouthe amonges vs of fewe or elles no man many day dorst be shewed" echoes snatches of pulpit verse lamenting the world's truthlessness, but similar protests are to be met with at every turn. "God be with trewþe, qwer he be. / I wolde he were in þis cuntre!" runs the refrain of an early fifteenth-century carol (*HP* 146); other writers imagine truth in exile ("Riȝtful dom is ouer-cast, / & trouþe is fer agon" [*HP* 327]), in prison ("trewthe is sperd under a lok" [*Reliquiae* 2:121]), or sleeping ("Pees now and speke softe, for truth is a-slepe" [quoted by Wenzel 1986, 184]). The ultimate source for these expressions seems to have been Augustine, whom Thomas Brinton, bishop of Rochester, cites in his last recorded sermon: "veritas ad tempus ligari, claudi, et occultari potest, sed non superari" [truth may for a time be bound, imprisoned, and hidden, but it may not be overcome] (2:497).[3] Similar sentiments are to be found in more ambitious lyrics like "De Veritate & Conscientia," "Truth Is Best" from the Vernon series (*RL14C* 168), or the early fifteenth-century "Treuthe, reste, and pes" from the Digby series (Kail 9–14),[4] and are given an extended airing in *The Simonie* (esp. C.409–44), and *Mum and the Sothsegger* (esp. M.171–205). Bishop Brinton was no radical demagogue, but if further proof were needed that these attitudes penetrated far beyond the obscure world of the popular preacher we have only to recall Gower's lines in the last book of the *Confessio Amantis*:

> And forto lokyn ovyrmore,
> Wher of the poeple pleigneth sore,
> Toward the lawis of oure lond,
> Men sein that trouthe hath broke his bond
> And with brocage is goon aweie,
> So that no man can se the weie
> Wher forto fynde rightwisnesse.
>
> (8:3029–35)

While the major Ricardian poets, in other words, were exploring the finer points of chivalric or religious truth, there were many in late-fourteenth-century England who were expressing profound disillusionment with those who claimed to rule in its name.

The mercers were not the only group in this period to proclaim their own truth and denounce the truthlessness of their rivals. John Ball, whose letters at the time of the Peasants' Revolt are a pastiches of sermon verses exhorted his followers to "stonde manlyche togedyr in trewþe, and helpez trewþe, and trewþe schal helpe ȝoue" (quoted by R. Green 1992, 194), and they in turn took "the trew communes" as their *wache worde*: "Et les ditz comunes avoient entre eux une wache worde en Engleys, 'With whom haldes yow?' et le respouns fuist, 'Wyth kynge Richarde and wyth the trew communes'" (*Anonimalle Chronicle* 139). The Lollards, opposed though they were to the florid demagoguery of the popular preacher, also developed a coded vocabulary in which truth played a prominent role; Anne Hudson has suggested that phrases like 'trewe prechours', 'trewe prestis', and 'trewe cristen men' (1985, 166–167) may have been regularly employed by members of the movement as a way of creating a sense of communal solidarity within the sect.

The introduction to the early Irish law book *Senchas Már* lists "the three periods in which 'the world is frenzied' as the visitation of famine, the onslaught of war and the dissolution of contracts" (quoted by F. Kelly 159), and throughout the Middle Ages there was a tendency for serious social disorder to be apprehended as a symptom of human faithlessness. We can see this, for instance, in the *Peterborough Chronicle*'s account of the anarchy of Stephen's reign or in Wulfstan's reaction to the resurgence of Danish power in Ethelred's, but the calamitous fourteenth century reveals a particular obsession with this idea. Thus the earlier Latin complaint (quoted in Wenzel 1986, 191),

> Heu, plebs conqueritur, quia raro fides reperitur,
> Lex viris moritur, fraus vincit, amor sepelitur,
>
> [Alas, the people are conquered, because good faith is rarely found; man's law is dead, deceit reigns, and love is buried]

becomes entirely recast in the fourteenth century as a denunciation of universal truthlessness:

> Men hem bimenin of litel trewthe,
> It is ded and ȝat is rewthe;

Lesing livet, and is above,
And now is biried trewthe and love!
(*Reliquiae* 2:121)

Even more striking examples of how earlier Latin aphorisms tend to be rephrased in this period into complaints against loss of truth are "ingenium dolus est" [cleverness becomes trickery], translated as "Trewþe ys turnyd into trecherye" (quoted by Wenzel 1986, 190), and "nullus erit amicus" [none shall be a friend], which becomes "Treuth may no man fynde" (*RL15C* 268 and n). A further interesting pointer to the way the rhetoric of social complaint was becoming increasingly focused on the quality of truth as the century wore on is offered by the Peterhouse version of *The Simonie*, which John Finlayson has argued to have been a late-fourteenth-century rewriting of a poem originally composed during Edward II's reign: "The betrayal of Truth is given greater prominence in the Peterhouse version, and in this text the betrayal of Truth through Pride is presented as the cause of spiritual and terrestrial devastation" (48–49).

A similar tendency can be observed in late-fourteenth-century romance. At the beginning of Chrétien de Troyes's twelfth-century *Yvain*, for instance, King Arthur is described as the pattern of prowess and courtesy (1–3), whereas the Middle English version characterizes him as "trew . . . in alkyn thing" (13), and an unflattering comparison between the courtly lovers of King Arthur's day and Chrétien's own contemporaries (21–28) is completely rewritten as a lament for lost truth in which love hardly features at all:

For þai war stif in ilka stowre,
And þarfore gat þai grete honowre.
Þai tald of more trewth þam bitw[e]ne
Þan now omang men here es sene,
For trowth and luf es al bylaft;
Men uses now anoþer craft.
With worde men makes it trew and stabil,
Bot in þaire faith es noght bot fabil;
With þe mowth men makes it hale,
Bot trew trowth es nane in þe tale.
(*Ywain* 31–40)

Similar shifts of emphasis are evident elsewhere in the same romance; when Chrétien shows us Lunet remonstrating with Yvain for his failure to keep his appointment with her mistress, for example, her measured admonition,

Si ne di je rien por clamor,
Mes tant di, que traïz nos a,
Qui a ma dame t'esposa. (2764–66)

[I make no formal complaint against you but I will go so far as to say that whoever married you to my lady has betrayed us]

is transformed into a ringing denunciation of Ywain's bad faith, "Þou es / Traytur untrew and trowthles" (*Ywain* 1625–26).

It is one thing to be able to show that the word *truth* was a "strong, difficult and persuasive word" in late medieval English usage and that a sense of its significance extended well beyond the social and intellectual elite of the kingdom, but if we are to establish the status of *truth* as a keyword in the Ricardian period, we must also be able to demonstrate that by the end of the fourteenth century it had acquired a considerable range of meanings, that some of these meanings were felt to be new and difficult, and that the overlaps between them were complex and potentially ambiguous. Undoubtedly, the most important overlap for our purposes was the one in the mercers' petition—one that R. A. Shoaf has articulated with particular clarity for Chaucer: "I propose that truth is less verification of the adequacy of word to thing than it is searching and cooperating for fidelity among persons, peace among men. . . . What is important is not getting it right but getting it true—best if you can do both, but, failing that, do the latter. I am not just here playing with the two meanings of 'trouthe'—verity and fidelity. I want to do much more, to suggest that the two meanings guard and preserve a wisdom we would do well to consider" (236). Much of this book will be concerned with seeking to unlock the cultural significance of the play between these two meanings, but before turning to this larger issue I shall first try to situate them within a general semantic history of the noun *truth* down to the end of the fourteenth century. In order to explore some of the ways in which its various senses evolved, we must defer for the moment any discussion of the underlying cultural changes that might have affected such evolution; in the first instance we shall be looking more for symptoms than causes.

Ricardian Truth: A Semantic History

By Chaucer's day the noun *truth* could claim a long and distinctive ancestry, and the late fourteenth century had inherited all the semantic complications that a prominent genealogy can bestow on such a word. In order to situate this complex term with any degree of precision in what J. D. Burnley has called the linguistic architecture of Chaucer and his contemporaries (2–4), we shall need a set of blueprints, and I propose here a schema based in the first instance on semantic fields, rather than semantic properties (such as objective/subjective or concrete/abstract), though fully aware that such fields must always seem somewhat arbitrary. As we might expect, the theoretical senses that they help us to categorize will rarely be quite so easily distinguished in practice. In the interest of simplicity, then, I divide the thirteen primary senses isolated by the *MED* (s.v. *treuth* n.) into four main areas of meaning:

1. *legal* senses: 'a promise, a pledge of loyalty, a covenant' (*MED*'s sense 2).[5]
2. *ethical* senses: 'fidelity, loyalty' (1); 'honor; integrity' (3); 'honesty' (4); 'goodness or rectitude of character' (5); 'trust' (7a); 'veracity, sincerity, candor' (12); 'rightness, justness, innocence' (13).
3. *theological* senses: 'divine righteousness' (6); 'belief, esp. in Christian dogma' (7b); 'a set of beliefs, a faith, religion, creed' (8a); 'the Christian religion' (8b–e); 'absolute truth, God or the Godhead' (9).
4. *intellectual* senses: 'correspondence to reality, accuracy, exactitude' (10); 'a fact, a factual statement' (11).

For the sake of clarity, in what follows I employ the following forms (at least where the primary sense appears to me relatively unambiguous): 'troth' for the legal senses, 'trouthe' for the ethical senses, 'Truth' for the theological senses, and 'truth' for the intellectual senses; when what is in question is the signifier rather than its signification I use the form *truth*.

Theoretically, the historical development of these four semantic areas is fairly easy to establish: the order of their emergence is well attested and the shifts that explain them present few formal problems. In practice, of course, since contextual ambiguity, "where a particular word may be taken in two different senses while the meaning of the utterance as a whole remains unaffected" (S. Ullmann 195), is a major factor in precipitating semantic change, we shall encounter many individual instances of borderline usage where precise meaning will be far from unambiguous. The legal senses are probably the oldest, reaching back into the word's Germanic prehistory; already in Old English, however, we find them involved with ethical senses, and a case can be made for the interdependence of both in *truth*'s proto-Germanic and even Indo-European roots. All four categories of meaning can be detected in the linguistic usage of Chaucer's day, but the ethical senses, as we shall see, had become predominant, while theological ones were still fairly recent, and the intellectual senses were very new indeed. For us, of course, intellectual senses of the word *truth* predominate and ethical senses are now very rare—almost the exact opposite of Ricardian usage, and a potential trap for the philologically naive. If for no other reason, a review of the semantic history of the word may help us to shed some of the contextually inappropriate associations we might bring to it, and to reanimate some of its original Ricardian connotations.

That one of the Old English words for 'troth/trouthe'—*treow*—should be a homonym of *treow* 'tree' is no accident for both are descended from the same Indo-European root (**dreu-wo*), an unsuffixed form of which (**dreu-*) is the ultimate ancestor of OE *treow/treowþ*. When the ballad hero Glasgerion swears "a full greate othe, / By oake and ashe and thorne" Child 2:138), then, he is echoing an immensely ancient conjunction between troth and wood. English cognates of *truth* include *dryad* (from Greek *drūs* 'oak'), *druid* (a Celtic 'tree-knower'), and the Germanic *tray* ('wooden board') and *trough* ('wooden vessel'). The association with wood among Western descendants of the I-E radical **dreu-* is so common that Hermann Osthoff argued that the original meaning of **dreu-wo* was 'oak', and that it acquired such senses as 'strength', 'firmness' (cf. Latin *durus*), and 'fidelity' by an obvious metaphorical extension. Émile Benveniste has more recently asserted that the development was in the opposite direction with some such original sense as 'firmness, solidity' evolving the meanings 'tree' and 'oak' from an adjectival form (i.e., 'the firm one'), and that the abstract, ethical senses, which are particularly common in the Germanic languages, are thus the more primitive: "The sense 'fidelity' found in Germanic, is descended directly from the Indo-European root, while that of 'tree' is a specialized sense which developed early and sometimes, as in Greek, survives alone" (1969, 108; cf. 1966, 301). The fact that 'tree/wood' senses are very widespread among Indo-European descendants, including Anatolian and Tocharian (Friedrich 21), tells against Benveniste, however, for the specialization he speaks of must have occurred so early as to be quite unprovable; moreover, we shall see in the next chapter that records of early legal practice offer a possible explanation for the way in which wooden objects may have been so closely associated with contractual rituals as to have acquired the legal and ethical senses found in virtually all Germanic languages.

Legal Senses

From the mists of philological prehistory, we emerge into the comparatively clear sailing of Old English and the other recorded Germanic languages. D. H. Green's investigation of the etymology of the OHG *triuwa* reveals a common thread in all its early Germanic cognates: "The semantic starting-point for this word appears to have been some such meaning as 'a mutual agreement or treaty on the basis of a promise between two parties', sometimes shading off to 'alliance' or to its result, 'truce' or 'peace'" (117). He finds traces of such senses, not only in Old High German, but in Gothic, Old Saxon, and Old Norse, in the medieval Latin *treuga*, and the Old French *trieve* (a probable West Germanic borrowing and the source of modern French *trêve*, 'truce'). For our purposes, of course, his most important evidence comes from Old English, where both *treow* and *treowþ* (from which are descended *truce* and *troth / truth*, respectively) clearly had such a meaning. Green is at some pains to stress both that the original function of *triuwa* was "as a legal term" and that the relationship it characterized "was all along conceived as essentially mutual," that is a formal agreement between equals rather than one between superior and subordinate (121). Even though, as Green shows, this sense of mutuality can sometimes break down, particularly when the term is used in a Christian context (363–65), it will be important to keep in mind the fundamental concept of reciprocity when we come to consider later senses of the word *truth* in English.

The legal senses of *treowþ/treow* 'troth' are well attested in Old English. The eleventh-century glosses in the Bodleian copy of Aldhelm's *De Laudibus Virginitatis* include "foedera: trywþa" and "pacto, .i. iure: treowþe, wise" (*OE Glosses* 1900, 13 and 73), and in biblical translation both *foedus* and *pactum* are often rendered by *treowþ*.[6] Though etymologically distinct, OE *treowþ* and *treow* seem, in Alfredian prose usage at least, to have enjoyed considerable semantic overlap, the choice between them being often a stylistic one (Bately 444). Both could clearly mean 'a promise or covenant', and might be used to translate either *foedus* or *pactum*; in Exod. 6:4–5, where the two words occur in close proximity ("Pepigique foedus cum eis . . . et recordatus sum pacti mei" ["and I made a covenant with them . . . and I have remembered my covenant"]), the Old English translator has rendered the first as "minne truwan" (*truwa* being a weak form of *treow*) and the second by "minra treowða," apparently more for the sake of stylistic variation than because of any great difference in meaning between the two forms (*treow* seems to be the only one used in verse, whereas in prose *treowþ* seems to be the commoner).

The legal ambiance of *treowþ* 'troth' is confirmed by its association with two terms of great importance in the Old English legal vocabulary: *wed* and *wær*.[7] However, to call *treowþ* a legal term is slightly misleading if this is taken to imply that it belonged to a restricted vocabulary used in exclusively legal contexts (a word like *nonfeasance* or *fungible*, for instance), or even that the sense 'troth' was peculiar to such contexts (as with the legal senses of words like *fee* or *construction*). David Mellinkoff is no doubt right to claim that "the Anglo-Saxon period is too early to properly speak of a language of the law" (46), yet *treowþ* and *treow* are clearly, to use his term, "law words," words used of an activity we would regard as legal in nature (the making of formal agreements), though not yet the province of the professional lawyer. In a period when, as Harold Berman puts it, "the peoples of Western Europe were not conscious of any clear distinction between legal institutions and other institutions of social cohesion such as religion or government or general custom" (1978, 553), it seems quite proper to describe as legal the diction of a passage like the following from *Genesis A*, where Abraham initiates circumcision to commemorate his covenant with God (K&D 1:71):

Abraham fremede swa him se eca bebead,
sette friðotacen be frean hæse
on his selfes sunu, heht þæt segn wegan
heah gehwilcne, þe his hina wæs
wæpnedcynnes, wære gemyndig,
gleaw on mode, ða him god sealde
soðe treowa, and þa seolf onfeng
torhtum tacne.

(2370–77)

[Abraham did as God commanded him, set the token of agreement, by the lord's command, on his own son, demanded that each man who was his servant or his retainer should bear the great sign; conscious of the symbol, he was glad at heart that God had given him actual 'troths', and then he received the noble token himself.]

We shall return later to the important distinction between *truth* and *sooth*, but for the moment we should notice that terms like *tacen* and *wær* indicate the Old English poet's assimilation of this scene into his own experience of legal contracts. In particular, the fact that a bargain struck between God and Abraham should involve a physical token conforms absolutely to his notion of proper procedure. The implications of this fundamental element in trothplighting will be explored in the next chapter.

There is no difficulty in establishing the continuity of these legal senses from Anglo-Saxon times down to the late fourteenth century and beyond (indeed, in the archaic phrase *to plight one's troth* and in the word *betrothal* they survive to the present day). Thus in the twelfth century, we find the *Peterborough Chronicle* attributing the anarchy of Stephen's reign to the failure of his barons to keep their troths with the king: "Hi hadden him manred maked ⁊ athes suoren, ac hi nan treuthe ne heolden. Alle he wæron forsworen ⁊ here treothes forloren" (55). And in the early-thirteenth-century the *Ancrene Wisse* renders Isa. 28:15 ("We have entered into a league [*foedus*] with death") as "we habbeð treowðe ipliht deað" (160). From the many examples furnished by the metrical romances of the thirteenth and fourteenth centuries, we might select the betrothal of Horn and Rymenhild, "Muchel was þe ruþe / Þat was at þare truþe" (*King Horn* 673–74); or the scene in *The Earl of Toulouse* where the heroine insists on helping one of her knights, "Thy couenaunt to fulfylle; / Y rede the holde thy trowthe!" (293–94). Among the Ricardian poets, this legal sense is clearly present in Bertilak's commendation of Gawain, "And þou trystyly þe trawþe and trwly me haldez" (*SGGK* 2348), or in Chaucer's Friar's description of the pact between his summoner and the devil: "Everych in ootheres hand his trouthe leith" ("Friar's Tale" 1404). As this last example implies, establishing a troth in this sense often demanded some form of ritual confirmation such as the shaking or slapping of hands. The loathly lady in "The Wife of Bath's Tale" makes her knight plight his troth "heere in myn hand" (1009), and Aurelius has evidently had Dorigen do the same:

> Ye woot right wel what ye bihighten me;
> And in myn hand youre trouthe plighten ye
> To love me best.
>
> ("Franklin's Tale" 1327–29).

Such traditional rituals could take several forms: though Sir Gawain and his host strike hands on their agreement to exchange winnings ("Swete, swap we so" [*SGGK* 1108]), they go on to seal the bargain with a ceremonial drink (1112). As we shall see in the next chapter, these gestures preserve legal formalities of great antiquity.

Though, in the fourteenth century, the sense of *truth* we have been discussing occurs commonly in the expression *to plight one's troth*, this was clearly not restricted, as now, to describing marital engagements, but could be applied generally to almost any agreement or contract: the knight, for instance, plights his troth to Piers when he offers to help him plow his half-acre (*PPl* B.6:34) and the three rioters in "The Pardoner's Tale" plight their troths to one another when they make a compact to slay death (702). For our purposes, however, this phrase, like the parallel expression *to keep one's troth*, is particularly interesting in that it suggests how ethical senses might have developed from an original legal term.

Ethical Senses

We have seen that *truth* might be used to mean simply a 'contract', and that two parties to an agreement might establish 'a troth' between them. From a very early date, however, they might achieve the same result by engaging *their troths*, the possessive pronoun and the plural form of the noun seeming to suggest that the agreement was thought of not as an independent entity to which they individually subscribed, but a combination of their separate consents. (The modern singular *truce*, in fact, has developed from *trewes*, a ME plural form of OE *treow*, an illustration of the process in reverse.) From this it would be but a short step to thinking of *truth* as a quality brought to the agreement by each of the parties—the quality, in fact, that makes the agreement workable. (Since ethical, as well as legal, senses of *treowþ* might be expressed in the plural, however, it is possible to argue the other way: that one's reputation for fair dealing was first conceived of as depending on the collective weight of one's previously honored troths.) The process may have been reinforced by a common linguistic tendency for the semantic border between the cause of subjective reaction and the reaction itself to become unstable; *my love* can be either the person I love or the emotion I experience, and *hope* might refer to whatever inspires optimistic anticipation (for example "her best hope") as well as the feeling itself. In this regard *trust* provides a good analogy for *truth*: a *trust* may be a commercial institution or the kind of confidence that might make investors willing to invest in it. An analogous semantic projection (which can clearly work in either direction) may account for the extension of the meaning of *truth* to include such an ethical sense as 'good faith'. The truth of those entering into an agreement has thus become attached to their attitude toward agreements in general—their reliability, their reputation for fair dealing, and finally their 'honesty'.

It may have been by some such series of associations that *truth* first began to extend its legal usage to what I have called the ethical senses of the word. The development occurs very early, however, and is evident in all Germanic languages except Gothic (D. Green 233–37). The oldest Anglo-Saxon glosses (the Épinal and the Erfurt), for example, gloss *perfidia* as *treulesnis* (*OE Glosses* 1974, 39). If Green is right we should expect the reciprocal ethical senses 'good faith, fair dealing' to be earlier than potentially hierarchical ones, such as 'fidelity, loyalty, faithfulness', but even these go back a long way. A particularly clear example is furnished by King Alfred's version of Augustine's *Soliloquies*: in a passage intended to clarify the way in which God can be apprehended, Reason asks Augustine whether he knows his servant through his inner or his outer senses; Augustine answers that he knows him through the outer, "ac ic wilnode þæt ic cuðe hys ingeþanc of minum ingeþance. Đonne wiste ic hwilce treowða he hæfde wið me" [but I wish that I might know his inner thoughts with my inner thoughts, for then I could know of his loyalty toward me] (59).

Admittedly, Old English seems to associate such ethical 'trouthe' with *treow* more often than with its cognate *treowþ*, though in practice drawing a clear distinction between the legal and ethical senses of either word can be a difficult matter. When Wulfstan in the *Sermo Lupi ad Anglos*, for example, exhorts his countrymen: "utan . . . ⁊ að ⁊ wed wærlice healdan, ⁊ sume getrywða habban us betweonan butan uncræftan" [let us keep carefully our oaths and compacts, and have some *truth(s)* among us without deception] (197–207), we must presumably render *getrywða* by some such gloss as 'good faith'; on the other hand, where he had earlier complained of "tealte getrywða æghwær mid mannum" [unstable *truth(s)* everywhere among men] (61–62), should we understand him to mean 'loyalties' or 'compacts'? A similar difficulty is presented by the passage from the *Peterborough Chronicle* quoted above.

One obvious relic of *truth's* legal heritage was the common asseveration "by my trouthe," which was still in regular use in the Ricardian period—it occurs, for example, no less than nine times in the dreamer's dialogue with the Man in Black in Chaucer's *Book of the Duchess*. While it had certainly by then lost much of its earlier weight—at one point the Man in Black uses it to make the dreamer promise to pay more attention: "'Swere thy trouthe therto'" (753)—it still carries echoes of a time when legal procedure demanded that contracts be bound with solemn oaths, and social pressure provided the sanction against breaking them. It is thus appropriate that "trouthe" should be juxtaposed with "honour" in the famous description of Chaucer's Knight,[8] or that Sir Gawain's "trawþe" should be emblazoned on his shield for all the world to see. Their society was still predicated on a system of honor, and a position in it was secured by those with an unsullied reputation for standing by their word, so that 'trouthe' in this sense was very much a matter of one's public image. Only by being seen to uphold one's own side of an agreement, a 'troth', would one preserve one's reputation for honesty, one's 'trouthe'.

Thus, the contextual ambiguity we noted in Wulfstan is still potentially present in Ricardian usage. In Troilus's rhetorical outburst, "Where is youre love? Where is youre trouthe?" (*Troilus and Criseyde* 5:1676), is he referring to Criseyde's broken promise or to her infidelity? The mention of her "biheste" one line earlier might incline one to the first interpretation, the reference to her "name of trouthe" in the next stanza to the second. An even more difficult example is offered by the famous lines in the "The Franklin's Tale":

> I hadde wel levere ystiked for to be
> For verray love which that I to yow have,
> But if ye sholde youre trouthe kepe and save.
> Trouthe is the hyeste thyng that man may kepe.
> (1476–79)

The legal sense seems clearly to be uppermost in the first instance—as it is in Aurelius's "Avyseth yow er that ye breke youre trouthe" (1320)—but what of the second? By associating *truth* with self-sacrifice, it might be argued, Chaucer pushes ethical considerations beyond the limits of an honor code, whether reinforced by formal oaths or not; indeed, D. S. Brewer has even gone so far as to argue that "*The Franklin's Tale* is explicitly about *trouthe*'s superiority to honour" (16). Undoubtedly the term is more generalized here, but before we rush to load it with abstract ethical connotations we might recall the words of Chaucer's swindling alchemist:

> Trouthe is a thyng that I wol evere kepe
> Unto that day in which that I shal crepe
> Into my grave, and ellis God forbede.
> ("Canon's Yeoman's Tale" 1044–46)

The Canon seems to mean little more by this hypocritical avowal than that he is not the sort of man to welsh on his debts. An even clearer illustration of the social ethos underpinning Arveragus's maxim is provided by the lines on oath-keeping in Robert Mannyng of Brunne:

> For hys loue þat deyde on þe rode,
> Forswere ȝow neuer for werldes gode,
> For ȝe wete weyl & haue hit herd
> Þat trowþe ys more þan al þe werld.
> (2761–64)

The ethical senses of *truth*, then, even in the Ricardian period, remain strongly tied to the quality of keeping one's given word. Criseyde loses her 'trouthe' (in practice, in this honor society, her "name of trouthe") by breaking her word to Troilus; Dorigen's 'trouthe' is preserved because she is prepared to keep hers to Aurelius. (Dorigen's case, of course, is the more complex because the demands of conflicting oaths jeopardize her honor whichever way she turns.)

At an earlier period, the element of fidelity to an oath seems to have been the essential ingredient of all ethical senses of the word, whether those to whom it was applied were involved in what D. H. Green calls horizontal relationships (in other words, dealings between social equals) or not. Even in the fourteenth century we should not automatically assume that where it is used to characterize vertical commitments (Christians to God, subjects to their king, servants to their masters, or, in terms of the medieval hierarchy, wives to their husbands), *truth* will denote nothing more than 'loyalty' in general, or even simply 'devotion'. Such commitments were often in practice reinforced with formal promises (baptismal vows, oaths of fealty, and so on), for, as Richard Southern puts it, "Medieval society was prolific in creating forms of association to which entry was obtained by some form of oath" (1953, 110), and I see no reason to suppose that Ricardian writers were not normally conscious of this when they used the word in an ethical sense. For Gower, indeed, the association between 'trouthe' as the highest moral good and the keeping of oaths is an absolutely natural one. He moves easily from the general assertion that

> Among the vertus on is chief,
> And that is trouthe, which is lief
> To god and ek to man also,
> (*CA* 7:1723–25)

to the advice

> Avise him every man tofore,
> And be wel war, er he be swore,
> For afterward it is to late,
> If that he wole his word debate.
> (1741–44)

This is not to deny that less limited ethical senses were in use in the fourteenth century, merely to warn against overlooking the possibility of narrower interpretation.

The wider senses of 'trouthe' are most easily detected in vertical relationships where the focus is on the behavior of a superior toward inferiors. There were of course hierarchical relationships bound together by the oaths of both parties; in England for instance the king's coronation oath was far from being a mere formality—"he schal uppon his covenant / Governe and lede," as Gower puts it (*CA* 8:3074–75). In practice, however, the troth which held superiors to their side of the bargain would rarely have been conceived of quite so narrowly. Even so, a more general and objective fourteenth-century ethical sense which appropriates to the word *truth* some of the connotations of noblesse oblige suggests that such relationships were still felt to imply a mutual commitment. This sense (though often overlaid with theological associations) is frequent in Langland, particularly in the "Visio." Reason's impassioned tirade, "'Reed me noȝt', quod Reson, 'no ruþe to haue / Til lordes and ladies louen alle truþe'" (*PPl* B.4:113–14), or Piers' advice to his volunteer-knight: "Loke [þow] tene no tenaunt but truþe wole assente" (B.6:38; cf. 15:310), suggest that *truþe* for Langland could mean something like 'punctiliousness in fulfilling one's social obligations'. One may detect a related sense in the Pearl-maiden's characterization of God, "al is trawþe þat he con dresse" (*Pearl* 495), when she introduces the parable of the vineyard. *Truth* in such passages comes close to meaning 'fairness' or even 'justice' (cf. *PPl* B.11:159 or 15:310), and has acquired, no doubt from neighboring theological senses, a new objectivity.[9] There may be no specific oaths implied in such uses, but the feeling of reciprocity remains strong. It may at times be possible to detect a similar ethical sense where obligation flows in the opposite direction, as in Gower's tale of Apollonius of Tyre where the shipwrecked prince is helped by a fisherman "onliche of his povere trouthe" (*CA* 8:650).

One clear indication of the employment of an enhanced ethical sense of the word *truth* in the Ricardian period is its application to situations that go well beyond the terms of any compact. While the ruthless logic of the folktale might be said to bind Gawain or Dorigen to rash promises they never expect to have to honor, no such compulsion binds Alceste. Indeed, the obligations of medieval marriage vows, like modern ones, explicitly stopped short of death: "I *N*. take the *N*. to my wedded housbonde . . . tyll dethe vs departhe" reads the new use of Sarum (*Manuale . . . Sarisburiensis* 48), dating from the late fourteenth century. Alceste is a heroine whose fidelity far outstrips the terms of any contract or any reasonable social obligation. Thus where Chaucer offers the 'trouthe' of "good Alceste" as a foil for Criseyde's faithlessness (*Troilus and Criseyde* 5:1778), elevates her above other women famed for their "trouth in love" (*Legend of Good Women* G.214 & 221), and associates her with "trouthe of womanhede" (*Legend* F.297), he is clearly using the word in an extended sense that goes further than 'integrity' or even simple 'loyalty'. Perhaps discomfort with this usage explains why Alceste is more often praised for her *bounte* than her *trouthe*:

> Now fele I wel the goodnesse of this wif,
> That bothe after hire deth and in hire lyf
> Hire grete bounte doubleth hire renoun.
> (G.508–10)

In view of the overall theme of *The Legend of Good Women* this choice is perhaps surprising and may indicate a preponderance of the older, narrower, ethical associations in Chaucer's verbal architecture. However, Gower too associates Alceste with 'trouthe' when he adds her story to the debate on the respective strengths of wine, women, and kings (from 1 *Esd*. 3–4) to prove that 'trouthe' surpasses all three:

Hou next after the god above
The trouthe of wommen and the love,
In whom that alle grace is founde,
Is myhtiest upon this grounde.
(*CA* 7:1945–48)

Whatever the precise interpretation of this curious episode, Gower like Chaucer is clearly using *trouthe* in a wider sense than simply 'fidelity'.

The importance of such elevated ethical senses of *truth* in Chaucer's work has been well argued by George Kane, but they are prominent in other Ricardian authors, too, and can clearly be discerned in key passages like the elaboration of Sir Gawain's pentangle (Burrow 1965, 42–45); indeed, the recognition that there are times when late-fourteenth-century writers endowed *truth* with some kind of enhanced signification is vital in helping to establish its status as a keyword. However, we should also acknowledge that more restricted ethical senses work equally well in a great many instances, and we should be tempted to reject them only on strong evidence.

I have spent so long on what I have called the ethical senses of *truth* in part because they are so unfamiliar (only the adjectival form—"I'll always be true to you, darling, in my fashion"—retains any echo of them today).[10] With the expression of the more elevated and disinterested ethical senses, however, we may seem to hear the reverberation of theological meanings which we will possibly find less alien. Chaucer's audience, on the other hand, probably found such meanings striking, for though their roots reach back some way their flowering is a fourteenth-century phenomenon and another symptom of *truth*'s Ricardian vigor.

Theological Senses

One comparatively minor ethical meaning of *truth* was 'trust, faith', and this sense offers us a bridge between the other senses we have been discussing and the new theological ones. Trust is the feeling which honest dealing inspires in those encountering it. In other words, *truth* developed an active ethical sense alongside its passive one: *my truth* might refer not only to my capacity for inspiring confidence in those doing business with me, but also to my own feeling of confidence in them.[11] It is not difficult to see how such a sense as 'trust' could be further extended to 'faith', and 'belief'. Thus John Barbour suggests that Edward I's death was brought about by his mistaken faith in an ambiguous prophecy: "Bot he wes fule, forouten weir, / That gaf treuth to that Creature" (4:222–23). So too Richard Rolle uses *trouth* to render Latin *fides* in the standard Pauline triad: "as many good thoghtes as we þynken in trouth and hoope and charite, so many pases go we to heuynward" (4, cf. 36). This extension of meaning was probably encouraged by association with the common ME verb *trowen*, and some writers do in fact link the words *trow* and *truth* rhetorically: a homily from the Thornton manuscript, for instance, calls "trouthe" the first virtue, "wharethurghe we trow anely in Godd" (Perry 10) and Dunbar writes, of "the twelf artickillis of the treuth: a God to trow" (17). The sense of *truth* as 'trust, faith' seems never to have been very common and may indeed have been more frequent in the north. The *OED*'s examples (s.v. *troth* sb. 3a) are all from northern texts or authors: Orm, *Cursor Mundi*, the Thornton Manuscript, Wyntoun, and (s.v. *truth* sb. 3a) Barbour—interestingly, its only post-medieval citation is from another northern author, Andrew Marvell; the *MED*'s examples (s.v. *treuth* 7a) are drawn from a wider area but several (particularly Chaucer, *Troilus* 1:584) are questionable.[12] Langland, however, may be using the word in this sense when he describes the gloss *in corde per fidem* given to the Psalmist's "mecum es" (22:4) as "a greet mede to truþe" (*PPl* B.12:294), and Pandarus's saw "to trusten som wight is a preve / Of trouth" (*Troilus* 1:690–91) is a possible Chaucerian instance, though not an unambiguous one.

From *truth* 'trust, faith' it is an easy step to the generalized meaning 'a system of belief' (*OED*, s.vv. *troth* sb. 3b/*truth* sb. 3b; *MED* s.v. *treuth* 8b). This meaning, also relatively uncommon, has a similar northern flavor; its earliest appearance is in the *Ormulum*:

> Forrþi þat teȝȝ [the Chaldeans] þatt time
> Ȝet unnderrstodenn littlesswhatt
> Off all þe rihhte trowwþe.
>
> (6951–53)

Its importance, however, lies less in its frequency than in the fact that it is the first indication of a new objective sense of the word: *truth* has become a quality that can be considered apart from those who embody it. Not merely 'my truth' or 'your truth' but '*the* truth'. As such it points the way to later theological and intellectual senses.

The more specialized sense of *truth* as 'Christian faith or doctrine', which becomes current from the middle of the fourteenth century, is indeed so natural an extension of the word's meaning that we might wonder why it does not occur earlier. Legal and ethical senses of *truth*, as we have seen, are easily assimilated into a Christian context: in D. H. Green's words, "[Old Saxon] *treuwa* as a state of affairs . . . flows from God—presumably because *treuwa* as a quality also characterizes him" (122–23). Moreover, the general sense of *truth* as 'faith' or 'belief' develops early in other Germanic languages (D. Green 124–25), and seems to have been a possible meaning of OE *treow*, if not of its cognate *treowþ*. Since it was generally recognized that, in Gower's words,

> Ther is a feith aboven alle,
> In which the trouthe is comprehended,
> Wherof that we ben alle amended,
> (*CA* 5:1734–36)

we might expect Christianity to have been called *the Truth* from a very early stage. That it was not may reflect the connotation of reciprocity that, as D. H. Green shows, continued to cling to the word for a very long time. It also reflects the stubborn survival of a term that was far less hampered by qualities of subjectivity or reciprocity, *soothfastness*.

In Old English biblical translation *soþfæstness* had generally been the word chosen to translate *veritas* and hence it had come to denote such things as spiritual reality, divine revelation, even the Godhead itself, senses which attach themselves naturally to the notion of eternal verity. These are qualities that today we could hardly begin to express without reference to the word *truth*. The *Old English Version of the Gospels* provide ample evidence of such senses. To take only some of the more obvious instances from the Gospel of John: "cognoscetis veritatem et veritas liberabit vos" ["And you shall know the truth, and the truth shall make you free"] is translated "ge oncnawað soðfæstnysse. and soþfæstnes eow alyst" (8:32); "ego sum via et veritas et vita" ["I am the way, the truth, and the life"], as "ic eom weg and soðfæstnys and lif" (14:6); and "spiritu veritatis" ["the Spirit of truth"], as "soðfæstnysse gast" (15:26). As late as the 1330s we can find a translator of Isa. 59:14, "iustitia longe stetit, quia corruit in platea veritas" ["justice hath stood far off: because truth hath fallen down in the street"], choosing the word *trouþe* to represent, not *veritas*, but *justitia*—*veritas* here being more naturally rendered by the word *soþnesse* (quoted in Wenzel 1986, 175).

Incontrovertible evidence that *truth* was supplanting *soothfastness* and had largely taken over the theological senses of *veritas* by the Ricardian period is provided by the Wycliffite Bible. This generally renders *foedus* and *pactum* as either "couenaunt" or "bonde of pees," but almost invariably renders *veritas* as "treuthe." The three quotations from John's Gospel given above, for example, appear in the first Wycliffite version as, "ȝe schulen knowe the treuthe, and the treuthe schal delyuere ȝou" (the second version has "make ȝou fre"); "I am weye, treuthe, and lyf"; and "a spirit of treuthe."[13] A particularly good illustration of this sense in Ricardian poetry comes from *St. Erkenwald*, which alludes to Augustine's mission to England: "Þen prechyd he here þe pure faythe & plantyd þe trouthe" (13). Though *soothfastness* had still not completely relinquished its hold on this semantic area, such senses for *truth* were widespread by the Ricardian period and can be found in every major writer. Chaucer, for instance, though generally translating *veritas* by *soothfastnesse* in Boethius, will sometimes use *trouthe* in specifically theological contexts—the refrain of his "Balade de Bon Conseyl" (taken from John 8:32), for example, "And trouthe thee shall delivere, it is no drede," or his translation of "et veritas in nobis non est" (1 John 1:8) as "and trouthe is nat in us" in "The Parson's Tale" (349). He does, however, acknowledge a semantic overlap when he alludes to John 18:38 ("Dicit ei Pilatus: Quid est veritas") at the beginning of his "Lenvoy de Chaucer a Bukton": "whan of Crist our kyng / Was axed what is trouthe or sothfastnesse" (1–2), but there is no such hesitation over the use of *trouthe* where the recently converted Valerianus hastens to share his new faith with his brother Tibertius in "The Second Nun's Tale": "Bileve aright and knowen verray trouthe" (259).[14]

To these various theological senses (the Christian gospel, spiritual enlightenment, God himself), we should add one more: *truth* in the sense of 'orthodox doctrine'. Gower contemplating the papal schism, prays, "God grante it mote wel befalle / Towardes him which hath the trowthe" (*CA* Prologue: 340–41), and a few lines later he looks forward confidently to the demise of Lollardy: "Bot whan god wole, it schal were oute, / For trowthe mot stonden ate laste" (368–69). Predictably enough, however, the Ricardian poet whose work embodies the most complex exploration of such 'Truth' is Langland.

To take only the first passus of the B-text of *Piers Plowman*, we find in Holy Church's explanation of the "merueillous swevene" and in her sermon on the text "whan alle tresors arn tried treuþe is þe beste" at least three theological senses. *Treuþe* is the Christian God embodied in the Trinity ("ther Treuþe is in Trinitee" [133]), though perhaps most closely associated at this point with its first person (the "fader of feiþ" [14] who opposes Satan, the "fader of falshede" [64]). It is also clearly Christian doctrine, the law of love: "Truþe telleþ þat loue is triacle of heuene" (148). To these objective senses must be added a subjective one: 'obedience to God's law', as in, "þo þat werche wel as holy writ telleþ, / And enden . . . in truþe" (130–31), or, "No dedly synne to do, deye þeiȝ þow sholdest, / This I trowe be truþe" (144–45). This sense extends to 'true belief', as in B.19 when Grace and Piers set out "to tilie truþe / And þe [lond] of bileue, þe lawe of holy chirche" (333–34). Langland's 'Truth' still carries with it older connotations of the rigid fulfillment of the terms of an agreement (what we may think of as the 'redde quod debes' sense, as in the pardon sent from Truth in B.7 or the debate of the four daughters of God in B.18), while at the same time denoting a theological doctrine based on the spirit, not the letter, of the law, "[Th]at is no truþe of þe Trinite but tricherie of helle" (198). This ambiguity—exemplified in the C-text's expansion of the text of Holy Church's sermon, "than treuthe and trewe loue is no tresor bettre" (1:135)—provides Langland with one of his most suggestive paradoxes. Thomas Usk seems to be exploring a similar paradox in the *Testament of Love*: "al this book (who-so hede taketh) considereth [how] al thinges to werchinges of mankynde evenly accordeth, as in turning of this word 'love' in-to trouthe or els rightwisnesse, whether that it lyke" (139). Such semantic complexity clearly arises from the overlapping of theological and ethical meanings, for *treuþe* in Langland is not only the New Law, but also, as we have seen, something close to 'impartial secular justice'.

The discussion of Trajan, the "trewe knygt," in the B- and C-texts offers a good illustration of the potential for misunderstanding in a similar semantic overlap. This is how the B-text describes Trajan's debt to Gregory the Great, who,

> "By loue and by lernyng of my lyuynge in truþe:
> Brouȝte me fro bitter peyne þer no biddyng myȝte."
> Lo! ye lordes, what leautee dide by an Emperour of Rome
> That was an vncristene creature, as clerkes fyndeþ in bokes:
> Nouȝt þoruȝ preiere of a pope but for his pure truþe
> Was þat Sarsen saued, as Seint Gregorie bereþ witnesse.
> (B.11:152–57)

In the C-text revision these lines become simply:

> "Loue withoute lele bileue as my lawe rihtfoel
> Saued me, Sarrasyn, soule and body bothe."
> Lo, lordes, what leute dede and leele dome y-used!
> (C.12:85–87)

Evidently Langland's motive in making these changes was to remove the ambiguous word *truþe*: Trajan's "lyuynge in truþe" in the B-text had obviously been intended to refer to his just administration of the law (an ethical sense), but, like the phrase "for his pure truþe," it was open to the possible misinterpretation that Trajan's salvation was owing to his orthodox faith (a theological sense quite opposite to what Langland intended). He makes his meaning quite explicit in the C-text by stating that Trajan was saved "withoute leele bileue," changing "[Gregory's] lernyng of my lyuynge in truþe" to "loue . . . as my lawe rihtfoel," and omitting the line that alludes to "pure truþe" altogether. One might add that he was able to leave "leautee" intact because it threatened no such ambiguity. This French term could certainly be used in alliterative verse as an approximate equivalent of 'trouthe', as when Bertilak alludes to Gawain's "untrawþe": "bot here yow lakked a lyttel, sir, and lewté yow wonted" (*SGGK* 2366); it seems, however, to have shared few of the English word's theological overtones.[15]

We have seen that, as it moved into the semantic territory formerly occupied by *soothfastness*, *truth* began to acquire objective senses, generally (though not exclusively) theological in nature. These seem to have prepared the way for the development of the final category of meaning we are to consider: *truth* as an intellectual concept, 'that which is in accordance with the fact', or 'the actual facts of the case'. For us these are the principal meanings of the word, but we should be aware that the teller of a tall story who insists that we have been told the absolute truth and the logician who discusses the truth function of a proposition are using the word in senses that would have been very strange in Chaucer's day; such senses were still most often conveyed by the word *sooth*.

Intellectual Senses

The distinction between *soþfæstness* and *soþ* in Old English is much the same as that between Latin *verum* and *veritas* (in principle, the distinction between 'truth' and 'the quality of being true').[16] Thus the Vulgate's "nec in iudicio plurimorum acquiesces sententiae, ut a vero devies" ["neither shalt thou yield in judgement, to the opinion of the most part to stray from the truth"] is paraphrased in the *Old English Version of the Heptateuch* as "ne beforan manegon soþes ne wanda" (Exod. 23:2), and "ille scit quia vera dicit: ut et vos credatis" ["he knoweth that he saith true, that you also may believe"] is given in the OE Gospels as "he wat þæt he soþ sæde þæt ge gelyfon" (John 19:35). The Vulgate itself, however, does not maintain a rigorous distinction between the intellectual senses of *verum* and *veritas* and it is worth noticing that OE translators sometimes render *veritas* by *soþ* rather than *soþfæstness* where the context is one of 'speaking the truth': thus "Si veritatem dico vobis, quare non creditis mihi" ["if I say the truth to you, why do you not believe me?"] (John 8:46), is given as "Gif ic soð secge" in both Ælfric's *Homilies* (Cook 216) and the OE Gospels (by the time of the Wycliffite version, significantly, this has become "if I seie treuthe.")

If the distinction between *soþ* and *soþfæstness* was at times a fine one in Old

English, that between *soþ* and *treowþ* was far clearer. Wulfstan begins the castigation of his contemporaries' *tealte getrywða* in his *Sermo Lupi ad Anglos* with the exhortation "gecnawað þæt soð is: ðeos worold is on ofste, ⁊ hit nealæcð þam ende" [know for a fact that this world is hastening to its end] (4–5). While history might disprove this particular *sooth* of Wulfstan's, the mere passage of time could never pose a similar threat to its author's *truth*. The first was open to objective verification, the second only to subjective judgment. Thus if Physiologus genuinely believes that mermaids sing well and merrily, then, in the earlier senses of the words, he speaks *truth* by claiming it for a *sooth*, and no amount of ichthyological observation can alter this. *Truth* here is opposed not to error but deceit; an honest reporter, after all, may be mistaken. It is *truth* in this sense that the antiquarian Horne Tooke could still describe in the late eighteenth century: "Two persons may contradict each other, and yet both speak TRUTH: for the TRUTH of one person may be opposite to the TRUTH of another" (607). For us, of course, Physiologus's honesty is largely irrelevant to the way we assess the truth of his assertion about mermaids; for us *true facts* are not honest, but tautological, ones.

In the late fourteenth century, *truth* was beginning to usurp the sense of *sooth*. By a natural synecdoche the acknowledged reliability of a speaker will come to be applied to that speaker's statements, so that *Physiologus spoke truth* might be taken to mean not simply 'Physiologus spoke like an honest man', but 'what Physiologus said was correct'. After all, a universal respect for *auctoritas* had meant that for the Middle Ages in general Physiologus's reputation for 'trouthe' would have seemed far from irrelevant to the 'truth' of his opinions. Often, in fact, it will be difficult to separate these two senses completely, and some theological contexts where both propositions are equally unassailable (God can be neither wrong nor deceitful) will make it quite impossible. Though some such mechanical shift may help to explain the appearance of objective theological senses in the first place, and thus provide a source for the new intellectual ones, the deeper cultural reasons for this shift seem to me far more significant (what makes *truth* a keyword in fact). Why should Chaucer's contemporaries have chosen to load yet one more piece of semantic baggage on an already overburdened *truth*, particularly when a more lightly laden *sooth* was still in full vigor? The laws of the linguist are not those of commerce and there is nothing surprising in the discovery that an apparently viable word can be driven out of a semantic market by another not obviously better equipped to trade on it. The specialization of the sense of the word *meat*, originally meaning 'food', at the expense of *flesh* is a well-known example of this kind of encroachment (L. Bloomfield 431–32), and inevitably it raises the same kind of extralinguistic speculation: "We may some day find out why *flesh* was disfavored in culinary situations" (441).

The significance of *truth*'s semantic encroachment upon *sooth* in the fourteenth century was stressed some time ago by Will Héraucourt—it reveals, he claims, "a revolution in the ethical sphere that can hardly be overemphasized" (81)—but his analysis is weakened, partly because he bases it on what he sees as a fundamental distinction between a theoretical, transcendent kind of truth (*sooth*) and a practical, pragmatic quality (*truth*), and partly because he is reluctant to go outside the language system to explain his *Umwälzung*. To argue that this semantic shift is driven by a new conception of 'truth' characteristic of the Renaissance seems to me to confuse causes and effects. Though I see it as less a shift from theory to practice than one from honesty to accuracy (the first a quality to be sought in people, the second in their statements), I entirely agree with Héraucourt's estimation of the importance of *truth*'s displacement of *sooth*; I would, however, prefer to see the new modes of verification and authentication that this implies as both the reflection as well as the stimulus of profound social changes. An attempt to articulate these changes will in fact be the concern of much of the rest of this book. For the moment, however, we have still to demonstrate the appearance of the new intellectual sense and illustrate some of its potential ambiguities.

By the mid-fifteenth century the establishment of a distinct intellectual sense of *truth* is well attested. The *Promptorium Parvulorum* (ca. 1440) gives Latin glosses for two separate meanings of *trowth*: the first, *veritas*; the second (for "trowth and levte"), *fidelitas* (492). To illustrate this new sense in context we might cite the courtroom scene in the *Tale of Beryn* (one of the earliest, and best, contributions to the Chaucerian apocrypha): the hero is on trial for murdering the father of a character called Machyn with a stolen knife, and his defense counsel tells the court,

Then were spedful for to knowe howe Beryn cam first t[h]o
To have possessioune of the knyff þat machyn seith is his:
To ȝewe vnknowe, I shall enfourm þe trowith as it is.
(3800–3802)

Such unambiguous examples are less easy to find in the fourteenth century, but King Athelston's command that Wymond be sent to the ordeal "To preue þe treweþe" (rather than *his* truth) seems fairly clear (*Athelston* 776). Similar is the sense in which Sir Gawain uses the word in response to Bertilak's inference that only important business could have drawn him out on his unseasonable journey: "for soþe, sir . . . ȝe sayn bot þe trawþe" (*SGGK* 1050); Daniel's explication of the writing at Belshazzar's feast in *Purity*, "And Phares folȝes for þose fawtes, to frayst þe trawþe" (1736); and Erkenwald's exhortation to the miraculous corpse, "Ansuare here to my sawe, councele no trouthe" (*St. Erkenwald* 184). On the other hand, many apparent examples of this intellectual sense which involve "saying," or "telling" the truth raise the possibility that this phrase may not have been an exact synonym for 'saying the sooth'. When Gawain asks, "þat ȝe me telle with trawþe if euer ȝe tale herde / Of þe grene chapel" (*SGGK* 1057–58), for instance, the phrase "with truth" may well carry the implication of speaking honestly or openly.

This problem is particularly acute in Langland. In the scene with Rechelesnesse which leads up to the first appearance of Trajan in the C-text of *Piers Plowman*, the dreamer, who has been complaining of the hypocrisy of the friars, is asked by Lewtee why he is scowling and replies, "Y wolde it were no synne . . . to seien þat were treuthe" (C.12:27). In the B-text (where the complaint is rather shorter) this had been, "If I dorste . . . amonges men þis metels auowe!" (B.11:86). A few lines later, Lewtee advises, "Ac be neuere more þe furste the defaute to blame; / Thouh thowe se, say nat sum tyme, þat is treuthe" (C.12:35–36). The B-text has here, "thouȝ þow se yuel seye it noȝt first" (B.11:104). In such passages, where what is being discussed is the morality of concealing, or rather not revealing, what one knows to be the 'truth', the sense in which *treuthe* is used is still not wholly divorced from ethical considerations. What Rechelesnesse and the dreamer offer (and what Leaute questions the value of) are what are sometimes called "home truths"—uncomfortable facts that might arguably be best left unspoken. Interestingly enough even *Mum and the Sothsegger* uses *trouthe* in this sense in a scene where the Commons is being reprimanded for not telling the king and his council about the true state of the country:

> For þere is no man of þe meeyne, more noþer lasse,
> That wol wisse þaym any worde but yf his witte faille,
> Ne telle þaym þe trouthe ne þe texte nothir.
>
> (M.158–60)

In Gower the phrase *pleine trouthe* seems sometimes to be used to convey this sense (e.g., *CA* 7:2442 and 3977).[17]

When what is at issue is the 'truth' of a tall story (B.13:304) or forensic 'truth' (B.14:288), however, Langland's normal word is *soþe*.[18] A particularly good example is provided by the dreamer's request of Conscience:

> kenne me þe soþe:
> "Is þis Iesus þe Iustere," quod I, "þat Iewes dide to deþe?
> Or is it Piers þe Plowman?"
>
> (B.19:9–11)

It is unlikely that Langland would have felt happy using *truþe* in such a context, and one of his favorite half-lines, "Truþe woot þe soþe," implies that he is far from regarding the two words as synonymous.[19] When the central character in *Pierce the Ploughmans Crede* tells the narrator, "I will techen þe þe trewþe & tellen þe þe soþe" (794), he is presumably claiming that the version of the creed he is about to offer will be both doctrinally reliable and verbally accurate. I have found no example in Langland to set beside Gower's,

> Forthi, mi Sone, tell me soth
> And sei the trouthe, if thou hast be
> Unto thy love or skars or fre,
> (*CA* 5:4726–28)

which is at least arguably tautologous. Even here, however, *truth* and *sooth* may well preserve distinct connotations, Genius implying that Amans is to tell the whole truth and nothing but the truth.

Ironically, in view of the inflated claims made by Héraucourt on his behalf ("eine Renaissance im Einzelmenschen" [82]), Chaucer's forays into the intellectual realm of *truth* are distinctly conservative. Unlike Gower, who provides some of the best examples of the new sense (e.g., *CA* 2:1452; 5:6561), Chaucer generally preserves a clear distinction between *trouthe*, as a subjective quality, and an objectively verifiable *sothe*. An excellent illustration occurs in his long gloss, taken from Trevet, on Boethius's *metrum* "Quisquis profunda" (Petersen 182–83): "Whoso wol seke the depe ground of soth [*verum*] in his thought . . . lat hym techyn his soule that it hath, by naturel principles kyndeliche yhud withynne itself, al the trouthe [*veritas*] the which he ymagineth to ben in thinges withoute" (*Boece* 3:met.11.13–24). Chaucer's choice of *trouthe* (where an earlier writer might have used *soþfæstness*) to render *veritas* here must surely have been influenced by the clearly subjective sense in which Trevet is using the word. On the other hand, where *veritas* is used to denote 'the facts', as it is when Boethius, speaking of the charges against him, says that he wishes to put the record straight for the sake of posterity ("cuius rei seriem atque veritatem, ne latere posteros queat . . ."), Chaucer translates "of whiche thyng al the ordenaunce and the sothe" (1:pr.4.165–66).

There are in fact very few incontrovertible uses of the intellectual sense of *truth* in Chaucer. Even two instances in the *Treatise on the Astrolabe* turn out to be more concerned with dependability than fact: "to knowe the verrey degre of eny maner sterre . . . sothly to the trouthe thus he shal be knowe" (2.17: rubric) and "this conclusioun is verrey soth, yf the sterres in thin Astrelabie stonden after the trouthe" (2.34:11–13). The sense here is one that still survives in the expression "out of true," and which the *OED* does not record before the seventeenth century (s.v. *truth* sb. 6): "agreement with a standard or rule; . . . *spec.* accuracy of position or adjustment." The same sense is perhaps to be found in Langland: "[Th]e pound þat she paied by peised a quatron moore / Than myn owene Auncer [whan I] weyed truþe" (*PPl* B.5:215–16). The two clearest instances of the intellectual sense come from Chaucer's "Tale of Melibee" (both translating French *vérité*): "the trouthe of thynges and the profit been rather founden in [Fr.: *par*] fewe folk that been wise and ful of resoun than by greet multitude of folk," and "certes, the trouthe of this matiere . . . nedeth nat diligently enquere" ("Melibee" 1068 & 1356). Pace the *MED* (s.v. *treuth* 11a), its use in the scene where Alla investigates a charge of murder against Constance is rather less clear than in the one from the *Tale of Beryn*, quoted above:

> This gentil kyng hath caught a greet motyf
> Of this witnesse, and thoghte he wolde enquere
> Depper in this, a trouthe for to lere.
> ("Man of Law's Tale" 628–30)

One possible implication of "trouthe" here, for instance, is that Alla is simply seeking to establish the reliability of the witness (as his subsequent action seems to suggest) rather than the facts of the case; another is that *trouthe* is being used in some kind of extended legal sense like a 'question of disputed integrity'—cf. "to trien a trouthe be-twynne two sidis" (*Mum and the Sothsegger* 2:85).[20] Other Chaucerian uses of the intellectual sense are even more ambiguous.

For the sake of brevity I have concentrated on the noun *truth* and its two main competitors, *sooth* and *soothfastness*. The general picture would probably not be significantly altered by a detailed examination of the history of the adjectives *true* and *verray*, the inclusion of less important rival words, such as *verity*), or discussion of antonyms, such as *treachery*, *error*, *falsehood*, *wrong* (*treason* is a special case, and will be discussed further in Chapter 6). It does seem possible, however, that the emergence of an intellectual sense of *true* preceded that of the noun *truth* and helped accelerate the process we have been discussing; this could have been prompted by an obvious contextual ambiguity about phrases such as "for trewe or fals report" (*Troilus* 1:593), whose sense is practically the same whether *trewe* means 'reliable' or 'factual' (see Dane 161).[21] Chaucer may be more willing to employ *trewe* in intellectual senses than its corresponding noun—the Nun's Priest's disclaimer, "This storie is also trewe, I undertake, / As is the book of Launcelot de Lake" ("Nun's

Priest's Tale" 3211–12) offers a particularly well-known example—but the dominant sense of *trewe* in his poetry remains 'honest, faithful, reliable': "A trewe wight and a theef thenken nat oon" ("Squire's Tale" 537). One can in fact find instances of the juxtaposed forms *trewe* and *sooth* connoting different qualities, as in the lines from "The Clerk's Tale," made much of by Héraucourt, "But sooth is seyd—algate I fynde it trewe, / For in effect it preeved is on me" (855–56), where transposition of the two words would clearly affect the sense (cf. "Man of Law's Tale" 169). There is an interesting example as late as the trial scene in the *Tale of Beryn* where the witnesses swear that "every word . . . / Was soth & eke trewe" (3151–52), which seems to imply that the evidence against him is presented as not only factually correct but in some way morally appropriate.

Before we leave this topic, however, I might point to one final sign that the word struck late medieval authors as difficult and ambiguous: their need to distinguish and qualify their uses of it. We have already seen the Chaucerian use of *verray trouthe* (n. 14), but even more striking is Langland's line, "ne wolde neuere trewe god bote trewe treuthe were alloued" (*PPl* C.14:212), which offers clear evidence that the poet was fully aware of *truth*'s semantic instability. The phrase *true truth*, which occurs as early as the Harley lyrics,

> Lut in londe are to leue,
> þah me hem trewe trouþe ȝeue,
> for tricherie to ȝere,
> (*Harley Lyrics* 12:19–21)

appears again in *Ywain and Gawain*, "bot trew trowth es nane in þe tale" (40). An analagous expression appears in *Athelston* where the four companions, "in trewþe trewely dede hem bynde" (24), and in the Göttingen manuscript of *Cursor Mundi*, whose owner promises that

> If it [the manuscript] be tint or dune a-way,
> treuli mi trouth i plight,
> Qua bringes it me widvten delay,
> i sal him ȝeild þat night.
> (17103–6)

Just as we might use *literal* or *actual* to point to an accepted meaning of a word we fear might be misunderstood, it seems that late medieval writers might employ the adjectives *verray*, *sooth*, or *trewe* when trying to keep their footing among the shifting and still evolving senses of *truth*. In the Ricardian period these adjectives are generally used to point up one of the older senses of the word, but by Lydgate's day things have changed: in the textual apparatus to *The Siege of Thebes* we find some scribes choosing to represent 'the actual facts' of Oedipus's birth by the phrase *the trewe ground*, others by *þe soth trouthe*, and yet others by *þe trewe trouþe*; one gives up and simply writes *the treuthe* (508).

This survey of the semantic range of *truth* in the late fourteenth century has been far from complete, but I trust that enough has by now been said to suggest its polysemous vitality for the Ricardian poets. In the remainder of this chapter I shall sketch out a broad cultural context in which the full significance of the emergence of intellectual senses of *truth* in this period may perhaps become clearer.

An Ethnography of Ricardian Truth

In Chinua Achebe's novel *Arrow of God*, one of the duties of Ezeulu, chief priest of the clan of Umuaro, is to eat a sacred yam at each new moon. Since twelve sacred yams are gathered each year and his consumption of the twelfth signals the beginning of the new harvest, Ezeulu acts, as it were, as a living almanac for his people. A crisis arises when an insensitive colonial administration prevents Ezeulu from performing his sacred duties by incarcerating him for two whole months so that the ritual calendar falls out of alignment with the lunar one. When it dawns on the villagers that the harvest upon which they all depend is to be delayed, one of Ezeulu's acolytes tries tactfully to suggest to him that he has lost count of the moons: " 'What! Are you out of your senses, young man?' Ezeulu shouted. 'There is nothing that a man will not hear these days. Lost count! Did your father tell you that the Chief Priest of Ulu can lose count of the moons? No, my son,' he continued in a surprisingly mild tone, 'no Ezeulu can lose count. Rather it is you who count with your fingers who are likely to make a mistake, to forget which finger you counted at the last moon' " (203–4). This scene offers a particularly graphic confirmation of the way in which, according to Ernest Gellner, the concept of truth in a small-scale agrarian community differs fundamentally from the truth of scientific-industrial societies. "Its notion of truth," writes Gellner, "is that of compliance with a norm, rather than that of echoing an extraneous fact. Truth is for it the fulfillment of an ideal, which in turn is molded by complex and plural concerns. This is wholly different from truth as satisfaction of the simple, isolated requirement, such as the collating and predicting of facts" (276).

Ezeulu and his hearers know perfectly well that the human truth of priestly ritual and the objective truth of the passing seasons are no longer in alignment, but where we would unhesitatingly privilege the latter they can see no easy way out of an appalling dilemma: "We know why the sacred yams are still not finished; it was the work of the white man," says one of the elders. "Shall we then sit down and watch our harvest ruined and our children and wives die of hunger? No! Although I am not the priest of Ulu I can say that the deity does not want Umuaro to perish. We call him the saver. Therefore you must find a way out, Ezeulu. If I could I would go now and eat the remaining yams. But I am not the priest of Ulu. It is for you, Ezeulu, to save our harvest" (207). Ezeulu's inability to find a way out, however, brings his people to the very brink of disaster. Such a logical impasse will be quite familiar to the cultural anthropologist, who is constantly faced with the problem that "the type of things that are said to be 'true' in traditional contexts, and the way people argue for their veracity, do not seem to square with ordinary ideas on truth and falsity" (Boyer 46). Lévy-Bruhl would no doubt have regarded Ezeulu's dilemma as typical of the prelogical mind, but Gellner is keen to alert us to the ideological bias of such an attitude. He first distinguishes two primary kinds of constraint upon what is held to be true (in other words, what receives social approbation), referential validity (is it correctly linked to nature?) and social loyalty (does it conform to normative conceptual expectations?). He then goes on to argue that our own readiness to adjudicate between these two kinds of constraint (almost always to the detriment of the second) is far from inevitable or universal: "The gratuitous assumption which we are challenging is that the speaker must himself be distinguishing the two activities, reference to nature and loyalty to social order — the supposition that their separation lies in the very nature of things" (47).[22]

To exemplify this point let us look at a recent instance of what Gellner would call multi-stranded thinking. Among Milman Parry's interviews with Serbo-Croatian epic singers is one with a man named Đemo Zogić, who recalls how he learned one of his favorite songs, "The Rescue of Alibey's Children," from another singer, Sulejman Makić:

> "I sat down beside the singer and in one night I picked up that song. I went home, and the next night I sang it myself . . ."
>
> "Was it the same song, word for word and line for line?'"
>
> "The same song, word for word, and line for line. I didn't add a single word, and I didn't make a single mistake." (Lord 27)

Zogić goes on to claim, "If I were to live for twenty years, I would sing the song which I sang for you here today just the same twenty years from now, word for word." The literal truth of these claims can be tested against recordings made of "The Rescue of Alibey's Children," not only in contemporaneous performances by Makić and Zogić, but also in a second performance by Zogić recorded by Albert Lord seventeen years later (28). What is much more surprising than the discovery that these three versions are very far from being "word for word" is the fact that Zogić himself could have predicted this:

> "Tell me this, if two good singers listen to a third singer who is even better, and they both boast that they can learn a song if they hear it only once, do you think that there would be any difference between the two versions?"
>
> "There would. . . . It couldn't be otherwise. . . ."
>
> "What are the differences?"
>
> "They add, or they make mistakes, and they forget. They don't sing every word or they add other words. Two singers can't recite a song which they heard from a third singer and have the two songs exactly the same as the third." (27)

What do we make of this blatant inconsistency? Lord argues that Zogić wasn't lying when he claimed to be able to reproduce another performer's song exactly—rather that for him "'word for word and line for line' [was] simply an emphatic way of saying 'like'" (28).[23] In Gellner's terms, however, Zogić is simply unaware of (or unimpressed by) the distinction between two kinds of truth: loyalty to a social order (a song should be true to its tradition) and reference to nature (one word is not the same as another). For Zogić there is certainly no compelling reason why our propositional truth should be separated out and granted precedence. As Isidore Okpewho has written of another oral performer, the Sudanese griot: "In the heroic 'world' that these bards celebrate, truth is equatable with glory. So long as the parochial or political interests of the group are upheld . . . the bard does not worry about sticking to the facts" (72). This insight may help to explain the kind of gratuitous self-contradiction which Zogić introduces into Makić's version of "The Rescue of Alibey's Children" and which Lord finds so puzzling (94–95). Indeed, it offers intriguing possibilities for investigating the internal inconsistencies with which so much emergent literature abounds.

The case argued by Gellner on anthropological grounds is cast in theological terms by Wilfred Cantwell Smith. Smith analyzes the main words for truth in Arabic to show how the modern Western world, though still "aware that earlier ages saw things differently" (14), has subjugated "realist" and "personalist" levels of truth to "an inert and impersonal observable" (13). Arabic does indeed have a word for propositional truth, *ṣaḥḥa*, but in Islamic society this is not apparently privileged over *ḥaqqa*, "what is real, genuine, authentic, what is true in and of itself by dint of metaphysical or cosmic status . . . a term supremely applicable to God," or *ṣadaqa*, "honesty, integrity, trustworthiness . . . being true both to oneself and to other persons and to the situation with which one is dealing" (7). Clifford Geertz's conclusion from a study of the word *ḥaqq* — that in Islamic law, "facts are normative: it is no more possible for them to diverge from the good than for God to lie" (189) — confirms Smith's view that Arabic, in Gellner's terms, draws no absolute distinction between reference to nature and loyalty to social order. Even more interesting, in view of the history of Middle English *trouthe*, is Lawrence Rosen's claim that the reason why *ḥaqq* in present day Morocco has come to mean "not only 'duty', 'claim', and 'obligation' but 'truth' and 'reality'," is because "the web of obligations that human beings create through their negotiated attachments to others is the central feature of their existence" (13).

The law is an obvious area for testing Gellner's hypothesis. Formal mechanisms for preventing and resolving disputes will claim to depend on social approbation, to function, that is, as interpreters of truth, so that if we find legal systems that assume very different standards of truth from our own, we may have reason to suspect that they are occupying a different kind of conceptual space. Thus, Smith's personalist truth expresses itself in Islamic law in rules of evidence that look very curious to the Western eye: not only are written documents "merely aids to memory," their contents admitted as evidence "only in so far as they are confirmed by the testimony of witnesses" (Schacht 193; cf. Geertz 190–91), but these witnesses must be of proven good character (*'adl*), a condition which has no real counterpart in Western jurisprudence. One has only to compare exclusionary rules in common law evidence (for example, "hearsay") with their Islamic counterparts to see how great a gulf divides the two systems: "Whether the witnesses are in fact *'adl* must be established by inquiry. Unbecoming, despicable acts, such as playing backgammon or entering a public bath without a loin-cloth, do not nullify the quality of *'adl* but nevertheless enable the *ḳāḍī* [magistrate] to reject the testimony of the person in question" (Schacht 193). Traces of an older attitude are still present in our common law (in the debate over whether the sexual history of his victim can be admitted as evidence in the trial of a rapist, for instance), but generally speaking modern lawyers, whatever their actual practice, will claim to see their principal job as exposing factual errors and inconsistencies in testimony rather than discrediting the moral worth of the testifier. As the anthropologist reminds us, however, this attitude to the witness as "an instrument of verification" is far from being the norm; "in other societies he is nothing of the sort: he helps to establish 'truth' because no 'verification' is possible" (Steiner 364).

The importance of human, as opposed to propositional, truth is even clearer in comparatively simpler legal systems. Among the Chagga of Southeast Africa, for instance, the word for 'truth', *lohi*, has, like Middle English *trouthe* and Moroccan *ḥaqq*, connotations of "the binding and the bound word" and is a central legal term: "A witness in court merely agrees to the words of the party under oath. He speaks *lohi*"; when an eyewitness, on the other hand, testifies as to the identity of the accused, his evidence belongs "to a reality of a different relevance" (Steiner 367). Though their court procedures are quite distinct, the jural importance of human truth among the Tiv of Nigeria is quite as marked. After reminding us that "Western jurists have a single standard of 'truth'—verifiability—and they have provided themselves with an elaborate mechanism for determining it" (1957, 47), Paul Bohannan argues that Tiv courts are concerned with two kinds of 'truth': *mimi* and *vough*. The first "means both the morally good thing and the socially correct thing, a distinction which is not easy to make in the Tiv language. What it does not necessarily imply, though it may do so, is the factually correct thing. If this aspect of 'right' is to be emphasized, the correct word is *vough*, which means 'straight or precise'" (49). Tiv judges, he goes on, "do not expect principal litigants to speak *vough*, but only to speak *mimi*. For principals the two may be opposed" (50). "'Truth' in Tivland," Bohannan concludes, "is an elusive matter because smooth social relationships are deemed of higher cultural value than mere precision of fact. We must not judge Tiv litigants or witnesses by our standards. They are not liars, as they are sometimes called: their truth has other referents than has European truth" (51). The Chagga, too, are sometimes said to be liars and for similar ethnocentric reasons: "Chagga concepts of truth apply to contexts covered by the European concept of lying," claims Steiner, and he cites as evidence "the talks preceding law cases, when clan members assemble and decide to stick to the version of their fellow clansman. All this is just talk, but the story to which they finally bind themselves is *lohi*" (368). That such an attitude to truth in traditional societies is not peculiar to Africa is confirmed by Michelle Rosaldo's observation that in disputes between Philippine headhunters, the parties "were not concerned with telling lies or telling truths. As always, what they claimed was 'true' depended less on 'what took place' than on the quality of an interaction where what mattered most was who spoke out" (214).

One of the more persistent canards of colonialism—and it is at least as old as the Spanish conquistadors (see Las Casas 280)—is that all natives are liars. E. M. Forster alludes to it in his picture of Ronny Heaslop, the city magistrate in *A Passage to India* who spends his days in court "trying to decide which of two untrue accounts was the less untrue" (50). In Achebe's *Arrow of God* we meet a district officer who tells his deputy: "I should mention that every witness who testified before me—from both sides without exception—perjured themselves. One thing you must remember in dealing with natives is that like children they are great liars" (38). In Ngũgĩ's *A Grain of Wheat* another district officer writes in his journal, "Remember the African is a born actor, that's why he finds it so easy to lie" (65). The calumny is even perpetrated by a black American visitor in Soyinka's novel *The Interpreters*: "You Africans, once you've told a lie, you feel bound to stick by it. Even when you are confronted with the evidence which even a child must see, you must lie, lie" (194). Although the general explanation for this attitude is, I believe, likely to be the colonialist's failure to conceive of truth's having "other referents,"[24] it should be recognized that in some small-scale societies the compulsion to speak the truth (in the Western sense) will seem less pressing in conversation with an outsider. J. D. Krige observes that among the Lovehedu of southern Africa, the chief and his advisers "generally know so much of the facts of the case that lying is of little avail," though there is a commonly held opinion that "any lie is good enough to deceive a European" (quoted by Colman 581).

When even the great Frederic Maitland could show himself insensitive to the possibility that for medieval people truth might have "other referents" ("our ancestors perjured themselves with impunity" [P&M 2:543]), I can hardly expect that this attempt to characterize our distance from the cultural norms of the Middle Ages in terms of the gulf that separated the Turtons and Burtons of British colonialism from their unfortunate subjects will meet with universal acceptance. Modern scholars have too often sought to recreate the Middle Ages in their own image, yet, "to ask why medieval writers claimed that what appears to us obviously 'invented' material was 'true' " is, as Ruth Morse has said, to remind ourselves "of the incommensurability of our cultures—however much ours owes to, and descends from, theirs" (2). Too often we have listened only to those who spoke for the official culture, to the educated Gallo-Roman Gregory of Tours leveling his charges of ubiquitous faithlessness against the barbaric Franks, or to the pious Saint Louis equally horrified by the perfidiousness of their descendants, forgetting how unrepresentative such voices are. For the Middle Ages in general truth was, as Aron Gurevich has put it, "anthropomorphous," a categorization entirely consonant with the normative, human truth described by Gellner and Smith: " 'Truth' meant something very different from the scientific 'truth' on which so much reliance is placed today: to the medieval mind truth had to correspond to the ideal norms. . . . In a society based on the principle of fidelity to the family, kindred, lord, etc., truth could not have a value independent of the concrete interests of the group" (1985, 178). Such a concept of truth was to linger on at the edges of official culture at least down to the Enlightenment, making an appearance, for instance, in David Sabean's account of the difficulties faced by officials investigating a bizarre animal sacrifice that took place in the Württemberg region in 1796: "[The commissioner] had a model of communication based on ascertainable facts, clear ideas, and a direct access to truth. For the villagers, truth was instrumental, and the specificity of the ideas not so important" (197). It would be unwise to claim that such attitudes are wholly extinct in the West even today.

Support for this way of viewing the mentality of the Middle Ages will occupy much of the first half of this book, but for the moment let us take as a test case the question of forgery. There is no doubt that in the early Middle Ages monks in major houses like Westminster, Canterbury, Winchester, and Malmesbury forged legal documents on a fairly impressive scale, and it is quite possible that as many as half the extant charters drawn up in the name of Edward the Confessor date from after the Conquest (Clanchy 1993, 318–19). Must we therefore disparage the moral standards of these creative scriptoria? Fritz Kern, for one, was convinced that "many a monk who fabricated charters for his house . . . thought he had won himself a place in Heaven," and that the decision to make a new forgery was often taken "to help truth and right to victory" (171). Michael Clanchy elaborates this view: "the distinction between fact and fiction in writing . . . would not have been as sharp to medieval people, although they were very conscious of the moral difference between truth and falsehood" (1993, 321). The subtlest reading of medieval forgery is that of Giles Constable, who draws on Smith's discussion of human truth to suggest that "people in the Middle Ages also saw what they wanted and needed to see, and believed to be true what had to be true" (24), arguing that "by this standard, a forgery designed to promote truth and justice would not be considered a forgery, in the pejorative sense, at all" (26).

If we ask ourselves, finally, what links all these muddiers of the clear water of truth—the priest Ezeulu, the Yugoslav gusle player, the Islamic *ḳāḍī*, the Chagga witness, the Tiv pleader, Ronny Heaslop's litigants, and the monastic forger—one obvious answer lies in an attitude to written records very different from our own. In much of what follows I shall be searching for clues to this particular mystery in the increasingly literate consciousness of the laity in fourteenth-century England—a consciousness upon which the study of customary law throws an especially bright light. I will offer only one brief illustration here. At the same time that the English word *truth* was beginning to gather to itself the new intellectual senses that would eventually overwhelm all the others, another noun with close semantic ties to it was first entering the language from the specialized vocabulary of legal documentation, the word *evidence*. Although the classical Latin *evidentia*, originally meaning 'clarity' or 'distinctness' had come to refer to 'a display' or 'manifestation' as early as the Vulgate, the peculiar modern English sense of 'information proving the truth of a statement or claim' seems first to have appeared in the Anglo-Norman terminology of thirteenth-century common lawyers, and, what is particularly striking from our point of view, seems originally to have referred exclusively to written documents.

"Our earliest records," writes James Bradley Thayer, "show the practice of exhibiting charters and other writings to the jury. These things, *par excellence*, used to be known as 'evidence' and 'evidences'" (104). Such a practice seems, indeed, to have been older than that of presenting the jury with the oral testimony of ordinary witnesses (Thayer 108). By the 1290s lawyers had begun to use *evidence* in something like the more general sense with which we are familiar (R. Palmer 1984, 157 and 228), but nonetheless the memory of its documentary origins was to survive to the end of the Middle Ages. Certainly, the restricted sense of *evidence* was still common in the law French of Ricardian courtrooms—"it was found by *nisi prius* in the country that the land was given by a deed which shown as evidence [*fut mys avant en evidence*]" (*YB 13 Rich. 2*, 25)—, and by this date was passing into English as well.[25] By the mid-fifteenth century, as its regular appearance in the *Paston Letters* proves, it had become thoroughly naturalized in the vernacular: "John Paston, squyere, schall delyuere . . . to the seid William Paston all maner of chartours, evidenc[e]z, monymentes, rolles of accomptes and courte rolles" (1:175).

The word *evidence* appears nowhere in the works of the Cotton-Nero poet, and is used only once by Chaucer: he says that he composed his *Treatise on the Astrolabe* after learning "by certeyne evydences" (1–2) of little Louis's mathematical aptitude (by which he seems to mean a letter or report card). It is used with some frequency by John Gower, however, and in many places its original cartulary sense is still quite clear; speaking of the significance of dreams, for instance, Genius says,

> Bot forto schewe in evidence
> That thei fulofte sothe thinges
> Betokne, I thenke in my wrytinges
> To telle a tale therupon.
> (*CA* 4:2922–25; cf. 1:1857)

In the same vein, Langland will sometimes refer to a textual authority as "an evidence," as where Rechelesnesse says

> ȝe se by many euydences
> That wit ne wihtnesse wan neuere þe maistrie
> Withoute þe gifte of god,
> (*PPl* C.11:285–87)

and then goes on to cite a passage from Augustine to support his argument (cf. C.8:262). Even though these Ricardian writers do use *evidence* in less restricted senses, there are clear signs that they still recognized its original association with written proof. I have sketched in the early history of the English word *evidence* here because it seems to me to offer a particularly elegant philological demonstration of the justice of Jack Goody's claim that "the shift to writing emerges as a driving force towards a more formal concept of evidence, and in a certain sense of truth itself" (154).

Michael Clanchy has described the long process by which the truth of written evidence came to be trusted, but the converse of this, the gradual erosion of the faith once placed in the truth of human beings, still invites detailed examination. Throughout the late Middle Ages, increasing reliance on written records forced people to confront not only the fallibility of human memory but, far more traumatically, the unreliability of human trouthe. Here, to conclude, are three otherwise unremarkable cases from St. Albans manorial court rolls (1269–1341) which show how written record and sworn verdict might be brought into direct conflict with one another in ways that cannot but have compromised local confidence in the ancient virtue of trouthe (cited by Beckerman 222–23): (1) Richard, defending himself against his brother-in-law Roger's attempt to reclaim a piece of land, says that his wife (Roger's sister) had been granted use of the land a dozen years earlier, but an inquest of local villagers rules against him — later, an unequivocal record of Roger's grant to his sister is unearthed in the rolls; (2) Robert and his wife, Margery, are granted use of a tenement by Alice and the transaction is entered in the rolls — twelve years later, when Alice sues to evict him from the tenement, Robert (unlike the modern archivist) is unable locate the record and a local inquest determines that no such grant had ever taken place; (3) Maud seeks to recover dower land leased by her late husband to Henry, but an inquest, citing as precedent the case of another widow called Joan fourteen years earlier, rules that according to local custom she must first wait for Henry's lease to expire — yet when the rolls are actually consulted it is found that Joan's recovery had in fact taken place immediately. In this last case, the written records proved unequivocally that the jurors had "completely misstated both the outcome of an earlier case and the custom of the manor" (223). There is no reason to suppose that these jurors (whose verdict was rendered on oath) were particularly corrupt or partial, and their example suggests how difficult it had become by the mid-fourteenth century to maintain an illusion of communal coherence founded on ethical truth in the face of the unwavering insistence of written evidence on a depersonalized intellectual truth. The final realization that these two kinds of truth could no longer be equated helped produce the crisis of confidence so vividly reflected in the work of the Ricardian poets.

In the following chapters, I hope to demonstrate that it was no coincidence that new intellectual senses of the word *truth* were appearing in the vernacular at the same time that a dramatic growth in lay literacy was leading to an increasing reliance on written evidence in the common processes of verification and authentification, nor that this growth should have been accompanied by a widespread loss of faith in the word of trusted neighbors—just such a loss as that lamented by the London mercers with whom we began: "for trouthe amonges vs of fewe or elles no man many day dorst be shewed." But though the subjugation of human to propositional truth (a process which, I have suggested, is reflected in *truth*'s Ricardian encroachment upon *sooth*) is bound up with the spread of literacy (a development whose impact Walter Ong, for one, has characterized in conceptual terms analogous to Gellner's),[26] this cannot be the whole answer by any means, and if we are to explore the problem in any serious way we shall have to delve far more deeply into the world we have lost. To appreciate the full significance of *truth* for Chaucer's contemporaries, and to understand fully the forces that made of it a keyword, we must first return to the root meaning of OE *treowþ* as a legal contract; only this time our focus must be on the jural and cultural context that gave it meaning.

2

Trothplight

> In that ago when being was believing,
> Truth was the most of many credibles.
> — W. H. Auden

SOMETIME IN THE MIDDLE OF THE eleventh century in the hamlet of Marmoutiers outside Tours a man called Baldonet entered the church of the local monastery of Saint Martin. Round his neck he had hung a set of bell ropes and on top of his head he carried four pennies; thus encumbered, he walked up to the high altar where he made an offering of his ropes and pennies. These curious actions were witnessed by at least twelve men (*Livre des serfs* 3–4). This much we know; a little more can be reconstructed with reasonable certainty: at the altar Baldonet would doubtless have sworn an oath; afterward he would probably have gone off to ring the abbey bells (Southern 1953, 100). In one sense there is no mystery about what he was doing: he was committing himself and his descendants to perpetual servitude — he was, in a particularly elaborate form, plighting his troth. But from another perspective his actions are as strange as any observed by an anthropological field-worker. They might legitimately be added to Gurevich's list of the "medieval 'absurdities' and 'incongruities' [that] stand in need of both explanation and an adequate degree of understanding" (1985, 8). In what follows I hope to clarify the cultural context of Baldonet's trothplight, but before reaching some sense of the social meaning of his actions, we will first consider them functionally, as part of the practical machinery of daily life in a society that had yet to learn to trust written records.[1]

The ceremony of Baldonet's enserfment serves as a useful point of departure for considering the formal nature of the folklaw contract,[2] for it was no different in essence from hundreds of others by which not only conditions of service but land transfers, sales of movables, even marriages, were concluded. The notary who records its details had no doubt about their function, for he introduces them with an unambiguous formula: "but in order that this his commitment of himself might appear the firmer and more obvious . . ." [ut autem haec sui traditio certior et evidentior apparet . . ."] (*Livre des serfs* 4). Its physical ceremony is what confirmed (a later medieval English lawyer might have said "clothed") Baldonet's contract in the eyes of the community.[3] Without its symbolic trappings, Baldonet's *traditio* (the term comes from Roman law and means literally 'handing over') would have been a mere *nudum pactum*, whose nakedness, though championed by the canonists, made enforcement difficult should the parties later fall out over it. The primary function of such clothing, as Richard Southern saw, was to impress "the occasion and its significance on the memory" (1953, 100).

If both parties to an important agreement are literate, or, more properly, live in a society where literacy is commonly accepted, they will probably decide to put their agreement in writing. The advantage of such a course will seem obvious to us: with proper safeguards, it provides unimpeachable evidence of the terms of their contract should either of them be tempted to challenge it later. But what happens in an oral society? The contract has no concrete existence outside the minds of those who enter into it or who witness it, so strict adherence to its terms will depend entirely on the good will of the parties themselves and the accuracy of their memories. Under these conditions, it becomes imperative that they use every possible means of fixing the agreement by whatever mnemonic device may assist its recall. In practice the number of these devices is limited, and though not every oral society will use all of them, or use them in exactly the same way, certain features appear regularly: witnesses are assembled, verbal formulas are repeated and oaths sworn, symbolic objects are exchanged and symbolic gestures made. The witnesses may be kinsfolk or disinterested onlookers; the oaths and formulas may be of varying degrees of particularity; the symbolic gestures may range from embracing a sacred relic to giving a simple handslap; and the objects may be of great value or mere tokens. The details vary but the rationale remains the same. Everything must contribute to make the contract an unforgettable event; in Brian Stock's words, "the ritual was the bond" (50). The record of Baldonet's enserfment offers a particularly vivid picture of the point where literacy and orality meet in a society whose mental furniture is still essentially pre-literate.

With literate hindsight, we will readily applaud the good sense of the preamble with which the Marmoutiers' notary introduced his account of Baldonet's *traditio*, a preamble which, if not unparalleled (Bäuml 1980, 249; Keynes 1990, 226), is remarkable for its length and detail: "As every picture fades with age, and if not touched up with new colors now and then becomes quite unrecognizable, so the record of every event, if it is not painted in the imagery of letters, as it were, vanishes, for, as every earthly thing is neighbor to corruption and every corporeal thing subject to time, so every memory of human deeds, as it draws toward oblivion, must fail at the last. Therefore, lest we mislead our descendants as to the intention of our acts, from which unknown harm may come, let us commit them to the durability of writing [durabilitati tradamus litterarum]. Be it known, then, by all our successors that a certain freeborn servant called Baldonet . . ." (*Livre des serfs* 4). For us, the mnemonic machinery that clutters up the actual *traditio* must appear primitive and clumsy alongside the articulate literate record which preserves it, but writing in eleventh-century Marmoutiers was clearly restricted to a very limited caste (a state which Havelock calls "craft literacy"), and as Michael Clanchy has well taught us, not everyone in such a society will grasp immediately the inferiority of living memory to written record. While we may accept uncritically the notary's confidence in the superiority of his pen-strokes to Baldonet's cavorting before the altar, Clanchy's work suggests that neither Baldonet himself nor most of his contemporaries would have shared our confidence. They would have seen no particular advantage in using written charters over a system in which "witnesses 'heard' the donor utter the words of the grant and 'saw' him make the transfer by a symbolic object" (1993, 254); indeed, many would probably have felt far more skeptical about the reliability of pieces of parchment than the evidence of tried and trusted *videntes* and *audientes*. One indication of the faith placed in the traditional system is its persistence in the popular imagination long after writing had become widespread. There is plenty of evidence that "dependence on symbolic gestures and the spoken word persisted in law and literature, and throughout medieval culture, despite the growth of literacy" (Clanchy 1993, 278), and we shall see how the traditional forms were to live on in metrical romances and folk ballads to the end of the Middle Ages and beyond. But this tension between two modes of evidence, two kinds of truth, was not felt solely by the uneducated and the provincial; it permeated the conceptual system of medieval society as a whole.

Before going on to consider some of the features of traditional trothplight in detail, however, we might speculate on why the subject has received so little attention from legal historians. H. D. Hazeltine is almost unique in claiming that "contract formed a very prominent feature of the English legal system prior to the Norman Conquest" (608); Sir William Holdsworth by contrast could detect "practically no doctrine of contract in Anglo-Saxon law" (2:82), and even the great Frederic Maitland thought that the law of contract held "anything but a conspicuous place among the institutions of English law before the Norman Conquest," (P&M 2:184). As late as the end of Henry III's reign, Maitland claims, "our king's court has no general doctrine of contract" (P&M 2:194), and A. W. B. Simpson's *History of the Common Law of Contract* hardly bothers to consider the period before 1290 at all. Given the postulates of modern jurisprudence such neglect is in fact quite understandable, and I should like to begin by considering some of the ways in which literate assumptions about the nature of law have distorted our view of the folklaw contract.

Trothplight as a Legal Institution

We have seen that the more "thinglike" (to adapt a term of Maitland's) an oral agreement can be made, the longer it will last in the memory. With the widespread acceptance of writing the law has come to depend upon the ready manipulation of abstract concepts, and so from the perspective of modern jurisprudence the very physicality of the rituals of oral trothplight can present a major obstacle to appreciating its legal premises. The common law has evolved an elaborate doctrine of contract based on the precise definition of individual rights and duties. Where, then, legal historians find what looks like an inability to conceptualize even a comparatively simple right, such as ownership, they will tend to dismiss the idea that anything but the most rudimentary notion of contract could ever have existed. To take sale as an example: in modern law the parties to an executory contract are placed under an obligation to follow a certain course of action in the future and this in turn means that such a contract is ultimately concerned with ownership, the *right* to possession, not possession itself. I can promise the right to possess my car, but I cannot promise the actual vehicle—*that* I can only transfer (an action in the present tense not an agreement in the future). The early law knew nothing of such distinctions: "What modern lawyers call ownership . . . is not recognized in early Germanic ideas. Possession, not ownership, is the leading conception; it is possession that has to be defended or recovered, and to possess without dispute . . . is the only sure foundation of title" (P&M 1:57).[4] From this point of view Anglo-Saxon contracts will appear virtually indistinguishable from the simple transfer of possession—as Maitland puts it, "the money was paid when the ox was delivered" (P&M 2:185)—and whatever took place beforehand was merely preliminary negotiation, binding upon neither party. To the lawyer such transactions will look more like conveyances than contracts (Ibbetson 1992, 2), and true sales will only become possible when contract law starts to exploit the abstract distinction between ownership and possession sometime in the fourteenth century (see Ibbetson 1991).

The legal mind will be tempted to see any confusion between such basic concepts as simply symptomatic of the habitual messiness of everyday language unrefined by professional definition. After all, most of us are far more likely to talk of selling our cars than selling the right to our cars, and only when something goes awry will we need a lawyer to show us how wrongheaded we have been. The Anglo-Saxon thegn, in other words, actually did own the estate he possessed; he just didn't happen to think of it that way. A difficulty arises, however, as soon as we start applying the concept of ownership to something that is not physically possessed, like a lent sword, a hired out horse, or a leased barn, or to something that can never be physically possessed, like an office or a service (lawyers call such things *choses in action*). Here is a problem that is more difficult to dismiss as merely terminological. Take the case of a man in the late thirteenth century who had acquired the right to be cared for in his old age by a monastery (something technically known as a corrody); to us this right will appear contractual (a right *in personam*, as the lawyers would say), yet if ever he had to go to law to defend such a right, our pensioner would have had to represent the breach of his agreement with the monastery as if it were a species of wrongful ejection from freehold land (as if, in other words, his rights *in rem* had been infringed).[5] It is in such circumstances that Maitland is drawn to speak of "thinglike rights," whose "thinglikeness is of their very essence" (P&M 2:125). Whether the mnemonic machinery of trothplight is a symptom of such thinking, or in some sense (as I prefer to believe) its cause, is a difficult question. What seems quite clear, however, is that early medieval law was very uncomfortable with the kind of abstract reasoning that underpins modern contract theory.

Only in the thirteenth century when the very nature of lordship was being placed under the legal microscope were common lawyers forced to draw a distinction between corporeal and incorporeal things, and thus to open the way to more refined notions of contract. This was particularly true of incorporeal hereditaments like the advowson, the right to appoint to an ecclesiastical living (see P&M 2:136). Henry Bracton, writing before the middle of the thirteenth century, is at pains to stress the elementary difference between the right to appoint to a church and the physical possession of the church itself, as if in the minds of his readers the two might be confused: "Though the church, as built of timber and stone, is corporeal, the right to present will be incorporeal, and hence it is one thing to give the church and another to give the advowson" (2:159–60). Evidently this was a matter of some importance, since it could lead to confusion between transferring the right of advowson and mere presentation to a church living (2:279). Only when the incorporeal nature of such rights had been clearly recognized could contract law, in anything like its modern sense, begin to develop;[6] thus, it is no surprise to find that "in all the oldest specimens" of the first truly contractual action at common law, the writ of covenant, "the subject matter of the *conventio* is land or one of those incorporeal things that are likened to land" (P&M 2:217).

The problem legal historians face when they try to reconcile the ancient forms of trothplight with modern concepts of contract is further compounded by what will look to them like a hopeless confusion between public and private law. The intellectual historian has little difficulty appreciating the profoundly contractual basis of early medieval society: "The nobleman was bound by several codes of law—as a Christian, a baron, a knight, a subject of the king; and he could suffer all manner of penalties for a breach of any of these codes of law. Into all these obligations he had entered by an individual contract in the ceremonies of baptism, homage, knighthood and fealty. If he was punished, even by being burnt as a heretic, he could reflect that he was being punished for breach of contract" (Southern 1953, 110). From the perspective of the lawyer, however, this stretches the idea of contract almost to the point of meaninglessness. As Maitland put it, early contract was "an unruly, anarchical idea," which "threatened to swallow up all public law," and needed to be "taught to know its place" (P&M 2:233). Medieval people themselves had no difficulty understanding "the idea that men can fix their rights and duties by agreement" (P&M 2:233): a statute of 1284 states that "enforceable covenants are infinite in number so that no list of them can be made" (see P&M 2:218–19), and even as late as the fourteenth century, though the formal scope of covenant was quite narrow, its conceptual scope remained very large (see M. Arnold 1976, 322–23). Some legal historians, however, have felt safer denying the very existence of contract than throwing open its doors so wide.

What is finally in question here is the universal applicability of modern legal categories. Are we to assume that early law is merely an unrefined and imprecisely articulated version of modern law, or does it perhaps have its own logic which our terminology is ill suited to rendering? Undoubtedly earlier notions of contract will appear unruly, even anarchic, from the point of view of modern jurisprudence, but only if we think of the social function of such agreements in terms of the obligations defined by our own notion of contract. Frederick Pollock's argument that "people who have no system of credit and very little foreign trade, and who do nearly all their business in person and by word of mouth with neighbors whom they know, have not much occasion for a law of contract" (P&M 1:43–44) is clearly circular: once contract has been defined in terms of a certain kind of economic system, it is thereby disqualified for use in any other context.[7]

Since Maitland's day, the work of cultural anthropologists has helped to refine this problem considerably: some striking parallels have been revealed between the legal systems of present-day traditional societies and the folklaw of medieval Europe. Max Gluckman, for instance, deduced from a study of the Barotse of Southeast Africa that the notion of executory contracts is foreign to traditional African law ("the passing of some property was necessary to establish an obligation")—a view shared, not only by the early Romans, as Gluckman himself points out (1974, 315), but also, as we have seen, by the Franks and the Anglo-Saxons. Similarly, Paul Bohannan notes that the Tiv of northern Nigeria dealt with certain lawsuits which modern Western jurisprudence would regard as falling within the sphere of contract as if they were matters of debt. Thus, an action to secure the return of a goat left with a neighbor for safekeeping would proceed as if the defendant 'owed' the plaintiff a goat (1957, 103–4); here, just as in the early common law, "the vast gulf which to our minds divides the 'Give me what I own' and 'Give me what I am owed' has not yet become apparent" (Maitland 31).[8] Much the same spirit underlies the Middle English proverb—a proverb that Chaucer, interestingly enough, puts into the mouth of his Man of Law ("Man of Law's Tale" 41)—"biheste is dette" (Whiting B214).[9] More remarkably, the Tiv might even subsume tort under the category of debt, so that someone who shot a neighbor's goat might be thought of as 'owing' it (105–w6). Even this apparent confusion between the categories of contract/debt and tort can be detected in early medieval English law, however; as Maitland puts it, "the non-payment of a debt seems regarded as . . . an unjust and forcible detention of money that belongs to the creditor" (Maitland 31).[10]

Put crudely, the early folklaw of Western Europe, whether Roman or Germanic, appears to share with traditional African law (or the traditional law of some African societies) at least two basic assumptions: that all solemn agreements must partake of the corporeal (be 'thinglike' in the sense I have been using the word here), and thus that any failure to honor them is a kind of tort, the breach of a duty *in rem*. One's word, that is to say, is no mere abstraction; it takes on some of the qualities of a piece of property to be defended against the world. It is surely some such conceptual economy that lies behind the conflation of the two earliest senses of truth: both troth (a contract—something lawyers think of as giving rise to a right *in personam*) and trouthe (the quality that enables one to make a contract, one might almost say the capacity to contract—something that looks much more like a right *in rem*). Some idea of what this might mean in practice is given by the case used to illustrate "disturbing a bargain" from a thirteenth-century treatise on holding manorial courts: the defendant is accused of having so disparaged the character of a would-be purchaser of a barrel of wine that the vendor was led to renege on their previous agreement (*Court Baron* 40–41). Here, what looks to us like an obvious contractual dispute is transformed into a tortious action against a third party. Even more curious is the way the action appears to combine contract/tort with slander (the plaintiff claims "to his damage of 40s. and shame of 100s.")—a conflation that renders troth and trouthe virtually indistinguishable.

The real question is whether it is then legitimate to call such agreements *contracts* at all. Bohannan, for one, is suspicious of any attempt to impose modern categories upon traditional law: "It would be possible," he writes, "to consider [Tiv 'lawsuits'] which concern 'releasing livestock' as cases of breach of contract. Little purpose would be served by doing so, for Tiv do not have a concept 'contract', and if we do so classify them, there is a grave danger of forgetting that we have applied the notion of 'contract' from our own culture" (1957, 104).[11] For Max Gluckman, on the other hand, this is a quibble. By confusing contract and tort with debt, he suggests, the Tiv merely reveal the immaturity of their legal terminology: "Since the Romans never evolved the kind of elaborate theory of contract and tort that modern Western law has evolved, the categories of modern law are likely to be more developed and refined than those available to the Romans . . . *A fortiori*, these modern categories will be more refined than those used by Tiv jurists" (1965, 211).[12]

Arguably the deepest pitfall awaiting all legal historians (or legal anthropologists) is the unthinking assumption of "a world always juristically like ours" (Milsom 1981, 149). If, however, medieval legal historians have sometimes seemed too ready to project their own two-dimensional model of ownership and possession back onto the less familiar order of medieval lordship, they can at least claim as an excuse that "all the seignorial words survived to serve a two-dimensional world" (150). Those studying earlier English law have rather less reason to fall into such a linguistic trap. Much Anglo-Saxon law has been preserved in the vernacular, but, unlike the law French of the twelfth century, few Old English legal words were used in exclusively professional senses; since, moreover, even fewer have retained their legal flavor to the present day (D. Mellinkoff 46–48), we remain free to borrow such terms as *folklaw* and *trothplight* if we wish to emphasize the distinctive character of Anglo-Saxon legal institutions. In this respect, Anglo-Saxon historians are far more fortunate than their Frankish colleagues, who must struggle with the straitjacket of Roman terminology into which the continental notaries forced their folklaw, and who must always "think twice," as Stephen White says, "before concluding that when a charter uses such terms as '*placitum*', '*iudex*', '*clamatio*', and '*judicium*', it establishes that a formal trial was held before a judge, at which formal pleadings were made by parties and which concluded with a formal judicial decision" (294).[13]

A more serious obstacle to understanding written accounts of the customary law of any traditional society, however, whether ninth-century Anglo-Saxon or twentieth-century Tiv, is the inherent incompatability of all written records with the operation of oral law. It is not simply that the craft-literacy of pre-Conquest England was ill adapted to recording contractual forms that had been developed to meet the needs of a predominantly oral society; the very fact that they are written down at all gives us the illusion that they operated in the same way as the legal forms with which we are more familiar. Literacy itself, as Goody reminds us, has been the "major contributory mechanism" in the evolution of modern jurisprudence (139), and we find great difficulty in imagining rules of law which are not written rules and do not function like written rules. This is why the fieldwork of modern anthropologists is of such value: it helps us to reconstruct the living custom behind the bare edicts of a Gundobad or a King Alfred, and to see how the omissions, inconsistencies, and ambiguities which would be marks of incompetence in a piece of literate legislation are merely signs of a legal system based on a quite different set of premises.

Though much that is obscure about Anglo-Saxon trothplight can be clarified by reference to other systems of customary law, this is not to imply that there is a uniform character to all preliterate law or that a specific institution found in one system can be assumed in all the others. There is, as Robert Redfield says, "no one 'primitive law' any more than there is one primitive society" (4). Just as the legal practices of the Tiv and the Barotse are quite distinct from one another, so too are those of the Anglo-Saxons from those of the Franks—and, indeed, those of individual Anglo-Saxon or Frankish tribes from one another (the Mercians from the West Saxons, for instance, or the Salians from the Ripuarians). On the other hand, since there is a limit to the number of methods of making formal agreements available to members of small-scale societies in which literacy is rare or unknown, there is bound to be some overlap in the kinds of legal forms and procedures they adopt.[14] As long as we keep in mind that comparable legal systems simply offer us useful illustrations of analogous forms that can never in themselves constitute proof of actual practice, we will be able to go some way towards filling in gaps and explaining obscurities in the records of Anglo-Saxon law.

Anglo-Saxon troths were, then, very different from the legally enforceable promises we recognize today, but there is little reason to think that they were any less complex for being the product of immemorial custom rather than jurisprudential definition, or any less effective because they were enforced in the first instance by the local community rather than the king's courts. Lawyers, as A. W. B. Simpson observes, "always find it difficult to grasp the fact that a system of adjudication can function without law to regulate matters which they are accustomed to being so regulated" (1981, 273), so we should not be surprised by the silence of most legal historians on the subject of trothplight. In actual fact, the small place occupied by contracts in the surviving legal records suggests that for the most part the system worked so smoothly that there was little reason to refer to them in writing at all. Indeed, one might go further and claim that the beginnings of a modern law of contract in the late thirteenth and fourteenth centuries, so far from marking an advance toward greater social order, as Sir Henry Maine would have it, reflect a breakdown of the established conventions governing personal obligations.

The Machinery of Trothplight

Tokens

It is time now to return to Baldonet and the most thinglike feature of his trothplight. When he entered Saint Martin's to perform his ritual of servitude, Baldonet did so with bell ropes around his neck, and holding four pennies on top of his head. These concrete symbols belong to a very large category of similar objects whose handing over registered the actual *traditio* visible, clothing the abstract trothplight with a thinglike physicality. Here, for instance, is how an eleventh-century Lombard formulary describes the legal transfer of real estate. Before accepting the charter, the buyer must hear the vendor agree to the terms of sale, recited aloud after the notary ("Dicis ita? — Dico"), and instruct the witnesses to touch the purchase money he is offering in exchange ("totos vos rogo tangere"). The formulary then continues, "if he is Roman he should say the same; but if the seller is a Salian, Ripuarian, Frank, Goth or Alemann: 'Place the charter on the earth and set on it a knife, a marked staff, a glove, and a sod from the land, and a tree-branch, and plowing-gear [cultellum, festucam notatam, wantonem et wasonem terrae et ramum arboris et atramentarium], and' (in Alemannic law) 'a *wandilanc*'. And let him lift [them] from the earth, and while he is holding the charter, speak the *traditio* as we have given it above" (*Leges Langobardorum* 595).[15] Jacques Le Goff has drawn attention to an article on *investitura* in Du Cange's medieval Latin dictionary that lists almost a hundred such symbols (237–87), and though this number can be culled slightly by distinguishing between symbolic objects and symbolic gestures (such as "per digitum," "per osculum," and the curious "canum venaticorum apprehensione" [by collaring hunting dogs]),[16] it is still considerable. As Gurevich remarks, "all sorts of things — sword, spear, hammer, club, chair, gauntlet, head-dress, key, etc. — have, over and above their pragmatic use, a symbolical meaning which is called upon in court and other juridical proceedings" (1985, 176).

Du Cange's list is very heterogeneous and Le Goff is surely right to query his attempt to classify it according to Roman legal precedent into (1) objects connected with the earth, such as clods or turf, (2) various staffs of command (scepter, twig), and (3) objects connected with the *ius evertendi* (right to uproot), particularly knives. While Roman law had largely outgrown its oral phase and literate jurists had thoroughly rationalized its traditional forms, the customary law brought into Western Europe by the Germanic migrations remained comparatively untamed. Where medieval symbols were to survive down to recent times they too would become systematized: in nineteenth-century Scotland, for instance, where lands were regularly transferred with "earth and stone," mills with "clap and happer," fishing rights with "net and coble," town houses with "hasp and staple," and so on (Walker 3:48 n. 10), we can sense the normative hand of the literate jurist tidying up ancient custom. We may be surprised to learn that betrothal, the one contract (along with marriage) still widely formalized today with a symbolic token was not in earlier times invariably sealed with a ring: in mid-sixteenth-century France, for instance, engagements were often confirmed by a *denier à Dieu* (N. Davis 1987, 47) and in England by a *bowed grote* [bent penny] (*Child Marriages* xlix n. 1). Even more homely tokens might, however, sometimes be pressed into service: in England we hear of carved knitting needles, spindles, and bobbins (Macfarlane 1986, 300), and in France of woolen belts, ribbons, flowers, fruit, even, on one occasion, a piece of cake (Flandrin 51–52, 56).

The symbols of trothplight resist systematic analysis because, with few exceptions, their significance is still local and contingent (cf. M. Bloch 1933, 289), depending upon whatever associative trick had been found to aid their mnemonic function. Thus, an account of livery of seisin made to two brothers in Wakefield in 1275 concludes, "and the Steward, holding a rod in his hand, of which one end was black and the other white, gave seisin to Richard with the white end, because he was fair in colour, and gave seisin to Thomas with the black end" (quoted by Homans 254). It is for this reason that many of these symbols (like the *wandilanc* in the passage quoted above) have remained mysterious to this day. To seek retrospectively to categorize such objects according to any kind of abstract principle is contrary to the whole spirit in which local custom endowed them with mnemonic power. In this world of thinglike abstractions the significance of Baldonet's bell ropes need have extended no further than the walls of Marmoutiers; in another monastery bell ropes might have provided a quite different kind of legal garment, recording, for example, the installation of an abbot (see Du Cange s.v. *investitura*: *per funes*) and, indeed, had Baldonet been English the actual objects of his trothplight would probably have been quite different—"as a symbol of his change of status he shall take up a sickle or a goad or the arms of slavery [*seruitutis arma*] of this kind" (*LHP* ch. 78.2c; 244).

One generalization about the objects in Du Cange's list does seem worth making, however. Almost a quarter of them are sticks (*festucae*), similar wooden objects (*per ramum*, *per lignum*), or implements of the same general physical characteristics (*per baculum*, *per fustem*, *per ferulam pastoralem*, *per hastam*, *per sceptrum*, *per virgam*). Other Indo-European cultures, moreover, make an association between such wooden objects and contractual obligations: just as the feudal bond of vassalage could be broken by publicly throwing down the *festuca*—there is even a verb *exfestucare* (Le Goff 259)—so too Achilles publicizes his breach with Agememnon by dashing a wooden scepter to the ground (Havelock 1978, 129–30). The material cause for such an association may well be sought in the practicalities of early technology: even in comparatively modern times "the most important material for making records [apart from parchment] . . . was wood" (Clanchy 1993, 123), and recent discoveries of medieval rune-staves from Bergen show that this technology could be remarkably adaptable (Liestøl). Such evidence offers a key to the problem, mentioned in the last chapter, of the ancient linguistic bond between the words *tree* and *truth*, which reaches back to their earliest Germanic origins and beyond. If the object itself was in some sense the bond, then it is easy to see how the legal sense of *treowþ* might have evolved from its ultimate source in I-E. **dreu-* 'tree/wood'; a parallel semantic shift is offered by OE *wed* which can refer to either a symbolic object or a bargain concluded by means of one. Interestingly, the term for the old Roman form of trothplight, the *stipulatio*, appears to derive from *stipula* 'a stalk, twig, or reed', a diminutive of *stipes* 'a tree trunk.'

Many of the symbolic objects on Du Cange's list have to do with the craft of writing that will in time spell the end not only of the old formal contract but the whole legal system that supported it. However, as Clanchy has pointed out, this does not mean that a *traditio* made *per chartam*, *per librum*, or *per pergamenum* was accomplished by simply registering the contract in writing, any more than by offering his four pennies on the altar Baldonet was simply 'paying' for his entry into the monastic community.[17] In the eyes of the non-literate these documents, like the pennies, were employed for their symbolic value, and, particularly in the North where the influence of Roman law was weakest, only gradually came to be accepted as a substitute for the formal trothplight. Thus our Lombard formulary has the charter placed on the ground and symbolically transferred together with the other objects used in the *traditio*; in Anglo-Saxon England we hear of title deeds being placed on an altar along with a sod of turf (Birch 1:405), and similar practices continued after the Conquest (J. Hudson 163–64). Regardless of their contents, mere possession of title deeds might at times be a matter of considerable procedural significance to litigants in Anglo-Saxon lawsuits: the principle that the possessor of title deeds was "nearer to the oath" than his or her rival sometimes seems to have been used to decide the important question of whether plaintiff or defendant should be required to swear an oath of exculpation.[18] In Susan Kelly's words, "the value of a diploma as a title-deed resided less in the information which it contained than in its function as a potent symbol of ownership" (44), and in the extreme case of the *carta sine litteris* the symbolic parchment need not have had anything written on it at all (Gurevich 1985, 173–74).[19] Equally vivid as an illustration of this elaborate interplay between the mnemonic machinery of traditional law and the notary's written document are the charters described by Clanchy (1993, 38–39, 258–59) and Le Goff (283) which have survived to the present day with knives or similar objects still attached to them. Clearly, in such a world even the literate had little confidence in their ability to enforce agreements by means of letters alone.

Conventional legal history has generally sought to explain the origin of such tokens in a kind of commercial utilitarianism which I believe is foreign to the spirit of traditional law. For Maitland the *wed* must originally have been a valuable object put in pledge to guarantee the payment of a debt (P&M 2:186), while Holdsworth imagines that it began as some form of security to ensure the appearance of the defendant at a trial (2:83).[20] The choice of tokens, I suggest, had originally less to do with physical value, than with mnemonic effectiveness and durability; one early Irish law text says that no object may be given as pledge which is subject to "rust, mouse, death, or clothes-moth" (F. Kelly 165). Of course, tokens might be expensive (like a modern engagement ring), but that was not their main point: they were seen, not as objects to put in pawn or set against bail, but as symbols to be witnessed; in certain circumstances richness of material might indeed make them more memorable, but equally it might be symbolically quite inappropriate, or even from a practical point of view disadvantageous—by rendering them more likely to be stolen, for example. No doubt the passage of time could transform a symbolic token into a practical commercial expedient—it is, for instance, possible to see how the "God's penny" with which one might close a bargain to buy goods from a merchant could become in time the mundane down-payment we know today (P&M 2:208), or how a marked staff [*festuca notata*], such as the one mentioned by the Lombard notary, might at length be "rationalized" into the tally stick familiar to medieval accountants (cf. *SPM* 133)—but we should be careful about projecting our own preconceptions about business practice onto an age when literacy had as yet made only limited inroads on far older forms of transaction.[21] When a draper in the fifteenth-century farce of *Maitre Pierre Pathelin* is cheated out of some cloth by a client who passes off the "denier à Dieu" as the actual purchase price, there is a particular appropriateness about the fact that this client should be a lawyer.

The most dramatic example of social reliance on tokens was physical mutilation. As we have already seen, the author of *Genesis A* has no difficulty imagining circumcision as a "friðotacen" (2371) of Abraham's covenant with God, but even mutilation that looks purely punitive can be argued to have had a mnemonic function. "Germanic law is fond of 'characteristic' punishments," writes Maitland; "it likes to take the tongue of the false accuser and the perjurer's right hand" (P&M 2:453). Certainly, there is poetic justice in the fact that when he fights the betrayer of King Athelwold's trust, Havelok should sever Godric's hand—"Hw mithe he don him shame more?" (2754)—but mutilation might also serve a quite practical purpose. Without a tongue one cannot swear a false oath, and the lack of a right hand will prevent trothplight on a Bible or holy relic. When there were no central records in which to verify a stranger's trouthe, what better method could an oral folklaw use to warn of the presence of a convicted perjurer? *The Tale of Beryn*, describing a woman who has made a trumped up charge of desertion against the hero while he is traveling abroad, adds the otherwise gratuitous detail that "hir tunge was nat sclytt" (3204), evidently to suggest a deplorable indifference to publicizing perjury among her own people.[22] With other offenses, there is clear evidence that mutilation was intended to memorialize dishonesty: King Edmund's third decree (ca. 945), for instance, sentences thieving servants to the loss of a little finger, "as a sign" [in signum] (ch. 4; in Liebermann 1:191). A more common mark of villainy was the loss of an ear (P&M 2:497–98): Gregory of Tours's old enemy Leudast, having had one of his ears slit for running away from his master, was forced to seek royal protection, "since he could get no authorization to cover up the mark made on his body" [cum notam inflictam corpori occulere nulla auctoritate valeret] (5.48; 1:368). The function of such mutilation was clearly still understood at the end of the Middle Ages: in early-fourteenth-century England, for instance, William le Noble's father, concerned "lest sinister suspicion arise hereafter," obtained a royal certificate to prove that his son's right ear had been "torn off in his minority by the bite of a pig" (Rothwell *EHD* 825).[23] It would be foolish to suppose that mutilation might not also be meant as a painful and humiliating punishment,[24] but understood on its own terms it may seem rather less barbarous than some commentators have made it appear; "thus may one correct and still save the soul," as one late Anglo-Saxon code says (2 Cnut ch. 30.5; Liebermann 1:334).

Not surprisingly, the potency of legal tokens in this "âge poétique du droit," as Michelet called it, is amply attested in the romances. One of the best examples comes from *Havelok*, where the hero, restored to his rightful kingship, makes over the estate of the usurper Godard to his old ally Ubbe:

And þe king ful sone it yaf
Vbbe in þe hond wit a fayr staf,
And seyde, "Her Ich sayse þe,
Jn al þe lond, in al þe fe."
(2517–20)

What is being described here is the legal ritual known as *livery of seisin*, by which land is visibly and audibly transferred from one person to another. Henry Bracton, writing not very much earlier than the date of this poem, says that the ceremony must be performed on, or in sight of, the land in question, preferably by the "hasp or ring" of the door of a house, "if there is no house on the land . . . let [livery] be made him in the manner commonly called 'by the staff and rod' " [quod vulgariter dicitur per fustum et per baculum] (2:125). Bracton recommends a written charter for additional security, but one was clearly not required by law. By the early fourteenth century, though a tenant might still be enfeoffed "without charter, by horn or spur or rod," this was coming to be regarded as "the old law" (Holdsworth 3:223),[25] but the practice was still known to Littleton in the late fifteenth century (P&M 2:83), and, when supplemented by a written deed, was to survive even longer. There are indications that symbolic livery of seisin was still being practiced in Burgundy in the late fourteenth century (Ligeron and Petitjean 289–91) and, despite the paucity of direct evidence, we may feel confident of its having survived well into the sixteenth century in England. Holdsworth quotes "the usual manner of delivery of seisin" from West's *Symboleography* of 1615: after the reading of the deed, "the feoffor or his Atturney must take a clod of earth or a bough or a twig of a tree thereupon growing, or the ring or haspe of the door of the house, and deliver the same with the said deed unto the feofee or his Atturney" (3:225). Feoffment with livery of seisin remained theoretically available to conveyancers until 1925, though in practice it must have become very rare after the 1677 Statute of Frauds required that all contracts to sell land be in writing (Hamburger 374); in Scotland, symbolic "sasine" would continue to be an essential part of conveyancing until 1845 (Walker 3:50).

Rods and staves could be used to mark other kinds of bargain than the transfer of land, of course. In the Auchinleck version of *Sir Beues of Hamtoun*, for instance, the king's appointment of Beves as his marshal is confirmed with a symbolic staff of office:

"Fet me," a seide, "me ȝerde of golde!
Gii, is fader, was me marchal,
Also Beues, is sone, schal."

His ȝerd he gan him þer take;
So þai atonede wiþ oute sake.
(3506–10)

There are, moreover, many other kinds of legal tokens on display in the romances. Probably the best known are the sword and spurs that betokened knighthood, "Horn he dubbede to kniȝte / Wiþ swerd and spures briȝte" (*King Horn* 499–500), or the glove which committed the knight to judicial combat, "Lo, here my gloue wyth þe to fyght! / Y undyrtake thys case" (*Earl of Toulouse* 1100–01). These tokens, and a host of other similar objects, take their place in the great medieval storehouse of mnemonic furniture, which the lawyers were certainly not alone in stocking. From the keys which identified the statue of Saint Peter over the porch of the church to the ale-stake which attracted customers to the tavern, the medieval world was filled with such props for the nonliterate.

Many medieval symbols must have been lost without trace, and only a tiny handful of legal tokens have survived to the twentieth century. Apart from wedding and engagement rings, there are a few embossed and adhesive stamps to preserve the once rich symbolism of seals and signets (see Clanchy 1993, 308–17), and at least to the First World War the "king's shilling" was still being used to enlist recruits in the army; no doubt a roomful of lawyers might put their heads together and come up with a few more (I have heard, for instance, of someone being asked to make a deposit of ten silver dollars in order to set up a trust fund in Canada), but they would be mere dusty curiosities. Thus the original effect produced by those medieval tokens we can still recognize is only to be recovered by a considerable effort of the imagination. What, for instance, are we to make of the statement (apparently attached by chance to a mid-tenth-century Anglo-Saxon ordinance on holding hundred courts) that a "Hryðeres belle, hundes hoppe, blæshorn: ðissa ðreora ælc bið anes scill' weorð; ⁊ ælc is melda geteald" [An ox's bell and a dog's collar, and a blast-horn—either of these three shall be worth a shilling, and each is reckoned an informer] (Liebermann 1:194; Whitelock *EHD* 394)? This sentence, now thoroughly opaque, was once clear enough to anyone for whom these objects had an unambiguous legal status.[26] The effort to recover their meaning is worth making, however, if we wish to penetrate what Gurevich has called the "semantic density of the social behavior of medieval people" (1985, 176). For the twentieth-century reader one avenue into this lost world is offered by the modern African novel.

An engagement of marriage is one of the few contracts still confirmed in the West with a symbolic token, but the scene in John Munonye's novel *The*

Only Son where the hero, Nnanna, first approaches his future bride, Ego, perhaps suggests something of the ritual formality that must once have surrounded betrothal. Nnanna, carrying a coconut, is introduced by his uncle to Ego's father: "There's a fruit we have found in your farm. Fortunately for us, neither you nor any of your kinsmen can eat it. We on the other hand love that fruit very much and wish to take it away" (69). Called from her hut, Ego displays great reluctance to accept Nnanna's proferred coconut (as "her mother had emphasized while coaching her for the great event"), even turning her back on him until reprimanded by her father; then, hissing disgustedly and with her face averted, Ego stretches out her hand and wrenches the coconut from Nnanna's grasp, "and with that the formal betrothal began."[27] A similar sense of ritual solemnity is conveyed though in a very different context in T. Obinkaram Echewa's *The Crippled Dancer*; here the compact is one of enmity rather than love: Erondu, the hero's grandfather, "reached towards the roof of the nearby house and broke off a mid-rib from a palm leaf on one of the mats, rubbed it into a signal twig and handed it to Izhima. 'De-Izhima,' he said solemnly. 'Here before the assembly of Njikara's children, I am handing you this twig as a signal. Tell Elewachi Owunna to stay away from me and what is mine. Tell him not to come near my compound or into it. Tell him if I see him near anything that belongs to me, he and I will bump heads in a way that will make him dizzy for the rest of his life. Tell him for me.'" (125). Munonye offers us a glimpse beyond the functional level when Nnanna's mother employs a piece of broomstick in a similar context: "That is my ogu and I have given it to you and your parents," she says, and the narrator adds, "Ogu is the moral force, that potent spur of righteousness, who drives the innocent against his aggressor" (76).[28] As a final illustration, though this time the token is a far more personal memento, there is a scene in Elechi Amadi's *The Slave* where the hero's grandmother, Nyege, submits a land dispute to the village council for arbitration: "Elders, if that land is proved to be his, I shall pay four hundred manillas. Take my pipe as a token" (23). Significantly, for all three novelists such tokens are associated with an older generation—a sign that in literate modern Nigeria their days are already numbered.

Gestures

Though the physical tokens of folklaw trothplight were, in practice, inseparable from the physical gestures that accompanied their deployment (Baldonet's pennies seal his compact only when they are offered on the altar, for instance, and his bell ropes, to judge from descriptions of similar ceremonies, only when he puts them to work by ringing the abbey bells), not every troth-plight required a material transfer, and in some the actual public gesture was its most conspicuous feature. Thus the early medieval dotal charter was sometimes referred to as an *osculum* after the kiss with which the betrothed couple marked the settlement of their dowry (P. Reynolds 56 n. 6). Other obvious examples include the kiss and the enclosing of hands with which the feudal lord confirmed a vassal as his "homme de bouche et de mains," the light blow (*collée*) administered by the priest to the aspirant to knighthood, even the shared drink which supplemented, and sometimes replaced, the God's penny in agreements between merchants. Such conventional gestures are found in other societies too: "I tried instinctively to seal the oath," says the narrator of Achebe's novel *A Man of the People*, "by touching my lips and pointing to the sky with my swearing finger" (145). But, as with tokens, these gestures might equally well be quite local and even improvised. White cites an instance from Baldonet's monastery of Marmoutiers in which the final settlement of a lawsuit, heard in the count's court, between the monastery and a man called Thibaud of Vendôme was marked in the following way: "To Thibaud's house there came a *villanus* who was trying to bet back a donkey of his which Thibaud's sons had taken from him. The members of the count's court then asked the prior to redeem the donkey for this peasant as a '*memoria*' of the act by which Thibaud and his wife and children had given up their quarrel with the monks and come to an agreement with them. He did so. Seventeen people witnessed this curious ceremony" (298). In the same vein is the story of William the Conqueror granting land to the abbot of Rouen, not only with the conventional *traditio* of a knife, but also by playfully offering to stab the prelate through the hand (P&M 2:87). Abingdon Abbey furnishes a further Anglo-Norman example: Giralmus de Curzun marked the resumption of his payment of tithes to the abbot, after a period when they had been in dispute, by publicly breaking the bolts of his barn with his own hands (cited by J. Hudson 160).

For the majority of routine transactions, however, a simple handshake (or handslap) seems to have sufficed.[29] We have already seen the plighting of troth in Chaucer associated with a handshake, and this gesture appears in the romances and the ballads as well. In *Athelston*, for example, when the king is tricked into an agreement by the villain, "Þanne þe Kyng his hand vp rauȝte. / Þat false man his trowþe betauȝte" (154–55), and in the ballad of "Young Beichan," the fair Susie Pye, who makes a rather better bargain with her lover, demands,

Give me the truth of your right hand,
The truth of it give unto me,

That for seven years ye'll no lady wed,
Unless it be along with me.
(Child 1:469)

The shaking or clapping of hands is of great antiquity—known for instance to the Romans and appearing very early in Germanic law (P&M 2:188–89). Though English royal courts, certainly after the thirteenth century, would not have recognized the handshake as sufficient in itself to clothe a contract, this was not the case in the local courts: "The special characteristic of the borough law of agreement, as contrasted with the common law of the fourteenth century, was its acceptance of the validity of the 'fides facta' as sufficient to bind a bargain. . . . The contract was formal, though a once elaborate ceremonial had been gradually reduced to the simplest of forms, a mere grasp of hands" (*BC* 2:lxxx). The stubborn survival of this gesture down to our own time suggests how vital a legal form it had once been (Lucke 294–96), even if busy judges in the late thirteenth century chose to deny it access to the king's courts.

Oaths

A further feature of Baldonet's trothplight was the making of a public declaration, for the witnesses are *audientes* as well as *videntes*. Possibly he would have taken part in a ritual dialogue (a survival of the Roman *stipulatio*) in which he publicly confirmed the terms of his agreement, and he may well have made a formal declaration as he placed his offerings on the altar: a little later in the century a Breton serf called Christianus is recorded as saying at this point in the ceremony, "by these four pennies I commit myself into the service of Saint Martin and his monks" (*Livre des serfs* 115). Finally, despite the fact that oaths were sometimes regarded with circumspection by the church (Silving 1343–44), it would have been most unusual had he not bound himself and his descendants in a solemn oath; some later English contracts involving land make specific mention of the oath, apparently with the hope of securing a procedural advantage in any subsequent litigation (Postles), but generally speaking this feature was so ubiquitous that any explicit reference to it would probably have seemed redundant. The *Livre des serfs* gives no actual example of an oath of servitude per se, but when it says that Baldonet bound himself "thus, namely by the rule [ea videlicet ratione], that not only he himself but also any children that might be born to him would serve in the capacity of serf under the perpetual authority of [the abbot] of Marmoutiers and the brothers of that house" (4), it is not difficult to imagine the actual words of Baldonet's commitment rendered here in indirect speech. Another formula found in the *Livre des serfs* suggests the rhetorical quality of an actual oath of servitude even more strongly: "namely thus, that alive he would serve us wherever we might command, and dead he would leave to us whatever he possessed" (22).

Oaths such as this were the cornerstone of the folklaw yet, as I have said, only in exceptional circumstances were they ever committed to writing. Such circumstances clearly lie behind one of the earliest specimens of French and High German to have come down to us, the Strasbourg oaths (Studer and Waters 24–25). When Louis the German and Charles the Bald made an alliance against their brother Lothair in 842, the problem of how to bind their followers in an oath for which they had no common language was solved with considerable ingenuity. Louis the German swore in French for the benefit of his brother's soldiers and Charles reciprocated in German. A simpler solution, to our way of thinking, might have been for both kings to swear in Latin, a language they would certainly have had in common, but such a trothplight could never have ensured the loyalty of their unilingual followers. In an oral society the precise words of the oath, at the moment that they are spoken, bind speaker and listener by virtue of an inherent performative power which resists translation or paraphrase.[30] That is why the mute, the deaf, and even the stammerer set the lawyers such a difficult problem: "It is clear that one who is dumb can neither stipulate nor promise, since he cannot speak or utter the words appropriate to a stipulation" (Bracton 2:286; cf. *LHP* ch. 78.6; p. 244). In some ways their position was analogous to that of an illiterate in modern Western society. Had the cleric who recorded Baldonet's entry into servitude tried also to set down in Latin the terms of any Frankish oath he might have sworn, Baldonet could quite properly have objected that he had agreed to no such thing.

To evoke something of the awe a formal oath, taken on a sacred object, might have held for the medieval swearer, I turn again to modern Nigeria. In one of Chinua Achebe's short stories, "The Voter," a party worker named Roof, having accepted a bribe to vote for the opposition candidate, is forced to confirm this treachery with an oath:

> The man nudged his companion and he brought forward an object covered with a red cloth and proceeded to remove the cover. It was a fearsome little affair contained in a clay pot with feathers stuck into it.
>
> "This *iyi* comes from Mbanta. You know what that means. Swear that you will vote for Maduka. If you fail to do so, this *iyi* take note."
>
> Roof's heart nearly flew out when he saw the *iyi*; indeed he knew the fame of Mbanta in these things. But he was a man of quick decision. What could a single vote cast in secret for Maduka take away from Marcus's certain victory? Nothing.
>
> "I will cast my paper for Maduka; if not this *iyi* take note." (*Girls at War* 16–17)

Later, faced in the voting booth with the problem of remaining loyal to his chief without breaking a solemn oath, Roof equivocates: "He folded the paper, tore it in two along the crease and put one half in each box. He took the precaution of putting the first half in Maduka's box and confirming the action verbally: 'I vote for Maduka'" (19). Roof's solution is one that Baldonet's contemporaries could have appreciated.

In *Havelok*, Earl Godric, summoned by the dying Athelwold, solemnly swears to protect the king's young daughter until she is old enough to marry. Like his Anglo-Saxon and Frankish predecessors, the king makes Godric swear upon sacred objects, and his oath too ("Withuten lac, withuten tel") has formulaic qualities:

A wel fair cloth bringen he dede,
And þer-on leyde þe messe-bok,
Þe caliz, and þe pateyn ok,
Þe corporaus, þe messe-gere.
Þer-on he garte þe erl suere,
Þat he sholde yemen hire wel,
Withuten lac, withuten tel,
Til þat she were tuelf winter hold,
And of speche were bold,
And þat she covþe of curtesye,
Gon and speken of luue-drurye,
And til þat she louen muthe
Wom-so hire to gode þoucte,
And þat he shulde hire yeue
Þe heste man þat micthe liue.

(185–99)

Later Earl Godric thinks he has found a way to reconcile his own dynastic ambitions with the terms of this oath when he stumbles across a hulking young porter called Havelok:

Þe king Aþelwold me dide swere
Vpon al þe messe-gere
Þat I shude his douthe[r] yeue
Þe hexte [man] þat mithe liue,
. . . .
Hwere mithe I finden ani so hey
So Hauelok is, or so sley?

(1078–85)

The whole subject of such equivocation will be explored more fully in the next chapter, but for now we may take these scenes from *Havelok* as illustrative of oath-taking at its most elaborate, suggesting something of the sacral power that the oath might exercise over the medieval imagination.

There is, of course, nothing exceptional about Godric's oath in *Havelok*, other than the detail in which it is described, for the plots of Middle English metrical romances regularly turn on the fulfilling or breaking of such oaths. In the romance world, stress on the virtue of absolute fidelity to one's given word is ubiquitous. The heroine of *The Earl of Toulouse* may speak for all:

Certys, yf thou hym begyle,
Thy soule ys yn grete paryle,
Syn thou haste made hym othe;
Certys, hyt were a traytory,
For to wayte hym [wyth] velany;
Me thenkyth hyt were rowthe!
(295–300)

We shall find a reflection of this attitude in rather more exalted company when we return to a closer examination of the Ricardian poets' treatment of troth-plight in Chapter 8. For the moment, however, I wish only to stress the central importance of the oath in the operation of the folklaw.

The very first of King Alfred's laws reads, "first, it is most necessary that we should instruct each man to keep faithfully his oath and compact" (Liebermann 1:46),[31] and a proclamation of his grandson Æthelstan made at Exeter circa 930 takes measures against hardened offenders, "because [their] oaths and compacts and guarantees are all overturned and broken . . . and we know of nothing else to trust in, except for this" [we nytan nanum oþrum þingum to getruwianne, butan hit ðis sy] (Liebermann 1:166). That all social intercourse depended finally on an ability to accept the sworn word at face value is underlined by the respect accorded to the concept of oathworthiness in the law codes. The West Saxon *Laws of Ine* (688–726), for instance, make oathworthiness ("gif he aðwyrðe bið") an important precondition to allowing a man accused of theft to clear himself by compurgation (ch. 46; Liebermann 1:108). As the first edict of Alfred's son Edward (899–924) makes clear, the alternative to compurgation (swearing an exculpatory oath along with a set number of respectable supporters) for those who had lost this oathworthiness was the ordeal: "Moreover, we decree that those who are, by common report, perjurers, or who fail to exculpate themselves by oath, or whose oaths are successfully challenged in court, shall never afterwards be oathworthy [þæt hy siððan aðwyrðe næran]; rather they shall be 'ordeal-worthy' [ac ordales wyrðe]" (ch. 3; Liebermann 1:140).[32] The edict issued by Æthelstan at Grately goes even further: it forbids burial in sanctified ground to anyone reputed to have sworn a perjured oath [*manað*] and thus to have forfeited his oathworthy status ("ðæt he næfre eft aðwyrþe ne sy"), unless he have special dispensation from his bishop (ch. 26; Liebermann 1:164).

The old assumptions upon which the folklaw depended lingered on long after the spread of literacy and the growth of a centralized judicial system had begun to undermine them. As late as 1613 we find the attorney general of Ireland insisting on the fundamental importance of oaths in terms which would not have seemed out of place in King Alfred's day: "An oathe is of such use and power in all affaires publique and private, as that every man's estate in particuler, and the state of the realme in generall, doth depend uppon the truthe and sincerity of men's oathes" (*Recusant Documents* 250). Though the Anglo-Saxon term "oathworthy" does not occur in legal circles after Bracton used it in the mid thirteenth century (3:71), the equivalent law French term, *franche leye*, survived into the fourteenth century (e.g., *YB 16 Edw. III (i)*, 61–63), and its English calque was still known in the early seventeenth (see *OED*, s.v. *Frank-law*). As should be obvious, this concept of oathworthiness underpinned ethical senses of the word trouthe itself, and the later phrase "worthi of trouthe" was virtually synonymous with the adjective "oathworthy": "suche peple [theves, comune women, and other mysdoers] withe oute consience mowe not of reson be vnderstonden worthi of trouthe nor to bere witnesse of trouthe in any cause wher ryght ys to be enquered" (*Anthology* 233). In such legal contexts, then, the idea of oathworthiness clearly remained important even after the actual term had fallen out of use: the Norman *Summa de Legibus* (of about the same period as Bracton) says that "all those convicted of perjury and bad faith, and those overcome in a judicial duel, and all whose loss of credibility is notorious [omnes increduli et publica infamia notabiles], are prohibited from acting as witnesses or as compurgators" (ch. 85.6; *CN* 2:203), and similar lists of exclusion are still to be found in English borough ordinances as late as the end of the fifteenth century (*BC* 1:49–51; Henry 57). In remote, tightly knit communities such prohibitions were to survive even longer; under the laws of the iron-ore miners of the forest of Dean, copied down in the late seventeenth century, for instance, while miners might deny by oath that they owed the king any taxes, "if the Miner bee found by his fellowship forsworne then the Miner shall be attaint against the King and shall never bee believed more agst any man" (*Book of Dennis* 77).

Since any hint of bad faith might compromise one's legal standing in the community, it was no small matter to accuse someone of perjury. One of the very earliest of the Anglo-Saxon codes, that issued by the Kentish kings Hlothere and Eadric (673–685), provides a fine of nineteen shillings for any such slander—twelve shillings to the king, six to the victim, and one to the man in whose house it was uttered (ch. 11; Liebermann 1:10–11).[33] Again, these attitudes long outlasted the Norman conquest. A chapter on the infamous "De Infams" in the late-thirteenth-century *Mirror of Justices* puts perjurers at the top of a list which includes, among others, grave-robbers, brothel-keepers, and corrupters of nuns (133–34). Fortescue, in the fifteenth century, bristles at the suggestion that those of any social standing would contemplate perjury; such a thing, he says, is unthinkable (*cogitare nequit*), "not merely because of their fear of God, but also to preserve their honor, and avoid both the public disgrace which would ensue, and the damage that their infamy would cause their heirs" (*De laudibus* 68). Even in Elizabethan England, nine hundred years after Hlothere and Eadric's code, wrongly to accuse someone of being "a false forsworne man" could cost one six pounds in the court of King's Bench (*SCD* xciv n. 3).

We have not yet finished with the role of oaths in the folklaw, for the full social implications of their use will only emerge when we come to consider their role in trial procedure in the next chapter. For the time being, however, let us return to the way contracts were established, rather than challenged.

Witnesses and Borrows

One final element, the presence of witnesses (Baldonet's *videntes et audientes*) needs little elaboration. Unless the parties were already well known to one another and the agreement relatively unimportant, witnesses were essential to the traditional contract. The elaborate ritual of a full-dress *traditio* was intended primarily for their eyes and ears; they were, in a sense, the living charters on which the folklaw recorded its contracts. Under certain circumstances, their support may have been all that was needed to compel observance of an agreement. Thus, the first step in enforcing the performance of a contract according to the *Pactus Legis Salicae* was to go the promisor's house "with the witnesses or with those whose duty was to establish the amount in question" [cum testibus vel cum illis, qui pretium adpretiare debent] (ch. 50.1; 190), and only when this failed were formal proceedings to be instituted in the mallberg (the local court) or before the count. In such an event, the strongest case that either party could make was by instrumental witness proof. From Anglo-Saxon England we have the form of an oath for one "who stands with another as a witness," and no litigant was in much danger of losing where a sufficient number of trustworthy witnesses were prepared to swear: "In the name of Almighty God, as I stand here, unbidden and unbribed [unabeden ⁊ ungeboht], as a truthful witness [on soðre gewitnesse] for N, so I saw with my own eyes and heard with my own ears that which I will say beside him" (*Swer*. 8; Liebermann 1:398).

Problems were likely to arise, however, where the contracting parties came from different communities, each with its own views of who might make a credible witness. In 962–963 King Edgar, apparently in an attempt to forestall disputes between Anglo-Saxons and Danes, sought to institute an official system of witnesses, ordering each borough to appoint thirty-six, two or three of whom should be present at every transaction: "⁊ swa geæþdera manna syn on ælcum ceape twegen oððe þry to gewitnysse" (ch. 6.2; Liebermann 1:210). Witnesses became particularly important when agreements were made outside the immediate community. According to Edgar, anyone failing to notify his neighbors that he was setting out intending to make a purchase, or failing to declare the purchase and the witnesses to it on his return home, risked forfeiting his bargain or even (if he were unable to cite proper witnesses) his life (ch. 7–11; 1:210–12). Analogous requirements had appeared in the late-seventh-century Kentish code of Hlothere and Eadric (ch. 16–16.3; 1:11). No doubt such provisions were intended to prevent disputes arising from accusations of theft or receiving stolen goods, but they serve to remind us that oral procedure can only have been effective as long as the administration of justice was largely a local matter and courts were not required to deal with strangers whose oath-worthiness could not be known.[34] The Salic law's chapter, "De migrantibus," which attempts to regulate the movement of strangers into established communities (*Pactus Legis Salicae* ch. 45; 173–76), offers a particularly striking illustration, but as late as the fifteenth century we can still hear echoes of a situation which had once informed the motif of the wanderer and the outcast in Old English poetry: a borough ordinance from Sandwich bars anyone who has "betrayed his lord in any way" from acting as compurgator, "as a Frenchman may have done in his own country from which he has fled to ours" (*BC* 1:51).

One further participant in the oral contract needs to be considered in this context: that is the *borh* [borrow] or guarantor of an agreement, whose role in the folklaw trothplight is one of the least understood. To stand borrow for someone was apparently to act as their surety and, at a later date, to risk penalty if they failed to honor their obligations. Æthelred's first code (ca. 1000), for instance, decrees that when the accused fails to turn up for an ordeal his *borh* is to be responsible for paying compensation to the accuser (ch. 1.7; Liebermann 1:218)—though it is possible of course that the borrow is here merely holding the bail money rather than paying it out of his own pocket. On the surface, this certainly appears to be a very different role from that of a witness, but I shall argue that the distinction is far more marked in literate law than it would have been under a traditional system. Certainly, older explanations of the origin of the *borh* need close examination: "We must remember," writes Maitland, "that in very old times the surety or pledge had in truth been the principal debtor, the creditor's only debtor, while his possession of the *wed* gave him power over the person whose *plegius* [i.e., borrow] he was. Hence it is that when we obtain details of the ceremony by which faith is 'made' or 'given' or 'pledged', we often find that the manual act takes place, not between the promisor and the promisee, but between the promisor and a third person who is sometimes expressly called a *fideiussor*" (P&M 2:191). What is really happening is something like this: Roger lends Ralph an ox and requires him to provide a borrow (Alan) for its safe return; when he comes for the animal Ralph brings with him a token—by Maitland's account originally an object of some value (P&M 2:186)—which he hands either directly to Alan, or to Roger who in turn passes it on. Should Ralph break the agreement that Alan is guaranteeing, the account runs, he will then forfeit the token. But in such a case why do we need Alan at all? Since, as Maitland concedes, Alan "does not accept any legal liability for the promise," Roger would surely be better off keeping the token himself; at least that way he could be sure of some compensation should he lose his ox. To hand it back to Ralph's borrow seems to make very little sense. Raoul Berger puts it somewhat differently: "no theory satisfactorily explains how the surety became liable by *taking* the staff from the creditor when the debtor bound himself by *giving* a pledge-symbol" (167). But Berger's own view that suretyship originated in the idea of hostage-giving, a view also supported by Holdsworth (2:84), does not get round this central problem very much better than an appeal to commercial expediency.

Only our difficulty in imagining a legal order erected on a set of premises quite different from those assumed by the modern lawyer prevents us from seeing a far simpler explanation. Borrows were originally the primary witnesses to contracts—people trusted by both parties to give a reliable account of what had been agreed should there later be a dispute—and the token was handed to them because it was their memory that would preserve the agreement and their testimony that might be needed to enforce it. Chapter 46 of the *Pactus Legis Salicae* (176–81) describes an elaborate ritual for transferring property. In the public court, the donor selects a middleman unrelated to him ("qui ei non pertineat") and before at least three witnesses throws a staff (*festuca*) into his lap; the middleman then returns to the donor's house and in the presence of three guests takes the property into his power ("in potestate sua"); finally, before twelve months are out the middleman, again in open court and with a further three witnesses, must throw the staff into the lap of the ultimate donee.[35] Paul Vinogradoff, on the evidence of a series of tenth-century memorandums from Medhamstead (Northamptonshire), shows that similar ceremonies involving middlemen certainly took place in England: "What responsibility was incurred by the sureties we do not know, but the principle itself is clear and important enough. Third persons intervene in cases of sale or exchange: they vouch for the validity of the title transferred" (160). These East Anglian middlemen are usually referred to as *festermen* (though the terms *borh* and *boruhhand* sometimes occur).

Later the borrow's role might develop into that of a full-fledged surety, personally liable for the good faith of the promisor, but, just as we cannot assume because the God's penny might later become a simple down-payment that this had always been its function, so here we should be cautious about reading backward from later developments. In fact, the institution of the "denier à Dieu" follows exactly the procedure described above; having closed the bargain, the purchaser hands the merchant a token penny, which is then entrusted to God to enlist him as borrow for the contract (in actual practice it was usually given as alms to the poor).[36] Similarly, when Baldonet lays his pennies and ropes on the altar of Saint Martin's, he is in effect making God the borrow of his agreement with the abbot.

Viewed in this light the otherwise puzzling reference in King Alfred's laws (ch. 33) to an agreement made by God-borrow—"gif hwa oðerne godborges oncunne ⁊ tion . . ." (Liebermann 1:66)—becomes quite intelligible (see P&M 2:191–93). It will of course present little difficulty to readers of Middle English romance where the appeal to God or his saints to act as borrow to an agreement or claim is common. One of the best examples comes from the *Gest of Robyn Hode* where the impoverished Sir Richard at the Lee is negotiating a loan from the outlaw:

> "Hast thou any frende," sayde Robyn,
> "Thy borowe that woldë be?"
> "I haue none," than sayde the knyght,
> "But God that dyed on tree."
> "Do away thy iapis," then sayde Robyn,
> "Thereof wol I right none;
> Wenest thou I wolde haue God to borowe,
> Peter, Poule, or Johnn?
> "Nay, by hym that me made,
> And shope both sonne and mone,
> Fynde me a better borowe," sayde Robyn,

"Or money getest thou none."
    "I haue none other," sayde the knyght,
"The sothe for to say,
But yf yt be Our derë Lady;
She fayled me neuer or thys day."
    "By dere worthy God," sayde Robyn,
"To seche all Englonde thorowe,
Yet fonde I neuer to my pay
A moche better borowe." (Child 3:59)

Sir Richard is in luck because Robin holds the Virgin in special regard, but the passage makes clear that though the appeal to a supernatural borrow may have lost some of its force by the late Middle Ages its function was still well understood. The outlaw assumes that only those unable to find respectable human borrows will appeal to God or "Peter, Poule, or Johnn," an assumption which Langland evidently shared: "For beggeres borwen euermo and hir borgh is god almyȝty" (*PPl* B.7:82). However, Robin clearly regards these figures as potential guarantors or unimpeachable witnesses rather than sureties in any conventional sense: after all, to pledge God or his saints, even metaphorically, offers a difficult concept. The same idea is quite explicit in Lydgate's lines:

þe goddis inmortal,
. . . .
Vn-to recorde with al myn hert I take;
And touchyng þis my borwys I hem make,
In witnessyng we ment[e] noon offence.
(Lydgate, *Troy Book* 1:1117–21)

But there are many similar instances (e.g., Chaucer, "Squire's Tale" 595–97, and Gower, *CA* 4:960–630).

That the responsibility for finding an acceptable borrow would, reasonably enough, have fallen on the prospective borrower did not necessarily mean that the borrow was therefore personally answerable for him or her. Whatever was to happen later, borrows seem originally to have been answerable primarily to themselves: their standing in the community (their trouthe) depended upon the reputation for impartiality that had recommended them for the job in the first place, and it was this that was put at risk. An Anglo-Saxon case from Medhamstead, where "a man who 'takes the *feste*' on behalf of the buyer appears at the same time as one of the *festermen* found by the seller," suggested to Vinogradoff "that the fact of being a *festerman* did not involve a one-sided partiality in favour of one of the parties concerned" (161). Even in the courts of Chaucer's London we can still observe the old system at work: when Joan Thurkell was sued by her landlord in 1386 for refusing to vacate his property, she claimed that two years earlier, in the presence of "a certain Robert Kent, who was acting for him," they had agreed on a thirty-year lease and sealed it with a God's penny; Robert Kent duly backed up her story and the landlord was thrown into prison for slander (*Calendar of Select Pleas* 124–25).

The importance of the borrow's duty to see that both sides lived up to their agreement is particularly marked when what has been agreed on is an appearance in court. We will naturally turn to what looks like a modern analogy, the surety who stands bail for a person accused of wrongdoing, and assume that the borrow's primary duty was owed to the court. However, an incident in Gregory of Tours suggests that the Franks may have viewed his role rather differently. Duke Guntram Boso, summoned to stand trial before King Guntram and his nephew King Childebert, gets Ageric, bishop of Verdun, to act as *fideiussor* for his appearance (9.8; 2:238); subsequently found guilty, Guntram Boso is killed by a mob while trying to escape the sentence (9.10; 2:244), yet later we learn that Ageric is struck with remorse for the fact that the duke had been killed whilst he was acting as borrow ("pro eo quod Gunthramnus Boso, pro quo fideiussor exteterat, interfectus essit) (9.23; 2:272). Clearly, Ageric does not feel himself answerable only to one side, as his modern counterpart might do; if he had a duty to the court to see that the accused answered its summons, he had also a duty to the defendant to see that he got a fair hearing. A similar situation arose in post-Conquest England when Count Alan of Brittany stood surety for the appearance of William of Saint Calais, bishop of Durham, before the king in 1088. A move to have the bishop arrested on his arrival produced an outraged reaction from the count, who, since he had already received some of Saint Calais's confiscated lands, might seem to have had little reason to side with the accused on this point: "I have brought him from his castle to the king's court after giving my word that if the king refused to do such justice as he could not justly refuse to one of his bishops, I would bring him safely to his castle. . . . And I strongly ask the lord my king that he should not make me belie my faith since he would not be able to count on me in the future" (*English Lawsuits* 1:100). As royal authority became more powerful and peremptory, the *fideiussor*'s scope for intervention became more and more limited, and gestures such as Earl Alan's began to look more and more old-fashioned.[37]

Personal suretyship seems to have played a particularly prominent part in the social life of medieval Ireland and Wales (Stacey) and a parallel to the kind of role I am claiming for the borrow is provided by the earliest type of surety recorded in Irish law, the *naidm*. D. A. Binchy argues that, in contrast to the *aitire*, who pledged his body (i.e., acted as hostage) and the *rath*, who pledged his goods, "the *naidm* pledged his 'honor' that the agreement guaranteed by him would be duly fulfilled"; Binchy also suggests that the *vindex* of early Roman law may have acted in a similar capacity (362). This notion of borrows as middlemen is unattractive to the modern lawyer because it appears to put them beyond, even above, the law. Yet, in Binchy's words, "the original surety was not designed merely to supplement or to facilitate the public administration of justice: he was rather a primitive substitute for it" (356–57). As Robin Chapman Stacey puts it, "suretyship is in many ways the quintessential institution of 'private' law" (44).

However difficult for the twentieth-century jurist, this insight turns out to have important implications for understanding the workings of the folklaw as a whole, Germanic no less than Celtic. As guarantor not only of private agreements, but also of appearances in court, the borrow threatens the very concept of public law by implying that justice itself was in some sense contractual, that, as an early Irish legal maxim has it, "law is founded on contracts" (F. Kelly 159). Folklaw litigation was far more like directed negotiation than imposed adjudication; rather than saying, if you harm your neighbor this is how you will be punished, the folklaw said, in effect, these are the kind of compacts you must make in order to restore the peace. Only some such assumption can explain Stephen White's curious observation that in the Marmoutiers records, "scribes did not distinguish clearly between people who judged cases and people who witnessed agreements" (293). Though most legal historians will readily concede that the modern distinction between civil and criminal law was far less marked at an earlier period, and that acts that today would lead straight to the police courts would in Anglo-Saxon England have been handled by private suit, rather fewer might be prepared to endorse Julius Goebel's suggestion that originally all adjective law was contractual: "Each step toward settlement depended upon consensual agreement—so the summons, the suspension of hostilities, the contract to observe the judgement, the final concord" (29). A detailed examination of procedure must wait till the next chapter, but I should like to conclude this discussion of trothplight by emphasizing its central importance in the resolution as well as the prevention of disputes.

Judicial Trothplight

"If one man accuse another," says the late-seventh-century Kentish code of Hlothere and Eadric, "three days after the provision of a borrow let them find themselves a mediator" [siþþan he him byrigan gesealdne hæbbe ⁊ ðonne ymb III niht gesecæn hiom sæmend] (ch. 10; Liebermann 1:10). However much they might be at odds over other matters, plaintiff and defendant first have to agree upon a *sæmend* before their dispute can even be heard. Such startling incitement to do-it-yourself justice is not, however, unique. The Salic law paints a similar picture: "Whenever the *raginburgii* sitting in the *mallobergo* investigate a case between two parties, the plaintiff should say to them: 'Speak the Salic law for us.' But if they are reluctant to do so, the plaintiff should say to them: 'Here I *tangano* you to speak the law for me according to the Salic law.' And if they are unwilling to speak it, seven of those *raginburgii* shall be assessed to pay 120 pence each (that is three shillings) before sunset [?] (this is a *schodo* in the *mallobergus*)" (*Pactus* 57.1; 215–16). As elsewhere in the Germanic codes, the compiler here resorts to Latinized forms of vernacular terms, because the Frankish words *mallobergus*, *raginburgii*, and *schodo* (usually glossed 'court', 'judges', and 'fine'), like the verb *tangano* ('challenge'), do not fit comfortably into the specialized terminology of literate law. This tactic, which is particularly marked in the case of the Salic law with its so-called malburg glosses, is symptomatic of a fundamental difference between the folklaw and more authoritarian legal systems. If the *raginburgii* had really been nothing more than 'judges' the compiler could have called them *iudices*. But what self-respecting *iudex* would ever turn control of the proceedings over to the plaintiff in this way? Why, moreover, should plaintiffs feel obliged to accept such a role, or defendants to concede it to them?

Like the Kentish *sæmendas*, the *raginburgii* look much more like mediators entrusted with conciliating the parties than judges appointed to decide between them. This would at least explain why they seem willing to confess themselves stumped by a knotty problem in a way that professional representatives of a modern legal system could never allow themselves to do.[38] Even more remarkable, however, is the suggestion that they could be fined if they failed to find satisfactory solutions — but then, apparently, even the local count (*grafio*) might be fined his full *wergeld* (quantum valet se redemat) for failing to intervene in a case after having been properly summoned by the plaintiff (*Pactus* 50.4).[39] To the modern legal mind the only possible explanation for such apparent encouragement to "sue the judge," as Marc Bloch puts it (1940, 2:373), must lie in an attempt by centralized authority to weaken regional autonomy by making local officials strictly accountable for their decisions, but there is little else in the Salic law to suggest such an attempt. In its earliest version, this most archaic of the Germanic codes presents itself as a *pactus* [sic] — an agreement between the nobles and the people on the best way of keeping the peace (*Inc.* 1), not as a set of rules handed down from above.[40] On the whole, it seems less likely that a central government was seeking to impose judicial restrictions that no judge would tolerate today, than that the *raginburgii* were constrained by a set of jural premises quite different from our own. The underlying assumption seems to be that judge and litigant were in some sense contractually bound (the one to provide a just solution, the other to abide by it), and that a failure by either side could incur penalty. To say this is, of course, to beg the question of what, beyond the pressure of local opinion, could make recalcitrant *raginburgii* and *grafiones* do their duty. Where such pressure failed, how could prominent members of the community be brought to respect any kind of sanction without the possibility of appeal to a higher authority? Where, if not to the king, was the dissatisfied litigant to turn?

The royal court did of course represent the ultimate source of justice, and it was certainly the final avenue of appeal for those who felt they had been denied fair treatment in their own community, but this is not to say that it stood at the top of a judicial pyramid, dealing with the serious cases and relegating others to lower courts. At its earliest stage, the folklaw worked from the bottom up and the king's court was merely the *mallobergus* writ large. Gregory of Tours tells how, after the decision of a local court to allow an accused murderer to clear his name by oath, the accusers, "not agreeing to this, placed their case in the hands of King Childebert" (7.23; 2:120); however, their action cannot be seen as marking a transition from private to criminal law, transferring to the king the role of prosecutor, for when no one appeared at the appointed time to plead against him, the suspect was duly sent home. As J. M. Wallace-Hadrill remarks of a dispute between two members of Theudebert's court, "it does not look as if the king's part in the matter was at all different from that of any other lord called upon to arbitrate between feuding dependants" (137).

Gregory of Tours reports hearing King Guntram, anticipating a possible feud between his two nephews, Childebert and Lothar, ask, "am I such a fool that I cannot mediate between them before the resentment spreads?" (9.20; 2:270), and Guntram's method, to placate the dissatisfied party with appropriate gifts, conforms absolutely to one of the basic premises of folklaw judgment as Berman describes it: "The answer is not to be found by asking the question: who is right? The answer is to be found by saving the honor of both sides and thereby restoring the right relationship between them" (1978, 589). By his own account, Gregory of Tours must have played just such a role in attempting to settle the famous blood feud of Sichar and Chramnesind (7.47; 2:152–56). The wronged party, Sichar, despite having been vindicated by a court in Tours ("in iudicio civium"), decides to take the law into his own hands and kills several members of Chramnesind's family; at this point Gregory himself tries to settle the dispute by offering to pay the offended party compensation out of his own episcopal coffers ("optuli argentum aeclesiae"), only to find that this time it is Chramnesind who turns to violent self-help. The feud is resolved, however (at least for the time being), by Gregory's paying Chramnesind out of church funds the half-compensation for which Sichar was now judged liable ("tunc datum ab aeclesia argentum, quae iudicaverant") — though the historian represents this as a quasi-legal move designed solely to bring about peace ("et hoc contra legis actum, ut tantum pacifici redderentur"). Much the same seems to happen in *Beowulf*, where Hrothgar recalls how he once resolved the feud between Ecgtheow and the Wilfings, apparently by paying Heatholaf's wergeld himself:

> Siððan þa fæhðe feo þingode;
> sende ic Wylfingum ofer wæteres hrycg
> ealde madmas; he me aþas swor.[41]
> (470–72)

Many centuries later, *The Awntyrs off Arthure* shows King Arthur acting in a similar role, offering rich lands from his own domain in order to prevent blood being shed in Gawain's territorial dispute with Galerun (664–89). We can even see the same principle at work in an actual Anglo-Saxon case: the early-tenth-century dispute over the ownership of Fonthill in Wiltshire. One of the parties, writing to ask King Edward to support his account of the previous tenure of the estate, adds: "gif hit elleshwæt bið, ðonne sceal ic ⁊ wylle beon gehealden on ðon ðe ðe to ælmessan ryht ðincð" [should it be otherwise, I must and will be bound by whatever seems right to you as a gift] (Harmer 32). Here, a litigant who is convinced of the justice of his cause apparently feels that an adverse decision should oblige the arbitrator to give him at least some recompense for the losses this might cause him.[42] There could hardly be a clearer illustration of the collaborative nature of Anglo-Saxon justice than this.

While appeal to the king represented the final chance to settle entrenched disputes, successful resolution seems to have depended as much upon respect for royal prestige as the power of royal sanctions. Asser, King Alfred's biographer, writes, "most obstinately driven on by their stubborn contentiousness, the parties would pledge themselves to accept the king's decision" [regis subire iudicium singuli subarabant], and, he implies, such was the king's wisdom that, "both sides would immediately hasten to carry it out" (92). But even a king as prestigious as Alfred could not guarantee that disputes would not flare up again: "If every decision which King Alfred gave is to be set aside," complains a frustrated litigant early in the next reign, "when can we be said to have settled?" [hwonne habbe we ðonne gemotad] (Harmer 31). Asser suggests that Alfred did try to intervene actively in judicial matters (and in this he may well have been following Charlemagne's example),[43] but, whatever the attitude of their Frankish contemporaries, his grandsons Æthelstan and Edmund and his great-grandson Edgar showed no great eagerness to divert legal clients to the royal court. Æthelstan recommends that anyone pressing a claim against his lord before the king should be fined the amount he is claiming if he is found to not have pursued the case through the proper channels first (2.3; Liebermann 1:152); Edmund will not allow the slayer a hearing ("ic nelle [þone] socne habban to minum hirede") until he has paid proper compensation as directed by his bishop (2.4; Liebermann 1:188–89); and Edgar refuses to see those who have not first been denied justice in their local court (ch 2; Liebermann 1:200). Even Cnut specifies that before approaching the king the litigant must first appeal to his own hundred (2.17; Liebermann 1:320).[44]

I have laid such emphasis on the way the process was driven from below, because this helps to explain one of the most striking symptoms of the contractual nature of folklaw justice: the composition tariffs that appear in all the early codes. That everything from a tooth to a human life had its price (as Louis Halphen puts it, "tout, jusqu'à l'existence humaine, est tarifé" [1948, 64]), and that payment of this price atoned for any injury, will become the ultimate example of trothplight's threat "to swallow up all public law" as soon as we are ready to accept that these tariffs were not imposed from above. There has been much discussion about whether they were inherited from a remote Germanic past, adapted from Roman law, or introduced by a civilizing Christian church, but few commentators seem to have doubted that, whether found, borrowed, or made, these tariffs resulted from an act of legislation, and that the king, whether acting alone or at the prompting of Christian missionaries, promulgated them for the benefit of his people. The problem with this view, however, is that it fails to show how the tariffs, or other provisions of the early codes, had, as Patrick Wormald puts it, any "actual value to judges sitting in court" (1977, 115)—though Wormald's own explanation, that the early codes were made for ideological and political show rather than forensic utility, seems to me unnecessarily ingenious. Only by ridding ourselves of the conviction that they represent "a set of rules enacted by a sovereign legislator and obeyed, more or less, by a subject people" (as T. M. Charles-Edwards suggests we do with the early Welsh laws [2]), will we be able to appreciate their true social significance.

We have only to try to imagine a reluctant king plagued by squabbling clients to see at once the attraction which an incontestable tariff might have held for him. The technology of writing offered beleaguered rulers a refuge from disgruntled litigants whining about such things as having to pay six shillings for cutting off a finger when someone in the next hundred had only had to pay four; the king could now point out that it was six shillings for a ring finger and four shillings for a middle finger (Æthelbert ch. 54.3 and 4; Liebermann 1:6) with a reasonable hope of putting an end to the matter. Wormald imagines that such tariffs may have been archaic at the time they were first written down (1977, 111–12), and must certainly have been so when they appear in the *Leges Henrici Primi* (e.g., ch. 93.1–37; 292–98), but their continued survival in continental custumals, where royal prestige is clearly not an issue, suggests otherwise. In the mid-thirteenth century, the Norman *Summa de Legibus* is still distinguishing between the amounts payable for a blow with the fist and one with the palm (ch. 85.9; *CN* 2:204), and as late as the fifteenth century a custumal from Guines in the Pas de Calais gives a tariff for several kinds of assault, including throwing wine in someone's face (*Livre de usaiges* 50). In the *Coutumes de Beauvaisis* (1283) Philippe de Beaumanoir describes precisely the kind of situation in which such information would have been most valuable: as an example of a case in which proof of the original wrongdoing is unnecessary, Beaumanoir offers, "as when I require of one of my men that he pay me the five sous he owes as compensation [d'une amende] for a blow which he gave another man in my jurisdiction, and he acknowledges the compensation but denies that it should be five sous" [mes il nie qu'ele n'est pas de .v.s.] (ch. 39.1155; 2:99).

All this has major implications for understanding the significance of folklaw contract. Rather than thinking of the rituals of trothplight as simply a way of rendering private agreements subject to central authority, we should see them as a formal expression of the primary social duty without which there could be no legal order, in much the same way that acceptance of the authority of the judicial system, of the rule of law, is the foundation of the modern state. Maine calls contract "the interposition of law to compel the performance of a promise" (1864, 303), and such inability to conceive of law apart from a system of political enforcement helps explain the difficulty that many legal historians have had with idea of contract in early law.[45] But this is to look through the wrong end of the telescope. From the perspective of the folklaw, enforcement was dependent on contract not contract on enforcement.

As the power of central authority grew, the distinction between *pactum* and *lex* became more marked. Only one Anglo-Saxon code, 3 Æthelred (ca. 1000), feels it necessary to point out that, "where a thegn has two courses, amicable settlement or legal process [lufe oððe lage], and he chooses the first, it shall be as binding as a court judgment" (ch. 13.3; Liebermann 1:232), but by the time of the *Leges Henrici Primi* (circa 1115) the point will bear frequent repetition. Among several statements which emphasize the growing gulf between "compromise settlements" and "judgments," the following is typical: "All cases . . . are to be decided with impartiality or, if circumstances permit, preferably settled by a face-saving agreement [pace honestande]" (ch. 3.1; 80).[46] It must have seemed to the clerical compiler of the *Leges Henrici Primi*, writing at a time when a more authoritarian justice system was just beginning to flex its muscles, that it was public law not private contract that needed, in Maitland's phrase, to be "taught to know its place." "Troth overrides the law [pactum legem vincit]" (ch. 49.5a; 164) is not simply a pious remonstrance against litigiousness; it is a plea for the waning power of the folklaw.[47] Writing a mere seventy years later, but in the very different jural climate of Henry II's last years, the author of Glanvill adds a significant qualification to this maxim: "*generaliter enim verum est* quod [for it is generally true that] conventio legem vincit" (10.14; 129).

In terms of Germanic folklaw at least, Maine's account of the rise of an enforceable law of contract fails to appreciate that such a movement marked a fragmentation not a refinement of older notions: contract and status did not stand in opposition to one another; they were intimately bound together. Only the communal honor accorded to oathworthiness and the shame attached to perjury can explain the system of trothplight we have been discussing, and it would be rash to assume that in its original form such a system was either irrational or ineffective. For Maine, however, the formalism of the folklaw contract was a denial of individual responsibility, so that the gradual stripping away, as he saw it, of extraneous ceremonial became a measure not only of social progress (1864, 165) but of moral refinement (298). Not surprisingly, then, he is skeptical of any claim that our ancestors accorded more importance to keeping faith than we do: "No trustworthy primitive record can be read without perceiving that the habit of mind which induces us to make good a promise is as yet imperfectly developed, and that acts of flagrant perfidy are often mentioned without blame and sometimes described with approbation" (303). Even as it stands this is a questionable assertion, but once we allow that our attitude to perfidy may be subject to the same kind of cultural bias as our attitude to truth, it becomes very dubious indeed. I am less interested in questions of comparative morality, however, than in seeking out the grounds for what Maine regards as our habitual reluctance to admit that "good faith and trust in our fellows are more widely diffused than of old" (297), a reluctance that the Saturnians of Chaucer's day would certainly have endorsed.

With hindsight we can see that the contractual machinery I have been describing in this chapter was doomed from the moment that acceptance of writing as the guardian of fallible memory offered authoritarianism one of its most powerful weapons, but its deterioration was slow (indeed, it is still not complete today), and the implications of that deterioration were only slowly recognized; one of the most profound of these was that objectification of truth whose linguistic traces we saw in the last chapter. When facts were inscribed solely in human memory, the truth of what was agreed was inseparable from the truth of those who witnessed the agreement. The system could not work at all without the presumption that the parties would act honorably, and, in theory at least, its elaborate ritualism was designed less to counter poor faith than to assist poor memory. This, as we have seen, is where charters first began to recommend themselves: Baldonet's clerk did not argue that his parchment was necessarily more credible than a human witness — merely, "because the life of man is but brief" (Bracton 2:108), more enduring. When King Offa set down a donation in writing in 785, he justified his action by explaining that "often, out of ignorance or even wickedness [ex ignorantia sive etiam ex improbitate], someone refuses to accept what was truly done" (Birch 1:342); the order in which Offa ranks these two dangers is instructive.

The passing of the folklaw may have been little regretted by those in authority, but its loss must have been felt by countless thousands whose memory, like an unretouched picture, has faded into obscurity. They at least might have appreciated the epitaph that Kern has left it, "something warm-bloodied, vague, confused, and impractical, technically clumsy, but creative, sublime, and suited to human needs; to that idea people gladly return, especially when the unwritten primitive laws of human conscience revolt against the cold callousness, as it seems to them, of written statute" (180). It might justly be objected that Kern ignores much that was narrow and cruel about his good old law, and it would certainly be difficult to find many modern lawyers prepared to share his nostalgia: "Unwritten law," snarls Mr. Justice Avory, "is the name given to the proposition that every man and woman is a law unto himself or herself, and that reverts us to a state of barbarism." Scholars, on the other hand, have less excuse for so open a parade of what E. P. Thompson calls "the enormous condescension of posterity" (1963, 12), and in the next chapter I shall be seeking to expose the caricature promoted by writers like Henry Charles Lea, whose bad old law is still very much with us today.[48]

3

The Folklaw

The custom of resorting to an oath in extreme cases, sanctified as it is by all religious antiquity, is apt (it must be confessed) to introduce into the laxer sort of minds the notion of two kinds of truth.

—Charles Lamb, *Essays of Elia*

ON MONDAY, MARCH 5, 1330, two freemen, William Johnson (Willem fiz Ion) and William Thomson (Willem fiz Thomas), stood at the bar of the itinerant royal court (the eyre) in Northampton. They wore loose tunics of sendal and were barefoot and bareheaded. Each was accompanied by two attendants, one of whom held aloft a wooden staff nearly four feet long topped with a crook, while the other held over his man a rectangular shield approximately four foot by three.[1] Presiding over the court was Chief Justice Geoffrey Scrope, and the observers included the local sheriff, several local knights, and at least two serjeants at law from Westminster (one, William Shareshull, himself to become a celebrated chief justice); finally, there were the two men who had initiated these proceedings, Thomas Staunton and the head of the Cluniac priory of Lenton. Staunton had summoned the prior by writ of right of advowson, and the question of who was entitled to present to the church living of Harlestone was about to be entrusted to the strong right arms of the two Williams (*Eyre of Northamptonshire* 2:546–61).

Earlier, there had been some discussion as to what should happen next. Someone recalled that champions swore oaths both at the bar and again on the field of combat: did this mean that the tenant's champion should swear in court and the demandant's reserve his counter-oath till they got outside (559), or ought there to be a double set of oaths? By the time the two Williams appeared at the bar of his courtroom, however, Scrope had ascertained the proper form: he ordered the prior's man to place his right hand on the Bible and with his left to take his opponent's right hand ("and he commanded him to hold the other's hand lightly, without gripping hard"), and to swear as follows: "Hear this, you whom I hold by the hand, and who let yourself be called by the Christian name of William fitz Thomas: the advowson of the church of H[arlestone] is the right of the Prior of Lenton and the right of his church of L[enton], and not the right of Thomas fitz Hugh of S[taunton]; and Thomas's ancestor William was not seized of that advowson as of fee and right in time of peace in the reign of King [Henry III], nor . . . [the oath continues as a point-by-point rebuttal of Staunton's original claim]; so help me God and the saints" (556). After William Johnson had kissed the book, he was ordered to change places with Staunton's champion, who then swore an oath that was the mirror-image of the first, except that it began, "Hear this, you whom I hold by the hand, who let yourself be called by the Christian name of William fitz John: you are a perjurer. And perjured because [qe vous estez pariours. E pur ceo pariours qe] . . ." The judge then arranged an escort for the two champions: each was to have a knight to carry his staff, another to carry his shield, and a third to guard his person. The two Williams can rarely have enjoyed such attention before, but then their pugilistic skills had suddenly turned them into valuable property: "justices," notes one of the commentators, "used to say to the parties that they should look after the champions like babes in the cradle" [com enfauntz enbercez] (560). Before leaving the courtroom, however, Scrope made one last appeal to the parties to reach a compromise ("negotiate with one another for a settlement from now until we arrive in the field"), and did his best to prevent unnecessary bloodshed by instructing the champions: "even if one of you is in a position to kill the other he must not do it if the other's master wishes to speak on his behalf" (557).

A little later, standing on the field of combat with their shields once more held above their heads (557), the two Williams prepared to swear their second set of oaths. Had things continued, they would have sworn something like, "Hear this, O justice, that I have neither eaten nor drunk nor done anything else nor caused anything to be done for me whereby the law of God might be abased and the law of the devil exalted, so help me God" (*Novae Narrationes* 29), but at this point Thomas Staunton lost his nerve. He offered to relinquish his claim to the advowson if the prior would pay the court costs; the prior agreed, and the battle was called off. What happened next, however, was more unusual and at this distance of time takes on a slightly farcical cast. Geoffrey Scrope was an old soldier and in his younger days had distinguished himself in the lists;[2] he had not gone through all this fustian ritual to be cheated of a good fight at the end of it. Turning to Staunton, he is reported to have said, "Thomas, you have put the king's court to great labor. The court will therefore have its pleasure [la court voet auoir son dedust]. The champions shall have at one another" (550). Accordingly, having traded in their horned *bastons* for simple white staves, the two Williams whacked away at one another for a good while ("e ferirunt ensembel bon pece"); Scrope then took their staves and shields away from them and set them to a spot of wrestling, which they apparently discharged very creditably (557). After a couple of rounds of this, Scrope called a halt to the bout (550), though before turning to his next case he awarded the two Williams their staves as a prize.[3] Something of an anticlimax perhaps, but it could have been worse: a judicial duel two hundred years earlier had had to be called off because "the two champions were so frightened of each other that they just sat down and refused to fight" (Galbraith 1948, 290).

There is about the account of the Northampton case an air of antiquarianism. We know of no such trial by battle having been joined within the previous thirty years (M. Russell 1983a, 432), and had the two Williams fought in earnest theirs would have been the last recorded civil case to have been decided by combat on English soil. True, appeals of treason resulting in combat to the death were occasionally waged under the aegis of the court of chivalry until the middle of the fifteenth century (as were criminal appeals at common law),[4] and a debased blood sport, pitting criminals who had turned king's evidence (approvers) against those whom they had informed on, survived to about 1500,[5] but trial by battle was clearly on the wane by the time Scrope marched his courtroom out to watch this abortive display. The very meticulousness of their records suggests an eagerness on the part of court reporters to capture the details of a process already falling into disuse, and the number of disagreements over points of procedure that are noted points the same way. Indeed, even the judicial setting of the Northampton case, an eyre court, appears old fashioned; the regular holding of eyres had come to an end in 1294, and this brief revival in 1329/30, perhaps orchestrated by Scrope himself, proved to be their swan song (Cam 1924).

All this might lead us to think of combat itself as an archaic process and to assume that the folklaw had turned to it as a convenient method of resolving disputes from the very earliest times. The prominence of the judicial duel in medieval literature seems to confirm this assumption, and as we read of Thierry splitting Pinabel's skull to prove Ganelon a traitor (*Chanson* 3926–30) or Lancelot knocking Mador de la Porte "grouelynge vpon the erthe" to clear Guinevere of a charge of poisoning (Malory 1:513), we readily imagine that combat was the archetypal legal procedure of the Middle Ages. It is not difficult to see why trial by battle with its ample opportunities for the dramatic portrayal of good's triumph over evil might have offered storytellers an attractive subject; after hearing how the wicked Sir Aldingar is struck down by an opponent who seems to be but four years old, we can well believe that "falsing neuer doth well!" (Child 2:46). On the other hand, it is less easy to see why actual litigants should have been attracted to it, and in fact there can be little doubt that its literary prominence has led commentators greatly to overestimate its general importance. In reality, as I hope to show, judicial combat was neither "an antidote to unlimited violence" (R. H. Bloch 63), nor "immune from the lessons of common sense" (Riedel 34), but a rare necessity reluctantly embarked on in exceptional circumstances. In the course of this chapter I wish to explore those less dramatic aspects of the Northampton case which seem to me far closer to the heart of folklaw process: the impulse toward compromise and reconciliation, the strong sense of local community, the judge's role as mediator rather than decision-maker, and, above all, the paramount importance of the judicial oath.

In his enormously influential *Ancient Law*, Sir Henry Maine offers us a faintly ludicrous "dramatisation of the origin of Justice": "Two armed men are wrangling about some disputed property. The Praetor, *vir pietate gravis*, happens to be going by and interposes to stop the contest. The disputants state their case to him and agree that he shall arbitrate between them, it being arranged that the loser, besides resigning the subject of the quarrel, shall pay a sum of money to the umpire as a remuneration for his trouble and loss of time" (1864, 364). This fortuitous praetor, whose intrepidity is even more conspicuous than his *pietas*, and these reasonable "wranglers," so improbably ready to lay aside their weapons, ring no truer than the entrepreneurial form of litigation in which they all connive. It is not, however, hard to see how Maine, by projecting backward his own experience of the adversarial process of the common law onto accounts of early Roman practice, was able to arrive at such a dramatization. Like Maine, many Anglo-American legal historians seem to have had great difficulty in imagining that some kind of "principle of equilibrium" (MacCormack 80) might ever have been adequate in itself to control the excesses of private warfare. Despite strong ethnological evidence that what Gluckman called "the peace in the feud" (1955) is common to many traditional societies, the largely unsubstantiated belief that trials originated as "substitutes for private out-of-court brawls" (J. Frank 80) has remained a truism of much legal scholarship down to our own day.

The dominant form assumed by modern common law procedure is agonistic: a contest between private parties or between the state and the criminal intended to maintain social stability by recompensing winners and penalizing losers in accordance with rigorously defined and applied rules. This form presupposes a society where conflict is endemic and only confined within tolerable bounds by the law's careful regulation. Such regulation, moreover, will only be effective where a powerful and centralized state is able to authenticate and enforce it; law becomes, in Roscoe Pound's famous definition, "social control through the systematic application of the force of politically organized society" (quoted by Roberts 192). As long as we are unable to conceive of law apart from our own essentially authoritarian model we will naturally imagine that its first glimmerings are to be found in the intervention of a state official between two armed men, and the history of jurisprudence will always appear as a "struggle between the rising power of reason and the waning supremacy of brute force" (Lea 101).

There are, then, at least three assumptions about the nature of traditional law which underpin our readiness to see trial by battle as its most typical process: (1) that the natural state of early society is agonistic and that early law will reflect its taste for confrontation; (2) that early law is authoritarian, its officers possessing the necessary power to regulate the instinctive violence of the litigants; (3) that early law is not only violent but superstitious, preferring the chance outcome of combat to the careful application of reason. I shall consider each of these assumptions in turn.

Aspects of Folklaw Jurisprudence

If it were indeed true that early society was more concerned with confrontation than compromise, we should expect the judicial duel to have taken pride of place in folklaw procedure, whereas in fact it was probably the least common way by which the folklaw reached its decisions. Since, however, it appears to confirm the belief of Lea and Maine that the earliest kind of law will merely impose rules of combat upon the endemic violence of primitive society, it has received disproportionate attention and its function and operation have been widely misunderstood. Ironically, the Germanic people most associated with trial by battle were those closest to the font of written law, the Lombards (J. Baldwin 615), while it seems to have been comparatively rare among the Franks, and may have been quite unknown to the Anglo-Saxons (P&M 1:39). The *Lex Salica* does not mention it, and in Gregory of Tours's *History of the Franks*, a mine of information of early procedure, we hear of only one challenge to a trial by battle (*Historiarum* 7.14; 2:108) and only one judicial combat which is actually fought (10.10; 2:346)—interestingly, both involve nobles rather than commoners. In England, trial by combat seems to have been introduced by the Normans, and barely a hundred years later Henry II was already seeking to reduce its scope (Van Caenegem 80–81). Battle may, in fact, have been most favored in situations where the litigants came from different jurisdictions, with neither shared customs nor common neighbors to reinforce witness proof: the very earliest reference to combat in Germanic law is in an edict of King Gundobad (474–516), appended to a set of laws intended, according to Gregory of Tours (2.33; 1:124), to regulate affairs between the Burgundians and the Romans (*Leges Burgundionum* ch. 80.2; 104–5), and William the Conqueror apparently turned to combat as a way of settling disputes between his own followers and the native Anglo-Saxons (P&M 1:89–90). V. H. Galbraith cites an interesting ninth-century case from Orléans where battle was resorted to "as a last resort when rival legal systems were in hopeless conflict" (1948, 288); and from late-thirteenth-century England we have an intriguing insight into the motives of the monks of Bury St. Edmunds in electing to defend their right to a manor by combat: "We were doubtful about the countryside [*patriam*], as friendly with [*familiarem*] and akin to [*affinem*] our enemies" (284).

The attitude to conflict and its resolution in traditional societies is far from uniform; as Redfield says, "some like litigation and some don't" (21). Nevertheless, in many there is a clear recognition of the dangers of confrontation and a corresponding premium placed on compromise and reconciliation. This spirit is clearly reflected, for instance, in the portrait of traditional law drawn by the modern West African novel: "It is the pride of Umuaro," boasts an elder in Achebe's *Arrow of God*, "that we never see one party as right and the other wrong" (100), and the spokesman for a village tribunal in *Things Fall Apart* says, "we have heard both sides of the case. . . . Our duty is not to blame this man or to praise that, but to settle the dispute" (66). A similar point is made in one of Soyinka's novels: "one thing our people are good at," remarks a character in his *Season of Anomy*, "is the formula that leaves no side of a quarrel in prolonged resentment" (114). The claim that many early Germanic societies would have applauded such sentiments will seem strange to those familiar with the Chronicle account of Cynewulf and Cyneheard's feud or the blood-boltered digressions in *Beowulf*; it may take a historian to remind us that "the world, private and official, stood ready to arbitrate" (Wallace-Hadrill 125), or that Germanic folklaw, "was not primarily a matter of making and applying rules in order to determine guilt and fix judgment, not an instrument to separate people from one another on the basis of a set of principles, but rather a matter of holding people together, a matter of reconciliation" (Berman 1983, 78). Even in a frontier society like Iceland, where life was as violent and justice as rough as it is possible to imagine, "arbitrated resolutions were some three to four times more frequent than adjudicated ones"—at least, once the initial impulse to vengeance had been resisted (Miller 1984, 100).[6] In more settled areas negotiated compromise seems to have provided the habitual mode of dispute-settlement, and was to prove very durable. Stephen White, who takes much of his evidence from Baldonet's monastery of Marmoutiers, finds it still operating in the Touraine in the eleventh century, and it was being practiced in Languedoc as late as the thirteenth: "arbiters were not there to judge according to rules; they were there to get the parties off the hook" (Cheyette 294). In England, as a number of commentators (White 308; Berman 1983, 74; Clanchy 1983b, 47) have pointed out, the *Leges Henrici Primi* offer some of the best evidence for the existence of this kind of legal order.

Two aspects of the folklaw's distaste for confrontation deserve mention: the frequency with which procedures ostensibly designed to produce clear winners and losers, such as battle and ordeal, were called off at the last minute, and the curious fact that even where the judicial machinery did produce a conclusive result, there seems to have been pressure on the winning party to act generously to the loser. We have seen that as late as Scrope's Northampton eyre, the court remained ready to abort the procedure in favor of a compromise to the very end ("negotiate with one another for a settlement from now until we arrive in the field"), and in fact no one can have been very surprised when Thomas Staunton did finally blink: even in the old days, as Maitland says, "there was much talk of fighting, but it generally came to nothing" (P&M 2:633; cf. M. Russell 1983b, 124). Indeed, even after battle had actually been joined, settlement still remained possible: of another advowson dispute from 1219, we learn that "the suit proceeded so far that the duel was pledged, and armed, and fought between them in the court of the lord king. But at length they were brought into agreement [tandem autem concordati fuerunt]" (*Rolls* 205–206). Galbraith gives several further examples (1948, 290), including one where "after many attacks and blows" a *concordia* was reached at the instigation of friends of the parties ("compellentibus amicis"). This was equally true on the Continent: from eleventh-century Anjou we find compromise settlements reached with judicial proof (by battle or ordeal) "étant même parfois en cours" (Halphen 1950, 190), and White shows the same thing happening in Touraine (295). In a record of 337 trials by ordeal from Varad in Hungary between 1208 and 1235, more than a quarter ended either in amicable settlement or in one or the other of the sides backing down, sometimes at the eleventh hour (Zajtay 545–47).

A graphic illustration of this attitude comes from an English dispute of the early eleventh century. Leofric, having sold an estate in Worcestershire in the presence of a number of witnesses, found that his right to sell was later challenged by Wufstan, who was claiming part of the land for himself. At the point when the dispute was about to come to formal witness proof, "spæcon ða Leofrices freond ⁊ Wulfstanes freond þæt hit betere wære þæt heora seht togæ[dre wur]de þonne hy ænige [sa]ce hym betweonan heoldan" [both Leofric's friends and Wulfstan's said that it would be better for them to come to an agreement than to keep up any quarrel between them] (A. J. Robertson 162). Doris Stenton has remarked on "how often a party who has been completely successful in the pleadings comes at last to a compromise" (1965a, 8); evidently it was better for both sides to save face with a voluntary settlement than to risk the continuing animosity that a formal decision might provoke.

Even after a formal conclusion had been reached, however, it seems to have been incumbent on the winner to behave graciously to the losing side. When the Mercian King Berhtwulf lost a property dispute with the bishop of Worcester in 840, the bishop gave him four fine horses, a ring, a platter, and two white drinking horns, with a further two horses, two flagons, and a gold cup for his queen (Birch 2:4). It would be easy to regard these as a bribe or as a cynical attempt to curry royal favor, but a passage in the *Leges Henrici Primi* suggests that what was at stake in such transactions was as much a matter of honor as material advantage: "If anyone makes amends to another for his misdeed or makes good the injury he has caused, and afterwards for the purpose of making a friendly concord with him offers him something along with an oath of reconciliation, it is commendable of him to whom the offer is made if he gives back the whole thing and does not retain any suggestion of the affront to himself" (ch. 36.2; 143). No decision which left either party feeling resentful could be certain to hold up in the long run. This is made quite explicit in the report of a Welsh case copied into the ninth-century Lichfield Gospels: "Tudfwlch the son of Llywyd and the son-in-law of Tudri arose to claim 'Tir Telych', which was in the hand of Elgu the son of Gelli and the tribe of Idwared. They disputed long about it; in the end they disjudge Tudri's son-in-law by law. The goodmen said to each other, 'Let us make peace'. Elgu gave afterwards a horse, three cows, three newly calved cows, only in order that there might not be hatred between them from the ruling afterwards till the Day of Judgment. A document afterwards: Tudfwlch and his kin will not want it for ever and ever" (quoted by Charles-Edwards 75). For a while the folklaw would manage to accommodate such documents, as it evidently still could in early-thirteenth-century Languedoc: "Even when a charter gave the prize to one side," says Frederic Cheyette, "the other was almost always paid off. No one left empty-handed" (293). In the long run, however, a system which sought to avoid the disruptive apportioning of right and wrong would not be able to survive the implacable dogmatism of letters. The *Leges Henrici Primi* represent the last stand of the old legal order in the king's courts. With Henry II, however, there is a new peremptoriness about royal justice: the king no longer writes to his *witan* exhorting them to settle disputes as seems most just to them — "swa rihtlice geseman swa him æfre rihtlicost þuhte" (A. J. Robertson 136); he commands his barons to do "full right" to their wronged tenants without delay — "praecipimus tibi quod sine dilatione plenum rectum teneas" (Maitland 67).[7]

The assumption that early law is authoritarian, its officers possessing the necessary power to regulate the potential violence of litigants, seems amply borne out by the *praecipe* writs, but as soon as we look back before the Norman Conquest we begin to recognize a rather different kind of legal order — one more aptly characterized by Peter Brown's term consensual (1975, 143). The role of the folklaw judge, as I suggested in the last chapter, was not to enforce but to conciliate, not to confront but to compromise. It is all too easy to find reflected in the early law a distorted image of our own jural sacred cows, but if, as Harold Berman has written, "a different and broader perspective is adopted — not the perspective of the Western legal tradition as it later developed, but the perspective of the legal concepts and legal institutions of non-Western cultures — the negative features of the earlier folklaw are less striking than its positive features" (1983, 77). Modern anthropological fieldwork suggests that in many small-scale societies the regulatory mechanism bears little resemblance to the authoritarian model, yet these societies seem in general quite capable of controlling their internal disputes and there is no evidence that the alternative to a strong, centralized judicial system will be a state of primal anarchy.

According to Paul Bohannan, societies that are not organized into politically centralized states ("a unicentric power system") are forced to evolve procedures for managing disputes between "two more or less equal power units," that is to say, "bicentric" procedures: "In such a situation, all troubles are settled by some form of compromise, more or less in accordance with a set of overt 'rules.' Instead of 'decisions' there are 'compromises.' In a unicentric system, it is possible to have judicial decisions and a recognized method of enforcement which presents problems merely of efficiency, not of substance. In a bicentric situation, nobody can be in a position to make decisions — it is organized so that there cannot be. The 'judges' must make compromises, and their compromises must be enforced from two power centers, which often — to a citizen of a 'state' — looks like no enforcement at all" (1965, 39). This "presence of order but absence of enforcement agencies" (Roberts 190) will create problems for those who wish to see universality in the norms of modern Western jurisprudence, but offers an attractive perspective on the folklaw of the Middle Ages. Bohannan's model helps clarify not only the Roman *legis actio sacramenti* dramatized by Maine, but much else that is puzzling about the folklaw of Europe. Maine has obvious difficulty with the role assumed by the judge in early law. He calls him an umpire, and implies that he is there to see that a properly regulated combat produces an undisputed winner, but at the same time he seems to glimpse another possibility, one his preconceptions force him to dismiss as simulation: "the magistrate carefully simulated the demeanour of a private arbitrator casually called in" (1864, 362).[8] Umpires belong in a unicentric system which can endow them with the authority to interpret and enforce the rules, but in the bicentric arena the arbitrator reigns supreme.

The third assumption about early law—that it is not only violent but superstitious, preferring the chance outcome of combat to the careful application of reason—also proves questionable on closer examination. We should not suppose that the folklaw was indifferent to factual evidence. On the contrary, it preferred its justice to be immediate and tangible: its favorite offenders were the murderer still clutching the bloody knife, the handhaving thief caught in possession of the stolen goods, the adulterous couple still sharing their warm bed. "It used to be," says *The Mirror of Justices* wistfully, that one could throw an arsonist "on the fire and burn him if one caught him freshly in the act" [freschement el fet] (135), and though this will look like mere lynch law from a modern perspective, it did in fact obey its own internal logic.

Students of literature will recall the bloody knife from "The Man of Law's Tale" and *Macbeth* but may be surprised to learn that it also appears in legal texts; there are some felons, says Bracton, who should be denied the chance to clear themselves by combat or jury trial, "as is the case when he shall have been taken standing over the body with his knife dripping blood [cum cultello cruentato], he may not deny the death; and this is the ancient constitution, for in this case there is no need of further proof" (2:386; cf. 404). Similarly, adulterers caught in one another's arms are a familiar enough literary type,

> Arise, arise, thou Littell Musgrave,
> And put thy clothës on;
> It shall nere be said in my country
> I have killed a naked man.
> ("Little Musgrave and
> Lady Barnard"; Child 2:245)

But they, too, turn up in legal sources. "If adulterers should be caught," says the *Leges Burgundionum* baldly, "let both the man and the woman be killed" (ch. 68.1; 95), a principle vividly illustrated in Gregory of Tours: "while they were sleeping, the husband returned," he writes; "he lit some straw, lifted his ax, and killed them both" (8.19; 2:186). A similar code of behavior was still operating in late-thirteenth-century France (Beaumanoir ch. 30.933; 1:472), and can be traced through to the later Middle Ages. The *Book of the Knight of La Tour-Landry* (written in the late fourteenth century) offers a good example: "And the good man douted hym that there was sum man with his wyff, and made semblaunt that he had slepte, and routed; and whanne they were doing the foule dede of synne, he hastely toke oute a long kniff and persed hem bothe thorughe into the bedde. And thus he sloughe hem bothe in doinge this orrible synne. And whanne he had done, he called his neygheboures and the officers of the lawe, and sheued hem what he had don; the whiche saide, all with one uoys, that hit was wel done to ponisshen hem in suche wise" (81–82). The reason for killing the lover in situ is clearly to provide unimpeachable evidence of the adultery, for as the author of the *Quinze joyes de mariage* (written only slightly later) remarks of an enraged husband who returns after an unsuccessful pursuit of the fleeing lover, intending to vent his anger on his wife: "that would have been a serious error, for he had no proof that they had done anything" (15:34–35; 87).

Such behavior may well look like mere lawlessness to the modern legal mind for self-help is contrary to everything that authoritarian law stands for, but these were nevertheless quite clearly judicial acts governed by well-established rules. Some early law codes, for example, specify that if the outraged husband kills only one of the guilty pair, he shall be held liable for the death (see H. Brunner 2:854–56), while Beaumanoir makes it a condition of his excusable homicide that the husband shall have given the adulterer fair warning before he takes action. In all such cases of manifest guilt it was particularly necessary for witnesses to be present (this was, of course, one of the advantages of raising the hue and cry). Thus in England as late as 1300 private suitors (known as *sacrabars*) in cases of manifest theft were held to be entitled to execute the hand-having thief, providing always that they were themselves the owners or custodians of the goods concerned, a confession had been extracted from the offender, and there were reliable witnesses to the deed (Kaye 751). The question of whether simple possession of stolen property was in itself sufficient to constitute a presumption of guilt exercised the ingenuity of royal justices through much of the twelfth and thirteenth centuries (Ireland 244–47).

Modern jurisprudence assesses degrees of criminal liability according to the intention of the agent (for us premeditation distinguishes murder from manslaughter), but for the folklaw the line was marked by concealment. Manslaughter and robbery were public acts, inherently less threatening to the stability of society than the murder and larceny that were committed in secret because there could be no argument about who was responsible. Anyone who kills a thief, say the seventh-century *Laws of Ine*, must announce with an oath ("aðe gecyðan") that he killed him fleeing from the crime ("fleondne for ðeof") and the dead man's kin must then swear that they have no case against the slayer; if, however, he conceals the killing ("gif he hit þonne dierne") and it only comes to light later, he is liable to pay compensation for his victim (ch. 35; Liebermann 1:104). Readers of the Icelandic sagas will be familiar with the way in which killers regularly announce their responsibility for a slaying to the next person they meet; "the honorable killer," as William Miller says, "always admitted his act" (1990, 249). Only where guilt was not manifest would disputes need to come to formal trial, and since such trials must ultimately become a contest between one party's word and another's they always held the potential to divide the community.

Even here, however—though, as Pollock says, "trial of questions of fact, in anything like the modern sense, was unknown" (P&M 1:38)—we should not suppose that factual evidence was treated with total caprice. In the Fonthill dispute, for example, the scratched face of a man seen fleeing through brambles from an attempted cattle-rustling is used as evidence against him: "ða he fleah, ða torypte hine an breber ofer ðæt nebb; ða he ætsacan wolde, ða sæde him mon ðæt to tacne" [when he fled a bramble ripped him across the face, and when he tried to defend himself it was held to be a token] (Harmer 32). The thief here had already been caught stealing once and was thus the kind of *tyhtbysig* 'much-accused' man whose legal status was ambiguous; by contrast, it would have been far more difficult to bring a respectable man to justice in such a bilateral context if his guilt was at all doubtful. Beaumanoir tells how he had once, as bailli of Clermont, conducted an investigation into the murder of a man killed at first light on a road out of town by a single blow to the head. Circumstantial evidence pointed to a local butcher as the culprit: he had dined with the victim the night before, his trade would have made him adept at delivering the right kind of blow, and he had been seen near the road at about the right time. The butcher, however, denied the crime and claimed to have an alibi. At this point a "rational" process would no doubt have investigated the alibi and sent the man for trial had it failed to hold water. Beaumanoir, however, proceeded quite differently. He asked the butcher whether he would agree to rest his case before a jury on the question of his truthfulness about the alibi, and the butcher unwisely said yes: "s'il estoit trouvés en mençonge de ce qu'il disoit, qu'il fust atains du fet et, s'il estoit trouvés veritables, qu'il en fust delivres. Il respondi: 'oïl'" (ch. 40.1243; 2:142). The alibi broke down and the man was eventually hanged, but not before a fierce debate among the members of the jury as to the legitimacy of this procedure; it is doubtful whether Beaumanoir would have got his conviction at all had he not been able to trick his man into what he chose to represent as "apertes presompcions" of guilt. There is no question here of the folklaw's being "impatient of too great an expenditure of logic" (Riedel 32); clearly, once the stolen goods had been sold, the bloody knife cleaned, or the lover had slipped away, something more immediately demonstrative than mere forensic argument was required to establish guilt or innocence in the eyes of the community.

From this perspective, it should be quite clear that folklaw procedure was not erected upon the "irrational" foundation of the judicial duel. Duels would not have been allowed where there was an open presumption of guilt, nor where unimpeachable witnesses could be marshalled against a plaintiff. They were rather the folklaw's last resort, employed only where two evenly balanced power groups remained completely intransigent in the face of all efforts to find grounds for compromise and reconciliation.[9] As an early Irish law text has it: "a duel should not be fought about certain things but about uncertain things" (quoted by F. Kelly 212). Thus, an edict of Louis the Pious (issued in 816) reads: "If anyone dispute with another in any kind of case and has witnesses whom he suspects of perjury brought against him, he is allowed to oppose them with other witnesses who he thinks to be better, that the wickedness of the worse witnesses may be overcome by the testimony of the better. But if both groups of witnesses disagree between themselves so that one side is totally unwilling to yield to the other, two men shall be chosen from among them, that is one from either side, who with shields and clubs shall dispute in battle" (*Capitularia* 268). Louis's decree adds that the loser shall forfeit his right hand as a perjurer and his fellow witnesses "redeem their hands" [manuas suas redimant] by paying fines. No one should doubt that such regulations were intended to make judicial combat seem as unattractive as possible, its outcome doubtful and its consequences, not merely for the principals, potentially painful. Gundobad's edict is similarly directed to discouraging combat by providing strong deterrents, not only for the loser but also the supporters: "all the witnesses for the side whose representative witness was defeated shall pay three hundred shillings by way of a fine" (*Leges Burgundionum* 80. 2; 104–05). Lea sees something sinister in this involvement of the witnesses, but the folklaw is not licensing the defendant to divert justice by merely "accusing an inconvenient witness" (120); it is simply making all those connected with the suit aware of their responsibility to reach an honest decision rather than push matters to a potentially disruptive trial of strength. From the early thirteenth century, when witness proof was giving way to the inquest or jury, we have similar evidence that battle was resorted to only after more measured methods had failed: "si autem dubitaverint juratores," says the *Très ancien coutumier de Normandie*, "per duellum causa illa terminabitur" [should the jury be in doubt, the case is to be decided by combat] (*CN* 1:93).

There is, however, a further dimension to the question of the folklaw's irrationality: it is usually assumed that what the victor in a judicial duel proved was his innocence (if he fought in a criminal appeal) or the justice of his claim (if the battle was a civil one), but this is not precisely correct. What he proved, strictly speaking, was the truth of his oath. Before taking the field, we might recall, the prior of Lenton's champion swore that Thomas Staunton had no claim to the advowson of Harlestone, and Staunton's champion then swore that his opponent was a perjurer ("Vous estez pariours. E pur ceo pariours qe . . ."). Evidently, this was standard procedure on both sides of the Channel. Here, for instance, from the prose *Lancelot*, are the oaths in a civil plea: "Maintenant furent li saint aporté, si jura Guidan que se Diex li äist et li saint, que li peres a la damoisele le avoit donee la terre don't ele le contralioit. 'Et se Diex m'äist,' fait Gueheriés, 'et li saint que vos estes parjures de cest sairement'" [Now the relics were brought, and Guidan swore that, as God and the saints might aid him, the lady's father had given him the land which she was disputing. "And, as God and the saints may aid me," said Gaheriet, "you are perjured by this oath"] (4:80). The formula hardly varies in an appeal of treason: "Si jura li senescax avant que il savoit bien que li vavassors estoit vers son seignor traïtres et mesire Gauvain jura aprés que se Diex li aidast et li saint, que il estoit parjures del sarement" [First, the seneschal swore that he knew for certain that the vassal was a traitor to his lord, and then Sir Gawain swore that, as God and the saints might aid him, he was perjured by the oath] (8:354).[10]

Such oaths were in fact indispensable in any judicial duel, as Chrétien de Troyes's Lancelot knew perfectly well:

> Sire rois,
> je sai de quauses, et de lois,
> et de plez, et de jugemanz:
> ne doit estre sanz seiremanz
> bataille de tel mescreance.
> (*Chevalier*, 4963–67)

> [My king, I know about actions and laws, and pleas and verdicts: in so doubtful a case, battle should not be joined without swearing oaths.]

From the early fifteenth century comes an anecdote about a Scotsman who appeals an Englishman of treason, without, apparently, having grasped this fundamental principle: "Whan þei schuldyn fyȝtyn aforn a iuge in here cause, þe iuge, as þe maner is, putte hem boþin to her oth. Whan þe Scot schulde sweryn, he seyde to þe iuge: 'Lard, Y cam nauȝt hidyr to sweryn. Y cam to fyȝtyn, for my chalanch was to fygtyn, and þerto Y am redy. But sweryn will Y noȝt, for Y made no chalanch to sweryn.' The iuge seyde but he wolde sweryn þat his apel was trewe ellys he schulde ben takyn as conuyct and tent tretour & ben hangyn and drawyn wythoutyn fyȝtyng. And so he was, for he wolde nout sweryn, wyttyng wel þat his apel was fals & mad only of malyce, as he was aknowyn er he deyyd" (*Dives* 1.i:255). Perhaps the author makes the appellant in this story a Scot to explain his ignorance of civilized procedure, for there can be no doubt that the universal and invariable function of the judicial duel, like that of every other folklaw process, was to authenticate the oath of one or the other of the parties. Since 'troth' and 'trouthe' are barely distinguishable in such a context, this fact is of great importance for the way we view the competing claims of ethical and intellectual truth in medieval society. For the remainder of this chapter I shall be dealing with this fundamental element of traditional law: How did the judicial oath work? What was it intended to prove? How was it verified? And what can it tell us about the attitudes of those who employed it?

The Judicial Oath

"Oath," says Pollock, "was the primary mode of proof, an oath going not to the truth of specific fact, but to the justice of the claim or defence as a whole" (P&M 1:39). This folklaw oath was thus quite different from that sworn in a modern courtroom: whereas present-day witnesses swear simply to tell the truth (the promissory or evidentiary oath), the oath in folklaw procedure invoked the truth of the parties themselves as a means of proving their claims (the assertory, decisory, or judicial oath). Such an oath did not initiate proceedings, it terminated them; it was not a preliminary to making one's case, but the culmination of it. This is true even where the proof employed was witness proof; witnesses were not expected to swear to the truth of their own account of events; they swore to the truth of the claim they were endorsing: "the original judicial oath was not incidental to testimonial evidence. Rather the reverse was the case; witnesses supported the oath" (Silving 1335).

Thus, in the archetypal folklaw situation, the court did not furnish the litigants with a set of weapons and wait to see which side would survive; rather, it put one of them to his or her oath (as King Mark does in Béroul's version of the story of Iseut's trial) and entrusted the outcome to divine providence. This pattern can still be found in the mid-thirteenth century: "There is an oath tendered by one party to the other in court, or by the judge to a party, upon which no conviction follows," says Bracton, "for it is sufficient that they await the vengeance of God" (3:342). Bracton's contemporary, the canonist Bartholemew of Exeter, suggests that such oaths were still common: "in ecclesiastical cases an oath should bring every dispute to an end, and in secular ones many disputes may be resolved with an oath. Those judgments which are popularly called manifest laws [*leges aperte* 'compurgation' (?)] are never concluded without an oath" (241). Even in the yearbook period we can still hear a distant echo of this pattern in the formula "Ready to aver" which concluded the pleadings and by which the parties showed themselves ready to submit the issue to proof.[11]

The most frequently quoted Anglo-Saxon legal maxim—though, ironically, it comes from an early twelfth-century forgery (the *Leges Edwardi Confessoris*)—is, predictably, "Bugge spere of side othe bere!" [Buy off the spear or bear it] (ch. 12.6; Liebermann 1:638–39), with its implication that the basic choice facing the offender is either to pay compensation or to risk a blood-feud. The seventh-century Kentish code of Hlothere and Eadric, however, offers a rather different choice: "Let him make peace with either money or an oath" [gecwime an feo oððe an aþe] (ch.10; Liebermann 1:10), and this maxim was still current in the early tenth century: "When will any dispute be settled," asks one of the parties in the Fonthill case, "if one can settle neither with money nor with an oath?" [hwonne bið engu spæc geendedu gif mon ne mæg nowðer ne mid feo ne mid aða geendigan] (Harmer 31). The implication here is that the standard alternative to paying wergeld is not taking up one's spear, but swearing to one's innocence. In Germanic folklaw, at least by the time we have adequate evidence, unsupported oaths seem to have been comparatively rare, but all other forms of trial—not only combat and ordeal, but compurgation, and even witness proof—turned on the public verification of an oath and may be thought of as merely elaborations of this basic form.

Though we may find it extraordinary that any litigant should ever have been allowed to win a case merely by swearing an oath, this is exactly what happens in many small-scale, primarily oral societies. The central incident in Elechi Amadi's novel *The Great Ponds* is just such a judicial oath. Two villages get into a violent dispute over the fishing rights to a neighboring pond and when their conflict threatens to disrupt the entire region the elders intervene to restore peace. After failing to reach a satisfactory compromise, these elders find themselves faced with the unpleasant task of deciding between the two villages:

> "There is only one way out, the gods must decide," Wosu said.
> "How?" Eze Iwai wondered. "A whole village cannot swear."
> "A whole village cannot swear of course, but a representative from either of the villages can swear on behalf of his village."
> It looked like a way out and the next day when the assembly met again this decision was announced by Eze Iwai. The decision was welcomed but each village insisted that the other should do the swearing. (84)

They wrangle over who is to swear, what god is to be sworn by, and what time period is to be set for verifying the oath; finally, a great warrior called Olumba is chosen to swear by Ogbunabali, the god of the night, that the pond belongs to his village, "If this is not true let me die within six months" (86). On the way home Olumba ponders his oath: "The Pond of Wagaba—who were its rightful owners? It was one thing to argue eloquently in public in favour of his village, and another to stake his life over the truth of his arguments. If the pond belonged to Chiolu, he would be all right. If not . . . ? He tried to recall all he knew about the Great Ponds. He remembered Eze Diali's speech during negotiations with Aliakoro. The chief had said: 'Time obscures many things, but time also establishes many things. That you have not challenged us for thirty years is proof enough that the Pond of Wagaba belongs to us.' Olumba wondered whether Ogbunabali the god of the night would recognize this time factor" (87). For the remainder of the novel we follow Olumba through his six-month ordeal and watch a great warrior slowly reduced to a shadow by the terrifying possibility of imminent retribution.

In another of Amadi's novels, *The Slave*, there is an attempt to settle a private quarrel with an oath:

> Aso had no witnesses outside his family to testify that the piece of land was his. Olumati had none either. There was only one way to resolve the matter; someone had to swear an oath.
>
> "Olumati, are you willing to swear that the land belongs to your family?" Minikwe asked.
>
> "No. I am new here. I am only going by what my late grandmother told me. If Aso thinks the land belongs to his family let him swear and take it." (99)

In this case, Aso dares not swear and the case is dropped. Like its Anglo-Saxon counterpart, traditional Nigerian society seems to have had a "clear understanding of the sacral virtue of an oath" (D. Stenton. 1965a, 17), a point made succinctly by the hero of Achebe's novel *Arrow of God*: " 'If a man is not sure of the boundary between his land and his neighbour's . . . he tells his son: *I think it is here but if there is a dispute do not swear before a deity*' " (98).[12] In present-day Morocco where the judicial oath is still commonly employed, most people apparently recognize the dangers of any "short-term gain others believe has been bought at the price of a false oath" (Rosen 35), and this kind of disincentive to perjury must also have operated in early medieval Europe.

Illustrated in this way, the notion that a court might acquit someone solely on the strength of an oath may come to seem less bizarre. In an oral society, or one with limited literacy, the difficulties faced by a court trying to assemble reliable evidence from which to deduce innocence or guilt are often enormous. The further back in the collective memory the evidence is sought, the more insecure and contradictory it will be, even in the smallest and most close-knit community. Natalie Zemon Davis's *Return of Martin Guerre* brilliantly illustrates how exclusively oral testimony could baffle a sophisticated tribunal investigating a question as elementary as the real identity of the accused (see 63); by the sixteenth century, French civil law no longer allowed judicial oaths in criminal cases, but when at one point the defendant proposes this way of settling the question (69), it is easy to see how an earlier tribunal might have jumped at such a solution.[13] The judicial oath is to forensic proof what the *traditio* by means of a staff is to the modern title deed; public, memorable, and above all incontrovertible, it rendered innocence as "thing-like" as ownership. Whether or not one chooses to see the judicial oath as reflecting the kind of "situational" thinking which has been claimed to be typical of nonliterate cultures (Ong 49–57), it certainly served to expose disorder to the public gaze, and to invite communal judgment on those who sought to justify themselves before their neighbors. Where no central authority busied itself investigating and punishing lawlessness, the folklaw could hardly have found a better way of exploiting the impulse toward consensual justice.

The course taken by a dispute submitted to the folklaw for resolution was shaped by three main factors: the degree to which guilt was manifest, the relative standing of the parties in the community, and the methods of proof traditional to the area. I have suggested that where there was a strong presumption of guilt the law was unlikely to offer the accused much shelter, but it is doubtful that a freeman would find the task of suing an earl a straightforward one, however clearly his opponent were in the wrong. The wealthy Icelander Hrafnkel openly admits to his poor neighbor Thorbjorn that he has killed his son, and is even ready to make restitution on his own terms, but regards the prospect of any formal proceedings between them with obvious distaste:

> "I will not accept these terms," said Thorbjorn.
> "What do you want then?" Hrafnkel said.
> Then Thorbjorn said, "I wish us to choose mediators between us."
> Hrafnkel answered, "Then you believe yourself of equal rank to me, and there is no way we can settle on such terms." (Gordon 65)

The folklaw set a price on every person's head and this price was easily converted into oath equivalents: if the wergeld to be paid for killing a churl was 200 shillings, for killing a thegn 1200 shillings, and for killing a king 7,200 shillings, then it follows that for a churl to sue a thegn he would need five other 200-shilling men prepared to swear alongside him (twelfhendes mannes að forstent VI ceorla að), and to sue a king, thirty-five others (Liebermann 1: 462–64). Since a king could clear himself with an unsupported oath if sued by thegn or churl, and a thegn could do the same if sued by a churl, such tariffs must generally have worked better as a shield for defendants than as a sword for plaintiffs.

In practice, of course, most disputes must have arisen between those of comparable rank, and here a second kind of status-marker came into play: whether or not the oaths of the parties were reliable, whether, in other words, the litigants belonged among the respected members of the community—the law-abiding (Odegaard) and the oathworthy—or carried the stigma of notorious perjury—the friendless, the much-accused, and the ordeal-worthy. It is worth noting in this context that where every trial verified an oath, every litigant who lost a case was automatically a perjurer; not only would this be a dreadful blow to one's honor, it could have devastating implications for one's future legal standing. Just how devastating may be judged from the provision in the *Leges Henrici Primi* that those who had lost their neighbors' trust (*incredibilis hundreto*) could be put to the ordeal for theft simply on the accusation of three of them (ch. 65.3; 208). Hence, feelings ran high, and there was considerable pressure to settle, not merely in those cases destined to be decided by judicial duel, but in every case which seemed likely to end up in an assertory oath: "Þa cwædon þa witan þe þær wæron," reads the account of a late-tenth-century Anglo-Saxon lawsuit, "þæt betere wære þæt man þene aþ aweg lete þonne hine man sealde forþan þær syþþan nan freondscype nære" [Then the elders who were present said that it would be better to set the oath aside rather than to give it, for after that there would be no chance of friendship] (A. J. Robertson 136). As late as twelfth-century London, the potential danger of pushing matters to a judicial oath was still recognized: "For if any one in the city should swear against his neighbour, whether concerning an inquest or an assize or concerning that wherein he has offended, great mischief might arise therefrom; for when the citizens are thus crowded together, whether at their drinking or elsewhere, they might kill each other and the city would never enjoy firm peace" (*BC* 2:56).

So diverse were local customs and so much was open to negotiation between the parties, that it is impossible to give a simple account of the progress of a typical folklaw case. I offer, however, an idealized diagram of the principles underlying folklaw litigation in the interests of clarifying what might otherwise seem a hopelessly random set of procedures (see Figure 1). It is based on English and Norman practice (though even here there must be many local exceptions and qualifications), and can only be transposed to other Germanic jurisdictions in the most general terms. Even then we must still remind ourselves that rules of court did not have for the folklaw the rigidity that they have in a modern legal setting; until hardened by literate record and enforced by an authoritarian system, they could do no more than provide a framework for bilateral negotiation, and were themselves always subject to modification in the face of local pressure.[14] This diagram may, however, be of some help as we trace the three main stages of the folklaw case (corresponding to what later law would know as initial, mesne, and final process).

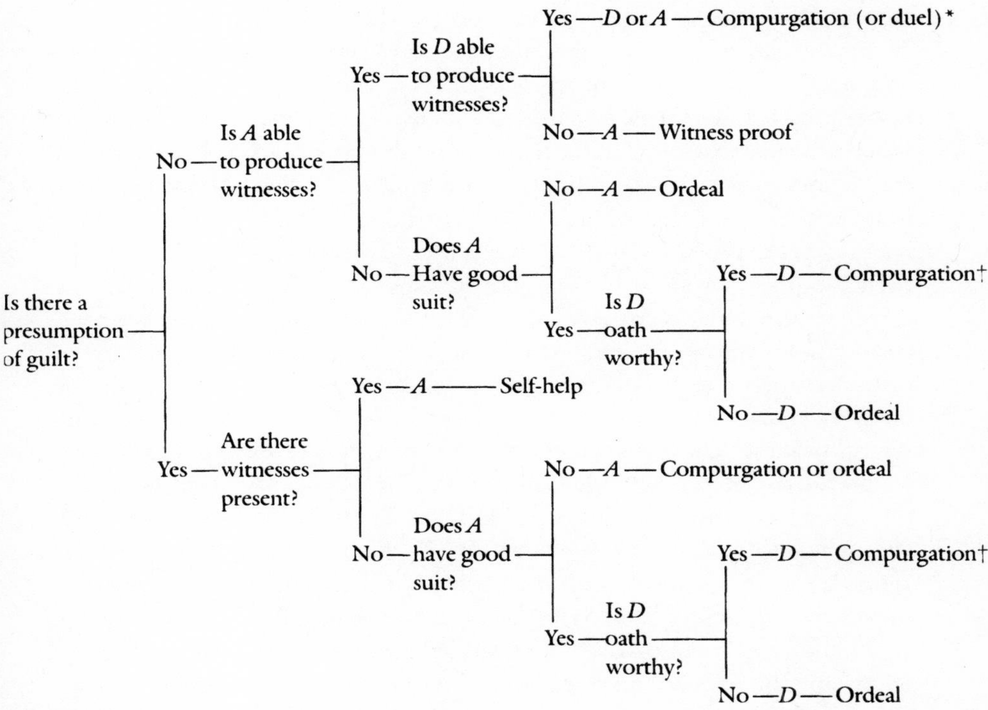

Figure 1. Folklaw litigation. *A* = accuser; *D* = one who denies the accusation; * = situation most likely to cause dissension; † = situation in which *A* might sometimes be put to the proof.

Where the parties were of equal social status and equally oathworthy, and where there was no question of manifest guilt, proceedings would begin with the plaintiff swearing an oath that the defendant had harmed him or her in some way. Such foreoaths might include the grounds for making the accusation; here, for instance, are two from an Anglo-Saxon formulary: "By the Lord, I do not summon N. either from enmity or malice or greed, but I know of nothing more true than what my informant told me and what I pronounce as a truth, that he was the thief of my cattle"; and "In the name of the almighty Lord, you promised me that what you sold me was sound, lawful, and warranted against subsequent claims, as witnessed by N. who was present with the two of us" (*Swer*.4 and 7; Liebermann 1:396–98). Since the final arbiter would be the community itself, plaintiffs needed, even at this stage, to show that they could muster communal support. Where possible they would produce material witnesses prepared to swear that they had seen and heard the event complained of, or, where the dispute concerned a contract, instrumental witnesses, who had been present when the original bargain was struck. "This is true," swears the witness to an assault in the Norman *Summa de Legibus*, "and I saw and heard it, and am prepared to decide this at law" [esgardium curie super hoc facere] (ch. 84.2; *CN* 2:199), and the instrumental witness in the Anglo-Saxon formulary swears: "In the name of the almighty Lord, as I stand here, a true witness for N., neither importuned nor bribed, I saw with my eyes and heard with my ears, that which I shall speak alongside him" (*Swer*. 8; Liebermann 1:398). When no such witnesses were available the plaintiff was expected to provide sponsors (the *secta* or *suit*, from which our terms *to sue* and *lawsuit* are derived) to guarantee that there was a genuine case to answer; the corresponding group of guarantors on the defendant's side, the compurgators or oath-helpers, were only employed at a later stage of the trial. No doubt many defendants faced with respectable witnesses would back down at this stage, but if they chose to deny the charge they would be expected to swear a counter-oath—in the example from the *Summa de Legibus*: "I did not cause this wound, and this man who offers himself as a witness neither saw nor heard [it], which thing I am prepared to prove by compurgation" (ch. 84.4; *CN* 2:199–200). In the more formal assemblies, a date would then be set, the parties would provide some kind of pledge or surety for their subsequent appearance, and the case would be adjourned. Provided both parties turned up on the appointed day (and an elaborate set of rules grew up to cover excuses for non-appearance, *essoins*), the case would then move from its initial into its medial stage.

This, though it is usually the least well documented, must have been the most lengthy and complicated stage of folklaw litigation. The first decisions here concerned the type of proof to be employed and which party was to be put to it—far less simple matters than we might imagine. Faced with devious, prevaricating, or intransigent litigants, the court could only appeal to custom in its search for a settlement, but custom was too malleable a tool to give firm shape to the arguments of the truly disputatious, and, particularly where both sides could produce respectable witnesses, the bicentric system must sometimes have come under severe pressure. As we have seen, it was just this kind of situation which Louis the Pious imagined might justify battle. Where both sides were of similar status but the issue less potentially explosive, the usual mode of proof chosen was compurgation; such questions as how many supporters would be needed and how they were to be chosen might still occasion much discussion, however. Where the parties were of unequal social status or one of them was held not to be oathworthy, the court would usually have settled on ordeal as the mode of proof, though again questions such as the type and severity of the ordeal would still need to be decided.

Modern commentators, who often seem to have difficulty believing that swearing an oath could have been a demanding way of proving one's case, assume that litigants would have fought for, rather than against, what Thayer calls, the "privilege" of going to the proof (10). The reality may well have been closer to what Rosen has observed in present-day Morocco, where the judicial oath is still employed: "I have myself not only seen many cases where one person refers the oath back to another: I have even witnessed a case in which a person maintained his claim all the way from the court to the mosque where the oath was to be taken only to stop on the doorstep, refuse to swear, and thus relinquish his preemptory right to conclude his claim successfully" (34).[15] In Morocco the rules for assigning proof are complex: the theoretical rule, claimed to have the authority of the prophet Muhammad, is that "the oath is incumbent on him who denies," but in practice it is "the one presumed most likely to know what is true about the matter at hand," whether plaintiff or defendant, who is usually challenged to swear; in any event, the party challenged always has the right to refer the oath back to his or her opponent (Rosen 33). Though, in the English folklaw too there seems to have been a general rule that defendants should be put to the proof (cf. P&M 2:603), the practice was again more flexible. In London, for instance, a defendant was free to "put himself himself on the oath of a plaintiff or *vice versa*" [a 'peremptory oath'], and traces of this survive at least as late as 1383 (*Calendar of Select Pleas* 15 and n.1).[16]

Above all, the litigants at this stage of the trial had to establish the nature and precise wording of the oath itself—a process that took place within a highly formal framework. As Robert Besnier has said, "an unorthodox plea is assumed not to be serious, and an unorthodox or inappropriate rejoinder is taken to be the work of someone who is in the wrong and who is being recalcitrant or evasive" (93). The *Leges Henrici Primi* divide oaths of exculpation into *iuramenta plana*, apparently brief oaths of general denial (including what is sometimes called a *thwertutnay* [a 'flat-out no'!]), and *iuramenta frangentia* or *fracta* (also known as *observantiae verborum*), more complex oaths, sworn clause by clause;[17] each would have been appropriate to particular offenses and particular offenders and would have demanded careful scrutiny by the opposing party. The Anglo-Saxon formulary offers the defendant accused of cattle theft a choice of four counter oaths (*Swer*. 3.1–4; Liebermann 1:396), and the plaintiff would have had to watch carefully to make sure that the one chosen exactly matched the offense complained of. We shall look more closely at this key point in the trial when we come to consider equivocal oaths a little later. Other formal matters that might be raised at this stage (such as the acceptability of essoins, the role and status of any sureties, attorneys, or other interested parties) offered equally fruitful grounds for dispute. A defendant, reluctant to go to the proof, could thoroughly muddy the waters at this point in the hope that the charge might be dropped before they cleared, and the legacy of this particular aspect of the folklaw can clearly be seen in interminable procedural bickering of the yearbooks in the fourteenth and fifteenth centuries.

In the final stage, which in the more elaborate tribunals would again have taken place on a later occasion (with ample opportunity for further wrangling over essoins), the oath of one of the parties was put to formal proof.[18] Where it proved sound the swearer was vindicated and his opponents would be forced to retract. The Norman *Summa de Legibus* vividly evokes the shame which attached to such a retraction: "he shall hold the end of his nose between his fingers [nasum suum digitis suis per sumitatem tenebit], and say: 'In that I called you thief (or murderer or whatever other crime he had been formally accused of), I lied, for this crime is not in you, and from my own mouth with which I said this, I have proclaimed myself a liar'" (ch. 86.3; *CN* 2:207). In most cases such failure to prove one's claim would result in a fine or even mutilation. If the oath of exculpation failed (or as the Anglo-Saxons said, "burst"), the swearer was subject to various penalties, and his opponent might expect compensation of some kind. Of the various formal proofs, I have already said something about the judicial duel, but compurgation and ordeal need to be discussed more fully.

Forms of Folklaw Proof

Compurgation

In proof by compurgation, the swearer had to have his oath ratified by a number of oathworthy supporters. "By the Lord," swears the defendant in the Anglo-Saxon formulary, "I am innocent [*unscyldig*] in either deed or word of the accusation which N. makes against me," and the oath of his companion who stands with him ("his geferan að, þe him mid standað") is, "by the Lord, the oath which N. has sworn is honest and unperjured [*clæne ⁊ unmæne*]" (*Swer.* 5 and 6; Liebermann 1:398). Similarly, the *Summa de Legibus* gives, "Concerning this oath which Thomas has sworn, he has sworn a sound oath [*salvum sacramentum*], so help me God and these holy relics" (ch. 85.2; *CN* 2:201). The one important condition attached to these supporting oaths, at least in theory, was that they should be sworn in precise form; any hesitation, omission, or deviation (known in English as *miskenning*) would result in the principal losing his case: "Note well," says the *Summa de Legibus*, that the compurgation is to be rejected "if any oath-helper [*coadjutor*] should be missing, or if he leave out or change any of the words dictated to him [*verba escariata*], or if he has to be called, summoned, or brought to the *disrainia*" (ch. 85.4; *CN* 2:202). A thirteenth-century English treatise lists the ways in which one can fail in one's law: "if the principal withdraws his hand from the book while he is making the oath, or fails to kiss the book, or does not say the words in full as they are charged against him, or if he has not the due number of compurgators, or if any of them makes a default" (*Court Baron* 17; cf. *BC* 1:51–52). Even where the oath was unsupported, the least sign of hesitation might be taken to indicate of guilt: in fifteenth-century Guines defendants swore a fivefold oath with their hand on the cross and lost their case if the hand trembled "even the least bit" ("qu'il tramble de la main tant seullement") (*Livre des usaiges* 73). In practice, however, one may doubt that very minor slips were invariably fatal (cf. Miller 1990, 248); the most tyrannical formalism generally belongs to the literate process of a later period.

Apart from a universal concern with miskenning (which was taken to indicate perjury), the rules about compurgation varied widely. In some places, for instance, the oath-helpers had to swear to the same oath several times, in others only once (cf. *LHP* ch. 64.1a–d; 202). There was a similar lack of uniformity in the number of oath-helpers required (P&M 2:601), two normally being the minimum, and twelve perhaps being regarded as standard, in England at least.[19] The process by which compurgators were selected was also far from uniform; often they were chosen by the principal swearer (sometimes from a group nominated by the court), but they might be nominated directly by the court or even picked by lot (*LHP* 430–35): with particularly serious cases in early medieval London, for instance, the aldermen (*prud'hommes*) bore the responsibility for their selection (Bateson 707), and Ipswich adopted the expedient of spinning a knife and choosing those to whom the blade pointed (Thayer 26). In practice, the actual number of sponsors and the way they were chosen would probably have varied according, not only to local custom, but also to the social standing of the litigants and the gravity of the charge.

It is important to distinguish oath-helpers from witnesses. While principals were expected to swear on the basis of their knowledge of the facts—"since every person is presumed to know best the truth of his own actions," as the *Summa de Legibus* puts it (ch. 123.1; *CN* 2:328)—oath-helpers attested to the good faith of the principals. Unlike witnesses, compurgators were not required to swear that they had seen or heard anything. What they were supporting was not primarily the factual truth of the defense, but the ethical truth of the defendant. A story from Gregory of Tours illustrates this perfectly.

When, in 585, King Guntram challenged the recently widowed Queen Fredegond to provide "clear proof" [*certa indicia*] that her young son Lothar was legitimate, she assembled three bishops and three hundred other dignitaries to swear an oath "that the boy had been fathered by King Chilperic" (8.9; 2:170). Of the three hundred and four people swearing to Fredegond's innocence that day, only one could have known the actual facts, yet Guntram unhestitatingly accepted the procedure as proof of her innocence. Since what was really on trial here was the queen's reputation, her honor, and since this was itself a function of communal attitudes toward her, it is entirely fitting that she should have sought to exonerate herself by a public demonstration of the community's confidence and that her accuser should have been satisfied with such a demonstration.

While a defendant might seek to produce oath-helpers to counter the plaintiff's witnesses, compurgation seems generally to have been regarded as less satisfactory than witness proof: "Where the law requires proof by three witnesses for simple homicide, and he cannot find witnesses," says an edict of the emperor Lothar, "we allow that he may swear with twelve oath-helpers, that cleared of the crime, he shall not lose his own life" (ch. 92; *Leges Langobardorum* 556). Faced with a plaintiff supported by respected witnesses, a defendant would have needed to gather a significantly greater number of respected oath-helpers to mount a successful defense. When Saint Eugenia, disguised as a male physician, is accused of sexual assault, the reeve is incensed at the idea that she might clear herself with an unsupported oath against the evidence of witnesses:

> Đ sædon þa hyred-menn þæt hit soð wære .
> and ealle mid aðe eugenian forlugan .
> Þa wearð se geræfa . þearle gebolgen .
> and axude eugenian . hu heo ana mihte
> ealle þa gewytan awægan mid aðe .
> (Ælfric, *Lives* 1:38; lines 221–25)

> [Then the servants said it was true, and falsely accused Eugenia with an oath. The reeve then became very angry and asked Eugenia how she alone could defeat all these witnesses with an oath.]

Probably, in fact, few defendants would have been allowed to clear themselves with an unsupported oath, and those few of sufficient status to make accusing them a doubtful undertaking in the first place.

The provision of private justice through social consensus is probably a fundamental element in the folklaw of most cultures, but compurgation demanded a particularly complex system of mutual trust to make it work. Despite the skepticism of earlier commentators like Lea, compurgation can only be explained in terms of a society that placed great value on the quality of personal trouthe. The system was open to abuse, of course, but generally speaking plaintiffs wishing to gather together an acceptable suit, or defendants in need of compurgators, would have found the task impossible unless they enjoyed a reputation for honesty and fair dealing; conversely, those asked to act as oath-helpers for a notoriously untrustworthy litigant would have risked their own reputation by assisting.

Earlier legal historians generally express little faith in such simple social pressure. Even Maitland, though conceding that "in the village courts . . . it would not be easy for a man of bad repute to produce helpers" (2:636), still concludes that "our ancestors perjured themselves with impunity" (2:543), and Holdsworth, though he too recognizes that "it would probably be difficult to get any considerable number of compurgators from the same neighbourhood and of the same rank [as] the accused to swear deliberately to be true that which the countryside knew to be false" (2:110), nonetheless suggests that it would have been easier with the older methods of proof "to meet a perjured claim by more detailed and particular perjury than to establish the truth" (1:311).[20] Recent commentators, however, have shown rather more faith in the effectiveness of compurgation. S. F. C. Milsom, for instance, suggests that "in the community situation, whether a community of neighbours who lived with each other or of merchants who dealt with each other, such guarantees of good faith probably ensured that only honest claims were pressed as well as that only honest denials were carried to wager of law and the like" (1981, 247–48). On the evidence of its use in church courts, R. H. Helmholz shows that, even measured by the crude standard of conviction rates, compurgation was at least no more ineffectual than the so-called rational modes of proof like jury trial (1983, 18–20);[21] he suggests, moreover, that we will only appreciate its efficacy once we have learned to resist the temptation to regard oath-helpers "primarily as triers of law and fact" and accepted their "'social' role in maintaining public peace" (1983, 24). What of course all commentators agree on is that the system worked best in a "community situation," that the threat of losing one's standing in the village, the hundred, the guild, or the parish was the major sanction against perjury and false witness.

While some scholars may have doubted the efficacy of compurgation, its popularity and durability suggest that medieval people themselves clearly appreciated its advantages. Not only was it the most widely distributed of folklaw proofs — in Lea's words, it "ruled from Southern Italy to Scotland" (34) —

it was also the most frequently employed. In England, indeed, compurgation was synonymous with the word *law* itself—to make (or wage) one's law, *facere/vadiare suam legem*, *gager sa ley*, meant to clear oneself with oath-helpers (or pledge to do so)—and in Normandy, the *Summa de Legibus* calls cases concluded by compurgation (*disraisnia*) *quereles simplices* (ch. 84.1; *CN* 2: 198), with the implication that all others (those ending in battle, inquest, or, at an earlier period, ordeal) belonged to a more exotic class of action. Judicial duels and even ordeals are scattered across the pages of romance, but in practice they were far less common than the compurgation for which we must search with a fine-tooth comb.[22]

The remarkable longevity of this process also attests to its utility. We shall see in the next chapter that it was still resorted to by the common law of Chaucer's day to decide some actions of debt, as well as for resolving a number of procedural logjams (P&M 2:634), and in the chaotic aftermath of the Peasants' Revolt parliament returned to it as an effective way of dealing with a rash of malicious prosecutions (6 Rich. 2, stat. 2, c.5; *SR* 2:31). Michael Bennett has noted an instance of its being used to settle a land dispute in Cheshire as late as 1412, despite the apparent availability of written evidence: "a mass having been celebrated [Sir Thomas] Grosvenor swore upon the body of Christ that he believed in the truth of the charters by which he claimed the disputed lands. His oath was then affirmed by fifty-eight of the other gentlemen present each 'raising his hand at the same time towards the Host as a sign of the veracity of the oath'" (25). In ecclesiastical courts, moreover, compurgation was widely used for dealing with criminal cases (Helmholz 1983), and it remained common in local courts to the end of the Middle Ages. Robert Henry sets an oath from Lydd in 1476 beside the Anglo-Saxon one quoted above to show that "the oaths of the defendants and of their compurgators were thus substantially the same from the tenth to the fifteenth century" (53). Such remarkable durability implies that the inferiority of compurgation to more modern methods of proof was not always obvious to those in a position to judge between the two.

Before leaving the topic of compurgation and witness proof, we might note one curious aspect of their legacy to the institution that, by the late Middle Ages, had largely replaced them (at least in the king's courts)—the jury. When Peter Idley, in the mid-fifteenth century, updated an old story from Robert Mannyng of Brunne about God's punishment of a litigant who had won his case by swearing a perjured oath in compurgation,[23] he evidently saw no reason not to transfer its moral to the situation of a false juryman:

> Anon as he hadde made his othe
> In open court before the Iugis audience,

God to whom periurie is grevous and lothe
Anon gave hem his mortall sentence.
(2750–53)

Modern courts require of their jurors an honest opinion not a guaranteed judgment and are quite prepared to forgive them their human fallibility should this opinion later prove mistaken. The Middle Ages seem to have made a far closer indentification between the truth of a jury's findings and the ethical truth of the jury itself. Only some such identification can explain why the opprobrium that attached to corrupt juries throughout the Middle Ages should regularly have been expressed in terms of perjury:

& þerfor ȝe questmen þat gon vp on questis,
For eny wraþþe or wynnyng do ȝe þat best is.
Loke þat ȝe swere truli & trewe tale telle,
Þat ȝe dampne not ȝour soulis & wend vn to helle.
("Lovedays" 144–47)

There is clearly more to such a passage than the simple feeling that dishonest jurymen had failed in their sworn undertaking to provide impartial justice; even Holdsworth (1:337) hardly goes far enough when he suggests that the older concept of jurymen as neighbor-witnesses explains why giving a false verdict made them guilty of "something like perjury" (see also Mitnick 203; R. Palmer 1984, 10). People still seem to have been able to conceive of a legal verdict in terms of its root meaning, a "trewe tale" (*voir dit* or *veredictum*), so that an erroneous verdict might almost be thought of as a kind of lie. Thus a late-thirteenth-century legal tract, *The Mirror of Justices*, regards it as an abuse "to insert into oaths the phrase, 'to the best of their knowledge,' so as to compel jurors to say what they opine, whereas the principal words of their oath are to the effect that they will say the truth [*qil voir dirrent*]" (173).

This curious viewpoint helps explain Bracton's virulent attack on attainted jurors as perjurers: "they incur perpetual infamy and lose the *lex terrae*, so that they will never afterwards be admitted to an oath, for they will not henceforth be oathworthy [quia de cetero non erunt *atheswurthe*]" (3:346). Statutes and law reports confirm this impression that jurors were felt to be somehow deciding cases *by* oath, not merely *on* oath. Thus the preamble to a chapter in Edward I's first statute of Westminster (1275) that institutes the action of attaint for land disputes reads, "Forasmuch as certain People of this Realm doubt very little to make a false Oath, which they ought not to do, whereby much People are disherited and lose their Right" (3 Edw. 1, stat. 1, c.38; *SR* 1:36); and the first statute of Edward III's reign (1327) extends attaint to cover "the false Oaths of Jurors in Writs of Trepass" (1 Edw. 3, stat. 1, c.6; *SR* 1:253). So, too, a yearbook report of a verdict in attaint from 1342/43 begins, "the jury [of attaint] said that the jurors of the petty jury had made a false oath, inasmuch as they said that the manor of Elledene was not given to the ancestor of John, son of Thomas de Brembleshete (uncle of Lawrence who now is plaintiff)" (*YB 16 Edw. 3 (pt i)*, 60–61). As late as the fifteenth century, a strong sense of shame still attached to such attainder: "the bodies of those jurors shall be committed to the prison of the lord king," says Fortescue, "their houses and buildings demolished, their woods cut down, their meadows ploughed up, and they themselves shall henceforth be infamous, and their testimony as to the truth shall nowhere be accepted" (*De laudibus* 60–63).

Ordeal

To those who had lost their oathworthiness or who could find few oath-helpers willing to support them, the folklaw offered one final opportunity for exculpation—the ordeal. Ordeal may have been an alternative to compurgation, but it was not, as is sometimes suggested (e.g., R. Bartlett 30), an alternative to oath-taking. Just like the other forms of folklaw proof, its purpose was in fact to authenticate an oath (P&M 2:600). Æthelstan's laws at Grately say that the accused is to "go to confession on the day when he must go to the ordeal, and then swear the oath that under the folklaw he is innocent of the accusation [he sy mid folcryhte unscyldig ðære tihtlan], before going to the ordeal" (ch. 23; Liebermann 1:162). And from early thirteenth-century Germany, when the institution was on the wane, we hear the accused invoking the power of the host to strike him dead, "if it is other than I have said and sworn" (quoted by Rubin 336). "O God," runs a prayer in an English form of the ordeal of bread and cheese, "knot up his gorge and choke off his gullet, that he may not swallow this bread and cheese, hallowed in your name, if he has unjustly sworn and denied the theft (or homicide, or adultery, or crime) of which he is accused, and held his oath at nothing, and called upon your name when it was not right to do so" (Liebermann 1:408). To be fair, such formulas are not typical: most prayers invoke the medium of the ordeal to expose either guilt in general or the specific crime complained of, not the perjury of the accused; on the other hand, since much of our knowledge about *judicia Dei* comes from the church officers who had to administer them, and since the ecclesiastical attitude toward judicial oaths was ambivalent, official forms may be somewhat disingenuous in this matter.[24] The importance of the judicial oath is certainly recognized in literary representations of the ordeal: it is a vital element in Thomas of Britain's account of Isolt's ordeal, as we shall see, and in the ballad of "Young Hunting" the murderer perishes in the fire after swearing that she had not seen her victim "since Moninday at morn" (Child 2:153).

Literary accounts of trial by ordeal usually portray it as a simple process producing unequivocal results in defiance of natural laws. In the romance of *Athelston*, for instance, Earl Egelond's stroll across hot coals leaves him "vnblemeschyd, ffoot and hand" (588), and when the falsely accused servant in "Young Hunting" is thrown into the fire,

> It wadna take upon her cheik,
> Nor yet upon her chin,
> Nor yet upon her yellow hair,
> To clense the deadly sin.
> (Child 2:153)

By contrast, when Egelond's accuser is put to the same test, "doun he ffel þe ffyr amydde; / Hys eyen wolde hym nouȝt lede" (*Athelston* 787–88), and Young Hunting's real murderer burns "like hollins grene" (Child 2:153). Sir Walter Scott, for one, was only too happy to take such dramatic displays seriously: the trial of Ysonde, he explains, "consisted in actually carrying a piece of red-hot iron in the naked hand from the choir to the altar through the whole length of a Gothic cathedral" (cited in *Sir Tristrem* 125). Alice's Queen of Hearts would doubtless have heartily approved of such a process ("Sentence first—verdict afterwards!"), but the reality proves to have been rather more complex.

Ordeals offered neither so daunting a challenge nor such unequivocal results as romance and ballad imply. Among the three hundred or so complete cases involving trial by hot iron recorded by the Varad register between 1208 and 1235, we find only seventy-eight convictions (Van Caenegem 68); even excluding cases settled out of court and comparing only those which actually went to trial, we find the ordeal acquitting nearly twice as many as it convicted (130 to 78). A story in the chronicle of Eadmer similarly suggests that "the ordeal of hot iron was so arranged as to give the accused a considerable chance of escape" (P&M 2:599): when some fifty survivors of the Anglo-Saxon nobility were sent to the ordeal for stealing the king's deer all fifty were acquitted—much to the annoyance of the king, William Rufus (*English Lawsuits* 122). From a study of crown pleas in the first quarter of the thirteenth century Maitland concludes that most defendants completed their ordeals successfully; in fact he finds only one recorded failure in the whole of that period (*SPC* 1:75 n. 3). Even those, like Peter the Chanter, whose opposition to ordeal led to its abolition at the Fourth Lateran Council (in 1215), seem to have been as much concerned with the fact that ordeal allowed the guilty to escape as that it convicted the innocent (J. Baldwin 629). If the ordeal was really so loaded against the accused how are we to explain such facts?

Two English accounts of ordeal by hot iron, one from just before the Norman conquest and one from after it (Liebermann 1:386–87 and 427–29), allow us to reconstruct a typical trial and to understand how such acquittal rates were possible. After a period of preparation which involved fasting and attending mass, accuser and accused, with an equal number of supporters, entered the church, where a burning brazier had been set up, and a track nine feet long (measured by the feet of the accused) and divided into three equal portions had been drawn; at one end of this track was placed a stand, and at the other there was a mark—presumably some kind of line. The priest then proceeded to bless the ordeal—and the earlier ordinance specifies that no one is to build up the fire once this blessing had begun (Liebermann 1:387). The iron, weighing between one and three pounds (depending on the number and severity of the accusations and the status of the accused) was then placed in the fire while mass was said. It was then removed from the fire and placed on a stand, where it sat cooling while a prayer was said, the opening of the Gospel of John was read, and holy water was sprinkled upon it and upon the accused's hand (Liebermann 1:387 and 429). The description at this point continues: "Let him hold (*teneat*) his right foot in the first division next to the stand and his left foot in the second one. Then let him transfer his right foot to the third division, when the iron may be thrown down and he should hasten to the holy altar. And let his hand be sealed up, and on the third day let it be examined to see whether it is festering (*inmunda*) or whole (*munda*; *clæne*) within the bandage" (Liebermann 1:387). I take this to mean that the accused had already placed one foot in each of the first two divisions (a natural stance for a right-handed person) before picking up the iron. If this is right, it would mean that he or she carried the iron merely a single step before throwing it down, but even if it is not, the maximum number of steps required could not have been more than three—a very far cry from "the whole length of a Gothic cathedral."

One's innocence was established, moreover, not by the fact that one's hand remained miraculously unburned, but by the far less remarkable process of normal healing: only evidence of exceptional physical trauma, *insanies crudescens* (Liebermann 1:429), was taken to indicate guilt. Such a criterion introduces a considerable human element into the *judicium Dei*, for though God may have been the final judge, the priest who muttered the prayers more or less quickly, who sprinkled holy water more or less liberally, who undid the bandaged hand more or less gently was hardly his passive intermediary. In any case, judgment of normal healing, as Peter Brown notes, is "as open-ended as a Rorschach test" (1975, 139), and in at least one Icelandic instance the supervising priest confesses himself unable to interpret the evidence conclusively (Andersson and Miller 209).

A major factor in any such interpretation must have been the attitude of the onlookers — the supporters on either side. A story in a late-tenth-century poem on Saint Swithun by Wulfstan Cantor (*Frithegodi* 150–54) tells how an implacable reeve forces an accused slave to undergo an ordeal despite his master's willingness to pay compensation on his behalf. The reeve has the fire so well stoked that the glowing iron is emitting sparks at the moment it is taken out ("scintillat et undique fervens") (342–43), and the terrified slave naturally accepts it with some reluctance (345–46). Long before the bandages are taken off his supporters have given him up for lost, but on the third day (through the miraculous intervention, the poet says, of Saint Swithun) the reeve and his party, despite the unmistakable evidence of a painful burn, immediately proclaim his innocence ("exclamat cum preside turba clientum / . . . 'vir hic inculpabilis est' ") (384–86)]. Clearly, the verdict of the ordeal is a curious amalgam of divine and human justice — the judgment of God manipulated to make it consonant with the communal will.

Such an account makes it obvious how the ordeal by hot iron could acquit a majority of those submitting to it, but it raises further problems. What Rebecca Colman calls "the discretionary power of local communities" (589) to manipulate the *judicium Dei* in accordance with their own preconceptions about a defendant's guilt or innocence led opponents, such as Peter the Chanter, to regard the whole process as downright fraud. Yet, as William Miller points out, "the fact that people rig ordeals does not mean that they do not believe in them" (1988, 203). A similar kind of "effortless mix of factual and legal / moral questions" (Hyams 1981, 100) can be observed in Chinua Achebe's novel *Arrow of God*: "There, in a fairly quiet corner of the *ilo*, sat Otakekpeli. This man was known throughout Umuaro as a wicked medicine man. More than twice he had had to take kolanut from the palm of a dead man to swear he had no hand in the death. Of course he had survived each oath which could mean that he was innocent. But people did not believe it; they said he had immediately rushed home and drunk powerful, counteracting potions" (196). Elechi Amadi confirms that "the results of an ordeal could sometimes be manipulated . . . a poison brew for an ordeal could be diluted or strengthened" (1982, 86).[25] Bronislaw Malinowski, long ago, observed that the Trobriand Islanders could express "horror at the idea of violating the rules," despite possessing "a well established system" for evading them (1926, 79–80), and as another modern Nigerian novelist, T. Obinkaram Echewa puts it, "even if our people are always saying that justice is like a brittle twig which cannot be bent, they are bending it, even while the words are still on their lips" (*The Crippled Dancer* 40). Paradoxically, then, "the vast bedrock of cunning with which medieval men actually faced and manipulated the supernatural in their affairs" (P. Brown 1975, 139) need not have precluded a profound faith in divine justice.

To believe that God's will is infallibly revealed in the ordeal and at the same time to recognize that the ordeal is subject to human manipulation looks to us like a classic breach of the law of noncontradiction (though this is not what most legal historians will mean when they call early process irrational). Certainly, this aspect of the ordeal exposed it to the scorn of educated commentators and representatives of authority alike. As Gottfried von Strassburg says of Isolde's exoneration by hot iron, "Thus it was made manifest and confirmed to all the world that Christ in His great virtue is pliant as a wind-blown sleeve [wintschaffen alse ein ermel ist]. He falls into place and clings whichever way you try him" (15733–36). According to Eadmer, William Rufus had expressed his frustration in failing to convict his fifty poachers in similar terms: "for the future . . . answer shall be made to my judgment, not to God's, which inclines to one side or the other in answer to each man's prayer [pro voto cujusque hinc inde plicatur]" (*English Lawsuits* 122). Yet to those small-scale societies which favor the kind of flexible face-to-face justice in which honor and personal reputation are intimately bound up with innocence and guilt, the kind of dispassionate inquiry into fact which we believe to constitute a higher form of jurisprudence will often seem equally repugnant. "Real justice," says the Nigerian novelist T. M. Aluko, is "impossible under a truth-inhibiting judicial system which [has] been imported from a foreign clime" (*Wrong Ones in the Dock* 185). Considering the judicial legacy of colonialism, we should hardly feel very smug about the superiority of our own "cold-blooded" process in such contexts.

Medieval trial by ordeal has been much misunderstood by those who have tried to reconcile it with the authoritarian model of law. The use of ordeal, even though normally restricted to those cases we should call criminal, was evidently still part of a bicentric system, demanded by the accuser or chosen by the accused, not a sentence passed down from above. Certainly, those who went to the ordeal did not usually enjoy the same kind of prestige as those who accused them (otherwise, the question of ordeal would hardly have arisen), but even the friendless could hope that their readiness to undergo voluntary pain and indignity might win them popular sympathy and offer tangible evidence of their belief in the truth of their cause.[26] As the Archbishop in *Athelston* remarks before offering Earl Egelond and his family a chance to prove their innocence by walking over hot coals,

> ȝiff þay be gylty off þat dede,
> Sorrere þe doome þay may drede,
> Ðan schewe here schame to me.
> (564–66)

The ordeal, then, was predicated on the assumption that a willingness to suffer pain would demonstrate the ethical truth of the accused.[27] The process has as much to do with expiation as exculpation (Colman). What Miller calls this "staged enactment of humiliation" (1988, 210) expresses the group's need to reestablish harmony even as it acknowledges the individual's need for vindication. The malice or cunning of the accuser, the pathetic agony, the noble stoicism, even the engaging quick-wittedness of the accused, and in particular the previous reputation of each party for fair dealing will all play a part in the communal drama and its final confirmation of guilt or innocence, rejection or acceptance, for which divine revelation will appear a perfectly reasonable explanation. To atone for disturbing the equilibrium of the community, to seek to regain one's former status in its eyes, is to confirm its sense of a divine purpose whatever the practical outcome might be.

A similar ethos may well have informed trial by battle; to undertake this painful and potentially lethal form of exculpation was to seek to prove one's ethical truth and defend one's honor to the world. Thomas Usk, late though his testimony is, provides a rare insight into the mind of someone prepared to fight such a judicial duel, and significantly the purgatorial nature of the ritual is precisely what attracts him to it. Languishing in prison and aware that his good name was in peril—"see ye not now, lady, how the felonous thoughtes of this people and covins of wicked men conspyren ayen my sothfast trouth" (29)—Usk was well aware that in trying to clear himself by judicial combat he risked defeat. For him that was not the point: "Many men in batayle ben discomfited and overcome in a rightful quarel, that is goddes privy jugement in heven; but yet, although the party be yolden, he may with wordes saye his quarel is trewe, and to yelde him, in the contrarye, for dreade of the dethe he is compelled; and he that graunteth and no stroke hath feled, he may not crepe away in this wyse by none excusacion. Indifferent folk wil say: 'ye, who is trewe, who is fals, him-selfe knowlegeth tho thinges'" (31–32). From this perspective, the trial was less an inflexible quest for factual certainty, than a public spectacle of self-exoneration where the real judgment lay neither with God nor brute force, but with the willingness of the community to accept expiation. Unfortunately for Usk, however, centralized authority had long since handcuffed such communal verdicts, and there is a dreadful irony in the fact that this man who had sought the mercy of judicial combat should in the end have been clumsily executed by the state, protesting his truth to the last (*Westminster Chronicle* 314).

Like compurgation, ordeal evidently served a valuable social function. By no means all Peter the Chanter's contemporaries shared his animus against the *judicium Dei*, and it retained its appeal in the popular imagination long after the Fourth Lateran Council's ban on clerical participation effectively put an end to it. In England, formal ordeal died out almost as soon as the ink was dry on the canon, but in other parts of Europe it lingered on for some time, and "Roger Bacon tells us that, half a century after the Lateran Council, there were still many men in various places saying prayers over hot iron and cold water and such-like things" (Southern 1953, 97). The English crown may have welcomed this opportunity to scotch the ordeal, but its passing was certainly mourned in other quarters: writing nearly a century later, the author of *The Mirror of Justices* declares flatly, "it is an abuse that proofs and purgations are not made by the miracle of God when no other proof can be had" (173), and literary accounts, like the fourteenth-century romance of *Athelston*, generally show justice well served by the ordeal. It survived unofficially in folk custom well into the seventeenth century, as Keith Thomas has shown (260–62 and 658), and its memory is still preserved in a traditional ballad like "Young Hunting," recorded in the nineteenth.

I suggested earlier that the precise wording of the oath to be tested, whether by ordeal or in some other way, was one of the most difficult of the questions to be decided at the medial stage of the trial, and I should like to conclude this chapter by suggesting how the negotiations surrounding the wording of the oath lay at the very heart of folklaw procedure, and how they form a vital part of its procedural legacy to the common law of the later Middle Ages.

Equivocal Oaths

In his account of the trial of Queen Isolt for adultery, Thomas of Britain says that before she was put to the ordeal of the hot iron the noblemen present "wrangled about her oath-formula [þrættu um eiðstaf hennar]" (*Tristrams Saga* 73); some, he adds, wanted to restrict and oppress her and others to assist her over this question ("sumir vilja þreyngja henni ok angra hana, en sumir vilja hjálpa henni um eiðstaffinn").[28] Charges of adultery must always have presented plaintiffs with a problem, for common decency would have proscribed some of the more graphic ways of wording the oath of exculpation,[29] and in this case the queen's social status must have made it an especially delicate matter. No doubt such oaths were particularly vulnerable to the kind of equivocation that Isolt subsequently employs, but in principle all those called upon to swear a judicial oath must have found themselves arguing for a wording which precisely fitted their own situation against opponents ever on their guard against possible chicanery. Casuistry plainly offered the only possible alternative to perjury for those who, knowing themselves to be guilty, were faced with having to swear to their innocence. When a malevolent steward formally accuses Amis of seducing Belisaunt, for example, the guilty couple ponder their options:

> "Ich haue þat wronge & he þe riȝt,
> Þerfore icham aferd to fiȝt,
> Al so god me spede,
> For y mot swere, wiþ-outen faile,
> Al so god me spede in bataile,
> His speche is falshede;
> & ȝif y swere, icham forsworn,
> Þan liif & soule icham forlorn;
> Certes, y can no rede!"
> Þan seyd þat leuedi in a while,
> "No mai þer go no noþer gile
> To bring that traitour doun?"
> (*Amis* 940–51)

Though the poet plainly considers the "gile" that Amis finally hits upon (that of getting his brother-in-arms and look-alike, Amiloun, to fight the duel in his place) as a dishonorable ploy, straightforward verbal equivocation seems generally to have been regarded as a perfectly legitimate tactic.

Isolt, for instance, has cleverly provided herself with material for her defense in advance. As in the ballad of "Clerk Saunders," where May Margaret uses her lover's sword to lift the latch of her chamber door and, having bound her eyes, carries him bodily to her bed, so that she may later swear, "her oth to save," that she had not let him in, nor had she seen him that night, nor had he set foot on her bedroom floor (Child 2:158–59),[30] Isolt lays the groundwork for an ostensibly watertight oath before the trial even begins. Since the ordeal is to take place on the far side of a river, Isolt has arranged that Tristran, disguised as a poor pilgrim, shall lift her from the boat; when they reach the bank, she hoists her dress and he falls on top of her—as the Scottish metrical version, *Sir Tristrem*, puts it, "next her naked side" (2251). Isolt is thus able to offer King Mark an oath that no man has come close to her naked except the king himself and the poor pilgrim who had helped her from the boat.[31] Unable to find anything wrong with this oath, Mark allows her to go to the proof, where she sets her hand to the red-hot iron without flinching and carries it with no sign of fear. As in *Athelston*, where Egelond's ordeal is shared by his two small children and his pregnant wife, Thomas makes much of the pathos of Isolt's predicament and goes to great lengths to stress the popular sympathy that it evokes. That her noble fortitude, rather than some dermatological miracle, should vindicate her in the eyes of the community is precisely what we would expect, and God predictably grants her reconciliation and concord ("sætt ok samþykki") with her husband (74). Unlike his successors, Béroul and Gottfried von Strassburg, Thomas sees nothing ironic in the fact that Isolt's equivocation should have brought about this most satisfactory of folk-law verdicts — honor appeased and dissension healed.

Other medieval narratives show a similar use of the equivocal oath in a legal setting. The hero of *Víga-Glúms Saga*, for instance, clears himself of a murder, of which he is in fact guilty, in the following way: "I call Asgrím to witness . . . that I swear the temple oath by the ring, and that I declare to the god that I was not there, and that I killed not there, and that I reddened not there spear point or sword edge [ek vark at þar, ok vák at þar, ok rauðk at þar odd ok egg] when Thorvald Barb was slain. Consider now my oath ye wise men who are present" (44–45; trans. Hollander 107). His opponents say they have never heard the oath given in quite this way before, but they can find no fault with it and Glum is acquitted; the odd wording of Glum's oath, however, proves on closer examination to conceal a grammatical quibble which lets him off the hook.[32] Perhaps the best-known English instance comes from Malory's account of Lancelot's combat with Sir Mellyagraunce. Here, Mellyagraunce's mistaken belief that the man who had left bloodstains on Guinevere's bed-sheets must have been one of the ten wounded knights in her chamber offers her champion Lancelot a chance to plead what customary law would have called a *thwertutnay* and to offer battle on this specific charge: "but as to that I saye nay playnly, that this nyghte there lay none of these ten wounded knyghtes wyth my lady Quene Gueneuer, and that wil I preue with my handes, that ye say vntruly in that now" (1:545). Predictably, the ensuing battle fully justifies this equivocation and restores peace between Arthur and his queen. Equivocation clearly offers both Glum and Lancelot, as it had done Isolt, a perfectly legitimate line of defense, and in a bilateral legal context the onus was evidently on their opponents to expose its flaws in court.

What all these stories suggest is a remarkably formalistic attitude to the interpretation of oaths. In fact there is ample evidence that such an attitude was widespread in the Middle Ages. We have already seen how Earl Godric tries to circumvent his oath to marry Goldborough to "Þe heste man þat micthe liue" in *Havelok* (199) by providing her with a bridegroom who, if not conspicuously noble, is at least exceptionally tall,[33] but such literalism is not restricted to romance. From one end of the Middle Ages we have Gregory of Tours's story of two servants who flee to sanctuary after marrying against their master's orders: they are lured out by his solemn oath that he will never separate them, only to find that he plans to bury them alive together (5.3; 1:282–84). From the other, comes the story of the warden of Haverfordwest, Rhys ap Thomas, who is said to have welcomed the earl of Richmond in 1485 by lying down on the ground and allowing the future king to walk over him, "soe to make good his promise to King Richard that none should enter in at Milford, onlesse he came first over his bellie" ("Life" 217–18).[34]

Equivocal oaths seem generally to have escaped the notice of legal historians, being apparently thought of as a literary or at least folkloric device rather than a reflection of actual judicial practice.[35] However, among the laws of Ine reissued by King Alfred there is a series of regulations concerning weapons lent either by their owner or by a smith who had been given temporary charge of them (ch. 19–19.3; Liebermann 1:60). Pollock's explanation that these were designed to counter "a rather common way of obscuring the evidence of manslaying" seems almost certainly correct: "one man would be ready to swear with his oath-helpers, 'I did not kill him,' the other, with equal confidence, 'No weapon of mine killed him.'" (P&M 1:54).[36] Pollock recognizes a degree of collusion here but does not explore its implications further. If the equivocal oath "no weapon of mine killed him" was in such common use that a royal order was needed to control it, how can the other party in the case (and we should remember that at this date even murder was a private action) ever have been taken in by it? Why was it ever accepted? Why did the accusers not demand a less ambiguous formula? Pollock would probably have replied that they were coerced or intimidated by the murderers, but the answer might equally lie in more disinterested communal pressure: if the community felt that the victim had deserved his fate and that the killing was long overdue, it might be ready to accept the defendant's equivocation against all objections by his opponent. Indeed, even the accusers themselves might have been willing to settle for such a formula as the price of not incurring a dishonorable feud.[37] Where they were not, their only recourse would have been to the higher authority of the king's court, and Alfred's directive may thus be read as an early sign of confrontation between authoritarian written law and older local oral custom.

By the late thirteenth century, when the earliest surviving yearbooks give us some insight into the way the issue was negotiated in common-law pleading (the equivalent under the king's law of the folklaw's "wrangling about the oath formula"), the litigants' room to maneuver had already become so limited by formal constraints that attempts at equivocation can rarely have escaped the scrutiny of opposing counsel or of presiding judges. When the plaintiff in a case from 1311, for instance, was confronted by the claim that the tenant's interest in an estate had already been established by an earlier plea, he tried to rest his case on the assertion that "these tenements never were in plea," only to be reprimanded by one of the judges, William Bereford: "Your answer is double; it means either that the tenant was impleaded but not of these tenements, or that he never was impleaded of these tenements" (*YB 5 Edw. 2 (1311)*, 67). Indeed, it is arguable that the whole arcane ritual of common-law pleading had grown up in order to prevent just such double pleading. Even in the fourteenth century we can still see how equivocal pleas might provoke a formalized procedural response: "non fecit predictam transgressionem" [he did not commit the aforesaid trespass], for instance, eventually fell into disfavor as a rejoinder to an accusation of trespass apparently because it provided a convenient loophole for those who had got others to do their dirty work for them; from the middle of the century it was replaced by the less ambiguous formula "in nullo est inde culpabilis" [he is in no way guilty of it] (*SCT* 1:xii).

Even by Bracton's day the principals' freedom to frame special pleas had been severely circumscribed, but, then, local juries might always try to temper the rigor of royal justice by returning equivocal verdicts. Clearly, it was the job of the judge to try to forestall such equivocation—"si autem incertum dixerint iudex examinare debet" (Bracton 3:74)—but it must still have gone on, for Bracton suggests that this kind of ambiguity—"si autem obscura dixerint et dubia ubi unica oratio duplicem habere possit intellectum" (3:73)—supplied grounds for challenging a jury's decision. A Cambridgeshire case from 1286 offers a good illustration of the kind of situation Bracton must have had in mind: the prior of Barnwell sued one of his tenants, Henry Tuillet, for building a wall which prevented his bailiff from gaining access to the property, and thus collecting the rent, but the jury found against him on the grounds that "Henry has not enclosed that tenement with that wall. For they say, that William, Henry's father, enclosed that tenement" (cited by Clanchy 1977, 189). This seems to have been literally true in the sense that the father had paid for the building of a wall on his son's estate, but equivocal in the sense that it implied the tenement had already been walled when the son took seisin of it; so incensed was the prior by this equivocation that he threatened to swear out a jury of attaint to convict the original panel, and Henry backed down (191–92).

If the question of equivocation is rarely raised explicitly by common lawyers, the canonists are far less reticent. The locus classicus is a maxim from Isidore of Seville's *Liber Sententiarum*, "quacunque arte verborum quisquis juret, Deus tamen qui conscientiae testis est, ita hoc accepit sicut ille cui juratur intelligit" (*PL* 83:634), a sentence translated by *Dives and Pauper* as, "what craft or sletþe euere ðu usist in þin speche & in þin oþis for desceyuyn þin euene cristene, God þat knowyth þi þouȝt & þin conscience takit it nout as þu menyst but as he vnderstondyt it to whom þu sweryst so in desyt" (1.i:235).[38] This maxim has about it an air of judicial admonition; it sounds like the kind of warning a judge might give suspected equivocators to remind them that God cannot be tricked as easily as their human opponents. Hardly surprisingly, Gratian has some difficulty with it, since it clearly makes the formal question of what the recipient of the oath understands, not the moral question of what the swearer intends, the acid test of equivocation (pt. 2, ca. 22, qu. 5, c. 11; 885–86).[39] Nevertheless, particularly in a somewhat modified form that simply removes any explicit mention of God from Isidore's equation, it can still be found in late medieval pastoral manuals and even survives to be employed by Thomas Cranmer in the mid-sixteenth century: "we wish always to observe this rule against such fraud: that he should be held to have sworn what the one to whom the oath was offered understands in the common manner of speech" (*Reformation* 217–18).

That such injunctions appear in pastoral manuals as well as legal textbooks proves that the question of equivocation was far from being merely academic.[40] Robert Mannyng of Brunne's popular *Handlyng Synne*, for instance, asks,

> Ȝyf þou swere to me for oght
> And a nouþer ys yn þy þoght,
> Wenyst þou þan þat þou swerst weyl
> Whan þyn oth to me ys gyle echedeyl.
> Nay, for as y vndyrstonde of þe,
> So shal þyn oth charged be.
>
> (2781–86)

Moreover, the matter is also raised in sermon exempla, such as the tale of a Derbyshire priest summoned before his local chapter to answer the charge of living with a concubine: his preparation for swearing the exculpatory oath that he was keeping no woman at home ("nullam mulierem haberet in domo sua") involves telling the woman in question to remain outside the house at the time scheduled for the trial. (Since this oath is to be sworn in compurgation, it is interesting that the priest appears to believe that his equivocation will ameliorate the perjury for his oath-helpers as well.) God, of course, is not taken in for a moment—though, with the kind of aberrant aim that modern feminists will immediately recognize, he hurls his thunderbolt, not at the equivocating priest, but at the poor mistress (BL, MS Addit. 33956, f. 826[b]; Herbert 633.82). Pulpit moralists certainly needed to be vigilant, for popular sentiment was quite ready to accept that even God himself might connive in the swearing of an equivocal oath: the episode of the miraculous harvest included in the story of the flight into Egypt in a single thirteenth-century manuscript of the so-called *Romanz de Saint Fanuel* (Chabaneau 378) has the Christ child make freshly sown wheat ripen instantly so that a farmer can mislead Herod's soldiers with the equivocal oath (sworn, ironically enough, "si m'ait Diex, qu'i ne menti") that he has seen no one pass that way since sowing time (printed in Reinsch 60–66). This story is understandably rare in the medieval apocrypha, but its popular appeal is amply demonstrated by its widespread survival in folktale and ballad down to modern times; in England it is preserved in the ballad of "The Carnal and the Crane" (Child 2:7–10).

The formalistic casuistry of the equivocal oath, as Gratian and Aquinas clearly recognized, depended upon a jural indifference to questions of intention. It is often said that medieval men and women acted "at their peril," that mens rea played no part in early medieval English law (Plucknett 1956, 463–65). Certainly, the early codes see the difference between an open and a concealed act (as in the original distinction between manslaughter and murder, for instance, or robbery and larceny) as being far more crucial than that between a premeditated and an accidental one; the law apparently regarded the deed indifferently, whether willed or not. The *Leges Henrici Primi* give several instances of accidental death being treated as rigorously as deliberate murder, though they do concede that if a man causes someone's death by falling out of a tree, the victim's relatives may expect no better compensation than to be allowed themselves to jump out of the same tree onto the killer (ch. 90.7a; 282). Generally, however, "it is a rule of law that a person who unwittingly commits a wrong must consciously make amends" [legis enim est, qui inscienter peccat, scienter emendet] (ch. 88.6a; 270). The occasional mention of reduced liability—for instance in the case of a man who kills another with a balance beam in the course of raising water from a well (Luitprand, ch. 136; *Leges Langobardorum* 166–67), or of one who kills another while holding his spear over his shoulder (Alfred, ch. 36; Liebermann 1:68)—is sometimes cited as evidence of local exceptions to this general rule, but it doesn't take much imagination to see how dangerous, in an age of formal proof, such provisions, however well intentioned, might turn out to be. A man bent on murder might easily with the help of a couple of strong accomplices contrive a deadly blow over his shoulder and then swear his oath of vindication with a clear conscience.

The canonists, schooled as they were in penitential doctrine, evidently felt little sympathy for the folklaw's reluctance to consider motive and intention, but, then, any legal system that relies on literate habits of mind is likely to find such reluctance outlandish. The common law, however, particularly in the sphere of private litigation, treated questions of intention with great suspicion to the very end of the Middle Ages: a lawyer in a case from 1419/20, for instance, objects to a written instrument being used as evidence of ownership on the grounds that it could show "only the private intent of a man," not his actual deeds (quoted by Thayer 109). Literacy appears to give people confidence in their ability to distinguish "the knower from the known" (Ong 46) and in a bureaucratic and authoritarian state will tend to promote a kind of jurisprudence that feels able to discriminate between deliberate and accidental acts. Significantly, then, consideration of intention first achieves legal respectability in England with the development of the law of treason in the fourteenth and fifteenth centuries. At a time when judges are still refusing to try the would-be felon's thoughts (see Holdsworth 3:373–74), they are declaring themselves quite ready to try the traitor's: "if a man imagines the death of the king, and does nothing more, he shall be drawn, hung, and disembowelled," says Justice Newton in 1441 (quoted by Bellamy 1970, 123). The alliance of literate consciousness with legal authoritarianism is most marked in the promulgation of the idea of institutional treason, as we shall see in Chapter 6, so there is nothing surprising about the discovery that the common law should first begin to consider intention in such a context. In other areas, such as private obligation, however, its significance was far less obvious.

The members of a small-scale, nonauthoritarian society will tend to pay lip service to a rigid formalism reinforced by tradition, in part because this is the only weapon the community has against offenders who swear their offense was accidental, and a general rule like *qui inscienter peccat scienter emendat* is precisely the kind of unforgettable maxim in which a society dependent on living memory will encode its law. On the ground, however, as Winfield (1926) has shown, its attitude will be infinitely more flexible and contingent: the compiler of the *Leges Henrici Primi*, indeed, seeks immediately to temper his stern maxim with the recommendation that "he ought however to be the more accorded mercy and compassion at the hands of the dead man's relatives the more we understand that the human race grows sick with the harshness of a cruel fortune and with the melancholy and wretched lamentation of all" (ch. 88.6b; 271). Justice may be a brittle twig which cannot be bent, but in practice people will bend it all the time. Such unacknowledged malleability was one of the first casualties of the bureaucratic authoritarianism of the king's law and contributed directly to the kind of equivocation and evasiveness by which local juries sought to temper the harshness of royal justice.

In the last two chapters I have tried to provide a conceptual framework for the legal senses of truth and to show how its ethical senses developed from the internal logic of a primarily oral culture—to show, in other words, how only a social equation of "trouthe and honour" could have allowed traditional law to build proof by oath into a system of local justice that operated effectively without recourse to writing. With the precocious centralized bureaucracy set up in Henry II's reign, however, the king's courts began to replace the old, oral, local process we have been looking at with a new literate and authoritarian rule of law, but they did so bound by the shackles of an intractable formalism which the folklaw had bequeathed to them—shackles, it should be added, they showed no great enthusiasm for breaking. In the next chapter we shall see how the old process was frozen by literate technology into a kind of formalized equivocation that often dispensed something very different from equitable justice (see Kern 179), how Isolt and Mark's "wrangling over the oath formula" developed into the arcane ritual of common-law pleading with its elaborate rules of count and denial, exception and replication, confession and avoidance, demurrer and traverse.

"No matter how supple the rule," says Goebel, "the rush of life is always swifter" (xxxvii), and it is quite legitimate to wonder whether the recorded decisions of the king's law were really any more effective in accommodating local contingencies than the protean maxims of the folklaw. It might indeed be argued that by the fourteenth century the esoteric maneuvers of professional pleaders had become the central preoccupation of a judicial system that, having lost almost all ability to respond effectively to the swift rush of human life, could only answer its clients' unflagging demand for justice with those collusive quibbles we call legal fictions. The burden of equivocation, in other words, had shifted from those who faced justice to those who claimed to dispense it, and the later Middle Ages were to usher in an era of legal casuistry that would continue unchallenged right down to Bentham's day.

4

The King's Law

Defending Counsel: I understand that if the oath is administered there is a strong possibility of prevarication, m'lord.
Judge: You mean he's a liar?
Defending Counsel: Only when on oath, m'lord. I am told he looks on the oath in the light of a challenge, m'lord.

—N. F. Simpson, *One Way Pendulum*

SOMETIME AROUND 1450, A LONDON goldsmith named Robert Ellesmere went to the house of a carpenter called William Searle to conclude an agreement to buy from him the leases on certain houses outside Aldgate for forty pounds. Robert arrived with two witnesses to meet William and his wife and to examine the written evidence of title William was to provide; he also brought a third person, George Houton, "a man of Counsell," to read over the legal documents for him. Houton told Robert that the title was sound, but suggested that he could probably get the leases for thirty pounds; Robert, however, is said to have replied that "he wolde geve xl li. rather than leve the bargeyn." What apparently happened next may best be told in George Houton's words:

Then I, the seid George, did spake and seid unto them, "Then ye be accorded?" Then I, the same George, geveng better erys to their speche, desired to knowe howe they were accorded.

Then seide the seid Robert, "I shall geve a grete some of money."

"What some?" I, the seid George, desired to wete.

And he answered me and seid, "xl li., and it most be purveyd agenst our lady day Annunciacion, at whiche tyme, it is accorded that the seid William shall delyver unto me," seide the same Robert, "all the seid evydences togeder with other evydences to be engrossed of the seid bargeyn. And yet," seide the same Robert, "I thank the godeman here, he puttyth me at my choyse whethir I woll have it or leve it at þe seid day."

"Then," seide I, the seide William, "be ye accordeth in the maner as Robert here hath rehersed?"

And he seid "Ye."

"Then, goo we drynke."

And so we did, unto the Swan, a brewhaus fast by Seynt Antoines [in Threadneedle Street], and then departed, &c.[1] (printed in W. T. Barbour 207)

This account is corroborated by both witnesses, evidently under oath, and one of them gives the further detail that the drink which sealed the bargain was bought "atte the coste of the saide Robert Ellesmere."[2] W. T. Barbour describes men like Ellesmere as making bargains "in their own simple way," unskilled "in the technic of the law" (118), yet his own example suggests a far from simple oral ceremony. On the contrary, it is a scrupulously performed trothplight, complete with formal language, ritual gesture, and even a respected borrow.

Among countless thousands that have passed into silent oblivion this trothplight has come down to us because it became the object of a lawsuit in the still youthful court of chancery: William Searle, confident no doubt that the king's courts would allow him to thumb his nose at such a contract for all its old-world ceremony, welshed on the deal, and an outraged Ellesmere, "havyng no remedie at þe common lawe, vnto his grete and importable hurt" appealed to the chancellor for justice. One can hardly read the details of such a case without acknowledging the extent to which literacy had compromised an ancient reliance on oathworthiness as the accepted norm; in this changed world the formalities of the old folklaw were no match for the cynicism of those familiar with the literate "technic" of the king's courts. Like many fifteenth-century chancery petitioners, Ellesmere had learned the bitter lesson that the common law offered little protection for those who trusted in the strength of their simple "trouthe" against the authority of written "evydences." Ellesmere himself seems to have been relatively well-to-do, but other chancery petitioners, like the two who sought redress against the "well lettred" John Lynford ("a gret styward, an auditour, & a myghty werker"), suffered under additional burdens; they describe themselves graphically as "ryght lewd & not lettred & so pouer þat þay may not apparay wyth the said John in no suyte ne tryall at the lawe" (*CPC* 2:xiii). Such representatives of the great mass of non-literate people clearly felt little confidence in the power of the king's common-law courts to defend persons of their stamp.

In this chapter I will try to outline the process by which, by the late fourteenth century, the common law had grown into a vehicle for such cynical exploitation. There are few real villains in this story, though undoubtedly individual judges could sometimes be cruel or corrupt; at root, there is only a grotesque formalism by which, following the profound sea change of Clanchy's shift to written record, the measured rituals of the folklaw are reduced to self-parody. Such an account of legal formalism must seem perverse to those accustomed to think of the rule of law as a fundamental protection for the marginalized and the exploited, those who believe, with Richard Posner, that "a punctilious legalism is the pariah's protection" (97), but, as I hope to show, in the context of the late Middle Ages such a view is difficult to sustain. By learning to look from the margins inward, we may come to see the literate unwieldiness of centralized law as itself marginalizing and exploitative, not only a symptom but also a contributory cause of profound cultural dislocation.

The medieval phase of the transition from a local, oral, and traditional culture to a centralized, literate, and progressive one began as soon as the Germanic invaders had become sufficiently settled to start to adopt those elements of written law and religion that still survived among the peoples they had overrun. The spread of literacy over the next half a millennium was at best slow and unsteady, but, as a number of recent scholars have argued, a marked increase in the power of writing to transform intellectual, political, bureaucratic and legal institutions occurred in the twelfth century (Illich and Sanders; Stock; Zumthor). Berman even goes so far as to claim that from a legal point of view this period witnessed a revolution as profound as those that were later to shake the Bastille and the Winter Palace. Not everyone, however, has been willing to subscribe to so dramatic a thesis. As Rosamond McKitterick asks, "rather than a sudden enlightenment, are we not observing in the history of western Europe after about 1000 an increase, extension and diversification of literate skills, the next stage in a continuous pattern from late antiquity to the early Germanic kingdoms?" (1989, 1). Susan Reynolds's emphasis on institutional continuity (1984), and Clanchy's picture of protracted rearguard resistance to literacy might equally be taken to suggest that the twelfth century is better thought of as a period of accelerated evolution rather than of revolution.[3]

The dissemination of literate habits of mind in the West, then, while continuous, has certainly not been uniform; periods of quiescence have been succeeded by periods of vigorous activity. If the advent of the "bookish text" (Illich) in the mid-twelfth century (hard on the heels of the emergence of Stock's "textual communities") offers evidence of one such period of activity, the rise of the new print culture of the sixteenth century (Eisenstein; N. Davis 1975) is clearly another.[4] In claiming that the half century following the Black Death—which witnessed, in England at any rate, a marked acceleration in the spread of vernacular literacy (C. Barron 1996, 221)—represents a further distinct stage in this process, I want at the same time to stress the way in which an increasing willingness to trust writing generated a corresponding crisis of authority, both intellectual and political. It is this crisis, whose roots reach back at least two hundred years, that makes the Ricardian period an important milestone along the route that leads from the world we have lost to the modern industrial state. I certainly do not wish to downplay the importance of the twelfth-century renaissance, but my concern here and in the next chapter is to recognize continuity as well as change, to emphasize the survival of the older folklaw into the fourteenth century and beyond), to expose the darker side of

Southern's great march from ritual to reason, and to write that Luddite history whose dim outlines must be sought in the shadows of those confidently articulate written monuments which have inevitably dominated our view of the period.

If the spread of vernacular literacy was a necessary cause of the semantic instability of the word *trouthe* for which I am claiming such significance, it cannot have been a sufficient one. Quite as important was the dislocation caused by a powerful centralized authority employing a highly literate bureaucracy to enforce a common law still profoundly local and oral in its structural assumptions—a law that, for instance, would not fully distinguish between criminal and civil jurisdiction until well after the end of our period. The king's courts insisted that his subjects recognize in written records the evidence of their own untruth but did so by a process still predicated upon the oath and reinforced by the values of the local community. Such institutionalized schizophrenia induced widespread skepticism about the administration of this centralized law, a skepticism which, as we shall see in the next chapter, finds its most dramatic literary expression in the outlaw tradition of Robin Hood and Gamelyn. For the moment, however, I wish to concentrate on the way the structures of the folklaw as they were converted to the purposes of written law produced a hybrid that wholly failed to provide satisfactory justice; I shall be building on M. T. Clanchy's admirable study of the social consequences of learning to trust writing, but by looking at the period which immediately follows the one he was most interested in, I hope to deepen and extend his insights into the structural shifts and social reactions this trust engendered.

The notion that justice is properly a local matter and the king's court only a last resort is sometimes to be met with in the official culture of the High Middle Ages, but in the main the dominant order had reason to be pleased with the direction taken by administrative and legal reform in the twelfth century, while those to whom increasingly centralized justice posed the greatest threat are also the least likely to have left us a record of their dissatisfaction. From the winning side, however, the story is one of ever widening royal jurisdiction, backed by an ever more complex bureaucracy and driven by the growing awareness of the kings themselves that "they could use [judicial] changes to enhance their own political power" (Davies and Fouracre 238). One has only to compare the section on the king's prerogative (*de iure regis*) in the *Leges Henrici Primi* (ch. 10; 108) with its counterpart in Cnut's laws less than a century earlier (2 Cnut, ch. 12; Liebermann 1:316) to see that this growth did not begin with the Angevins; nevertheless, it is with Henry II that we are most likely to associate the beginnings of a new order. When Henry came to the throne (1154) royal justice was still, as Berman says, "extraordinary justice, not regular professional justice administered by permanent courts" (1983, 441), yet the next thirty-five years were to witness those administrative developments which are often credited with shaping that distinctive legal order we call the common law. At the heart of Henry's reforms lay the recognition that literate officials could use legal institutions in ways his predecessors had scarcely dreamed of: "through the technology of writing," says Clanchy, "the king's right as overlord of all freemen to redress the wrongs of undertenants could be effectively enforced for the first time" (1983a, 155).

The question of why specific developments in England led to a native legal system that was eventually strong enough to resist the more mature traditions of Roman law lies outside the scope of this study. However, English society differed from that of the rest of Europe in a number of important ways which cannot but have influenced the course of Henry II's bureaucratic reforms and constrained his freedom of action; these may be worth dwelling on here, if only to counter crudely professionalist theories of judicial reform which tend to lay heavy stress on the administrative genius of the king and his individual ministers. Whatever may be the case in other societies, Alan Watson's claim that it is "above all, lawyers thinking about law, not societal conditions, that determines the shape of legal change" (537) will not, I believe, hold true of early medieval England. It is fundamental to my position that the common law developed piecemeal, guided by unquestioned assumptions and political contingencies, rather than by the jurisprudential scheming of a group of farsighted royal administrators. In Susan Reynolds's words, the legal developments of the twelfth century were more a result of "varying political circumstances than because of radical rethinking" (1984, 57).

The Norman Conquest had had two profound effects on the way the country was to be governed. First, by marking the division between rulers and ruled with that most powerful of cultural institutions, language, it made possible the concept of a national law, a law common to the whole kingdom. In an earlier era the principle known as "personality of law" (Halphen 1948, 59–62) meant that no king, not even one as powerful as Alfred, would seriously have considered subjecting a Mercian or a Northumbrian to the laws of his own West Saxons. But Anglo-Norman kings stood aloof from their English-speaking subjects and could bring to the task of providing a national law far greater detachment.[5] It is no accident that the common law as it grew in confidence should have settled on French as its official language (cf. Woodbine), nor that the only other European country as legally and administratively advanced as England should have been Sicily. Like England, Sicily with her foreign rulers developed absolutist policies very early (S. Reynolds 1984, 50–51), and in both countries a precociously centralized authority was to provoke violent reaction (298–301). Second, by weakening the connection between property and jurisdiction (Milsom 1981, 20), the Conquest had allowed the king to claim a monopoly in criminal cases (and to interpose himself between vassal and overlord in civil ones) in a manner which continental magnates could not but have regarded as an intolerable threat to their prerogatives (Clanchy 1983a, 143). No doubt more immediate events helped smooth Henry's path (the anarchy of the previous reign must have made his subjects readier to accept increased royal authority, and his rivalry with Becket may have seemed to them a credible excuse for strengthening secular administration), but such events merely contributed to a process already under way.

If the Conquest was to generate the impetus toward centralized law and the conditions under which it might flourish, the distinctive form of this law was determined by even older forces. Norman and Angevin kings had, for instance, inherited from their Anglo-Saxon predecessors a tradition of written vernacular law and even a rudimentary system of judicial writs (Van Caenegem 30–32; Keynes 1990, 244–48) unmatched among the Franks. Yet at the same time, England entirely lacked anything to compare with the notarial system that still preserved the forms of Roman law at a local level in southern France and Italy (Clanchy 1993, 304–7). Given the conservatism with which all largely oral societies tend to regard their legal customs, the fact that the English had learned to use writing to record and administer their folklaw without ever developing a professional legal caste guaranteed that any common law envisaged by the king would conform to existing structures, and prevented, in Maitland's words, "the jurist from having it all his own way and making the law too fine a thing for common use" (P&M 1:220). If the English common law owes its precociousness to the fact that Henry found ready-made literate foundations to build upon, its owes its distinctiveness to the fact that these foundations were laid down on a bedrock of oral custom before the civilians and canonists had rediscovered Justinian.

Much has been made of the bureaucratic innovations, particularly the system of returnable writs, which fueled the expansion of the royal courts in Henry II's reign, but it is less often stressed that the form of justice these courts dispensed underwent no fundamental change. In England, as in Europe generally, however, "the new world of the twelfth century was more legally articulate, but court procedures did not change all that much, and it is far from clear that they were supposed to" (Davies and Fouracre 238). In fact, the enormous jurisdictional shift set in motion by Henry's legal innovations could hardly have been predicted and was probably largely unintentional (Van Caenegem 32–33). S. F. C. Milsom has even argued that what has often been regarded as a deliberate policy of promoting the king's right to determine all disputes over land title began as nothing more than an attempt to shore up established custom; his insistence that the earliest royal writs (right, mort d'ancestor, and novel disseisin) were "conceived as mechanisms by which the customs were enforced upon lords and their courts, and that the transfer of jurisdiction which in fact followed was neither intended nor foreseen" (1976, 36) helps to explain much of the subsequent procedural complexity of the early common law. The arcane writ system, far from being a sign that Henry's judges had made the bold leap into a brave new world of written law, is merely symptomatic of their desperate attempt to save customary appearances in the face of accelerating literate technology. Where Maitland believed that English folklaw procedure disappeared from the king's courts with "marvelous suddenness" in the twelfth century (P&M 2:458), Milsom is far less dogmatic: "the Year Books [from the 1290s on] are dark because still in the shadow of the old monolithic law suit" (P&M 1:lxx).

Where this shadow, thrown by the jural practices of an oral, small-scale society, fell across courts transformed by the technology of writing, it had two major consequences for the quality of justice these courts dispensed. First, writing froze legal procedure, even procedure that was no longer appropriate or just, into a set of inflexible rules justified by an appeal to tradition that quickly became tyrannical. Where oral process had once been free to remember those judicial forms that seemed most equitable, literate process was forced to abandon equity to the mercy of a formalism it felt powerless to alter and which it could only circumvent by egregious legal fictions. In Fritz Kern's words, a law which "itself remains young, always in the belief that is old" was ousted by a law in which "the dead text retains power over life" (179). Second, writing allowed litigation to be removed from its local context, where oathworthiness, personal honor, and standing in the community might be decisive factors in the judicial process, to a detached setting where neither party was well known and the rich scoundrel might expect as good a hearing as the honest pauper—or rather, given the notorious avarice of professional lawyers, a better hearing. We will tend to assume that liberty to appeal to a higher, more remote court must inevitably serve the interests of objective, detached judgment—that, for instance, tenants can expect little justice where their landlord sits on the bench (cf. Bonfield 518–20)—and that those who complained about such liberty did so because the threat to local prerogatives weakened their freedom to pursue private ends. But the advantages of disinterestedness will only count for something where the higher court can bring superior forensic techniques to bear on the case; when both share jural assumptions evolved in a local context, the distant court may well lose in procedural equity whatever it gains in judicial detachment. Many centuries were to pass before the common law evolved rules of evidence and standards of proof comparable with those the civilians had built upon the foundation of Roman law (W. Ullmann 1946). In the meantime, cases at Westminster were settled in accordance with formalistic rules that, whatever purpose they might once have served in a local setting, were now good for little but to insulate the law from the real world and to promote the interests of an ever more inflexible legal bureaucracy. It is hardly surprising that many people came to regard such law as arbitrary and those charged with administering it as corrupt.

Criminal Law

Let us begin with some fairly simple cases from the second half of the thirteenth century; they are taken from the *Placita Corone*, described by Alan Harding as a "handbook for accused felons, telling them how to resist the verbal trickery of judges" (1973, 78). The report of the proceedings against Nicholas de C for cattle theft (17–18) may well be based on an actual case, but in any event the process is entirely typical; Nicholas has been brought to court by the sheriff along with two cows which he is suspected of having stolen (in this report, trial "by one's body" refers to trial by battle and trial "by the country" means jury trial).

Justice: Nicholas, the good people of this district complain grievously that their horses, oxen, cows, pigs, sheep and lambs have been stolen and that you are in the habit of selling cattle which you never buy: and, as to how this can be, we have a weighty suspicion and serious presumption that you never came honestly by these cattle.

Nicholas: Sir, if there is any man willing to make suit against me alleging that I came by these cattle dishonestly, I am ready to defend them as my own property, lawfully purchased at the fair at C, on the day of the fair, &c., by my body or by whatever means the king's court may adjudge me to prove it.

The justice asks why Nicholas has kept the cows indoors rather than letting them graze in the open and is told that they were being fattened for Martinmas—an answer he finds satisfactory. He then suggests that Nicholas will have no objection to proving his honest title before "the country."

Nicholas: Sir, it seems to me that I have no need to do that because I am ready to defend [it] by my body, or by whatever means the king's court may adjudge, as my own, lawfully purchased, property.

Justice: Nicholas, you are here in custody, and attached in the king's court, on account of your possession of these cattle, and on suspicion of the theft of other animals in this district. In respect of this suspicion, no man is proceeding against you except the king: and you cannot defend yourself against the king by your body, or in any manner other than by the country. Consequently you are bound to pursue this course, if you think it fitting.

Nicholas: Sir, I am a stranger in these parts and less known to these good people than I would need to be. Hence I dare not trust myself to their verdict in respect to this suspicion, which has been raised against me without reason.

Justice: And how, then, do you wish to acquit yourself of this presumption and this weighty suspicion?

Nicholas: Sir, by my body, if any man makes suit against me, and in no other way.

The judge then orders him to be imprisoned on short rations until he is ready to change his plea. "And be it known," says the *Placita Corone* of a similar case, "that he will never be hanged so long as he gives such a reply—provided he be not defeated in battle—but will be kept in prison as long as the king lives. And if the king dies he will be released" (23).

The first thing that strikes one about this account is that though it describes what we would think of as a criminal trial it treats it as essentially a private contest. It was at this date still possible for felony appeals to be brought by a private party, and such cases show an obvious blurring of the line between what we think of as civil and criminal law (Harding 1966, 62–63), but even here where the crown acts as prosecutor the outlines of the old face-to-face folklaw procedure remain quite distinct. In reality Nicholas may have been indicted by a presenting jury ("the good people of this district"), but the memory of a time when larceny was regularly a civil action is still strong enough for him to regard it as properly a matter between himself and an injured party ("is any man willing to make suit against me?"). Technically, of course, he is being sued by the king, but the folklaw substructure makes of this king not an incorporeal abstraction but a stand-in for the flesh-and-blood appellant who might be challenged to trial by battle and whose accusations, like those of any other neighbor, must lapse with his death—in such a world, even criminal process will incline to the ancient principle that an *actio personalis moritur cum persona* (see *SCKB* 1:xlii–xliii). The justice is thus cast in the awkward double role of both prosecuting lawyer and judge; insofar as Nicholas's accuser is the king, the justice is prosecutor ("the king will not do battle, and no more will I" [23]), but insofar as Nicholas is accused by his neighbors, the justice is intermediary ("how, then, do you wish to acquit yourself?"). Even were he not constrained to it by a conservative tradition, we might expect anyone placed in this difficult position to be only too ready to conceive of justice as primarily a matter of punctilious observance of procedural rules. In fact, such an attitude was fundamental to the early common law in all its aspects: "You will do as others have done in the same case, otherwise we do not know what the law is," as one fourteenth-century lawyer was to put it (*YB 18/19 Edw. 3*, 378–79).

One apparent consequence of bureaucratic centralization was an increased severity in the administration of the law, for the literate hardening of procedure spelled the end of the folklaw's protean ability to adjust to local contingencies. Even that most adversarial of folklaw processes, trial by battle, must sometimes have ended in an honorable draw, but when royal justices needed winners and losers for their records and a noose awaited every loser however gallant, little honor can have clung to battle's later incarnation. Another case in the *Placita Corone*, the account of Hugh de M's trial for theft (16–17), suggests how inflexible thirteenth-century justice had become. Hugh is accused of stealing a horse, "feloniously as a felon," by an appellant who is prepared to support the accusation "with his body." Hugh is an unlettered man and asks to be advised "by some learned person" as to how best to defend himself; the judge predictably denies his request ("for who can tell us more about your doings than you yourself"), advises him to tell the truth like a good and faithful man (*com bon et leaus*), and promises to be as merciful as he can "according to the law." Thereupon Hugh confesses the theft but pleads that it had been a first offense to which he was driven by extreme poverty. Wherein lay the judge's capacity for mercy is unclear for the inevitable consequence of such a confession is the gallows (*et suspendatur*). The folklaw too might resort to the death penalty for theft (though it seems often to have preferred symbolic mutilation),[6] but the practice of making the accuser (the "sakeber") responsible for carrying out the sentence (P&M 2:496) must have discouraged malicious prosecution and sometimes led to last-minute reprieves. A late survival of the principle that *ille qui sequitur faciat justiciam* [whoever prosecutes shall carry out the judgment] in the royal courts concerns a conviction for rape from Edward II's reign: faced with the prospect of having to blind and castrate her attacker with her own hand, the victim understandably chose to withdraw the charge (*Eyre of Kent* 134–35).[7] Hugh's accuser might have thought twice about starting proceedings had he not been able to turn his man over to the impersonal machinery of the king's justice for punishment.

In the third place, as we might expect, this trial is almost entirely concerned with questions of legal procedure rather than of fact. Apart from briefly satisfying himself about the suspicious circumstance of Nicholas's keeping his two cows indoors, the justice is only interested in formal questions, in how he can bring Nicholas to answer the accusations in an appropriate manner. The game has clear rules: the justice cannot force Nicholas to undergo jury trial as long as he is willing to defend himself by combat; Nicholas will not have to fight as long as his accuser is the king. Stalemate. What is immediately obvious, however, is that these forms have very little to do with getting at the facts (unlike, for instance, modern rules of evidence); they exist because under an oral system of face-to-face justice they had offered some hope of fair play by discouraging the overly litigious and protecting those of good name. Superficially the following exchange from the *Placita Corone* might resemble a modern cross-examination, but in reality it is nothing of the sort:

> "Are you a good and honest man [boens et leals]?"
> "Yes, indeed," said he . . . , "and I am ready to defend myself by my body against this accusation."
> And the justice continued: "I say are you good and honest?"
> and the thief said, "Yes, sir, I am."
> And the justice said: "How do you wish to prove it?"
> and the thief said: "By the country, to be sure."
> And the country came, and said he was a thief and had committed such a theft for which he had been indicted, and several others: so he was hanged. (23–24)

The justice is not seeking to establish a factual case against the accused, merely to maneuver him into an untenable position; "and in such a way he was tricked" [et issint fust il deceu], as the *Placita Corone* puts it. We may begin to appreciate why medieval pleading was so ritualized and formulaic when we realize how serious were the consequences of such verbal slips; the accused opened his mouth at his peril. The judge tries a similar trick in a case of excusable homicide: "Thomas, what was the name of the man you killed in premeditated attack, feloniously as a felon?" To which Thomas wisely replies, "Sir, if you please, I have never been a felon and never did mischief to living man in premeditated attack" (19).[8] Evidently, a false move at this point would have hanged Thomas, just as surely as stumbling over the oath formula in an old folklaw trial would have done—"be it known that a man will never be hanged so long as he does not admit his guilt by his own mouth" (22)—only here there is no suggestion that the slip was taken to be a sign of divine intervention.

Fourthly, Nicholas's guilt is judged, as it would have been under the folklaw, as much by his common reputation as by his specific actions. This is, in other words, really a trial of the trouthe of the man not the truth of the accusations made against him, and hence, it is still possible to see it in terms of personal honor: "if he is a thief or if he is doubtful of the jury," says the *Placita Corone*, "[the accused] will say, if he is sensible, that for reasons of family pride [pur hounte de sun linage] he would rather die in prison than be hanged" (23). Whether one is an honest man or a notorious felon depends on what one's neighbors say one is, and Nicholas's fear of the verdict of the country ("I am a stranger in these parts and less known to these good people than I would need to be") is doubtless entirely justifiable. To assume that jury trial was at this period what it was later to become, an investigation into the facts of the case and hence a counterweight to the extreme formalism of the lawyers, would be mistaken. There is no indication that medieval jurors were expected to make an objective assessment of evidence previously unknown to them—indeed, quite the reverse. They were chosen because of their probable knowledge of the parties and the circumstances surrounding the case; in criminal cases at least, rumor, hearsay, and surmise must have been their stock-in-trade. The time when, as Milsom puts it, jurors lost "their character as the witnesses who supplied the facts, and became persons to whom a case was presented and who had to decide on what they heard in court" (1981, 424) still lay very far in the future (see Musson), but as we have already noticed a major step along this path was the introduction during the thirteenth century of written evidence in criminal trials. In view of the legal implications of the emergence of a new objective sense of *trouthe* in the fourteenth century, the fact that the very term *evidence* seems first to have been applied to documents, "put in 'to inform the jury'" (P&M 2:628; see also Thayer 104–12) is striking.

Though the administration of the law was becoming more complex, the principles of evidence and the concept of proof underwent no dramatic transformation. The horizons of the fourteenth-century criminal jury remained parochial and its decisions clouded by local prejudice. While it might treat a respectable neighbor with conspicuous leniency it still showed little pity for the outsider, the impoverished, and the friendless. Here, for instance, are two entries in the report of an early fourteenth-century commission, the London Trailbaston of 1305/6: "John of London, dwelling in Colmanstrete, is indicted *coram rege* for suspicion of ill, because, [though] well clad, spending much, and leaving town for two or three weeks and returning, he practises no trade" (*Calendar of London Trailbaston* 76.127). John got off because he said he lived at Gracechurch and the sheriff had got the wrong man, but Peter of Montpellier, "taken for suspicion of larceny because he came into the goldsmithery of London to sell a silver saucer broken in pieces," was not so lucky: "asked how he came by it says that he bought it upon Cornhull and did not steal it and pleads not guilty. Jury say that he stole it. So *hanged*" (64.65). Few aspects of common law are more veiled in mystery than the deliberations of the medieval jury (cf. M. Arnold 1974), but is difficult to feel confident that these particular jurors accorded the case against Peter the kind of careful factual analysis it had clearly lacked at the hands of the king's justices. For all their esoteric procedures, the king's courts do not seem to have brought superior forensic techniques to bear on the cases they removed from local jurisdiction; they merely magnified the worst elements in the old folklaw (its narrowness and formalism) while binding its best qualities (flexibility and a preference for mediation) in a literate straitjacket.

To suggest that medieval criminal jury trial was a court of rumor and hearsay seems at odds with the claim, sometimes made, that juries were courts of conscience. In fact these claims are not irreconcilable. The same jury that could condemn a man on no better grounds than that he was a known troublemaker and had no respectable friends in court might show conspicuous leniency toward a good neighbor whose offense, while undeniable, was felt to be venial. The basic assumption of course was that "each should judge his neighbor as he would himself be judged in a like case at another time" (*Mirror* 9). Like the (no doubt apocryphal) Australian jury that is said to have found a local sheep-stealer "not guilty, so long as he returns the sheep," medieval English juries seem to have felt that their task was to judge the criminal as much as the crime; indeed, there is even "evidence of jurors acting as mainpernors or pledges for the future good behavior of [acquitted] defendants" (Musson 138). Since, however, the actual process had become inflexible, justice was often forced to rely on fiction, and as Milsom puts it, "jurors made unacceptable rules produce acceptable results by adjusting the facts" (1981, 422). The king's law had inherited the old folklaw principle that the court had no business deciding questions of intention or trying to judge states of mind, but without a corresponding freedom to adjust procedure to local contingencies this principle threatened to hang the accidental homicide and the man who killed in fair fight as high as the smiler with the knife under the cloak.

In neither England (Hurnard) nor France (N. Z. Davis 1987) did the courts have any official authority to spare the killer who had acted involuntarily or under provocation; this was felt to be properly a matter for royal clemency alone. English juries could, however, make sure that such clemency would be forthcoming by certifying that the killer had done everything possible to avoid fighting, had struck the fatal blow only when all avenues of escape had been closed, and preferably had made use of some simple implement found lying to hand rather than employing a deadly weapon brought for the purpose. This they accordingly did with suspicious regularity.[9] In 1384 jurors had gone so far as to claim that the victim "'in his madness and of his own volition' had run upon the knife drawn by John in self-defence and had thus killed himself" (*PJP* 398). A thirteenth-century jury had gone one better: they reported that a cornered archer had "held his loaded bow in front of him, his assailant having no respect for the arrow in the bow, rushing on it and disembowelling himself" (cited by Hurnard 302). Even the threat of an international incident could not deflect a jury in 1379 from finding that two men accused of murdering the Genoese ambassador had acted in self-defense: "the justices, an impressive array comprising Cavendish, Bealknap, Tresilian, Skipwith and Fulthorp, asked them how this could be. They said they were wholly ignorant. Questioned further they stubbornly offered the same answer" (Bellamy 1970, 167). Such license was not necessarily extended to juries in other kinds of case, however: members of one fourteenth-century jury found themselves called "malvays ribauds" for trying to enter a special verdict of self-defense in a case of assault and battery, for, as the irate justice explained, "You are charged on nothing but whether he beat him or not" (*SCT* 1:xiii). By giving verdicts (*vere dicta*) such as these, medieval juries were clearly keeping alive the old folklaw prerogative of speaking the truth in its ethical, rather than its intellectual, sense.

In this same vein, Thomas, the homicide in the *Placita Corone* who manages to avoid confessing that he had killed "feloniously as a felon," goes on to claim that he had been attacked in his own house (an echo of the old folklaw offense of *hamsocn*), that at first he had put up no resistance, and that only when he had been struck several times "with a Welsh knife" and feared for his life, had he wounded his assailant in the right arm with "a little pointed knife which [he] carried," a wound that was unfortunately to prove fatal (19). The justice is frankly skeptical about these details ("vous avez mut embeli vostre parole et vostre defens enflori"), but the jury readily confirms them. No doubt they had no wish to see the king hang a good neighbor merely for killing, as Thomas himself puts it, "un wischous homme et plein de deceyte et de mal engins et ne mye creable de bon renon ne de bone fame" [an unprincipled man, full of fraud and trickery, completely untrustworthy and of ill fame]. From the king's point of view, and from the point of view of those legal historians who are kings' friends, juries that passed such verdicts proved themselves partial at best, shameless perjurers at worst,[10] but their behavior is amenable to more a generous interpretation. As Thomas A. Green has argued, high acquittal rates for theft and murder and the jury's readiness to accept transparent pleas of self-defense in part sprang "from deeply engrained notions of how social harmony was to be maintained through composition with, rather than ultimate rejection of, the offender" (64), while "those few who were condemned had especially offended against the standards of the community" (33). Again, in view of our characterization of the conflicting senses of *trouthe*, it is interesting to find Green writing that, "from the outset of the common law period, trial juries were prepared to voice a sense of justice fundamentally at odds with the letter of the law . . . [they] remained free to say the 'truth' as they knew it" (52).

The final point to be made about Nicholas's trial is that it is hardly in modern terms a trial at all. It is really only a preliminary hearing: it decides nothing and the final resolution is deferred until Nicholas is ready to change his plea. The painful procrastination of medieval process (far more marked, of course, on the civil side) was one of its most distinctive features. In part this was the legacy of the folklaw's preference for negotiated compromise over imposed decision, but it was also something woven into the very structure of the early common law—the equivalent of Isolt and King Mark's "wrangling over the oath formula," an activity which, as I argued in the last chapter, lay at the heart of folklaw procedure. What Milsom says of medieval contract litigation is, mutatis mutandis, true of all other forms of action: "if the answer must be a blank denial, legal refinement and indeed common sense can only go to work on the claim: the law will be largely about the obstacles which have to be surmounted by a plaintiff before he can put the defendant to make the answer" (1967, 5). It is no surprise then to find that even the simple felony cases described by the *Placita Corone* were intended to show "what delays [the accused] will be able to cause before having to reply" [quels delays il purra fere avaunt respouns] (22), nor that the last we hear of Nicholas the cattle thief, he is trying to buy himself more time by turning informer (20–21).

With the growing power of the crown in the fourteenth century the problems exemplified by these thirteenth-century cases grew still more acute. The old county courts, which in the thirteenth century had enjoyed a "symbiotic relationship" with the king's court (R. Palmer 1982, 306), became increasingly marginalized as more and more of their business was appropriated by itinerant royal justices and their clerical underlings; this inevitably led to a far greater dependence on formalized written communication, and in turn rendered criminal justice even less responsive to local needs. One symptom of this is what Holdsworth calls the "extraordinary and irrational set of rules" (3:618) that grew up around the written indictments upon which the whole process depended. Thus a fourteenth-century Nicholas, whose indictment said simply that he "abduxit vaccas" [carried off cows], might have got away scot-free because it had left out the word *felonice*, or because it did not use the phrase *cepit et abduxit*, or because it did not specify the number of cows nor their market value;[11] he might even have got off had the indictment misspelled his name. Interestingly, defendants who relied on such formalistic quibbling seem to have been more rather than less successful as the century wore on (Musson 118–19; *PJP* lxxiv).

Furthermore, the increased use of writing led to the private element in thirteenth-century criminal process becoming institutionalized in a particularly disruptive form, the commission of oyer and terminer. As Harding has shown, "the writing down of criminal accusations as bills [in the late thirteenth century] opened up new procedural possibilities, just as the writing down of civil claims as writs had done" (1975, 77). The oral plaint had virtually restricted to the county courts those who wished to make the king's "known concern . . . for public order" (75) an excuse for employing his common law against their neighbors, but the new written bills redirected such local feuds through Westminster where they elicited judicial commissions whose impartiality was open to serious question (79). The new process fostered a dramatic growth in trespass actions (trespass was the medieval equivalent of modern tort), for, unlike the appellant in a felony case, the plaintiff who alleged trespass *contra pacem* and *vi et armis*—becoming "as it were, a private prosecutor for the crown" (M. Arnold 1987, 515)—could hope for a tangible benefit in the form of damages by the action. Thus, in the fourteenth century one might even try to represent a felony such as rape as a private trespass in order to enable the injured party to obtain compensation (*YB 13/14 Edw. 3*, 64–65; see Putnam 1950, 274 n. 320). The popular reaction to these developments will occupy much of the next chapter, but for now I want merely to stress the way in which it perpetuated the overlap of private and public jurisdiction that we saw in the *Placita Corone*: "it must have looked at the beginning of the fourteenth century," writes Harding, "as though the English judicial system was being reorganized around the bill and the commission of oyer and terminer, both ambiguous in being civil and criminal at once" (1975, 79). Perhaps the most dramatic effect of such ambiguity was the way it turned the old folklaw punishment of outlawry into a weapon which neighbor could use against neighbor; not for nothing was the fourteenth century to make heroes out of Robin Hood and Gamelyn.

One important fourteenth-century development affected civil and criminal proceedings alike: the rapidly increasing flow of statute law.[12] Though royal edicts of various kinds had been regularly issued since before Henry II's day, it was not until the middle of the thirteenth century that recording techniques had become sufficiently advanced to begin to make their regular use in court practical (Richardson and Sayles 1934, 205–6). Up to this point the literate distinctiveness of statute law is largely missing, mostly because the handful of authoritative royal decrees had simply become part of an oral heritage: "the assizes of Henry II have worked themselves into the mass of unenacted law," writes Maitland, "and their text seems already to be forgotten" (P&M 1:176). The reign of Edward I (1272–1307) was marked by what Theodore Plucknett called "one of the greatest outbursts of reforming legislation in English history until the nineteenth century" (1956, 27), but nonetheless Edwardian lawyers had still to depend on their own private collections (or recollections) rather than on official public records. Even in the next century, the evidence suggests that "reference by the court to an official copy of a statute was decidedly unusual, and that the court did not possess a copy of its own for ready reference" (Plucknett 1922, 104). Some idea of the difficulties faced by those who needed authoritative texts for courtroom use is suggested by a case from 1314 where the claim that a particular statute "was no statute, for it was never sealed" was met with the response: "You will find in the rolls of Sir Gilbert Roubery that the king commanded that it be firmly kept, and if you direct a writ to Sir Gilbert, he will certify you to that effect" (cited by Plucknett 1922, 23). One could hardly ask for clearer evidence that, even on a bureaucratic level, the tensions between memory and written record continued beyond the terminus Clanchy sets for himself.

Though chancery, the royal secretariat, had begun to keep a regular record of statutes by 1299, it would still be a "good many years" before its collection could be called "in any sense complete or peculiarly authoritative" (Richardson and Sayles 1934, 213). The Exchequer did not attempt an official compilation until 1354 (218), though we do hear of a collection of statutes, kept in a bag, which the king's remembrancer made available for reference in 1342 (208). These facts, symptomatic as they are of increasing centralization, serve to remind us how deeply oral the common law was even at this late date. However literate the legal administration had become by 1307 (when Clanchy's study ends), much of the law that it administered was still preserved in living memory, as it had been in Glanvill's day. For some time yet, forensic tradition would maintain its authority in court, as when a judge in 1341 announced "that the strongest argument he knew against [a particular interpretation] was that Hengham [d. 1311] who made the statute read it another way" (cited by Plucknett 1922, 51). Even Chaucer's Man of Law, we might recall, had every statute since the conquest "pleyn by rote" ("General Prologue" 327) — a mammoth task compared with the six statutes a lawyer at the beginning of Edward I's reign was expected master (Thorne 1959, 88), but still not an impossible feat. At first glance, the situation would seem to have changed radically by 1376, when Sir Peter de la Mare, speaker of the Good Parliament, met Lord Latimer's denial that his actions had contravened the laws of England by producing a statute book — "and the said Sir Peter had a book of statutes ready to hand, and he opened it and read out the statute before all the lords and the commons, so that it might not be denied" (*Anonimalle* 86) — but ironically no statute relevant to Latimer's situation has ever been found and some modern scholars have doubted its very existence (183).

Once written law began to receive some measure of bureaucratic support, however, there was far greater incentive to kings and parliaments to pass statutes. Though in the long term this was to have a beneficial effect, for the late Middle Ages it may well have caused as many problems as it solved. In the early 1300s judges might still modify or even disregard the plain words of an act when they seemed likely to produce improper results. For instance, when Chief Justice Bereford realized that the careless wording of a clause in *de donis* allowed the heir of the grantee of an entailed estate to alienate it against the grantor's wishes, he simply "read these missing words into the statute and gave effect to them in his judgment" (Bolland 1921, 60). After the middle of the century, by contrast, "the terms in which an act was phrased had gained greater importance than they had earlier and could not easily be augmented without parliamentary action" (Thorne 1942, 45). The tone was set by Justice Shareshull in 1346: "we cannot take the statute further than the words of it say" (cited by Plucknett 1922, 88). Not for another two hundred years were there any signs that the intention of the makers might "form the justification for extending a statute beyond its words" (Thorne 1942, 59). Moreover, quite apart from its general tendency to add to an already complex court process by giving the lawyers more procedural niceties to argue over,[13] the incorrigible formalism of late medieval attitudes to legislation tended to turn any act, however well intentioned, back on itself. This seems to have been particularly true of attempts to limit procedural abuses by statute. Here for instance is Plucknett's description of the results of a series of statutes of jeofail, which begin in 1340: "These statutes adopted the policy of enacting that certain minute slips in enrolling should not for the future invalidate the record. They began with slips of spelling, and proceeded by cautious stages to defects slightly less trivial. The result was disastrous. By excusing some slips, the others were by implication rendered still more grave, with the inevitable result that pleadings as a whole became still more dependent upon minute accuracy for their effect than they were before" (1956, 397)."[14] Charles Plummer's account of the effects of early-fifteenth-century attempts to limit forgery by statute strikes the same note: "Forgery of documents seems to have been common; and when statutes were passed against this practice, advantage was taken of these statutes to throw suspicion on genuine title-deeds" (Fortescue *Governance* 31). Perhaps the most significant result of the plethora of new statutes in the fourteenth century, however, was the renewed interest it fostered in the making of law and the sources of royal authority (Barraclough). The degree to which the political crisis at the end of Richard II's reign was brought on by such concerns will be discussed at the end of Chapter 6.

Private Law

In moving from comparatively simple criminal trials in which folklaw elements are still clearly present to more purely civil actions, we notice at once an enormous increase in procedural complexity. There are two obvious reasons for this. In the first place, the subjects of disputes between neighbors will of themselves tend to be more varied and complex than single felonious acts and thus less amenable to legal formulation. This means that medieval defendants were often forced to try to modify the inadequately formalized pleas made against them or to qualify the bare responses they were expected to make in return; civil process, in other words, was constantly seeking to stretch ill-fitting forms to cover awkward facts. Where the accused criminal was reduced finally to a bald denial of guilt, the civil litigant came to rely on a battery of exceptions and special pleas intended to clarify the matter at issue. In the second place, civil litigants were as a rule more likely than accused criminals be represented by counsel (Seipp 1995) and this inevitably led to far greater legal sophistication and a greater exploitation of procedural loopholes. Such loopholes, in an institution as dominated by rigid formalism as the medieval common law, were legion. A third reason—that the impact of literacy on the civil side of the common law was substantively more evident than in felony cases—will be discussed at the end of this chapter.

What has already been said of a kind of structural procrastination built into the legal system becomes even clearer when we consider the civil side. The months spent by the folklaw plaintiff trying to get an opponent into the local court,[15] and the hours then spent trying to get him or her to agree on the nature of their disagreement, were transformed by the bureaucratic machinery of the king's law into years of exchanging documents and caviling over their form and content. What J. A. Baker has aptly called "the possible moves in the recondite games of legal chess" (1990, 205) became so numerous that play might be spun out almost indefinitely, the attacker's hopes of pinning down an elusive opponent constantly frustrated by a defender only too happy to settle for a stalemate.[16] Thus at each of the three stages of a medieval lawsuit defendants were given every encouragement to drag their feet: after the initial process they had a range of available excuses (*essoins*) to allow them to defer their physical appearance in court; after the mesne process a variety of maneuvers (*exceptions*) which allowed them to evade or qualify the case pleaded against them; and even after the final process, when a decision had at long last been reached, a number of countermoves (such as swearing out a *writ of error*) to invalidate the whole business. As Harding says, "it was seemingly impossible in English law to bring a campaign of litigation to a decisive end" (1966, 138).[17]

Verbal equivocation, the "wrangling over the oath formula" that must have occupied so much of the oral trial, became frozen by literate formalism into a quite absurd game of legal riddling. Mistake was no defense against the pleader who sought to nonsuit an opponent for an injudicious choice of words, while a literal interpretation, no matter how alien to common sense, would always override a plea based on intended meaning. Writing transformed the folklaw's traditional concern with miskenning into a monstrous obsession with meticulous verbal precision at every stage of proceedings: as a 1344 yearbook notes, "if the person who is demandant omits in his process any part of his demand included in the original writ, the whole is discontinued" (*YB 18/19 Edw. 3*, 152–53).[18] The word *praecipe* written twice at the beginning of a writ, the name Margery appearing in another document as Margaret (*YB 13/14 Edw. 3*, 108–0) or Anastasia spelled later as Anstancia, a fishmonger referred to in one place as *piscenario* and in another as *piscario* (*YB 14 Edw. 3*, 234–35 and 136–37), or the phrase "quod ei reddere debeant" used of two creditors rather than one (*YB 17 Edw. 3*, 146–47) — all such oversights might easily jeopardize an otherwise good case.[19] Plainly, medieval judges had nothing remotely resembling a modern "slip rule" (whereby courts are able to discount minor clerical errors) to fall back on. In a 1377 prosecution under the Statute of Labourers, for instance, a local jury committed a shepherd called Robert Penne to prison for failing to honor a contract to serve one William of Thelnetham for a year, but carelessly gave its reasons in the following form: "that the aforesaid William made a covenant with the said Robert to serve him at the said day, place, and year and he did not come" (*SCKB* 7:8). Robert duly appealed on the grounds that the verdict plainly said that "the said William made a covenant with the aforesaid Robert to serve Robert" (8), and the court promptly threw out the case against him. I doubt that any of Edward III's serjeants at law would have seen in such slips of a clerk's pen a sign of God's intervention, yet this is surely the suppressed original of the endless wrangling over these matters of form (cf. Esther Cohen 61–67).

This kind of verbal quibbling permeated legal thinking so thoroughly that it could easily become hardened into a procedural principle. The curious form that allowed a younger son to plead the illegitimacy of his elder brother for the purpose of barring him from an inheritance offers a good illustration. Though English custom, reinforced by the Statute of Merton (1236), declared unequivocally that the later marriage of his parents could not retroactively legitimize a bastard, any younger brother who had brought an action at common law in the thirteenth century to recover property from an elder on the grounds that he was illegitimate would have been bound to lose, for confirmation of illegitimacy was a matter for the canon lawyers, and they, in contrast, had ruled that marriage *did* confer retroactive legitimacy on children born out of wedlock. On this issue the two systems of law were, as William Bolland says, "in direct conflict" (1925, 89). In the fourteenth century, however, the common lawyers found a very simple way round the impasse. The trick was for the younger brother to plead that the elder had been born before the marriage of their parents but to say nothing directly about his legitimacy. The timing of the birth and the wedding could properly be established by a local jury and as long as no one breathed a word about bastardy the canon lawyers need never be involved with the matter. Common law judges could then rule that no child born before the marriage of his parents should succeed to the family estate, and, according to their own lights, justice would have been done. An elder brother barred from an estate by such a quibble might justly wonder where the difference lay between having his birth labeled illegitimate and having it described as anterior to his parents' marriage, but in the eyes of the judges this difference was crucial.

One important corollary to its rigid observance of the principle that "form ought to be as much followed as substance" (*YB 13/14 Edw. 3*, 108–9) was the common law's predisposition to treat factual slips far more leniently than procedural ones. No doubt it had inherited this attitude from a folklaw process forced to come to terms with the frequent aberrations of living memory. In late medieval proof-of-age cases, for example, the formal requirement that local juries "tell signs to prove the time of the birth, as that the same year there was a great thunder, tempest, or pestilence, and the like" (Thayer 19) was often satisfied with a nonchalant inventiveness on the part of the jurors themselves. Thus, in the first year of Henry VI's reign an Essex man named Richard atte Hoo testified that he particularly recalled June 22, 1400, the day that Walter Pechard was baptized, because on that very day, John Waryn had hanged himself with a noose at Great Teye. The circumstantial details of this sad event would be easier to credit if over the next two years a second juror had not deposed that John Wargon had hanged himself with a noose at Little Laver on October 18, 1401, the very day Thomas Enfield was baptized; a third, that John Wareyn hanged himself at Thorpe on June 4, 1402, precisely the day of Walter Howse's baptism; and a fourth that John Warde's hanging occurred at Layer Marney on August 14 of that year, which also just happened to be John Marny's baptismal day. While there may well be "a substratum of fact" here somewhere, as R. C. Fowler has claimed, and "about the beginning of the fifteenth century some man, with a name like John Waryn, hanged himself somewhere in Essex" (103), for these four witnesses the ethical truth of their testimony clearly depended less on a meticulous regard for factual accuracy than on the general truth of the claim that they were being asked to substantiate.[20] As long as they felt sure that Pechard, Enfield, and the rest were indeed twenty-one years old, they found no difficulty reorganizing their memories to accommodate this fact.

All legal systems are faced with having to toe the fine line that separates form from substance, or, if one will, the demands of law from the ends of justice, but the hybridized common law of the fourteenth century seems to have had remarkably little time to spare for this particular problem. One does not have to search far in fourteenth-century yearbooks to find legal arguments so grotesquely formalistic that they cannot but have appeared to laypeople as both a mockery of common sense and a travesty of justice. The exceptional judge might sometimes appeal to a pleader's honor or good faith when faced with an especially flagrant piece of casuistry, but he had every reason to expect the kind of answer Chief Justice Bereford received in 1319: "It is not right that conscience should prevent you giving us our legal due" [Il ne covient mye pur conscience qe vous lessez qe vous nous facet ley] (*YB 12 Edw. 2 (pt. 1)*, 84)—a response which, predictably, forced Bereford to back down. A couple of fourteenth-century illustrations may stand for all.

In 1340 the Earl of Lancaster sought to recover property from a tenant who had defaulted on his feudal dues. In the original writ this property had been described as a "toft" (homestead) but the tenant replies that it is in reality a fish pond. In view of some of the quibbles we have already seen, so blatant an error might be expected to have been disastrous for the earl's case, but we have here entered an upside-down world in which mere facts pale into insignificance beside the forms by which they are pleaded; though courts seem to have assumed that allegations made in pleading could not ordinarily be rebutted "merely by attacking their details" (Sutherland 190), they were extremely reluctant to extend this indulgence to any detail that was felt to be an essential part of a set form. As we shall see, this was to lead to the absurd situation where a case that would have been lost through a scribal error might be won on the basis of a blatant falsehood in which the court actively connived. At any rate, while the judges in this case see nothing wrong with calling a fish pond a toft, they treat the formal slip exposed by the tenant's second line of defense with far less leniency. He holds the fish pond/toft jointly with his wife Alice, he says, and since the original writ does not mention Alice it is automatically invalid. Now that, says Justice Stonor, would indeed have been an excellent plea, had he not already raised the question of the fish pond, for when he objected to the term toft he did so on his own behalf and not jointly in the name of himself and his wife. Remarkably, this oversight costs the tenant his case, for the court holds that he has denied himself the possibility of subsequently pleading joint tenancy by the form in which he made his first plea; "his mouth," as Justice Shareshull puts it, "is stopped by his own supposition" [par son supposer demene sa bouche est estope]" (*YB 14 Edw. 3*, 234–37). The principle at work here is one known to modern lawyers as estoppel (the legal doctrine that prevents parties denying the truth of statements they have themselves previously made) and is one that presumably grew out of the need to limit interminable debate in an oral context (analogous in this respect to "rules of order" designed to regulate business meetings and committee discussions in our own day). Applied with the literalism of a judgment such as this, however, the rule will clearly offer a rich source of formalistic casuistry. This was especially true when the estoppel rule was transferred from oral pleading to legal documents.

To take an example from the Ricardian period, the yearbooks for 1389 record a case arising out of a land grant which was drawn up by a careless attorney in the following form: "I have given and granted to Cristine my daughter and her heirs for her marriage all the lands and tenements which I have in a certain vill . . . and if it should be that the said Cristine should die without heir of her body then [the land is to revert]"; Cristine does indeed appear to have died childless and the reversioner (perhaps her elder brother) duly claimed his estate, only to be met with the argument that the entail was invalid. There is no doubt that what the donor *intended* was to give the lands in tail to his daughter and her direct descendants, but he foolishly omitted the words "of her body begotten" after the phrase "to Cristine my daughter and her heirs." Even though the subsequent clause, "if it should be that the said Cristine die without heir of her body" made quite clear that that is what he meant, the estoppel rule gave the first clause precedence over the second, allowed the son-in-law to declare himself Cristine's heir (though not of course "of her body"), and claim unrestricted title to the land (*YB 13 Rich. 2*, 25–31).[21] In both this and the previous case estoppel takes on a dangerously inferential cast: one is bound not merely by what one says but by the implications of what one has failed to say. This principle might have been useful to a King Mark trying to deal with the equivocations of his wife, but rigorously applied in a world of writs and charters (and meticulously divorced from all consideration of the writer's intention) it quickly becomes tyrannical.

It is hardly surprising, under the circumstances, that baffled litigants should sometimes have been moved to take out their frustration on the legal instruments themselves. Violent attacks on writs and charters crop up regularly in court cases (e.g., *SCT* 2:180–81 and 394–95), but one particular form taken by such attacks gives an especially vivid sense of the outrage experienced by those who felt that their rights were being eroded by written records. On June 17, 1355, in Ficket's Field, just across from Chancery Lane, a certain John of Offham waylaid a widow called Nicola Godechepe, with whom he was involved in a lawsuit about an advowson that Nicola was claiming on behalf of her son. At the time she was apparently on her way to Westminster armed with copies of "a certain charter . . . and a certain quitclaim," which she may well have just obtained from the nearby Rolls House. John and some of his cronies set upon her and forced to her eat not only the offending charter and quitclaim but also "the seals of charters and muniments" as well (*SCKB* 6:118–19). This bizarre assault, however, is not without parallel (though most others seem to have been directed against officials seeking to enforce written mandates rather than against private litigants): Maitland gives an example from as early as 1250 (P&M 2:507), while Bertha Putnam describes "making a bailiff eat his warrant" in a later case as "a not uncommon device" (*PJP* lxxiv). Incidents such as these clearly reflect a world in which written records could still provoke suspicion, resentment, and, as we shall see again in the next chapter, even ritualized violence.

Perhaps the most dangerous legacy of the old folklaw process to the later common law was its insistence that every trial must ultimately come down to a single point of disagreement between the parties—this final stage was known as its issue. To illustrate the difficulties this might create for later law let us return to the thirteenth century. The *Brevia Placitata*, of roughly the same date as the *Placita Corone*, is a handbook describing the moves in civil cases where a plaintiff has purchased a royal writ against the defendant. In the case used to illustrate a writ of debt (100–102), a plaintiff claims that he had lent the defendant ten marks to be repaid on a set day, and that when he came for his money the defendant failed to appear. The defendant claims to owe nothing because he had earlier sold the plaintiff twelve marks' worth of wheat for which he had still not been paid. The plaintiff denies that the two debts are related, but the defendant argues that he had in fact borrowed the money in order to guarantee he would be paid for his wheat since he knew the plaintiff to be a slippery character ("tant plein de wandie"). The plaintiff continues to insist that the two debts must be treated separately: "[he] has come to this court to answer [our] demand by writ, and [we] are neither summoned nor attached to answer his demand of which he requests judgment" (102). The judge agrees, pointing out that the defendant is quite free to bring his own suit for the twelve marks: "You have an action against him just as he has against you, if you wish" [purchacet vus sur ly si cum il ad sur vus si vus volez]. In an oral setting such distinguishing of claim and counter-claim may have helped to simplify debate, and in a local court where the loser could bring a counter-action reasonably quickly no great harm would have been done; once, however, such a counter-action had to be channeled through chancery with all the consequent expense and delay, this proscription of complex issues might easily put honest defendants at a serious disadvantage.

There were graver consequences to the stubborn survival of the single issue, however. The rule had first arisen from the ubiquitous use of the judicial oath in oral process. When trial means testing an oath, such oaths must obviously be kept simple if disputes are to be resolved, and for the same reason only one of the parties must be put to the oath. Under such conditions, and as long as assertion and denial exactly mirror one another, a successful oath (by either party) will yield a clear verdict. The old pattern of assertion and denial, refined to a single issue, as Milsom has shown, remained embedded in the structure of the common law long after the passing of the old folklaw, and this was to have a profound effect on the balance between form and substance in the actual courtroom. The principle that the issue must always be single placed a potent weapon in the hands of any lawyer who wished to prevent extraneous facts being brought to bear on his client's case. In the example given above, for instance, the claim that both parties had incurred reciprocal debts is formally inadmissible; the facts alleged can never be either proved or disproved—they must simply be shut out of all consideration. Thus, what went on in a fourteenth-century common-law court was often quite the opposite of the "getting at the facts," which, crudely speaking, is what most people would assume modern judicial procedure is all about; "keeping out the facts" might almost be a fairer characterization. "When a fact is discussed in the Year Books," writes Milsom, "the argument is not about its substantive effect in law but about how it is to be pleaded, and, in particular, whether it should not be contained in the general issue. . . . [We see] a kind of looking glass world in which the legal relevance of facts is uncertainly reflected in discussion about whether they can formally be disclosed" (1967, 15). If the later common law finally began to unpack the general issue, he concludes, it was because lawyers "could not quite stop each other talking about what actually had happened" (19).

The homeostatic quality of oral law allows it to adapt to changing social conditions without threatening its confidence in its own immutability, but the updating of written law is a far more uncomfortable process. Henry Maine distinguished three principal ways by which outdated law might be brought into harmony with social needs: legal fiction, legislation, and equity (1864, 24). Of these, legislation, as we have seen, was often misdirected or ineffectual in the fourteenth century, while the earliest solid influence of equitable theory on the common law is generally regarded as a fifteenth-century phenomenon (associated with the rise of the court of chancery); legal fiction, however, if not yet raised to its highest art, was beginning to come into its own at this period. Lawyers seeking to unpack the general issue by means of either special pleading or special actions might easily find themselves forced to employ such legal fictions, but many simpler and more striking examples show the curious effect of repressive formalism on the legal representation of actuality. One particularly important fourteenth-century fiction, the feoffment to use (by which property owners could temporarily transfer ownership of their estates in order to escape certain kinds of legal limitations and liabilities), has led Robert Palmer to remark not only on the rapid growth of "an extreme artificiality about the law, a gap between law and life," but also on the degree to which "individuals had internalized a most strange view of their world" (1984, 219).

The assumption "which conceals, or affects to conceal, the fact that a rule of law has undergone alteration, its letter remaining unchanged, its operation being modified" (Maine 1864, 25) grew commoner as literate habits of mind led to court procedure becoming more and more ossified. Such an assumption will often mean in practice that litigants are forced to connive in blatant falsehoods in order to evade jurisdictional rigidities. The "forty-shilling rule," for instance, was intended to keep debt litigation for trivial sums out of the king's courts, but as long as the plaintiff was prepared "to count untruthfully to bring his case within the jurisdiction" (Milsom 1961, 260) he might still sue for a smaller sum. A seller who was owed, say, thirty shillings, might enter forty on the writ in hopes that the defendant would join issue on the correct amount, or might sue for thirty and throw in a fictious debt for ten, trusting that the defendant would deny the one but not the other (258–61). Neither method can have been without risk since an unscrupulous defendant might try to take the general issue on the whole sum, but only the premise of some such fiction can explain why "a suspiciously high proportion of counts . . . allege sales for just 40s" (258).[22] A similar fiction involved the marshalsea court, which was originally constituted to hear cases connected with the royal household and was limited in its jurisdiction to breaches of the peace occurring within twelve miles of the king's own person (McIntosh 727). The records of this court for 1358 suggest the rather surprising fact that the local people of Havering in Essex, where Edward III spent most of the summer and fall, managed to curb their lawless impulses on all but two particular days during the whole of this period; presumably, a simpler explanation is that these days had been "identified by the court as ones on which the king was definitely at Havering and were then used by the parties as 'safe' " (730).

Not only the court's freedom to hear certain types of case but the litigant's freedom to advance certain kinds of argument might depend on the use of fictions. The basic principles of medieval pleading seem to have encouraged such a practice. Since the court expected pleas to be specific rather than general, but at the same time required them to be refuted in substance rather than in detail, the parties were free to invent whatever details might give them a procedural advantage, knowing that these details would not normally form a basis for the final issue—knowing, in other words, that they would not ultimately be forced to stand by them. Under some circumstances it might even be safer to provide a totally fictitious account than to plead a true one. In 1330, for instance, a defendant charged with obstructing the plaintiff's right to present a new parson to a church living argued that the last parson presented by the plaintiff was still alive and still in office; this was apparently true, but disastrous to his case for it conceded the greater part of his opponent's claim. The reporter shakes his head over this procedural blunder: "he could safely have alleged some total stranger as parson, and said that he had the office at the presentment of someone else, who had nothing at all to do with it [qe vnqes nauoit reins], for issue cannot be taken on this material" (quoted by Sutherland 191 n. 25). By suppressing an inconvenient truth, the defendant could easily have thwarted his opponent's claim that the living was vacant, without at the same time trading away the issue of the plaintiff's right to present.

By the late fourteenth century, these kinds of fiction, which came to be known as "giving color," were becoming standard. Unless they intended to challenge its legal basis (demurrer), defendants had in general to choose one of two possible responses to a plaintiff's charge: they could deny it outright (traverse) or they could admit it but plead additional material (confession and avoidance); in neither case would the jury normally learn more of the plaintiff's position than was contained in the original count. Thus a plaintiff with a dubious claim to a manor who sued the putative owner for ejecting him, might try to manage proceedings so that the defendant was forced to fight the case solely on the legality of the ejection and not over who had the sounder claim. In order to expose the plaintiff's case to further examination, the defendant must make allegations about the circumstances of this claim which the plaintiff would then be forced to answer. As in the case discussed above there was no necessity for such allegations to be based on fact. Such "giving color" appears to have arisen around 1330 (Sutherland 187) and became commonplace in the fifteenth century. The incongruity, pointed out by D. W. Sutherland, that "statements that were wholly false and known to be so should operate to turn the course of proceedings whose intent was to find facts and do justice" (184) cannot have escaped contemporaries. No doubt the belief that the trouthe of an oathworthy litigant should always prevail over the sooth of circumstantial details allowed many fourteenth-century judges and lawyers to use legal fictions "with honesty and honor" (192), but as the relentless progress of literate habits of mind drove trouthe and sooth ever closer together such a belief must have become more and more difficult to maintain. Moreover, even if individual lawyers saw themselves "doing their best as good and true men" (193) with forms they felt powerless to alter, can we be sure their opponents' clients would always have agreed with them?

Fourteenth-century common law was in a state of transition—close enough to its oral roots to retain vestiges of its old homeostasis, but increasingly immobilized by legal book-learning. One of the more amusing legal fictions of the period was the *vi et armis* condition in trespass actions, which was stretched to cover the most unlikely offenses so that the plaintiff might assert breach of the king's peace; Milsom cites one case in which the buyer of a cask of wine "left it for later collection, and complained that in the meantime his seller, against the king's peace and with force and arms, to wit with swords and bows and arrows, drew off some of the wine and substituted water" (1965, 502).[23] Though, around 1370, lawyers could still silently agree to drop the *vi et armis* condition in trespass, such instances of organic development were becoming rarer, while procedural fictions were growing commoner and more outrageous. For sheer legal deviousness, however, there is little in the fourteenth century to match such fifteenth-century devices as the notorious bill of Middlesex, by which wholly fictitious accusations of trespass were used to secure the persons of those whom one wished to sue for something entirely different (Blatcher), or the elaborate procedure known as common recovery, designed to allow one to break an inconvenient entail. The details of this labyrinthine process, whose roots reach back before Richard II's reign (Elphinsone 287), need not detain us here, but we might note that it required the services, as fictional middleman, of a professional perjurer (the "common vouchee"), who, along with his cousins, the hired compurgators known as "knights of the post," was to serve the law faithfully right down to Dickens's day.[24] It is perhaps no coincidence that the century which first raised legal fiction to such an art should also have witnessed what S. E. Thorne has characterized as a revolution in legal education (1959, 96), nor that by the end of that century we should find the ancient skills of the oral pleader giving way to a new system of "paper" pleading (Holdsworth 3:640–48).

We have seen how literacy, by supporting bureaucratic centralization and entrenching procedural formalism, profoundly altered the character of the law, and how, moreover, the typically more complex civil cases were proportionately more severely affected by the straitjacket of legal formulas. There was, however, a further way in which writing impinged on civil cases, for, unlike most felony trials, both real and personal actions might easily turn on the possession and interpretation of written evidence.

Legal Instruments

The clerk of Marmoutiers who recorded the ceremony of Baldonet's enserfment in the mid-eleventh century makes quite clear that he saw the function of his record as being to preserve the memory of the event more durably than flesh-and-blood witnesses could do. In the short term the parchment might act as an aide-mémoire for those named in it, but even after they had perished it could still stand as their representative and continue to attest to a ceremony long out of mind. Though Baldonet might as easily have become a serf without it, his new masters clearly felt happier with the extra security this written record gave them. Evidently, however, the document itself was not legally binding in the same sense as the ceremonial handing over the bell ropes and the head money was. At what period, then, did contracts such as Baldonet's demand a written instrument in order to make them valid? When did acknowledgment of such an instrument (by signature, mark, or seal) become the act that actually bound the parties to the conditions recorded in it? When did contractual procedure technically recognize, in Clanchy's terms, the change from memory to written record, or, as the modern lawyer would put it, when did written contracts cease to be evidentiary and become dispositive? The answer is obviously important to our inquiry into the nature of the shift from troth to truth. Unfortunately, for England at least, it is far from clear, though we can at least be certain that the question was still contentious in the fourteenth century.

Most of the energy of the common law in its formative stages was directed to questions of land tenure. From as early as the seventh century written records had been kept of gifts of land, usually gifts from the laity to the church, but it is quite clear that these Anglo-Saxon charters were evidentiary in nature and intended to complement traditional rituals of seisin. For instance, a fairly common introductory clause, while suggesting that transactions should be committed to "most trustworthy writings and documents to avoid uncertainty in future time," is careful to stress that "the word alone is sufficient" [quamvis solus sermo sufficeret], and one such charter mentions that the donor has placed sods of earth from the lands in question on a copy of the Gospels (Birch 1:156). One effect of the increasing use of written records, however, was to obviate the requirement that the ceremony of transfer take place on the actual land where the witnesses could view its boundaries in person, since these might be described in detail in the document itself (Thorne 1936, 349–52). From here it would have been but a short step from witnessing a symbolic act to simply witnessing a dispositive document, but this step was not taken. The common law came into being at a time when "the transaction was complete without the charter" (353), and by replacing local witness proof with trial by a panel of knights of the shire it guaranteed that this state of affairs would continue, though in a somewhat different form. While conservatism preserved the old ceremonies of transfer by staff and rod, and prudence suggested that a written record should be kept of them, the importance of local witnesses gradually declined (359–60), and there was a corresponding rise in the importance accorded to publicizing one's physical possession of the land in question.

Throughout the late Middle Ages, a written charter might provide useful corroboration that title to land had passed, but the vital thing for the recipient was to establish actual livery of seisin. This was something concrete a judge could ask a jury to verify, no mere matter of assessing a donor's intentions. As we have seen, courts treated questions of intention with great suspicion, even apparently when they were expressed in a witnessed document; indeed, in a case from 1419/20 it was specifically objected that "this deed is only the private intent of a man, which can be known only by writing" (quoted by Thayer 109). Thus a judge in 1338 suggests that there are two valid defenses against anyone who claims a deed "as being by way of feoffment": one is to deny the deed, and the other to show "that livery of seisin was not made in such a manner that [the title] passed by that deed (so that you make use of it as being in the nature of a feoffment, when in fact you were never seized)" (*YB 12/13 Edw. 3*, 62–63). What such seisin had come to mean may be illustrated from the incidents which set in motion the Whilton dispute: in the spring of 1265 William de Whelton seised his second son, Nicholas, in the manor of Whilton by placing his hand on the door hasp and handing him a branch of a cherry tree. He then left Nicholas in total possession of the property for fifteen days, during which time his son fished the manor's fish pond, burned its firewood, and received oaths of loyalty from its tenants. All this was not enough however; Nicholas had not plowed the land, appointed a bailiff, received rents, nor freed any serfs, and his failure to establish such irreversible seisin was to involve his descendants and the descendants of his elder brother Roger in a lawsuit that would last for the next 116 years—this despite the fact that Roger had written him out a formal quitclaim from the very beginning (R. Palmer 1984, 31–33).[25]

If in the sphere of real property (at least property in fee simple), legal documents were still broadly evidentiary in the fourteenth century, in the area of private contractual obligations they were beginning to take on a rather more dispositive character. The main evidence for this is the requirement that certain kinds of action could only be maintained with the support of appropriate documentation ("specialty"). Before the end of Edward I's reign (1307), writes Maitland, "the man who relies upon a covenant must produce in proof some 'specialty' (*especialté, aliquid speciale*); the production of 'suit' is not enough. Thenceforward, however, it is only a short step to holding as a matter of law that a 'deed'—and by a deed (*fet, factum*) men are beginning to mean a sealed piece of parchment—has an operative force of its own which intentions expressed, never so plainly, in other ways have not. The sealing and delivering of the parchment is the contractual act" (P&M 2:220). There are, however, some important qualifications to be made to his account.

In the first place, Maitland seems to imply that the question had virtually been settled by the end of the thirteenth century, whereas, even in covenant cases, it was clearly still being debated in Edward II's courts. Indeed, the Waltham carrier case of 1321 is sometimes cited as a landmark in this respect. An action, brought against a carter who had failed to observe an oral agreement to carry a load of hay from Waltham to London, was supported with the argument that "one cannot have a writing for every such little covenant" [homme ne poet pas de chescun tiel petit covenant faire escript]. To this the judge replied witheringly: "The law will not be changed for a cartload of hay," and went on to explain that "a covenant is neither more nor less than an agreement between parties which cannot be taken to law without specialty [a sealed writing]" (*Eyre of London* 2:287). From this date, Baker says, "informal agreements had been shut out from the central courts and the development of a law of consensual contracts stifled by the formal requirement of a seal" (1990, 363–64).[26] Questions were still occasionally raised even in the second half of the century, however, for some judges were apparently having second thoughts about the rigidity of their own rule: "this action of covenant of necessity is maintainable without a specialty," says a judge at the end of Edward III's reign, "because for such a small matter a man cannot always have a clerk to make a specialty" (quoted by McGovern 1971, 1169). Typically, however, their solution was not to change the rule, but to foster a new procedure (the action of *assumpsit*) whose effect was primarily to circumvent it.

Second, we should not be too quick to take the new formal requirement as evidence of a conceptual shift. No doubt it had originated in response to purely practical considerations such as the difficulty of dragging a suit of neighbors to Westminster — a problem that had led to good suit itself becoming a fiction), and which in turn meant that "an action on an unwritten covenant had come in reality to depend on the plaintiff's own bare word" (Baker 1990, 363). A. W. B. Simpson argues that the sealed instrument was regarded as evidentiary throughout the yearbook period (1987, 15–17) and that a covenant "cannot be taken to law without specialty" does not necessarily mean that the document itself was regarded as dispositive — merely that it was a formal requirement for those intending to bring an action of covenant in the king's courts. In an analogous situation, the forty-shilling rule can hardly have meant that royal judges did not regard debts for smaller sums as not being debts at all merely because they were not actionable in their courtrooms. The king's law was not incapable of imagining how oral agreements might be binding; it simply insisted that any litigation involving them be taken elsewhere. In other jurisdictions parol agreements were certainly recognized; manorial courts were far less restrictive in this matter (*Court Baron* 113–18), while a dispute involving an oral contract between merchants might more appropriately be settled in the court of the fair or borough where it had arisen. One very important class of oral agreements, those which created consensual marriages, properly fell under the jurisdiction of the church courts (Helmholz 1974).

Finally, covenant was not the only form of action by which contract disputes might be heard, and some of the others reveal an ambivalent attitude to written records. The most important was debt—a far broader concept than in modern law. As long as a specific amount of money (the "sum certain") was at issue, plaintiffs might use debt in many situations which would now be regarded as contractual. And in debt, the progressive and the customary lie side by side. Where plaintiffs could produce a written bond, they would sue in debt *sur obligation*, in which case the instrument itself would be accepted as proof. Such bonds, at least by the fifteenth century, seem to have taken on a clearly dispositive cast (A. W. B. Simpson 1987, 95–98), but, ironically, they support only one side of an action whose other pillar stands firmly on an ancient faith in the sworn word. Where the agreement that gave rise to the debt was an oral one plaintiffs would sue in debt *sur contract*, but defendants were then free to prove their *nihil debet* by the time-honored method of compurgation. The archaic and unfamiliar nature of such proof has led some commentators to assume that the award of compurgation in debt was virtually a perjurers' charter, and there is some contemporary support for such a view: "God forbid," says Chief Justice Bereford early in Edward II's reign, "that [the defendant] should get to his law [i.e., compurgation] about a matter of which the country may have knowledge, for then with a dozen or half-a-dozen ruffians [ribauz] he might swear an honest man out of his goods" (*YB 2&3 Edw. 2*, 196).[27] However, although there was undoubtedly room for abuse, this view is easily overstated. Langland, for instance, seems to have regarded the abuse of this process as a failing typical of Sloth rather than Avarice:

> If I bigge and borwe auȝt, but if it be ytailed,
> I foryete it as yerne, and if men me it axe
> Six siþes or seuene I forsake it wiþ oþes.
> (*PPl* B.5:423–25)

Interestingly enough, for a Yorkshireman to be called a "perjurer in all pleas of debt" was considered grounds for an action for defamation in 1318 (*SCD* 33). Some recent authorities have shown more charity toward the integrity of medieval and later compurgators (e.g., Baker 1971, 228–30), but, nonetheless, the force of Milsom's point that compurgation, which had evolved in a community situation, was inevitably weakened by the fact that "neighbours could not be dragged to Westminster" is undeniable (1981, 67; cf. P&M 2:636).

By the end of the fourteenth century some litigants who were unable to find adequate remedies for breach of contract in covenant and debt were beginning to turn to trespass, or, as we would say, tort (A. W. B. Simpson 1987, 199–247)—a sure sign that the older actions were failing to provide satisfactory remedies. Once trespass had shed the procedural requirement that it must originate in a disturbance of the king's peace, a wide variety of personal actions (known collectively as trespass on the case) became attached to it; among these was one called *assumpsit* which enabled those who had suffered loss as the result of the improper execution of a consensual contract to sue for its recovery at common law. The incompetence of ferrymen whose cargo went to the bottom, of innkeepers who lost their guests' belongings, of smiths who killed the horses they were shoeing, of doctors whose remedies made their patients worse—these were the kind of blunders for which a plaintiff might seek relief on the grounds that the defendant had undertaken (*assumpsit*) to act quite otherwise. The very first action of this type is usually said to be the case of the Humber ferryman,[28] dating to the middle of the fourteenth century (1348), though the actual word *assumpsit* seems not to have been regularly used before 1373. By 1400 the action of assumpsit was clearly established, but only over the course of the next two centuries was it to broaden into the major avenue of contract litigation that legal historians regard as contributing directly to modern common-law contract. Moreover, in its early phase it suffered from one serious limitation: reflecting, no doubt, its trespass origins, it could only be employed where an actual wrong had been committed (what the lawyers call misfeasance), not where there had been a failure to perform a positive duty (nonfeasance)—in other words, where there had been a bungled attempt to carry out a contract, not where the contract had simply been set aside altogether. The doctrine that "not doing is no trespass" (Milsom 1954) was to hamstring this branch of common-law contract to the end of the Middle Ages.

Generally speaking, those who suffered harm as a result of relying on parol agreements that were never honored had no remedy at common law in Chaucer's day. That this was a far from satisfactory state of affairs is suggested by the spread of equitable jurisdiction in the fifteenth century. The petitioner of Richard II's reign who sought help from the chancellor because, "for this, that he has no special or any writing of the aforesaid covenant, action fails him at the common law" (*CPC* 2:ii), was to become a typical figure in the fifteenth-century court of chancery, the only royal court prepared to countenance parol contracts (W. T. Barbour 160–68). Robert Ellesmere, with whom we began this chapter, makes one of this company. Like the development of assumpsit, the introduction of equity into late-fourteenth-century chancery procedure was in part a response to the common law's inflexible attitude to informal contracts (Avery 134–35), yet, again like assumpsit, only in the fifteenth century was this new avenue of litigation to provide any real prospect of relief for those who had failed to get their agreements put in writing. In what may well be a parallel development, fifteenth-century ecclesiastical courts were also entertaining suits involving parol agreements that gave rise to a debt (despite being specifically prohibited from doing so by Henry II's Constitutions of Clarendon) under cover of their general responsibility to discipline perjury, *fidei laesio* (Helmholz 1975). Common-law judges began complaining about this threat to their jurisdiction from 1400 onwards (A. W. B. Simpson 1987, 145–46), but too few records survive from earlier centuries to allow us to assess the magnitude of the shift with any precision. It is clear, however, that such attempts to close what Morris Arnold calls the "odd gap between law and morality" in the legal treatment of promises had made little headway by the end of the Ricardian period and that for the fourteenth century as a whole common-law contract remained a "curiously retarded" institution (M. Arnold 1976, 321).

The Shift to Written Contract

The fossilization of English contract law occurred at just the time that written agreements were taking on an unprecedented importance in many people's lives. The social and political organization of late medieval England, the period lasting roughly from the death of Edward I to the accession of Henry VII, has frequently been categorized by the term bastard feudalism—a description that has generated almost as much debate as the term feudalism itself. Some historians have endorsed Helen Cam's view that it connotes a "parasitic institution," far removed from "the atmosphere of responsibility, loyalty and faith which had characterised the relationship of lord and vassal in the earlier middle ages" (1940, 225), while others, taking their cue from K. B. McFarlane, insist that it should be understood "not as a kind of feudalism, however modified, but as something essentially different while superficially similar" (1943/45, 162)—neither more nor less debased than the institution it succeeded. Even as he argues for this ostensibly reasonable position, however, McFarlane is forced to recognize that Cam's views are more in tune with the temper of the period itself than his own: "Being men of their time, they believed that the evils with which they contended showed a contemporary falling off from a more perfect past" (179). Typically, however, he himself has little use for such Saturnian sentimentality: "in thinking so they were usually wrong" (179). Within the historical establishment, McFarlane's air of cool objectivity has generally won more converts than Cam's censoriousness, but those prepared to allow that it may sometimes be necessary to forgo the pose of Olympian detachment in order to try to understand the past on its own terms may well feel that his account, too, has its limitations.

The one characteristic of bastard feudalism that both Cam and McFarlane were agreed on was that it was based upon a new kind of contract between lord and dependent—a contract "no longer secured by land" (225), in Cam's words, or, as McFarlane puts it, one "divorced from tenure" (162). But McFarlane then goes on to make the curious assertion that the "peculiar instruments" of this system "were not the charter of enfeoffment but the indenture and the letter patent" (164). No one, of course, would deny the importance of the indenture of retinue in the political organization of the later Middle Ages, but McFarlane's comparison with the charter of enfeoffment is ill-conceived, since these two kinds of documents were far from being legally commensurate with one another, nor could one truly be said to have replaced the other. McFarlane's remark is a little like saying that the peculiar rituals of feudalism were not livery of seisin but the manual act of homage and the oath of fealty. By the thirteenth century, charters of enfeoffment (as opposed to charters of confirmation),[29] would be drawn up when title to a free tenement passed out of the direct line of descent, and, as we have seen, though they might be used to supplement livery of seisin were not a legal substitute for it. Such charters, then, would be retained by a family for generations because they attested to its tenurial rights. Each time the tenement passed from father to eldest son, on the other hand, the new tenant had to establish his personal right by performing an act of homage and swearing an oath of fealty to his lord, and in just the same way homage had to be reestablished between the new lord and his tenantry whenever the demesne itself was inherited or alienated. Thus the significance of homage, unlike enfeoffment, was restricted in the first instance to the lifetime of the parties. Though the terms of enfeoffment were frequently, if not universally, recorded in writing, this was far less commonly the case with homage,[30] but about the end of the thirteenth century a kind of quasi-homage, lifetime retainer, began to assume documentary form with the indenture of retinue. We might say, then, that the "peculiar instruments" of bastard feudalism were not homage and fealty but written indentures; when McFarlane draws a comparison between the systems in terms of two kinds of document, he is revealing a literatist bias that might be more difficult to defend today.

Clanchy's work, in particular, should have prepared us to recognize that the peculiarity of bastard feudalism lies not in its employment of one kind of legal document as against another, but in its supplanting the ancient bonds of the commemorative act of homage and oath of fealty by the newer constraints of a written covenant.[31] Scott Waugh has recently characterized the indenture of retinue in just such terms: "The contract, like homage and fealty, was the meeting point of two aims: the lord's quest for service and the client's quest for protection or promotion. Thus, like feudal lordship, contractual lordship depended upon a conditional reciprocity between service and rewards, as well as on the ideal of a lifetime association between lord and client, but it expressed these ideals in precise legal formulae that, it was hoped, would protect both parties" (818). The replacement of the ancient trothplight of lord and vassal with a ragged piece of vellum is one of the most conspicuous examples of the objectification of troth underpinning the Ricardian shift from trouthe to truth that is the central theme of this book. Thus, it is my contention that there is a direct connection between this fundamental mechanism of bastard feudalism and the Saturnian malaise that even McFarlane is forced to recognize in the later Middle Ages.

It would be convenient to be able to claim that the indenture of retinue, so characteristic of late medieval political relationships, was simply the ancient formula of homage committed to the new medium of writing, but unfortunately the story is not quite so simple. The main objection is that by the thirteenth century homage was bound up with the hereditable tenement held in knight's service and was thus conceptually quite distinct from any kind of negotiated contract for a limited term. Bracton is the loudest spokesman for this kind of exclusive homage, specifically denying that homage may arise from "a fee or a rent paid out of a chamber" (2:231), or "from a tenement held for a term" (2:232). Nevertheless, the very force of his denial suggests that some people were already coming to think of such arrangements as entailing a kind of homage, and even he was forced to concede that "Rodknights," whose duty was to ride with their lord from manor to manor, and holders of similar private serjeanties, sometimes performed homage (2:231). By *Britton*'s day his position would probably have looked distinctly old fashioned: "when anyone is to do homage for a chamber pension, such as a servant does to his lord (as his servant, not as his man) the words shall simply be . . ." (*Britton* 2:38). Only conservatives like the author of *The Mirror of Justices* were still insisting on the narrow meaning of homage: "One should also hold a contract to be void in the case of homage done in contravention of the law [contracts suppose auxi faus en homage pris en fraude de la lei], as if I receive your homage in respect of any other service than the service which issues from a knight's fee [de fieu de haubert]" (75); significantly, this passage occurs in the context of a discussion of written contracts.

I am not of course arguing that around 1300 the holders of hereditary knight's fees and their lords simply started replacing the time-honored rituals of homage with an exchange of sealed indentures, for clearly the two systems were conceptually distinct and continued to function alongside one another to the end of the Middle Ages. On the ground, indeed, the continued vitality of older patterns of lordship well into the fifteenth century has led Christine Carpenter and others to modify the classic account of indentured retaining considerably.[32] Nonetheless, as hereditary estates were alienated and traditional duties commuted it is clear that there was a growing tendency for homage to be replaced by written contracts for life-service, sharing many of the features of the older oral agreements. The major substantive difference, of course, was that the indenture carried with it no suggestion of heritability. Indeed, it was probably the fear that lifetime retainers might try to represent their service as hereditable that led Bracton and others to deny that homage might be performed on a contract for services, and the ultimate success of their campaign may be seen in the popularity of the fifteenth-century proverb "service is no heritage" (Whiting S169).

It would be easier to argue for a continuity between the oral trothplight of homage and the written indenture of retinue if we knew more about the words that were actually used in the original ceremony. Unfortunately our knowledge is sketchy at best. We can, however, be reasonably sure that the bare texts preserved in the legal treatises tell only half the story. Here, for example, is Bracton: "[The tenant] ought to place both his hands between the two hands of his lord, . . . and say these words: 'I become your man with respect to the tenement which I hold of you (or 'which I ought to hold of you') and I will bear you fealty in life and limb and earthly honour (according to some, but according to others, 'in body and goods and earthly honour') and I will bear you fealty against all men (or 'all mortal men,' according to some) saving the faith owed the lord king and his heirs'" (2:232). On the surface this looks to have little in common with such elaborate indentures as the one drawn up the earl of Norfolk and Sir John Segrave, detailing the precise duties owed by the knight right down to whether he was himself to be responsible for providing the oats and hay for his own horses on campaign (Denholm-Young 167–68). When we turn to *Britton*'s account of homage, however, it becomes clear that what Bracton offers us is merely a skeleton form: "I become your man for the fees and tenements which I hold and ought to hold of you, *and particularly for such a tenement named by certain quantity and certain bounds, and for such fees*" [italics mine] (2:37–38). The author of *The Mirror of Justices* is even more explicit: "'I become your man of such a fee,' *so that the quantity of the fee be expressed and specified and certain, and the lord may know how much and in what manner he must warrant to his tenant, and to how much he obliges his fee by the warranty, and the tenant may know for how much he becomes his lord's man*" [italics mine] (117). Indeed, even Bracton hints at some fuller form of the words of homage when, after giving the words of the oath of fealty that accompanied the act of homage, he remarks, "and some add the following to the oath, and properly, that faithfully . . . he shall do his service to his lord and his heirs, according to the agreed terms" [terminis statutis] (2:232). Bracton's "agreed terms" must surely have been the result of a process of "oral negotiation between lord and man" similar to that which J. M. W. Bean has suggested lies behind the earliest indentures of retinue (1989, 66). In other words, the act of homage seems to have been accompanied by an oral recital of the rights and duties on either side, and such recitals might easily have provided the model for the written indentures whose sealing would eventually supplant the older rituals (just as the act of livery of seisin was eventually rendered obsolete by the charter of enfeoffment).

There are two features of the surviving indentures of retinue that suggest an origin in the oral rituals of homage and fealty. The first is the stubborn survival of a nominal association between military service and land tenure. Two of the earliest indentures (from 1297) make this association very clear. When Robert de Tothale agreed to serve John de Grey in peace and in war for the term of his life (Jones and Walker 39) he was granted six marks a year from the manor of Yapham in Yorkshire in language that is strongly reminiscent of a charter of enfeoffment ("dominus Johannes dedit, concessit, et hac presenti carta sua confirmavit"), and when Sir John Segrave made a similar agreement with Roger Bigod, earl of Norfolk in exchange for the manor of Lodden in Norfolk such a charter is specifically mentioned: "with all the appurtenances in fee together with the advowson of the church, as is contained in the charter of enfeoffment which the said Sir John has by the gift of the earl" (Denholm-Young 168). A slightly later indenture (from 1310) suggests a further stage in the evolution: Lord Mohaut promises Sir John Bracebridge a lifetime annual rent of ten pounds from his vill of Walton on Trent for performing military services, and the indenture then registers the names of twenty-six tenants, both bond and free, and the sums of money due from each (M. Jones 391). Bracebridge, then, appears to have been little more than a rent farmer, and if such might be the basis for military service there would seem to have been little reason not to pay the retainer directly from general chamber revenues. But this never became standard practice: the retaining fee "usually took the form of a rent charge, payable in two instalments, assigned on one of the lord's manors or receiverships. . . . It was also quite common in the case of favoured retainers, for the lord to alienate a whole manor to his servant for the term of the latter's life" (Jones and Walker 24). This tenuous link between service and land holding seems to preserve a dim memory of feudal homage for knight's service. Even Bracton had been prepared to allow that homage might arise from a rent paid out of the chamber, always providing there was "a tenement from which a rent may issue" (2:231).

The second indication of a link between indentured retaining and the ancient ritual of homage is the occasional hint that the sealing of such indentures was accompanied by the swearing of oaths, in much the same way that homage had regularly been confirmed by an oath of fealty. When Hugh le Despenser retained Sir Peter de Uvedale in 1316, for instance, Sir Peter swore "to observe and perform the aforesaid services well and truly in the manner specified with his bare right hand laid physically on God's holy gospels" [sur les seintz Evangelies Dieu corporament touchez de sa mayn destre toute neuve] (Jones and Walker 56), and the sealing clause leaves the impression that the parties regarded this oath as the real dispositive act: "in witness of truth [en tesmoignaunce de verite], the aforesaid parties have set their seals to this indenture interchangeably." A similar impression is conveyed by those indentures which introduce the sealing clause with the phrase "ad maiorem securitatem" (40) or "a grendre suerte" (63), as if the oath was regarded as the primary act of verification and the sealing an additional safeguard. Reference to swearing oaths on the Gospels is still to be found as late as 1400 (122–23), and one of the earliest indentures to be drawn up in English (in 1426) preserves unmistakable traces of its oral roots: "For the whiche covenauntz whele and trewly to be holden and perforned on the behalf of the said Thomas as he has plight his troth to the said sir Richard. In the witnenes herof the parties beforesaid to the parties of this endentures entrechaungeably have set ther seals" (147). Of this and similar indentures that make reference to pledges of faith ("le dit monsire Thomas a plevy sa foy" [132–33]), Michael Jones and Simon Walker remark that "no details of what this act involved are given" (30), but at the very least it must have involved swearing an oath to observe the conditions of the agreement and quite possibly included a public recital of these conditions. Indeed, it would hardly be surprising to discover that the sealing of all such indentures was accompanied by the swearing of oaths or that the instruments themselves were regularly thought of, much as John Gower describes Florent's formalization of a parol agreement, as a kind of written oath: "Under his seal he wrot his oth" (*CA* 1:1487).[33]

What might it have meant in terms of people's working relationships with one another that the old rituals of oral trothplight were being ousted by this exchange of sealed instruments? Scott Waugh's claim that the new system of contractual lordship resulted in a "highly flexible system of retaining" (818) is true only as long as we are able to conceive of it as simply the result of a useful cartulary innovation. As soon as we think of it, on the other hand, as merely a further stage along the road from memory to written record, we are in a position to recognize that one kind of flexibility was being purchased at the expense of another. Anyone who has witnessed the replacement of tenured faculty by part-time and limited-contract teachers in the modern university will have some idea of the kind of flexibility Waugh is talking about, and, more important, whose interests were best served by it. It is thus unsurprising to find Christine Carpenter observing of Richard Beauchamp, earl of Warwick (1401–1439), that "the only losses to Beauchamps' affinity were men that he himself threw over" (1980, 518). The earliest charters of enfeoffment and certification are remarkably vague about the precise nature of the knight's service: "With few exceptions they are composed on the assumption that those who hear them will understand what is meant by the service of a knight, and that disputes about this duty will be settled by the peers of the fee and not by the terms of any written document" (F. Stenton 170). Even after the ancient machinery of feudal service had become too unwieldy to meet the lord's immediate military and domestic needs, the services of the mercenary soldier and the feed servant had been secured by oral trothplight under a system arguably far more flexible than anything governed by indentured covenants.

As the dissemination of literacy led more and more people to commit their agreements to writing, this in turn made possible greater complexity in the framing of such agreements. That terms of service were now being written down, however, was certainly no guarantee that they would remain uncontentious, especially since, at least in this transitional phase, "indentures rarely covered every detail of the relationship between lord and man with absolute precision" (Bean 1989, 65)—a recipe for disaster in an age when the enforcement of covenants relied on a meticulous respect for form. One has only to follow the thirty-seven year legal battle between Oldcotes and d'Arcy that began with the drawing up of an apparently unambiguous indenture between the two around November 1, 1272 ("Oldcotes" 64) to recognize that the mere existence of legal instruments might quite as easily fuel dissension as damp it down. The legal fiction known as feoffment to use, for example, though generally hedged about with a variety of written documents, from indentures and deeds poll to last wills (Bean 1968, 151–52), was a constant source of dissension in the fifteenth century; by the end of Henry VI's reign "ninety per cent of the total business of the equitable court of chancery was concerned with feoffments to use" (Avery 132). Narrow legalism and rampant litigiousness are hardly conducive to flexible social arrangements, and both bulked very large in the life of late medieval society. That these might be as much an effect of the spread of literate habits of mind as its cause should not be difficult to appreciate in a period such as our own which has seen an analogous shift in modes of communication accompanied by a similar enthusiasm for litigation.

The extreme formalism of medieval common law always worked to the advantage of those who could afford lawyers capable of prolonging cases to the point where their opponents became exhausted, so that the increasing use of written covenants to govern social relationships could hardly fail to concentrate yet more power in the hands of the rich.[34] The author of *Mum and the Sothsegger* complains about precisely this kind of abuse:

> Thus laboreth þe loos among þe comune peuple
> That þe wacker in þe writte wol haue þe wors ende;[35]
> Hit wol not gayne a goky a grete man forto plede,
> For lawe lieth muche in lordship sith loyaute was exiled,
> And poure men pleyntes / penylees a-bateth.
>
> (1580–84)

The poor men whom the author speaks of here should certainly not be thought of as the dregs of society; the author has just complained about how such tactics have served to haul "þe howslord oute atte halle-dore," and drag him "clene fro his dees / he dysneth þere nomore" (1570–73). It would be dangerous, on the other hand, to assume that the kind of developments I have been discussing were manifest at only the higher social levels. To show how thoroughly the literate revolution had permeated all orders of society I should like to conclude this chapter with a very different kind of written contract that began to make its appearance at about the same time as the indenture of retinue but at the very opposite end of the social scale—the maintenance contracts by which late medieval peasants sought to bind their children to care for them in their old age. Such documents must appear far more outlandish to the modern eye than the indentures of retinue, for, as Alan Macfarlane has remarked, "to find the essence of 'contract' in this central crucial parent-child relationship, rather than a relationship based on status, is very extraordinary, and in no way fits with any conceivable model of peasant society" (1978, 143).

Ideally, the transfer of property from one generation to the next in the English medieval village seems to have occurred, not when landholders died, but when their retirement from active labor coincided with the marriage of their heirs. At this point, responsibility for the property was handed over to the young couple in exchange for a promise to maintain the parents for the rest of their life. In practice, of course, a host of circumstances might demand modification of this ideal pattern, but a good sense of its traditional working is provided by a Suffolk court case from 1227: "The jurors say that the aforesaid [Anselm] gave the aforesaid Alice, his daughter, to Hugh, and it was proposed [*prolocutum*] between them that he [Anselm] would give him half of all his acquisitions in Illegha [Monks Eleigh] and that they would dwell together in one house, so that the same [Anselm] would dwell in one room and they in another. And the same [Anselm] went out of the house and handed over to them the door by the hasp, and at once begged lodging out of charity [*caritative*]" (quoted by Homans 153–54). This is clearly an oral trothplight, sufficiently publicized within the village for a jury to be able to report its details. While such ceremonies must have continued throughout the Middle Ages, toward the end of the thirteenth century they were coming to be supplemented by written contracts, formally registered in the manorial court rolls. In one such contract from Essex in 1320, a son receives seisin of his mother's tenement on the following conditions: "said John will find for said Petronilla for said Petronilla's lifetime reasonable victuals, in food and drink, as befit such a woman, and moreover said Petronilla will have a room, with wardrobe, at the eastern end of said messuage, to dwell therein during said Petronilla's lifetime, and one cow, four sheep, and a pig, going and feeding on said half-yardland as well in winter as in summer during said Petronilla's lifetime for her clothing and footwear" (quoted by Homans 145).[36] Less than a hundred years separates the retirements of Anselm and Petronilla, yet the arrangements made by each seem to belong to different worlds.

Whether such maintenance contracts served to weaken the family ties between parents and children is finally an unanswerable question. One can point to the moral warnings against thankless children in writers such as Robert of Gloucester and Robert Mannyng of Brunne (cited by Homans 154–57); one can show that parents often went outside their own kin when contracting for support in their old age (and guess that such contracts might sometimes have led to land passing out of the family); one can find instances where these contracts became commodified (even on occasion being sold by one contractee to another) and led to parents and children falling out over them (Hanawalt 1986b, 233–34), but such facts are inconclusive. Even where there is statistical evidence, such as Elaine Clark's finding that before 1350 about half the East Anglian pensioners she studied negotiated contracts with their own children, whereas after that date less than a quarter did so (315), it can be interpreted in more than one way. Nonetheless, it is tempting to set these statistics alongside other demonstrable changes in village relationships (such as the decline of the system of personal pledging and the rise in trespass litigation) that occurred at the same period and read them as symptomatic of what Edwin Dewindt has called a "weakening village cohesiveness in the face of a growing spirit of particularism" (263): "Something was missing from the picture after the 1350's that had been very much in evidence before. It was a kind of commitment — almost a 'family' commitment — to the community as a whole, where the individual members of the society were bound together by several and far-reaching ties of responsibility which they strove to honour" (274–75). While the growing importance of literate technology in manorial life (see Beckerman 219–26) was clearly not the sole cause of this weakening, we should certainly be prepared to recognize that, as in the case of maintenance contracts, it can have done little to make traditional relationships either more flexible or more humane.

From the late thirteenth century onward, truth — a narrow and formalistic kind of truth — was ousting trouthe as surely in the law as it was in the language, and both the indenture of retinue and the maintenance contract help us to understand why legal contract is so useful "a paradigm of the uses of literacy in social and intellectual development" (Goody 146). Writing of the Ricardian social crisis in the "Lak of Stedfastnesse," Chaucer turns naturally to legal terminology: the written bonds (*obligacioun*), which have replaced "mannes word" (line 2), and the fraudulent agreements (*collusioun*), by which neighbor wrongs neighbor (10–12), are both seen as contributing to a world in which "trouthe is put down" (15). When he concludes by exhorting the king to "do law" and "love trouthe" (27), he may perhaps be forgiven for failing to see an inherent contradiction in such advice. If the king's law might one day learn to frame workable solutions, in Chaucer's day it was plainly making the situation progressively worse.

In this chapter I have concentrated on procedural developments in fourteenth-century common law in order to suggest the oddly displaced roles of evidence and proof, of truth and fiction, of law and fact, in the institution which determined the shape of people's agreements and disputes. In the following chapters I shall be looking at ways in which centralized law sought to redefine social loyalties by turning old, local folklaw virtues into new crimes against authority. Local solidarity, once encouraged by such institutions as the frankpledge, came to be looked on as dangerous conspiracy, and the communal protection afforded by earlier notions of warranty and good lordship (Hyams 1987) was redefined by such offenses as maintenance and champerty to appear like reprehensible partisanship. When those in power abused the law as openly as those they accused of abuse (Winfield 1921, 154–57), it is little wonder that they provoked fierce opposition. Perhaps the greatest irony of all lay in the eagerness with which the king's law embraced outlawry — one of the oldest of folklaw sanctions and "a weapon," as Maitland says, "as clumsy as it was terrible" (P&M 2:581)—to deal with such opposition.[37] In the next chapter I shall argue that the crisis of authority—reflected in Chaucer's nostalgia for the vanished stability of the old trouthe or Langland's mordant venality satire with its constant harping on legal abuse (see Yunck)—is most directly evoked in the gleeful brutality with which Robin Hood and Gamelyn treat the king's officers. I shall seek to show that the outlaw tradition can only be understood in the light of a genuine and documented late-medieval resistance to central authority which many historians would dismiss as mere endemic lawlessness, but which I prefer to characterize as a last-ditch appeal to older legal strategies. In our period the most extreme, though far from the only, example of such resistance is the Peasants' Revolt.

5

Folvilles' Law

It is not a basketful of law-papers, nor the hoofs and pistol-butts of a regiment of horse, that can change one tittle of a ploughman's thoughts.

— R. L. Stevenson, *Travels with a Donkey*

LATE IN THE AFTERNOON OF JUNE 24, 1336, Peter, sixth abbot of the Cistercian house of Vale Royal in Cheshire, was riding through a place called Green Delves on the outskirts of the village of Exton in the county of Rutland. He was on his way home from visiting Edward III at the royal hunting lodge in King's Cliffe where he had been seeking the king's support in a troublesome legal dispute he was having with some of the villeins on his abbey's manors of Over and Darnhall. These villeins had denied their servile status and defaulted on their customary duties, and, though Abbot Peter had established his rights more than once in the county court, they had refused to accept its decision and even managed to get the queen on their side. Moreover, when he had attempted to enforce the court's decision, the village ringleaders had simply taken what they could of their movables and decamped. It must, then, have been a rather nervous abbot who saw approaching him along the high road "a great crowd of the country people" of Darnhall, particularly since some of his own men had fallen a little way behind the main party. The details of the fight that followed are confused: the abbey's own account suggests that, despite the loss of one of their servants, the monks at first got rather the better of it (particularly after their cellarer, "like a champion sent from God to protect his house and father," came galloping up from the rear to join the fray), but that the intervention of a crowd of locals ("those bestial men of Rutland") led to the abbot's being "ignominiously taken" (*Ledger-Book* 40–41). Abbot Peter was, however, freed by the king the next day and rode home leaving his attackers in chains, "and in the greatest misery," in the nearby city of Stamford.

As I have presented it here this incident is typical of what many historians would regard as the endemic lawlessness of the later Middle Ages: unruly subjects ignoring established legal channels and resorting to violence to settle their differences. But even the abbey's own version (the villagers of Darnhall have not left us their side of the story) leaves us with a number of unanswered questions. How did the fight start? Why should "a great crowd" of armed countryfolk have had such difficulty overcoming a party of unarmed monks? What made the local people intervene on the side of the villagers? Why, having captured the abbot, should they have carried him off to the king? And why, despite the killing of an abbey servant, should the king's court have subsequently released the villagers, even sending an order (which Peter felt quite justified in ignoring) that the abbot should return any of their property he might have seized as compensation for the death? The answer to some of these questions is suggested by looking at the Exton brawl in its larger context; once we try to piece together the case against Vale Royal we begin to see that its monks may not have been quite the innocent victims nor the men of Darnhall quite the lawless aggressors that the abbot's account would have us believe. I shall argue, finally, that their fracas is symptomatic of a wider conflict between two legal orders (what I have called the folklaw and the king's law) which raged throughout the fourteenth century and which was to come to a head in the Peasants' Revolt.

The origins of the dispute over the status of the villagers of Darnhall and Over does not (or at least not as far as it concerns Vale Royal) reach back to the time when Baldonet carried his bell ropes into the abbey of Marmoutiers. Vale Royal was a recent foundation (sixty-five years old at the time of the Exton brawl), which, despite its royal endowment, had been chronically short of money throughout its brief history; perhaps their penury made the monks particularly oppressive landlords, but there is evidence that relations between the villagers and the abbey were strained from the very start (*VHCE Cheshire* 3:156). The villagers of Darnhall resented being treated as villeins and soon went to complain to the king [Edward I], "carrying with them their iron ploughshares" (*Ledger-Book* 121). We should have no difficulty recognizing these plowshares; they are folklaw tokens—in the minds of their owners at least, legal evidence of free status. It would not have been surprising had the king, who must have felt some proprietary interest in an abbey he himself had founded, been unimpressed by such tokens, but, though he is alleged to have rejected their appeal with the memorable words, "as villeins you have come, and as villeins you shall return,"[1] other evidence suggests that he may actually have behaved rather more circumspectly.[2] Nevertheless, it was the memory of this dramatic judgment (and the record of its confirmation by a justiciar of Chester thirty years later) that seems to have been the abbey's main proof against the claims of its disgruntled tenants. It had, however, a far more potent weapon up its sleeve—the ability to manipulate legal process right up to the very highest courts in the land.

It will be worthwhile at this point to give a synopsis of the events leading up to the Exton brawl, for, as even the abbey's own record shows (*Ledger-Book* 37–42), the villagers of Darnhall and Over had turned to violence only as a very last resort. They begin proceedings by complaining to the justiciar of Chester that though free "from aforetime by charter of the lord the king," they are now being treated as villeins by the abbot (37–38). We do not learn what kind of reception they receive from the justiciar, but on their return home they are thrown into prison until they acknowledge their servile status and swear not to complain again. Despite this oath (exacted presumably under duress), they now send a deputation to see the king (then "in the Northern parts") in person, but this party ends up in Nottingham jail and escapes hanging for theft only at some financial cost to the village (38). They then present a petition in Parliament at Westminster, which leads to the king's sending a new justiciar to look into their case; by the time the villagers present this justiciar with a second petition, he has been sufficiently impressed by "the charters of the lord the king which the Abbot publicly produced" to send them back to the abbey for punishment (39). Undeterred, the villagers complain to the king at Windsor against both abbot and justiciar, and the king deputes the earl of Chester (the six-year-old Black Prince) to do them justice. "Encouraged and comforted by this" (did they hope this earl might prove a second Randolf?),[3] they once more take their case to the Cheshire county court "with the aid of some persons skilled in the law" (39). Again they lose. It is at this point they flee with "such of their goods as they could carry" to complain to Queen Philippa (39–40). And it is her intervention on their behalf which forces the abbot to visit the king and queen in person, with the results we have already seen.

What strikes one at once about this account is not the lawlessness of the abbey's tenants but their touching faith in legal process.[4] Three times they seek justice at a county level and three times in the royal court. Moreover, after the Exton brawl it is they, rather than the abbot, who seem the more eager to accompany the local Rutland men to see the king; later, when all but three ringleaders have been starved into submission, these last resisters are finally arrested trying yet again to bring bills against the abbot in the county court (*Ledger-Book* 41–42). Even then the villagers' faith in royal justice remains strong enough for one stubborn tenant to sue the abbot and the cellarer "because they had violently despoiled him of his goods at Exton"; predictably, he too later "submits" to the abbot. This represents nine separate attempts to get justice from the king or his officers, yet this from those whom we would normally be asked to regard as lawless: people who spend money on lawyers; who try to gather their own written evidence; who travel to Nottingham, to Westminster, to Windsor, and to Stamford in search of a hearing. They gain the king's ear; they even seem to gain his sympathy. Yet none of it does them any good. If the villagers turn finally to violence it is only in desperation. Their first impulse when legal means fail is flight: "when the bondmen were informed of this, they all fled, taking with them such of their goods as they could carry, and secretly withdrew themselves by night" (39). Even their part in the Exton brawl is far from clear. Who really started the fight? Was the abbot's servant really acting in self defense? Did "those bestial men of Rutland" really come to the aid of the aggressors?

Questions like these, however unanswerable, are raised by the glaring inconsistencies of the surviving account, yet such questions have too often in the past been silenced by our easy assumption that men like the abbot of Vale Royal "doubtless stood on sound law" (Coulton 136). I have no doubt that for their part the villagers too believed their law to be sound. In an earlier dispute (1329) they had claimed that "it was not lawful for the abbot to punish them for any offence, except by the assessment of their neighbours" (*Ledger-Book* 31), and some idea of the kind of legal order they stood for is suggested by the charter of the borough of Over with its mention of "a cuckstool and pillory and such other kind of judicial instruments the which belong unto a free borough" (188).

At its heart the struggle between abbey and village was a struggle between rival jurisdictions, and the villagers' appeal to the common law, naive as it may appear to us, was simply a recourse to what they must have seen as disinterested arbitration. In a similar dispute between the abbot of Leicester and the villagers of Stoughton in the 1270s (memorialized in verse, presumably by a member of the monastic community), the tenants are represented as saying, "Nulli servire volumus: dum possumus ire, / Ibimus ad regem qui nobis vult dare legem" [none of us wants servitude; whilst we still can, we shall go the king who is happy to grant us our law] (Hilton 1941, 95). Such touching faith in ultimate royal justice was still alive a hundred years later when it betrayed Wat Tyler's followers to Richard's empty promises at Smithfield. So, too, when the representative of the Leicestershire villagers arrives at the king's court, he learns the harsh reality from a professional pleader:

> Tu male discernis, reus es quia dominum spernis.
> Cum domino certare tuo non consilium do,
> Rustice: victus eris dominum qui vincere queris.
> (Hilton 1941, 95)

> [You are sadly mistaken; you are to blame for rejecting your lord. I don't advise you to contend with your lord, peasant! It is you who seek to defeat your lord, who will be defeated.]

Not without irony the poem concludes its gloating description of the abbot's inevitable victory with the tag "Uncore a la curt le rey, usum menie la ley" [In the king's court custom still rules the law].

We may see a structural inevitability in the common law's alignment with the forces of literate authority against those of oral custom, but the naive villagers of Darnhall and Over can only account for their failure in terms of local corruption: "The abbot had spoiled them of their goods, exceeding £100 in value, with which he had so corrupted both the justiciar and all the chief people in Chester that the justice-place was not open to them" (*Ledger-Book* 39). More fundamental than any such corruption, however, was the inability of literate legal process to deal adequately with customary rights, with the kinds of question which only the folklaw could properly address. Not for nothing did the victorious abbot reinforce his final victory with those old folklaw devices, the oath and the token: "And so it came to pass that, touching the holy gospels, they all swore they were truly the bondmen of the abbot and convent, and that they would never claim their freedom against them and their successors. And for many Sundays they stood in the choir, in the face of the convent, with bare heads and feet, and they offered wax candles in token of subjection" (41). At the other end of the kingdom these same patterns were being repeated at a far grander house, St. Albans Abbey, and we shall see later how the resentment they generated was to simmer on until Wat Tyler and John Ball provided it with a temporary release in the early summer of 1381.[5] For the time being, however, I wish to stress that resentment of the king's law was far from restricted to the lowest levels of society.

There is an interesting footnote to the story of the Exton brawl: one of the abbot's assailants on that day was William de Venables, a man who was at the time involved, along with his brother Thomas, in an unsuccessful lawsuit with the abbey over fishing rights; some idea of the brothers' status is given by the fact that one of those who later stood surety for Thomas was a Monsieur Hugh de Venables (*Ledger-Book* 125). Abbot Peter's triumph over the Venables brothers, however, was to be short-lived. Four years later he seems to have met his end, alongside his redoubtable cellarer, in a violent attack on his abbey, and one of those required to make satisfaction to his successor for his death "and for other trespasses and injuries inflicted upon the said abbot and convent and their monastery" was Thomas de Venables (164). In this phase of the struggle between the king's law and the folklaw, we should not be too quick to assume that the gentry and peasantry would automatically have found themselves on opposite sides of the fence.[6]

Rival Modes of Dispute Settlement

A mere five miles from Exton at the time of the brawl lived two men who may well have enjoyed hearing of the attempt to rattle some of Abbot Peter's teeth:

Richard, parson of the village of Teigh, and his brother Eustace. Indeed it is tempting to imagine that they or some of their friends were among the "bestial men of Rutland" who intervened on the Cheshire villagers' behalf; they seem to have relished a good fight, and certainly they had no great love for upholders of the king's law. In January 1326 Eustace had ambushed and killed a local parvenu, Roger Bellers, a baron of the exchequer (Stones 1957, 119), traveling at the time with a retinue more than fifty strong (Knighton, *Chronicon* 1:433), and in 1332 Richard, according to Henry Knighton (1:460–61) had organized the kidnapping and ransom of an even more senior judge, Sir Richard Willoughby, a future chief justice of King's Bench (Stones 1957, 122). These were the high points in the career of the two most prominent of the celebrated Folvilles—leaders of a band whose exploits were to become proverbial in the fourteenth century. Generally deplored by modern historians, the "crimes" of Eustace and Richard seem to have struck contemporaries in rather a different light, for when William Langland alludes to them (R. Bowers), he recalls them as blows struck in defense of the right. Describing the weapons given by Grace to aid men in their battle with Antichrist, he writes:

> And some to ryde and to recouere þat [vnriȝt]fully was wonne:
> He wissed hem wynne it ayein þoruȝ wightnesse of handes
> And fecchen it fro false men wiþ Foluyles lawes.
>
> (*PPl* B.19:245–47)

In view of these lines, we may wonder whether E. L. G. Stones does not understate his case when he asks, "is it not possible that many people took a fairly light-hearted view of the Folvilles' crimes and were far from friendly to the powers who sought to arrest them?" (1957, 133).

The world of the Folvilles is slightly easier to penetrate than that of the villagers of Darnall. They were after all members of the gentry, a class far more likely than the villein's to employ writing and attract written notice: John, the eldest of the Folvilles, appears in fact to have been a conventional enough country gentleman—though his appointment as keeper of the peace (Stones 1957, 118) should not be read as a sign of exemplary, or even consistently law-abiding, behavior. We might suppose that their two most famous targets were chosen because they were conspicuously corrupt members of the judicial profession (Willoughby, for instance, was later arraigned "by clamour of the people" for having "perverted and sold the laws as if they had been oxen or cows" [*YB 14/15 Edw. 3*, 258–59]), but there is also a strong local factor in the Folvilles' choice of victim. Both Bellers and Willoughby were neighbors, the first had estates in Leicestershire, and the second, a manor just across the border in Nottinghamshire. In both cases it seems likely that animus engendered by local feuding had been heightened by what was seen as their unfair recourse to the king's law. Bellers had earlier "threatened and wronged" the Folville brothers, says Knighton (himself a Leicestershire man and probably working from local tradition). The chronicler evidently felt little regret at the judge's murder; in fact, he calls Bellers "an oppressor of the priesthood and his other neighbors" (ed. Lumby, 1:433). The chance survival of a contemporary lampoon in macaronic verse makes clearer the grounds of Bellers's unpopularity: it accuses him, not only of being "neuer weri" of "falsnes" ("Versus" line 4), but (insult to injury) of acting "with the king's power and under cover of the law" [tum cum vi regis tum cum velamine legis] (line 9).

When the brothers' second judicial victim, Sir Richard Willoughby, had the temerity to ride into Folville territory, it was with the ostentatious backing of the king, for he was serving on a commission of oyer and terminer—ironically enough an institution intended to dispatch royal authority to the lawless provinces. As Knighton sees it, this was merely a red rag to a bull: "In the year 1331, judges sat on trailbaston commissions throughout the whole of England [trailbastons were a particularly hated form of oyer and terminer] and outlawed many everywhere in the kingdom. For which reason, a royal judge, Richard Willoughby, was after Christmas captured on the road to Grantham by Richard Folville, rector of Teigh, who was fierce, bold, and given to violence. And he was led to a certain band of confederates [socialem comitivam] in a nearby wood and there compelled to pay ninety marks [Willoughby claimed it was 1,300] to save his life, having sworn an oath to keep their counsel ever after" (*Chronicon* 1:460–61). We may never be able to establish Richard Folville's motives precisely—was he paying off an old debt with a local rival, expressing his contempt for royal justice, or merely indulging in a spot of profitable brigandage (or perhaps a mixture of all three)?—but there does survive a remarkable poem in MS Harley 2253 which suggests that the factor stressed by Knighton may not have been insignificant.

Had "The Outlaw's Song of Trailbaston" been written in English rather than Anglo-Norman it might now be better known, but this attack on the operation of the king's law—"trop est doteuse la commune loy" (line 56)—gives us an invaluable insight into the world of one of its victims. It was clearly written very shortly after the establishment of trailbaston commissions by Parliament in 1305. The author, who, since he writes in French, must have been a man of some social standing, represents himself as an old soldier who has been ruined by the legal chicanery of his enemies—men, he says, who would never have dared attack him in person (line 78). Even his own servants use the law against him:

Sire, si je voderoi mon garsoun chastier
De une buffe ou de deus, pur ly amender,
Sur moi betera bille, e me frad atachier,
E avant qe isse de prisone raunsoun grant doner.
(9–12)

[Sir, if I choose to correct my lad with a blow or two for his own good, he'll slap a summons on me and have me arrested, and before I can get out of prison there'll be a large sum to pay.]

Since he has no money left for legal costs, his very life is now at stake (lines 75–76), yet, he protests, he is neither murderer nor thief (95–96) — even though the law has certainly driven others to a life of crime (44–48). He proclaims his innocence (82) and complains of the unjust outlawry that keeps him (just like William of Cloudesly in the later ballad) from his home and family (lines 30, 71, 94), but he has no doubt that the real villains are the royal judges and the justice they dispense:

Spigurnel e Belflour sunt gent de cruelté;
Si(l) il fuissent en ma baylie ne serreynt retornee.
Je lur apre[n]droy le giw de Traylebastoun,
E lur bruseroy l'eschyne et cropoun,
Les bras et les jaunbes, ce serreit resoun;
La lange lur toudroy e la bouche ensoun.
(35–40)

[Spigurnel and Belflour are cruel men; if they were under my jurisdiction they'd not escape. I'd teach them to play at Trailbaston: I'd tan their backs and their backsides, their arms and their legs, as would only be just. I'd cut out their tongues, and their testimony to boot.]

Both Henry Spigurnel and Roger Belflour were actual judges (see Aspin 77 n. 35), the former a man of some prominence (Holdsworth 2:557), and it is particularly interesting that the outlaw would like to inflict on them the old folklaw punishment for false accusation (P&M 2:453). He concludes the poem by saying that it has been written on parchment the better to preserve its memory ("pur mout remenbrer" — an echo of the old cartulary formula), and that he intends to drop it on the high road for people to find (lines 99–100), presumably because this is a plaint that will fare better in the court of common opinion than under the common law. The gesture of seeking to turn back the course of literate authoritarianism with this scrap of parchment is not without its irony.

We shall be returning to this interesting poem later, but for the moment I want to look at the trailbaston commission from the other side: from the point of view of the commissioners. The records of the Lincolnshire trailbaston of 1305 contain little reassurance for those who might assume that the charges of "The Outlaw's Song of Trailbaston" are merely rhetorical exaggeration. Let us take, for instance, the case of Sir Ralph Friskney who is hauled up before the commission on four separate charges. Like the speaker in the "Trailbaston" poem (and, incidentally, Eustace Folville), Sir Ralph was an old soldier; he was also evidently a local rival of one of the commissioners, Sir Edmund Deincourt.

Two of the charges concern contempt for the king's law and its officers: one is a general complaint that he has been intimidating jurors ("Early Trailbaston" 164.44) and that when indicted before Sir Edmund, he had threatened them in life and limb by calling them villeins and false men ("ipsos rusticos et falsos vocando"); the second is more elaborate (163.42). He is accused by a royal purveyor, William de Wormelay, of having attacked him out of long-standing enmity ("odio antiquo"),[7] but the details of the case, as a local inquest reports them, are not quite so simple. On December 21, 1300, Wormelay had come to Boston in Lincolnshire to buy grain for the king and found a suitable purchase at the house of a John de Thumby. John, however, no doubt for sound commercial reasons, was unwilling to sell, and put his grain under lock and key, whereupon Wormelay on his own authority commandeered it by setting his seal over John's door ("ostium domus sigillo suo signavit"). John now goes for help to Sir Ralph, presumably because he is a man with a reputation for defending local interests against officious bureaucrats, and things rapidly get out of hand: after remonstrating with Wormelay, Sir Ralph knocks him to the ground, and his servants then pull his hood over his head, throw him into a nearby pond, and trample on his warrant. Finally, Sir Ralph goes back to John's house where he destroys Wormelay's seal "in contempt of the king" [in contemptum domini regis]. So flagrant an act of defiance is not, however, unique even among the fifty or so cases printed from this particular commission: in one, for instance, a man is outlawed (in absentia) for having refused to pay a royal bailiff what he owed (160.29), and in another two men and a woman are convicted of beating a royal justice in Stamford market place (161.32) — the man was apparently investigating poaching on the king's estates at the time ("ad inquirendum de malefactoribus venationis domini regis"). Similar cases are to be found in other trailbaston rolls.[8]

As Richard Kaeuper observes, "vigorous though a defendant might be, the odds remained clearly in favor of any plaintiff who had gotten a commission" (1979, 773), and on both charges Deincourt and his fellow commissioners find Sir Ralph guilty and commit him to prison. For beating William de Wormelay he has to pay forty shillings to regain his freedom—the exact sum complained of in "The Outlaw's Song of Trailbaston":

> Quaraunte souz pernent pur ma raunsoun,
> E le viscounte vint a son guerdoun,
> Qu'il ne me mette en parfounde prisoun.
> Ore agardez seigneurs, est ce resoun?
> (13–16)

> [They take forty shillings for my ransom, and the sheriff comes for his reward for not putting me in a deep dungeon. Now think about it, sirs: is this just?]

To set this complaint alongside the terse note at the bottom of the account of Sir Ralph's trial is instructive: "Et predictus Ranulphus committatur gaole. Dampna xl s. unde clericis j marca et marescallo dimidia marca" [and the aforesaid Ralph is committed to prison. Fined forty shillings—including a mark for the clerks and half a mark for the marshal] ("Early Trailbaston" 163.42). One might note that half of Sir Ralph's forty shillings went to paying court officials. But at least he was luckier than Henry le Bercher, accused of refusing to pay a royal bailiff (160.29): Henry failed to appear in court, perhaps because of the expense, and the note in his case reads simply "exigatur et utlagetur" [called for, then outlawed]. Read in this context the criticisms of the "Trailbaston" poem do not seem farfetched.

The remaining two charges against Sir Ralph Friskney concern the behavior of his men and in some ways bring us even closer to the world of Eustace Folville and his band. The more general (164.45) concerns his having maintained as members of his household ("ad robas suas tamquam familiares") two notorious criminals ("communes malefactores in feriis et mercatis")—apparently the kind of men Chaucer would later describe as market-beaters ("Reeve's Tale" 3936); what was worse, these were men who had previously been indicted before Sir Ralph when he had acted as keeper of the peace for the king. Again, the more specific charge (163–164.43) might lead us to qualify this impression of organized crime. John de le Fendik accuses Sir Ralph of sending his servants (one of whom is one of the *communes malefactores* of the previous case) to break into his house, threaten him, beat his wife, and intimidate him into paying fifteen shillings to settle his differences with their master, but the inquest finding suggests that this violence was not entirely unprovoked. The fight had started when some flax that John and his wife had left to dry on the king's highway had been run over by Sir Ralph's men with a cartload of timber, an event which seems to imply not only that extortion had not been their first business of the day, but also that they may even have felt a certain provocation in acting the way they did. Moreover, the payment of fifteen shillings had been arranged by an intermediary ("per quemdam Radulfum Cokewald intereuntem et exorantem") who looks to have been trying to bring about a peaceful settlement between neighbors rather than acting as local agent for a protection racket. Again, this trailbaston roll contains several complaints of similar unwilling settlements (148 n. 36), which force us to consider whether what is there made to look like violent extortion may not in reality represent the folklaw's failure to impress its preference for peaceful resolution on the contumacious and intransigent.

The offenses Sir Ralph Friskney is accused of here bear a marked resemblance to those contained in Peace's petition against Wrong in the Meed episode of *Piers Plowman*:

> He mayntenep hise men to murþere myne hewen,
> Forstalleþ my feires, fiȝteþ in my Chepyng,
> Brekeþ vp my bern[e] dore[s], bereþ awey my whete,
> And takeþ me but a taille for ten quarters Otes;
> And yet he beteþ me þerto and lyþ by my mayde.
>
> (B.4:55–59)

Moreover, just like a number of the cases in the 1305 Lincolnshire trailbaston report, the progress of Peace's lawsuit displays a marked tension between judicial and extracurial modes of dispute settlement (the role played by Ralph Cokewald as mediator between Sir Ralph and John de le Fendik is approximated by the character of Wisdom in Langland's poem), and illustrates the kind of social disruption that such tension might breed. Despite his name, Wisdom's activities are represented as thoroughly disreputable:

> [Th]anne gan Mede to me[k]en her, and mercy bisouȝte,
> And profrede Pees a present al of pure[d] golde.
> "Haue þis [of me, man]," quod she, "to amenden þi scaþe,
> For I wol wage for Wrong, he wol do so na moore."
> [Pees þanne pitously] preyed to þe kynge
> To haue mercy on þat man þat mysdide hym ofte;
> "For he haþ waged me wel as Wisdom hym tauȝte,
> I forgyue hym þat gilt wiþ a good wille."
>
> (B.4:94–101)

Such out-of-court settlements, Langland implies, make a mockery of justice—less a valuable alternative method of resolving disputes than an invitation to shameless venality. In this particular case only an uncharacteristically principled judiciary (for the time being, at least, the king is ruled by Reason and Conscience) prevents the rule of law from becoming hopelessly compromised:

> "Nay," quod þe kyng, "so me crist helpe,
> Wrong wendeþ not so awey [er] I wite moore.
> Lope he so liȝtly [awey] lauȝen he wolde,
> And [ofte] þe boldere be to bete myne hewen."
> (B.4:104–07)

A similar point is made in a Lollard depiction of a lord who maintains "his men to bete pore men & do wrongis by loue daies holdynge, & meyntenynge of causes þat riȝt and lawe may not haue his cours" (Wyclif, *English Works* 243).

Though Langland is hardly any more consistent on this topic than on most others—elsewhere he observes that the king's law is ruthless in demanding its pound of flesh even where one of the parties is willing to make concessions (B.17:305–9)—much of the time he is strongly opposed both to the operation of less formal modes of dispute settlement in general, and to the lovedays that "doþ men lese þoruȝ hire loue þat lawe myȝte wynne" (B.3.159) in particular. Given his unwavering hostility to professional lawyers and his apparent support for men like the Folvilles, this suspicion of the traditional loveday (cf. B.5:420–21; 10:19–22, 311–12) appears on the face of it somewhat surprising. Langland's is far from being a solitary voice, however, and a similar distrust of lovedays is expressed by a number of his contemporaries, including Chaucer.[9] If anything, the genial Chaucer's distrust of lovedays (see "General Prologue" 258–61) seems even more curious than that of the mordant Langland.

Typically, Chaucer and his fellow Ricardian poets display a profound respect for just that spirit of generosity, toleration, and forbearance that the loveday was supposed to embody. Indeed, John Burrow regards the "sober acceptance of things as they are" as an essential attribute of the ideal of 'high eld' that he would place at the very heart of Ricardian poetry (1971, 129):

> For in this world, certein, ther no wight is
> That he ne dooth or seith somtyme amys.
> Ire, siknesse, or constellacioun,
> Wyn, wo, or chaungynge of complexioun

Causeth ful ofte to doon amys or speken.
On every wrong a man may nat be wreken.
("Franklin's Tale" 779–84)

When due allowance has been made for differences in individual temperament (cf. Yeager), this Ricardian ideal might be argued to perpetuate an ancient faith in the superiòrity of love over law (see Alford 1988a, 91) that, as we saw in Chapter 2, had once been exemplified by the traditional maxim *pactum legem vincit*.

In the fourteenth century, writers of popular romances and lyrics were still expressing admiration for the kind of mediated settlement (the old term was *saughtelinge*) that *The Peterborough Chronicle* had described in its entry for 1140 (recte 1141): "Þa feorden þe wise men betwyx þe kinges [Stephen's] freond ⁊ te eorles [Ranulf of Chester's] freond, ⁊ sahtlede sua ðat me sculde leten ut þe king of prisun for þe eorl ⁊ te eorl for þe king: ⁊ sua diden. Sithen þerefter sa[ht]leden þe king ⁊ Randolf eorl at Stanford, ⁊ athes suoren ⁊ treuthes fæston ðat her nouþer sculde besuyken other" (58). When Gwynevere appeals to Arthur to step in and end the judicial duel between Gawain and Galeron at the end of *The Awntyrs off Arthure*, for instance, she alludes to the popular acclaim that arranging "here saȝtlynge" (line 661) would win him:

Woldest þou, leve lorde,
Make þes knightes accorde
Hit were a grete conforde
For alle þat [here] ware.
(634–37)

It is clear that such *saughtelinge* typically involved the use of a mediator or go-between, for when Arthur learns that Ywain and his cousin have called off their judicial battle in *Ywain and Gawain*, he asks "Wha had so sone made saghteling / Bitwix þam þat had bene so wrath?" (3682–83). *Ywain and Gawain*, in fact, ends with a particularly elaborate *saughtelinge* in which the maid Lunete brings about a reconciliation between hero and heroine, by tricking her mistress Alundyne (unaware at this point that the knight with the lion is the husband she has renounced) into swearing "to saghtel þe knyght with þe liown / And his lady of grete renowne" (3917–18). It is worth noting that such settlements invariably end in a trothplight. Clearly it was regarded as a laudable act to bring about such a *saughtelinge* between enemies, and one of the Vernon lyrics also makes of it a Christian duty (cf. Matt. 5:9): "And men vnsauȝte loke þou assay / To sauȝten hem þenne at on assent" (*RL14C* 149).

By the late fourteenth century, as these quotations imply, the use of the term *saughtelinge* seems to have been mainly provincial and noncourtly (it appears in Langland and the Cotton-Nero poet, for instance, but not in Chaucer or Gower), but the traditional ideal of amicable settlement it represents appears to have been universally understood nonetheless; Gower, for instance, concludes the prologue to his *Confessio Amantis* by lamenting his country's want of a second Arion:

> And every man upon this ground
> Which Arion that time herde,
> Als wel the lord as the schepherde,
> He broghte hem alle in good acord;
> So that the comun with the lord,
> And the lord with the comun also,
> He sette in love bothe tuo
> And putte awey malencolie.
> (1062–69)

Why was it, then, that an institution that Gower here turns to as the solution to his country's ills might be seen, in its formal guise at least, by Langland and others as a vehicle for bribery and intimidation?

There has recently been a great deal of useful historical research into informal methods of dispute resolution in the late Middle Ages, but few historians have been prepared to endorse Thomas Heffernan's conclusion (based primarily on literary rather than documentary evidence) that "by the late fourteenth century in England, the practice of holding lovedays, while in principle an efficient extra-legal custom, had long lost its efficaciousness and had become a burlesque" ("Lovedays" 175). By contrast, the chorus of approval, particularly from those who work on the records of local gentry, is almost unanimous: Ian Rowney, for example, writes of arbitration as "offering an honourable and cheap compromise, substituting satisfaction for victory and bypassing the rancour and humiliation of legal defeat" (376); Edward Powell calls it "an antidote to the elaborate formalism of the common law," and "a well designed, adaptable procedure notable for its flexibility, simplicity and speed" (1983, 55); Simon Payling's work on the Nottinghamshire gentry leads him to conclude that arbitration, at its most effective, could "quickly and cheaply provide compromise solutions acceptable to both disputing parties" (147); and David Tilsley infers that the Cheshire gentry saw "the intervention of a mediating influence as consistently holding the best chance of a lasting settlement" (70). While there is some recognition that arbitration had its limits—even Powell concedes that it was "not always effective in resolving violent conflict" (1984, 28)—few English historians seem ready to give much credit the skeptical view of lovedays to be found in contemporary literary accounts. One notable exception is Michael Clanchy, who speculates that "in the later Middle Ages procedure by love seems to have become as embroiled in faction as the ordinary processes of law" (1983b, 61).

How are we to account for this discrepancy? One explanation is certainly to be sought in the obvious fact that not all social groups were equally well served by the loveday; as Ian Rowney notes, it never "greatly assisted the poor and needy, remaining essentially intra- rather than inter-class based" (368). Arbitration, in other words, whether among the gentry or at a manorial level (see Clanchy 1983b, 59–60; Bonfield 530–34; Williamson), worked best in a communal situation where both parties were of roughly equivalent social status and equally susceptible to pressure from shared neighbors. Even here, the intervention of an outsider or superior in the mediation process could easily lead to suspicions of partiality and undue pressure: William Paston, for instance, having already reached what he regarded as a satisfactory resolution of his dispute with Walter Aslak (1427), claimed that he was forced to resubmit it to arbitration because, "þe seyd Walter by hese sotill and vngoodly enformacion caused þe seyd Duke [of Norfolk] to be hevy lord to þe seyd William" (*Paston Letters* 1:10). Where there was any significant difference in power or status between the parties the pressure to conciliate could very quickly become one-sided and oppressive. A dispute between Lord Roos and Robert Tirwhytt, a justice of King's Bench, in 1411 offers an interesting example. Evidently anticipating that an impending arbitration would go against him, Tirwhytt had tried to ambush Roos on his way to the loveday, only to call down the wrath of the king and the lords spiritual and temporal on his head; Parliament awarded that Roos should choose his own arbitrators, and these predictably set about arranging a public humiliation for the upstart judge. Tirwhytt was required to provide two barrels of claret, two fat oxen and a dozen fat sheep for a feast at Melton Roos where he was to make the following declaration: "My Lord the Roos, I knowe wele, that ye been of such birth, estate, and myghte, that if yow had lyked ye myght have comyn to the forsaid Loveday in such array, that I schoold have been of no myght to have mad no party; . . . 3et, for as myche I am a Justice, that more than an other comun man scholde have had me more discrely and peesfully, I knowe wele that I have failled and offende yow, My Lorde the Roos, wherof I beseke yow of grace and mercy, and offre yow v c. mark to ben paied at youre will" (*RP* 3:650). The same kind of pressure might also be exerted lower down the social ladder: in a case from 1388 concerning disputed servile status, the putative serf claimed that arbitrators forced him to agree to pay his former lord a thousand pounds for his manumission ("and there by duress of imprisonment you forced him to submit himself to the arbitrament of the same persons . . ." (*YB 11 Rich. 2*, 169).

Secondly, it is clear that by the late fourteenth century the ancient equilibrium between law and love had shifted decisively in favor of law (cf. Carpenter 1992, 637), and that traditional constraints on social disorder were being removed from the communal to the judicial arena. No doubt the turning point, as Clanchy suggests, had been the legal reforms of Henry II's reign, which had "had the long-term effect of weakening and straining the bonds of affection existing in feudal lordship and kindred loyalties and putting nothing as adequate in their place" (1983b, 62). The common law may in fact have shown itself suspicious of amicable settlement earlier than other medieval legal systems; we have already noticed that Glanvill added the significant qualification *generaliter enim verum est* to the old maxim *pactum legem vincit*, and in Bracton we find only one passing allusion to the loveday—and that, significantly enough, advice that participants make sure that they keep open the possibility of subsequent litigation should attempts at arbitration fail (cited by Clanchy 1983b, 59). By contrast, the *Regiam Majestatem*, "the Scottish Bracton," has a lengthy discussion of arbitrators and arbitration procedure (105–11), drawn in part from Azo, a civilian well known to Bracton himself. Whatever the reason, it is clear that in the late Middle Ages few of those who feared for their chances in an amicable settlement had much compunction about going to law to try and circumvent it.

Moreover, the king's justices were often only too happy to accommodate them. In 1312, for instance, John of Hardwick complained that in the course of his lawsuit with William of Flent, they had agreed, "by an indenture made between them, on a certain loveday when they would submit themselves to the arbitration of arbitrators. Yet while that loveday was pending, this same William came to Westminster, in our absence, and recovered against us . . . contrary to our agreement and contrary to his own deed"; accordingly, John brought a writ of conspiracy against William only to have his case thrown out of court on the grounds that "no deed made in the country can extinguish in such case the jurisdiction of the King's Court" (*YB 5 Edw. 2 (1312)*, 215). Despite the fact that courts paid lip service to the notion that arbitrated settlements were binding on both parties, fourteenth- and fifteenth-century yearbooks abound in cases where such settlements are challenged, sometimes with the most blatant legal quibbles. The year 1388/89, for instance, supplies two cases in which litigants refuse to admit that an arbitration has occurred (*YB 12 Rich. 2*, 159–61, 164–66), a case in which it is argued that a writ brought in London may not be compromised by arbitration in Cornwall (*YB 12 Rich. 2*,

37–38), and another in which the absence of one of the arbitrators is given as a reason for not being bound to observe their award (*YB 12 Rich. 2*, 70–71). In light of such potential challenges it is hardly surprising that, as Edward Powell points out, "arbitration procedures in late medieval England" came to "bear the unmistakable imprint of legal thought and practice" (1984, 34), nor that in some cases "arbitrators were men of law who followed legal timetables and adopted legal thinking to determine legal issues" (38)—rather *lex pactum vincit*, it seems, than the other way about.

The notion that after 1350 prosecution and arbitration were mutually exclusive strategies has been challenged by Powell in two important articles (1983; 1984), but his own evidence only serves to show how thoroughly the traditional preference for conciliation over litigation had been undermined. By his account disputants were merely offered complementary means to the same end, making their choice as the advantages of cost, speed, or conclusiveness recommended one course or the other. Evidently, the notion that *pactum*, trothplight, offered a different order of conflict resolution no longer entered the picture. One particular reason for this is worth dwelling on here, for it offers a neat illustration of the central thesis of this book as a whole. The final concord arrived at in the medieval loveday was a trothplight between the parties, and hence fell into the same vexed legal category as all other compacts and agreements. Like any other covenant in late medieval England, it came to be accepted, that the terms of an arbitration could not be defended or challenged in court unless they had been set down in writing: the test case here seems to have been De Wetenhale v. Arden (1346) in which a ruling that it was not the local custom for a man to have to produce written proof of an arbitrated settlement, was overturned on a writ of error (*Source Book* 181–82); this was evidently standard doctrine by 1383 (*YB 7 Rich. 2*, 2–4), though it was still being argued early in the fifteenth century (Simpson 1987, 27). Such a rule helps to explain not only "the enormous growth of documentary evidence for the practice [of arbitration] which takes place after 1350" (Powell 1983, 62), but also the widespread standardization of arbitration procedure in the late Middle Ages (1984, 33). Thus, the documents regularly associated with arbitration soon came to follow a well-defined pattern: mutual bonds or recognizances binding the parties to respect the arbitrators' decision, formal statements of claim by the parties themselves, and finally a detailed record of the actual award.[10] Traces of the old folklaw flexibility do certainly survive—as where arbitrators faced with the fair apportioning of a disputed estate between two sisters wrote down the details of each portion on separate slips of parchment, enclosed each in a ball of wax, and then offered them to one of the sisters to choose (cited by Payling 157)—but by and large amicable settlement was in danger of becoming almost as institutionalized and formalistic as legal process itself. The breakdown of traditional mechanisms for resolving disputes (or rather their co-option by the machinery of the king's law) provides yet one more instance of the deadening effect of the combination of vernacular literacy and centralized authority on the dynamics of folklaw trothplight.

The Lincolnshire trailbaston cases, of course, predate the full impact of this breakdown, but nonetheless clear signs of future trouble are already present. No longer are the king's courts a last resort for those who cannot be brought to settle their disputes locally; they have become merely another, and quite routine, front on which to carry on the fight. The dominant impression left by the Lincolnshire trailbaston report is that the fires of endemic local feuding were stoked rather than damped by the intervention of the king's law. Everywhere we hear of fights provoked "ex inimicitia perhabita" (cases 1, 5, 6, 12, 21) or "odio antiquo" (8, 19, 21), and it was obviously in the best interests of those who sought a hearing before such commissions (or better yet to get themselves appointed as commissioners) to represent their old enemies as ruthless gangsters, hardened criminals, and violent extortioners. It would not be difficult from Sir Edmund Deincourt's evidence to paint Sir Ralph Friskney as a small-time Eustace Folville, yet within a year the roles of judge and accused were to be reversed, with Deincourt cast as the malefactor and Friskney sitting on the commission of oyer and terminer appointed to look into his case (149). There is nothing unusual about this; indeed Bertha Putnam regards the tendency to alternate between "committing . . . crimes and helping to punish criminals" as entirely characteristic of the period (1950, 137), and Nigel Saul has noted the ability of the late medieval gentry to "switch roles with apparently effortless ease," appearing "first as poachers then as gamekeepers; first as lawbreakers, then as lawmakers" (1990, 40). Richard Kaeuper argues that "a sizeable majority of the commissions . . . seem to have reflected in large measure the countryside disputes of the gentry" (1979, 752), and it was clearly but a short step from such judicially stage-managed feuding to the out-and-out partiality of a John de Molyns rigging a special commission to acquit him of a triple murder in 1327 (W. Jones 317). Not without reason, Kaeuper concludes that "on balance the commissions seem to have contributed more to countryside disorder and suspicion of the legal mechanism than to order and confidence in the king's justice" (784).

This then was the world which made heroes of the Folville brothers, men who carried on their disputes not under cover of the king's law but in open defiance of it. One of the Folvilles' local enemies was Sir Robert Colville of Castle Bytham, just across the border in Lincolnshire. In 1331 he had led an unsuccessful assault on Eustace's house which cost several lives (*VHCE Rut-*

land 2:152), but when he returned to the village nine years or so later circumstances had changed. Eustace was away (perhaps serving the king in Flanders), and a commission had been appointed to arrest his brother Richard as a notorious suspect; Sir Robert entered Teigh as a keeper of the peace, a member of the king's commission, and in the company of the undersheriff. Richard put up a good fight, barricading himself in his own church and defending himself with his bow. He had killed one man and wounded several others, before Sir Robert's men finally broke down the door, dragged him out into the village street, and cut off his head (Stones 1957, 117). It is not difficult to find in the circumstances of Richard Folville's death evidence for the argument that, as Clanchy has put it, "royal power contributed to disorder and that the judicial authority of the crown was a public nuisance" (1974, 78).

One should, of course, resist the impulse to romanticize the Folville brothers, or Sir Ralph Friskney, or William de Venables and the villagers of Darnhall and Over. All were no doubt quite as capable of cynical violence as their opponents. Nor should we imagine that every footpad who waylaid a royal official in the fourteenth century was really fighting to keep alive his ancient rights; there is, for instance, no reason to suppose that the Richard Brierley, who took ten pounds from Chaucer in September 1390, was anything other than the "notorius latro" the records describe him as being (*CLR* 477–89).[11] But the point I wish to stress is that this violence flourished in the vacuum left by the disintegration of the folklaw, that the dislocation of customary modes of dispute settlement was forcing neighbors to resort to a judicial system which magnified rather than resolved their differences, and that this in turn led them to blame, not without reason, the system itself—or at least its representatives and procedures. The evidence for this is inevitably anecdotal but its cumulative weight is persuasive (*SCKB* 6:xxvi–vii).

Consider, for example, the career of Sir William Shareshull, chief justice of King's Bench. In 1329, while still a serjeant at law, he was violently assaulted near St. Paul's wharf (Putnam 1950, 4), and four years later, when he had become a justice of Common Pleas, two knights, Sir William and Sir Richard Harcourt, assaulted his servants and goods at York (4); three years after that his assizes in Wiltshire were threatened by "armed gangs of murderers and robbers" (63); the next year, his houses at Bromsgrove were attacked by a "large group of malefactors including a vicar and two chaplains" (5); and in 1345, the monks of St. Swithun's disrupted his courtroom (147). In 1347 there was a particularly serious disturbance at Tredington: "a large number of evildoers, who for many misdeeds against the peace are outlawed, . . . contemptuously prevented [Shareshull and his and his fellow officers] from entering the [court] and holding their sessions, and placed pennons (*pensellos*) of the arms of some of their number on the walls of the [court] in sign of maintaining their rebellion, . . . and would in no wise render themselves to the law of the land" (*CPR* 1335–48, 386). In the 1350s two of his properties were broken into, one by a parson, the other by a knight (Putnam 1950, 147); and in 1358 a number of men were arrested for making threats against him, one of them a clerk who is reported to have said that he "would gladly strike" the judge (148).[12] Clearly, not everyone at the time would have agreed with Putnam's estimate of Sir William as a champion "of law and order, of right-doing, of economic and social stability" (148), and it is perhaps not surprising that Shareshull seems to have decided to take early retirement in 1361.

Lest we should be tempted to imagine that Shareshull's career was untypical, let us consider a selection of King's Bench cases from the middle of the century: in 1339 two men force a terrified royal coroner to take refuge in a house in Westminster, threatening him in life and limb (*SCKB* 3:cxxxi); in 1340 a knight's wife accosts a justice of King's Bench on his way to the courtroom "with abusive words," calling him "false and faithless" [falsum et infidelem] (*SCKB* 5:121); in 1343 a man goes to the house of a chief justice in York and attacks him "with outrageous words [verbis enormibus], vilifying him many times in the presence of many bystanders there" (*SCKB* 6:29); in Louth in 1354 a knight assaults a judge on his way out of court and accuses him of speaking wickedly and falsely ("qil dit malement e fausement") (*SCKB* 3:cxxxv); in 1357 a woman waylays a justice of Common Pleas on his way to a meeting of the barons of the Exchequer, and calls him "in front of a fair-sized crowd [populo non modico audiente], a false traitor to the king and faithless [falsum proditorem ipsius regis et infidelem], fit to be drawn and hanged" (*SCKB* 3:cxxxvi). Nor were such attacks on the judiciary always merely verbal. The judge in Louth, for instance, was also subjected to "various hostile assaults" by the knight, who, "with drawn sword before all the people would have killed him, whom he took violently by the throat, if he had not been prevented by others" (*CPR* 1354–58, 166);[13] and the same justice of Common Pleas who had been insulted by a woman in 1357, was on his way to a privy council meeting two years later when he was stabbed in the belly with a knife "and attrociously wounded . . . so that his life was despaired of" (*CPR* 1358–61, 280). On a lighter note, when a clerk of the court called William of Thorpe (later to become a judge), was on his way to a sitting of King's Bench in 1318, a band of assailants merely knocked him down, kicked him, and threw piss over him ("vrinam super ipsum proiecerunt") (*SCKB* 4:79). Many of the assailants in such cases are knights, but resentment against the judicial profession clearly permeated all orders of society, from men like John Braundys who greeted the news of the approaching sessions in Berkshire in 1375 with the words, "Iche defie alle the kynges Justices" (*PJP* cxviii), or the early-fifteenth-century London scrivener who shouted, "Thou shalt do me lawe, maugre yn thyn hert," while giving his local sheriff a good shaking (Riley 595), right up to the highest in the land. When a justice of the peace called Sir William Sturmy indicted one of the earl of Devon's retainers for murder in 1391, the earl "swore on the cross of his chapel that the said William Esturmy should answer with his body, accusing him repeatedly of being a false traitor to him [luy appellaunt souent faux treitour a luy], and said that he should have respite no longer than this day" (*SCKC* 78). Quite as impressive as the number of these incidents is the sense of moral outrage they convey: *traitor*, as we shall see in the next chapter, was a highly charged term in fourteenth-century England.

Still more striking are those cases where challenges to the authority of the law were supported by a whole community. Perhaps the most spectacular instance took place in 1344, when the arrival in Ipswich of a commission of oyer and terminer, presided over by the formidable Shareshull (Putnam 1950, 66), led to the murder of one of the commissioners and a spontaneous rebellion against the king's authority. People of all ranks, we are told ("tam de maioribus quam de mediocribus et minoribus"), brought presents to the murderers, "such as food and drink and gold and silver and sang so many songs of rejoicing in their honour there that it was as if God had come down from Heaven" (*SCKB* 6:37). Furthermore, the citizens marched to the town hall, summoned the commissioners (including Shareshull), held a mock trial, and fined them in absentia, "in contempt of the king and in mockery [in dirisionem] of the king's justices and ministers in his service." When asked later why they had not kept better order, the bailiffs said that they were weak and old and powerless to act without the support of "the more substantial men" of the town (38). Thereupon, in a graphic demonstration of the relative power of the king's law and the folklaw, the court of inquiry removed from office these representatives of the local community ("electi . . . per totam communitatem eiusdem ville") and replaced them with the king's man: "the bailiffs delivered up their wands to the court, and the custody of the town is handed over by the king's court to John Haward, the sheriff, who was sworn to look after the town well and faithfully to the king's profit" (38). The Ipswich incident was not unparalleled, however. At Lincoln in 1334 royal justices were so intimidated that they had had to set up their court outside the city (*SCKB* 6:xxvi). When a royal bailiff in Edward II's reign had tried to arrest some Northampton men he found himself fleeing for his life, pursued by townspeople shouting "At him! At him! He's the king's man!" [A luy A luy, Il est ou roy] (cited by Kaeuper 1979, 748). And at Oxford the hue and cry was set up on some servants of a king's attorney: "clamantes semper cum magno hutesio: Sle, Sle, Sle" (*PJP* cxi).

So serious was resistance to royal authority in the fourteenth century that it might be claimed without a great deal of exaggeration that the country was in a state of near civil war. The author of "The Outlaw's Song of Trailbaston" warns that "si Dieu ne prenge garde, je quy qe sourdra guere" [if God doesn't help us, I believe war will break out] (line 4), yet, ironically, it was this same threat that had led to the trailbaston commissions being set up in the first place; the king saw in them an answer to "riots and outrages which were like the outbreak of war and in defiance of royal authority" (cited by Kaeuper 1979 737, n. 14). As Kaeuper says, such a statement makes it harder to dismiss as hysteria such dire predictions as Peter Langtoft's: "If this turbulence is not stopped, general warfare may be the result" (736) — predictions that did not diminish as the fourteenth century progessed. It is important to remind ourselves that outside the southern counties the king's authority over his own subjects was precarious at best; as Ralph Higden, himself a northerner, dryly remarks, when kings go "to þe norþ contray, a goþ wiþ gret help and strengthe" (Sisam 150).

Outsiders' Law

It is, however, one thing to show that the king's law and its officers were held in contempt (and not merely by disgruntled individuals but by whole communities), it is quite another to claim, as I have been doing, that its opponents espoused their own "rival system of justice" (Stones 1957, 135) — that Folvilles' law, in other words, was the opposite of mere lawlessness. The evidence for this, since our communities so rarely speak for themselves, must be largely inferential.

In the first place, it is noticeable that opposition to the king's law flourished at the margins of society, in areas where the power of literate authority was weakest and where we should expect the old ways to be preserved most strongly. By the fourteenth century this opposition is marginal in two senses: it grows stronger the greater the distance from Westminster; furthermore, even in Lincolnshire or Cheshire, its natural territory is at the edge of society, where it can quickly take to the forests and wild places when threatened by the power of central law. As John of Bridlington puts it, "Inter silvestres leges pennis volitabunt" [amongst the forest folk the laws shall fly on feathers] — a reference, his glossator explains, to the law of the bow and arrow, "which is the way such people fight" (Wright, *Poems*, 1:137 and 140). Thus the speaker in the "Outlaw's Song of Trailbaston" has been driven by the inequity of the king's law:

antre bois, suz le jolyf umbray;
La n'y a fauceté ne nulle male lay,

En le bois de Belregard, ou vole le jay
E chaunte russinole touz jours santz delay.
(17–20)

[amid the trees, in a fair shade, where there is no falsehood or wicked law; in the woods of Belregard, where the jay flies free and the nightingale's "song" is never deferred.]

"Come with me," he says to others who have fallen foul of the common law, "Al vert bois de Belregard, la n'y a nul ploy / Forque beste savage e jolyf umbroy" [to the green woods of Belregard, where there is no "order" but the wild creatures and the fair shade] (lines 54–55). And he concludes by telling us that his poem "fust fet al bois, desouz un lorer, / La chaunte merle, russinole e eyre l'esperver" [was written in the woods, beneath a laurel, where only the blackbird and nightingale "sing" and only the sparrowhawk "circles"] (lines 97–98).[14]

A striking parallel to this sylvan picture occurs in a threatening letter sent to a Yorkshire parson in 1336 which concludes in parody of a royal writ, "Given at our castle of the North Wind in the Greenwood Tower in the first year of our reign" [Donez a nostre chastiel de Bise en la Tour de vert en lan de nostre regne primer];[15] the letter is cited as evidence in a King's Bench case, and the court takes seriously such flouting of royal dignity ("tangit regiam dignitatem et preiudicium domini regis") (*SCKB* 5:93–95). There is, moreover, ample evidence that the so-called fourteenth-century gangs (the Folvilles are only one of a number of such bands to have been identified)[16] existed much of the time in this shadowy forest world. When the Folvilles captured Sir Richard Willoughby, they took him, according to Knighton, to "a nearby wood," and a later indictment says that he was moved "from wood to wood" until the ransom money was handed over (cited by Stones 1957, 122); two of the Folville associates on that occasion, John Coterel and Roger Savage, were later traced "to the wild forest of the High Peak, Derbyshire," but, warned of the sheriff's approach by one of their spies, managed to escape (Stones 1957, 127). In 1361 Sir William Coningsby "with many others in his company" arrived at daybreak at the house of the parson of Langar, who was involved in a lawsuit with one of Coningsby's servants, and dragged him off to Sherwood where they forced him to pay a fine (*SCKC* 47). Much later in the century, another band leader, William Beckwith of Yorkshire "was forced to flee to the forest" when confronted by a trailbaston commission led by John of Gaunt in 1390, and a second commission a year later was said to have driven him "to the densest part of the forest" (Bellamy 1964/65, 257–58).

Some insight into the way these bands managed to survive on the edge of society is provided by an indictment against another man associated with the Willoughby kidnapping, Sir Robert de Vere, constable of Rockingham castle and keeper of Rockingham forest: "Sometimes twenty armed men, sometimes thirty, come to Vere at the castle, and they leave at dawn, or during the night. He shuts the gates on the side facing the town, and they can leave secretly, by a postern. Those bringing victuals to the castle are not allowed to enter, lest they should come to know those armed men" (quoted by Stones 1957, 124). John Bellamy has traced the movements of John Coterel and his band in 1331 and 1332, and suggests that "he never stayed more than a month in any one place though he periodically revisited the places where he was most assured of a friendly welcome. . . . There are several reports of food being taken to [his gang] in the woods" (1964, 702). Similarly, when a posse was sent after the band that disrupted Shareshull's sessions at Tredington in 1447, a royal proclamation to the effect that "all of the county should aid in the arrest" was studiously ignored by the local inhabitants, who seem on the contrary to have been happy to "cherish and nourish the evildoers and outlaws to the utmost" (*CPR* 1345–48, 386–87). Though Bellamy does not allow his "Coterel gang" the kind of sympathy I have been indulging in here, even he admits that "no man claimed in court he was forced to shelter members of the gang. . . . The impression given is that in many quarters the gang was not only respected but reluctantly admired" (1964, 717). We seem very near to what E. J. Hobsbawm has called "social banditry." The Folvilles and their kind appear to conform closely to his definition of men, regarded by the state as criminals, but "considered by their people as heroes, as champions, avengers, fighters for justice" (Hobsbawm 17); as I have been at some pains to suggest, they may also have shared something of the social bandit's aspiration "to establish or to re-establish justice or 'the old ways', that is to say fair dealing in a society of oppression" (55).

If marginality is one characteristic of fourteenth-century adherence to the folklaw, a strong sense of community, of fellowship, is another. We have already seen Knighton calling the Folville band a *socialis comitiva*, and similar terminology appears in official documents—one indictment, for example, refers to Eustace Folville as a *capitalis de societate* (cited by Stones 1957, 131). Centralized authority clearly regarded local solidarity with a great deal of suspicion. Indeed, one of the additional directives which led to the older commissions of inquiry developing into the new trailbastons was an instruction to the commissioners to investigate those who might have made formal agreements with known malefactors—"pactum fecerunt cum malefactoribus" ("Early Trailbaston" 144)—and the experience of the first trailbastons led to Parliament's passing the ordinance of conspirators (Harding 1984, 189–90;

see also W. Jones 316). For the author of the "Trailbaston" poem this is merely a further spur to malicious prosecution:

Si je sei compagnoun e sache de archerye,
Mon veisyn irra disaunt: "Cesti est de compagnie
De aler bercer a bois e fere autre folie.
Que ore vueille vivre come pork merra sa vie."
Si je sache plus de ley qe ne sevent eux,
Yl dirrount: "Cesti conspyratour comence de estre faus."
(85–90)

[If I'm a sociable fellow and can draw a bow my neighbor will go around saying, "He's a member of that band that goes poaching in the woods and doing other mischief. Let him now choose between death and the life of an outlaw."[17] If I know more law than they do, they'll say, "This conspirator begins to be untrustworthy."]

There is plenty of evidence that the outlaw bands thought of themselves as unified confederacies. Roger Savage, for instance, leader of a band that, as we have seen, worked with the Folvilles on occasion, sent a letter to the mayor of Nottingham in 1332 demanding thirty pounds "ad opus societatis" of *gentz sauvages*, and twice that sum was demanded of Sir Geoffrey Lutterell (whose son-in-law, incidentally, was a chief justice of King's Bench) by "la companie sauvage" (Bellamy 1964, 706–7). The threatening letter cited above purports to have been sent by "Lionel, roi de la Route de Raueners" [king of the band of robbers] (*SCKB* 5:93), a title which suggests a degree of organization within the group. Perhaps the best evidence of such cohesion, however, comes from a poem cited in evidence against a band (*covina*) of eighty Yorkshiremen, who for six years (1386–92) had dressed "in one livery of a single company by corrupt allegiance and confederacy" [in vna liberata de vnica secta per falsam alligianciam et confederacionem] and prevented any sheriff, escheator, "or other royal minister of whatsoever rank" from doing "anything that it is his duty to do within the domain of Cottingham" (*SCKB* 7:83–85). The poem is said to have been recited publicly in Beverley, Hull, and other Yorkshire towns, a region which the band evidently regarded as its special territory (its "soken"). The confederates liken their ties to one another to membership in a religious order,

Among this frers it is so,
and other ordres many mo,

whether [þ]ei slepe or wake,
and [y]et wil ilkan hel vp other
and meynteyn him als his brother,
bothe in wronge and righte.
And also wil [we] in stond and stoure
meynteyn owre negheboure
with al oure myghte.

They are prepared to defend the band's honor against any insult to it, from whatever quarter:

but hethyng wil we suffre non—
neither of Hobbe nor of Johan,
with what man he be.

They insist that a slight to one is a slight to all:

who so dose vs any wrang
in what place it falle,
yet he might als wele,
als haue I hap and hele,
do again vs alle.[18]

Similar loyalties were displayed by the members of a Gloucestershire gang that besieged a church in 1389 (acting, interestingly enough, on behalf of the author, John Trevisa): when ordered to disperse by the sheriff's bailiffs they shouted back that they would answer to no one but John Poleyn, their leader (Saul 1981, 165–66).

Words like *societas* and *compagnie* are clearly loaded terms in this context, as is the English word *fellowship*. All imply the existence of oaths of mutual loyalty taken in defiance of established authority: "*ffelows*, or knytt to-geder in wykkydnes" is the way the mid-fifteenth-century *Promptorium Parvulorum* renders the Latin word *complices* (158). The phrase "good felawe," familiar from Chaucer ("General Prologue" 395 and elsewhere) and Gower (*CA* 5:7752–56), takes on a certain menace when seen in this light. Originally used with no pejorative overtones,[19] by the late fourteenth century this phrase was often associated in official culture with taverns and debauchery,[20] perhaps because, as David Aers has noted, alehouses might easily foster "solidarities and a culture hardly in harmony with the one recommended to plebeians" (38).[21] Interestingly, a number of the Lincolnshire trailbaston cases concern fights in taverns, and at least one involves a local group attacking unpopular outsiders ("Early Trailbaston" 157.21). Harding has suggested that "communal oaths of obedience to established authority" were always "in danger of becoming oaths of communal solidarity against the authorities" (1984, 190), and it does not take much imagination to see how easily the good fellowship of the tavern might move from Falstaffian parody to genuine threat. If the distance between a "kyng of felawys" in an alehouse and a "roi de la route de raveners" in the woods was small enough to worry the authorities, they must have felt that their worst fears had been realized when the rising of 1381 produced leaders like John Littestere "qui se 'Regem Communium' appellabat," or Robert Westbrom "qui se regem fecerat" (Walsingham, *Historia* 2:6 and 11), not to mention a John Ball rallying his followers behind "Johan Trewman and alle his felawes" (2:34), or a Wat Tyler swilling beer in the presence of Richard II himself (*Anonimalle* 148; cf. Pearsall 1989, 68).

A third characteristic of folklaw survival is suggested by just such parodic gestures. Mockery is always likely to find a place in folklaw procedure, loosely defined, since oral law is much concerned with honor, with one's standing in the community, and public shaming will therefore offer it a potent means of enforcing communal standards. Gregory of Tours mentions that Childebert II had had some would-be assassins mutilated and then set at large to endure public ridicule, "ad ridiculum laxaverunt" (10.18; 2:372–74), but less brutal mockery had also formed part of the old law: according to the *Leges Burgundionum*, for instance, anyone caught stealing a hunting dog was sentenced to kiss the dog's *posterior* in the presence of the whole community (ch. 97; 112–13). In the late Middle Ages the folklaw's natural weapons were the pillory, the stocks, the cuckstool, and the tumbrel. Though the *Statutes of the Realm* contain a set of regulations, of uncertain date, concerning the use of such implements (1:201–2), these do not appear to represent either a parliamentary or a royal decree: all the offenders mentioned in it are urban (bakers and ale-sellers who use inferior ingredients, unhygienic butchers and cooks, merchants who give false measure, and so on) and it was evidently meant for the use of borough rather than royal officers (cf. *PPl* B.3:76–81). The Guildhall Letter Books give us several examples of the "judicium pillorii" in late medieval London: a man who swindles two trusting women is condemned to "stonde here vpon þe pillorye thre market dayes, eche day an hour, wiþ a Weston [whetstone] aboute hys necke in tokene of a Lyere" (Chambers and Daunt 95),[22] while a forger of legal documents and a collier convicted of giving short measure receive similar sentences, the first with "on of his fals lettres" hanging round his neck (96), and the second, "his sakkis brent vndur hym" (101). Naturally, such folklaw sanctions applied in the countryside as well as the town: "The ale-tasters present that Agneta the widow brewed and sold contrary to the assize. Therefore command is given that she do ascend the tumbrel with distaff and spindle" (*Court Baron* 100). That these legal remedies might be felt to be in competition with royal justice is implied by a pointed couplet that follows a long passage on the abuses of the king's law in two of the versions of *The Simonie*: "But bi Seint Iame of Galice, þat many man haþ souht / Þe pilory and the cucking-stol beþ imad for noht" (A.475–76; cf. C.427–28). In the third, this couplet follows an attack on royal tax collectors (B.427–28).

There is a very fine line separating such punishments from the later ridings, rough music, Lady Skimmingtons, and charivaris which "in their boisterous mixture of playfulness and cruelty" sought "to set things right in a community" (N. Davis 1984, 42). The Guildhall Letter Books, for instance, record that in 1423 a notorious bawd was sentenced to be led from prison to the pillory on three market days "with pypys or oþer opyn Minstralsy . . . þe cause why proclamed" (Chambers and Daunt 103), and it is not difficult to read into these bare phrases the kind of ritual that was to be witnessed by the young John Stow over a hundred years later. He tells of a draper called Atwood who went off to work leaving his wife playing backgammon with a chantry priest: "but returning to fetch a Pressing iron he found such play to his misliking, that he forced the Priest to leape out at a window . . . The priest being apprehended, and committed, I saw his punishment to be thus: he was on three Market dayes conueyed through the high streete and Markets of the Citie with a Paper on his head, wherein was written his trespasse: The first day hee rode in a Carry, the second on a horse, his face to the horse taile, the third, led between twaine, and euery day rung with Basons, and proclamations made of his fact at euery turning of the streets" (1:190). Inevitably, official culture came to regard such methods of communal self-regulation with suspicion, and they were increasingly associated with lawlessness and misrule. Yet even in their later manifestations charivaris can be shown to have followed well-established patterns; in general, they were very far from the disorderly riots their victims usually represent them as being (Cashmere).

Medieval instances of opponents of the king's (or archdeacon's) law resorting to parodic ritual can offer some of the best evidence for the existence of a rival system of justice. When the people of Sellings, Kent (ca. 1304), mounted the representative of an ecclesiastical court on a horse "with his face to the tail and inhumanely compelled him to hold the tail and ride, with songs and dances, through that town" (cited by Hahn and Kaeuper 85), they were clearly affirming their allegiance to an older legal order (see R. Mellinkoff). So too were the citizens of Boston in Lincolnshire, when, in a grim variation on the traditional mounting on the tumbrel, they left the dead body of a man called Stephen Ryngolf in a cart for three days "so that everyone could see it" (*1341 Royal Inquest* 129.1196); Ryngolf seems to have been an unsavory character, conspiring with the sheriff to bring false indictments against his neighbors (96–97) and bribing the coroner to cover up a murder he himself had committed (98), so this display looks very much like folklaw rough-justice meted out to an unpopular crony of the king's officers. Some sense of the public shame such rituals were intended to occasion is given by a mid-fifteenth-century chancery petition in which a royal forester complains of Sir John Griffiths that "in despite, shame, and reprofe of the seid suppliant, [he] brake the Kinges parke at Barton, and there slowe and caried awey by nyghtes tyme two grete buckes, and the hedis of them set at Kynges Bromley, oon upon the yate of the seid forster, and another upon the butte in myddes of the town, with a scornefull scripture of rymes wryten in Inglish sowed in the mouthes of the buckes hedis" (*CPC* 2:xxxiv).

Private quarrels, particularly between local gentry and ecclesiastics, were always liable to take on a parodic dimension. When Sir William de Clifton fell out with the rector of one of the churches of Vale Royal Abbey over the payment of some tithes, "he obliged the rector's cart, laden with hay, to stand for a month and more in the field, and out of the rector's draught-horse he mockingly made a hunting palfrey for himself" (*Ledger-Book* 34); since one of the people named as a supporter of Sir William in his campaign against the rector is a certain Adam le Harper we might guess that rough music also played a part in the proceedings. A similar piece of mockery was reported to the Lincolnshire trailbaston, where a row between Sir Philip Darcy and the prior of Nocton had led to the knight's cutting off the tail of a horse on which one of the priory's canons rode and getting a boy to kiss the horse "in posteriora [*sic*] parte" ("Early Trailbaston" 158.24). More elaborate was the visit of three men who went to threaten a church farmer in Hackney, probably in 1327: they delivered him an ultimatum from their "convent," dressed up in monks' habits and calling themselves Brother Muf, Brother Cuf, and Brother Puf (Kaeuper 1979, 734–35).

At a later period the charivari came to be directed against authority figures—George I, for instance, mocked as "a damned cuckoldy rogue and a dog" by rioters in Hertfordshire (Ingram 108)—and E. P. Thompson has argued that such public charivaris express the alienation experienced by people who still retain the remnants of their own communal law in states where the authorities claim to monopolize the legal system (1972, 310). Ritual skirmishes between folklaw and king's law can be found long before the industrial revolution, however; David Underdown has described such public charivaris in seventeenth-century England, and something similar might even be detected in the later Middle Ages. The king himself, as the peasants' misplaced trust in him in 1381 shows, was still revered in the popular imagination as the wellspring of justice, but no such deference was felt for his officials. When local resistance, in the spirit of Thompson's public charivaris, spilled over into quasi-political parody it often appropriated official forms, as in the mock trial held by the citizens of Ipswich (mentioned above), or the threatening letter sent by the king of the "route de raveners" in the form of a royal writ. The terms of a trailbaston commission of 1332 imply that such parodic letters, "quasi sub stilo regio," were in fact commonplace (Stones 1957, 134), and when this bandit-king demands forfeits for "being against us and our laws" [*countre nous et noz leys*] (*SCKB* 5:93), we may sense the presence of a genuine rival system beneath his parody. William of Bulkeley, a Cheshire band captain, not only prevented the holding of the earl's court in 1375, but proclaimed his own court "with the usual assize of bread and ale" (Hewitt 107), and in the late 1380s a Yorkshireman called William Beckwith is even said to have summoned his own parliament "called 'Dodelowe'," which was held on several occasions "in subversion of the law" (Bellamy 1964/65, 256).

In 1439 William Love and other tenants of the royal honor of Tutbury complained to Parliament of the depredations of a Derbyshire gang led by a gentleman called Piers Venables. A number of the old themes are present (Venables' gang, we are told, wear his livery, they "kepyn the wodes and strange contrays," and they prevent bailiffs, clerks, and other officers from holding proper courts), but one phrase in the petition stands out: Piers is said to have behaved "like as it hadde be Robyn hode and his meyne" (Holt 150).

A number of historians have pointed out that the outlaw tradition we have been discussing is vividly embodied in two literary works of the period, the *Gest of Robyn Hode* and the tale of *Gamelyn*. That these works have been shown to contain parallels in contemporary legal records is of great importance in confirming their verisimilitude (e.g., Shannon; Kaeuper 1983), but there is no need to repeat this work here. What I should like to stress however is the pervasive presence of the folklaw in both poems, for where other commentators see their treatment of legal issues as a matter of attacking specific abuses, I would prefer to emphasize their general dissatisfaction with the dominant legal order. Certainly, criticism of the institution of the king's law was generally imperfectly articulated and often expressed itself as criticism of specific aspects of that law, but, as Maurice Keen has pointed out, in an age when the idea of "law itself was ultimately unassailable, protest against abuse must be to some extent specific" (1987, 128). The nostalgic commitment in both these works to an older legal order reveals their sense of a more profound conflict. The medieval outlaw, like Hobsbawm's other "social bandits," lived according to a clear legal code—"God's law and the common custom, which was different from the state's or the lord's law, but nevertheless a social order" (149). The rivalry of outlaw and sheriff takes place in a world turned upside down, a world in which the real robbers are those whose rapacity is cloaked in the official law; as an early-fourteenth-century preaching manual puts it, "Sithyn law for wyll bygynnyt to slakyn, / . . . Robbyng and reuyng ys holdyn purchas" (quoted by Wenzel 1978, 178).[23] Faced with the ubiquitous perversion of royal justice, the outlaw poems proclaim their faith in an older order, and the pervasive presence of the folklaw informs what Douglas Gray has called their "sense of an alternate realm and 'rule'" (1984, 31).

In the *Gest of Robyn Hode* (where "gode felawe" has yet to become a pejorative term—is used indeed in contrast to the shady association of great prelates and "the hyë sherif of Notyingham" [Child 3:57, sts. 14–15]), the supreme folklaw virtue of good faith is constantly contrasted with the treacherous behavior of the official representatives of morality and public order. Robin is willing to lend the destitute stranger Sir Richard at the Lee four hundred pounds with no better security than the Virgin Mary as "borwe" (sts. 65–66) because his test has shown the knight to be "true inowe" (st. 43). When the same test later proves the monk of St. Mary's Abbey a liar (st. 247) Robin feels no compunction about robbing him. Though Sir Richard uses the borrowed money to repay the abbot of St. Mary's a loan which he had secured with his estates (st. 120), the abbot continues to use the law to try to obtain the lands which have so narrowly escaped his grasp (st. 253). Sir Richard in contrast amply repays Robin's trust in him by bringing the full sum, with interest, on the appointed day (st. 270), though bound by no written instrument to do so. The sheriff of Nottingham, kidnapped (like Sir Richard Willoughby) and released after solemnly swearing never to harm his captors in the future (sts. 202–4), is put to the test in a public archery contest: "I wyll wete the shryuës fayth, / Trewe and yf he be" (st. 287); needless to say, the sheriff fails:

> And wo be thou! thou proudë sheryf,
> Thus gladdynge thy gest;
> Other wyse thou behotë me
> In yonder wylde forest.
> But had I the in grenë wode,
> Under my trystell-tre,
> Thou sholdest leue me a better wedde
> Than thy trewe lewtë.
>
> (sts. 297–98)

As in other outlaw ballads, *Adam Bell, Clym of the Clough, and William of Cloudesly*, for instance, the sense of comradeship is strong. Robin refuses to leave the wounded Little John to the sheriff's men (st. 306), and Sir Richard opens his castle gates to his old benefactor in time of need (st. 311). Hardly surprisingly, the king finds Robin's men "more at his byddynge / Then my men be at myn" (st. 391), for an example of the good faith of crown servants is furnished by the High Justice's refusal, after Sir Richard unexpectedly turns up to pay off his debt, to refund the abbot the money he has already been paid to seize the knight's estates (sts. 94 and 123). Everywhere open generosity is amply rewarded and narrow legalism punished: Sir Richard pays back the penny-pinching abbot his exact sum (st. 121), but gives the free-handed Robin an extra twenty marks, "for your curteysy" (st. 270). The whole poem is built on such contrasts, and when Robin boasts to the sheriff of "our ordre . . . / Vnder the grenë-wode tree" (st. 197), there is a strong sense that the entire system which the sheriff represents, not merely individual abuses of it, is confuted by this picture of "a kind of alternative commonwealth and morality" (Gray 1984, 17).

The tale of *Gamelyn* places greater emphasis on the inequities of a common law (which makes an outlaw of a disinherited younger son and a sheriff of the brother who has cheated him) than it does on the virtues of the folklaw. Yet here too there is a striking contrast in the value placed on good faith by the two brothers: "The knight þought on tresoun and Gamelyn on noon" (line 165). This is most obvious in the scene where Gamelyn, having returned in triumph from a wrestling match and defied his elder brother's authority (by throwing the porter who was barring the gate to him down the well), is tricked into submitting to be bound. Having mollified him with a promise to make him his heir, the brother continues:

> Tho þou þrewe my porter in þe draw-welle,
> I swor in þat wraþþe and in that gret moot
> That þou schuldest be bounde boþe hand and foot;
> Therfore i þe beseche brother Gamelyn,
> Lat me nought be forsworn, brother art þou myn.
> Lat me bynde þe now boþe hand and feet
> For to holde myn avow as i þe biheet.
>
> (372–78)

Gamelyn understands at once the obligation under which such an oath puts his brother—"Thou schalt not be forsworen for þe loue of me" (line 380)—and trustingly allows the fetters to be placed round his wrists and ankles, only of course to find himself bound in earnest. When, with the help of his father's old servant Adam Spencer, he is freed from this treacherous confinement, he responds by beating his brother "aȝein þe kinges pees" (line 548) and is forced to flee to the woods: "Better is vs þer loos þan in town ybounde" (line 606).

Later in the story, after Gamelyn has been "made maister outlawe and crouned her kyng" (line 694), his brother, who has become "scherreue and sire" (line 697), has him indicted and begins formal outlawry proceedings. When Gamelyn turns up to answer the charges he is arrested and imprisoned, and is only released on the mainprise of a third (middle) brother, Sir Ote. It thus becomes a matter of honor for Gamelyn to keep his word and appear in court in order to release Sir Ote from his liability; as he tells his outlaw band back in the forest, "we moote be þare; / For i am vnder borwe til þat i come" (lines 794–95). Gamelyn's arrival at the county court with his men at his back provides the climax of the romance. The theme of judicial parody, of a rival system of justice, is quite explicit in this scene: "For i wil be iustice þis day domes to deme. / God spede me þis day at my newe werk! (lines 826–27). The carnival atmosphere, the sense of a world turned upside down, is caught by the poet's word "bourde":

Whan Gamelyn was iset in þe iustices stede,
Herkneþ of a bourde þat Gamelyn dede:
He lete fetre þe iustice and his fals broþer,
And dede hem come to þe barre þat oon wiþ þat oþer.
(857–60)

The humor of hanging not only the justice and the sheriff but the twelve jurors — "to weyuen wiþ ropes and wiþ þe wynd drye" (880) — may be a bit strong for the modern palate, but it does convey vividly the sense of outraged custom. In *Adam Bell, Clym of the Clough, and William of Cloudesly*, however, the tally is even higher:

Fyrst the justice and the sheryfe,
And the mayre of Caerlel towne;
Of all the constables and catchipolles
Alyue were left not one.

The baylyes and the bedyls both,
And the sergeauntes of the law,
And forty fosters of the fe
These outlawes had y-slaw.
(Child 3:28)

In both *Adam Bell* and *Gamelyn*, as in the *Gest of Robyn Hode*, the folklaw world of oath, borrow, and wed is contrasted with the untrustworthy machinery of the king's law, but here armed opposition is put before sylvan escapism. The violent end of the royal officials in these poems was to have more than one real-life counterpart in the peasant rising of 1381.

To mention the Peasants' Revolt in such a context is to risk reviving an old debate over the connection between Robin Hood and the followers of Ball and Tyler (see Hilton 1976, 6–8 and 236–72). Nevertheless, the rebellion of 1381 clearly exhibits some of the same characteristics of resistance to the king's law (particularly local cohesiveness and ritual parody) that we have already noted. A la longue durée, I would argue, the Peasants' Revolt has more to do with the clash of two legal orders and the resistance of oral custom to literate authoritarianism, than it has with restrictive employment or unfair taxation; these merely fanned into flame a fire which had been smoldering long before the Black Death created a shortage of labor. As a manifestation of long-established popular discontent with the direction of social change, the revolt may have merely been the tip of the iceberg. Though the demand for justice was a recurrent theme among the rebels, they showed a marked hostility to the institution of literate, centralized law (Harding 1984; Maddicott 1978, 61–64; Prescott, 133–36) and I shall conclude this chapter by first illustrating this hostility and then discussing its significance.

The Peasants' Revolt

All the major chronicle accounts of the revolt report the hatred of the peasants for the representatives of the king's law. From the very beginning, according to *The Anonimalle Chronicle*, the peasants "intended to kill all the men of law [toutz les gentz de la ley], and all the jurors, and all the royal officials they could find" (135), and when they reached London they made a proclamation to that effect (144). Walsingham ascribes to Wat Tyler the view that they "should be given a commission to behead all lawyers, escheators, and everyone who had had either a legal training or dealings with the law by virtue of his office [in lege docti fuere, vel cum iure, ratione officii, communicavere]. He certainly believed that with all legal experts dead everything would henceforth be left to be run by the decree of the common people" (*Historia* 1:464).[24] Nor was such hostility restricted to words alone; Knighton reports that the rebels attacked jurors' houses and that wherever they found either city jurors or common-law barristers ("iuratos quoque ciuitatis et iuris regni apprenticios quoscunque") they immediately put them to death (*Knighton's Chronicle* 217). *The Anoni-*

malle Chronicle confirms this attack on the houses of jurors and "questmangers" and adds that the Marshalsea prison was stormed and all those imprisoned for debt or felony released (140). The rebels burned to the ground the house of John Butterwick, undersheriff of Middlesex, and wrought havoc with the Temple in Fleet Street, already a popular lodging for lawyers (Hilton 1973, 194). Prominent among victims of the uprising were Simon Sudbury (the chancellor), Sir Robert Hales (the treasurer), Sir John Cavendish (chief justice of King's Bench), Sir Richard Imworth (marshal of the King's Bench) and Roger Legett, a well-known lawyer (Harding 1984, 179–80). When a deputation of peasants arrived from St. Albans hot on the heels of this rampage they were given to believe that "most of the lawyers had perished and the remainder, as they judged, were bound to perish" (Walsingham, *Historia* 1:468).

There are, moreover, some familiar themes in this antijudicial uproar. Though a new poll tax sparked the first murmurs of dissent, trailbaston commissions sent to enforce compliance were what fanned them into open rebellion in both Kent and Essex. Of the Kent trailbaston, *The Anonimalle Chronicle* tells us that the commissioners arrived with a great number of indictments "pur fair le roy riche" (136), while in Essex the head of the commission, Chief Justice Robert Bealknap, found himself called "traitour al roy et al roialme" in his own courtroom (135). According to Michael de la Pole two years later, animosity against "the lesser servants of the king, such as the sheriffs, escheators, collectors of subsidies and others of the same type" was the main cause ("sours & cause principale") of the whole revolt (*RP* 3:150; Dobson 362). There were, too, the familiar complaints against outlawry; Walsingham says that the charters extorted from the king promised his subjects freedom from all sentences of outlawry (*Historia* 1:467), and *The Anonimalle Chronicle* reports that Wat Tyler's demands included that "there should be no law but the law of Winchester and that henceforward outlawry should be totally removed from all legal process" [qe nulle lay devroit estre fors la lay de Wynchestre, et qe nulle ughtelarie serroit en nulle processe de laye fait de ore en avaunt] (147). This allusion to the law of Winchester has been much discussed,[25] but whatever interpretation is accepted, most commentators will agree that the rebels were seeking a return to an older legal order.

The most striking, if not entirely unprecedented, aspect of the peasants' assault on the law, however, is their rage against its literate machinery (cf. Justice 40–48), which clearly shows that the rebels resented the malfunctioning of the king's government "not as some abstraction of political philosophy, but as a powerful force working in their daily lives" (Kaeuper 1988, 371). They destroyed archives and legal documents with all the fervor of luddites smashing weaving frames. At Lambeth, for instance, they "set fire to all the registers and Chancery record rolls" that they found in Sudbury's house (*Anonimalle* 140), and at the Temple "they took all the books and enrolled records which were in the barristers' cupboards, carried them out into the road, and burnt them" (141). Knighton confirms the destruction of legal records at the Temple and adds the vivid detail of peasants smashing open the lawyers' record chests with axes (*Knighton's Chronicle* 217). Walsingham even discusses motives: "they decided to burn all rolls and old court records, so that, with the memory of ancient things discarded, their lords would henceforth be quite unable to maintain any rights against them" (*Historia* 1:455). Nor was such destruction confined to London. At Canterbury "they burnt charters, records and writings in the house of justice" (Dobson 208), and at Cambridge an old woman called Margery Starre stood in the market square crying "Away with the learning of clerks, away with it!" as she threw university archives onto a bonfire (quoted by McKisack 417). Walsingham describes the records of his own abbey of St. Albans being burned in the town square next to the cross (*Historia* 1:474) and tells how the rebels demanded the muniments of the sister house of Bury (2:4). R. B. Dobson asserts that the records of Cambridgeshire Assizes held after the uprising leave us in no doubt "that the destruction of manorial court rolls and other documents could be a regular rather than intermittent objective of the insurgents (xxvii), and the scale of the damage is confirmed by two subsequent statutes (5 Rich. 2, stat. 1, c.8 and 6 Rich. 2, stat. 1, c.4; *SR* 2:21 and 27), which make provision for those who had lost legal documents in the uprising. Inevitably, this widespread destruction of charters became a pretext for further litigation (e.g., *SCT* 1:395; Grieve 39; Beckerman 226), and in several cases defendants claimed that they had been forced to destroy legal records at the time of the uprising (*SCT* 1:lxiii–lxiv, n. 467).

Walsingham evokes something of the oral mentality of some of the rebels when he records their demand for "a certain ancient charter . . . on which there were capital letters, one gold, the other blue" (*Historia* 1:475) — a demand the prior is (or pretends to be) at a loss to be able to satisfy (cf. Justice 256–58). The particular animus shown in both Kent and Essex toward documents sealed with green wax (Brooks 260) offers an even more vivid illustration, for, as the Harley "Song of the Husbandman," dating from the beginning of the century (*HP* 6–8), shows, the unlettered had long ago learned to recognize the hated Exchequer writ carried by the taxman by the color of its sealing wax:

> ȝet comeþ budeles, wiþ ful muche bost:
> "greyþe me seluer to þe grene wax;
> þou art writen y my writ, þat þou wel wost!"
>
> (37–39)

Walsingham even suggests a more general hostility toward literacy when he reports that "they compelled masters of grammar to swear that they would never in future teach children this skill" (*Historia* 2:9), and concludes, "it was dangerous to be recognized as a cleric, but far more dangerous for anyone to be found with an ink-horn hanging by his side, for such men hardly ever escaped their hands." Similarly, the Anonimalle chronicler reports that John Ball's proclamation against lawyers also extended to their clerks: "toutz qe savoient brief ou lettre escriver" [all who know how to write writs and letters] (144).

These details might seem to imply that opposition to literacy, like opposition to the king's law, was a fundamental element in the revolt—as Susan Crane has put it, "the widespread burning of documents suggests that to the rebels writing appeared innately to be an instrument of oppression" (205). Steven Justice, however, has recently mounted an eloquent challenge to such an argument: "The insurgent animus against the archive," he writes, "was not the revenge of a residually oral culture against the appurtenances of a literacy that was threatening because alien and mysterious" (41). Justice reminds us that many of the insurgents were themselves literate and that most if not all must have understood perfectly well the way letters functioned. While his study provides us with a salutary warning against the too easy assumption that peasant culture in 1381 was uniformly oral or that its attitudes toward literacy were invariably hostile, the widespread destruction of rolls and charters in the revolt remains an inescapable fact. Justice, indeed, comes very close to my own position when he argues that "the rebels believed that *trewþe*—contractual faithfulness; mutual supervision, protection and enforcement; the whole range of rights and responsibilities and penalties properly overseen by the 'common assent and judgment of the whole community'—had been *supplanted* by bureaucratic and judicial writing" (188), though I suspect he might be reluctant to go as far as to claim that the very operation of *trewþe* in this sense was fundamentally incompatible with the spread of a documentary mentality. In any case, Justice's point that, pace Walsingham, it was primarily certain kinds of legal document, not writing in general, that incited peasant fury is well taken.

Rosamond Faith has given a good illustration of just how peasant resentment against specific legal records might be enflamed when she points to the marked increase in the years leading up to the revolt in requests from rural communities for certified copies of Doomsday entries.[26] For peasants resisting the impositions of exploitative landlords one defense had been to show that they were living on "ancient demesne" (that is, lands whose customs were unalterable by virtue of having once belonged to the king), and, naturally enough, those who knew themselves to be in this enviable position looked to find proof of their status in the oldest legal record known to them: "the belief that the king's own tenants—or tenants on lands which had once been the king's—were owed special protection continued among the peasantry, many of whom continued to place their trust in Doomsday Book" (Faith 51). Such trust, however, seems largely to have been misplaced. Even where Doomsday returned favorable answers the lawyers had generally found ways of discounting its significance (50), but in most cases its answers were disappointingly negative (52), often for the remarkable reason that "many of the places involved had been royal property *before* the Conquest, in some cases long before" (54). The most dramatic example given by Faith, though it dates from after the revolt, concerns the tenants of four manors belonging to the abbey of Chertsey (57), whose claim to be living on former royal lands could not be supported by Doomsday; however, modern archivists (better equipped than medieval chancery clerks) can show that these manors were last in royal hands (the hands of King Frithuwold) four hundred years before the Doomsday Book was compiled. The abbot of Chertsey's tenants, and many others who shared their predicament, must have been bitterly frustrated by a literate world whose most authoritative product refused to confirm what they knew in their bones to be true. When local customs could depend on a living memory that went back eight hundred years, no wonder the records that contradicted such memory and the lawyers who defended them drew the wrath of those who still lived by the folklaw and its traditions.

I have said that two of the characteristics of adherence to the folklaw (cohesiveness and ritual parody) are prominent in the Peasants' Revolt. What separated this outbreak from those that preceded it, however, was not only its scale but its metropolitan character. Certainly the majority of the rebels were socially marginal—peasants, hedge-priests, lesser tradesmen, people about whom we can discover little more than their names, finally driven to violence by the increasing oppression of literate authority—but the revolt of 1381 was not marginal in any topographical sense: apart from sporadic outbreaks in the north and west, the main resistance came from Essex and Kent, areas where the king's writ had long run unopposed. Arguably in such areas the burden of central law, unmitigated by local custom, fell most heavily on the least advantaged. Perhaps the lack of the safety valve provided by the greenwood in more remote areas contributed to the seriousness of the southern uprising; but most probably, as J. R. Raftis has hinted (1986, 15), it was the weakening of customary tenure, most pronounced in the south-east, which led to greater acuity on the part of the peasants about the real source of injustice and oppression, and gave their resistance far clearer focus than had earlier been possible.

Evidence is abundant for the tendency of the rebels to form sworn confederacies and fellowships in defiance of authority. The phrase *magna societas* is scatterd thoughout the legal records of proceedings following the rising, a fact which has led some historians to see the peasants as organized into one Great Society. More probably, however, as Rodney Hilton has argued (1973, 215), the records imply a number of "large companies" or "great bands," whose members, as Walsingham describes it, "jungentes dexteras, fidem acceperunt ab invicem et dederunt" [clasping their right hands, gave and received mutual vows of fidelity] (*Historia* 1:471). A particularly full account is given before an inquest in Scarborough: "The accused unanimously swore to maintain each of their individual complaints in common; and, as enemies and rebels to the lord king, they rose in various fellowships and bands against the king and his liegemen, making and wearing a livery of hoods for that purpose" (Dobson 291). As Alan Harding has pointed out, the legal terminology of maintenance and conspiracy, in which such accusations as these are couched, dates back to the end of the thirteenth century, when ironically it was used to describe "the activities of the lords, rather than of the servant class on which [it was] now projected" (1984, 188).

Lest finding traces of carnival riot in the violence of the Peasants' Revolt should look like a trivialization, we might notice that at least one contemporary, the Monk of Westminster, describes how drunken peasants smashed up Archbishop Sudbury's Lambeth manor with cries of "A revel! A revel!" ("et ista perpetrantes . . . 'A Revelle! A Revelle!' exclamarunt") (*Westminster Chronicle* 2). The examples of parodic ritual turned up by the Peasants' Revolt are among the most revealing instances of fourteenth-century folkaw survival to be recorded, perhaps because, as A. W. Smith has suggested, social struggle "is likely to expose to view really deeply felt traditions" (251).[27] We might begin, however, with one ritual which is ironic only in its anachronism. The sworn confederates, whom Walsingham describes demanding the blue and gold charter from his prior, had earlier marched to one of the abbey's manors and granted themselves "seisina" of traditional rights in the fields and woods, "per ramos arborum" [by the branches of trees] (*Gesta* 3:303). That these rebels against the abbey's authority should seek to cloak their actions in the legitimacy of the old folklaw form of "livery of seisin" is particularly revealing. One of the rights the St. Albans peasants had asserted was the right to hunt small game (*warren*) and in token of this ("in signum libertatis et warennae sic adeptae") they then marched back to the abbey with a rabbit fixed on a spear; that folklaw ritual is shading into anti-authoritarian parody here becomes still more obvious when we find them setting up this transfixed creature on the abbey stocks. A similar parading of impaled trophies turns up elsewhere in the

Great Revolt, and at Chelmsford legal instruments were made the object of public mockery: about forty writs were saved from a bonfire of exchequer documents, "to be displayed stuck up on long poles 'en commune chemin'" (Grieve 38).

A far grimmer parody took place at Bury St. Edmunds. There the peasants marched to the stocks holding aloft the transfixed heads of the prior and Sir John Cavendish, chief justice of King's Bench, whom they had captured in nearby villages: "When they arrived there, as a token of the previous friendship between [the two men], and in mockery of them both, they placed their heads set on the points of spears next to one another with the greatest disrespect, as if they were whispering to each other or exchanging kisses. Finally, tiring of such games, they put the two heads back over the stocks" (Walsingham, *Historia* 2:3). The popular hatred which great lords engendered by their courtship of the king's officers is vividly illustrated in this grim Punch-and-Judy show, but that such indignities should be heaped upon the legal representative of a government which displayed the heads of its traitors on pikes is savagely ironic. No doubt John of Gaunt would have been subjected to similar cruel mockery had the peasants caught him at the Savoy; as it was, they resorted to another ancient vehicle of folk parody, the effigy: "Then, so that they might omit no kind of dishonor, but rather inflict every imaginable insult on the duke, they took one of his most valuable garments, called a 'jakke', put it on a spear, and set it up as a mark for their arrows. And when they were unable to do much damage to it by shooting, they took it down and hacked it apart with axes and swords" (Walsingham, *Historia* 1:457). There remains one final instance of ritual parody in Walsingham's account of the revolt, but though in many ways the most interesting, it cannot be fully understood without a brief sketch of its background.

Richard, abbot of the ancient and wealthy Benedictine monastery of St. Albans, was a contemporary of Abbot Peter from the remote and impecunious Cistercian house of Vale Royal, and both men faced similar difficulties with recalcitrant tenants. However, if Richard's tenants were more numerous and better organized, they were pitted against a far more formidable opponent, and one who could afford to retain as his steward a royal justice, John de Cambridge (Maddicott 1978, 30). The focus of the St. Albans dispute was the right of the abbey's tenants to grind malt at home in their own hand-mills as opposed to having to pay to have it ground at the monastic mill, and in 1328 the townsmen had been close to establishing this right when an unfortunate incident put them at the abbot's mercy. A brawl between townsmen and monks resulted in two deaths and offered the abbey the opportunity it needed to bring its legal guns to bear. In 1331 a trailbaston commission, headed by none other than the abbey's own steward, Justice Cambridge, found a number of townsmen guilty of disturbing the king's peace, and the price of their liberty turned out unsurprisingly to include destruction of the hand-mills. The alliance of Abbot Richard and Justice Cambridge—what J. R. Maddicott calls, the "combination of territorial lordship and judicial authority" (1978, 36)—had proved too much even for the burghers of a wealthy town like St. Albans, and in 1332 they were forced to deliver their millstones to the church, "in token of their complete renunciation of their milling-rights" [in signum purae renunciationis multurae suae] (Walsingham, *Gesta* 2:255). True to the folklaw nature of such tokens, Abbot Richard had these millstones cemented into the floor of the monastery parlor, where visiting tenants in years to come might find a permanent reminder of their legal obligations.

Fifty years later, when the St. Albans rebels destroyed the legal records in the abbey muniment room, they also vented their fury on a legal record of a quite different kind: "But meanwhile the rioters, entering the cloisters with their tools, tore up the millstones which had been placed in the floor in the doorway to the visitors' parlor as a record and memorial [*munimentum et memoriam*] of the proceedings between the monastery and its villeins in Abbot Richard's time, carried them out, and delivered them to the common people. And right there they broke them into tiny pieces, giving one piece to everybody, just as the blessed bread is habitually broken and shared out in the parish church; thus, seeing these same fragments among them, they acknowledged themselves, as it were, satisfied in their earlier lawsuit with the abbey" (Walsingham, *Historia* 1:475). Walsingham, of course, had ample motive for making the rebels' actions appear sacrilegious, and the fact that this event took place just two days after the feast of Corpus Christi (see Aston 1994, 29) may have contributed to the particular parodic cast he chooses to give it. Nonetheless, the ritual potency of this remarkable scene cannot be wholly explained away as mere monastic propaganda. In its powerful sense of communion and, above all, in its vivid evocation of a disappearing world of oral custom, this attack on the St. Albans' parlor might serve to epitomize fourteenth-century resistance to the relentless growth of the king's law. If nothing else, its assertion of communal values may help us understand why, when the peasants rose against the lawyers in 1381, John Ball exhorted them to march with "Johan Trewman and alle his felawes" (Sisam 161) and to "stonde manlyche togedyr in trewþe, and helpez trewþe, and trewþe schal helpe ȝowe" (quoted by R. Green 1992, 194). It will come as no surprise to learn that when the rebels resolved to devise a "wache worde" for themselves they should have lighted on the phrase "trew communes" (*Anonimalle* 139).

6

Truth and Treason

It is the will of God that all should guard their little cabins from the treachery of law.
—J. M. Synge, *Playboy of the Western World*

On March 16, 1347, while Edward III's army was shivering beneath the grim walls of Calais, back in England a Norfolk knight named Sir John Gerberge was engaged in a rather different kind of military exploit. From the wording of his later indictment it would be easy to believe that Gerberge had offered a major threat to the stability of Edward's home front ("against his allegiance usurping to himself royal power within the king's realm, the lord king himself being in foreign parts" [quoted by Bellamy 1970, 62]), but the reality proves somewhat different. At Royston, on the Hertfordshire-Cambridgeshire border, Sir John had waylaid a Lincoln merchant called William de Botelisford and held him to ransom for ninety pounds. A little over a month later, near Dunstable, he ambushed and killed a man called William Catesby and his servant.

Sir John Gerberge seems to have been fairly typical of the kind of gentleman-bandit we met in the previous chapter, and we may surmise that had these two incidents occurred on his home territory, near Great Yarmouth, the king's law might have shown some circumspection in its dealings with him. Three years earlier, when William Shareshull had led a commission to Great Yarmouth to investigate Philip de Reppes and 305 others accused of "having ridden with banners displayed . . . taking men and imprisoning them till they made ransoms . . . and perpetrating homicides, arsons, and other evils against the peace," he had prudently decided to offer them the king's pardon, and, in fact, Gerberge and three of the men indicted with him for the Royston and Dunstable ambushes are specifically named in this pardon (*CPR* 1343–45, 323–26). Operating away from his home base and with a criminal record, as it were, Gerberge and his gang were not so lucky the second time, but what makes his case noteworthy is that because he was alleged to have ridden along the king's highway wearing *cote armure* and with a drawn sword in his hand he found himself on trial not for a simple felony but for treason (Bellamy 1970, 61–63).

I very much doubt that when Sir John reached down his armor on that March morning he seriously considered the possibility that he might find himself on trial for treason. His own notion of treason was probably quite different from the one being promulgated by Edward III's justices, and he may very well have been outraged to hear himself called traitor in the court of King's Bench. Like its principal antonym, *truth*, the word *treason* had a far wider range of meanings in the fourteenth century than it does now, and changes in its meaning were proving a source of potential ambiguity for contemporaries. *Treason*, in other words, just like *truth*, may be regarded as a fourteenth-century keyword. Incontrovertible evidence for such ambiguity comes from the preamble to Edward III's Statute of Treasons (1352), the first official attempt to define the offense: "Whereas divers Opinions have been before this Time in what Case Treason shall be said and in what not . . ." (25 Edw. 3, stat. 5, c.2; *SR* 1:319). No doubt, like the parliamentary petitioners who agitated for statutory definition in 1352, Gerberge would have argued that when the king's judges claimed that by wearing his *cote armure* he was levying private war and hence committing an offense against the state, they were giving treason a legal construction far beyond the term's generally accepted meaning. Gerberge's case was in fact one of those which had prompted the petitioners to object against people being arrested "for various offences not generally recognized as treasonable" [desconues a la Commune estre Treison] (*RP* 2:239).

Contemplating the confusing array of offenses that might be called treason before 1352, even the redoubtable Maitland was reduced to describing it as "a crime which [had] a vague circumference, and more than one centre" (P&M 2:503). At the risk of oversimplification I shall here be concerned with just two of its centers: a personal conception of treason in which the offense was committed against someone who had good reason to trust the traitor, often because they were bound to one another by oath, and an institutional view of treason according to which it could only be committed against someone in political authority, particularly the king, his immediate family, or his judicial officers. Given the fact that political relationships were frequently defined by oath in the Middle Ages, this distinction will sometimes be difficult to draw in practice, yet an overall pattern is quite clear. The law, by trying to insist that treason should be defined as any challenge to the king's sovereignty, found itself in conflict with some deeply held traditional ideas about the nature of social order. Our own notion of state treason was evidently still unfamiliar in the mid-fourteenth century, and its subsequent dissemination offers a measure of the success of central authority in its continuing struggle against traditional loyalties — a counterpoint to the dwindling importance of ethical senses of *trouthe*. The story of this dissemination and an analysis of some of its underlying causes will be the main concern of this chapter.

I shall begin by trying to characterize the older concept of personal treason and contrast it with the later institutional treason with which we are more likely to be familiar today; I shall then seek to show how this older concept remained potent in the political life of the late fourteenth century, informing resistance to the autocratic tendencies of Richard's governance in the Merciless Parliament, in the trial of Richard Fitzalan, earl of Arundel, and in the process of the king's deposition; finally, I hope to be able to show how these two rival concepts of treason provide the focus for a struggle between two political orders, one essentially oral and, even in the late fourteenth century, still retaining traces of an older reciprocal mode of association characterized by the oath, the other resolutely documentary and striving to exercise authority from above through its control of the bureaucratic machinery of the state. This struggle was inevitably to resolve itself into a constitutional battle over the nature and sources of positive law.

Concepts of Treason

Let us start with an example of treason on which both Gerberge and his judges would have had no difficulty agreeing. Ten years after the Battle of Hastings, Roger, earl of Hereford, and Ralph, earl of East Anglia, approached Earl Waltheof of Northumbria to discover whether he was prepared to join them in a rebellion against King William. Here is how Orderic Vitalis describes Waltheof's reply:

> Every man in every nation must keep complete faith with his own lord. King William has received my oath as between lord and vassal, and given me his own niece in marriage that I might remain ever faithful to him. He has also bestowed on me a rich earldom and numbered me among his close companions. How can I be unfaithful to such a prince, unless I should wish entirely to betray my good faith? I am known throughout many regions and great would be my dishonour, alas, were I publicly to be reputed an impious traitor (*proditor sacrilegus*). No good song is ever sung of the traitor. All nations curse the apostate and the traitor like a wolf. . . . English law punishes the traitor with beheading and deprives all his children of their proper inheritance. May my honour never be stained with wicked treason (*proditione nefaria*), and may such shameful infamy never be broadcast through the world on my account! (*English Lawsuits* 17).

Such sentiments, recast in alliterative verse, would not have been out of place in the mouth of a Wiglaf or a Byrhtwold, and they clearly spring from the ethos of the old Germanic comitatus — an ethos that bound lord and man in a nexus of reciprocal obligations knotted with oaths of loyalty (see Magennis). There seems, in actuality, to have been more than a whiff of the old Anglo-Saxon *hæleð* about Waltheof: he had at first fought stubbornly against the conqueror and the fame of his capture of York from the Normans in 1069 was to live long in popular memory (Scot 179); his subsequent marriage to one of William's kinswomen was no doubt intended to cement his reconciliation with the new king, but the Hyde chronicler's dark forebodings about this union make it sound not unlike the ill-fated wedding of Ingeld and Freawaru (*English Lawsuits* 21).

However much Waltheof's idea of treason may have looked backward to a heroic past, it was still very much alive over two hundred years later when Edward I sent Sir Simon Frazer, one of Robert Bruce's captains, to the scaffold for treason in 1306. The author of one of the Harley lyrics (*HP* 14–21) employs the archaic term *lord-swyke* to describe Frazer's crime (162),[1] and represents the man himself, like Bruce's other supporters, as a perjurer:

> To þe kyng edward hii fasten huere fay;
> fals was here foreward so forst is in may,
> þat sonne from þe southward wypeþ away.
> (41–43)

The fact that Frazer "wes four siþe for-swore" is plainly seen as the cause of his undoing — "& þat him brohte to grounde" (174–76) — and the poet regards it as only fitting that Frazer should have been paraded through the streets of London with a garland of green leaves on his head (green was the color traditionally associated with falsehood), "ffor he shulde ben yknowe . . . for treytour" (118–20). Whatever incipient notions of state treason may have been in Edward I's mind when he ordered the execution, the popular imagination clearly still saw Frazer's crime as primarily the personal betrayal of an oath of allegiance. As we shall see, treason from this perspective was only incidentally the hierarchical offense of a subject against the king; it was first and foremost the breach of a mutual agreement. As one feudal law code (ca. 1200) puts it, "for the law . . . holds that the king owes as much faith to his liegeman and his liegewoman as they owe to him" (*Assises* 625–26).

Wherever treason meant personal betrayal, the greater the debt of gratitude owed, the more heinous the treason. The obvious corollary to this, however, was that kings like Heremod in *Beowulf* who gave their followers no cause for gratitude had little reason to expect their blind devotion. As long as treason remained an offense against the individual not the institution, one might always seek to justify it on the grounds that the individual had by some transgression or default forfeited the right to continued loyalty. The Anglo-Saxon oath of fidelity (*hyldað*) contained a quite clear exceptions clause, allowing retainers ample grounds for withdrawing from a contract they no longer felt to be mutually honored: "wið þam ðe he me healde, swa ic earnian wille, ⁊ eall þæt læste, þæt uncer formæl wæs, þa ic to him gebeah ⁊ his willan geceas" [so long as he stands by me as I shall merit, and performs everything that was in our understanding when I submitted to him and accepted his will] (*Swer.* 1; Liebermann 1:396). As the *Leges Henrici Primi* make clear, such exceptions clauses were no empty formality: "If a lord deprives his man of his land, or his fee by virtue of which he is his man, or if he deserts him without cause in his hour of mortal need, he may forfeit his lordship over him" (ch. 43.8; 152–53). The hold-oath evidently defined a bilateral commitment which imposed binding conditions on both parties; as such, it stands in marked contrast to the kind of public loyalty oath a modern citizen might be required to swear. By Edward I's day the Anglo-Saxon hold-oath, as we shall see, had turned into the far less egalitarian Anglo-Norman oath of fealty, yet the ethos to which it attested still lingered on in the popular imagination.[2]

The swearing of the hold-oath would have been accompanied by the solemn ritual of *manrede* (later, the Norman act of homage),[3] but that the rupture of the kind of bond it created was perfectly possible is confirmed by the provision of a parallel set of rituals for dissolving homage—the *diffidatio*. Where, for instance, homage was symbolized by the public *traditio* of a rod, a *festuca*, its renunciation led naturally enough to the public throwing down or breaking of this rod (*exfestucatio*)—a gesture which can be traced back to the Homeric age (Havelock 1978, 129–30) and which could still be observed in France as late as 1602 (Ligeron and Petitjean 292). Marc Bloch has demonstrated conclusively that such acts constituted a recognized legal formality that was intended to obviate the shameful charge of treason. He cites a scene from *Raoul de Cambrai* where Bernier, one of Raoul's squires, is finally driven by his master's assaults on him and his family (they have included burning his mother to death in a nunnery) to renounce his homage (1912, 199); Bernier throws down three hairs from the ermine cloak he is wearing with the words, "Vassal, I defy you! Never say that I have betrayed you" [Vassal! je vos desfi! / Ne dites mie je vos aie traï] (*Raoul* lines 2138–39). That Raoul's own squire should address his former master as 'vassal' may look ironic,[4] but we should not take this to suggest that such formal 'defiance', in its old sense, was no more than a legally sanctioned vehicle for challenging authority. Bloch cites other instances where it is the lord not the vassal who performs the act of exfestucation (1912, 196), and there are recorded instances of actual kings—Henry III, for instance (P&M 1:303)—defying their own subjects—clear evidence of the originally bilateral nature of the ceremony of homage and the obligations it entailed.

What distinguished *diffidatio* from *proditio* was precisely what distinguished manslaughter from murder, or robbery from larceny, the fact that it was a public act, performed with no trace of the dangerous concealment that threatened the very foundations of the folklaw. "When the vassal renounced his homage," writes Bloch, "the throwing down of the staff, it seems, could only take place in the presence of the rejected lord" (1912, 196). The public nature of the *diffidatio* might help to explain the otherwise puzzling history of William the Conqueror's subsequent dealings with Earl Waltheof as Orderic Vitalis relates it. After the failure of the rebellion, he tells us, Earl Ralph fled to Brittany, abandoning his English fiefs to the king, and Earl Roger spent the rest of his life in a Norman prison, whereas the noble Waltheof, whose only crime had been to agree to a terrible oath ("conjuratione terribili") not to reveal the conspiracy he had refused to join, was beheaded. This punishment is all the more surprising in light of the usual treatment of highborn rebels at this time: as Maitland says, "for two centuries after the Conquest, the frank, open rebellions of the great folk were treated with a clemency which, when we look back to it through intervening ages of blood, seems wonderful" (P&M 2: 506); indeed, despite the civil unrest under Stephen, John, and Henry III no other earl was executed for treason on English soil for more than two hundred years (Bellamy 1970, 23). While the chronicler may have underestimated the extent of Waltheof's involvement in the rebellion (but see Scot 205), or while the apparent discrepancy between the punishments meted out to Roger and Waltheof may simply have been due to Norman realpolitik, the possibility remains that William had feared Waltheof's secret concurrence more than Roger's open defiance and had regarded it as by far the graver crime.[5]

Thus, to the idea that treason was the dissolution of a personal bond of allegiance, generally sealed with an oath, the folklaw added the important qualification that such dissolution will be treasonable only when it is covert. Beaumanoir—who grants to private war between gentlemen, at least where the proper formalities have been observed, far more scope than an English commentator might have done—makes stealth the prime attribute of treason: "Anyone wishing to make a verbal declaration of war on another should not speak equivocally or covertly, but rather plainly and openly so that he to whom the declaration is spoken or sent may know that he must be ready to defend himself. Any other course of action would be treason" (ch. 59.1675; 2:358). He goes on to say that a formal defiance must be made in the presence of witnesses, so that, if necessary, their testimony can later be adduced to refute the charge of treason" — "car en cel cas il est mestiers de prouver la desfiance pour soi oster de la traïson" (2:359). Indeed, so important is this element for Beaumanoir that he is prepared to argue that murder (that is, surreptitious killing) is always treason, though treason, of course, is not always murder (ch. 30.827; 1:430).

By this standard Sir John Gerberge's crime bears little resemblance to treason. Not only was he breaking no oath, so far as we know, to either Botelisford or Catesby, but by riding along the highway with drawn sword and wearing *cote armure* he was behaving in a manner that was anything but surreptitious. Of course, as his indictment makes clear, the justices of King's Bench regarded his behavior as treason against the king, not against Botelisford or Catesby, but this hardly helps things. Neither of Gerberge's victims, it seems, was a royal officer or active on the king's business at the time of the assaults, so his actions could not have been construed as, even indirectly, a threat to the king himself, and Gerberge might properly have wondered how his oath of allegiance to the king proscribed offenses against private citizens. True, he was in breach of the king's peace, but then so was everyone convicted of a felony, or even a trespass, at this time.

We are left finally with the argument that in waging private war without his king's permission Gerberge was breaking the law of arms and was thus guilty of treasonable lese majesty (Bellamy 1970, 62–63). Such a charge might indeed have been leveled against him had he ridden at the head of a body of armed men with banners unfurled and with cannon or siege engines in his train, as contemporary manuals of chivalry make clear.[6] The poet of *Wynnere and Wastoure* describes private citizens usurping the king's prerogative by leading just such a "rowte in his rewme so ryall to thinke" (line d128) — behavior he appears to regard as treasonable even under English customary law:

> For this es the vsage here and euer schall worthe
> If any beryn be so bolde with banere for to ryde
> Withinn þe kyngdome riche bot the kynge one
> That he schall losse the londe and his lyfe aftir.
> (130–33)

But Gerberge's "rowte" appears to have consisted of no more than a handful of servants,[7] and in any case there is an enormous gulf between displaying banners and merely wearing one's *cote armure* or between dragging siege engines about and simply holding a naked sword in one's hand. Quite apart from the question of whether such a case should not properly have been decided by the Court of Chivalry rather than King's Bench, it seems clear that the king's judges were here conniving in a blatant legal fiction in order to extend their own authority. By doing so, however, they were putting the whole system of traditional loyalties in jeopardy, and in 1352, as we have seen, Parliament proved that it was not prepared to allow servants of the crown to accuse a man of treason merely because he had fetched down his armor to teach a recalcitrant neighbor a lesson.

The Statute of Treasons, as Bellamy has shown, came into being "as a direct result of the royal judges trying to extend the common law of treason" (1970, 100), and thus represents a deliberate attempt by Parliament to restrict this dangerous growth of royal prerogative. Had it been passed a few years earlier, it might well have saved Gerberge's skin: "And in the event a man of this land should ride, with arms displayed or covered, together with armed men, against another in order to kill him, rob him, or hold him to ransom, it is not the intention of the king and his council that treason should be judged in such a case, but rather felony or trespass according to the traditional usage of the law of the land" (*RP* 3:239). Why Edward III should have agreed to this retrograde piece of legislation is uncertain for it was plainly in his own interest for his judges to continue to expand the scope of treason: not only would this have provided the crown with increased powers to deal with local disorder, but it would have swelled royal coffers with the revenues that came from forfeiture of the traitor's lands, for in the case of a simple felony such lands were merely forfeited (the technical term is *escheated*) to the felon's lord (P&M 1:351–52). Probably Edward was willing to forgo these advantages in order to keep Parliament happy; its cooperation was vital if he wished to continue financing his expensive French wars. Whatever his motives, he bequeathed a dangerous legacy to his grandson.

It would hardly be an exaggeration to claim that the overriding political issue in the last two decades of the fourteenth century was the legal definition of treason. In Richard's questions to the judges, in the actions of the Lords Appellant, in the response to Thomas Haxey's petition, in the fall of Gloucester, Arundel, and Warwick, in the quarrel between Hereford and Norfolk, and finally in the process of deposition, the issue of treason is omnipresent. We shall even find traces of it in the Great Revolt of 1381. It is a comparatively straightforward matter to take the wording of the Statute of Treasons and measure the actions of Richard and his enemies against it; to adumbrate the struggle between a parliamentary definition of treason (embodied in the original 1352 statute) and a royalist one (presented in Richard's 1397 revision) as one between those who saw the sanction of forfeiture as a way of swelling royal coffers and keeping the opposition in line and those who saw this as an intolerable threat to baronial independence; to consider the narrow significance of terms like *accroaching*, *compassing*, and *misprising* as weapons in the lawyer's armory; to weigh the merits and limitations of various actions like *attainder*, *impeachment*, and *appeal* in the prosecution of treason cases; to watch, in other words, the events of Richard's reign unfold through the eyes of a modern legal or constitutional historian. But what of the other side? What did laypeople mean by the word traitor, and are we really to believe that the popular understanding of treason was entirely irrelevant to the political crises of Richard II's reign?

However the constitutional historian might wish to gloss it, no literary scholar would have much difficulty defining the word *traitor* at this time. It meant primarily someone who had betrayed a trust, particularly the kind of trust that might be expected to exist between members of the same family or household. As Chaucer puts it in "The Parson's Tale," "he that wikked conseil yeveth is a traytour. For he deceyveth hym that trusteth in hym" (line 639). Much the same conception of treason had been found in two legal treatises written a century or so before Chaucer. *Britton* had said that "treason consists of any mischief which a person knowingly does, or procures to be done, to anyone to whom he pretends to be a friend," and had offered as an example: "as by procuring the death on anyone who has allied himself with him [*se affiera de luy*]" (bk. 1, ch. 9.2; 1:40). Similarly, *The Mirror of Justices* stresses that "treason can only be committed between those allied, and they may be allied by blood, affinity, homage, oath, or by hire" (21). Most of the situations in which the word was used by the Ricardian poets conform to these definitions. Thus, in *Sir Gawain and the Green Knight* one reason for the hero's discouragement of his hostess's advances is his fear of being "traytor" to her husband (line 1775), and in "The Reeve's Tale" the word is used of someone who betrays a host's trust by seducing his daughter (line 4269). In Gower's "Tale of the False Bachelor," a servant who marries a sultan's daughter on the strength of a secret token stolen from his master is described as a traitor (*CA* 2:2762), and there is a similar instance of the word applied to a dishonest servant in "The Merchant's Tale" (line 1785).

Though the breaking of a specific oath of allegiance seems not to have been an inevitable element in this personal treason (no such oath would have bound close blood relatives to one another, for instance), it clearly helped define the offense where there was otherwise room for doubt and certainly increased its seriousness. Thus, "The Parson's Tale" describes priests who break "hire avow of chastitee, whan they receyved the ordre" as "the special traytours of God" (lines 892–94), and in "The Knight's Tale" Palamon interprets his cousin Arcite's interest in Emily, not obviously in itself a betrayal of their cousinship, as a breach of their compact as brothers in arms:

"It nere," quod he, "to thee no greet honour,
For to be fals, ne for to be traitour
To me, that am thy cosyn and thy brother
Ysworn ful depe, and ech of us til oother."

(1129–32)

A particularly interesting example occurs in *The Earl of Toulouse* where the hero, at war with the Emperor Dyoclysyan, captures one of the emperor's men, Sir Trylabas, but offers to release him without ransom on condition that he arrange for the earl to see the empress:

Than answeryd Syr Trylabas,
"Yn that couenaunt in þys place
My trowthe y plyght thee;
Y schall holde thy forward gode
To brynge the, wyth mylde mode,
In syght hur for to see."

(217–22)

When Trylabas, upon his release, suggests to the empress that they should use the earl's visit as an opportunity to set a trap for him, she accuses him of contemplating "tratory"—specifically, "syn thou haste made hym othe" (line 297). Since Trylabas is assisting his country's enemy by arranging the tryst, this incident pits institutional treason against personal treason, but the poet leaves us in no doubt as to which he sees as the graver offense (cf. 413–20).

It may seem that the distinction I am drawing between institutional and personal treason is little different from the one to which lawyers refer when they talk of high (or great) and petty treason. The first official appearance of this pair of terms is as late as the Parliament of 1423 (Bellamy 1970, 229), though the term *haute traisoun* alone had been used by the appellants in the Merciless Parliament of 1388. Edward III's Statute of Treasons, however, if it had not employed these actual terms, had certainly drawn a distinction between two kinds of treason. The first involved crimes against the king, his immediate family, his judicial officers, and the symbols of his power, and resulted in forfeiture of the traitor's lands to the crown. The second resulted only in forfeiture to the lord, as with any simple felony: "moreover, there is another kind of treason, as for instance when a servant kills his master, a wife her husband, or a layman or priest kills a prelate to whom he owes faith and obedience; and such manner of treason confers the forfeited escheats on the traitor's own feudal lord" (*RP* 2:239). Though there may be no contemporary authority for labeling these two classes of treason *high* and *petty*,[8] such terminology was generally employed by later commentators and has been adopted by most legal historians. The real question, however, is whether all fourteenth-century ideas about treason can be adequately classified under these two headings.

In the twelfth century the fundamental feudal crime had not been treason at all, but felony. The French term *felonie* was originally used exclusively to designate a breach of feudal obligations and only later did it develop, at least in England and Normandy, into "a general name for the worst, the utterly 'bootless' crimes" (P&M 2:466), those that might be prosecuted at the king's suit. In the early twelfth century, "mere common crime, however wicked and base, mere wilful homicide, or theft, is not a felony; there must be some breach of that faith and trust which ought to exist between lord and man" (P&M 1:304; cf. Goebel 249–50). Something of this old sense still survives as late as *Havelok*, where the poet uses the word to characterize the betrayal of the rightful heirs to the thrones of England and Denmark; by this date, however, it had to be reinforced by the synonym *tresoun* if it was not to be misunderstood:

> he woren with wronge ledde
> Jn here youþe, with trecherie,
> With tresoun, and with felonye.
> (2988–90; cf.444 and 1091)

As the meaning of *felony*, a word "expressive to the common ear of all that was most hateful to God and man" (P&M 2:466), became generalized to cover all crimes in which there was an element of underhandedness (murder, rape, larceny, arson),[9] there seems to have grown up a need to be able to distinguish those made particularly abhorrent by virtue of the fact that they had violated some sacred trust (in much the same way that we now feel the need to distinguish between simple and aggravated assault, or between first- and second-degree murder), and for this purpose the law borrowed another French word, *traïson* — a term that appears to have originated in the early twelfth century as a "semilearned synonym" for *felonie* (Dessau 193).

A good illustration of how this might have worked in practice is offered by a case in the *Placita Corone* (21–22) in which a servant, said to have been particularly trusted by his master, is accused of feloniously and traitorously wounding him ("com felon et tretre"). There is little about this case formally to distinguish it from any other felony trial: the servant's plea is that he had acted in self-defense after his master had given him so savage a beating for staying out all night with a girl that he feared for his life ("je dotay sa felonie"), and he appeals to the jury to decide whether such an act should be judged treason or not ("si un tel fet seit a juger pur treyson ou non"). The jury returns a guilty verdict (though not simply on the basis of the wounding but also because he is found to have robbed his master), and he is sentenced to be hanged *com felon traytre*. If the fact that this particular felony had been aggravated by treason meant that the servant's punishment was made more severe in some way (e.g., by drawing), we are not told about it (cf. W. Barron). Though it is not a murder trial, this case seems superficially to correspond to the kind of 'petty' treason described by the 1352 statute, "quant un Servant tue son Mestre." There is however a significant difference.

What makes the *Placita Corone* case treasonable is that it involves a breach of trust ("because he had more trust and faith in him [pur creance et pur feaute] than in any other of his servants"); *treason* is here, as it were, restoring to *felony* associations it had lost in the course of becoming generalized to cover any unamendable crime. But 'petty' treason, as Edward III's statute defines it, is clearly a hierarchic offense, a crime committed exclusively against one's social superiors. I suspect that in fact those who drafted the statute had not really intended to define 'petty' treason at all, merely to give examples of certain crimes, commonly called treason, that fell outside the scope of institutional treason; nevertheless, the way in which they characterized the offense is symptomatic of the growing authoritarianism of the law. As Paul Strohm has written, this development "recognizes the political character of . . . ostensibly non-political institutions, asserting that the master in his shop and the husband in his household and the priest in his parish participate analogically and symbolically in the regality of the king" (1992, 125).

The *Chanson de Roland*'s account of the struggle between "Carles li reis, nostre emper[er]e magnes" (line 1) and the archetypal traitor Ganelon leaves us with so powerful an impression of ultimate royal justice that we are apt to forget that even in the high Middle Ages its authoritarian version of the feudal equation did not go unchallenged. *Raoul de Cambrai*, whose bloody history exemplifies the moral that "a bad king brings disgrace on many a fine man" [par malvais roi est mains frans hom honnis] (line 650), is only one of a number of *chansons de geste* belonging to the "cycle des barons révoltés" that treat a vassal's defiance of an unjust lord with open sympathy (see Calin 113–43). Several examine the question of whether the vassal owes absolute loyalty to an unjust overlord; some explicitly describe instances of "feudal betrayal in which the *loiaus om*, the faithful vassal, fights against the traitor" (Dessau 194); and one particular group (which includes *Ogier le Danois* and *Girart de Roussillon*, as well as *Raoul de Cambrai*) portrays "treason committed by a lord . . . with what is incontestably a juridical motivation" (Dessau 194). One English work to convey some sense of this ethos is the Anglo-Norman *Fouke le*

Fitz Waryn, which survives only in a prose epitome (ca. 1330) of a late-thirteenth-century verse romance. Fouke falls foul of King John when the king grants a rival one of the Fitz Waryn estates without holding a proper hearing, and his speech of defiance makes very clear the reciprocal nature of its view of vassalage: "Sire roy, vous estes mon lige seignour, e a vous su je lïé par fealté tant come je su en vostre service, e tan come je tienke terres de vous; e vous me dussez meyntenir en resoun, e vous me faylez de resoun e commune ley, e unqe ne fust bon rey qe deneya a ces franke tenauntz ley en sa court; pur quoi je vous renke vos homages" [Sir King, you are my liege lord, to whom I am bound in fealty as long as I remain your man and your tenant, but you, who should support my rights, have failed me both in right and in common law. No good king ever denied justice to his free tenants in his own court, and therefore I withdraw your homage from you] (*Fouke* 24). Though, as we saw in the *Leges Henrici Primi*, unlawful disseisin was regarded as an adequate reason for a vassal to renounce his homage, Fouke here lays far more emphasis on John's subsequent failure to allow him to defend his right at law; interestingly, there is a similar emphasis on failure to provide justice in a mid-thirteenth-century list of six situations which justify a vassal's defiance found among the laws of the Latin Kingdom of Jerusalem (*Assises* 1:442).

As long as political relationships could still be viewed as essentially contractual, arising from "a legal bond with mutual rights and duties," people would continue to expect what Walter Ullmann calls "some kind of equilibrium between lord and vassal" (1966, 64). While we may not be surprised to find this sense of equilibrium articulated in early texts like Glanvill (9.4; 107), we should note that it can still be clearly recognized in legal treatises from the end of the thirteenth century. Philippe de Beaumanoir, who completed his *Coutumes de Beauvaisis* in 1283, expresses it succinctly: "we say, and our custom holds it true, that for as long as the vassal owes his lord faith and loyalty according to his homage, so too the lord owes them to his vassal" (ch. 61.1735; 2:383). Bracton had made a very similar point (2:233). Consequently it was still possible at this period to conceive of treason as a crime committed by a superior against an inferior: the author of *The Mirror of Justices* argues that it is quite as possible for a master to betray his servant as the other way about: "Treason can only be committed between those allied. . . . And just as one of the allies, or persons related by blood or marriage, can commit this offence of treason against the other, so *vice versa* [en mesme la manere se fet pecchie al revers]. . . . And in the same way that a person who takes my property and is seised thereof can commit treason against me, in like manner can I offend against him" (21).[10] Though this personal and reciprocal concept of treason, so foreign to the modern imagination, was increasingly threatened in the fourteenth century by the efforts of a centralized bureaucracy to entrench the rights of an impersonal crown, I shall be arguing that we can still find traces of it even as late as the constitutional upheavals of Richard II's reign. There is at any rate no dearth of evidence that its older associations continued to cling to the word *treason* in popular usage throughout the Ricardian period.

We have seen that those who had betrayed the trust of a fellow member of their household, family, or affinity, particularly where such trust had been reinforced with oaths, were regularly referred to as traitors in Ricardian usage, but much more significant are those cases where the treason is committed against those who are demonstrably lower in the established hierarchy than the traitors themselves. Thus, in "The Man of Law's Tale" Donegild's plotting against her daughter-in-law, Constance, is described as "traitorie" (line 781), while *Gamelyn* provides a similar description of an elder brother's falsehood toward a younger: "the knight þoughte on tresoun and Gamelyn on noon" (line 165). Even more striking is Pandarus's fear, in the third book of *Troilus and Criseyde*, that he is acting as a traitor toward Criseyde, for not only does the treason here run counter to a hierarchy based on seniority but also to one based on gender:

> But wo is me, that I, that cause al this,
> May thynken that she is my nece deere,
> And I hire em, and traitour eke yfeere!
>
> (3.271–73)

So, too, in *Ywain and Gawain*, where a husband who has broken a solemn promise to his wife is called in public "Traytur untrew and trowthles" (1626) by her maid, and in *The Legend of Good Women*, where the word *traitor* is regularly used of men who have abandoned women to whom they have sworn to be true (R. Green 1988, 15–17). In the feudal context, we find a clear example as late as Malory, where King Mark with his "groundyn glayue" is described as a "fals traitour" to his own vassal Sir Tristram (1:562). A country in which a king could be still described as a traitor to one of his own subjects had not yet lost all memory of a time when mutual oaths of loyalty might be imagined as an effective curb on the arbitrary exercise of political authority.

A recognition of the broader semantic field of *treason* in the vernacular may help us to understand what the peasants of Essex meant by accusing Sir Robert Bealknap, chief justice of Common Pleas, of being a "traitour al roy et al roialme" in his own courtroom in 1381 (*Anonimalle* 135). No doubt, like others who objected to the presence of traitors on the bench (such as the woman who in 1357 accosted another justice of Common Pleas on his way to court, calling him "a false and faithless traitor to the king himself, fit to be drawn and hanged" [*SCKB* 3:cxxxvi]), they were turning their own frustration with the systemic inequities of the king's law against those whose job it was to administer it, but the form taken by their denunciations is revealing nonetheless. When peasants called Bealknap a traitor it can hardly have been for his part in carrying out the king's will and defending the authority of the crown; it must rather have been for some imagined breach of trust or supposed failure to uphold an obligation. The most obvious grounds for making such an accusation must surely have been that he was felt to have broken his solemn oath of office.[11] Evidence for this kind of thinking, as so often when we search for an expression of the conservative position, is to be found in *The Mirror of Justices*.

The author of *The Mirror of Justices* begins his list of those offenses punishable by death with the crime of *laesa majestas*, but (once we are past a conventional enough opening paragraph in which offenses against the king's person and his family are listed) it is a *laesa majestas* that few Roman lawyers would have recognized (cf. Lear 3–48). After a brief excursus on crimes against the majesty of God, such as heresy and sorcery, he turns immediately to its earthly manifestation: "Item, of those who commit the crime of *laesa majestas* [le crim de majeste], and first of perjury" (16). Perjury, it soon appears, is at the heart of everything that we should characterize as political or judicial corruption, and hence strikes at the very basis of the king's regality: "For all those who perjure themselves by betraying their faith to the king commit this sin, as do ministers of the king who have sworn to do right and perjure themselves on any point" (16).[12] Though the author nowhere employs the actual word *treason* in his characterization of *laesa majestas* (as we have seen, he defines treason itself in exclusively personal terms), this is evidently the nearest he can come to imagining what we have been calling institutional treason. But it is plainly institutional treason seen from below, not above. If there is irony in the fact that, while the 1352 statute defines even petty treason as a hierarchical offense, the author of *The Mirror of Justices* should try to represent high treason in such personal terms, the response given by the Kentish rebels to the king's messengers in 1381 is no less ironic. Asked for the cause of their dissatisfaction, these men, whom the state clearly regarded as archetypal traitors, replied that "they had risen in order to save [the king] and to destroy those who were traitors to him and to his realm" (*Anonimalle* 138). Their cry was to be echoed by Kentish insurgents seventy years later: "and we were disposyd azenst oure Soveraigne lorde, as God forbede, what myzt his traytours helpe hym?" ("Declaration" 267). As we shall see, even the Lords Appellant may have shared this viewpoint.

The Mirror of Justices' list of those whose perjury threatens the king's majesty is a long one and contains some whose offense hardly seems serious enough to warrant the death penalty (such as sheriffs "who overburden their hosts with too many folk, horses, or dogs"), but we shall scarcely be surprised to learn that the author includes corrupt judges in his list: "Into perjury against the king fall all those officers who refuse plaintiffs remedial writs of possession, attaint, or other writs of common form, or otherwise delay or sell right, and those who wrongfully delay or disturb right judgments and their execution, and all those who wrongfully execute tortious judgments, and all those who exercise their privileges and franchises tortiously or excessively" (18). Some of these offenses he may indeed have regarded as capital ones, for he later lists, with evident relish, the names of forty-four judges whom, he claims, the good King Alfred had "hanged as homicides for their false judgements" in a single year (166). In popular usage, the word *traitor*, as we have seen, was virtually synonymous with *perjurer*, and it does not take a great deal of imagination to see how disappointed litigants might come to feel that the judge who ruled against them had been a traitor to his oath of office. Some sense of the powerful animus such a feeling could engender is conveyed by Walsingham's description of the parody of a traitor's death inflicted on Sir John Cavendish, chief justice of King's Bench, by the angry peasants of Bury St. Edmunds in 1381.

Treason in 1397

Bearing in mind this vernacular sense of the word *traitor*, let us now turn to the trial of Richard Fitzalan, earl of Arundel, before Parliament in 1397. Here, if anywhere, we should expect to find the accused having to defend himself against a statutory definition of his crime, yet, even though Richard had prudently got Parliament to modify the 1352 statute in anticipation of the trial (Bellamy 1970, 114), the game seems to have been played out under a far older set of rules. In order to understand it fully, however, we must first trace the history of King Richard's troubled relationship with Arundel back to the previous decade.

When Arundel, in the spring of 1384, had complained before Parliament of the evil government of the kingdom, he provoked an extraordinary reaction in his young sovereign: "the king flushed at these words and flew into a great rage; looking upon the earl with a grim expression, he said to him, 'if you are claiming that this is my fault, and are laying the blame for the evil state of the kingdom at my door, you are lying in your teeth. You can go to the devil!' Hearing this, they all fell silent, and not one of the onlookers dared say a word" (*Westminster Chronicle* 68). By 1397, no doubt because of the course taken by the political events of 1386–1388, this oversensitivity to the slightest hint of criticism had grown into a morbid obsession with the threat of treason which was effectively gagging any formal attempt to offer him advice. Thomas Haxey's petition concerning the excessive expense of the royal household, for instance, elicited the following remarkable recognition of the king's prerogative from a particularly submissive Parliament: "It was declared that if anyone at all, whatever his status or condition, should encourage or incite the commons of Parliament, or any one else, to remedy or reform anything which concerns our person, our rule, or our regality, he should, and shall, be held a traitor" (*RP* 3:408). Such a statement, going far beyond any possible interpretation of the 1352 definition of what I have called institutional treason, is of a piece with what Nigel Saul has recently represented as a conscious campaign by Richard in the 1390s to invest himself with "the mystique of majesty and to set him apart from lesser mortals" (1995, 863) in the manner of his continental counterparts.

Any insult offered to Richard's majesty by Haxey's petition in 1397 was, however, trivial compared to the threat that had been mounted against the king's authority by the "great and continual council" instituted by Parliament in 1386 to supervise the affairs of state—a council on which Arundel, along with the duke of Gloucester, had been a prominent member. Richard's reaction to the setting up of this commission was covertly to submit a set of written questions to a panel of common-law judges in a transparent attempt to get them to declare its supporters traitors:

> In the first place they were asked, Whether that new statute and ordinance and commission made and promulgated in that last Parliament held at Westminster was derogatory to the regality and prerogative of our lord the king?
>
> To which question they unanimously replied, That it was derogatory, especially as it had been contrary to the king's will. . . .
>
> Item, they were asked, What punishment do those deserve who compelled or induced the king to consent to the making of the said statute, ordinance, and commission?
>
> To which question they unanimously replied, That they deserved to be punished as traitors (*ut proditores*). (Chrimes 376–77)

As soon as the existence of this set of questions and answers came to light in the late summer of 1387, a showdown between Richard and the leading commissioners became inevitable: it triggered, in S. B. Chrimes's words, "a race to see whose heads should roll first" (386) and led directly to the muster at Harringay, the battle of Radcot Bridge, and the triumph of the five appellants over the king's advisers in the Merciless Parliament of 1388.

Predictably enough, among those condemned to death by this Parliament were Sir Robert Tresilian, chief justice of King's Bench, and a lawyer called

John Blake, who seem between them to have been responsible for framing the actual questions (the remaining judges who had sat on the panel, almost the entire senior judiciary, were banished to Ireland). That the appellants' charge against these men was one of treason may not have seemed as preposterous to their contemporaries as it apparently did to Chrimes (387), for their offense might well have looked to many like a version of that *laesa majestas* expounded by the author of *The Mirror of Justices* almost a hundred years earlier (cf. Favent 10). Moreover, Richard had certainly not helped things by trying to keep his approach to the judges secret, so the appellants were able to claim that Blake and the others had "imagined and compassed" (the formula in retrospect looks ironic) that the commissioners "should have been taken and murdered falsely, traitorously, and wickedly" (*RP* 3:240). From the point of view of Gloucester, Arundel, and the other appellants, the attempt of Blake and his master Tresilian to suggest that those who had helped set up the commission were traitors had been fittingly answered by showing how the judges were, in a still widely recognized sense of the term, no less traitors themselves.

By the time Richard felt strong enough to bring Arundel to trial in 1397, then, there was already a long history of personal animosity between the two men,[13] shaped in part by their conflicting understanding of the nature of treason. According to Adam of Usk, who was an eyewitness at the trial, Arundel was charged with four counts of treason: for establishing the commission of 1386, for holding a Parliament to the prejudice of the king, for sentencing the courtiers James Berners and Simon Burley to death, and for raising an army against the king at Harringay (12–13). The actual trial procedure, that of appeal by eight nobles, was a curiously archaic one for Richard to have chosen under the circumstances, if only because, as Plucknett has pointed out, "impeachments and appeals were essentially opposition weapons" (1953, 154); quite possibly, Richard, never one to waste the opportunity for a theatrical gesture, intended it as a deliberate parody of the parliamentary appeals in which Arundel himself had participated nine years earlier.[14] In the event, however, Arundel managed to redirect the focus of the actual trial, such as it was, away from the charges prepared against him, and onto a quite different kind of treason.

Here is Adam of Usk's eyewitness account of the courtroom battle between Arundel and his accusers:

> When the articles had been expounded to the earl, he, firmly denying that he had ever been a traitor, claimed the protection of the pardon granted to him earlier, protesting that he would never forgo his king's indulgence (*gratia*). But the duke of Lancaster said to him, "Traitor! that pardon has been revoked." The earl answered, "Indeed you lie! I have never been a traitor!" Then the duke said, "Why did you procure yourself a

pardon then?" The earl replied, "To silence the tongues of jealous rivals like you. And as far treasons are concerned, you are surely more in need of pardon than I am."[15]

Then the king said to him, "You must answer the appeals." The earl replied, "I see well enough that those men brandishing their appeals are accusing me of treason. And indeed they are all liars! I have never been a traitor! I continue to claim the protection of my pardon, which you granted me within the last six years on your own initiative, and after you had come of age and were your own master." Then the king said, "I granted it on condition it should not be used against me." Then the duke of Lancaster said, "So the grant is invalid." The earl replied, "Indeed, I knew no more about that treason than you who were overseas at the time."

Then Sir John Bushy said, "That pardon has been revoked by the king, the lords, and by us, his honest commons (*fideles plebeios*)." The earl replied, "Where are these honest commons? I don't see how you and your henchmen here can have gathered for any honest purpose, since the honest commons of the kingdom are not with you. But they, as I know, are very concerned for me, and you, I know well, have always been dishonest (*falsus*)." And then Bushy and his supporters cried out, "Look, my lord king, how this traitor is trying to stir up trouble between us and those commons of the land who have remained at home!" The earl replied, "You are all liars! I am not a traitor!" (13–14)

Reading this spirited defense, one might be forgiven for wondering who is really on trial here: Gaunt, Bushy, and even the king himself all find themselves facing serious allegations, but, as Arundel doubtless recognized, it was the question of the revoked pardon that was to prove most damaging to the royalist position.

There can be little doubt that what Richard wanted from his show trial was a public demonstration of Arundel's treason, and he must have found the earl's resolute refusal to admit to the crime extremely galling. On the very steps of the scaffold his accusers were still urging him to proclaim himself a traitor, and Walsingham reports that they even tried, without any success, to get his chaplain to admit that treason was one of the sins for which he had sought absolution in his final confession (*Annales* 217). By contrast, Arundel's fellow appellant, the earl of Warwick, had been gratifyingly eager to grovel to the king: "moaning, sobbing, and howling like a miserable old crone, he confessed that, as a traitor, he was guilty of everything contained in the appeal" (Adam of Usk 16) — an admission that Richard is reported to have said that he valued above all the forfeited estates of Arundel and Gloucester (Walsingham, *Annales* 220).

Warwick's confession, however damaging to his reputation (see Goodman 72), did at least save his neck, whereas Thomas of Gloucester, the last of the senior appellants, was never even offered the chance to save himself. Richard prudently had him murdered in prison at Calais before he could stand trial. In a transparent attempt to save appearances, Richard then had his written confession, which had been taken down in prison in the presence of a judge called William Rickhill (Tait 205–8), read out before Parliament, where it was apparently, quite wrongly, construed as an admission of his treason — Adam of Usk refers to it as "certas confessiones in scriptis redactas super dictis prodicionibus commissis" (15).[16] By far the most striking thing about this confession is that it never employs the words *treason* or *traitor* at all, and, as Walsingham suggests, Richard seems to have set out deliberately to misrepresent the tenor of this inconvenient document in Parliament (*Annales* 221). It would be interesting to know whether Gloucester had studiously avoided the word *treason* for fear that it would mean his certain death, or whether, assuming that he was doomed anyway, he had stubbornly refused to give the king the satisfaction of being able to show that he had died a self-confessed traitor.

Any satisfaction Richard had been able to derive from Warwick's craven confession, then, must have been more than offset by the intransigence of the two other senior appellants, and particularly by the brilliant coup achieved by Arundel at his trial. The king seems to have been anticipating just such a move when he had earlier had it proclaimed that Gloucester, Arundel, and Warwick had been arrested, not for any past wrongs, but for new crimes, committed against him after the time they had been granted charters of pardon for their old offenses ("postquam de veteris delictis obtinuerunt chartas perdonationis de eodem"); though he promised to disclose the nature of these new crimes at the next meeting of Parliament, he was evidently bluffing, for, as Walsingham remarks, "events were to prove this proclamation totally false" (*Annales* 206–7).[17] Having failed to come up with even enough evidence to convince a particularly docile commons of Arundel's new treasons, Richard was forced to the unpleasant expedient of getting Parliament to revoke his pardons. Walsingham's comment on the readiness of the spiritual lords to comply with this breach of faith on the part of their king probably expresses the popular reaction: "not considering that the revoking of this kind of favor was totally incompatible with the person of the king, since mercy is the foundation of the royal throne and whoever removes the king's mercy removes the underpinning of that throne" (*Historia* 2:224). Listening to Arundel's defense Richard must have felt that his worst fears had been realized.

All the chronicles make the earl's reliance on his royal pardon the centerpiece of his defense for the very good reason that it had enabled him to turn the tables on the king.[18] As John Gower puts it is his *Cronica tripertita* (*Latin Works* 314–43):

> Rex prius accusat, et Equs scelus omne recusat,
> Pretendens regisque sigilla sub ordine legis
> Cartam monstrauit, qua tucior esse putauit:
> Non fuit absque nota, prius est concordia nota.
> (2:125–28)

[After the king's accusation, Arundel denies any crime and, holding out the king's seals, valid in law, he showed the charter by which he believed himself to be quite safe. It was not unnoticed that their reconciliation had been publicly acknowledged earlier.]

If one were able to ask someone in the fourteenth-century what word best described a private person who, after publicly pardoning an offender, later sued him for that same offense, there is a fair chance that the answer would have been *traitor*, but while it was still certainly possible to accuse a royal officer of treason, even Richard's enemies seem to have had difficulty thinking of the king himself in precisely these terms. Under the folklaw, a certain mystique, which can still be detected in the lives of notably upright later kings like Saint Louis, had attached itself to the sanctity of the king's word. By the late fourteenth century this had combined with an increasingly authoritarian view of kingship to make *treason* seem a self-contradictory term to apply to the monarch himself. Even the articles of Richard's deposition, though they frequently accuse him of perjury, cannot quite manage to call him a traitor. Nevertheless, everything that constituted the idea of personal treason—betrayal of trust, breach of one's word, underhanded behavior—could be observed in Richard's treatment of Arundel, and the earl's defense deliberately exploits this taint of personal treason to undermine the charge of institutional treason that had been leveled against him. At one point, indeed, he does come very close to calling the king a traitor, when he hints to Gaunt that Richard's caviling about the terms governing the pardon was treasonous: "Indeed, I knew no more about that treason [de illa prodicione plus nescivi] than you who were overseas at the time."[19]

Though the articles of Richard's deposition certainly mention the revoking of Arundel's pardon (ch. 21; *RP* 3:418), we find there, perhaps not surprisingly in view of the manner of Gloucester's death, rather more emphasis on the king's equally perfidious treatment of his own uncle. The thirty-second article (ch. 49) tells how, in 1388, Richard of his own accord and in the presence of many witnesses, had sworn on the holy sacrament placed on the high altar at Langley to pardon Gloucester for all his offenses, "yet afterwards, notwithstanding an oath of this kind, the king had the duke dreadfully and cruelly murdered for his supposed crimes, thus incurring the damnable guilt of perjury" (*RP* 3:421). Moreover, to this double treason of a broken oath and an offense against a kinsman, Richard, so an earlier article tells us, had added a third ingredient, duplicity: after pardoning Gloucester, Arundel, and Warwick, we are informed (ch. 21), he had for many years, like Chaucer's smiler with the knife under the cloak, treated them in a cheerful and friendly manner ("vultum hillarem & benignum exhibuisset"). Walsingham makes much of the devious manner in which Richard set about getting the three arrested by inviting them to a feast which, he says, would have been more infamous than Herod's, had all gone according to plan (*Annales* 201), though in the event only Warwick was naive enough to accept the invitation; and the second part of Gower's *Chronica tripertita* describes how the king, "pretending peace, under the guise of feigned amity, cunningly tricked the three noblemen" (*Latin Works* 320). *Britton*, we might recall, had defined treason as "any mischief which a person knowingly does, or procures to be done, to anyone to whom he pretends to be a friend."

By stressing Richard's faithlessness and duplicity, the apologists for Arundel and Gloucester were clearly trying to make the charges of treason rebound upon their originator, but from the king's point of view, of course, such an attempt simply missed the point. If the response to Haxey's petition, with its suggestion that the slightest criticism of royal policy was potentially treasonable, looks to us like the most extreme statement of Ricardian prerogative, the brief reenactment of the law of treason made in the same Parliament (21 Rich. 2, cc.3–4; *SR* 2:98–99), presumably in preparation for the appeals against Arundel, Warwick and Gloucester, raised a far more cogent constitutional issue. Bellamy seems inclined to downplay the importance of this statute, arguing that its scope was particular not general and that it added only two new items to the act of 1352 (1970, 114), but the justification offered for its repeal in Henry IV's first Parliament suggests that it had been taken seriously enough at the time: "divers Pains of Treason were ordained by Statute, in as much as that there was no Man which did know how he ought to behave himself, to do, speak, or say, for Doubt of such Pains" (1 Hen. 4, c.10; *SR* 2:114). Of the four grounds for charging someone with what is here called "high" treason, compassing the king's death and levying war on him were, as Bellamy says, already well established, but plotting to depose the king or planning to renounce one's homage to him ("chescun qi compasse & propose . . . ou de luy deposier ou desuis rendre son homage liege") were certainly not. No wonder they caused consternation among contemporaries, for they struck at the very heart of the feudal equation, making it quite literally unthinkable for a vassal to bring a king to account for failure to honor his contract with his people. By making the ancient procedure of *diffidatio* illegal, in other words, the act of 1397 finally turned what had once been, at least in theory, a reciprocal agreement into an entirely one-sided obligation.

Lest we should be tempted to imagine that the act of 1397 merely set the seal on what was already a well-recognized principle, we should recall the fifth item in Gloucester's written confession: "Also, in that, that I among other communed for feer of my lyf to yiue up myn hommage to my lord, I knowleche wel that for certain that I among other communed and asked of certeins clercs, whethir that we myght yive up our homage for drede of our lyves or non; and whethir that we assentyd thereto for to do it, trewlych and by my trowth I ne have now none full mynde thereof, bot I trowe rather ye than nay" (cited by Tait 206–7). Interestingly, the legitimacy of an actual *diffidatio*, of feudal defiance, does not seem to have been in question for Gloucester; he did not apparently imagine that merely to plan "desuis rendre son homage liege" could be construed as a treasonable act in itself. Rather, for him, the issue had been whether fear for one's life (doubtless his own predicament after learning of the judges' replies to Richard's questions) was a sufficient reason for taking so momentous a step. Even more interesting is his claim to have consulted "certeins clercs," for this clearly implies that he and his fellow appellants had felt the need of the support of written record before embarking on a course of action that unwritten custom had long endorsed. We must assume that Gloucester's clerks were able to reassure him, for, despite his tortuous syntax, he seems clearly to be confessing, not just to considering renouncing his homage, but to agreeing actually to do so: "and whethir that we assentyd thereto *for to do it* . . ."[20]

Despite the early promise of Magna Carta's remarkable sixty-first article, Gloucester's clerks are unlikely to have found much support for their master in common-law treatises.[21] There is little in England to match the unambiguous assertion of the early-thirteenth-century *Sachsenspiegel*: "the vassal must and shall resist his king and his judge when they are unjust, and help to restrain them at all times, even if they should be his kinsman or his overlord, and in this he is not acting against his oath" [unde ne dut dar an weder sinen truwen nicht] (3.78.2; 260). Apart from Bracton's *De legibus* (and its epitome *Fleta*), no English manual seems to have had much to say about situations such as Gloucester's, and even then the most promising passage in Bracton is of questionable authenticity: "The king has a superior, namely, God. Also the law by which he is made king. Also his *curia*, namely the earls and barons, since the earls are called the partners, as it were, of the king and he who has a partner has a master [qui socium habet, habet magistrum]. And therefore, if the king should be without a bridle, that is without law, they ought to put the bridle on him, otherwise they too would be unbridled like the king" (2:110).[22] Maurice Keen claims that by the late fourteenth century, "though it was not regarded as treason to defy a private person, to levy war against the king in his realm was so regarded, for the king was not a private person, but public majesty" (1965a, 233). Nevertheless, the best support for this claim comes from the Paris parlement and, while the *diffidatio* may indeed have been a dead letter in France after the middle of the century (Cuttler 31), there is room to doubt that the French and the English would necessarily have seen eye to eye on this question. As Ernst Kantorowicz remarks, "the doctrine of the ruler as a *lex animata* . . . seems to have fallen on particularly barren ground in England before the age of Queen Elizabeth" (1957, 147).

If Gloucester's clerks might have found slim pickings among the books of law, there were always the historical precedents. The two greatest triumphs of baronial opposition to royal despotism in the thirteenth century, Runnymede in 1215 and Lewes in 1264, had both begun with the issuing of a formal defiance, but even if we should suppose that such distant events were no longer readily recalled, the deposition of Edward II was still fresh enough in memory. The 1397 parliamentary accusation against Gloucester and Arundel makes it clear that this was indeed where the appellants had turned for their written evidence: "And the said duke and the earl of Arundel and Warwick, following their traitorous plan and assault aforesaid, by a common agreement amongst them, caused the records in your treasury from your great-grandfather King Edward's time to be searched to discover how your said great-grandfather should have been deposed"; nor apparently was their search futile for the record continues, "and they showed you, most redoubted lord, written reasons for his deposition" [et monstrerent en escript . . . les Causes de demyse de sa Coroune] (*RP* 3:376). Whatever the precise nature of this written evidence,[23] it would presumably have told them that Sir William Trussell, speaking as *procurator* on behalf of a number of prelates, earls, barons, and others, had informed Edward that he was revoking and rendering up his homage and fealty to the erstwhile king, thereby freeing and acquitting them "in the best manner decreed by law and custom" (*Rotuli parliamentorum Anglie* 101). Some record of this event seems to have been known at the end of the century when William Thirning, chief justice of Common Pleas, speaking as one of the "procuratours" for the Lords and Commons in a parliamentary assembly,[24] formally yielded up to Richard "Homage liege and Feaute, and alle Ligeance, and all other bondes, charges, and services that longe ther to" (*RP* 3:424) — after which defiance, says Adam of Usk, "he was no longer to be held by them as king but as the private lord, Richard of Bordeaux, a simple knight" (31). With hindsight, we may interpret the form taken by the appellants' resistance to Richard's tyranny as futile adherence to an outmoded feudal concept of treason, but many at the time must have seen their actions as defending the traditional order against a royal policy that showed signs of dangerous innovation.

"The concept of high treason," as Walter Ullmann pointed out, will always be intimately bound up with "the prevailing thesis of government and law" (1978, 137), and it is perhaps inevitable that our investigation should have brought us into the domain of medieval political theory. If the crisis of treason that I have been discussing really is a counterpart to the Ricardian crisis of truth, then it too must represent a significant shift in attitude; but the claim that Richard II treated the exercise of political authority in a radically new way will certainly not be accepted by all historians. We are forced, then, to consider whether Richard was indeed, as Anthony Steele thought, "the last truly medieval King of England" (8), or whether, as V. H. Galbraith maintained, "there is something new here: a conception of royal power which is not that of Edward II or of Henry III, and which consciously or unconsciously looks forwards rather than backwards" (1942, 235). How much weight, in other words, can we really attach to Walter Ullmann's claim that, "although separated by nearly 200 years from John's reign, the government of Richard II would prove once again that the nature of his conflict with Parliament was in essence not so different from that which characterized John's with his barons" (1978, 182).

The Nature of Kingship

A good starting point for this discussion is Ullmann's characterization of the two contrasting medieval concepts of kingship as "theocratic" and "feudal": "First there was the king by the grace of God—the theocratic king *par excellence*—who, because he alone had received the power to rule from God, stood above his subjects (symbolized by the elevated throne), who could not call him to account; secondly, next to this theocratic function every medieval king was also a feudal lord. . . . As a theocratic king his will alone counted, while as a feudal king he had entered into contractual relations of an individual nature with his tenants-in-chief and thereby had become one of them. In this feudal capacity he did not stand above the kingdom, but was a member of the feudal community itself" (W. Ullmann 1966, 66–67). In no medieval state was kingship seen as exclusively theocratic or exclusively feudal, of course, and the constitutional history of any given state can easily be represented as a struggle between these two competing theses. Viewed against such a broad backdrop as this, the barons on Runnymede may well have looked to Ullmann not so very different from the Lords Appellant; both were attempting to force the king to acknowledge the feudal side of his office, even though by Richard II's time this had become somewhat modified by notions of a constitutional or limited monarchy. Once we try to recast Ullmann's two categories in terms of an oral/literate dichotomy, however, some interesting patterns begin to emerge.

What bound the feudal kingdom together was a tool of social cohesion that seems to be omnipresent in medieval oral culture, the oath. The people swore to keep faith with their king, and he in turn swore to keep faith with them. How deep a part of the English social structure this remained even in the late Middle Ages is easily shown by comparison with France. S. H. Cuttler's claim that "injured majesty was the central, all-encompassing aspect of treason in later medieval France, and that betrayal, though primordial, was but a subordinate one" (238), could not have been made of England with anything like the same confidence. Marc Bloch, who would have observed nothing of the sort in his own country (at least, not after the end of the Carolingian period), was naturally struck by the fact that in England, "the king could demand the oath of fealty of his vassals' vassals" (1931, 186). In fact, such oaths were required even of those who stood outside the system of vassalage altogether. *Britton* tells us that all males of twelve years and over had to swear fealty to the king when they were admitted into a tithing at the annual view of frankpledge and gives the form of this oath as follows: "Hear this you, *N*, bailiff, that I, *P*, from this day forward will be faithful and loyal [*feal et leal*] to our lord *E*. king of England and his heirs, and will bear unto them faith and loyalty [*foy et leauté*] of life and limb, of body and chattels, and of earthly honour, and will neither know nor hear of their hurt or damage, but I will oppose it to the best of my power; so help me God and the Saints" (1:185). A glance back to the Anglo-Saxon hold-oath will show that this formula is markedly more one-sided, containing no exceptions clause whatsoever. Indeed, as Maitland points out, the promise made in an oath of fealty to the king was "so unconditioned that it becomes known as the oath of ligeance or allegiance" (P&M 1:299). Even the corresponding oath of fealty sworn between vassal and lord was qualified only by the phrase "saving my faith to the oath that I have made to such a king" (*Mirror* 117–18), and demonstrates clearly how much more hierarchical political relationships had grown since the Conquest.

In addition to these routine oaths of allegiance, English kings might sometimes require more specific oaths from their subjects. Again, this would have seemed odd in France. In 789, and again in 793 and 802, Charlemagne had given a dramatic example of what F. L. Ganshof calls the feudal tendency "to think of power in contractual terms" by attempting to make every single one of his subjects, twelve years and older, swear an oath of allegiance to him (117); in so doing he was apparently reviving an ancient Merovingian practice, but the tactic proved ineffectual and soon fell out of use. Certainly, no French king later than the tenth century would have ever dreamed of making such a demand of his people (M. Bloch 1933, 336). English kings, however, continued to do so to the very end of the Middle Ages. Doubtless this was frequently counterproductive, if only for the reason said to have been given by Rhys ap Thomas in a letter to Richard III (though the language looks suspiciously modern): "I am persuaded, that these pressings of vowes and othes upon subjects, noe way held in suspect, hath often times wrought even in thos of soundest affections, a sensibilitie of some injurie don to their faith" ("Life" 200).[25] Certainly, Richard II's attempts to make everyone in the kingdom swear to uphold certain statutes and ordinances favorable to his own prerogative were widely unpopular and were specifically mentioned in the articles of his deposition (Clarke 103–5; C. Barron 1968, 14–16). The attempt, however misguided, confirms nonetheless that even this most autocratic and perfidious of kings recognized how much sacral power the oath still retained among his subjects.

If the late medieval oath of fealty differed from its Anglo-Saxon predecessor in its lack of any explicit mention of the terms upon which loyalty was due, this is not to say that those who swore it felt that the king was entirely free to make whatever demands upon them he chose. Though Richard II may have been unwilling to recognize the fact, his subjects understood that the counterpart to their own oaths of allegiance was the solemn oath that he had sworn to them at his coronation. At every medieval coronation, while the ceremonial anointing emphasized the theocratic nature of kingship, separating the king from his subjects, associating him with the priesthood, and granting him precedence over those who did not enjoy this right (Schramm 115), the swearing of a coronation oath confirmed its feudal element: "king and subjects in all Western countries were bound together by oath at the accession of every new King" (183). Nevertheless, the emphasis accorded each element in this oath varied from one country and from one era to another and serves as a useful measure of the feudal (one might almost say, oral) residue in any given national conception of kingship.

Initially, there seems to have been little substantial difference between the English and French coronation oaths. Both were based on the so-called *tria precepta* whereby the king promised that he would strive to maintain the peace, to control wrongdoing, and to exercise justice and mercy. Sometime before Edward I's coronation in 1272, however, and perhaps as early as Henry II's, a fourth promise—to maintain the rights of the crown unimpaired—seems to have been added to the English oath. So general a set of undertakings, coupled with the vassal's unconditional allegiance, placed very few formal constraints on the king. The document outlining his complaints against the barons that Henry III submitted to Louis IX's arbitration in 1264, for instance, was endorsed with the note: "especially as the lord king cannot do or grant the aforesaid things [the baronial demands] against his oath which he took at his coronation; and similarly, on the other hand, his subjects cannot take the aforesaid matters upon themselves, or interfere with them against the oath of fealty which they made to the lord king" (Treharne and Saunders 257). Apart from the much later addition of a similar provision concerning the crown's rights at Charles V's coronation in 1364 (Richardson 1949, 54–55 and n. 59), the French ceremony continued to demand what Bernard Guenée calls "the same vague traditional oath" (172) to the end of the Middle Ages, but with the coronation of Edward II in 1308 its English counterpart underwent a radical revision.[26]

The original promises to strive to keep the peace and to exercise justice and mercy were retained in this new oath, but explicit reference to maintaining the rights of the crown unimpaired was dropped and the second of the original *tria precepta*, the promise to control wrongdoing, was changed almost beyond recognition. Here is what Edward swore instead:

> The bishop asks: Sir, do you wish to grant and keep and by your oath confirm to the English people the laws and customs granted to them by the ancient kings of England, your rightful and godly predecessors, and namely the laws, customs, and freedoms granted to the clergy and the people by your glorious royal predecessor, Saint Edward.[27]
> The king replies: I grant and promise these things. . . .
> The bishop asks: Sir, will you agree to maintain and keep the rightful laws and customs which the commons of your realm shall have chosen,[28] and, as far as you may, defend and enforce them to the honor of God?
> The king replies: I grant and promise these things. (Hoyt 237 n. 6)

Such an oath was clearly intended to provide those wishing to curb the royal prerogative with far more ammunition than its precursors had done, and when the earl of Lincoln presented the king with a set of articles condemning his favorite, Piers Gaveston, for treason later the same year, he concluded it with the significant request that the king should accept the decision of the people and act upon it, "as he is sworn in his coronation oath to keep the laws which the people shall choose" (cited by Richardson and Sayles 1963, 468). That the king by his coronation oath was felt to have sealed with his people a contract that he might disregard only at his peril is confirmed by the fifth of the so-called articles of Edward's deposition: "Item, whereas he is bound by his oath to do right to all, he has not chosen to do this . . . nor has he kept the other articles of the oath that he made at his coronation, as he was bound to do" (*Foedera*, new ed. 2:650).

The coronation oath devised for Edward II was also employed, with only minor variations, at the coronations of his son and great-grandson, but its far greater prominence in the articles of Richard II's deposition suggests that by the late fourteenth century it had come to be regarded in some quarters as a cornerstone of the constitution with the potential to offer genuine protection against autocratic and arbitrary rule. Indeed, as early as June 1388 Richard's oath had come into public focus when the Lords Appellant had reenacted this part of the coronation ceremony to mark the end of their dispute with the king. Though both Richard and the nobles had sworn oaths on the earlier occasion, says Thomas Favent, "nevertheless, what was in effect the same oath in the same manner and form as at the coronation, together with the oaths and homage of the nobles, was solemnly renewed, partly because it had first been taken when the king was a minor, and partly in order to dispel any secret reservations and avoid any wavering, as much on the king's part as on the part of the nobility" [tum propter cordium scrupulas et titubaciones tam penes regem quam penes proceres euellendas et evidandas] (24; cf. *Westminster Chronicle* 342). In view of this twice-sworn oath, Richard could hardly have expected much clemency from those who accused him of perjury in 1399.

The archbishop of Canterbury, the newly restored Thomas Arundel, initiated proceedings against him in Henry IV's first Parliament by preaching a sermon on the three qualities essential to the government of any kingdom (respect for justice, the law, and the orders of society); though the précis of it given in the rolls of Parliament contains no specific reference to Richard's coronation oath (*RP* 3:415), Adam of Usk reports that the primate had spoken of how Richard "strove to overthrow the whole law of the realm to which he was sworn" (32). On the next day the thirty-three articles of Richard's deposition were read out before Parliament.[29] They were recorded (or rather, their "tenor" was recorded) in the parliamentary rolls, where they were introduced with a text of Richard's coronation oath (omitting, somewhat curiously, its first clause).[30] Of these articles, three explicitly mention actions which had contravened this oath (9, 17, 22), another three simply describe actions said to have been in some way contrary or deleterious to the laws, statutes, customs, or liberties of the land (10, 16, 26), and a further eight specifically link allegations that Richard had acted against the laws, customs, or statutes of the realm with the charge of perjury or oath-breaking (3, 11, 13, 18, 27, 29, 30, 33). If we add to these, three articles which accuse Richard of breaking particular agreements, such as the pardon to Arundel (4, 12, 32), and four others which describe him falsifying records (8, 24), dissimulating his intentions (25), and failing to pay his debts (14), then the cumulative effect is a devastating portrait of an utterly faithless monarch, whose cynical disregard for the obligations of his coronation oath had rendered him patently unfit to rule.

The parliamentary record of Richard II's deposition is not without its convenient fictions, but there is every reason to take seriously its itemizing of the king's failure to observe the terms of his coronation oath. Contemporaries clearly regarded this oath as anything but an empty formality. As E. Talbot Donaldson has convincingly argued, Langland's well-known lines "Thanne kam þer a kyng; knyȝthod hym ladde; / Might of þe communes made hym to regne" (B.Pro:112–13) must have been written with Richard's coronation in mind and reflect the strong impression made upon the poet by the actual circumstances of the oath (116–18).[31] Likewise John Gower, in "O deus immense," (*Latin Works* 362–64), written toward the end of the reign, was led by the king's excesses to reflect on the binding power of his coronation oath: "Laus et honor Regum foret obseruacio legum / Ad quas iurati sunt prima sorte vocati" (7–8; cf. *CA* 7:3078–83) [The praise and honor of kings should be the keeping of the laws to which they were sworn when called by their first duty].[32] A poem in MS Digby 102, composed shortly after Henry IV's accession, makes the point even more starkly (Kail 13): "Eche kyng is sworn to gouernaunce, / To gouerne goddis puple in riȝt" (3:137–38). As late as 1450, the Kentish rebels are still challenging the theory that the king is above the law in just these terms: "the contrarie is trew and elles he schuld not have beene swerune in his Coronacione to kepe hit" ("Declaration" 266). Perhaps the most striking statement of this view, however, appears in Thomas Hoccleve's *Regement of Princes*, written for the future king Henry V:

> Tho othes that at your creacioun
> Shul thurgh your tonge passe, hem wel obserue;
> Lat no coloured excusacioun
> Yow make fro hem slippe aside or swerue;
> Holde vp hir lyf, lat hem nat in yow sterue;
> It is nat knyghtly from an oth to varie;
> A kyng of trouth, oweth bene exemplarie.
> (2192–98; cf. 2899)

This seems to run counter to the suggestion made in many other such *specula principum*, including one of Hoccleve's own sources, the *Secretum Secretorum*, that "it is not convenient to the dignyté and magisté of a kynge for to swere, and whan he doth it he doth derogacion to his honour" (*Secretum* 43). Whatever Henry's reaction may have been, it is not difficult to imagine which advice Richard II would have found the more congenial, and Hoccleve is evidently here trying to alert a future king of England to the dangers of repeating a predecessor's mistakes.

There is of course nothing new about political confrontation between a king and his magnates being couched in the language of faithlessness and perjury. The document submitted by the barons to Louis IX's arbitration in 1264 makes just such charges against Henry III (Treharne and Saunders 258), and a baronial apologist was to describe the battle of Lewes, which followed the breakdown of this arbitration, in similar terms:

Gladius inualuit, multi ceciderunt,
Veritas preualuit, falsi fugerunt.
Nam periuris restitit dominus uirtutum,
Atque puris prestitit ueritatis scutum.
(*Song of Lewes* 23–26)

[The sword waxed strong, many fell, the truth prevailed, and the false fled. For the Lord of hosts withstood the perjured, and the shield of truth stood before the pure.]

Nor, as we have seen, was Richard II's deposition the first time a specific allegation of failure to observe the terms of a coronation oath had been laid at the door of an unpopular king. What is new, however, is the way in which this oath had become a text; the king's promises had been fixed by writing into a set of inflexible conditions so that what was once a purely oral undertaking had begun to take on the appearance of a written contract. Though Henry II and earlier kings do seem to have been provided with a written copy of the oath for use in the ceremony, its principal purpose was to serve as a physical token of his solemn pact with his people (Richardson 1960, 172); like Baldonet's head money and bell ropes, it was laid upon the altar in a solemn gesture clearly still rooted in a world of living memory. Even in the late thirteenth century this relic of the oral trothplight had still fully to enter the age of written record: "We have good reason to believe that at each coronation the king had a written form of the oath before him," says H. G. Richardson, "yet these writings having served their purpose were not carefully preserved" (1960, 172).

With Edward II's coronation, however, all that changed. Not only was the text of his oath officially recorded on the close rolls and his original coronation roll carefully preserved in the government archives (a precedent that was to be followed for the coronations of Edward III, Richard II, and Henry IV), but what seems to have been an actual roll used by a participant in the ceremony, and even what looks to have been the original service book, still survive today (Richardson and Sayles 1935/36, 131–33; Richardson 1938, 10–11). Though we no longer possess a copy of the service book used at the coronation of Edward III, by the early 1380s it had been superseded by the magnificent *Liber Regalis* (compiled either for Richard II's coronation or for Queen Anne's). This volume is still kept in Westminster Abbey and preserves a text that was to become "the standard for centuries thereafter" (Richardson 1960, 112). What is perhaps even more striking than the care with which this text was preserved, is the fact that some trouble was taken to publicize it; according to H. G. Richardson and George Sayles, the text of the coronation oath must have been known to a wide circle by the latter part of the fourteenth century (1935/36, 141). As we have seen, the official parliamentary record of the articles of Richard's deposition was prefaced by a copy of the actual oath sworn by the king, and this oath is significantly referred to as the one customarily used at coronations, "such as is contained more fully in the pontificals [*in Libris Pontificalium*] of the archbishops and bishops" (*RP* 3:417). In some quarters at least, the text of the coronation oath was clearly being regarded as a kind of official job profile which every king must agree to and which could then be cited in dismissal proceedings against him should he fail to observe its requirements.

I have been arguing that the movement from the old oral trothplight to the formal written contract was one of the most important factors in the Ricardian crisis of truth, and it is therefore particularly significant to find signs of such a movement at the very heart of the political system. There is nonetheless an enormous difference between entering the text of a king's coronation oath in an official register and drawing up an indentured agreement with a retainer. While the indenture of retinue, the foundation on which the whole edifice of bastard feudalism stood, was essentially progressive (heralding a transition from medieval *Gemeinschaft* to modern *Gesellschaft*), the use of writing to enhance the political potency of the king's coronation oath was fundamentally reactionary—an attempt to breathe new life into a fast-fading institution. By espousing a system of contractual retaining, fourteenth-century magnates were throwing in their lot with the clerical elite and the increasingly powerful judiciary that reinforced it; by adhering to traditional ideals of feudal kingship, on the other hand, they were making a last stand around the tattered standard of a good old law that the royal bureaucrats had changed almost beyond recognition. That the shield-wall with which they sought to protect it was constructed of ink and parchment should not be allowed to disguise the inherent anachronism of the whole enterprise. If, as I have been suggesting, the Ricardian crisis of truth was the product not simply of the rapid spread of literacy but of the way in which such literacy was employed to enhance and extend centralized political authority, we will expect to find signs of the perennial battle between oral and written law growing hotter at the end of the fourteenth century.

The Sources of Law

For most constitutional historians the struggle between the king and his magnates will appear primarily as a struggle for control over the machinery of legislation. On the one hand, there was law from above (a matter of royal ordinances issuing directly from the king) and, on the other, law from below (parliamentary statutes originating with the knights of the shire). While, in practice, most legislation was hybrid, with the king granting parliamentary petitions and Parliament ratifying royal decrees, the theoretical question of where the ultimate responsibility for passing new laws lay remained as a potential source of friction down to the seventeenth century. To us, viewing it with the benefit of hindsight, this picture, however obscure in some of its details, will seem clear enough in outline, but it cannot have been nearly as easy to recognize in the fourteenth century. Indeed, since England was still to emerge fully from the long shadow cast by the ancient idea of the king as lawfinder, the very terms in which we couch the question would have sounded odd to many people. It is not the job of either king or Parliament to *make* the law, they might have said; their task is simply to *administer* the laws we have inherited as justly as possible. When most medieval people thought at all about substantive law (the kind of law that spells out the actual rights and duties of individual members of society) they thought of it as something permanent and unalterable; the only law they would have regarded as subject to human interference, and even then to only a very limited degree, would have been what we should call adjective law (that is, the legal rules and procedures by which rights are defended and duties enforced). For such people, the constitutional struggle between king and magnates would have appeared primarily, not as a battle to decide who should make the law, but rather as a contest between those who were bent on changing the law and those who were sworn to preserve it.

Even King Alfred, that most learned of Anglo-Saxon lawgivers, had felt obliged to minimize the novelty of his own legislation: "I dared not be so bold as to set very much of my own down in writing, since I could not know how it would be received by our descendants" (49.9; Liebermann 1:46); his method was rather, he says, to cull the best from the laws of such illustrious predecessors as Ine, or Offa, or Æthelberht. A similar attitude is attributed to an even older and more illustrious king; in Laȝamon's account of his dying words, Arthur bequeaths the kingdom to his heir:

> Ich þe bitache here / mine kineriche.
> and wite mine Bruttes / a to þines lifes.
> and hald heom alle þa laȝen / þa habbeoþ i-stonden a mine daȝen.
> and alle þa laȝen gode / þa bi Vðeres daȝen stode.
>
> (C.14273–76)

[I bequeath my kingdom to you here: defend my Britons as long as you live, and preserve for them the laws that have been kept in my time, and all the good laws that were kept in Uther's time.]

It is a mark of the power of this model in the popular imagination that, even before 1308, many chroniclers seem to have assumed (apparently erroneously) that the king's coronation oath contained some reference to preserving the ancient laws and customs of his realm (see Hoyt).

Where keeping the laws of one's forebears was the mark of a good king, the making of new laws was always liable to be regarded with suspicion. Here, for instance, is how Henry II, revered by most legal historians as the founder of the English common law, appeared to Ralph Niger: "His greed was never sated, but having abolished the ancient laws, he issued new ones each year, and called them assizes" (168). Edward I, Plucknett's "English Justinian," fares little better:

> Nostre roy de Engletere,
> Par le conseil de sa gent,
> Wolde a nywe laghe arere
> And makede a muchele parlement.
> . . . .
> Joe ne say mes ke dyre,
> Mes tot y va tribolay
> Curt and laghe, hundred a[nd] syre;
> Al it god a duvele vay.
> (6:9–12 and 21–24; in Aspin 62)

> [Our English king, by the advice of his men, wished to make a new law and summoned a great Parliament. . . . I hardly know what to say, for all is turned upside down: court and law, hundred and shire, all is going to the devil.]

Edward's judges come in for similar criticism:

> Nummosque colligentes,
> Pauperes despiciunt,
> Et novas leges faciunt,
> Vicinos opprimentes.
> (Wright *Songs*, 230)

> [Hoarding up gold, they spurn the poor, and make new laws to crush their neighbors.]

Suspicion of any kind of legal innovation seems to be as typical of oral and traditional cultures as reliance upon positive law is of literate and progressive ones. While societies are in a state of transition from memory to written record, however, the threat that writing poses to their customary law will often appear far less serious than the promise it holds out of being able protect such law against change. Thus, the same people who are most disturbed by the profound effects of literacy on legal institutions may, ironically, be the very ones most eager to see the law written down. The author of *The Mirror of Justices* is relentless in his condemnation of Edward I's legislative reforms, yet he begins his treatise by saying that he had been moved to take up his pen by the realization that those who ought to govern the law "would never agree to customary rights being put in writing" for fear of weakening their own powers (1). The first three in the long catalog of abuses with which he ends the work are the king's claim to be above the law, his administration of the law through a clerical elite rather than through Parliament, and the fact that "the laws and customs of the realm, together with their justification, are not set down in writing so that they might be known and followed by all" (156). This perspective is admirably summed up by the author of the early-fifteenth-century poems in MS Digby 102:

> In alle kyngdomes, here lawe is wryten;
> For mede ne drede, þey chaunge it nouȝt.
> In Engeland, as all men wyten,
> Law, as best, is solde and bouȝt.
> Eche ȝeer newe lawe is wrouȝt,
> And cloþe falsed [false cloþed (?)] in trouþe wede,
> Fern þer was lawe; now nes it nouȝt.
> We ben newe fangyl, vnstable in dede.
>
> (13:25–32; in Kail 56)

However much the literate machinery of the king's law contributed to the Ricardian crisis of truth, the fact remains that many of those most disturbed by what they saw as universal faithlessness would have felt that the answer lay in more rather than less written law.

The English law (as Glanvill and Bracton, both apologists for the king's law, seem quite happy to admit) was unwritten law, but even before Magna Carta, those who sought to resist the inroads of centralized justice had recognized that written documents might be useful to them in their struggle to protect the old law from the arbitrary changes of unjust kings. Henry I, Stephen, and even Henry II reassured opponents by issuing coronation charters affirming their willingness to protect the laws and customs of their predecessors (Hoyt 241–44), but Magna Carta must have appeared to render such guarantees obsolete. At regular intervals, thereafter, but with particular insistence from 1258 to 1265 (Maddicott 1984) and from 1297 to 1305 (Rothwell), barons and gentry were to remind the king of his duties under Magna Carta and urge him to reconfirm the charters. Their success in the *Confirmatio Cartarum* of 1297 led to the first official enrollment of Magna Carta and the provision that sealed copies of the charters should be deposited in cathedral churches throughout the land and read to the people twice a year.

Inevitably, these efforts came to nothing, and when first Henry III and then Edward I reneged on their commitments, it was for flouting a written compact that contemporaries castigated them. Thus, "Vulneratur karitas," a lament for the state of the kingdom, apparently written shortly after Simon de Montfort's death at the battle of Evesham (1265) and preserved in a thirteenth-century collection of legal texts, complains, "In presenti tempore non valet scriptura, / Sed sopita veluti latent legis jura" [Nowadays, written documents are powerless, but legal rights are veiled as if in sleep] (14:9–10; in Aspin 153). Similar disillusionment is expressed in "De Provisione Oxonie," written at the very end of Edward I's reign:

> La purveance est de cyre,
> Jo l'enteng e byn le say
> And is yholde to neȝ þe fyre
> And is ymolten away.
> (6:17–20; Aspin 62)

> [The provision was made of wax, as I understand and know well; it was held too near the fire and has melted away.]

As Harry Rothwell says, "somewhere between 1297 and 1311 'The Charters' ceased to be a sufficient slogan: a chapter in our history ends" (319), for though they continued to enjoy a kind of half-life to the end of the century—featuring prominently in Edward III's parliaments and cropping up twice in the articles of Richard II's deposition (chs. 44 and 46; *RP* 3:420–21)—it is clear that at the beginning of the fourteenth century the battle lines were being redrawn. The conservatives, having found the charters tactically ineffective, now sought to rally their forces around the coronation oath. When Archbishop Stratford, one of the deposers of Edward II, rebuked Edward III in 1341, it was first of all for disregarding "the law of the land which you are obliged by your coronation oath to protect and maintain," and only then for acting "encountre la graunt chartre" (Robert of Avesbury 325). Royal administrators, on the other hand, were beginning to appreciate the enormous strategic advantage that being able to dictate the very substance of law itself gave them.

Throughout the thirteenth century the king's claim to be able to make law had been stubbornly resisted by two lines of argument. The first—that he was there not to make but to preserve the law—had begun to atrophy with Edward I's victory in the struggle for the charters, so the reference to the laws of Edward the Confessor in Edward II's coronation oath was, quite literally, a paper victory. If, after 1308, the laws of England were no longer strictly speaking unwritten laws—for, as Richardson has shown (1949, 60–64), Edward II was swearing to uphold an actual code—even the prestige of his saintly predecessor could hardly furnish this legal archaism (now, ironically, known to be a forgery) with any real political or juridical weight. The second line of argument conceded that changes in the law might sometimes become necessary but assigned the responsibility for making such changes, not to the king alone, but to the king acting in consultation with his nobles. This, too had ancient roots: "then I, Alfred, king of the West Saxons, showed these [laws] to my whole council [*eallum minum witum*], and then everyone said they would be pleased to keep them" (49.10; Liebermann 1:46). Such traditional thinking gives added significance to Bracton's interpretation of Ulpian's famous maxim "quod principi placuit, legis habet vigorem" to mean the king's pleasure after due deliberation in council. "The importance of Bracton's constitutionalist qualification of the dangerous word *placuit*," writes Kantorowicz, "cannot be minimized" (1957, 152);[33] it points forward to the constitutional arrangement which Fortescue's *Governance of England* would distinguish from the simple *ius regale* of France by calling it a *ius politicum et regale*. A continuing commitment to this ideal of a constitutional or limited monarchy helps explain why the "duketti" of 1397, were so widely detested, for autocratic kings might always try to use compliant counselors to give a gloss of constitutional respectability to their unpopular decisions.[34] In the struggle between king and magnates in late medieval England, control over the council might appear as at least as important a prize as control over Parliament. An attempt by the magnates to set up a "great and continual council" was after all what had prompted Richard's questions to his judges in 1387, and, as D. R. Clementi has shown, he seems to have been particularly concerned that they should discredit an apparent precedent for this action from early in Edward II's reign.

When the articles of Richard II's deposition claimed that the king, "unwilling to keep or preserve the just laws and customs of the kingdom . . . said specifically, and with a completely straight face, that the laws were in his mouth (or, on several other occasions, in his breast), and that only he himself might change or make the laws of his kingdom" (ch. 33; *RP* 3:419), we might be forgiven for thinking that little had changed since the author of *The Song of Lewes* had complained: "Dicitur vulgariter: ut rex vult, lex vadit; / Veritas vult aliter, nam lex stat, rex cadit" [It is commonly said, "As the king wills, the law goes"; Truth wills otherwise, for the law stands, the king falls] (871–72). But in fact the nature of royal law-making had changed fundamentally by the end of the fourteenth century. This change has been admirably summed up by Geoffrey Barraclough: "Although under Edward I there is unparalleled definition of substantive law, this is a different thing from the definition that was to follow. . . . It was legal definition, definition of what the law was. Subsequent definition, on the other hand, was definition not of the law, but of the law's sphere. It was a definition of functions. In the last resort, it is fair to say, it was political where Edward I's work had been legal. It sought to define powers, and one of the powers which it sought to define was the legislative power" (81). Barraclough rightly sees such change as underlying the political crises of Richard II's reign, but we should not take this to imply that the king himself was solely, or even mainly, responsible for it. It reflects deep-seated structural shifts to which the autocratic Richard clearly responded more enthusiastically than his grandfather, but which must inevitably have provoked a political confrontation at some point whoever was occupying the throne.

Arguably, the first real attempt to define the law's sphere, actually to make substantive law, in England, was Edward III's Statute of Treasons.[35] "While as yet the felonies were being left to unenacted common law," wrote Maitland, "treason became in 1352 the subject of an elaborate statute" (P&M 2:502). Yet this legislation, as we have seen, was drafted in response to conservative pressures and passed by a far from autocratic or progressive king. "The predominant and characteristic legislative process under Edward III," writes Richardson, was "that of basing statutes upon a common petition" (1949, 73) — in other words, law from below — and some idea of the conservatism of Edward's parliaments is conveyed by Maude Clarke's observation that they made more prominent reference to Magna Carta than any of their predecessors (245); Edward, indeed, went so far as to cite the obligations placed on him by his own coronation oath when he attempted to clean up judicial corruption in 1346 (*SR* 1:30). Yet, even in this atmosphere, the Statute of Treasons exhibits clear signs of the increasing power of centralized royal authority: in some ways its most revealing clause is the one that makes it treason to kill "the Chancellor, the Treasurer, or any of the king's judges, of either bench, or judges in eyre, or in assize, or any other justice assigned to commissions of oyer and terminer, while in the performance of their duties" (*RP* 2:239).

At its heart, institutional treason was judge-centered law,[36] designed to promote the interests of the royal bureaucracy by fostering the symbiosis of the king and his judiciary. In 1352, parliamentary misgivings about cases like Gerberge's, reinforced by Edward III's own conservative sympathies, had offered Shareshull and his fellows a less-than-satisfactory opportunity for its promulgation, but the accession of a naturally autocratic young king in 1377 offered their successors a far better prospect. One early indication of the new atmosphere was the redrafting of Edward I's prohibition against *scandalum magnatum* (3 Edw. 1, stat. 1, c.34; *SR* 1:35) in order to extend the list of those protected from dangerous rumormongering to include "the Chancellor, Treasurer, Clerk of the Privy Seal, Steward of the King's House, Justices of the one Bench or of the other" (2 Rich. 2, c.5; *SR* 2:9), but it was to be Arundel and Gloucester's provocative attempt to impose a commission on Richard in 1386 that would offer the king's judiciary its first real chance to extend its own prerogative. When Richard put to his judges the question "whether or not the lords and commons can impeach in Parliament officers and justices for their offences, without the king's will," they unanimously replied that they could not (Chrimes 379–80), and added ("gratuitously," as Chrimes points out) "that if anyone does to the contrary he is to be punished as a traitor."

It is sometimes suggested that Richard II favored the civil law over the common law (e.g., Tuck 151–52), and certainly his policies would have been easier to justify from a civilian's bookshelves than from a common lawyer's; as Keen puts it: "faced with the problem of resistance, [the civilians'] natural inclination was to ask whether rebellion did not create more problems than it solved" (1965b, 123). Nonetheless, we should not underestimate the degree of cooperation between the king and his judiciary in the last quarter of the fourteenth century. The "questions to the judges," which were to send Tresilian to the gallows for promoting his master's interests, may be the best known, but they are far from the only instance of this. Confronted by the appellants in February 1388, Richard turned straight to his judges: "at which time the justices, and serjeants, and others expert in the law, and also experts in the civil law, were commanded by our lord the king to give their advice to the lords in Parliament" (*RP* 3:236). And when he had indisputably regained the upper hand in 1397 he made a point of resubmitting the questions of 1387 to a new panel of judges and serjeants. Notwithstanding the fact that at least two members of this panel (Clopton and Thirning) owed their appointments to the former appellants, they promptly confirmed the findings of their predecessors, though not without a little understandable equivocation (Chrimes 389). When we observe Justice Clopton acting as legal consultant at the trial of his former patron, the earl of Arundel (*RP* 3:377), or Justice Rickhill roused in the middle of the night and sent off to Calais to take down Gloucester's confession, we can hardly suppose that their relationship with the king was even remotely an arm's length one. As late as 1369 judges had still been able to toy with the idea that the king might be sued like a private person (P&M

1:516; Kantorowicz 1957, 163–64), but by the last years of Richard II's reign such notions had been firmly consigned to the realm of legal fantasy.

Nothing conveys more vividly the threat posed by this alliance of king and judiciary to traditional institutions than the allegations made in the articles of Richard's deposition that he had abused the literate machinery of the law. While his opponents were engaged in a futile attempt to bind him by oath to observe legal archaisms they believed could be enshrined in written record, the king and his advisers were attempting to liberate the real political potential of literate technology. The success of the Lancastrian putsch suggests that Richard's experiment was premature, but there is no mistaking the consternation it caused among his contemporaries. The deposition articles furnish numerous instances of Richard's inconstancy and duplicity, not only in his word, but, more significantly from our point of view, "in his writings" [in scripturis suis] (ch. 42; *RP* 3:420). The twenty-fourth article (ch. 41), for instance, accuses him of having had "the rolls of the records which concerned the state and government of his kingdom destroyed and erased . . . in order to benefit and support his own evil rule," and the eighth (ch. 25) of having had "the rolls of Parliament altered and deleted at his pleasure" in order to legitimize the establishment of his own commission to deal with parliamentary petitions.

Other articles accuse the king of having reneged on his written undertakings, and here we are given a particularly clear glimpse into the way written record was dismantling Ricardian trouthe. As Thomas Hoccleve, himself a royal bureaucrat, would remind the future Henry V, kings had to be particularly circumspect when committing their promises to writing:

> And syn a princes oth, or his promesse,
> Whan þei nat holden ben, him dishonure,
> His lettre and seel, whiche more open witnesse
> Beren than þei, good is take hede and cure
> That þei be kept; writinge wil endure;
> What a man is, it prest is for to preue;
> Outhir, honure hit shal him, or repreue.
>
> (*Regement* 2367–73)

Richard's use of written documents certainly appeared to make his own perfidiousness "prest for to preue." We have already seen how he had gone back on the pardons granted to Arundel and his fellow appellants—and the fourth article (ch. 21; *RP* 3:418.) of his deposition makes quite clear that these were written pardons: "tam Cartam de dicta Pardonatione generali quam Cartam Pardonationis postea sibi concessam." As if to add insult to injury, Richard even compelled those suspected of sympathy for the former appellants to sue for fresh pardons and to pay heavily for what must have seemed to them very flimsy guarantees indeed (chs. 23 and 24). In the same vein, he is also accused of breaking a written undertaking ("per Literas suas patentes") to Hereford to protect the duke's interests while he was in exile (ch. 29), and of failing to repay loans despite having promised faithfully in writing to do so ("non obstante quod idem Rex per singulas Literas patentes promisit bona fide . . .") (ch. 31).

One article, however, the twenty-first (ch. 38), stands out from all the others, as exposing the bureaucratic underpinning of Richard's new monarchy: "The king, striving to crush his people and ingeniously acquire their goods for himself, so as to load himself down with superfluous wealth, caused the people of seventeen counties to be forced to submit themselves to the king as traitors, in sealed documents [ad submittendum se Regi tamquam Proditores, per Literas sub sigillis eorum]; by which device he had great sums of money granted to him by the priests and people of those same counties to enable them to keep their king's good will." These are the famous "blank charters," justly deplored in contemporary chronicles (see Clarke 105–14); though they may not have been literally blank, they were certainly, as Caroline Barron has shown, "couched in terms which gave the king *carte blanche* over the lives and possessions of his subjects" (1968, 13). One could hardly ask for a better illustration of the literate foundations of institutional treason than this. Where the old personal treason had once been defined by mutual oaths of loyalty, its far more potent successor was truly the product of one-sided written instruments. Richard's contemporaries saw clearly enough that in this case the medium was as dangerous as its message, for in one of those memorable parodic gestures the folklaw turned to at times of crisis, they celebrated the success of the Lancastrian revolution by submitting Richard's charters to a traitor's death: "all the blank charters by which the king's subjects throughout England had submitted themselves to Richard's pleasure under their own seals were carried publicly to London on the points of spears and burnt, together with their multitude of seals, as though there had been a new conquest of the land" (Adam of Usk 42). It was, of course, to be a short-lived triumph; though the usurpation may have looked to some like a reverse for the forces of literate authoritarianism, their ultimate victory could never really have been in doubt. Henry of Bolingbroke and his supporters were hardly less open to charges of perjury than their opponents (Sherborne); they were quite as aware of the value of written record, and, if anything, they were even more astute in the business of generating literary propaganda (Strohm 1992, 75–94). As Gervase Mathew observes, Henry himself "seems to have shared the same conception of kingship as Richard and pursued the same policy in administration" (167); predictably enough, the lessons of Richard's deposition would not be lost on later Lancastrian kings.[37] In the long run, its Ricardian crisis would prove to have changed the meaning of *treason*, like that of its antonym *truth*, almost beyond recognition.

7

Charter and Wed

. . . still if he wrote it I suppose thered be some truth in it . . .
— James Joyce, *Ulysses*

In the autumn of 1432 a man named John Lydeyard was involved in a lawsuit with a certain Thomas Seyntcler. Lydeyard was claiming by right of his wife certain Oxfordshire manors once held by her forebear Roger St. John, who had died without issue. The tenant, Thomas Seyntcler, on the other hand, claimed that Roger's manors had been left to a certain Peter St. John, and thence to his own family, citing a Chancery document, a postmortem inquisition of 1353, that stated that Peter St. John was "a cousin and the nearest heir of the aforesaid Roger, being more than forty years of age" at the time (*SCKC* 97–98). This document, safely locked up in the Tower of London, was the key to Seyntcler's defense and it was crucial that Lydeyard find some means of discrediting it. Accordingly, he bribed an Exchequer clerk called William Broket to turn forger in order to bring its legal authority into question.

Robert Danvers, Seyntcler's lawyer, however, proved to be more than a match for Lydeyard and before the case could even come to trial he had managed to expose the forgery and thoroughly discredit his opponent. Incensed that anyone could have imagined that he himself might stoop to forgery ("the aforesaid Robert has been greatly defamed by persons in many parts of the realm who blame him"), and suspecting some skulduggery on Broket's part, Danvers had contrived to send the Exchequer clerk a letter over Lydeyard's name asking "whether any of the clerkes of the Tour in any wyse myght aspie you in rasyng of the seyd record, and whether you have tolde your counsell to any of your felowes that is aqueynted with Davers, etc." and the poor man fell right into the trap: "as touchyng the clerkes of the Tour Credo quod non vidit [I believe he saw nothing], etc. And as touchyng the counsell Nemini loquebar nisi quod scitis [I have spoken only to those you know about] etc." (*SCKC* 99). Danvers promptly hauled Broket up before the King's Council, where he confessed to everything and was duly relieved of his post. Lydeyard's case naturally enough collapsed, and Danvers went on to enjoy a highly successful legal career, becoming a serjeant at law in 1444 and a justice of Common Pleas in 1450.

An air of archaism clings to a number of the details of this story. If the lawyer's tone of moral indignation seems rather strong by modern standards, it is perhaps no more than we might expect in an age when trouthe and honor were still so closely identified with one another. The status accorded written evidence also appears somewhat exaggerated from our perspective, particularly as we are made all too aware of the still rudimentary systems of registration and authentification underpinning it. Finally, the subterfuge employed by Danvers to expose Broket's dishonesty reminds us that in a period of limited literacy the widespread use of amanuenses and messengers made the private letter a far from secure medium (cf. E. S. Cohen). But, for all this, we are unlikely thus far to find anything strikingly unusual in the story of Lydeyard's attempted forgery. What is distinctly odd, however, is the form that this forgery took. William Broket's public confession, made after he realized that the game was up, reveals that "with his fingernail he erased the number *XL* contained in the said inquisition . . . and with fresh ink he wrote again the said number and blotted it [cum nouo incausto renouauit et blottauit], in order that in this point it might appear especially suspect" (100). The document in question is still to be seen in the Public Records Office and examination under ultraviolet light confirms the truth of Broket's statement (Hector pl. 4): he did indeed do nothing more than erase the Roman numeral forty and then write it back in over the erasure.

In one sense, of course, Broket had forged nothing, but his tampering, had it been successful, by casting doubt on Peter St. John's age at the time of the grant, and hence his fitness to inherit and bequeath the estate, would have severely compromised Seyntcler's defense. This forgery was thus, I suggest, a kind of literate counterpart to the equivocal oath—its form, so alien to the modern imagination, reaching back to an age when an ambiguous truth was the first refuge of anyone trying to avoid an unequivocal falsehood. Behind it lies the same kind of superstitious reluctance to tamper with the form of a charter that had once attached to the form of words used in an oath. The case, in other words, provides an excellent illustration of how even the landowning class of late medieval England had still not fully made the imaginative leap into our world of written record: the picture of William Broket furtively scraping away two letters with his fingernail and then hurriedly writing them back in again, is a vivid reminder that this was a world where written documents might still be regarded as potent artifacts.

A similar impression is conveyed by a late-fifteenth-century report, written by one of the principals, of a protracted dispute between a Lancashire gentleman called Robert Pylkington and a rival claimant to one of his manors called John Aynesworth. Pylkington had begun this report in 1493, "be the advycez of his counsayle lernyd accordyng to his evydencez be the comaundement of my lord Husse that tyme chefe jugge of Englend, at kyllyngworth at the furst shewyng of owr evydencez both the parties, for a substanchall recorde" (*Report* 29). The formal display of documents described here ("the furst shewyng of owr evydencez") had occurred during a preliminary skirmish that had apparently gone in Pylkington's favor: "we layd afor the lordes owr evydencez, but the said John schuld have layde forth furst his evydencez be cause he began the trowbull, but yet he hade so grete favor that the said Robert shewed furst his evydencez and be the grace of God and gud ryght was well alowyd with all the curte at that tyme &c., accordyng to his lyne of blode and discent. And then the said John layd forth his evydence, and then my lord Husse lokyt on but a lytyll whyle and then cast thaym away from hym and said thay were enturlynyd" (33). We know from Langland that any sign of interlining was supposed to invalidate charters in the eyes of the law:

> A chartre is chalangeable bifore a chief Iustice;
> If fals latyn be in þat lettre þe lawe it impugneþ,
> Or peynted parentrelynarie, parcelles ouerskipped.
> The gome þat gloseþ so chartres for a goky is holden.
> (*PPl* B.11:303–6)

Quite properly, then, when the case was finally brought before a jury (in 1497), the judges were careful to direct its attention to this particular defect in Aynesworth's "evidence": "His ruggenall [original] dede was haldon up with the jugges that all the pepull myght see and poyntyd with the jugges handes how hit was enturlynyd in so mone dyvers placys the jugges said thay see never none so mych enterlynyd and be calde a pole dede and said they couth not alow that dede for gud, but put hit to the discressiones and consiensez of the xii aforsaid" (*Report* 42). Unfortunately, this particular jury's consciences were not so tender that they were prepared to make their neighbor Aynesworth look like a *goky*, and Pylkington, much to his indignation, lost the case.[1] Nonetheless as he describes the squabble over which party should first present its "evydencez," or Chief Justice Hussey's peremptory dismissal of the "enturlynyd" charter, or the royal judges' parading of Aynesworth's "ruggenall dede" around their courtroom for all the people to see, we get a strong sense of the talismanic authority that still clung to legal instruments even at this late date.

It would be easy to conclude from cases such as Seyntcler's and Pylkington's that even in the fifteenth century people were still conscious of the novelty of writing and approached charters and deeds with a kind of awe that centuries of familiarity have robbed them of for us, but I shall argue that the real reasons are far more complex. For one thing, as those who stuck charters on poles during the Peasants' Revolt and again in the aftermath of Richard's deposition saw all too clearly, written instruments were a physical embodiment of the power of the ruling elite and the authority of the king's law; for another, they still partially inhabited a world of wed and borrow where the solemn rituals of trothplight continued to imbue them with an aura that had long attached to all such contractual tokens. In the fourteenth century the written word could be objectified, fetishized, and demonized in ways that are largely foreign to us, and this chapter will attempt to reconstruct some of the associations it must still have possessed for Ricardian England.

Writing as Talisman

Narratives recording the first exposure of nonliterate people to writing often emphasize their sense of awe at its magical properties. Peter the Martyr (*De Orbe Nova* 3:8), for instance, tells of one of the first Spanish settlers on Hispaniola sending an aboriginal messenger across the island with a present of roasted rabbits for a fellow colonist; since an inventory (written on the leaf of a local tree) had been sent along with this gift, however, its recipient was able to ascertain that the messenger had consumed part of his consignment en route: "When the mayster had looked a whyle on the leafe in the presence of the seruaunt, he sayde thus vnto hym. Ah soonne, where is thy faythe? Coulde thy gredye appetyte preuayle so muche with the as to cause the to eate the connies commytted to thy fydelytie? The poore wretche trembelynge and greatlye amased, confessed his faute: And therwith desyred his mayster to tell hym howe he knewe the treweth therof. This leafe (quod he) whiche thou browghtest me, hath toulde me all" (Arber 174). While it might seem to us that this story offers a particularly nice illustration of the way writing can disrupt traditional loyalties by forcing an uncomfortable confrontation between ethical and objective truth, for the author it reveals nothing more than the gullibility of the aboriginal inhabitants and the utility of writing as an authoritarian tool: "It is to bee lawghed at what owre men haue perswaded the people of the Ilande as towchynge this leafe. The symple soules beleue that at the commandement of owre men, leaues do speak and disclose secreates . . . And thus they meryly deceaue these seely soules and keepe theym vnder obedyence: In so muche that they take owre men for goddes." Peter's pose of superior condescension toward the naive nonliterate is of course entirely typical of such accounts.[2]

A similar description of "the feelings of an untaught people, when observing for the first time the effects of written communications" is given by John Williams, an English missionary to Rarotonga in the Cook Islands in 1827. He tells how once in the course of building a church he found he had left his square at home and dispatched a local chief with a message for his wife written in charcoal on a chip of wood. The chief undertook this errand with the utmost skepticism, but on finding that delivery of the chip duly elicited the missing implement, "[he] leaped out of the house; and, catching up the mysterious piece of wood, he ran through the settlement with the chip in one hand and the square in the other, holding them up as high as his arms would reach, and shouting as he went, 'See the wisdom of these English people; they can make chips talk, they can make chips talk!' . . . It was a circumstance involved in so much mystery, that he actually tied a string to the chip, hung it round his neck, and wore it for some time" (J. Williams 102). One does not have far to seek in fourteenth-century England for what at first glance look to be counterparts to this Rarotongan chief's phylactery.

Let us take, for example, the case of Roger atte Hacche who in 1382 paid a man called Roger Clerk twelve pence as a down payment on a cure for his wife, Johanna, "then lying ill with certain bodily infirmities" in London. Clerk sold him "an old parchment, cut or scratched across, being the leaf of a certain book, and rolled it up in a piece of cloth of gold, asserting that it would be very good for the fever and ailments of the said Johanna; and this parchment, so rolled up, he put about her neck, but in no way did it profit her" (Riley 465). In court it transpired that Roger Clerk, who was "in no way a literate man," believed, or claimed to believe, that the parchment contained the words, "Soul of Christ, sanctify me; body of Christ, save me; blood of Christ, drench me; as thou art good Christ, wash me," but upon examination it was discovered that "not one of those words was found written thereon."[3] Clerk's punishment was to be ridden through the streets of London accompanied by rough music and with the offending parchment, a whetstone, and two urinals hung about his neck (466), but whether he would have had to undergo these indignities had the parchment indeed contained the alleged prayer is far from certain for such objects seem to have been a perfectly regular feature of medieval life. A Yorkshire ghost story, set in the time of Richard II, for instance (James 415), tells of a nervous tailor setting out to keep an appointment with a restless spirit and offering the neighbor who had promised to accompany him "part of my writings ("partem de scriptis meis") which I wear about me for night fears" (416) to protect him; in the event, the neighbor's courage having failed him, the tailor arrives at the trysting place protected only by the "four gospels and other sacred words" that he has upon him (417). Luckily, all goes well and he manages safely to release the spirit, which then repays the favor by advising him that on his return home he should be sure to go to sleep with his best writings on his head ("optima sua scripta in suo capite") (418). That the author of this particular ghost story was apparently a monk of Byland Abbey suggests that such talismanic use of religious texts was not in itself necessarily frowned upon by the church, and in fact no less an authority than Thomas Aquinas had been prepared to speak up for talismans. Writing of whether it is wrong to hang holy scriptures about the neck ("utrum suspendere divini verba ad collum sit illicitum"), Aquinas assures us unequivocally that as long as we wear only sacred words and do not wear them out of vanity, "such tokens are lawful" (2a2æ.96.4; 40:83).[4]

Not that everyone would have approved, of course: the Wycliffites, predictably enough, regarded talismans as idolatrous—"it is supersticious to hang wordis at þe nek," says one lollard tract bluntly (*Apology* 92)—though a more common complaint was that the practice smacked of magic. Certainly, written artifacts were sometimes put to somewhat sinister uses: in 1371 a man named John Crok was arrested for having in his possession a bag containing the head of a dead Saracen, a book, and "some paper scrolls, painted in various ways" (*SCKB* 6:163); he was acquitted because no one could be shown to have suffered any actual harm from these fearsome objects, but the court made sure that before his release both the bag and its contents were burned. Against such a background, we may appreciate why the author of *The Mirror of Justices* should have included "carrying the evangelists and charms on their necks" in a list of the species of divination and sorcery that merit excommunication (16), but such an objection was still insufficient in most people's minds to relegate talismans to what Eamon Duffy has called "the devotional underground" (278). An early-fifteenth-century exemplum from Northern Italy tells of a clerk, famous for his expertise in making talismans ("peritum in experimentis et famosum") who is asked by a lady for a magic scroll that will open locked doors; he fobs her off with a useless piece of paper ("scripturam sine virtute"), though not, as J. A. Herbert assumed, simply because he hoped "thus to cure her of faith in magic" (656), but, rather more interestingly, because he disapproved of the purpose to which she intended to put his scroll—to help her make clandestine visits to her lover (BL Addit. MS 27336, f. 29[a]).

The handful of such talismans to have survived down to modern times claim to be effective against an enormous range of misfortunes; indeed, there seems little"—short of the condition of mortality itself, against which "no chartyr may help, byll, scrow, ne clawse" (K. Brunner 28, st.7)—that the appropriate roll of parchment might not ward off. One, for instance, offers its bearer protection "fro hys enmys, fro soden deth, fro poysoun, fro wykyd bestis, fro fyre, fro water, fro thondyr and liȝtenyng, fro feuerys, fro all maner of parellys and fro all maner desesys that be withyn the body of man or woman fro the hede to the fote" (Förster 219). Another promises that

> þe day þat þou beryst it vpon þe or lokist þer-vpon, þou shalt haue þise gret giftis þat folowyth: The furst is þou schalt die no soden deth; The seconde is þou schalt not be hurte nor slayne with no maner of wepyn; The iij^{d} is þou shalt haue resonabull godis & helth vn-to þy lyuys ende; The iiijth is þyne enmys shall neuer ouyr-com þe; The vth is no maner of preson nor fals wytnes shall neuer greve þe; The vjth is þou shalt not die with-oute the Sacramenttes of the Chirche; The vijth is þou schalt be defendid from all maner of wykkid spirites, tribulacions, & dissesis, & from all infirmitees & sekenes of þe pestilence; The viijth is yf a woman be in trauell of childe lay þis vpon her wombe & þe childe schall haue Cristendom & þe moder schall haue purificacion. (quoted by Bühler 274)

There is no question of such claims not being taken seriously: one of the rolls studied by Curt Bühler, for example, "from the severe usage it has evidently undergone (as its present, largely illegible, state makes evident), may well have seen service as a 'birth girdle'" (274).[5] Even these extensive lists do not exhaust all the possibilities, however. Writing "Seynt Iorge our lady knyghth" on a "bylle" and hanging it on the mane of one's horse, for instance, could apparently protect it from nightmares (Gray 1974, 57), while *vita vasta anima*, written on "pur parchment with the blode of an owle also mole" and buried under a woman's door, would make her "in a whill daunce naked and take it awaye" (Robbins 1968, 6–7).[6]

By the late fourteenth century the use of writing for magical purposes had a very long history in England. There is a well-known story in Bede of a Northumbrian warrior called Imma who was held captive by the Mercians; his brother, a priest called Tunna, believing him to be dead, said regular masses for his soul, as a result of which no fetter was able to hold him. His captors, naturally enough puzzled by this phenomenon, asked him "whether he had on his person any loosening charms [*litteras solutorias*] such as are told of in stories" (4.22; 402). The charms referred to have usually been assumed to be runic but R. I. Page has suggested that *litteras* here could equally well refer to letters written on a slip of parchment or to "a document containing the whole charm" (23). He cites in support an Old English charm for obtaining favor: "If you wish to go to your lord or to the king or to another man or to a meeting, then bear these 'staves' [*stafas*]. Each of them will then be gracious and kind to you"; the staves in question consist "partly of individual letters . . . partly of meaningful words and gibberish letter groups" (22). It might, I suppose, be possible to attribute to a late-seventh-century Northumbrian warrior the same kind of superstitious awe of writing that our early-nineteenth-century missionary claimed to have observed in Rarotonga, though I think even this would be stretching things; but for Ricardian England, where even members of the unfree peasantry must have had some familiarity with the way literacy functioned (cf. Clanchy 1993, 46–50), such a claim is quite impossible to sustain.

It was not even true, for example, that only nonliterates like Roger Clerk and Roger atte Hacche were likely to put their trust in the salutary effects of wearing a piece of written parchment. No doubt a guarantee of not being "hurte nor slayne with no maner of wepyn" held a particular attraction for professional champions, so we need not be surprised when, during the course of preparations for a duel in a writ of right case of 1355 over the ownership of Salisbury castle between the bishop of Salisbury and the earl, the judges discovered "in the coat of Shawel, who was the bishop's champion, many rolls of prayers and charms" [plusors rolles des orisons et sortileges] (*Abridgements* 29 Edw. 3, p. 12b). But lest we should suppose that only unlettered bruisers like Shawel could have put any reliance in such things, we might recall that a few years later Thomas of Gloucester's regulations for the conduct of duels (regulations drawn up for use in the Court of Chivalry and clearly intended for wellborn combatants) require that each party swear not to carry into the lists "ne stone of vertue, ne herbe of vertue, ne charme, ne experiment, ne carocte, ne othir inchauntement" (*Monumenta* 1:317). Perhaps the most dramatic instance of a literate person's being associated with such talismans in this period, however, occurs in Favent's account of the death of Chief Justice Tresilian after the appellants' rebellion in 1388: "And when he had arrived at the place of execution to be dispatched, he was unwilling to ascend the ladder, but as he climbed, goaded with clubs and whips, he said: 'As long as I bear certain things upon me I cannot die.' They stripped him at once, and found certain charms [*experimenta*] with certain signs drawn on them in the manner of heavenly letters [*carecterum celi*], and one had the head of a devil drawn on it and several had been inscribed with the names of devils. When these had been taken from him, he was hung naked, and to make completely sure he was dead, his throat was cut" (18). This story was known as far away as Bordesley Abbey in Worcestershire, where a monk called John Northwood, after copying the talismanic "Letter of Charlemagne" (see Bühler 271 n. 12) into his commonplace book, noted "in þis wrytyng ar to names ho-so nemyth hem. þ[t] day he schal not dye þey he were hongud on a tre. And þis," he adds, "was preuyd by. syr Robard. tresylyan" (*Worcestershire* 154). Whether or not the story had any real substance is of course quite another matter, but the fact remains that it was told of a very prominent member of the royal administration in late-fourteenth-century England and credited at the time by a member of an important Cistercian abbey that possessed a substantial library (Blaess).

Tresilian's story suggests that whatever power written documents might command as talismans at this period could hardly have depended simply on the naive awe of the impressionable illiterate. Not that a credulous deference to the written word was never a factor, of course—"þes leude pepull wenyth," observes John Mirk, "thus I se a pryst do, and þys he sayde; wherfor I may do ryght soo: he ys letturt, and seth yn his boke what hym faylyth and owyth to do" (192)—merely that it is not sufficient in itself to explain the fetishization of documents in the fourteenth century. Indeed, even the accounts, given above, of the first reactions of people who have had no previous experience of the operation of literacy may be suspected of exaggerating this element in their behavior.

In his well-known description of the reaction of the Nambikwara to his offer of pencils and paper (339–45), Claude Lévi-Strauss differs radically from Peter the Martyr or John Williams in laying stress on the morally detrimental effects of exposure to writing: "[they] dimly perceived that writing and treachery were entering their world in unison" (345). Nonetheless, as Jacques Derrida has taught us, his account is scarcely less ideologically loaded than theirs—merely substituting for the paternalistic rhetoric of the colonist the romantic stereotype of Rousseau's noble savage. We do not have to accept uncritically Derrida's fanciful notion of an "archi-écriture" to recognize the justice of his observation that the Nambikwara's rapid comprehension of the function of writing "presupposes the prior existence of structures which make it possible" (185), nor to acknowledge the force of his challenge (prompted by Lévi-Strauss's dismissive reference to the Nambikwara's simple decoration of their utensils): "how far can we legitimately deny that these dots and zigzags on their gourds are to be called writing?" (161–62). An instinctive grasp of the communicative function of writing is not really surprising given the fact that many traditional cultures appear to live far denser symbolic lives than we do ourselves and that our writing is arguably little different in essence from many of the symbolic systems with which they are likely to be familiar. As a character in Achebe's *No Longer at Ease* remarks, "Our women made black patterns on their bodies with the juice of the *uli* tree. It was beautiful, but it soon faded. If it lasted two market weeks it lasted a long time. But sometimes our elders spoke about *uli* that never faded, although no one had ever seen it. We see it today in the writing of the white man" (115). Thus, when Soyinka recalls seeing in his youth a talisman that consisted of "a sheet of paper with strange diagrams and words which seemed . . . distortions of some biblical names from the Old Testament" (*Aké* 188), we need not feel surprise at learning that its owner was no illiterate villager but an anxious candidate for a government exam. Such faith in the potency of the written word is very far from being simply a function of its technological novelty, and, as anyone at all familiar with the ritual life of modern Judaism will know, can survive in a thoroughly literate milieu. Clearly, one source of this potency, as Lévi-Strauss was at pains to stress, is an almost universal association between writing and authority; if writing has not always been necessary for advancing knowledge, he notes, "it is perhaps indispensable for asserting authority" (344).

The Authority of Writing

In the late Middle Ages, England was emerging from more than a millennium of craft-literacy in which the oath-book had been one of the primary emblems of the power of both church and state. In just the same way that scraps of parchment might be used talismanically so too might complete copies of the Gospels themselves: "þe gospel writun is not to be worschipid," warns the Wycliffite tract quoted above, and goes on to explain that, "we how not to honor þe gospel þus, þat is to sey, þe henk, or þe parchemyn, and þe figeris; wening werkyng to be gostly in hem, or þe spirit of God, or þe godhed; noiþer þat swilk writing bi hem silf drif a wey fendis, or seknes, or kep fro harmis, as sum not vndirstonding wel gostly þingis demun" (*Apology* 91). The Gospel of John appears to have been particularly prone to such use: "to whome thynkest thou spake he these thynges: the flesshe profyteth nothynge at all / it is the spiryte that quyckneth and gyueth lyfe?" writes Erasmus; "veryly not to them whiche with saynt Iohans gospell, or an agnus dei hangynge aboute their neckes, thynke themselfe sure from al maner of harme" (113).[7] When Roger atte Hacche sought to cure his wife's ailment with a piece of holy parchment, then, it is likely that he was merely seeking to tap into the same source of power that was widely employed to seal verdicts, testimonies, and contracts with oaths sworn on the Evangelists.

This power is well evoked by a sixteenth-century note on the last page of one surviving early oath-book, the Red Book of Darley: "This booke was sumetime had in such reverence in darbieshire that it was comonlie beleved that whosoever should sweare untruelie uppon this booke should run madd" (Ogilvy 180–81). Something of the awe surrounding an oath sworn on the Bible is occasionally evoked even by mundane legal documents such as this deposition from Kent (1416): "and that thes poyntes be trewe all [and] sume, we seyne, so helpe vs gode and halydome, as we wil answere before gode atte daye of doome, and for mede of owre soles; in discheyinge of a mannes ryght, we make this testimone in owre lives, because we ben men of grete age; We be owre oone will with owte corarcturr[e] haue touched the booke" (Flasdieck 55). Though the inexorable spread of vernacular literacy was beginning to demystify even sacred writing for the late-fourteenth-century laity (as Lollard polemic amply demonstrates),[8] it could evidently still command considerable awe among the people at large.[9]

This popular awe of sacred writings offered the church a powerful weapon. The author of an early-fifteenth-century poem on legal abuses exploits the immanent power of the oath-book in his warnings against perjury:

> & whan he goþ [to] boke forward on his fete,
> þer up on to swere fals he schal wel wete,
> þat he forsakiþ [&] lessiþ for his fals entent,
> Alle þe gode weys & pilgremage þat euere he rode or went;
> and whan þat he on þe boke leyth forþ his hond,
> Þer on to forswere him he schal vnderstond,
> Þat he lesiþ alle his gode werkis wit[h] his hondis wrought,
> & to sauacioun of his soule þei serve him of nought;
> & þerto he forsakith alle þe gode wordis of god,
> Þat bene wretin in þat boke be þei euene or od;
> & when þat he afterward haþ kissid þe boke,
> For any þank of god þar hym neuere loke.[10]
> ("Lovedays" 64–75)

While some of the sensational consequences attributed to perjury at an earlier period may make warnings such as these appear rather tame, it is nonetheless important to remind ourselves that the "Britoun book, written with Evaungiles" that blinds Constance's perjured accuser in "The Man of Law's Tale" (666–72) would have been no romantic archaism for many of Chaucer's contemporaries. Earlier in the century Robert Mannyng had told the story of a rich Londoner who sought to win a lawsuit "aboute a lytyl land" (2701) with a poor rival, by swearing a false oath (apparently in compurgation):

> And god toke veniaunce apertly
> Þat alle hyt saye þat stode hym by,
> For whan he hadde hys oth swore
> And kest þe boke hem alle before,
> Vp ne ros he neuer more
> But lay ded before hem þore.
> (2715–20)

And an exemplum added to the *Speculum Laicorum* (attributed to John of Howden), early in the fifteenth century, tells of a cynical perjurer whose rash boast that the hand with which he had touched the book was as sound as the other provokes God to scorch both hand and arm with infernal fire (Herbert 410.ix; BL Royal MS 7.C.XV, f. 132b).

The close identification of medium and message implicit in such stories is strongly reminiscent of the medieval cult of the saints, who might themselves, of course, be evoked as guarantors of solemn oaths. Indeed, it is not difficult to understand how owning or even simply touching the book of a saint's life might be felt to provide the devout with access to the saint's power in just the same way as the Bible might be seen as establishing a physical link with God himself. The early-thirteenth-century *Seinte Marherete*, for instance, gives as one of the items in the martyr's final prayer: "Ich bidde ⁊ biseche þe, þet art mi weole ⁊ wunne, þet hwa-se-eauer boc writ of mi lif-lade, oðer bi-ȝet hit iwriten, oðer halt hit ⁊ haueð oftest on honde, oðer hwa-se hit eauer redeð, oðer þene redere bliðeliche lusteð, wealdent of heouene, wurðe ham alle sone hare sunnen for-ȝeuene" (46). God immediately grants this request, assuring her that all sinful creatures who put their lips to the "boc of þi pine" will, indeed, have their sins forgiven them (48). John Capgrave's *Life of St. Katharine* offers an even more vivid example, describing the discovery of the original book recording her martyrdom in terms that recall the invention of the true cross. The priest who unearths this buried treasure is led to the spot by a bizarre vision whose eucharistic overtones are unmistakable: in his dream "a persone honest, clothed in precyous shrowde" commands him to eat "a boke ful elde / Wyth bredys rotyn, leuys dusty & rent" (81–86) and, though he complains that "þese leuys derk & dyme . . . wyll brek my chaules & my throte" (94–97), he finds them surprisingly "swete, ryth as it hony wer" (107). A similar play on the eucharistic implications of literary consumption is found in the concluding section of Mechtild of Hackeborn's *Booke of Gostlye Grace* (589–91).[11]

From such remarkable representations of the physical book as these it is but a short step to one of the strangest emblems of the sacral power of the written word in the fourteenth and fifteenth centuries: the widespread image of the suffering Christ as a crucified charter or book spread out upon the writing desk of the cross and lettered with the ink of his blood. The ubiquitous topos of God as author—not merely the literal author of Holy Scripture, but also the figurative author of the great book of nature—had long meant that the image of the physical book had had a strong appeal for the medieval schoolman (Curtius 310–32). The effect of portraying God, not as the inscribing agent, but as the inscribed artifact involves something rather different and very much stranger to the modern imagination, a "movement between metaphor and referent" that as Miri Rubin has justly remarked is "dizzying" (306).

The crucified book seems to have found far more favor in private meditation and popular homily than in scholastic circles, where no doubt it was felt to smack of a kind of superstitious covenantalism.[12] A well-known example of its private use is found in Richard Rolle of Hampole: "More yit, swet Ihesu, þy body is lyke a boke written al with rede ynke: so is þy body al written with rede woundes. Now, swete Ihesu, graunt me to rede vpon þy boke, and somwhate to vndrestond þe swetnes of þat writynge, and to haue likynge in studious abydynge of þat redynge. . . . And, swete Ihesu, graunt me þis study in euche tyde of þe day, and let me vpon þis boke study at my matyns and hours and euynsonge and complyne, and euyre to be my meditacioun, my speche, and my dalyaunce" (75).[13] A similar use of this figure can be traced back at least to the letters of Peter of Blois in the early thirteenth century (208), however, and by the end of that century it was turning up in vernacular prayers to the Virgin.[14] There is an interesting example in the mid-fourteenth-century *Meditations on the Life and Passion of Christ* (1527–34),[15] and its appearance in the so-called Digby play of *Christ's Burial* (*Late Medieval Religious Plays* 149) shows that it could still command much of its old devotional power at the end of the fifteenth.[16]

The *Meditations on the Life and Passion of Christ*, with its sophisticated interweaving of this image with that of the *liber cordis*, a figure first made popular by Saint Bernard (see Leclercq 68–69), shows that the crucified book was employed as a focus for pious meditation within a thoroughly literate, if hardly scholastic, milieu, but such a claim cannot be made with nearly such confidence of its use in sermons, preaching manuals, and materials for popular instruction. Here the writer's purpose was clearly to exploit the reverence in which books were still widely held by the laity in order to impress upon them the solemnity of Christ's crucifixion and enliven for them the theology of the redemption — though at the same time this tactic was clearly dependent upon their having at least some comprehension of the way in which literacy functioned and of how images might be read and interpreted like letters on a page. As H. Leith Spencer puts it, "by studying Christ crucified (perhaps by meditating upon an image of the scene), the ignorant people receive their first lessons in spiritual literacy" (141). This tradition, savoring more of the grammar school than the hermit's cell, also reaches back to the first half of the thirteenth century,[17] but seems to have held a special fascination for the later Middle Ages.

The figure of the crucified book or charter evidently offered the preacher a particularly striking image. For example, the *Fasciculus Morum*, a popular early-fourteenth-century preacher's handbook, written by an English Franciscan, not only gives an exposition of the figure itself ("Christ, when his hands and feet were nailed to the cross, offered his body like a charter to be written on. The nails in his hands were used as a quill and his precious blood as ink"), but also suggests how the preacher might fully exploit its the dramatic impact on a lay audience: "Notice that a charter that is written in blood carries with it extreme reliability and produces much admiration" [nota quod carta conscripta sanquine vehementer solet importare securitatem et magnam admiracionem]" (212–13).[18] A sermon preached by Friar Nicholas Philip at Newcastle on Good Friday 1431, in which the comparison of Christ's passion to "a boke of scripture and wrytyng" (Little 248) forms the second of the sermon's three main divisions, gives the figure of the crucified book a more extended treatment. "The passion of Jesus Christ, which is the book of the laity [que est liber laicorum], can be known by the letters of the alphabet," says Philip, and then proceeds, in the best modern tradition (cf. Spencer 247–49 and 335–41), to explicate it meticulously letter by letter.[19] Though recorded in an odd mixture of Latin and English, this sermon would presumably have been preached in the vernacular and must have made a vivid impression at the time: "9ª littera est .k. qui denotat his knokyng', quando illi poppid hym and betten his chekis" (253).[20] So graphic an icon of God as a book can only have been fully effective in a society that had still not lost all inclination to regard books as objects imbued with magical power.

Of all the many treatments of the crucified book or document in Middle English, the fullest and most graphic appears in a very popular late medieval poem known as *The Charter of Christ*. This poem has come down to us in two main forms: one, the short version, contains the bare text of the charter itself (a conditional deed, drawn up in quasi-legal form, granting an estate in heaven to true believers); the other, longer version sets this deed within a narrative account of how it came to be drawn up, sealed and witnessed at the crucifixion. The legal language of the various texts of *The Charter of Christ* suggests that it may well have originated among the clerical dependents of a great estate, either ecclesiastical or secular, though whether its circulation was restricted to such milieu is far less certain. There are, in fact, a number of suggestive parallels between the *Charter* and the talismans we looked at earlier.[21] The opening lines of the long *Charter* in the B- and C-texts, for instance, read like an advertisement for its talismanic properties:

> He þat wyll rede ouer þis boke
> & with hys gostly high þer-in loke
> To [o]þer scole thare hym noȝt wende
> To sawe hys saule fro þe fende
> (*Minor Poems* 2:637)

Copies of the more portable shorter version offer even stronger evidence of the poem's talismanic appeal, with one text promising its possessor an indulgence of twenty thousand and thirty years (and six days) from purgatory (Spalding 15). No doubt hope of similar assistance had led someone (perhaps a monk) in 1400 to have the whole text of the shorter version carved on his gravestone in Kent, where it was later noted by the Elizabethan antiquary William Lambarde (Spalding xx).

Only the longer version of the charter (which survives in three distinct, though clearly related, texts) explicitly exploits the metaphor of the crucified book, however. In what is probably its earliest form (the A-text) the long *Charter* describes how Christ is forced to write out the deed on his own body since he can find no more permanent writing surface:

> Ne myȝte I fynde no parchemyn
> ffor to laston wel and fyn
> But as loue bad me do
> Myn owne skyn y ȝaf þerto
> (A.51–54; in Spalding 22b–24b)

The parchment itself is prepared by being beaten, washed, and stretched out to dry on the cross:

> To a pyler I was plyȝt
> I tugged and tawed al a nyȝt
> And waschon in myn ovne blod
> And streyte y-streyned vpon þe rod
> Streyned to drye vp-on a tre
> As parchemyn oveth for to be
> (A.75–80; 26b)

The ink is supplied by the blood streaming from Christ's nose, and the scourges are used as pens; all three versions give the curious detail, apparently derived from Mechtild of Hackeborn, of the number of letters (i.e., wounds) used to write out the charter:

> Hou many letters þer-on ben
> Red and þou maist weton and sen
> ffive thousand CCCC fifty and ten
> Woundes on me boþe rede and wen[22]
> (A.87–90; 26b)

The seals used to seal it are the spear and the iron nails, and, as for sealing wax:

The selyng wax was dere abouȝt
At myn herte rote it was souȝt
And tempred al wiþ vermylon
Of my blod þat ran a-doun
(A.143–46; 32b)

The B-text adds the further detail that the particular magnificence of this charter is exemplified by its having no less than five seals appended to it:

ffyue selis were sett there on
ffadir son god and man
the fythe that y louyd meste
that y come of holy goste
And there-fore þou myste well yse
that y am a man of grete poteste
(B.231–36; in Spalding 64a–66a)

It is difficult to read these remarkable passages without recognizing that such conflation of the power of the written word with the physical body of God himself could only have occurred in a culture where books and charters were regularly fetishized as objects of awe and mystery.

While a sense of awe deriving from a talismanic association of the written word with divine power explains much of the effect of the various texts of *The Charter of Christ*, there is another less obvious kind of dynamism at work here, one that derives from their role as records of contract between God and humanity. We have seen in earlier chapters how the physical token was gradually replaced by the indenture as a method of memorializing agreements from the twelfth century onward and how the two systems of oral trothplight and written covenant operated uneasily alongside one another throughout the Middle Ages. But, despite our ingrained bias in favor of technological evolution, we should not suppose that the influence flowed all in one direction, and I want next to examine how the older model might have affected the way writing was received in the late Middle Ages. Before looking at how some of the cultural capital that had once been invested in the wed came to be transferred to the charter, however, I shall first try to illustrate the continuing vitality of the old system to the end of our period and elucidate the role it played in late medieval social intercourse. Since, with only a few exceptions, the physical tokens themselves have not survived (or where they have survived cannot be positively identified), much of our evidence will inevitably be literary.

Writings and Tokens

When Margaret Paston tells us that her husband "set more by hys wrytyngys and evydens than he dede by any of his moveabell godys" (*Paston Letters* 1:333), she reminds us that techniques for duplicating and registering charters remained rudimentary to the end of the Middle Ages, and that people went to a great deal of trouble to safeguard original documents (see Marsh). In assiduously preserving legal instruments for posterity, however, medieval people were merely acting much as their forebears had done in carefully passing down valuable weds and tokens from one generation to the next. Many extant medieval artifacts owe their very survival to modern times because, as important symbols of tenure, they have been carefully conserved by successive owners. In a purely oral society, of course, all such tokens would eventually have been swept up with the detritus of history, but particularly when reinforced by inscriptions and written records they have sometimes proved unexpectedly durable. Medieval hunting horns and drinking horns, for example, are a comparative rarity in museum collections, but almost all those we do still possess turn out to have had a symbolic importance for the families that once owned them: the Ulph Horn in York Minster, the Savernake Horn acquired by the British Museum in 1975, and the Pusey Horn, now in the Victoria and Albert Museum (with its inscription, "King Knowde [Cnut] gave William Peuse / This horne to holde by the land"), are all well-known instances (Cherry). In the late fourteenth century such horns had not yet become mere antiquarian curiosities. In 1361, for instance, William Stanley had defended his hereditary forest rights in Wirral by producing just such a charter horn in open court (Stewart-Brown 107), and in the course of a long feud (1387–1392) over a forestership in Knaresborough, William Beckwith had broken into his rival's house and carried off "a silver mounted horn" in triumph, presumably because it symbolized the office he was claiming (*CPR* 1391–96, 551). Though many similar artifacts having reached the end of their mnemonic lifespan must have been quietly discarded, some idea of their original effect on contemporaries can still be recovered from medieval narrative. Romances are an obvious place to look for these symbolic tokens; no less than the rituals which invested them with significance, the stories associated with them offered a practical means of preserving their semantic potency for successive generations (as is still true of mementos and keepsakes in our own day). Indeed, the natural congruency of ritual and narrative in this aspect of oral culture helps account for much of the prominence of enchanted objects in medieval romance.

Predictably, then, the romances are filled with legal tokens, though they have often been camouflaged by thick accretions of myth and folktale. When Malory's Arthur, for instance, proves himself "rightwys kynge borne of all

Englond" (37) by pulling a sword from a stone, he is demonstrating his right to possess a symbol of dominion that under more conventional circumstances might simply have passed to him at a coronation. The motif of the encumbered title-sword makes a number of interesting appearances in English and French romance. The foundling hero of the early-thirteenth-century *Chevaliers as devs espees* succeeds in ungirding an enchanted sword from around the waist of a nameless damsel, who had acquired it by chance from a dead man in a ruined chapel. After various adventures, he finally learns of his parentage from his mother whom he meets immediately after drawing a second sword, this one accompanied with a letter threatening him with death unless he proves to be the most chivalrous of knights (lines 7197–7203). Having learned that he is called Meriadeuc and that the dead knight was his father Bleheri, he marries the helpful damsel, Lore of Caradigan. A somewhat later thirteenth-century romance, *Beaudous* by Robert of Blois, offers another example of the motif. On his death-bed a king, whose heir is his only daughter, makes his barons promise that she shall marry only that knight who is valiant enough to be able to unsheathe his sword *Honorée* (lines 693–96). The land is conquered by an opportunistic rival, and even a journey to Arthur's court, "to seek a knight who could draw the sword and by his lineage, prowess, and nobility come where he might marry her and deliver her land" (lines 719–24) fails to provide a champion until the arrival of Beaudous. The young man of course defeats the pretender, marries the heiress, learns his true lineage, and proves himself a worthy successor.

There is an obvious common element in such representatives of the encumbered sword motif. In every case the achiever of the sword is a young man of obscure parentage whom it aids in the recovery of his rightful lands. The sword establishes the young knight as legitimate claimant to a title, usually by proving his lineage, though sometimes (as in *Beaudous*) by establishing his right to the hand of an heiress. With this in mind, there are at least two further weapons which, though protected by neither stern warning nor magic, should, I believe, be included in this romantic armory: the broken sword in *Sir Degaré* and the self-forged sword in *Sir Gowther*. *Sir Degaré* begins with the hero's being left on the doorstep of a hermitage by his mother, who has been abandoned by her fairy lover. Brought up by foster parents, the boy eventually discovers his mother by means of a pair of magic gloves (which will fit only one hand) and receives a broken sword for his patrimony:

Þe swerd sche fet forht anon riȝt,
And Degarré hit out pliȝt.
Brod and long and heui hit wes:
In þat kyngdom no swich nes.
Þan seide Degarré forþan,

"Whoso hit auȝt, he was a man!
Nou ich haue þat i[n] kepe,
Niȝt ne dai nel ich slepe
Til þat i mi fader see,
ȝif god wile þat hit so be."
(705–14)

Predictably, Degaré's father, with whom he later finds himself jousting, recognizes the sword with its missing point and is duly reconciled with his son.[23] By contrast Gowther, the son of an Austrian duchess, has no legitimate claim to his dukedom because he has in reality been fathered by a fiend. It is surely therefore significant that

Be that he was fyftene yere of eld,
He made a wepon that he schuld weld
(No nodur mon myght hit beyr):
A fachon bothe of styll and yron.
(136–39)

Sir Gowther provides an antitype to the encumbered sword motif—the illegitimate heir forced to fashion his own title.

The use of weapons as symbols of tenure is well attested in England, at least at an earlier period, though in general swords are rather less well represented than knives (Clanchy 1993, 37–41, 156, 258–59; Le Goff 283; P&M 2:88). At least three such knives have survived to modern times, two in Durham Cathedral (Clanchy 1993, 39 and 258) and one in Trinity College, Cambridge (Le Goff 283); all are from the first half of the twelfth century and all have broken blades. A knife might be useful because it could be readily identified with its owner (one of the Durham ones was probably Stephen of Bulmer's carving knife [Clanchy 1993, 258]), and if anything, a broken blade might be more mnemonically effective than an undamaged one, for the two pieces might be used, like the two halves of a tally stick or indenture, for purposes of authentification.[24] Clanchy, in fact, has found evidence that such knives might be deliberately and ritualistically broken to mark a livery of seisin (1993, 258–59). The significance of this for understanding the broken sword in *Sir Degaré* is obvious:

Certes ich am fader þine!
And bi þi swerd i knowe hit here:
Þe point is in min aumenere.
(1057–59)

If knives are the more numerous, there are certainly enough swords to prove that they too might serve as evidence of title. In the mid-1150s Durham Priory became involved in a dispute over the manor of Heatherslaw, and though the prior and one of the monks claimed to have witnessed its conveyance two or three decades earlier by means of its owner's sword, they had carelessly misplaced the weapon and subsequently lost their case (Clanchy 1993, 39–40). Clanchy has argued that we should understand in the same light a story of Earl Warenne brandishing "an ancient and rusty sword" before the king's justices in 1290 and challenging his *quo warranto* proceedings with the words: "Look at this, my lords, this is my warrant!" (36). Finally, there is one surviving weapon, the Conyers falchion, which as recently as 1860 was still being produced by the Conyers family to prove their right to hold the manor of Sockburn from the bishop of Durham (Cherry 112).

By now the cultural affiliation between the enchanted sword Arthur draws from the stone and such rare survivals as the Conyers falchion should be clear: both are title-swords—important, and far from merely symbolic, instruments of legal tenure.[25] The magical protection extended to the sword in the stone is not, I would argue, its original raison d'être but a later accretion, the result of a natural tendency, particularly in traditional societies, to attach taboos and talismanic properties to objects of great cultural importance. Such a functional account is unlikely to hold much charm for those literary scholars who have been drawn to either Freud or Frazer for expositionary models of the encumbered sword motif.[26] But even the restrained claim of Alexandre Micha, who sees a literary rather than a ritual descent from the Vergilian Golden Bough, seems to me tendentious; why should "une mission divine à remplir" represent the original motif and "un trône terrestre à conquérir" be its later rationalization (42) rather than the other way about? Our tendency in such contexts to stress the symbolic properties of magic rather than the magical properties of symbol strikes me not only as anachronistic, but ultimately as less useful for the purposes of literary analysis (cf. Vinaver).

For the moralizing elaborators of the Grail legend, magic and mysticism may have been more useful allies than customary law, but elsewhere in medieval romance the legal substratum remains quite distinct. The "holyn bobbe" (*SGGK*, line 206), for instance, that the Green Knight carries as a sign that he travels "in pes" and seeks "no plyȝt" (266), though it made John Speirs think of "an old vegetation god" (225), is perfectly comprehensible as a legal symbol.[27] A branch of living wood seems to have been a local English variant of the white baton carried by heralds on the battlefield, universally recognized after the mid-fourteenth century as the sign of a noncombatant (Keen 1965a, 110). Thus, only after he "brake a braunche in his hande and [brayde] it swythe" does Edward III's envoy ride between the two armies in *Wynnere and Wastoure* (line 121), and even a Saracen go-between in the *Sege of Melayne* recognizes the legal import of such a token:

> The messangere bare a wande
> Of ane olefe in his hande,
> In takynnynge he come of pece.
> (1211–13)

Indeed, without a universal acknowledgment of such signs, the laws of war in the Middle Ages could hardly have functioned at all. Among others were the public unfurling of banners to signify open hostility (see *Wynnere and Wastoure*, line 52),[28] and the handing over of a drawn sword to signify surrender:

> There þey openyd þer ȝatys wyde,
> Syr Garcy came down þat tyde,
> Wyth a drawyn swyrde in hys hande,
> And wyth a keye of golde clere,
> And ȝyldyd vnto Syr Emere,
> Hyt sygnyfyed all the lande.
> (*Bone Florence* 1222–27)

Knighton tells us that the defenders of Calais against Edward III in 1347 had presented him with two such drawn swords: the first to signify that he had conquered the city "vi et armis" and the second that they put their lives in his hands; though Knighton makes no mention of a token key, he does add that the citizens carried ropes in their hands as a sign that the king might hang or spare them as he chose (*Knighton's Chronicle* 84–85). In the military sphere, as in so many others in the fourteenth century, however, these traditional symbols were being augmented and replaced with written instruments—the drawn sword with a treaty of surrender, for instance, and the staff of the noncombatant with a letter of safe-conduct (see Keen 1965a, 127–30 and 197–206). Their use remained widespread to the end of the Middle Ages, nonetheless, and on the battlefield at least, continental lawyers were forced to allow that "words and signs had the same force that legal instruments had in ordinary law" (117). Indeed, one such medieval sign, the white flag of parley, has survived right down to the twentieth century.

More familiar to a modern reader will be the tokens given by lovers to affirm their love, yet even here a cursory survey will reveal how much more potent such tokens were in a medieval context than is common nowadays. For us the offer of a trifling gift to a member of the opposite sex need be little more than a gallant or sentimental gesture; for people in the Middle Ages it was often an action fraught with significance. In *The Earl of Toulouse*, the empress's gift of a ring produces a paroxysm of joy in her secret admirer:

> My dere derlynge,
> On thy fyngyr thys was!
> Wele ys me, y haue thy grace
> Of the to haue thys rynge!
> Yf euyr y gete grace of þe Quene
> That any loue betwene vs bene,
> Thys may be oure tokenyng.
> (402–8)

In the event, this gift proves to be the extent of the queen's extramarital indiscretion, yet later, faced with the prospect of imminent death, she still feels obliged to reveal the sin to her confessor (1076). What underlies her sense of guilt is the recognition that such a gift might easily be taken to imply a compact. It is surely for this reason that in Froissart's account of Edward III's flirtation with the countess of Salisbury, the lady should go to such lengths to avoid accepting a gift from her sovereign: by employing the cunning expedient of wagering a precious ring on the outcome of a chess game that he then contrives to lose, the king manages to trick her into accepting the ring, but next morning she calls her maid to return it to him; since Edward refuses to take it back and the countess will have no part of it, this royal token finally ends up in the possession of the lucky go-between (Froissart 2:184–87). Just how charged with meaning even the most innocent-seeming gift might be is suggested by a dilemma posed by a fifteenth-century collection of *demandes d'amour*: when a lady traveling out of town borrows a horse from one of her admirers and a cloak and hat from another, we are asked to decide "whome she is more holden too and whiche she shulde loue better." The correct answer, it transpires, is the lender of the cloak and hat, "be cause she may not worshipe more hym than to were his own clothes, ande no more may he hyr; and hit shewithe welle that she louethe hym better whan she puttethe his clothes nexte hyr herte in arayinge hyr body" (*Winchester Anthology* 103ᵇ).

Love tokens such as these belong in the world of aristocratic courtship, a world it is still possible to penetrate because it was recorded in (indeed, if Huizinga is to be believed, was shaped by) the literature of courtly love. The posy rings that Chaucer's Troilus and Criseyde *entrechaungen* to mark the beginning of their love, or the "broche, gold and asure, / In which a ruby set was lik an herte" that Criseyde sticks in her lover's shirt (*Troilus* 3:1370–72), can still be recognized as contractual tokens. Not only have actual examples of such medieval posy rings and heart-shaped brooches survived to the present day, but we can sometimes recognize the love lyric or verse epistle that an eager suitor composed to be sent along with them (R. Green 1983). A paucity of written evidence from the other end of the social scale, however, should not lead us to suppose that the use of tokens was any less common at the very humblest levels of society. A Harley lyric which imagines the Man in the Moon as a wretched peasant who has been caught stealing brushwood by the village hayward offers a rare glimpse into this obscure world: "He haþ hewe sumwher a burþen of brere, / Þarefore sum hayward haþ taken ys wed" (lines 23–24; in Turville-Petre 33). As in Langland's exemplum of the merchant caught trespassing in a field of wheat who must surrender his hat, hood, or gloves to the hayward (*PPl* C.13:45–47), this wed was no doubt a readily identifiable chattel or piece of clothing whose function was to ensure its owner's subsequent appearance in court. The stanza that follows is obscure, but the poet is apparently trying to lure the Man in the Moon home by proposing a clever plan to have the hayward himself stand surety for him (by getting him drunk and putting him in a compromising position), thereby recovering the wed from the village bailiff and removing the threat of legal action (cf. Menner 10–12). Unfortunately, the Man in the Moon proves too stupid to see the advantage of such a ruse—"Þe lostlase ladde con nout o lawe" (line 36)—and refuses to budge.

Such identification symbols demonstrate with particular clarity the subjective quality of the meaning invested in token objects, for their effectiveness clearly depended on a close association with those for whom they spoke. This is why rings, jewels, drinking vessels, gloves, and articles of clothing are so often employed to identify messengers, strangers, and long-lost friends in medieval romances and traditional ballads. Among a wealth of examples, a few must suffice here. Setting off to win his spurs, King Horn is given a precious ring by his lady Rymenhild (*King Horn*, lines 563–76) and when he returns seven years later disguised as an old palmer he reveals himself to her by dropping this ring into her wine goblet (1159–62); similarly, Amiloun marks his parting from his brother-in-arms Amis by giving him one of a pair of identical gold cups (*Amis and Amiloun*, lines 313–24) and when later, disfigured by leprosy, he arrives at Amis's gate it is by means of the cup that he is recognized (2005–124). A rather less dramatic instance of such use of tokens occurs in *Floris and Blancheflour*, where Floris, hot in pursuit of his lady, is helped on his way by a kindly host who directs him to a friend further along the road:

> We arn bretheren, and trouthes plyȝt:
> He can þe wyssh and rede aryȝt.

Þou shalt bere him a rynge
Fro myself, to tokenynge,
Þat he help þe in boure and halle
As it were my self befalle.
(503–8)

Traditional ballads often convey an equally strong impression of the subjective property of such tokens. In "The Lass of Roch Royal," for instance, the heroine is tricked into betraying her identity to her lover's jealous mother by means of their love-tokens:

Have you not mind, Love Gregory,
    Since we sat at the wine,
We changed the smocks off our two backs,
    And ay the worst fell mine?
(Child 2:216)

And in "Child Maurice" "a glove . . . lined with the silver grey" sent by a son to arrange a meeting with his mother (Child 2:266) is misinterpreted by her husband as a love-token from a secret admirer, with inevitably tragic consequences.

It might seem that there was little, other than a question of functional efficiency, to distinguish written documents from symbolic weds; this, after all, is how they were often distinguished by contemporaries. Gower's "Tale of the False Bachelor" (*CA* 2:2501–781) offers a particularly good example of how easily the simple wed might miscarry. Outside Cairo, on the eve of a battle against the caliph of Egypt, the sultan of Persia makes provision for the security of his only daughter:

The Soldan in gret privete
A goldring of his dowhter tok,
And made hire swere upon a bok
And ek upon the goddes alle,
That if fortune so befalle
In the bataille that he deie,
That sche schal thilke man obeie
And take him to hire housebonde,
Which thilke same Ring to honde
Hire scholde bringe after his deth.
(*CA* 2:2606–15)

On his deathbed the sultan gives this ring to one of his captains (the Roman emperor's son), but he in turn foolishly entrusts its secret to his squire, who then steals it and uses it to deprive his master of his rightful bride:

> His Bacheler it hath forthdrawe,
> And axeth ther upon the lawe
> That sche him holde covenant.
> The tokne was so sufficant
> That it ne mihte be forsake,
> And natheles his lord hath take
> Querelle ayein his oghne man;
> Bot for nothing that evere he can
> He mihte as thanne noght ben herd,
> So that his cleym is unansuerd,
> And he hath of his pourpos failed.
> (*CA* 2:2697–707)

We should not suppose that the legal weight accorded this "so sufficant" token is entirely a matter of romance hyperbole, for as I have been at some pains to suggest, Gower's world had yet fully to transfer its allegiance from the machinery of preliterate trothplight to that of the written indenture. Yet Gower pointedly underlines the functional disadvantages of the mute token in this story by contrasting it with the efficacy of written communication. What finally brings the squire's treachery to light is a letter which the brokenhearted suitor causes to be written as he lies on his deathbed (2:2731–32), a letter that leads to the squire's being arrested by the Persians,

> And forto seche an evidence,
> With honour and gret reverence,
> Wherof they mihten knowe an ende,
> To themperour anon thei sende
> The lettre which his Sone wrot.
> (2:2751–55)

When this letter reaches Rome the emperor duly sends off an army to bring the false bachelor to justice.

While their far greater denotative precision certainly helps to distinguish charters of enfeoffment and letters of surrender from broken swords and bunches of keys, there is a further obvious, but vital, difference between the two types of semantic vehicle, and a tendency for the transitional culture of the late Middle Ages to elide this difference goes some way to explaining the physical potency of the written word in our period. In the case of the charter the message is intrinsic, enabling someone who had not been present at the actual livery of seisin, who knew nothing of either of the parties, nor anything about the property transferred, to grasp the essence of the transaction merely by reading the document, whereas for the wed meaning is self-evidently extrinsic and must be actively projected onto it both at the original *traditio* and at each new "reading." Beyond the circle of those who attended the ceremony (or at the least those who could still recall such people to mind), the rod, the roof tile, the piece of turf must remain mute objects, and even within this circle they will only continue to bear meaning through continuous human reinvestment. This simple fact underlies many ancient rituals: bounds must be beaten every year, for instance, if succeeding generations are not to forget where the jurisdiction of the parish ends. Even the bread and wine of the Eucharist, tokens of Christ's compact with his followers, might be seen to function in this way: "do this for a commemoration [KJB: 'in remembrance'] of me" (Luke 22:19) — an insight to which we shall return when we come to consider the rise of Lollardy at the end of this chapter.

By and large, the literate citizenry of the late twentieth-century Western world has formally dispensed with such semantic vehicles, but some trace of them still survives in things like sporting memorabilia, family keepsakes, holiday souvenirs, and veterans' trophies: a ball that scored the winning run, a child's first pair of shoes, a piece of rock brought back from the Great Wall of China, a brass shell-casing from the Great War, these objects have meaning for their owners alone, but by the same token the inherent quality of this meaning will be quite different from that conveyed by words on a page. By virtue of its very potentiality such meaning must always be far more dynamic than documentary information can ever be; it remains inextricably enmeshed in the human lifeworld, only recoverable through active human intervention. The Middle Ages would certainly have understood our taste for such mementos: Ragnar Lodbrok's son Ivar, contemplating a raiding expedition against Rome, is said to have asked the distance of an old pilgrim, only to be shown two pairs of iron-shod shoes that the man had worn out on the journey back — "and," adds the saga writer, "the tokens of this are to be seen to this very day" (*Saga* 234). Such personal mementos were, however, only a small part of an extensive and readily recognized semantic system. Many medieval tokens, like the palmer's "signes of Synay and shelles of Galice" in *Piers Plowman* (B.5:521), had a conventionally assigned value that was widely understood, while still others, like the keepsakes exchanged by lovers or the personal articles sent with messengers to authenticate their messages had an intentionally restricted meaning. Somewhere in between lay the countless weds and tokens of everyday exchange that have now passed into cultural oblivion; while the general semantic import of many of these would have been obvious to all, the details they preserved would have been accessible to only a few. One has only to think for a moment of the very different kinds of information conveyed by a wedding ring and a marriage certificate to recognize the gulf separating the two systems.

Since engagement and wedding rings remain potent symbols in private life to this day, the immanent power that still resides in them may help us understand the potency of all such contractual tokens in earlier times. Just as a spouse, even today, might easily read into the loss of a wedding ring an ill omen for the future of the marriage, so a medieval king who dropped the scepter at his coronation might seem to have threatened the safety of his very kingdom. In fact, there is every reason to suppose that a close identification between symbol and symbolized generated a reverence for tokens in general that went far beyond anything likely to be met with in twentieth-century Western culture. The reason why counterfeiting or clipping the king's coin, for instance, was punished with far greater savagery than most other simple felonies seems to have been because "any tampering with the king's image and superscription on seal or coin was assimilated to an attack upon his person" (P&M 2:505 and was thus regarded, as a fourteenth-century case in King's Bench puts it, as "a special form of treason done to us" (*SCKB* 4:102). In a French letter of remission from the same period we hear of a man convicted of seeking to do harm to his sovereign by spitting on a coin and scratching it with a knife (Marchand 263). For the nonliterate, in particular, transferring to written artifacts the respect that was regularly accorded to physical tokens must have seemed natural enough. We learn from the Wycliffite tract cited above that "men seeng þe letter or selle of a lord, may bow him, or do of his hod" [*Apology* 91]). Such signs of respect are noteworthy, not merely because they attest to the perception of an aristocratic power residing in letters and seals, but also because they offer a clear illustration of a widespread sensitivity, far more dynamic than anything we are likely to encounter nowadays, to the potential importance of physical objects as carriers of meaning. They reflect, in other words, the continuing cultural prestige of what I have called "thinglike" troths. It should not be difficult to appreciate how, in a period of transition, such prestige might carry over from oral wed to written instrument.

The royal pardons purchased by medieval homicides to protect themselves from subsequent legal action offer a particularly obvious example of the way even mundane documents might acquire a talismanic status. In an age when verification of legal records in a central registry was a cumbersome, time-consuming, and expensive business, people might naturally be expected to have taken great care of original documents, but the necessity of carrying one's charter of pardon on one's person at all times seems to go well beyond the demands of normal safekeeping; in fact, it turns out that one's very life could depend on it (Hurnard 66). "Know that if a man has committed a felony and been outlawed for it, and he has purchased the king's charter," says the *Placita Corone*, "if he is sensible, he will carry the charter always on him [si il fet cum sages, il portera la chartre tout diz prest] to vouch for him, whatsoever may come to pass. For if he can be caught without his charter he can be beheaded as an outlaw, according to the law" (25). A vivid illustration of the practical consequences of this is provided by the sad case of Richard Sapling, who spent the winter of 1307/8 in the damp dungeon of Norwich Castle with his precious pardon clutched in his hand; when the commissioners for jail delivery turned up the following August the sodden document had become quite illegible, and though its royal seal was still intact poor Sapling was confined to his dank cell for seven more years while officials tried to authenticate it (cited by Hanawalt 1979, 38–39). Obviously, as Naomi Hurnard notes, "it was worth while getting a worn-out charter renewed and only prudent to get a lost one replaced" (66). Though their loss might not have had quite such dramatic and immediate consequences, many other legal documents would have been equally difficult, if not impossible, to replace, and charters of all kinds were jealously guarded by their owners.

In such a world, it is no wonder if documents were sometimes still thought of as somehow symbolizing, rather than merely recording, the legal facts to which they attested. In 1470, for instance, one of the judges in the case of a man accused of feloniously stealing six boxes of charters and muniments gave as his opinion that "[charters] are real property and it cannot be felony because they are not real chattels but are real in themselves [*realx en ex mesme*]" (*YB 10 Edw. 4*, 124). Some commentators have rationalized decisions such as this as merely an expedient way for the court to avoid having to impose the death penalty for a felony (P&M 2:499), but J. F. Stephen may very well have been right to believe that charters were actually regarded as "either realty or savouring of realty" (3:143).[29] The curious argument (unanimously accepted by the judges in the 1470 case) that because real property cannot be stolen neither can the title deeds associated with it reflects, I suggest, the stubborn survival of an ancient belief that deeds were not so much evidence of ownership as symbols of possession.[30] In another of the Byland Abbey ghost stories, cited earlier, the spirit of a woman walks by night because she had in life unjustly handed over to her brother certain charters and thus enabled him to evict her husband and children from "a toft and croft together with its appurtenancies in Ampleforth" after her death. Her spirit can never find rest, she says, until her brother returns these charters to their rightful owner (James

422). Apparently, it was the simple possession of these documents, rather than any specific information they might have recorded, that was the issue here.

Considered from this perspective, the immanent power of the various texts of *The Charter of Christ* we discussed earlier resides not merely in the preeminence of the grantor but in the momentous nature of the trothplight to which they attest. All forms of the *Charter* turn Christ's body into a specific deed of enfeoffment conveying the seisin of heavenly bliss to humanity, and a glance at the detailed instructions—beginning "fit autem donatio in scriptura per haec verba"—given by Bracton (2:111–19) for drawing up such instruments will confirm that the authors have gone to considerable lengths to make this identification as exact as possible.[31] Not only do they echo the most obvious linguistic features of such deeds—with *sciant presentes et futuri*, for instance, becoming "Wete now al þat ar here / And after sal be" (short *Charter*, lines 1–2; in Spalding 8)—but they follow the proper diplomatic form in considerable detail. Thus the A-version of the long *Charter* is careful to specify the donor—"I ihesu crist with blody syde" (100; 28b)"—and the donee—"to þe mankynde" (110; 28b). As Bracton recommends, it employs both the triplet *dedi*, *concessi*, and *confirmavi*—"I make heron confirmament / That I haue granted and y-ȝeue" (108–9; 28b)—and the doublet *habendam et tenandam*—"To haue & to holden withouten mysse" (112; 28b). What Bracton calls the *modus* is rendered as "In a condicioun ȝif þou be kynde / And my loue-dedes haue in mynde" (113–14; 30b), while the *causa* becomes

ffre to haue and fre to holde
Wiþ al þe purtinaunce to wolde
Min erytage þat is so fre
ffor homage ne for fewte
No more wole I aske of þe
Bot a four leued gras to ȝelde me.
(115–20; 30b)

After a brief allegorization of this token payment of a quatrefoil or true-love knot (a peppercorn rent, as it were), there comes a proper warranty clause (cf. Bracton 2:117–19):

Thaw þou be falle and gretly mystake
Mi dede wol I not forsake
ȝif þou amend[e] and mercy craue
Thyn erytage shalt þou haue
(131–34; 30b–32b)

and, following a description of the seals, a list of witnesses:

Hiis testibus Matheus and Iohan
Luk Mark and many on
And namely my moder swete
(169–72; 34b)

The short *Charter* even adds one final diplomatic detail: "This was geuen at Calluery / the first day of the great mercy" (33–34; Spalding 4).

Here, as in the *Fasciculus Morum* and in the Vernon lyric cited above (n. 20), Christ's body is far more than simply a book to impress the unlearned; it is a potent legal symbol sent down from heaven to demonstrate God's commitment to save the human race. The biblical source for such an idea is clearly Col. 2.14, a text alluded to by Chaucer when he added to his translation of Deguilleville's lyric the detail that Christ

wrot the bille
Upon the crois as general acquitaunce
To every penitent in ful creaunce.
("An ABC" 59–61)[32]

The legal ramifications of this text are explored by Jacob de Voragine: "this dette here thappostle calleth Cirographe/ or oblygacion/ the which Jesus Cryst bare and attouchyd it to the crosse/ Of which saynt Austyn saith/ Eue toke of the fende synne by borrowynge by vsure/ and wrote an oblicacion/ she leyde it for pledge/ And the vsure is augmented and grewe vnto all the remenaunt of the lignage/ Thenne toke Eue of the fende synne/ whan ayenst the comandement she consented to hym/ she wrote thobligacion/ whan she put hir hande to the tree ayenst the deffence of god/ She delyuerd pledge/ whan she made Adam to consente to the synne/ And thus thusure grewe/ and augmentid vnto the remayne of all the lignage" (*STC* 24873, fols. xvi^{v}–xvii; cf. *Stanzaic Life* 6381–424). The implied covenantalism of such a reading may well have earned it a cool reception in university cloisters, but in a pastoral context, as we shall see in Chapter 9, this kind of theology continued to exercise a powerful hold over the popular imagination for it was deeply rooted in enduring notions of the identity of trouthe and troth.

It would, however, be a serious mistake to assume that medieval people universally accorded written documents the same kind of reverence they had once invested in the symbols of trothplight, or even that they inevitably recognized the superiority of one medium over the other. Not everyone living in a period when literate technology is ousting the older forms will give letters their unqualified approval. "Letters are good because they never forget any of the messages you put in them," says a character in *White Man of God*, a novel by the Cameroonian writer Kenjo Jumbam; "there is only one thing I do not like about them. They deliver their messages to anybody, even to people for whom they are not meant" (82). Doubtless, it is some such suspicion of their semantic profligacy that explains why letters often miscarry in medieval romance: Donegild's interception of the letters that pass between Constance's guardians and her husband Alla in both Chaucer's "Man of Law's Tale" (line 724–802) and in Gower's "Tale of Constance" (*CA* 2:931–1050) is an obvious example; in their analogue, *Emaré*, these undependable missives (lines 508–603) are set in marked contrast to the gown which accompanies the heroine everywhere on her travels and by which she is finally recognized by her husband. In all three poems, and in Nicholas Trevet (Chaucer and Gower's source), the seriousness of using writing to misrepresent the king's spoken word is underlined by the charge of treason leveled against the heroine's mother-in-law and by the savagery of her punishment: "For sche it hadde wel deserved / Thurgh tresoun of hire false tunge" (*CA* 21298–99). "In oral culture," as Stock reminds us, "a forger was not a person who altered legal texts; he was a traitor. He betrayed the relationship not between words and things but between men" (60).

A similar suspicion of the epistolary medium is evinced in one of the oldest English romances, *Sir Beues of Hamptoun*. At one point the trusting hero delivers a letter which, like the one Claudius sends with Hamlet to England, contains instructions for arranging his own death, despite having been given a chance on the road to learn the truth:

Terri on Beues be-held
And seȝ þe boiste wiþ a scheld.
"Me þenkeþ, þow ert a masager,
Þat in þis londe walkes her;
Icham a clerk and to scole ȝede:
Sire, let me þe letter rede,
For þow miȝt haue gret doute,
Þin owene deþ to bere aboute!'
Beues seide, ich vnder-stonde:
'He, þat me tok þis letter an honde,
He ne wolde loue me non oþer,
Þan ich were is owene broþer."
(1321–32)

At another point, a forged letter deprives Beves's lady, Josian, of her bodyguard and enables a wicked ravisher to carry her off (lines 3137–54). We encounter a further instance of the romance's mistrust of the ease with which writing may disguise true intentions when the king in *Athelston* lures Eglond to his court with a letter inviting him to attend the knighting of his two sons (187–96). Here, as in the other examples, the duplicity of the impersonal written message is deliberately contrasted with the honest good faith of the human messenger.

When we read it against the kind of attitude to letters reflected in popular romance, the "Litera Criseydis" of the last book of Chaucer's *Troilus* takes on a particular poignancy. The agonizing indecision in which Troilus is left by Criseyde's carefully crafted epistolary evasions is brutally resolved by the discovery of his parting love-token to her pinned to Diomede's "cote-armure":

As he that on the coler fond withinne
A broch that he Criseyde yaf that morwe
That she from Troie moste nedes twynne,
In remembraunce of hym and of his sorwe.
And she hym leyde ayeyn hire feith to borwe
To kepe it ay! But now ful wel he wiste,
His lady nas no lenger on to triste.

(5:1660–66)

Far more than Boccaccio's, Chaucer's handling of this scene accentuates the contrast between the slipperiness of the written word and the solidity of physical tokens,[33] suggesting that even those who moved in the thoroughly literate world of the Ricardian court need not have been entirely immune to the more popular suspicions and prejudices of the wider culture.

I hope that by now enough has been said of this particular aspect of the cultural stock onto which vernacular literacy was grafted in the late Middle Ages. While from our perspective letters of the alphabet might appear to function quite differently from physical tokens, this cannot have been how they struck everyone at the time and traces of the superimposition of these two semantic systems can still be detected even as late as the fifteenth century. This may help explain not only the fetishizing of written artifacts in the Middle Ages but also the remarkable prominence of legal documents and of writing in general in the work of Ricardian poets.

That Chaucer and his fellow authors are peculiarly sensitive to the actuality of the written word is no new discovery. Critics have long been struck by Chaucer's preoccupation with the conflict between authority and experience and the way this makes reading so "obtrusive" (Josipovici 98) an activity in his work. The prominence of images of writing and books in his poetry has also been noted (Neuss; Christianson), as has the imagery of legal documentation in Langland (Hughes; J. Simpson 250), and some critics have made a start on exploring the dynamic tension between literacy and orality in Ricardian poetry that such imagery seems to reflect (Gellrich 1995, 195–272; Harwood; Scase). Rather than reiterating this work here, I want to turn briefly to a passage by one of Langland's earliest and most successful imitators, the author of *Mum and the Sothsegger*. In the remarkable concluding section of this poem, the awakened dreamer, having learned the importance of speaking out against the evils of misrule, opens a bag, "for[to] conseille þe king,"

> Where many a pryue poyse is preyntid withynne
> Yn bokes vnbredid in balade-wise made,
> Of vice and of vertue fulle to the margyn
> That was not y-openyd þis oþer half wintre. (1343–47)

As it stands, the catalog of assorted legal instruments that follows is more than four hundred lines long, but since the poem lacks an ending and the passage includes a lacuna of two folios, it must originally have run to over six hundred. From the poet's bag tumbles a quite extraordinary assortment of documents: "a quayer of quitances" (line 1348), "a penyworth of papir" (1350), "a volume of visitacion of viftene leves" (1353), "a rolle of religion" (1364), "a paire of pamphilettz" (1370), "a copie for comunes of culmes foure and twenty" (1388), "a scrowe for squyers" (1489), "a writte of high wil y-write al newe" (1498), "a raggeman rolle þat Ragenelle hymself / Hath made" (1565–66), "a forelle . . . þat frayed is a lite" (1586), "a librarie of lordes" (1626), "a copie of couetise" (1683), "a [title] of testament[z]" (1697), "a poynt of prophecie" (1723), and "a cedule soutelly indited / With tuly silke intachid right atte rolle-is ende" (1734–35).

Two things are particularly striking about this passage: the first is the physical solidity of the documents themselves; the second, the marked discrepancy between the medium and its message. Almost without exception these densely material documents bear eloquent witness to the universal inconstancy and duplicity of those in authority—only the "copie for comunes" (1388) and the "poynt of prophecie" (1723) concern the common people, and even they register dangerous rumor-mongering and foolish belief in old prophecies. Indeed, with a perceptiveness that even his master Langland can hardly match, the *Mum*-author comes close to identifying the true cause of his Saturnian malaise in the disruptive potential of literacy itself: bishops who "lien on þe lettrure" grow rich from the fines paid by "lemmans and lotebies" (1351–52); poor men who go to law against the great are soon proved "wacker in þe writte" (1581); rich men can intimidate the poor, since "To strue a man with [strength] þe status been so made" (1593); and if "of euery writte withoute wronge þere were amendes made" (1608), it would "chaunge al þe chauncellerie and cheuallerie amende" (1613). If for the *Mum*-author "lawe lieth muche in lordship sith loyaute was exiled" (1583), we are left with the strong impression that at root this is due to an unholy alliance between unprincipled authority and literate technology. The material solidity of his actual documents, reminiscent of the reassuringly solid weds of the old trothplight, supplies an ironic counterpoint to this depiction of universal faithlessness.

Though it would be going too far to suggest that writing is demonized in the concluding section of *Mum and the Sothsegger*, the term demonization can be appropriately applied to the early-fourteenth-century Anglo-Norman "Lettre du prince des envieux" (Aspin 143–48), a parodic antitype of the texts of *The Charter of Christ* that we looked at earlier. Where Christ had offered his own body as a charter in which the faithful could read the terms of their own salvation, however, the devil here employs mundane parchment and ink to convey to the rich and powerful the exclusive right to deceive and oppress the poor:

E ke afermé seit ceste covine
Mun sel j'ai mis de fausime
Par unt jeo lur conferm et grant
Ke ja ne tient covenant
A nul, pur escrit ne serment,
Mes tuz dis decevent la gent.
(43–48)

[And to make this contract binding I have set here my seal of falsehood, with which I confirm and grant that they need never honor any covenant with anyone, whether written or sworn, but continually defraud the people.]

This documentary travesty of the old trothplight may serve to reinforce the obvious point that admiration for the social consequences of the spread of literate technology was far from universal even among the literate themselves.

While some people in the late Middle Ages were still trying to make room for writing within the symbolic economy of the old wed, and others, having measured writing against this economy, were finding it wanting, still others, growing attuned to the semantic detachment that inhered in all written communication, were developing a new attitude to the truth of the tokens themselves. If, in some circumstances, the cultural potency of the token might be carried over to parchment, in others the depersonalized semiology of the charter might have the effect of draining the familiar wed of its ancient authority. This must have been an important, if unrecoverable, element in many broken troths of the period (an aspect of that externalization of trouthe for which I am claiming such significance), but in one important social movement in Ricardian England, the rise of Lollardy, its presence is quite clear.

Lollardy and Literacy

Among all the symptoms of a critical confrontation between the new documentary culture and the older ethos of the oral trothplight in the late fourteenth century perhaps none is more dramatic than the rapid spread of Lollardy. I shall not be concerned here with a detailed theological investigation of the movement itself, but only with those aspects of it that illustrate the general cultural shift from which I believe it drew its inspiration. John Wyclif's views reveal a strong affinity with those of the eleventh-century theologian Berengar of Tours, and I shall be arguing that "the recognition of different levels of understanding between *litterati* and *illitterati*" that Brian Stock sees as having informed the earlier heresy (524) can profitably be transposed, mutatis mutandis, to the later.

Despite the very obvious differences between the societies for which Berengar and Wyclif wrote, they shared one important characteristic: Berengar's views, as Stock convincingly shows, had been fostered by the newly emerging Latin textual communities on the eve of the twelfth-century renaissance. So too those of Wyclif's followers, I suggest, could only have flourished in the new environment of vernacular and secular literacy that characterizes late-fourteenth-century England. Indeed, it does not take much imagination to recast the Lollard strongholds that quickly sprang up in London, Leicester, Bristol, Northampton, and Coventry, complete with their conventicles, schools, and underground links with Oxford (A. Hudson 1988, 73–81), as later vernacular manifestations of what Stock has labeled "textual communities" (cf. Rubin 326). While much valuable work has been done on the role of literacy in disseminating Wyclif's ideas (A. Hudson 1994; H-J. Martin 177–81), my focus here will be rather different; I want to examine the way the kind of thinking literacy encourages informed some of the central tenets of Lollard belief and how the very fabric of the heresy itself reflects an emergent literate consciousness. This perspective, I hope, may bring us closer to understanding why, in Margaret Aston's words, "it was as a vernacular literate movement that Lollardy had gathered momentum and it was as a vernacular literate movement that it was suspected and persecuted" (1984, 207).

Berengar of Tours's challenge to traditional thinking on the Eucharist in the middle of the tenth century did not occur in a vacuum. It was merely one instance (admittedly the most notorious) of a much wider concern with the problem of "the status of a physical object having religious associations during an age of increasing literacy" (Stock 244); images and relics, just as in Ricardian England, offered other focal points for this concern. "For the unlettered, still largely attached to oral traditions," writes Stock, "the concrete representation of the Eucharist and its associated rituals were the norm" (265); the priest's bare assertion that a piece of bread was the body of Christ need have posed no problems for those unprepared to make, what he memorably terms, "the hermeneutic leap from what the text says to what they think it means" (522). With increasing literacy, however, came skepticism, analysis, and demystification; the priest's words demanded interpretation before they could be accepted—as Langland puts it, "goddes body myȝte noȝt ben of breed wiþouten clergie" (*PPl* B.12:85). For Stock, the opposing positions taken by Berengar and Lanfranc over the interpretation of the Eucharist do not offer us a straightforward fit with the distinction between literate and oral cultures (241); both, he argues, by virtue of their interpretative claims reveal a profoundly literate underpinning. Nonetheless, it seems quite clear with hindsight that Lanfranc's position is essentially communalist (that is to say, he seeks to save appearances by offering an intricate rationalization of the unexamined assumptions of a vast majority of nonliterate believers for whom token and betokened still maintained their timeless synergy), whereas Berengar's is idiosyncratic, anticipating the increasing emphasis on individual justification in a progressively more literate society (cf. 297). If it is true that, "like the transition from oral to written tradition as a whole, the change in mentality shifted the criteria of belief from the community to the individual" (Stock 252), then Berengar's rhetorical "I" points very much more steadily than Lanfranc's "we" (Cramer 222–36) toward an increasingly literate future.

So far as his position can be reconstructed from the fragmentary nature of his surviving works, Berengar held that "the bread and wine . . . are converted into Christ's body and blood not sensibly (*sensualiter*) but intellectually (*intellectualiter*)" (quoted by Stock 276). Like his predecessor Ratramnus of Corbie, he seems to have understood the Eucharist allegorically or symbolically: "it was apprehended by the senses as bread and wine; it was the body and blood of Christ only *in figura*. Put in other terms, the bread and wine were symbols of the body and blood of Christ" (270). That at any rate is how his views were represented by his opponents and how they passed down to posterity. However much Wyclif might have attempted to distance himself from Berengar (e.g., *De Apostasia* 79),[34] he himself came quickly to be associated with this particular heresy. As early as 1381, for instance, the chancellor of Oxford William Barton was writing in rebuttal: "the true body and blood of Christ are not only virtually, or figuratively [non solum uirtualiter seu figuraliter], but essentially, substantially and corporally present" (*Knighton's Chronicle* 275). The chronicler Thomas Walsingham certainly saw Wyclif as "reviving certain condemned opinions of Berengar's" (*Historia* 1:450) and many of his contemporaries would have agreed with him (A. Hudson 1988, 286–87 n. 47).

Wyclif's own views on the Eucharist, unlike Berengar's, have been preserved in a number of complete tracts, the most important of which, for our purposes, is his *De Eucharistia Tractatus Maior*. From the outset *De Eucharistia* makes clear that Wyclif was prepared to consider the consecrated host, not as the actual body of Christ, but as its sign or clothing—"non corpus Christi sed eius signum vel tegumentum" (16). Those who hold that the physical bread on the altar is identical with Christ's body, he says, are failing to distinguish between the signifier and the signified—"non distinguentes inter illam figuram et suum figuratum" (217). He mocks those clerics who have no difficulty recognizing the figures on coins ("ymagines auri et argenti") yet cannot distinguish between the real nature and the outer form (the *quidditas* and *forma*) of the host (182–83); "what," he asks, "may be more shameful in a prelate than that he diligently labor over the character of a seal or a charter, and not over the real nature of the consecrated host?" (183). And in a remarkable passage, intended to counter the argument that his views will cause the people to lose faith in the Eucharist, he makes quite clear the debt his position owes to a self-consciously literate mentality:

> The following concrete example will demonstrate how bare and absurd is the argument that if it were to remain bread it might signify the substance of bread more than the body of Christ: When scribes scribble letters, phrases, and statements on a material surface, these remain as a material overlay and by their accidents signify [reading *significant*] the overlay itself. And yet these accidents, set down in order to convey meaning to those who by skill and other natural qualities understand letters, signify in a far more fundamental and noteworthy manner than the material forms signify themselves, insofar that what the layperson takes as a natural signification is of worth to the cleric. So much the more should the quality of faith lead the faithful to understand through the consecrated bread the true body of Christ. (144)

It would be difficult to think of a clearer example in support of Ong's contention that "writing separates the knower from the known and thus sets up conditions for 'objectivity', in the sense of personal disengagement or distancing" (46), than this logical reduction of the central sacral Truth of the Christian Middle Ages to a symbolic representation. Without the spread of vernacular literacy it is very doubtful that Lollardy could have made any headway in its campaign against an epistemology which, in its refusal to distinguish between signifier and signified, had provided, as Rubin notes, "the basis for sacramentality" (326).

When Berengar had first made his proposition, the great mass of the people were unlettered and the *litterati* had found it prudent to adopt the highly intellectualized interpretation of the Eucharist that Lanfranc had erected against him. In the short term, this must have looked like a shrewd move. Throughout the high Middle Ages, as Rubin has brilliantly demonstrated, the church skillfully exploited the superstitious appeal of a real presence to promote its own interests among the unlettered; indeed, as Keen has recently argued, Wyclif's own campaign against the doctrine of transubstantiation may well have drawn on his sense of moral outrage at its "shoddy claim for physical, sacerdotal magic" (1986, 14). By the late fourteenth century, however, the old Berengarian threat had become far more difficult to contain. For an increasing number of laypeople who had acquired vernacular literacy (and indeed for some nonliterates who grasped the essential function of letters) the analogy of signifier and signified offered a clearer way of understanding the Eucharist than either the naive identicalism (as it now appeared) of the oral imagination or the sophisticated rationalization of the scholastic (cf. *Plowman's Tale* 1221–24). Offered a choice between God-as-bread on the one hand and accident-as-substance on the other, they opted for what looked like a reasonable third path: "þat þe hoost, wenne hit is sacrud, is Cristus body in figure and verey breed in his kynde" (*English Wycliffite Sermons* 2:363 [cf. 3:161–62 and 247]). With hindsight, such a choice seems an inevitable consequence of the spread of literacy, and it was being made by contemporaries like "John the Paper," well beyond the ambit of Wyclif or Hus: in 1440 Jean dit Papier appeared before the ecclesiastical court in Troyes charged with claiming publicly that "in the sacrament on the altar and in the holy sacrament which is taken in procession on the feast day every year [i.e., at Corpus Christi] there is no body of Christ but only its memorial [*rememoracio*]," which opinion cost him a public penance and a year in prison (*Inventaire* 273, cf. 270–71). In England by the late fourteenth century such views were evidently circulating freely.[35]

At the end of the *De Eucharistia* Wyclif says that he had openly taught the laity that the host was a figure of the body of Christ and the means by which he might be remembered and imitated (305). However, the claim that the bread and wine of the Eucharist memorialized the body and blood of Christ (represented its meaning as a wed might be said to represent trothplight, in other words, or as pen-strokes represent the meaning of the words they record) soon became a dangerous one to make in public, and this aspect of Lollard belief is sometimes better demonstrated from the complaints of their opponents than from their own vernacular writings. The first of the *Confessions* ("the vernacular text," Anne Hudson tells us [1988, 282], "with the strongest claim to be regarded as Wyclif's own," and one that owes its very preservation to the anti-Lollard chronicler, Henry Knighton) offers what is probably the clearest statement of it: "as a man leeues for to þenk þe kynde of an ymage, wheþer it be of oke or of asshe, and settys his þouȝt in him of whom is þe ymage, so myche more schuld a man leue to þenk on þe kynde of brede" (*Selections* 17).[36] The allegation in *Friar Daw's Reply* that Lollards regarded the bread of the Eucharist "but as a signe & not verre Cristis bodi" (line 846; in Heyworth 99) is borne out by *Wycklyffes Wycket* (a tract of uncertain date surviving only in sixteenth-century prints): "all the sacramentes that be lefte here in earthe be but myndes of the body of Chryst for a sacrament is no more to say but a sygne o[r] mynde of a thynge passed or a thyng to come" (quoted by A. Hudson 1988, 289 f. 62). For the most part, however, the Lollards themselves fell back on a coded phrase, that "þo sacrament of þo auter is verrey Cristis body *in forme of brede*" (T. Arnold 3:484 [cf. 3:106, and Wyclif, *English Works* 357]).[37]

Ironically, some of the best evidence for the claim that the overlap of literate consciousness with oral trothplight lay behind the popularity of Wycliffite views of the Eucharist, comes from the orthodox response to another Lollard doctrine: their mistrust of the popular veneration of images. Here, objections to the fetishization of relics, images, and even, as we have seen, scraps of parchment, by those who "wenen þat þeos ymagis doun verreyly þe myraclis of hemsilf" (*Selections* 87), were met by the argument that, properly used, images were merely mnemonic prompts enabling the worshiper to recall to mind a saint's good deeds—an argument in itself perfectly acceptable to moderate Lollards who seem to have been prepared to allow them the status of "signes or tokones," to be used by the nonliterate "as clerkis don her bokis" (*Selections* 23). Thus, Bishop Pecock was similarly opposed to the notion that "an ymage hath withinne him vertu" (*Repressor* 157), yet defended images as "seeable rememoratijf or mynding signes and tokenes" (165), whose operation he illustrated by the following analogy: "If a marchant or eny other man haue myche nede forto bithenke upon a certeine erand . . . it is weel allowid and approued bi resoun that he make a ring of a rische and putte it on his fynger, or that he write sum seable cros or mark or carect with cole or chalk in the wal of his chaumbre or hal, or that he hange up bifore his siȝt sum hood or girdil or staf or such other thing, or that he make a knot on his girdil or on his tipet, as alle men wolen herto consente" (166). Pace V. H. H. Green (168),

Pecock's own position on the Eucharist did not follow "closely along the ordinary orthodox lines," however, for like the Lollards themselves, he too was prepared to represent it as "a remembrauncing tokene, or signe of witnesse" (*Donet* 35). Pecock characterized the operation of the sacraments in general in terms that Wyclif himself could hardly have taken exception to: "Mankinde in this lijf is so freel, that forto make into him sufficient remembraunce of thingis to be profitabli of him remembrid he nedith not oonli heereable rememoratijf signes (as ben Holi Scripture and othere deuoute writingis), but he nedith also therwith and ther to seable rememoratijf signes . . . And also, if heereable rememoratijf signes hadden be sufficient to Cristen men into al her nedeful goostli remembrauncingis, wherto schulde Crist haue ȝeue to Cristen men vndir comaundement seable rememoratijf signes, as ben hise sacramentis of the Newe Testament?" (*Repressor* 209; cf. 220). That Pecock, in all other respects so bitterly opposed to Lollardy, should have slipped into this particular error shows how seductive such an interpretation could be in an age that had still not forgotten the cultural force of the wed and the trothplight.

One final tenet of Lollard belief that is particularly relevant to this discussion (and indeed to the theme of this book as a whole) was a deep suspicion of oaths, for behind the circumspection with which these "true priests" and "true men" treated the common identification of trouthe and troth lay a sensitivity to the slipperiness of language characteristic of the emergent lay literacy that underpinned the movement as a whole. "Siþ Crist is þe firste treuþe and hatiþ lesyngis, algatis þre treuþis shulden men sue and fle wisely þre lesyngis," writes a Lollard homilist; these three truths are ethical truth ("þe treuþe of lif"), theological truth ("treuþe of bileue"), and, finally, verbal precison: "men shulden haue treuþe in wordis and fleth falsed þat is in wordis" (*English Wycliffite Sermons* 3:247).

Chaucer's Harry Bailey offers strong evidence that disapproval of swearing was commonly taken to be a sign of Lollard tendencies:

> The Parson him answerde, "Benedicite!
> What eyleth the man, so synfully to swere?"
> Oure Host answerde, "O Jankin, be ye there?
> I smelle a Lollere in the wynd," quod he.
> ("Man of Law's Tale" 1170–73)

The oath in question here will no doubt strike the modern reader as more of an imprecation than an asseveration, but to many people in the Middle Ages this distinction would probably not have seemed a very important one (cf. *Plowman's Tale* 253–56), and, at one level, Wycliffite distaste for swearing was simply a natural consequence of a general reverence for the literal teaching of the Bible, a perfectly consistent response to Matt. 5:33–37: "Again, you have heard that it was said to them of old: Thou shalt not forswear thyself: But thou shalt perform thy oaths to the Lord. But I say to you, not to swear at all; . . . But let your speech be, Yea, yea; No, no: for whatsoever is more than these, cometh from evil." Wycliffites were certainly not the only people in the Middle Ages to be troubled by this apparently unambiguous injunction (Silving 1343–44). At a deeper level, however, there seems to be something far more interesting going on.

We have seen that customary law reflects its oral origins by treating oaths with an absolute formalism. Reluctant to make "the hermeneutic leap from what the text says to what they think it means" courts treated the form of an oath, indeed any set formula, with what often looks to us to be a preposterous literalism. In this respect they were merely reflecting a tendency of medieval people in general to resist stubbornly any attempt to force them to distinguish between signifiers and signifieds. There is a historical irony in our way of commonly referring to this tendency as literal-mindedness, for in actuality it seems an obvious symptom of the preliterate imagination; the modern term, however, attests to the fact that discrimination between the two modes of understanding would be inconceivable without the kind of consciousness literacy fosters.

Anyone who has read at all widely in medieval literature will be familiar with instances of people treating apparently metaphorical utterances with a solemn literalism that in a modern context cannot fail to appear comic—though there is every indication that at the time they were taken seriously enough. In the *Buke of the Howlat*, to pick but one example, Sir Richard Holland tells us that when Robert the Bruce died without having had the chance to fulfill a vow he had made, "with all the hart that he had" (444), to go on crusade to the Holy Land, his faithful lieutenant, the earl of Douglas, took his mummified heart "clos in a cler cace" (469) all the way to Jerusalem and hurled it at the first Saracen army he could find:

> Amang the hethin men the hert hardely he slang,
> Said: "Wend on as thou was wont,
> Throw the batell in bront,
> Ay formast in the front,
> Thy fays amang."
>
> (490–94)

Holland does not record the reaction of the Saracens. The dissemination of literacy does not necessarily put an end to such literal-mindedness (as the approving tone of the literate record I have just quoted proves); in a period when access to literacy is still limited strong traces of what Ong calls "residual orality" may continue to appear in literate individuals, particularly those still closely in touch with the popular culture. Writing of the function of metaphor in the speech of Menocchio, the late-sixteenth-century miller of Friuli, Carlo Ginzburg notes that, "in his mental and linguistic world, marked as it was by the most absolute literalism, even metaphors must be taken in a rigorously literal sense" (62). The spread of literate habits of mind, however, meant that fewer and fewer people were able to ignore the uncomfortable fact that experience had now become "separable, if not always separated, from ratiocination about it" (Stock 531).

Whenever Ida of Louvain (d. ca. 1300) recited the words "Verbum caro factum est," she is reported to have tasted the word as actual flesh on her tongue (cited by Bynum 67); and, as Caroline Walker Bynum amply demonstrates, this kind of literalism, encouraged by the orthodox interpretation of the Eucharist, could elicit the most remarkable physical responses to the imagined presence of God's body in the mass. In the face of such an attitude, the Lollards' skepticism about the real presence appears all of a piece with their distrust of oaths. In reacting against the universal custom of asseveration, they were betraying a similar sensitivity to the potential gap between words and meanings, between utterance and intention: "Crist techiþ in þe gospel to have oure wordis þus, ȝhe, ȝhe, and nai, nay, wiþouten ony ooþ. Þere he doubliþ his wordis, as if he wolde seie,—Ȝif ȝe seie ȝhe in ȝoure soule, seie ȝhe wiþ ȝoure mouþ, and be ȝe trewe men" (T. Arnold 3:84). Postmedieval treatises on equivocation make quite clear how much such scruples owe to literate introspection.

The Jesuit recusant Henry Garnet,[38] for instance, argues that there are four categories of proposition: mental, vocal, written, and mixed. What he means by this last category will be clear from the following quotation:

> The essence or whole nature of every proposition, as we learne out of Aristotle, is in the mynde; and voyces and wrytinges are ordayned as instruments or signes to expresse that proposition which is in the mynde. Therfore as I may expresse all in word or all in wryting, and the proposition of the mynde remayneth the same, so may I by an other kind of mixte proposition expresse part and reserve part, and yet the proposition of the mynde beyng not altered at all. Besides there may be a mixture of a written and vocall proposition: as if I should, intendinge to speake this proposition, "God is not vniuste," loose sodainely my speech before I had spoken the last worde, or of sett purpose holdinge my peace, exhibite the last worde in wryting,—who doubteth but all that were but one proposition, whose verety were to be adiudged according to both partes togither? (Garnet 12–13)

As a consequence of such a line of reasoning, someone interrogated under oath was allowed enormous scope for casuistry. For instance, in 1606 John Ward, an

English Catholic priest trained on the Continent, denied that he was a priest and denied that he had ever crossed the seas; when the court produced evidence that he was lying on both counts, Ward coolly replied that he had mentally reserved the words *of Apollo* after "priest" and *Indian* before "seas" (quoted by Sommerville 160).

Equivocation of this kind stands in marked contrast to the verbal quibbles that characterize customary legal process for the obvious reason that, as a contemporary Protestant lawyer remarked, the latter could be "easily discovered if the impostor bee suspected, but hee which useth mentall reservacion cannot possibly bee detected" (*Recusant Documents* 251). As such it was utterly foreign to the ethos of oral trothplight: "for if it once take roote in the hartes of the people, in a short time there wilbee no faith, no troth, no trust, and consequently all commercing and all contracting will cease, and all civill societies will breake and bee dissolved" (254). Wyclif's Protestant descendants, horrified by such Jesuitical subterfuge, portrayed it as a new thing, a threat to the very fabric of their commonwealth (253), but in reality it was far from being new. It had been known to the church in Wyclif's day and quite possibly even in Berengar's.

In December 1402 or 1403 (Snape 357–58), a suspected Lollard called Richard Wyche, having fallen foul of the bishop of Durham (initially over the question of biblical authority for the mendicants), refused to swear an oath that he would henceforward observe the canon law, and was thrown in prison. He has left us an account of his subsequent ordeal in the form of a long letter to a fellow Lollard. After several weeks of questioning and ineffectual attempts to persuade him to change his mind, a knight, whom Wyche judged to be a respectable man (*solidus homo*), appeared in his cell and offered him a deal:

> "Richard, surely you can find it in your conscience to obey the law of the catholic church insofar as it concerns you?"
>
> "Certainly," I said, "since I know that the law of God is the law of the catholic church, and God forbid that I should not obey the law of God insofar as it concerns me."
>
> "You say well," he said. "You shall keep that in your heart, and let that be your oath, and you shall swear it with that reservation in your heart [iures tu istud in corde tuo limitatum]."
>
> "You say well," I said. "But you well know that, if I am given an oath to swear by a judge, I am obliged to accept it according to the judge's intention and not my own."
>
> "You may be certain," he said, "that my lord will accept this oath from you, for my lord has sent me to you to negotiate the oath with you." ("Trial" 534)

On these terms, Wyche and the unnamed knight come to an agreement (Wyche calls it a *pactum*). The very next morning, however, when he is given the written form of the oath he is to swear, he discovers to his horror that not only is it far more specific than anything he had been led to expect, but that it is so worded that he can find no way to qualify it in his conscience.

For a member of a sect that professed to shun oaths, Wyche's behavior in this trial might appear somewhat incongruous, but his shocked reaction to the breaking of his pact with the knight shows that it was not a lack of respect for the sacral power of the oath that prompted the aversion, but rather its reverse: a heightened awareness of the dangers inherent in so solemn an institution brought on, no doubt, by his literate sensitivity to the slipperiness of language. There remains a strong sense of residual orality in his letter; we are forcefully reminded, for instance, of the ancient equation of truth and honor when Wyche comes close to accusing the knight of having broken his word and almost provokes a fight; "are you saying that I negotiated with you in bad faith?" demands the knight darkly (539). Wyche and the knight evidently remember their pact differently. Though we can never know where the truth really lay, what *was* known, and what was implacably resistant to any form of accommodation or compromise between them, was the written text of the oath itself. Their confrontation is thus emblematic of the theme of this book as a whole, but the confusion of their roles (the Lollard appealing to the given word and the knight to a written document) should serve to remind us that this crisis of truth, however clear its outlines might appear to us in retrospect, was confused and disturbing to those who lived through it.

Over three hundred years earlier, Berengar of Tours had had a similar battle with a Lateran Council that had demanded, not only that he assent to the orthodox eucharistic formula, but that he "promise to interpret it in the sense in which it was understood by the council and not otherwise" (Southern 1948, 46). Berengar, as Wyche's inquisitors were quick to remind him, had submitted to the council's oath, but Wyche himself, at least by his own account, was made of sterner stuff: still refusing to swear, he was declared excommunicate and a heretic (541). Before he leaves this particular stage, however, he offers us one final glimpse into his enigmatic world: "I never thought to swear that oath," he tells his correspondent, "and yet it seems to me that if I had willingly sworn that oath I should not have been bound to observe it" (541). The reason, we learn, is that the written form that had been tendered to him had begun with the words, "I Richard Wyche, of the county of Worcestershire . . ." and this particular Richard Wyche, he triumphantly informs us, had been born in another county altogether.[39] It was the kind of quibble that the king's judges were faced with every day, but it is somewhat startling to meet with it in this particular company.

How Richard Wyche escaped from the bishop of Durham's prison is something of a mystery,[40] but we do know that he lived to fight another day (he finally died at the stake in 1440). The thought that it may have been this quibble that allowed the devout Lollard to slip through the hands of his inquisitors is a pleasant, though probably unwarranted, one. At any event, it offers a graphic illustration of the permeability of the boundary between *lered* and *lewed*, between the world of the old oral trothplight and that of the new written charter. We shall be meeting further examples of such permeability in the next chapter.

8

Rash Promises

In an old song one of the parties—I believe both—says "I will give thee the Keys of Heaven." No court would listen to any suit that was founded upon such an undertaking.

—A. P. Herbert, *More Uncommon Law*

AT THE VERY END OF THE FIFTEENTH century in Champagne a bachelor called Claude Nonette was amusing himself among a group of young women at the house of his master, a trader in oil. One of them said to him in play, "My darling love, give me something to drink," and Claude, parodying the traditional gesture of sealing a bargain with a drink of wine, offered her a cup of water, saying, "Here, drink this in the name of marriage." The cup was taken, not by the woman who had first asked for the drink, but by another called Nicole Loyseau. Nicole, having duly drunk from the cup, seems to have informed the startled Claude that she now regarded herself as formally betrothed and when he refused to acknowledge the engagement brought an action for breach of promise against him in the ecclesiastical court in Troyes (*Inventaire* 309). Hardly surprisingly the court found that Claude had not intended to bind himself to Nicole and dismissed the case. However, what is striking about this incident is that Nicole had clearly "believed that she could force the young man to marry her . . . and that Claude, without even attempting to debate his intentions, was afraid that he might indeed be forced to [do so]" (Flandrin 56). Medieval literature is full of similar rash or ill-considered promises, and too often modern critics have taken them no more seriously than the canon lawyers of Troyes. In this chapter I shall be trying to look at them from the point of view of Nicole Loyseau and her friends. If we are to catch any echo of those unfamiliar whisperings in the oil trader's back room, however, we must first learn to close our ears to the insistent accents of Gratian and Baldus.

To some readers it will seem absurd even to think of considering so patently fictional a motif as the rash promise from a legal point of view. In an influential article on Chaucer's "Franklin's Tale," Alan Gaylord observed that it had been "intriguing inquiring what basis for an action Aurelius might have had and what remedy he might discover if he sued Dorigen for breach of contract (i.e., failure to commit adultery) in civil or ecclesiastical courts," but that he had "since concluded that such research provides more recreation than relevance" (357). The question continues to present itself, however, if only for the reason that medieval authors themselves frequently raise it. In the case of "The Franklin's Tale," for instance, there is, as Roland Blenner-Hasset noted some time ago, "an air of legality in the poem" (791), and Chaucer's use of legal terminology inevitably prompts us to speculate, in Alfred David's words, on "what would have happened if one of the characters had insisted on his rights" (190). Like Gaylord, I am quite aware that there is something more than a little ludicrous about trying to drag a literary character like Dorigen through the courts, but all the same the exercise is far easier to defend than, say, asking how many children Lady Macbeth had. The law, however imperfectly, attempts to define and enforce standards of socially accepted behavior; to ask how a fourteenth-century lawyer might have viewed Dorigen's predicament is thus to attempt to uncover something about accepted attitudes to promises and bargains in Chaucer's day. The real problem is to know which lawyers to ask and what we are to make of their answers.

For many commentators the most natural place to turn will be to the second part of the *Summa theologiae*. True, Aquinas was not a lawyer, but his knowledge of the Digest and the Decretals was extensive and his treatment of the nature of private obligations, though primarily the work of a moral theologian, has obvious legal implications. Aquinas does not discuss contracts per se (though he does have much to say about sacramental contracts like baptism and marriage, which are hardly typical), but in the course of his discussion of vows and oaths (2a2æ.88–89; 39:158–235) he lays the groundwork for a coherent contractual theory founded squarely on the sanctity of the given word. This sanctity he regards as absolute as long as three conditions are met: "whoever swears to do something is bound to do it, insofar as truth [*veritas*] may be fulfilled and so long as two companion qualities are present, namely judgment and justice [*judicium et justicia*]" (89.7; 222). Oaths which fail to meet the test of truth are false (*mendax*), those lacking judgment are rash (*incautum*), and those without justice are wicked or unlawful (*iniquum sive illicitum*) (89.3; 210).[1] As a moral theologian Aquinas is concerned with the circumstances under which a person can be released from the terms of an oath without sin, but it is not difficult to see how his three conditions might be applied to the legal question of which contracts are to be held void or voidable and to such perennial problems of contract law as mistake, fraud, and illegal consequence. In general, most of the answers he adumbrates will look reassuringly familiar today for the very good reason that, as James Gordley has shown,

Aquinas is a vital link in a jurisprudential chain reaching from the nineteenth-century theorists of contract law right back to the Romans. Though the Romans themselves had had no coherent theory of contract to bequeath to later commentators, medieval schoolmen reinterpreted discrete rules from Justinian in the light of the moral imperatives of the church and rationalized them according to the new Aristotelianism of the schools to produce an account of promises and vows whose outlines can still be detected in what remains of an integrated doctrine of contract in the late twentieth century.

Aquinas would have had little difficulty accepting such a truism of modern contract law as that no one can be bound by an agreement intended to effect something either impossible or illegal; he would clearly have treated a contract intended to effect an impossibility as void on the grounds that it lacked *judicium*, and one whose consequences were illegal as failing to meet the test of *justicia*. Thus, he remarks of Herod's rash promise to Salome that their agreement would have been legal "if its attendant condition had been understood, namely that she might only request what it would be right to give" (89.7; 39:222). In only one important respect does the medieval theologian reveal an attitude to promises that would seem distinctly odd to a modern lawyer: speaking of duress, he says that, though an oath extorted by force may be void as regards the party to whom it is made, it must still be honored because it has been made in God's name—"such an obligation cannot be annulled in the court of conscience, since one ought to suffer temporal loss rather than break one's oath" (89.8; 224). The view that enforced consent is still consent (since, presumably, the promisor has in some sense chosen the lesser of two evils) should serve to remind us that even here, on the airy uplands of medieval reason, the logic of contractual obligations was built on premises we might find difficult to accept today.[2]

Once we descend from these uplands into the misty valleys of actual forensic argument we will encounter ideas still more alien to our way of thinking, yet the descent must be attempted if we are to get any closer to popular ideas about contract. To assume, on the basis of what we find most familiar in Thomist analysis, that medieval people in general thought about contractual obligations in the same way that we do is extremely dangerous. At the best of times working lawyers and their clients are unlikely to have much use for jurisprudential conjecture, but in the Middle Ages, when the gap between *lered* and *lewed* was more clearly marked than it is now, the gulf between legal theory and the concerns of actual litigants was correspondingly far greater. As in the breach of promise case between Claude Nonette and Nicole Loyseau with which we began, when we turn to the records of actual lawsuits (even those heard according to the rules of civil or canon law),[3] we will sometimes discover traces of an approach to promises that looks very curious indeed to the modern eye. If there is any truth in the suggestion that a French ecclesiastical case from 1499 can tell us as much about the attitude of Chaucer's audience to rash promises as all the subtle analysis of the *Summa theologiae*, then a similar claim made with reference to the common-law cases of Ricardian England should be far easier to defend.

There are two obvious reasons for this. The first, and less interesting, is that *de iure* almost the whole area of contract litigation in England fell within the jurisdiction of customary rather than written law. In theory, this had been settled as early as Henry II's Constitutions of Clarendon (1164), which specifically denied the claim that because a bargain had been made with God as witness, any dispute arising from it should be decided by God's officers in an ecclesiastical court (P&M 2:198); by Bracton's day even contract disputes between clergy and laity came under common-law jurisdiction (4:265). In actuality, disputes over secular contracts were sometimes decided by the courts Christian—the archdeacon in Chaucer's "Friar's Tale," for example, hears cases "of contractes and of lakke of sacramentz" (1308). Indeed, because the procedural requirement of a sealed instrument meant that the common law writ of covenant was unavailable to many potential litigants, this practice seems to have been on the increase in the fifteenth century.[4] For the same reason, the court of chancery was sometimes prepared to hear contract disputes, particularly (as shown by Robert Ellesmere's petition with which we began Chapter 4) those arising from parol agreements. Nevertheless, most actions for breach of contract in late medieval England would have been heard either before the central common-law courts (brought under the old actions of debt and covenant or the newer one of assumpsit), or by local, borough, and franchisal courts, which often followed customary procedure of even greater antiquity.

The second reason is that de facto English customary law in the late Middle Ages, though certainly not unaffected by the written law of the canonists and the civilians, still exhibits clear evidence of the traditional forms and attitudes from which it was constructed. Unfortunately, common lawyers seem in general to have been reluctant to analyze the law they administered, their natural tendency being rather toward unreflective conservatism than principled innovation. "Sir," says Chief Justice Fortescue in 1458, "the law is as I say it is, and so it has been laid down ever since the law began; and we have several set forms which are held as law, and so held and used for good reason, though we cannot at present remember that reason" (quoted by Holdsworth 3:626). One oft-cited exception to their habitual reticence occurs in a case from 1344/45 where the issue, a particularly thorny one for the fourteenth century, turned on the evidentiary status of a written deed in conveying title to land (*YB 18/19 Edw. 3*, 376–79). The tenant, who is seeking to prevent the court's recognition of the deed, receives some encouragement from one of the three judges, William Shareshull, who cites the supporting decisions of two distinguished predecessors, Bereford and Herle. Shareshull adds, however, that "no precedent is of greater weight than what is just" [nulle ensaumple est si fort come resoun], which prompts an immediate objection from the tenant's lawyer: "I think you will do as others have done in the same case or else we do not know what the law is." Though neither of the other two judges seems ready to concur—Hillary: "[Law] is the will of the Justices"; Stonor: "No; law is what is just" [ley est resoun]—the tenant's lawyer nevertheless wins this point for his client. In the final analysis, it appears, neither just dealing nor judicial ruling is any match for established custom.

It will be seen at once that the law being discussed here is primarily adjective law; the greater rights of the principals are completely subordinated to the procedural priorities of their lawyers, yet curiously, from a modern perspective, no one in court seems capable of separating the two. This reverence for procedure, with a corresponding lack of interest in larger substantive issues, is one of the most striking characteristics of medieval customary law. With the obvious exception of Bracton, medieval common lawyers had even less time for jurisprudence than their modern counterparts. If we were able to ask one of Richard II's serjeants, Thomas Pinchbeck for instance, for his definition of a contract we would probably be astonished by the pragmatism of his reply. The cases and dooms recorded in his "termes" and even the statutes engraved on his memory would have dealt almost exclusively with matters of procedure, and Justice Herle's is typical of the kind of definition Pinchbeck might have expected to find in his yearbooks: "covenant," said Herle in 1321, "is nothing but a verbal agreement between parties which cannot be proved [at law] unless expressed in a sealed writing" (*Eyre of London* 2:287). As the early Tudor writer Christopher St. German says, "yt ys not moche argued in the lawes of Englande what dyuersyte is bytwene a contracte/ a promyse/ a gyfte/ a lone/ a bargeyne/ a couenant/ or suche other/ for the intente of the lawe ys to haue the effecte of the mater argued and not the termes" (228). Though we might have an easier time among the canonists and the civilians, the underlying assumptions of English customary law may well prove, as I have suggested, to have rather more to tell us about popular attitudes to promise-keeping than the sophisticated analysis of the Romanists. Exposing these assumptions is no easy matter, however, for they cannot be found neatly summarized in contemporary legal treatises—"the bookes of the lawe of Englande treate lytell therof," St. German says, "for yt ys lefte to the determynacyon of doctours" (229). When we try to deduce substantive law from the arguments of actual lawyers and the rulings of actual judges, we are forced to pry into what Sir Henry Maine called "the envelope of its technical forms," to search out the substantive law "secreted in the interstices of procedure" (1883, 389), and to reconstruct, in Milsom's evocative phrase, "a routine of life" behind the formal workings of archaic actions (1965, 496). The nature of this task may be made somewhat clearer if we first approach medieval covenant cases by way of common-law contractual theory in general.

When the Oxford jurist Sir Frederick Pollock (1845–1937) and the great American judge Oliver Wendell Holmes (1841–1935) began discussing the fundamental principles of common law contract in the late nineteenth century, the shape of their debate was determined in part by values that had survived unexamined from the law's earliest period. Forced to reconcile the legal forms that reflected such values with the sophisticated analysis of continental jurists, their dispute came inevitably to focus on the vexed question of the psychological element in contractual obligations. Perhaps nothing about the common law is more puzzling to the layperson than its long-standing reluctance, particularly in this area, to meddle with psychology: "the law has nothing to do with the actual state of the parties' minds," writes Holmes; "in contract, as elsewhere, it must go by externals and judge parties by their conduct" (quoted by Gilmore 40; cf. Holmes 463–64). Holmes's dictum, of course, was hardly unassailable even in his own day, and he was no doubt prompted to make it partly in response to Pollock's advocacy of the so-called "will theory," which treated contract as a psychological fact arising from the mutual consent of the parties. Holmes himself espoused what is often referred to as the objective theory (particularly associated Samuel Williston), which held that contract was rather to be seen as a social fact created by the operative use of language (see Hart 95–96). This objective theory, I shall argue, preserves traces of a far older attitude to contract than the psychological one, but, quaint though this may appear to an age as obsessed with psychology as our own, it has not yet lost all respectability in Anglo-American courtrooms, if only because its rival raises some very obvious practical difficulties.

As the current disarray of contract theory suggests, neither position has proved entirely satisfactory, the will theorists being unable to show how parties can be said truly to have willed a binding agreement if they subsequently fall out over it, while the objectivists find great difficulty explaining why fraudulent or mistaken contracts should not be honored. Pushed to its logical extreme, the psychological theory would allow just about anyone who felt himself to have made a bad bargain to try and recoup his losses at law; by the same token, the objective theory, though able to narrow the scope for litigation considerably, can offer little protection for the weak or the gullible. In practice, few adherents of either school would go to such lengths: will theorists are generally prepared to allow that contractual relations should be governed by certain formal constraints, and objectivists are ready to concede that the intention of the parties is not wholly irrelevant to the establishment of a contract between them. At the very least, most would say, both parties must intend that their agreement be legally binding in order to make it enforceable,[5] though whether the parties must also intend the consequences of their agreement is a more difficult question and one more likely to provoke debate.

I have already had several occasions to touch on the question of the role of intention in early medieval law (in discussing equivocal oaths in Chapter 3, for example), but the issue becomes even more critical when we consider contractual obligations. It may be best then to begin this discussion of rash promises with a discussion of the customary law's attitude toward intention in general.

The Role of Intention

As a rule of thumb, the more dependent any given system of law is upon formalism, the less time it is likely to have for questions of motive and intent. I suggested earlier that the European folklaw's highly formalized attitude to intention is seen most clearly in the way it imposed strict liability in those cases that we would call criminal; in principle at least, absence of *mens rea* was no defense against a felony charge: "qui inscienter peccat, scienter emendet" (*LHP* ch. 88.6a; 270). Such a principle is evidently common to other folklaw systems as well. Readers of Karen Blixen's *Out of Africa* may recall her account of the legal complications that resulted from an accidental shooting on her farm and the jural principle she adduces from them: "whether you lie in wait for your enemy and cut his throat in the dark; or you fell a tree and a thoughtless stranger passes by and is killed: so far as punishment goes, to [the Kikuyu] mind, it is the same thing" (100). Her observation is generally supported by the anthropologists: Gluckman, for instance, cites Richard Thurnwald to the effect that "a Kikuyu who hurled a spear through a lion which had pinned another man to the ground would be held responsible for the murder because his spear went through the lion and his comrade" (1965, 112).[6] A similar attitude is also to be met with in the Nigerian novel: in Echewa's *The Land's Lord*, for example, a village court finds a man responsible for a shooting death even though he was trying to wrest the weapon away from its owner at the moment of its discharge (58–59), and in John Munonye's *Obi* the hero is forced into exile for his part in a kinswoman's death even though its immediate cause is the incompetent medical treatment she had received (209). In the same way, Anglo-Saxons were apparently answerable for even their most involuntary actions and could be held liable for the outcome of chains of causation that no modern court would take seriously for a moment. The *Leges Henrici Primi*, for instance, apportion some of the responsibility for the death of a traveler to the companion who invited him on the journey, even where the actual killing was done by the victim's own enemies, and hold that the owner of a sword is in part responsible for the wound it makes, even when the wounding was caused by a third party's knocking it from the peg on which its owner had hung it (P&M 2:471).

On the other hand, this principle should not be overstated. African customary process does sometimes acknowledge reduced liability for an unintentional act (e.g., Rattray 289–90). Of the exile of Okonkwo, the hero of Achebe's *Things Fall Apart*, for killing a clansman the narrator remarks, "the crime was of two kinds, male and female. Okonkwo had committed the female, because it had been inadvertent. He could return to the clan after seven years" (87). A well-known Anglo-Saxon example is King Alfred's provision of a reduced penalty from the man who accidentally kills another while holding a spear on his shoulder (ch. 36; Liebermann 1:68). In general, however, it seems to have been felt that such adjustments are best left to local discretion rather than legal definition: this is precisely what Clause 53 of Æthelred's sixth code with its clear distinction between deliberate wrongdoing and something done involuntarily ("unwilles oþþe ungewealdes") encourages by suggesting that someone acting under duress ("nydwyrhta" [in self-defense?]) always deserves to be treated leniently ("se bið gebeorhges ⁊ þy beteran domes symle wyrðe") (Liebermann 1:258). In practice, the local community would usually have been able to modify the harsher effects of the principle of absolute liability for those of its members who were felt to be the victims of circumstance, just as later, local juries would enter fictional verdicts of self-defense in order to prevent the king's judges from hanging good neighbors. Whatever practical adjustments might be made to accommodate local contingencies, however, the principle of absolute liability for offenses such as homicide was retained to the end of the Middle Ages and beyond (see Holdsworth 2:52), and what Maitland says of the early law's attitude to involuntary killing would have been as true under Richard II as it had been under King Alfred: "such manslayers as one would not wish to hang are not acquitted, but are recommended to the 'mercy' of judges and princes, for the *rigor iuris* holds them answerable for all the effects of their actions" (P&M 2:472).

That such a rigorous legal standard reflects the law's excessive formalism rather than its appetite for exemplary punishment becomes clear as soon as we realize that the court's refusal to consider the psychological factor could be as much of a handicap for the accuser as the accused. "He meant to kill me" was no more admissable a plea than "I didn't mean to kill him"; medieval judges were clearly bound by the principle that, as Holmes was later to put it, the law "must go by externals." A case from 1343/44 shows just how severely this principle might restrict the law's reach: the prior of Merton brought an action against some men who had helped their friends evade arrest, but since he was unable to prove that an actual arrest had ever occurred he failed to get his conviction; for the court, it was not enough for him to argue that he had intended to arrest the fugitives, since, as the defendants' lawyer remarks, "in this case he has no act which can prove his will" [mes issi nad il nulle fait qe puit prover sa volunte]. The yearbook annotator underlines this point by recalling another case where a man who had brought a writ of trespass against someone who, he claimed, had obstructed those wishing to come to his market had had his plea dismissed on the grounds that the will of another person cannot be divined, "le brief sabati pur ceo qe autri volunte ne puit estre trove" (*YB 17/18 Edw. 3*, 464–65). Such cases might seem to contradict the fourteenth-century legal maxim that "the will is to be taken for the deed" (see P&M 2:476 n. 5), yet this maxim seems in practice to have been applied to failed attempts to commit a felony (e.g., a leaving for dead) rather than to alleged intentions to commit one in the future (*Source Book* 42–54; cf. Bolland 1921, 61–62). The law was far happier handling a waylaying or a lying in ambush than premeditation or malice aforethought; even malice, says Maitland, "creeps into the records and law books" with "no strong emphasis on the intention" (P&M 2:469 n. 1). The absence of any malicious intent is, of course, raised as a defense in the fourteenth and fifteenth centuries (with varying degrees of success), but it is not until 1470 that we find a lawyer prepared to proclaim openly that "in felony the intent and will of a man shall be construed" (cited by Seipp 1995, 27 n. 75).

When the criminal law had shown such suspicion of questions of motive and intent, we should hardly be surprised to find that resistance was at least as great on the civil side, for, in Milsom's words, "absence of fault would naturally lead a jury to absolve a criminal defendant from punishment more readily than to deprive a civil plaintiff of compensation for his injury" (1981, 299). As the hero of Achebe's *Arrow of God* remarks, "a man might pick his way with the utmost care through a crowded market but find that the hem of his cloth had upset and broken another's wares; in such a case the man, not his cloth, was held to repair the damage" (176). The question of whether a given act was willed or not does sometimes arise in court, however, just as it does in felony cases, and for an analogous reason: though the community regarded well-intentioned defendants as no less liable merely because they had taken reasonable precautions against causing harm, the king demanded additional penalties of the negligent or the ill-willed for having put his judges to avoidable trouble. In other words, while accident was no defense against strict liability, evidence of evil intent might be used to distinguish those trespass cases in which the king had an interest (that is, cases that might involve punishment and fine in addition to simple restitution or compensation); as Morris S. Arnold neatly puts it: "on the tort side, if you did it, you had to pay for it; and if you did it with a wicked motive, you had to pay the king" (1987, 520).

In one case from 1379, discussed at some length by Arnold, a defendant tries to mitigate the charge that in the course of carrying out repair work he had caused some slight damage to the plaintiff's house, which adjoined his own, by claiming "that the act had been without malice on his part and that the damage had been caused unintentionally and 'against his will'" (1979, 369; see *YB 2 Rich. 2*, 69–70 and xix–xxii). In a modern courtroom such a defense might be advanced for the purpose of establishing reduced liability on the grounds that the defendant had taken all reasonable care, but as Arnold shows, such is not the issue here: "in pleading lack of wrongful intention," the defendant was not seeking "to escape the duty to compensate, but to avoid imprisonment and its attendant fine" (370). Probably a similar motive led the defendant in a 1384 case concerning an injury suffered by a nine-year-old boy in the course of a game to claim that "the harm suffered by the said Gregory was done in play, not willfully or maliciously [sine voluntate et absque alia malicia] on the part of the said William" (*YB 12 Rich. 2*, 126). Though the defendant's first line of defense had lain elsewhere (that by agreeing to the game the plaintiff had also agreed to accept its risks, a defense still known to modern law as *volenti non fit iniuria*), this particular argument was presumably intended to prevent the case sliding across the somewhat vague boundary that distinguished a mere private wrong from an offense punishable by the crown.

Before turning to the specific question of the role of intention in the formation of contracts, it is worth asking ourselves what lay behind the law's reluctance to raise the issue of intention. Most commentators seem to regard it as a purely legal matter, simply a sign of immature forensic technique: "ancient law," says Mary Bateson, "could not discuss the question of intent because it had not the machinery wherewith to accomplish the inquiry" (*BC* 2:xl), and even Maitland suggests that the early law, "finds grave difficulties in its way if it endeavors to detect and appreciate the psychical element in guilt and innocence" (P&M 2:474). Behind such views lies a need to believe in the evolution of ever more supple and discriminating legal techniques: "Today," says William McGovern, "we are bold enough to try to determine not merely a man's intent but his motive. Medieval law was less sure of its powers" (1968, 61). What such explanations all seem to imply is that no medieval lawyer or judge could really have doubted the potential importance of intention as a factor in assessing legal liability but that, recognizing their own forensic unhandiness, they simply chose to ignore it or speak of it only obliquely. But what if we seek to account for the law's silence as a sign of something very much stranger to the modern imagination — a dim memory of something we might call unintentional guilt?

If the folklaw of many societies seems uncomfortable dealing with intention this is partly because it sees even unconscious acts as reflecting some kind of hidden purpose and its own role as stopping short of questioning the mysteries of the offender's personal deity. Attempting to limit the disruptive effects of a transgression was one thing, but probing the luckless transgressor's own private doom was quite another. This is easy enough to appreciate in the case of the Greek *daemon*, the Igbo *chi*, and even the Norse *fylgja*. In England, however, Anglo-Saxon *wyrd* became early depersonalized into an abstract fate: only the faintest echo of the ancient power of its Old Norse cognate *Urðr* still clings to it by the time Sir Gawain tells his guide that he must press on to the Green Chapel, "Worþe hit wele oþer wo, as þe wyrde lykez / hit hafe" (*SGGK* 2134–35). To claim, then, that the medieval common law's suspicion of intention retains faint memories of this power will seem absurdly far-fetched to many. Even E. R. Dodds' modest claim that "early Greek justice cared nothing for intent — it was the act that mattered" (3), has recently provoked a stern reproof from Bernard Williams.[7] Before dismissing such a hypothetical residue out of hand, however, we might ask ourselves how it was that medieval courts should have been prepared to put animals on trial or seen fit to require compensation of inanimate objects? After all, no one can ever have supposed that the pig that ate the baby or the oak that fell on the carter had acted from malice aforethought.

For England, unfortunately, what little information we can glean about animal trials comes from literary sources rather than conventional legal texts. In *Sir Beues of Hamtoun*, for instance, when the hero's horse kicks the king of England's son to death,

Þe king swor, for þat wronge
Þat Beues scholde ben an-honge
& to-drawe wiþ wilde fole.
Þe barnage it nolde nouȝt þole
& seide, hii miȝte do him no wors,
Boute lete hongen is hors.

(3567–72)

(In the event Beves accepts voluntary banishment rather than see his horse so punished.)[8] English legal sources offer no such evidence of the ascription of culpability to animals as the *Sachsenspiegel*'s provision (3.1.1; 195) that all living creatures present at a rape were to be beheaded (presumably they were felt to be at fault for not raising the alarm), and no early instance of the full-dress animal trials that are first recorded in Northern France in the thirteenth century and were later to turn up in the Low Countries, Germany, and Italy (Esther Cohen 110–11);[9] we can nonetheless glean from the medieval common law's treatment of the owner's liability for damage done by animals something of the popular attitudes that such trials embodied. Early law seems generally to have assigned liability solely to the offending animal itself and held its owner free of any direct responsibility for its wrongs (G. L. Williams 9–11 and 265–69); we hear of animals punished by death, mutilation, and even banishment, while their owners enter the picture only where they have actively assisted in the crime or sought to protect the criminal. The owner's responsibility went no further than seeing that the animal was punished or at the least handed over for punishment. Thus a judge in Edward III's reign could still argue "that if my dog kill your sheep, and I freshly after the fact tender you the dog, you are without recovery against me" (G. L. Williams 273), and the defendant in a case of sheep-worrying from Wye in Kent in 1360 protest "that as soon as he knew that the abovesaid dog was a malefactor and doing such damage, he killed that dog" (cited by R. Palmer 1993, 249 n. 78). It is easy for us to assume that when, in the second half of the fourteenth century, the common law first provides remedies against owners who incite their dogs to attack, or those who continue to keep dogs they know to be vicious (R. Palmer 1993, 228–51), the lawyers are beginning to recognize the principle that guilt should be attributed only to rational creatures, yet the forms of action in themselves require no such explanation; they are entirely consistent with the earlier principle that only those owners who can be shown to have been accessories before or after the fact can be forced to answer for the crimes of their animals.

The business of punishing inanimate objects, which will look even more bizarre to the modern mind, is well attested in medieval England. At an earlier period, when death was caused by a cart or a mill wheel, the offending object seems to have been forfeited to the victim's family as a kind of *wergeld*, but by the thirteenth century this deodand, as it was called, regularly fell forfeit to the crown.[10] The king was expected to put the proceeds of such deodands to charitable use, but a case which created something of a stir in legal circles in 1388 shows that this was far from inevitable. When a man was killed by a fall of rock in a tin mine in Cornwall, Richard II tried to make this the excuse for donating the mine to two of his chamber valets; not surprisingly the mine owners complained that their sovereign was only entitled to the offending lump of rock, not to the whole mine, and to their credit the king's judges, after a great deal of judicial debate, agreed with them (*YB 12 Rich. 2*, 19–20). Of course, it is merely an assumption that when the king's judges confiscated a guilty cart or mill wheel they saw themselves as exercising justice upon it—they are as silent about the underlying justification for their actions here as elsewhere—but then the explanation that would see them as preserving an impenetrable archaism merely for the sake of its charitable consequences is no less of an assumption. Given the common law's suspicion of all questions of motive and intention throughout the Middle Ages, I see no reason for regarding one explanation as inherently less probable than the other.

We have seen that at common law questions of motive and intent hovered in the wings in felony cases and tort litigation while the central drama of the defendant's innocence or guilt was played out by more important members of the cast, but we have still to explore what role they might have played in the sphere of contractual obligations. Did the law take an equally objective view of contract, or was it prepared to recognize a psychological element in the formation of agreements between individuals? If not, how could it begin to take account of such common contractual problems as fraud, misrepresentation, or mistake? As I hope to be able to show, the principle still familiar to lawyers as *volenti non fit iniuria* (the principle that one cannot expect redress where harm has resulted from an arrangement to which one has voluntarily subscribed) had a far wider application under medieval common law than it does today; indeed, it covered the whole sphere of private obligations and could as easily be invoked against the victim of a badly framed formal contract as against the victim of a sporting accident.

The Intention to Be Bound

When we turn to the treatment of contractual obligations in medieval literature, we notice at once a marked consonance between the lawyer's approach to the intention of the promisor and the poet's. Strictly speaking, the term *rash promise* should probably be restricted to gratuitous offers—obligations binding, if at all, on only one party, as opposed to bilateral contracts based on a quid pro quo or, as the common lawyer would now say, upon consideration. Such offers, though less common than what we might term rash bargains, are always taken seriously where they do occur and are worth looking at, because they raise with particular clarity the question of whether the promisors really intend themselves to be legally bound.

When Sir Orfeo, in quest of his wife Dame Herodis, stumbles upon the fairy kingdom where she is being held, he represents himself to the king as a wandering minstrel and offers to play for him. The sweetness of his harping elicits a classic rash promise from the king:

> Menstrel, me likeþ wel þi gle.
> Now aske of me what it be,
> Largelich ichil þe pay:
> Now speke, & tow miȝt asay.
> (*Sir Orfeo* 449–52)

This promise is entirely gratuitous, for the poem makes it perfectly clear that the king could not in any sense be said to have commissioned Orfeo's performance: "Ich, no non þat is wiþ me, / No sent neuer after þe" (lines 423–24). The canonist, the civilian, and the common lawyer would have agreed, though not all for the same reasons, that such a promise should be called a *nuda promissio*, but each would have had a very different way of dealing with it.

In the fourteenth century, only among the canonists does it seem to have been generally accepted that *ex nudo pacto oritur actio*—that promises made with none of the proper legal formalities were legally binding (Kemp 22–23); as long as their performance did not lead to sin, promises formed an *obligatio juris naturalis* that could not be evaded, and ecclesiastical courts undertook to enforce them by means of a process, known as a *denunciatio evangelica* (Coing 233–38), which in extreme cases could lead to excommunication. This antiformalist position is entirely consistent with church teaching. Medieval canon law had grown out of penitential doctrine, and though many of the earlier penitentials are surprisingly indifferent to the psychological dimension,[11] the spread of the practice of private confession after the Fourth Lateran Council in 1215 provoked more and more interest in the spiritual sources of sin and the remedies to be sought within the sinner's own conscience. Since it was a commonplace that one could sin in thought as well as word and deed, the canonists could hardly have avoided consideration of motive and intention in their legal deliberations (Berman 1983, 189–90). Predictably, then, the canonists' theory of contract fell squarely on the psychological side of the objective/psychological divide, and in principle formal questions must always have remained secondary. Since God saw the innermost thoughts of the heart, it could hardly matter what robes were used to clothe the naked promise: "promises must be kept," says Hostiensis, "even if they are naked according to the law . . . for God makes no distinction between a simple utterance and an oath" (quoted in P&M 2:195 n. 2).

Fourteenth-century civilians would also have seen the fairy king's promise as naked, but for them this would have been a good reason for discounting it. In their scheme of things contractual nakedness meant the absence of a sufficient *causa*: "where there is no cause," says Baldus, "there can be nothing caused; therefore a naked pact offers no grounds for an action" (quoted by Zimmermann 552). A promise made without a proper cause, they would have argued, cannot give rise to an action at law because it offers no reason for believing that it was meant to be taken seriously. The civil lawyer's doctrine of cause clearly represented a major step along the road toward a psychological theory of contract. One made a promise because one had some definite end in mind: "the final cause is the object of the intellect," writes Baldus, "as the image is the object of vision or a port is the object of navigation" (quoted by Gordley 52). Although liberality was one of two broad categories of cause governing promises (the other was exchange), Baldus would have found the kind of unreasoned liberality displayed in *Sir Orfeo* quite easy to exclude, and the fairy king's *nuda promissio* would have been voidable on the grounds that it arose from mere foolishness. Such lack of *causa* should be distinguished from what a common lawyer would now mean by saying that the promise lacked consideration.[12] The test of consideration is, in principle at least, a formal or objective one: Orfeo could not claim in a modern court that the king had made a binding contract to reward him for his music, because the harping had preceded the promise of reward; such a claim, in their terms, would fail because it was grounded in what is technically known as past consideration. Where the medieval civilian's *causa* can be located in the promisor's mind, the modern doctrine of consideration claims to concern itself solely with the actual words or deeds of the parties.

The kind of thinking that lay behind the doctrine of *causa* (but not of modern consideration) was quite alien to the fourteenth-century common lawyer, whose own conception of contract was entirely objective. The fairy king's *nuda promissio* would not have been legally binding on Orfeo, not because it lacked a *causa*, but because it had been made with none of the necessary formalities. Cases such as this never came before the common-law courts in the fourteenth century for the simple reason that they would have failed to meet the procedural requirements of any of the available actions. Without being able to produce a sealed instrument, Orfeo could not have sued in covenant; unable to prove that he was owed an agreed sum of money, he could not have sued in debt; and lacking evidence of any actual damage done to him, he could not have sued in trespass. This does not, however, justify us in concluding that common lawyers would have denied that such promises were binding in and of themselves. The evidence is inevitably negative, but Morris Arnold, for one, is prepared to offer as one "reason for believing that the idea embodied in the word covenant had no limitation . . . that no one ever raised the point that the promise was made without consideration" (1987, 510). Fourteenth-century common lawyers would no doubt have agreed with the canonists that in principle all *pacta sunt servanda*, but, unlike confessors, judges clearly felt they had no business prying into the recesses of the promisor's mind: "No one, except God, can know whether that seisin was with your knowledge or not," remarks Justice Willoughby in a case from 1346, "for a person's will cannot be the subject of an averment [i.e., verification by a jury]" (*YB 20 Edw. 3 (pt. 2)*, 396–97). As a consequence, common-law judges dealt only with those promises that, having been made in the recognized legal form, could be properly confirmed by witnesses or by an inquest. Formally, a rash promise was no different from any other and the law would have regarded the promisee who failed to make sure that the proper procedures had been observed as neither more nor less foolish than the imprudent promisor.

To show that informal, gratuitous promises were not actionable in the secular courts is quite different from suggesting that medieval people were under no social pressure to honor them. One indication of the seriousness with which they were regarded was the way in which they were associated in cases like *Sir Orfeo*'s with the principle of noblesse oblige. When the fairy king learns the harper's choice of reward he objects:

"Nay!" quaþ þe king, "Þat nouȝt nere!
A sori couple of ȝou it were,
For þou art lene, rowe and blac,
& sche is louesum, wiþ-outen lac."
(457–60)

But Orfeo promptly reminds him of his duty to honor his promise, and the king hesitates no longer:

"O, Sir!" he seyd, "Gentil King!
Ȝete were it a wele fouler þing
To here a lesing of þi mouþe:
So, Sir, as ȝe seyd nouþe
What ich wold aski haue y schold;
& nedes þou most þi word hold."
Þe king seyd, "Seþþen it is so
Take hir bi þe hond & go."
(463–70)

The particular claim that a broken promise makes one a liar ("To here a lesing of þi mouþe") rings oddly on the modern ear and may serve to remind us once again of the rather different standards governing medieval ideas of truth.[13] The real problem with the promise in *Sir Orfeo*, it seems, is not that it is gratuitous, but that the king, like Herod with Salome, has foolishly attached no conditions to it. By contrast, *Ywain and Gawain* provides a good example of a gratuitous promise in which the promisor exhibits a legalistic circumspection in his choice of words; the hero is here promising his lady that he will return from his quest before the end of twelve months:

> Bot, madame, þis understandes,
> A man þat passes divers landes,
> May sum tyme cum in grete destres,
> In preson or els in sekenes;
> Þarefore I pray ȝow, or I ga,
> Þat ȝe wil out-tak þir twa.
>
> (1519–24)

Ywain's careful insertion of an exceptions clause here shows clearly that he expects to be held to the exact terms of his promise, however one-sided.

The promise made by the fairy king in *Sir Orfeo* may be ill-considered, but it is at least, from our perspective, cast in the form of a promise. While the civilian might claim that the king's words lack a sufficient *causa* and the common lawyer that they have no formal clothing, there can be no doubt that they do constitute an offer of some kind. In Robert Henryson's fable of "The Fox, the Wolf, and the Husbandman," on the other hand, the modern reader will doubt that there has been any kind of genuine offer at all: "The volff . . . mot haue ȝou all at anis!" cries an angry plowman to his unmanageable oxen (line 2244). Not even in fifteenth-century Scotland, one might think, could anyone seriously have imagined that such an imprecation need be taken literally, let alone that it might form the basis for a legal action; "God forbid, schir, all hechtis suld haldin be," as the plowman says a little later (2276). Indeed, the very seriousness with which it is treated by the wolf and his companion, the legalistic fox, contributes much to the fable's comic effect. Nevertheless, Henryson does make the plowman's malediction the basis of a burlesque lawsuit, and prompts us to speculate on the legal and social meaning of unintended promises for his readers.

Everyone in the fable, including the narrator, refers to the plowman's curse as a promise (a *hecht*),[14] yet most people nowadays would instantly recognize that there is a glaring difference between the two illocutions. One need hardly be a twentieth-century speech-act theorist to see the fundamental distinction: "a promise," as Aquinas had said, "is the offer to do something for someone, for it would be a threat rather than a promise if one said that one was going to do something to them" (2a2æ.88.2; 39:162). How is it, then, that Henryson's plowman fails to appreciate this distinction? When John Searle makes promising his paradigmatic illocution (54–71), he gives what he terms the essential condition of all promises as follows: "[The speaker] intends that the utterance . . . will place him under an obligation to do [a certain act]" (60). Among his subsidiary conditions, Searle lists the speaker's intention to perform this act, and the speaker's intention to produce in the hearer the knowledge that the utterance constitutes an obligation. Searle's analysis, whether or not one accepts its details, offers irrefutable evidence that the twentieth-century mind makes an intuitive association between promising and intending to promise. For most of us, an unintentional promise is a contradiction in terms.[15] In the Middle Ages in general, however, the mental faculty most readily associated with promises was not intention but will. This may look like a quibble (yearbook editors, for instance, regularly translate *volunte* as 'intention'), but even everyday modern usage preserves a distinction between the two qualities. To will something to happen is not the same thing as to intend it to happen, nor is to be willing to do something the same as to intend to do it. Will in such phrases implies a choice or commitment (a sense still present in expressions like *will power* and *strong-willed*), where intention implies simply a plan or design. A promise, says Aquinas, arises from a purpose of the will (*propositum voluntatis*), which is itself a consequence of deliberation (2a2æ. 88.1; 39:160). When later he says that "the obligation of a vow is occasioned by one's own will and intention" [ex propria voluntate et intentione] he seems to associate the will with the act of vowing and the intention with the course to which it subsequently commits the votary (2a2æ. 88,4; 39:168). Similarly, when he speaks of baptism — a sacrament that the canonists regarded as fundamentally contractual — he says that it demands "the will by which one intends a new kind of life" [requiritur voluntas qua intendat vitæ novitatem] (3a.68.7; 57:102).[16]

While for the canonists and the civilians *voluntas* and *intentio* were being drawn closer to one another, for the common lawyers *will* continued to express a kind of objective quality we might almost render as 'consent' or even 'freedom to consent'. This can be illustrated by the vexed issue of the contractual capacity of married women. Contrary to popular belief, it is very difficult to find an unequivocal statement of the medieval common law's position on this question,[17] but, had they been asked to rule on it, judges in the fourteenth and fifteenth centuries might well have agreed with the argument offered by a Tudor justice for denying that married women were free to make contracts: the wife, said Justice Luke in 1536, "has no will, for the will of the woman depends on the will of her husband" (quoted by A. W. B. Simpson 1987, 547).[18] Such a doctrine must have had only limited practical consequence, at least for contract law. Of a slightly earlier claim that "if my wife buys things to keep my household, such as bread, and I have no knowledge of this, I shall not be charged although they are used in my household," Simpson astutely remarks that "this has all the air of a somewhat unworkable doctrine" (548).[19] Speaking of those occasions on which a husband might indeed be forced to honor his wife's contracts, he suggests that, "whatever the theory, the law was that the husband could be bound by prior authorization or subsequent ratification" (549). Will in this sense, then, is clearly more than a kind of mental formulation underpinning certain types of behavior; it is itself a species of legal capacity or authority, capable of being conferred or abrogated at the decision of another person.

Such an account of the role of will in common-law contract runs counter to the claim sometimes made (e.g., Gaylord 357) that as a married woman Chaucer's heroine in "The Franklin's Tale" lacks the legal capacity to make a contract with Aurelius. Not only does Dorigen's husband plainly endorse Aurelius's claim after the fact (1474–78), but Arveragus had explicitly renounced any control over his wife's will at the time of their marriage:

> Of his free wyl he swoor hire as a knyght
> That nevere in al his lyf he, day ne nyght,
> Ne sholde upon hym take no maistrie
> Agayn hir wyl, ne kithe hire jalousie,
> But hire obeye, and folwe hir wyl in al.
> (745–49)

In this, Dorigen's position stands in stark contrast to Griselde's:

> But as ye wole youreself, right so wol I.
> And heere I swere that nevere willyngly,
> In werk ne thoght, I nyl yow disobeye.
> ("Clerk's Tale" 361–63).

As Griselde later tells Walter, "Whan I first cam to yow . . . / Lefte I my wyl and al my libertee" (655–56).[20] While we may allow that the common lawyers might have been prepared to argue, in principle at least, that the wife lacked the will to enter into contracts without her husband's consent, in this particular case Arveragus is clearly bound not only by his "subsequent ratification" but by his own "prior authorization" to recognize his wife's contract.

To return to Henryson's fable and the question of whether his promise of the oxen, though clearly unintended, might be said in some sense to have been willed: for Aquinas, promising may well have been a deliberate (one might almost say an intentional) act, but it will hardly seem odd in a post-Freudian world to claim that the medieval popular imagination might feel that an impulse of the will need not always be conscious.[21] Is it not possible that one might have been held responsible for the form of one's own utterances whatever one's professed intentions, and that a speaker who, however thoughtlessly, happened to utter a curse in the form of a promise was still felt to have willed the obligation it entailed? Another way of putting it might be to say that one was felt to be answerable for the performative power of one's own words even when one had had no intention of making them perform anything, just as one was answerable for a wound caused by one's own sword even when someone else had knocked it down from its peg.

In actuality, of course, medieval people would have found the burden of such immanent responsibility for every single thing they said or did quite intolerable had they not been able to rely for support on a universal respect for legal formalism.[22] The first of the plowman's two objections to the wolf's claim to his oxen is that his imprecation had possessed none of the formal characteristics of a binding promise: "'Gaif I my hand or oblissing,' quod he, / 'Or haue ȝe witnes or writ for to schau?'" (2278–79). These are legal arguments (and, interestingly, when he points out that he has put nothing in writing he anticipates the one condition that modern law will recognize as the basis for an action on a gratuitous promise). His second objection, however, is based on status. Kings, he says, might be obliged by their position to keep their word under all circumstances (one thinks of the fairy king in *Sir Orfeo*), but poor folk labor under no such disadvantage; they are fully entitled to hide behind the proper legal forms:

> Ane leill man is not tane at halff ane taill.
> I may say and ganesay; I am na king.
> Where is ȝour witnes that hard I hecht thame haill?
> (2298–90)

This attitude seems to me a natural enough consequence of having to live in a world where, to borrow Searle's terminology, expressives and commissives were inextricably entangled; it offered people a measure of protection against the dangerous capriciousness of their own language with its potential for unleashing performative forces when least expected. Behind it lies something like the "system of truth" that Brian Blakey derives from Béroul, a system whereby "one was not bound to be truthful, unless one had sworn to be so" (28–29).

Such a system was apparently familiar enough to *true* Thomas Rymer, to judge from his angry outburst when the Queen of Elfland offers him "the tongue that can never lie":

"My tongue is mine ain," True Thomas said;
"A gudely gift ye wad gie to me!
I neither dought to buy nor sell,
At fair or tryst where I may be."

(Child 1:326)

The principle that all promises must be kept might be all very well for priests (like Henryson's fox-friar) and gentry (like his wolf), but clearly a simple plowman was free to hide behind the convention that promises need only be taken seriously when made in the established form.

An instance of an unintended gratuitous promise that will be far more familiar to most readers than the one in Henryson's fable occurs in Chaucer's "Friar's Tale." The essential situation here is very similar, with a carter and his enmired draft horses replacing the plowman and his wayward oxen, and a curse that consigns the animals to the devil rather than to the wolf:

"Hayt, Brok! Hayt, Scot! What spare ye for the stones?
The feend," quod he, "yow fecche, body and bones,
As ferforthly as evere were ye foled,
So muche wo as I have with yow tholed!
The devel have al, bothe hors and cart and hey!"

(1543–47)

Chaucer's story draws upon a rather different literary tradition than Henryson's, however. All the closest analogues of "The Friar's Tale" are sermon exempla, where we might expect the preacher's natural concern with salvation to give far more prominence to the spiritual state of his characters than in the popular fable. By setting his tale in the context of the mutual antipathy of the friar and summoner, Chaucer heightens the effect, for behind this antipathy lies the old rivalry of the confessional and the consistory court, of private absolution and public correction.

While the question of intention is studiously ignored in Henryson's fable, the whole plot of "The Friar's Tale" turns on it: much of the humor derives from the literal-minded summoner's inability to see something quite obvious, not merely to the reader, but (by a nice irony) to the devil himself—the importance of the swearer's intention in such situations. The distinction I have been discussing between scholastic and popular attitudes to promises is, in fact, far more marked in Chaucer than in his analogues where the effect of the curses had generally depended not on intention but on sincerity. In one of the two surviving fourteenth-century English versions of the tale (see Nicholson), the devil refuses to act upon the curses of a poor cowherd and a harassed mother, since "they do not curse from the heart" [non maledicunt ex corde] (Bryan and Dempster 272); the teller of the other, the Benedictine preacher Robert Ripon, repeats this justification, but goes even further, offering as one of the lessons of his exemplum that "one should not commend anything to the devil, since by chance it can happen that such commendation will come to pass" (Owst 1961, 163 n. 2). Indeed, the further back we go in this tradition the fewer the moralists we will encounter who pay lip service even to the importance of sincerity: thus a chapter *de cavendis imprecacionibus* in the *Gesta Romanorum* relates a story from Gervase of Tilbury of a man who rashly wills his squalling infant to the devil in order to warn us against subjecting members of our family to any such imprecation, however irritating we may find them (542–44), and similar stories are to be found in Caesarius of Heisterbach (cited in Gurevich 1988, 189). The historian Joinville tells us that any member of his household who said "the devil take it!" got a beating, "for it is a very sinful manner of speaking to consign to the devil men or women who have been given to God from the time of their baptism" (*Vie* ch. 687; 228).

Larry Scanlon has justly observed that the force released by this kind of cursing "seems beyond the speaker's conscious control" (153), whereas Chaucer clearly viewed the matter, as most people would do nowadays, in terms of intentionality: "'Nay,' quod the devel, 'God woot, never a deel! / It is nat his entente, trust me weel'" (lines 1555–56). The point is made twice more in the tale. When the horses finally extricate themselves from the mud with the carter's blessings, the devil remarks dryly that he had earlier "spak oo thing, but he thoghte another" (1568). Later, after the old widow has sent the summoner to the devil, together with the pan he had extorted from her, the devil is very careful to establish her real intentions: "is this youre wyl in ernest that ye seye?" (1627). At such moments, when not only the characters within the tale but the materials from which it has been shaped so clearly reflect the characteristic late medieval interplay of *lered* and *lewed*, we are made particularly aware of what Ong has termed the "psychodynamics" of oral culture (30–77)—its firm roots in the physical world and its distrust of mental introspection.

Compared with the homespun moralizing of its analogues, "The Friar's Tale" reveals considerable jural sophistication. This is particularly clear in the climactic final confrontation where, by making the heartfelt malignity of his victim's curse a sufficient cause of the bailiff's damnation, the analogues retain clear traces of the traditional view of the immanent instrumentality of the spoken word and reflect the general tendency of oral cultures to treat language as "a mode of action and not an instrument of reflection" (Malinowski 1927, 312). Chaucer, however, as befits a clerkly maker, "disperses the mystery and moral ambiguity of the curse" (Scanlon 153) by providing a far more empirical account of the summoner's damnation, one that might have stood up to legal analysis even in Bologna. His damnation is not a direct result of the widow's curse, intentional or otherwise, for her words can make no performative claims upon him. She is, however, quite within her rights to consign her own pan to hell, and if the summoner should happen to be carried off along with it he has no one to blame but himself. Before claiming his prize, then, the devil, like a meticulous canon lawyer, must first establish that the old woman intends to give him the pan, and next satisfy himself that the summoner has no intention of relinquishing what he regards as his rightful property:

> "Nay, olde stot, that is nat myn entente,"
> Quod this somonour, "for to repente me
> For any thyng that I have had of thee."
> (1630–32)

Were it not for the prominence of "entente" among its rhyme-words (see Murtaugh), Chaucer's emphasis on intention in this tale might easily pass unnoticed, so intuitively do we associate promising with this mental faculty; in the fourteenth century, however, as we quickly see when we compare it with its analogues or try reading it against a background of customary legal doctrine, such an emphasis reveals a considerable degree of analytical sophistication. Had Chaucer been setting out to refute Chief Justice Bryan's famous dictum that "a person's intention shall not be tried, for even the devil can have no knowledge of a person's intention" [car le Diable n'ad conusance de l'entent de home] (*Abridgements* 17 Edw. 4, pasc. 2), he could hardly have done better than to start with this illustration of the fallacy of its major premise.

If promises made in anger offer an obvious source of difficulty for any lawyer who is reluctant to take account of intention, those made in play will hardly prove much easier to deal with. Where the promises we have looked at so far have been unilateral or gratuitous ones, the playful promises of medieval literature are often found in the context of some kind of mutual exchange, and hence constitute what we might call rash bargains rather than rash promises. This complicates the picture considerably. In the first place playful exchanges will furnish an appearance of consideration or a quid pro quo and hence bear a closer formal resemblance to binding contracts than gratuitous promises; secondly, they are likely to add to the fundamental question of whether the promisors intend themselves to be bound the secondary issue of whether they truly intend the consequences of their promises.

Unintended Consequence

Medieval customary law, as we have seen, preferred to deal with states of affairs rather than states of mind, and this made it a particularly clumsy instrument for dealing with mistake or fraud. While it was quite ready to listen to claims that an express warranty had been broken, it was very uncomfortable with claims of misrepresentation and preferred devoting its time to regulation of the seller's activities before a dispute arose to obtaining relief for the unwary purchaser afterward. Thus, most commercial situations were governed by elaborate and widely recognized rituals and conventions the purpose of which was to render them as objective and unambiguous as possible. The guild guaranteed that its members did careful work, used pure materials, gave accurate measure, and charged fair prices, but buyers would only have had themselves to blame if they made a purchase, whether of a loaf of bread or a silver goblet, without checking that it had its maker's stamp on it; similarly, courts would enforce agreements that had been entered in their official records, but woe betide any promisee who had failed to check that the correct details of the agreement had been properly enrolled.

Walton H. Hamilton has shown that the maxim *caveat emptor* is more fittingly applied to the commercial system of more recent times when, by and large, the burden of proving the soundness of goods has shifted from vendor to purchaser. We may think it cumbersome that medieval people habitually swore oaths that their goods were sound, sealed bargains by shaking hands, or offering pennies to God, or drinking tankards of ale, and brought along trusted friends to witness the discharge of debts, but such activities would have seemed unremarkable to them. Probably the system worked well enough in general: "credit, not distrust," says Hamilton, seems to have formed the basis of most commercial dealings (1162). This might appear to be at odds with the claim that medieval people acted at their peril, or that "a man [had] himself to thank if he [was] misled by deceit" (P&M 2:536), but in reality the two are but opposite sides of the same coin. Buyers had little need to beware as long as they observed the proper formalities, but these they certainly ignored or neglected at their peril. On the other hand, while sale of goods was a routine, even commonplace, transaction, more exotic kinds of agreement must always have held the potential for exposing the parties to deceit. Thus, while *caveat emptor* may not have been a typically medieval warning, *caveat pactor* certainly was.

The paradigmatic situation here is the exchange-of-winnings game that occupies the third fit of *Sir Gawain and the Green Knight*. This is indubitably based on a formal contract between Gawain and his host, even if its form is that of the ancient trothplight rather than that of the more modern indenture: their *couenauntez* are made in front of witnesses, confirmed with a handslap and an oath —"Swete, swap we so, sware with trawþe" (line 1108)—and sealed with a drink—"Who bryngez vus þis beuerage, þis bargayn is maked" (1112); for good measure, the terms are reconfirmed before they part for the night (1123). Similar rituals are performed when the bargain is renewed on the second evening (1403–9), and repeated, though less prominently, on the third one (1677–78). Gawain, of course, has no idea when he makes this bargain that his very life depends on the punctilious observance of its terms, but it is difficult to see how so formal a compact could ever have been invalidated without appealing to the intention of the parties, without, in other words, establishing that for Gawain no such serious consequences had been intended by this Christmas game.

In modern law, of course, the enforceability of a contract such as Bertilak's might be challenged on the grounds that it is nothing more than a kind of wager,[23] but this would not have seemed a valid objection in the Middle Ages. Medieval common lawyers would have had little sympathy for the nineteenth-century notion of an "idle wager," whose enforcement was simply "a waste of the court's time" (Treitel 393). Nor would it have been much help to point to the comparatively trivial objects of this particular bet: though the spoils of a hunt or a flirtation may look to us like mere sporting trophies of no value in themselves, "it never seems to have been argued during our period that wagering contracts were bad at common law, either on the ground of mere frivolity or on the ground that their enforcement was contrary to public policy" (A. W. B. Simpson 1987, 534). Indeed, even in more modern times three kisses would hardly look out of place among some of the things proposed as consideration in regular contract cases. It is, moreover, but a short step from a compact to exchange winnings to one, like the bargain between the summoner and the devil in "The Friar's Tale," to share them (1533–34),[24] and this would have constituted an absolutely unremarkable form of medieval obligation.

In 1442/23, no doubt because he had failed to have their agreement put in writing, a Yorkshireman called William Parker was forced to take his case against Gilbert Bedenall to the chancellor's court rather than to the court of Common Pleas, and thus we learn more than we might normally do about the circumstances of their dispute. It appears that six years earlier the two men had sunk "theyr comon silver and golde in Mercerware to the price and value of xl S. and more pakked in fotepak and in hors pak . . . unto theyr bother oeps [profit]," but that, though their common stock now stood at thirty-four pounds, Parker, or so he claimed, had received no part of it, "whare by their covenaunt he shuld have the half" (cited in W. T. Barbour 182–83). A similar dispute, also between Yorkshiremen, came before chancery ten years or so later: John Carter of Beverley complained "that where [he] and Roger Kidall were possessed ioyntly of ix^{c} Stockfisshes and an C iiij^{xx} Saltfisshes þe which [were] putte in to a hous to have ben uttered and sold to their bother use and profite . . . the forseid Roger . . . noon accompte nor profite therof, ner of any parcell therof, will yelde to your said Oratour" (W. T. Barbour 199).

A comparison of the elegant game played by Gawain and his host with such mundane arrangements as these might seem somewhat strained, yet the merchant's haggling carries as great a share of the metaphorical burden in the exchange of winnings scenes as the courtier's persiflage. "Tas yow þere my cheuicaunce, I cheued no more," says Gawain as he delivers the firstday's kiss (1390), and Bertilak receives his next day's consignment with, "'Ȝe ben ryche in a whyle, / Such chaffer and ȝe drowe" (1646–47). Mercantile language is especially prominent in the final day's exchange:

> "Bi Kryst," quoþ þat oþer knyȝt, "Ȝe cach much sele
> In cheuisaunce of þis chaffer, ȝif ȝe hade goud chepez."
> "Ȝe, of þe chepe no charg," quoþ chefly þat oþer,
> "As is pertly payed þe chepez þat I aȝte."
>
> (1938–41)

For all that the exchanges are described as a *layk* (1111 and 1125) and the bargains are said to be made in jest (1404 and 1409), the poet's choice of metaphorical vehicle recalls a more sober world where obligations are discharged with *feez* (1622) and payment is required *bi lawe* (1643).

Another, rather more courtly, parallel to the compact made between Gawain and his host is the institution known as brotherhood in arms. Indeed, in some ways brotherhood in arms was an aristocratic counterpart of the commercial trading partnership, for, as Keen has shown, beneath its chivalric trappings lay a perfectly businesslike arrangement. Thus, when the great French knights, Bertrand du Guescelin and Olivier de Clisson, swore mutual brotherhood, each subscribed to a set of written terms and conditions that included: "Item, we wish and consent that you shall have half of all the profits and rights which may fall to our lot, both from prisoners taken by us or our men in war, as from lands ransomed" (Keen 1962, 6). Such documents survive only rarely, but another drawn up in 1421 between two English esquires, John Winter and Nicholas Molyneux, who were on campaign in France at the time, suggests that among the lesser gentry brotherhood in arms may have been an even more commercial institution: "Item, all goods that shall, by the grace of God, be won by them or between them, and that may be spared, shall be sent to London and safely deposited in a chest placed in the church of St. Thomas Acon, which chest shall have two keys, one for Molyneux and the other for Wynter" (McFarlane 1963, 309). Many literary scholars will find it difficult to think of idealized pairs like Palamon and Arcite, Amis and Amiloun, or Eger and Grime in terms of such commercial expediency, yet as Keen reminds us, it is "unwise to assume that anything that writers of medieval romance took seriously was a matter of indifference in practice" (1962, 1).

Formally, then, the compact made between Gawain and his host would have been quite unexceptionable and would indeed have closely resembled others in the workaday world with which the poet's audience would have been perfectly familiar. The real question is whether a medieval common-law court would have been prepared to accept the defense that an agreement in due form had not been entered into seriously by one of the parties. We know from poor Nicole Loyseau's experience with the ecclesiastical court in Troyes that canon lawyers would probably have done so, but, in view of what has been said about their attitude to intention, and in light of their general reluctance to admit such analogous defenses as mistake or fraud,[25] we must doubt that common lawyers would have had any truck with the argument that there were sound legal reasons for voiding a contract merely because it had been made in play. In a parallel situation, a fifteenth-century plaintiff who had foolishly allowed himself to be persuaded to seal a bond when he was drunk had had such serious doubts about his chances at common law that he took his case to the chancellor: "and afterwardes he made me drynke ale and wyne and he tolde me hyt was wyne of Surre where Sarsons dwelleden and bad me drynke ynow therof, and y schull be the better ever whiles y lyve. . . And ther they made me selee God wot y wyst ner what" (*CPC* 1:xxix–xxx). There are, of course, other difficulties with Gawain's contract with Bertilak (not the least being the concealed penalty clause which nearly costs him his life), but I suspect that many medieval readers would have been less impressed than we are by Gawain's general punctiliousness in observing the terms of a bargain made in play and would have been correspondingly more critical of his final slip.

If Gawain could hardly be expected to recognize the hidden condition that was attached to his exchange of winnings game with Bertilak, still less could he have foreseen, when first he agreed to play it, the course that would be taken by his beheading game with the Green Knight. As Robert Blanch and Julian Wasserman point out, Gawain confirms his agreement to play the beheading game with all the proper legal formalities (600–602); indeed, the traditional rituals of trothplight are even more elaborate here than in the exchange of winnings game, for on this occasion Arthur himself acts as borrow and the ax that is hung up in his hall as a "trwe tytel" of the bargain (line 480) seems, at least in part, to function as its wed (Blanch and Wasserman 601). From the outset the Green Knight makes it quite clear that he is seeking to play a game—"I craue in þis court a Crystemas gomen" (283)—and Arthur's courtiers evidently understand the challenge in just this way:

> Ryche together con roun,
> And syþen þay redden alle same
> To ryd þe kyng wyth croun,
> And gif Gawan þe game.
> (362–65)

No one, on the other hand, appears to regard the fact that the compact had been made in play as a reason not to honor it, even though some members of the court are later prepared to blame Arthur for his lack of circumspection at the time (682–83). It is, however, difficult to see how either Gawain or his king could have acted any "warloker" (677), given the reasonable assumption that a man who has had his head cut off is unlikely to have much interest in enforcing the covenant he has just made—a particularly obvious illustration of the principle that an *actio personalis moritur cum persona*. The poem itself recognizes this: not only does Arthur wryly predict that, "if þou redez hym ryȝt, redly I trowe / Þat þou schal byden þe bur þat he schal bede after" (374–74), but even the Green Knight implies that Gawain will have no further reason to seek him out after the first blow has been struck—"And if I spende no speche, þenne spedez þou þe better, / For þou may leng in þy londe and layt no fyrre" (410–11). In other words, everyone understands that an agreement to exchange successive lethal blows is inherently impossible to fulfill.

Gawain's compact with the Green Knight is not the only agreement in Ricardian narrative to raise the question of impossibility. In Chaucer's "Franklin's Tale," Dorigen agrees (again, in play) to an assignation with Aurelius on condition that he remove the rocks along the coast of Brittany.[26] In both modern and medieval law a valid contract must not be objectionable as intended to effect an impossibility, though it should be pointed out that neither Gawain nor Dorigen make impossible contracts in quite this sense: they agree to perform actions that are perfectly possible in themselves (Gawain, that he will allow his head to be cut off; Dorigen, that she will sleep with Aurelius), but to which ostensibly impossible conditions are attached (that the beheader shall first have submitted his own neck to the ax; that the rocks along the coast of Brittany shall first have been removed). Of the two, Gawain's position would seem to be the stronger since, unlike Dorigen, he himself does not impose the impossible condition, and at the time the bargain is concluded there is an obvious inequality of knowledge between the parties (the Green Knight's failure to declare an ability to survive without a head might well be regarded by a modern court as misrepresentation). It seems quite clear that neither would have agreed to their respective contracts had they known that the conditions would in fact prove to be possible (neither, in other words, really intended to be legally bound), so that these stories illustrate precisely the kind of agreement that those who espouse a completely objective account of contract will find most difficult to deal with.

The Romans had sensibly regarded impossible agreements as void from the outset and the maxim *nemo obligatur ad impossibile* [no one can be bound to do an impossible thing] passed down to the common lawyers via the civilians. Bracton, quoting Justinian virtually word for word, writes, "if the condition be impossible, as if I should say, I give you that thing, if you can touch the firmament with your finger [si coelum digito tetigeris], the donation is not valid, and the condition is regarded as void" (2:71). Given that contracts intended to effect an impossibility or dependent on self-evidently impossible conditions are very rare in real life, it is somewhat surprising to find them discussed at all by medieval lawyers (particularly by medieval common lawyers). Nonetheless, discussions of such contractual impossibility (and not merely in its comparatively more common guise of supervening impossibility—the situation that arises when a change in circumstances renders an originally feasible agreement subsequently unworkable) are to be found even in the yearbooks (see A. W. B. Simpson 1987, 29–30 and 107–08).

Though common lawyers may have been prepared to recognize the impossibility rule, however, they still sought to constrain its application within the narrowest possible limits. In 1478, for instance, a builder, who had been sued for his failure to honor an undertaking to build a house, defended himself by claiming that though he had arrived to do the work the plaintiff had ordered him not to proceed; the court refused to accept this defense, but suggested that the defendant would have done better to have said that the plaintiff had refused him permission to come onto his property (cited by A. W. B. Simpson 1987, 25–26). Presumably the judges felt that, while it was still possible to build a house against orders, it was quite impossible to build one on land to which one had been denied entry. Like the Thomist attitude to duress, such a restricted view of contractual impossibility suggests far greater jurisprudential respect for the sanctity of the given word than would be the case today. Most people nowadays would hardly feel any more compunction about breaking an impossible promise than one extracted under pressure, but medieval people may not have shared our equanimity in such matters.

Justinian had provided an interesting counterexample to his illustration of contractual impossibility, one that Bracton also employs: "if it is put this way, 'If I do *not* touch the sky with my finger,' the stipulation will then be valid, because it is unconditional [quia pure facta est] and can be sued on at once" (2:286). In practice, later Roman law had demonstrated a rather more flexible attitude to mistake than this example suggests, but that common lawyers should have taken it as marking the limit of contractual impossibility is particularly significant: an impossible contract, they are at pains to stress, is not one that is merely self-contradictory or absurd—it is one that is literally unperformable (cf. *YB 12 Edw. 2 (pt. i)*, 83–84). An illustration similar to Justinian's is offered by a yearbook annotator in the report of a case from 1310 in which Chief Justice Bereford ruled against a man who was trying to get out of a disadvantageous agreement: "Note that the law will suffer a man of his own folly [de sa folie demene] to bind himself to pay on a certain day if he do not make the Tower of London come to Westminster" (*YB 3&4 Edw. 2*, 200). Bereford himself had apparently justified his decision by citing a maxim that already enjoyed some popularity among the common lawyers, *volenti non fit injuria* [an injury cannot be done to one who wills it].[27] As St. German was later to put it, "for it is oftentymes sene in the lawe/ that the lawe doth suffre hym to haue hurt without helpe of the law that wyll wylfully renne in to it of his owne acte not compelled therto and aiugeth it his foly so to renne into it/ for whiche foly he shal also be many tymes without remedy in conscience" (185). Since St. German is plainly referring to the court of chancery when he speaks of a "remedy in conscience," it seems that in England at least even civilians might have had some sympathy for the view that those who are foolish enough to promise to do something in return for not doing something they couldn't have done anyway don't deserve the law's protection.

Bereford seems to have assumed that civil lawyers would have treated the claims of the unwary promisor rather more indulgently than his own colleagues, for he follows his maxim *volenti non fit iniuria* with the aside, "even if the written law says [tut die ley escrit] that 'no one can be bound to do an impossible thing.'" St. German certainly suggests that the doctrine of impossibility carried rather more weight among the civilians and canonists than at common law. Discussing the question of whether a tenant should be held liable for damage done "by sodayne tempest or by straunge enemies," the common-law student takes issue with the doctor's assertion that "the lawe semyth nat reasonable that byndeth a man to an impossybylyte": "no man shall be compelled to take that bonde vpon hym but he that wyll take the lande/ and yf he wyll take the lande: it is reason that he take the charge as the lawe hathe appoynted with it/ and that yf any hurte growe to hym thereby; it is thrughe his owne acte and his owne assente/ for he myght haue refusyd the lease yf he wolde" (186). This example, of course, concerns what lawyers call supervening impossibility, but it will help to bridge the gap between jurisprudential theory and actual forensic practice.

A case from 1366, discussed by both A. W. B. Simpson and Morris Arnold,[28] conforms precisely to the situation imagined by St. German: a tenant who had promised to leave leased premises in as good condition as he had found them justifies their dilapidation as being due to a "sudden adventure" or "adventure of God"—possibly Langland's "southwestryne wynd on satirday at eue" (*PPl* A.5:14)?. Interestingly, had the owner sued on a writ of waste he would almost certainly have lost, since the principle that a tenant could not be held liable for damage (waste) for which he was not even indirectly responsible seems to have been well established by this time (Holdsworth 3:380), but the position was far less clear where a writ of covenant was involved. Just like St. German's Student, the plaintiff's lawyer in this case had argued that "a party to a private contract could by express covenant exempt himself from strict liability if he wished to do so" (A. W. B. Simpson 1987, 32), and this view seems to have been the one favored by the court. "The Year Book report, typically, is inconclusive; but the justices who spoke were clearly inclined to the view that the general covenant to repair would bind the defendant to do even what common right would not, and that the tenants here should have made an express exception in their covenant for sudden happenings. But regardless of who prevailed, the interesting point is the characterization of the role of promise on which the discussion proceeded: its office was to chip away at commonly held assumptions about how the world was ordinarily ordered. It was a private law and you owed it specific obedience" (M. Arnold 1987, 511). The principles here are quite clear; once the parties to an agreement had given formal expression to their will, the law required specific performance of them, no matter how detrimental the unexpected consequences of such a willed agreement might later prove to be: *volenti non fit iniuria*.

Such a principle seems to remove any grounds either Gawain or Dorigen might have felt they had for complaining that their contracts were impossible. Both had unambiguously willed their agreements (in the sense of having gone through a set of recognized contractual formalities),[29] so that when these agreements become unexpectedly subject to what we might call supervening possibility they find themselves in a similar position to the man who had agreed not to move the Tower of London to Westminster. In other words, while Dorigen's impossible condition, like the Green Knight's, might be sufficient to void her contract in theory, the simple fact that Aurelius does remove the rocks and the Green Knight does keep his appointment completely undercuts the grounds for any such objection.

What is most striking about all this to the modern eye is the way the common law stands foursquare behind the principle that *pacta sunt servanda*. It was, to quote Morris Arnold again, "a juridical world in which the idea that promises must be kept [was] a bedrock assumption" (1987, 510). No hair-splitting over consideration or quid pro quo here: the order of the day was *caveat pactor* and whatever one agreed *de sa folie demene*, one was stuck with. As John Gower puts it,

Avise him every man tofore,
And be wel war, er he be swore,
For afterward it is to late
If that he wole his word debate.
(*CA* 7:1741–44)

Only a psychological account of contract can justify voiding an agreement merely because one of the parties had believed its conditions to be impossible at the time it was made, but, as we have seen, insofar as medieval common law had any coherent theory of contract it fell squarely on the objective side of the objective/psychological divide. What Gaylord characterizes as the "kind of fanatical literalism" which "cannot take 'entente' . . . into account at all" (347), in other words, is precisely the kind of thinking on which a medieval serjeant would have most prided himself.

In this regard the common lawyer found himself opposed, not only to the canonist (whose account of contractual obligation, as we have seen, was a fundamentally psychological one), but also to the civilian. From as early as the thirteenth century continental lawyers were broadly in agreement that a meeting of minds (a *consensus ad idem*) was essential to any valid contract, and by the fourteenth century they had elaborated certain hints they found in Justinian into a theory of contract that required of the parties both a common intention (*animus*)[30] to be legally bound and a mutual understanding (*consensus*) about the nature of the agreement they were making.[31] Indeed, in France, even the customary lawyers, influenced by what A. Esmein calls the canonists' "interprétation fausse mais féconde du droit roman" (34), began to accept that contracts depended primarily on the consent of the parties and that formal acts, like the *paumée* and the *denier à Dieu*, were merely ancilliary to such consent (37–43). Thus substantive French law (as opposed to the quite different jural world occasionally revealed to us by litigants like Claude Nonette and Nicole Loyseau) provides what we should now regard as a far more rational account of contract than anything to be found north of the Channel. A good illustration is seen in Christine de Pisan's treatment of safe-conducts in her *Book of Fayttes of Armes and of Chyualrye*; safe-conducts were covered by the law of arms and thus came under the civilian's jurisdiction (moreover, Christine's immediate source here is a canonist Honoré Bouet), so that when she discusses the status of an artfully framed safe-conduct that specifies immunity for the outward, but not the return, journey, she offers a predictably strong endorsement of the written law's antiformalist position. She denies that such an ambiguous safe-conduct could justify a man in arresting his enemy as soon as he sets out for home, for "the lawe wol not that the malyce of the frawdylouse deceyuer take soo straytly the symplenes of hym that gooth thus vpon and vndyr the termes of gode feythe"; and the justification she offers is strongly reminiscent of the standard canon-law refutation of equivocal oaths: "Soo ought to be vndrestande the saufconduyt thentent of hym vnto whome it is yeven" (244).[32]

Though traces of such thinking can be found in Bracton with his talk of an *animus donandi* and an *animus recipiendi* (2:62), this seems to be an example of his own habitual insistence on "the mental factor," as Maitland puts it (P&M 2:499), rather than the reflection of any kind of general attitude at Westminster. When a lawyer at the end of Edward I's reign suggested that his opponents were dissembling their real reason for having made a distraint, he was sharply reprimanded by the judge, "are you able to divine their will" [poez vous conustre lour volunte]?" and found himself openly laughed at (*derisus*) in court (*YB 33–35 Edw. 1*, 326–27). Common lawyers were more likely to speak in terms of agreement than consent: "there can be no perfect bargain unless both parties are agreed," says a pleader in Edward IV's reign (1467), and the context makes quite clear that he means by this that the parties shall have acted in such a way that their formal agreement may be verified by a third party. The case, in fact, is the one that gave rise to Chief Justice Bryan's famous pronouncement (which, incidentally, he characterizes as a "comen erudition") about the devil's inability to fathom human intention, and the judge was supporting a pleader's contention that an offer made in the form "you shall have the goods if they still please you after you have seen them" was insufficient in itself to conclude the bargain. Brian argued that until the buyer certified the seller that the goods did indeed please him his intention was unknowable and the contract could not be regarded as a "matter of fact" (*Abridgements*: 17 Edw. 4, Pasc.2). As St. German's Student, repeating what was evidently still a common law platitude in the early sixteenth century, puts it: "Yt ys secrete in hys owne conscyence whether he entendyd for to be bounde or naye / And of the entent inwarde in the herte: mannes lawe can not Juge" (231).

None of this is meant to suggest that we should regard the high culture of

Ricardian England as in some way mysteriously immune to modern notions of intention and responsibility—indeed I hope that what I have said about canon and civil law has demonstrated that such notions were readily available to it—but what I have been trying to do here is show how the clerkly makers were writing within a broader culture that was founded on far less familiar attitudes and assumptions, on a "routine of life" to borrow Milsom's phrase, very different from our own. My hope is that a recognition of this broader culture may lend added point to literary discussions of such themes as "game and ernest" or "entente" in the work of the Ricardian poets. It can hardly be accidental, for instance, that when Chaucer came to describe Troilus's attempts to divine his lady's true feelings for him, he should have turned to the image (and it was one, incidentally, that he did not find in Boccaccio) of a written contract:

> Though ther be mercy writen in youre cheere,
> God woot, the text ful hard is, soth, to fynde!
> How koude ye withouten bond me bynde?
> (*Troilus* 3:1356)

As readers reflect on how the *Canterbury Tales* concern themselves with "the difficulty of penetrating (without a magic mirror) the motives governing one person's behaviour towards another" (Blamires 63), or how *Troilus and Criseyde* is preoccupied with "the unreliability of stated intentions and the difficulty of interpreting them" (Archibald 192), they may find it helpful to consider the ways in which late medieval society at large was wrestling with similar problems.

Illicit Consequence

It is time, finally, to turn to the difficult question of the importance of promise-keeping in relation to the promisor's other legal obligations. The principle that promises must be kept may have been a bedrock assumption, but what happens when a promise commits the promisor to perform an illegal or immoral act? This situation provides the crisis of a number of medieval narratives: Chaucer's "Franklin's Tale," where Dorigen can keep her promise to Aurelius only by committing adultery, is probably the best known, but *Sir Amadace*, where the hero must kill his wife in order to honor a rash bargain, or *Amis and Amiloun*, where he must kill his children, provide even more dramatic examples. Can the study of medieval customary law tell us anything about such situations as these?

Of course, like their modern counterparts, medieval lawyers would have regarded any agreement to commit an illegal act as unenforceable; in Thomist terms, promises such as Herod's to Salome are void because they fail to meet the demands of *justicia*. Indeed, since, as Alford (1977) has taught us, the distinction we are quite willing to draw between legality and morality would have puzzled most medieval lawyers,[33] they had if anything even more scope for raising the defense of illicit consequence than we have. As Robert Mannyng of Brunne puts it,

> Noþeles y seye hardely
> 3yf þou vowe to do foly,
> As a man to bete or slo
> Or to take hys gode hym fro,
> . . . .
> God wyle nat þou holde hyt so
> þat þou þy vowe yn wykkydnes do
> (2803–10)

or, in Chaucer's words, "the lawes seyn that 'alle bihestes that been dishoneste been of no value'" ("Tale of Melibee" 1229). Thus, even the customary law would have objected to a formal agreement that sought to bind the parties to break one of God's commandments. In a remarkable case heard by a Yorkshire manorial court in 1337, for instance, a Robert of Rotherham sued John of Ithon for failing to deliver "a devil tied with a thong" [diabolum ligatum in quodam ligamine] for which Robert had paid fourpence, according to "a convention made between them" sealed with a halfpenny earnest money (*Antiquarian Repertory* 2:395). The court duly decided that "such a plea should not lie between Christians," and the reeve sent them both off with a fine.

On general principles, then, Aurelius could hardly have expected much of a hearing, even in the king's courts, if Dorigen had decided not to honor their compact to commit adultery. Generally speaking, common lawyers took little professional interest in adultery—since the law sensibly presumed that all children born within wedlock were legitimate (*YB 1 Hen. 6*, 25) not even inheritance or land tenure were affected by it—so we should not expect to find many analogous lawsuits at Westminster. The closest I know of is an amusing case from the seventeenth century, where an upholster sued a client for not giving him a fair price for four gilt hangings. On learning that his counsel planned to refer to these hangings in the pleadings as *quatuor pictas pellices*, the poor litigant would have done well to check the man's Latinity, for the correct word was *pelles* ('skins') not *pellices*. Accordingly, he lost his case because, as his opponent's counsel was quick to point out, "*quatuor pictas pellices* is four painted whores and the providing of them for the defendant is unlawful" (cited by A. W. B. Simpson 1987, 509).

Though an agreement to perform an illicit act would certainly have been regarded as void from the outset, the subsequent immorality of one of the parties in performing an otherwise perfectly licit agreement did not, it seems, offer quite such obvious grounds for voiding their contract. A 1390 dispute over the terms of a lease (brought in trespass because the defendants had used force in trying to evict the lessee) offers a particularly vivid illustration. The property in question, which belonged to the bishop of London, was situated in St. Paul's cemetery, and the bishop's men had tried to recover it after he had discovered that his tenant was keeping "immoral women and prostitutes, habitually engaged in the art [usules a ce art]" there. The plaintiff responded with an argument analagous to the one used in 1366 to counter a defense of supervening impossibility, that if these were to be the grounds for breaking his lease the defendants should produce written proof of so specific a condition; remarkably, the defendants' counsel dared not press the point (*YB 13 Ric. 2*, 154). Though he was perhaps being overcautious, counsel's reaction here suggests how powerful a countervailing moral force might be generated by the universal respect for the sanctity of formal agreements. When we find that a man accused of keeping a brothel on church property could outface his episcopal landlord with the defense that this activity was not specifically forbidden in his lease, we are forced to recognize that the comparative morality of promise-keeping may have been a little more complex than at first it might appear.

Despite a steady stream of edicts from a succession of English bishops (Sheehan 1978b), and the best efforts of generations of archdeacons to try to make sure that they were obeyed, the church seems to have had its work cut out for it attempting to regulate the sexual behavior of its flock throughout the Middle Ages. Only by the beginning of the twelfth century was it able to establish the vital bridgehead of ecclesiastical participation in the secular rituals of marriage (Sheehan 1978a, 27), and even at the end of the fifteenth its hold over this territory was still far from secure. About 1217 Bishop Richard Poore of Salisbury, whose decrees Michael Sheehan regards as having set the standard for subsequent English marriage law (1978b, 414), commanded that marriage should be celebrated, "without any laughter or joking, and not in taverns, at public revelry, or feastings, lest a man might jocularly bind wreaths of rushes or some other base (or even precious) material about the hands of young women in order to make love to them the more freely, imagining that since he is in jest he may be able to escape the honour of matrimony" (*Councils and Synods* 2.i:87). Just how partial a view of secular marriage this decree presents, however, may be judged from a frequently used English pastoral manual, the *Summa Confessorum* of Thomas of Chobham, which is almost exactly contemporary with it; Thomas states quite unequivocally "that a man and a woman can contract a marriage by themselves, without a priest and without all others, in any place, so long as they agree to a permanent way of life" (Sheehan 1978a, 23).

What appear at first glance to be moralizing complaints against sexual license can often be read as protests against traditional forms of marriage that bypassed the church altogether.[34] Yet despite the church's best efforts to undermine the appeal of secular marriage, many people still evidently preferred to exercise their traditional freedoms. The author of *Dives and Pauper* attributes to the seventh-century Pope Boniface III the complaint "þat Englych peple despysyn þe lawys of wedlac" (2:64), and if the Harley lyricist's description of the consistory courts is anything to go by ecclesiastical officiousness in this matter was still deeply resented seven hundred years after Boniface:

> Ʒef ich on molde mote wiþ a mai
> Y shal falle hem byfore ant lurnen huere lay
> Ant rewen alle huere redes.
> (4:4–6; in Turville-Petre 28)

In the course of a tirade against the church courts, the otherwise rather strait-laced author of *The Plowman's Tale* objects, "A simple fornicacioun, / Twenty shillings he shall pay" (669–70), and writing in the middle of the fifteenth century Bishop Pecock represents it as a common (though regrettable) belief "that fleischli comunyng bitwixe a syngil man and a syngil womman doon bi her fre consent is no synne" (*Repressor* 155; cf. *Dives and Pauper* 1:76). Whatever the views of the canon lawyers, then, many medieval people might well have felt that an unmarried Dorigen would have been obliged to honor her oath to Aurelius however sinful its consequences; sexual irregularity, in other words, would have carried far less of a social stigma for them than oath-breaking.

Dorigen's marital status, however, complicates the problem considerably, for in fulfilling her oath to Aurelius she must break her marriage oath to Arveragus; as Gaylord says, "the conflict is between two promises, one of which must be broken if the other be held true" (337). There can be little doubt that the canonists would have seen any act of adultery as a contravention of the marriage oath; indeed, the English term *spusebreche* 'adultery' clearly derives from the notion of breaking a *sponsum* or 'marriage vow'. The first of the three benefits of marriage, according to one of the commonplaces of church teaching (derived ultimately from Augustine) was *fides*, which William of Shoreham renders by the word *treuþe*: "Treuþe hys þat þer no gile be / Þourwe spousebreche maligne" (1:1998–99). There is a similar recognition that adultery involves a breach of *trouthe* in Gower's ballade sequence "Traitié . . . pour essampler les amantz marietz" (*French Works* 379–92); as Quixley's early-fifteenth-century translation renders it:

> Grete merueille is, and myche ayhein reson,
> That when a man hath taken vnto wyue
> A woman, at his owne eleccion;
> And after that his trouth breketh belyue
> And dayly, as longe as he is alyue,
> Newe loue seketh, as þat he were a beste,
> A mans trowth to breke it is nat honeste.
>
> (5:1–7)

Clearly, then, Dorigen's *trouthe* will be compromised whichever course she chooses, but, even though no canon lawyer would have had a moment's hesitation deciding which of her two promises had to be sacrificed, three qualifications should be made to this apparently cut-and-dried situation.

First, whatever the theory, the church's most pressing practical concern was with irregular or bigamous relationships, not with passing infidelities. Gratian offers what at first glance looks like a classic analysis of Dorigen's situation where he quotes Isidore to the effect that "an oath which rashly commits one to wickedness should not be kept, as when someone might promise eternal faith to remain with an adulteress" (pt. 2, ca. 22, qu. 4, ch. 13; 878), and later cites Augustine's view that "a woman who having broken her conjugal commitment keeps faith with an adulterer is certainly wicked" (ch. 21; 880). But these maxims touch on a situation that is significantly different from the one in "The Franklin's Tale," and one that in an age of widespread secular marriage posed a far deeper threat to the church's campaign to control matrimonial relations. The promise to remain true to a second lover, if permitted to retain any of its sacral character, might seem to legitimize bigamy or worse, and for this reason church courts treated with "special repugnance" the man who, having lived in adultery with a woman, went on to marry her after the death of his first wife (Helmholz 1974, 94; cf. Sheehan 1978b 420). Casual adultery, especially in those who, like "The Adulterous Falmouth Squire" (Furnivall 123–32), made a habit of it, could certainly rouse the church's ire, but faced with a choice between winking at a passing infidelity and risking a permanent breakdown of marriage the pastoral manuals are clearly anxious to foster a spirit of toleration (cf. William of Shoreham 1:2115–21). The author of *Dives and Pauper* treats situations such as Arveragus and Dorigen's with surprising leniency: a husband who knows of his wife's lechery, "suffryth hyr in hyr synne and medelyth with hyr aftir . . . or forȝeuy[th] it hyr & reconcylith hyr to hym," has no grounds for formal complaint, he says (2:74); and if, as Dorigen's would have been, "þe fornicacion . . . be pryue & may nout ben prouyd [the husband] schal nout forsakyn hyr opynlyche ne he is nout bound to forsakyn hyr pryuelyche as anemyst þe bed" (2:75).

Secondly, there is the question of the actual formulas sworn by the marriage partners, and how they (as opposed to their clerical mentors) might have understood them. Although the precise wording of the marriage oath could be a matter of great significance,[35] it is surprisingly difficult to establish precisely what the church would have required a typical couple to swear to in late fourteenth-century England.[36] Some generalizations are possible, however. The binding formula was normally no stronger than "þare to I plyght my trowth" (*Manuale . . . Eboracensis* xvi); certainly, there is nothing in medieval England approaching the extravagance of this one from sixteenth-century Arras: "I promise and swear to you, on the faith I owe to God, on the christening and baptism that I received at the font, on the body of our lord Jesus Christ which rests here within the church, on all the saints and the holy evangelists who are read and recited by the whole world of Christendom, on my share of paradise and on the damnation of my soul, that . . ." (cited in Molin and Mutembe 117 n. 118). Moreover, the oaths were sworn, not on the altar, but at the doors of the church, well away from the most sacred part of the building.[37] Finally, explicit reference to sexual constancy is generally found, if at all, not in the actual oaths, but in the priest's interrogation of the couple's consent which preceded them: "Will you [*vis*] . . . forsake all others and hold only to her/him as long as you shall both live?" (*Manuale . . . Sarisburiensis* 47). The general impression made by all this is that the church was seeking to prevent the members of its flock from compounding the sin of adultery with the far worse one of perjury,[38] and many people may well have chosen to believe that the fidelity the priest had made them swear to meant primarily a commitment to permanent cohabitation rather than to unwavering sexual constancy.

The final point to be taken into account was "the tenacity of the belief that people could regulate their own matrimonial affairs, without the assistance or the interference of the church" (Helmholz 1974, 31). One indication of this belief, Helmholz has suggested, was the readiness of couples to attach conditions to their marriage contracts (51). Many of the conditional parol contracts he cites have an air of dreary predictability about them ("I will marry you, if you let me sleep with you," "If you get pregnant, I will marry you"), but some, such as the following from Rochester (1443), are rather more surprising: "She confesses that she contracted marriage with him about four years previously, under this condition however, that he should be able to act with her as a man ought to with a woman. And afterwards within a fortnight, she tried him, and because he could not she dismissed him and contracted with Thomas Ricard" (53). In another, from Canterbury (1420), a man makes his marriage contract conditional on his wife knowing how to "brew, bake, and weave both linen and wool" (56 n. 109). Such contracts might lead us to take more seriously the condition Dorigen attaches to her marriage contract with Arveragus — that he "take no maistrie / Agayn hir wyl" ("Franklin's Tale" 747–48) — or even the one that Walter requires Griselde to agree to — "And nevere ye to grucche it, nyght ne day" ("Clerk's Tale" 349).[39] Interestingly, Panormitanus (b. 1389) regards as completely invalid a contract made "on condition that if [the wife] should commit adultery he might withdraw from the marriage" (Helmholz 1974, 55 n. 103).

My reason for raising these points is not, finally, to suggest that either Chaucer or his audience, had they subjected Dorigen's dilemma to the cold light of legal logic, would have reached a decision seriously at odds with church teaching, but rather that this dilemma might not have presented itself to them in quite the same terms as it does to us. For the Middle Ages, promises constituted a kind of private law (both canonists and common lawyers referred to them as such), and many people might have felt that it was up to Dorigen and her husband, not to some outside authority, to try to resolve the conflicting obligations that bound her.

From this perspective the narrative logic of "The Franklin's Tale" shows a striking resemblance to what John Burrow has observed in *Sir Gawain and the Green Knight*: "The hero, caught in some impossible predicament where he cannot conceivably reconcile his various obligations, perseveres with the course of conduct dictated by whichever obligation the author regards as 'higher.' . . . This demonstrates in a striking way his dedication to some important virtue. Then when the demonstration is sufficient . . . the tester suddenly relents, releases the hero from his higher obligation and allows him to fulfill the lower" (1965, 164). The archetypal example of this narrative structure is, of course, the story of Abraham and Isaac. Under such a schema, Aurelius becomes the tester of Dorigen's dedication to *trouthe* — the higher virtue which cannot be reconciled with her marital fidelity — and his exhibition of generosity at the end represents the sudden volte face that allows her to fulfill this lower obligation. If we are in any doubt as to whether the private law of *trouthe* or the public law of ecclesiastical marriage is the more potent shaping force behind the plot of "The Franklin's Tale," we might ask ourselves which course of action is represented as the more painful for Dorigen and her husband — keeping her oath to Aurelius or breaking it. Sir Gawain and Dorigen are not the only late medieval English narratives to subjugate more familiar moral imperatives to the tyranny of the oath; in both *Sir Amadace* and *Amis and Amiloun*, where the cruder artistry of the popular romance exposes a disposition of forces far better camouflaged by Chaucer and the Gawain-poet, the clash between ostensible moral duty and private oath-keeping is even more dramatic.

In *Sir Amadace*, the impoverished hero accepts assistance from a mysterious white knight on condition that his helper shall be entitled to half of anything he may win. Some time later, when success in a tournament has won him the hand of a beautiful heiress, his former benefactor appears and demands his all-too-literal half. Amadace demurs but the white knight insists:

"Butte thenke on thi covenand that thou made,
In the wode, quen thou mestur hade,
  How fayre thou hettus me thare!"
Sir Amadace sayd, "I wotte, hit was soe,
But my lady forto sloe,
  Me thinke grete synne hit ware."
Then the lady undurstode anon
The wurd that was betwene hom,
  And grevyt hur nevyr the more.
Then sayde: "For his luffe that deut on tre,
Loke yore covandus holdun be:
  Goddes forbotte ye me spare!"

(721–32)

As in the other examples of this plot-type, as soon as the white knight is convinced that Amadace is prepared to sacrifice his wife, he calls off the test and everything ends happily. Nevertheless, the poem makes clear that Amadace has made the right choice by putting his obligation to his former benefactor before even his wife's life.

Even more bizarre is an incident in *Amis and Amiloun*, where the oath to be honored is one of brotherhood in arms:

Trewþes to-gider þai gun pliȝt,
While þai miȝt liue & stond,
Þat boþe bi day & bi niȝt,
In wele & wo, in wrong & riȝt,
. . . .
Fro þat day forward neuer mo
Failen oþer for wele no wo:
Þer-to þai held vp her hond.

(146–56)

Amis is informed by an angel, who visits him in a dream, that only the blood of his own two children can heal Amiloun of his leprosy (a disease, incidentally, which Amis's own act has brought on him). Again, the hero is under no illusion that in keeping faith with his sworn brother he is committing a sin:

> Þan þouȝt þe douk, wiþ-outen lesing,
> For to slen his childer so ȝing,
> It were a dedli sinne;
> & þan þouȝht he, bi heuen king,
> His broþer out of sorwe bring,
> For þat nold he nouȝt blinne.
>
> (2245–50)

This time the deed is actually done (the occasion is Christmas, with its reminder of Herod's massacre of the innocents), and not only is Amiloun duly healed, but the children, as if to justify Amis's decision, are miraculously restored to life. So gaudily painted a deus ex machina makes the sleights of hand which provide a happy ending in "The Franklin's Tale," *Sir Gawain and the Green Knight*, and even *Sir Amadace*, look somewhat anemic, yet the underlying logic is identical in all four: oathworthiness is tested by an extreme moral dilemma which only an unwavering adherence to *trouthe* can resolve.

While I would not wish to overstress these parallels, romances like *Amis and Amiloun* and *Sir Amadace* offer some very useful pointers to the older imperatives that underlie the narrative structure of their more self-conscious cousins like *Sir Gawain and the Green Knight* and "The Franklin's Tale." Chaucer and the Gawain-poet, however, show a far clearer recognition of the gap that was beginning to open up in the late fourteenth century between the morality and the law of promise-keeping, and their concern with explicitly legal issues reveals a far greater sensitivity to the complexities of Ricardian *trouthe*. Faced with the impossible task of accommodating the ancient formalist troth to the analytical truth of the new textuality, both turn instinctively to an idealized fairy-tale past—to a world where the equation of truth and honor can still be made to seem unproblematical and the assaults of petty legalism to break harmlessly against the chivalric virtues of courtesy, generosity, and noblesse oblige. As with the fairy king in *Sir Orfeo*, the less Dorigen is legally bound by her promise, the more honor she is finally able to demonstrate by keeping it.

The Franklin's espousal of such an ethos may well appear sentimental to the modern eye, yet even Chaucer's mentor Boccaccio was not wholly immune to it. A native of the land that had raised the study of Roman law to a science, and himself a student, though apparently an unenthusiastic one, of canon law in his younger days, Boccaccio might be expected to have had little interest in a dilemma such as Dorigen's, yet his story of the "amorous knight" Tarolfo in *Il Filocolo* is close enough to "The Franklin's Tale" to have been argued to constitute Chaucer's direct source. This story, offered by a character called Menedon as his contribution to a game of love questions, is designed to elicit discussion on which of its three main characters has behaved most honorably. In the debate that follows, the *magistra ludi*, Fiammetta, answers Menedon with an argument that is only implicit in Chaucer: "You wish to say that the husband did nothing generous in giving up his wife, since he was bound by law to do so because of the lady's oath—and this would certainly be the case if the oath were binding" [la qual cosa saria così, se il saramento tenesse] (*Opere* 1:408). Sworn without the knowledge of her husband, she says, and in direct contradiction to the higher vows of her marriage, the lady's oath is demonstrably flawed, yet Fiammetta does not use this flaw as a way of exposing the "moral absurdity" (to borrow Gaylord's term) of respecting all such rash promises, but rather to represent strict adherence to the sworn word, even where the law can offer one a loophole, as the nobler course.

Chaucer's perspective is not, of course, precisely identical with Boccaccio's here; the issues raised by "The Franklin's Tale" appear to have had considerably more urgency for him than they did for the Italian. The fact that the husband in Menedon's story was under no legal obligation to Tarolfo would probably have seemed far more self-evident to Boccaccio's audience than to Chaucer's, and for this reason the English poet is forced to weaken the lover's legal claim in his own version of the tale (Tarolfo, for instance, actually produces his flourishing midwinter garden, where Aurelius produces only the illusion of vanished rocks). How otherwise could Arveragus have exercised any freedom, in either its modern or medieval sense? As John Burrow has written: "[Dorigen] has to honour an agreement made on her part 'in play,' and fulfilled on the part of Aurelius 'agaynst the proces of nature.' Either consideration might now be thought sufficient to invalidate Aurelius' claim upon her: that she did not really mean it, and anyway she was not to know that Aurelius would resort to magic. Yet Chaucer recognizes these arguments only in so far as their availability makes Dorigen's truth the more notable and praiseworthy" (1965, 25). Though Chaucer may recognize such arguments, they must have seemed far less compelling, not only to the common lawyers of his time, but also to many of their clients. Like the Breton lay he tells, however, the jural world the Franklin represents was already passing, for, just as surely as the expanding documentary culture was undermining the foundations of Ricardian *trouthe*, so too the juridical premises of unwritten custom were being forced to yield to the analytic rigor of the Romanists. This makes the dilemma of Chaucer's version not only less academic than Boccaccio's, but also, in the naive optimism of its solution, far more richly Saturnian.

9

Bargains with God

I can't change truth. I'm not God! I'm not even sure that he could. I don't think God can change truth!

—Tennessee Williams, *Suddenly Last Summer*

SOMETIME IN THE LATE TWELFTH century a boy named Henry, the son of a certain Uhtred of Ulchel (probably Ulleskelf just south of York), lost his eyesight and his grief-stricken parents vowed St Thomas à Becket a penny if the saint would cure him (*Libellus* 423). Any modern reader who feels that a penny was a rather modest price for such a miracle is making an anachronistic assumption that this sum was simply payment in advance for the saint's favors; what Henry's parents were really pledging was not money in the sense of a unit of value at all, but a quite specific coin intended as a token to mark the sealing of their contract with the saint. To this end they had symbolically bent it over the boy's eyes when they swore their oath ("super oculos pueri denarium ad Sanctum Thomam cum voto incurvaverunt"). Such "bowed groats," as we have seen, were widely used to seal bargains of all kinds, but their use in plighting troth with saints seems to have been particularly common in England (Finucane 94–95). The mnemonic function of their bending is clearly alluded to in an account of one of Saint Cuthbert's miracles (*Reginaldi* 229–31): the suppliant, who had suffered a nasty riding accident, sealed his vow to visit the saint's shrine on Farne Island with a token penny which had been "bent to help him identify it" [recurvato ut eum dinoscere posset]. What really lay behind such offerings, then, as Duffy has suggested, was "some notion of a contract, in which the pledged coin was an 'earnest penny'" (184). The saint's real payment would come later, with the client's actual worship before his shrine, when the penny would be added to a mountain of similar votive objects left to provide concrete proof that the vow had been performed. These contracts were undoubtedly felt to be binding on both parties, and votaries clearly expected to receive something in return for their pledges.

When, after two years, the great Saint Thomas had still failed to provide a cure for young Henry's blindness, the penny that his parents had destined for Canterbury, was recycled to mark a second vow, this time to Saint Godric, whose shrine at Finchale, three miles northeast of Durham, was considerably closer to home. Much to the delight of the local monks their own homegrown saint finessed the famous Becket by restoring Henry's eyesight and they record with some glee in their book of miracles that "the father offered [to Saint Godric] the penny which he had bent for Saint Thomas" (*Libellus* 423). Somewhat disingenuously they speculate that the more prestigious saint may have declined the cure in order to offer the chance to a fellow member of the heavenly city ("in coeli gloria concivis"), but there seems to have been some concern that the southerner had been poaching on their territory. When, a few years earlier, a former servant of St Thomas had traveled from York to Canterbury in search of a cure, his old master had appeared in a vision and, despite his pleas not to be referred to another saint ("noli me de te alium Sanctum transmittere"), ordered him back north to visit Saint Cuthbert, Godric's senior partner at Durham; apparently even Becket was wary of offending so venerable a figure: "I wish to do nothing against my fellow knight Saint Cuthbert, for he is one of the most powerful members of the heavenly host" (*Reginaldi* 262).

In many traditional societies the relationship between supernatural beings and their followers is construed in essentially contractual terms. Bound to the god's service with rituals that often (like Uhtred's bowed groat) bear a marked formal resemblance to those of purely secular trothplights, worshipers will expect the devotion they pledge to be reciprocated in quite practical ways. The arrangement is thus bilateral: "the deified spirits of his ancestors look after his welfare," Achebe writes of the typical Igbo; "in return he offers them sustenance regularly in the form of sacrifice" (*Beware Soul Brother* 66). The mutually beneficial partnership of God and votary leads to a degree of familiarity unthinkable in the modern West and worshipers will often see nothing incongruous about exploiting this partnership for personal advantage; indeed, "in such a reciprocal relationship," says Achebe, "one is encouraged (within reason) to try and get the better of the bargain" (66). On the other hand, gods who fail to provide their punctilious followers with adequate rewards are felt to have broken their side of the agreement and may expect to find their influence diminishing. At the end of Achebe's *Arrow of God* the villagers desert to the new Christian god because they blame Ulu, their patron deity, for a disastrous harvest; in doing so they are following a well-established tradition: "we have all heard how the people of Aninta dealt with their deity when he failed them. Did they not carry him to the boundary between them and their neighbors and set fire on him?" (28). In a short story by another Nigerian writer, I. N. C. Aniebo, it is ironically the Christian convert who, afflicted by a debilitating illness, comes to see that he has made a bad bargain: "Christianity had failed him in his greatest hour of need and there was no doubt that he would go back to the old gods as soon as he got well again" (*Of Wives* 39).

In Europe, such well-known stories as Gregory of Tours's account of the conversion of the Frankish king Clovis (2.30–31; 1:116–120), or Bede's description of the conversion of the Northumbrian king Edwin (2.12–13; 175–87) suggest that the Germanic invaders practiced a similar brand of pragmatic theology. It is expressed with particular candor by Edwin's pagan chief-priest, a man called Coifi: "I frankly admit that, for my part, I have found that the religion which we have hitherto held has no virtue nor profit [*nihil utilitatis*] in it. None of your followers has devoted himself more earnestly than I have to the worship of our gods, but nevertheless there are many who receive greater benefits and greater honors from you than I do and are more successful in all their undertakings. If the gods had any power they would have helped me more readily, seeing that I have always served them with greater zeal. So it follows that if, on examination, these new doctrines which have now been explained to us are found to be better and more effectual, let us accept them at once without delay" (2.13; 182–83) Typically, in official Christian tradition, only pagan gods are the subject of such crude consumerism — Frey's failure to protect the interests of his priest Hrafnkel, for instance, costs him dear in future sacrifices (Gordon 79) — but it would be altogether surprising if the new religion had been able to obliterate it overnight, and accounts like the Finchale record of Saint Godric's triumph over Saint Thomas attest to its continuing vigor, albeit contained and rechanneled, long after Bede. Even in Ricardian England, as we shall see, popular preachers such as John Mirk were still catering to their parishioners' need to believe in a *deus pactor*. We should be careful not to take such views as typically a mark of low culture, however, for anyone tempted to assume that only ignorant peasants were still making bargains with God in the late Middle Ages should recall Louis XI's remark on learning of the English invasion plans late in 1474: "Ah, Holy Mary, even now when I have given thee fourteen hundred crowns, thou dost not help me one whit" (quoted by Scofield 2:114).[1]

Covenantal Theology: Vernacular and Academic Traditions

John Mirk, an Augustinian canon of the monastery of Lilleshall in Shropshire, composed his set of sermons for the feast days of the saints sometime in the late 1380s (Fletcher 218), perhaps intending them for the pulpit of St. Alcmund's church in Shrewsbury (221). For anyone whose view of medieval theology derives from the disciplined rationalism of the schoolmen this "outstanding example of the popular festival sermon-book" (Owst 1926, 245) comes as something of a shock, but its author, who also compiled a Latin *Manuale Sacerdotis* (Owst 1926, 55), can hardly be dismissed as some unschooled rustic. He was sufficiently abreast of current issues to be preaching against Lollardy within ten years of the Blackfriars Council (Fletcher), and his house at Lilleshall was certainly no remote and impoverished foundation. Though much reduced by the Black Death, it was still able to entertain the greatest in the land, and Mirk himself may well have been present when King Richard and Queen Isabella stayed there in 1398 with a retinue which included five dukes, four earls, and three bishops. He may also have helped minister to John of Gaunt when the duke fell sick and spent two days at Lilleshall later the same year; so grateful was the king's uncle for the treatment he received that he and his wife Katherine enrolled as members of the abbey fraternity (*VHCE Shropshire* 2:76).

Mirk's world, like that of other popular preachers in the Middle Ages (Owst 1961, 110–34), teems with spiritual forces. Closest to home are those "þat walketh aftyr þat þay ben ded and buryet yn holy plase" (281). One of his most charming stories concerns a man who lived next to a church and was in the habit of saying a *de profundis* for the souls every time he passed by the graveyard: "Then, on a day, hyt happonet so þat he was persewet wyth enmys, þat he flogh homward; but when he come ynto þe chyrch-ȝeorde, he þoght: 'Now ys tyme forto say "De profundys,"' and knelut adowne, and sayde. And anon þerwyth all þe chrych-ȝeorde rose full of bodyes, yche on wyth an ynstrument yn hys hond of his craft, and dryuen aȝeyne his enmyes" (269–70). Most revenants, despite Mirk's reassurance that their visitations were "no wexyng of þe fend," were far less welcome, however, and the local man whose "spyryte ȝede nyghtes" because he had died while under the abbot's curse for stealing his ox, "soo feeryd þe parysch þat aftyr þe sonne goyng downe þer dyrst no man go out of his yn" (281).

Then there are the superhuman forces that battle for the souls of the living. On one side are the devils, who, reminded of the horrors of the harrowing of hell, are especially difficult when there is thunder about: "Then þay meryþe warres; þay makyþ tempestys in þe see, and drownyþe schyppes and men; þay makyþe debate bytwyx neghtburs and manslaȝt þerwyth; þay tendyþe fyres, and brennen howses and townes; þay reryth wyndys, and blowyþ don howsys, stepuls, and trees; þay make wymen to ouerlye hor children; þay makyþ men to sle homselfe, to hong homself oþyr drowne hom in wanhope, and such mony oþyr curset dedys" (150). But even in fair weather constant vigilance was necessary, as the nun who inadvertently swallowed a devil with a piece of lettuce she had picked by the roadside learned to her cost: irritated at receiving a nasty bite, he sent her into a dead faint — a dire warning to all those who neglect to say grace before meals (*Early South English Legendary* lines 597–614).[2] On the other side are the saints in heaven, whose massed support on All Hallows' Day (as Mirk learned from Jacob de Voragine) is particularly efficacious: "know well þat þis day your prayers schull be sandyr herd of God þen anoþer day, for þis day all þe sayntys of Heuen yfere praythe for vs; wherfor ȝe schull know for certeyne þat all þe sayntes praying at ones schull be raythyr herd then on othyr too by homselfe" (267). Earthly saints, too, could offer practical assistance: the unfortunate lettuce-eating nun, for instance, was restored to her wits by a local holy man, and Mirk tells a story of how Saint Thibaud, finding a soul trapped in a block of ice that some fishermen had brought to cool his feet, calmly set about saying masses for it, "and þen was þe yse molten away, and so þe soule holpen" (271). The "extravagant dualism" (Owst 1961, 93) of writers such as Mirk, retaining as it does strong echoes of a pre-Christian past, had, unsurprisingly, been still more marked in earlier times; the Old English prose *Solomon and Saturn* had even gone so far as to represent the battle of good and evil as a shape-shifting duel between "se Pater Noster" and "ðæt deofol" (Hill 1988).

People in Mirk's day evidently still retained much of that "tremendous sense of the intimacy and adjacency of the holy" that Peter Brown finds characteristic of an earlier period (1975, 141). Saints were not remote, awesome beings, but the familiar spirits of ancestors, always glad to hear from their old acquaintance. In Mirk's words: "for þe seyntes þat now ben yn Heuen wern summe tyme, as we ben now, of oure flesch and oure blode and our forme fadyrs. Wherfor þay haue compassyon of vs, and byn fayne forto get any prayers of vs þe whech þay mow presend God wyth yn oure name" (267). By praying to them we pay, what Caxton's translation of the *Legenda Aurea* charmingly calls, in a phrase picked up by Eamon Duffy, "the dette of entrechaungynge neyhbourhede"; for, as he explains, "the sayntes make of vs feste in heuene . . . And therfor it is ryght . . . that we make feste of them in erthe" (*STC* 24873, fol. 346). Hardly surprisingly, local saints were likely to prove more sociable than foreigners: Mirk makes much of Saint Winifred, who had been brought to Shropshire from North Wales when the first abbot of Shrewsbury acquired her bones, "for þay hade no seynt wyth hom forto ben hor patron and berer of hor prayers to God, as oþer abbotes of þe cuntre hade" (179). Even closer to home (though clearly rather less prestigious) was the obscure Saint Alcmund, over whose bones Mirk seems actually to have preached: "He also takyþe al þe prayers of Goddys seruantes þat byn yn his chyrch, and offerþe hom vp befor þe hygh mageste of God. For ryght as a temporall lord helpyth and defendyth all þat byn parechons or tenantys, ryght soo þe saynt þat ys patron of þe chyrche helpyth and defendyth all þat byn paryschons to hym, and don hym worschyp halowyng his day, and offyrne to hym" (241–42). Before smiling at Mirk's naïveté, we might ask ourselves whether his advice springs from an impulse so very different from that which made Edward I write to the pope and seventeen cardinals urging them to canonize Thomas Cantilupe, "so that his friend on earth could be his patron in heaven" (Finucane 175); or even that which inspired Richard II to lobby for the canonization of his great-grandfather, Edward II. Many historians represent this lobbying as little more than a calculated move in the king's campaign against the former appellants, but even Richard can hardly have been indifferent to the advantages of having a saint in the family, especially one so deeply in his personal debt.

It is easy enough to see why Mirk's parishioners invoked the saints, but why did the saints respond? What was in it for them? "The saint," says Duffy, "desired honour from his clients" (183), and this honor was proffered in the form of worship. Saints were clearly pleased to have prayers directed toward them—"fayne," as Mirk puts it, "forto get any prayers of vs" (267)—and evidently felt that one good turn deserved another. The Virgin was especially generous in this regard—willing to be our advocate, says Chaucer, for as "litel hire" as "an Ave-Marie or tweye" ("An ABC" 103–4). Mirk tells of how she so enjoyed listening to Saint Fulbert repeat her "five joys" that once, when he was "negh ded of þe swynasy [quinsy]," she appeared to him and said, "'Fylbert, my seruant, hyt wer euell ydone þat þy throt schuld suffyr lengyr þys penance, þat haþe so oft gladyd me wyth my v joyes.' And þerwyth toke out hyr swete pappe, and mylked on hys þrote, and soo ȝode hur way. And anon, wyth þat, he was hole as a fyssh" (110). And on another occasion, when a devout cleric prayed that he might be allowed to see her before he died, the Virgin sent an angel with the message: "Syr, for þou seruyst our lady welle to pay, scho wyll þat þou haue þi prayer" (234). For those in extremis who had not built up credit in advance, saints might always be prepared to accept a vow of future devotion. Right here in Shrewsbury, says Mirk, three men were sitting chatting, when a spider came out of the wall and bit them in the neck; they didn't think much of it at the time, but later the bites festered and two of them died. The third sent his mother to offer a candle at Saint Winifred's shrine and bring him back some of the water in which her bones had been washed. Finding this water soothing, he made a vow to the saint "þat, yf he myght haue lyfe and hele, he wold make an ymage of syluyr and offyr to her. Thus he amendyd yche day aftyr othyr ynto þe tyme þat he was hole; and þen he dud make an ymage of syluyr as he behette, and went thydyr, and offryd hit vp to þe scryne, and become her seruant euyr whyl he lyvyd aftyr" (181). The silver image left at

Saint Winifred's shrine might have represented one of a number of things: the site of the miraculous cure (though a neck would have offered the silversmith a rather greater challenge than the more usual eyes, breasts, teeth, ears, and assorted limbs); the cause of the affliction (though a silver spider would have been distinctly odd among the model animals, ships and carts, and the actual weapons, commonly left at shrines); or a figurine of the restored patient himself.[3] Again, we should be careful about assuming that this image was simply appropriate payment for a miracle duly performed; like the penny vowed by Henry of Ulchel's parents, it might better be thought of as a token of the compact made between patient and saint—in this case, that he would "become her seruant euyr whyl he lyvyd aftyr."

Osbern Bokenham's account of how he was led to begin his *Legendys of Hooly Wummen* with a translation of the life of Saint Margaret offers a parallel case. He informs us that the saint's foot (minus the heel and big toe, which belonged to the nuns of Reading) was in an Augustinian priory near his birthplace in East Anglia,[4] and that travelers who touched this foot with a brooch or ring before setting out could invoke the saint's protection should any misfortune befall them on the road by pledging to leave the object at her shrine on their return. His own experience on the way back from Rome five years earlier had shown the wisdom of this precaution, he tells us, for, lost in a fen near Venice,

> sone aftyr I had be-hyht the ryng,
> Wyth wych I towchyd at my partyng
> Hyr foot bare, to bryngyn ageyn,
> I was releuyd ryht sone certeyn.
> (167–70)

Bokenham's ring is thus no mere reward for being rescued from a fen but a token of his continuing relationship with a saint whom he trusts will help him "purchase / Of [his] mysleuyng a pardounn of grace" (231–32) when he comes to die.[5] By writing her life, no less than by returning to East Anglia to worship at her shrine, he was fulfilling his side of a bargain to which the token ring bore witness.

Underlying such stories is a clear assumption that, just as in human affairs, dealings with the supernatural will be regulated by trothplight. In the normal course of things one would expect most bargains to be struck not directly with God but with his saints, who often proved themselves to be as particular and capricious as any human bargainer, and who, like Achebe's Igbo deities, might fall out of fashion whenever their powers appeared to be on the wane (Shinners 137–38), but medieval people clearly felt that behind such local and contingent bargains stood the ultimate contractual relationship, the bond between the faithful and God himself. This was perhaps natural enough for adherents of a religion whose holy book frequently figured God's dealings with his chosen people in terms of a covenant, but I suspect that many traditional societies find such covenantal theology appealing. Among present-day Moroccans, for instance, "attachments to Allah himself are viewed as contractual in nature. . . . He is the ultimate embodiment of this relational reality" (Rosen 13). We might ask ourselves whether when people in medieval England spoke of their God as Truth they were not sometimes expressing a similar attitude.

The interweaving of human and divine contracts is nicely illustrated by Mirk's story of the woman who renounces a long-standing love affair after hearing a sermon on the "horrybull paynes of helle yordeynt to all þat vsyth lechery" (287), only to recant when her old lover promises, "be we heraftyr of won assent, as we haue ben befor, and I wyll plyght þe my troþe þat I woll neuer leue, but hold þe allway" (288). They both end up in hell—the woman presumably for her backsliding and her lover, as he rather churlishly points out to her, for his promise to keep her company: "and yf þou hadyst holden good couenant wyth hym þat þou madyst, þou myghtyst haue sauid vs bothe. But I behette þe þat I wold neuer leue þe. Wherfor go we now boþe ynto þe payne of hell þat ys ordeynt for vs boþe!" (288). The guarantee of salvation for those that keep their covenant with God is theologically more problematical than damnation for those who break it, but Mirk offers such a guarantee quite explicitly in a sermon written for the feast of the circumcision (we should recall that circumcision, instituted *in signum foederis inter me et vos* [Gen. 17:11], was often taken to be a foreshadowing of Christian baptism): "For a good seruand þat hath a good maystyr, he maketh but onys cownant wyth hym, but soo holdeth forth from ȝere to ȝere, hauyng full tryst yn his maystyr þat he woll for his good seruyce reward at hys ende and at his nede. Now right soo Goddys seruandys maketh couenant wyth hym, onys at þe fonte whan þay be jcrystenet. And soo holden forth hor couenantys, hauyng full tryst yn hor God þat he woll at hor endyng be hor socoure, and ȝeuen hom auauncement in his court of Heuen" (44–45). Given the anxiety felt for human truth in the late fourteenth century, however, we should hardly expect to find such faith in divine truth unproblematic, and, as we shall see, neither Langland nor the Cotton-Nero poet gives the impression that covenantal theology is quite the simple matter Mirk would have us believe.

Perhaps the most striking aspect of Mirk's view of divine covenants (as with their common-law counterparts) is its formalism. After telling us about the five joys of the Virgin, he asserts, "Then schull ȝe know well þat he schall neuer fele þe soroues of hell þat woll deuotly yche day grete hur wyth þes v joyes yn erthe" (109–10). Even more remarkable is his story of the evil woman whose only good deed was to have a daily candle burned before an image of the Virgin (61–62). Mirk pays lip service to the creed that *qui vero malo, in ignem eternam*, but deep down he cannot really bring himself to believe that all these candles bind the Virgin to nothing. Accordingly, when the woman dies, devils arrive to haul her off but are stopped at the gates of hell by two angels, who complain that she has not had a proper trial. The devils reply that "hur nedyd no dome, for scho had neuer don good dede yn hyr lyue," but the angels insist that she be brought before the Virgin: "But when hit was fond þat scho dyd neuer good dede, scho most nede goo to hell. Then sayde oure lady: 'Scho fonde a serge befor me brennyng and wold euer whyll sho had lyued; þen wyll I be as kynd to hur as scho was to me.' Wherfor scho bade an angell take a gret serge and lyght hyt, and bade hym sette hit so brennyng byfor hur yn hell, and commaunde þat no fende schuld be so hardy forto come nygh hit, but let hit brenne þer for euermor. Than sayde þe fendes þat hit schuld be a hoge confort to all þat ben yn hell; wherfor þay had leuer leue þat soule, þan do such an ese to þe soules þat ben in payne" (62). The Virgin duly instructs an angel to return the woman's soul to its body, and the woman, realizing what a narrow escape she has had, leads an exemplary life thereafter.

It is not only the Virgin, however, who assumes this traditional role of the trickster on our behalf. Christ himself, according to an ancient piece of soteriological lore, took on human shape in order to trick the devil into overstepping his rights. This is why, says Mirk, Christ was circumcised: "þen when þe fend sygh Cryst ycircumcised as othyr werne, he wende he had taken þat penaunce yn remedy of orygnall synne, and soo knew hym not by anoþer synfull man. For yf he had knowen hym redely þat he had comen forto by monkynd out of his bondam, he wold neuer haue tysut mon to haue don hym to deth. This was also þe cause, why oure lady was wedded to Ioseph, forto deseyue þe fende, þat he schuld wene, þat he was hys fadyr, and not conseyuet of þe Holy Gost" (46). Like the human beings they manipulate, Mirk's supernatural forces (the devil, no less than God and his saints) are bound by a web of contractual rights and obligations. After the Fall, the devil had held all humanity in thrall, but, tricked on Calvary by his clever rival, he could now claim as his fee only those Christians who broke their covenant with God. With this proviso, however, his title was perfectly sound and if the Virgin occasionally resorted to a lawyer's trick to steal a soul from him, neither she nor her son had the authority to challenge this basic right.

That Mirk should still be preaching the theory of the "devil's rights" three hundred years after Anselm's refutation of it, suggests how deeply it was embedded in traditional consciousness. Boso, Anselm's interlocutor in the *Cur Deus Homo*, implies that this theory was the standard one in the late eleventh century: "we usually say [dicere solemus] that . . . when the devil killed God, against whom he had no case, he justly lost the authority he had wielded over sinners, for otherwise God would have committed a violent injustice against him, since he had just title to the human race" [quoniam iuste possidebat hominem] (1.7; *Opera* 1.2:55–56). At no point, however, does this theory seem to have formed a coherent dogma, though its various manifestations all reveal a markedly dualistic attitude to the redemption in which human beings appear as dependents, vassals, debtors, slaves, prisoners, or simply possessions — the prize in a contractual dispute between Christ and Satan. In its strong form, still present in Mirk, God must resort to trickery, a kind of legal equivocation, to wrest humanity from an opponent whose title is apparently otherwise unassailable; in its weak form Satan's title is flawed because he won Adam's allegiance with a false promise (that he would be like God) and Christ's primary task is to expose this flaw.[6] An intermediate position makes the devil's title sound, but the means by which Christ cancels it, simply a matter of paying him what he is owed. Both Scripture and the authority of Saint Augustine could be adduced in support of this intermediate position, and it continued to maintain a place in pastoral, if not academic, theology, throughout the Middle Ages; it is, indeed, implicit in the motif of *The Charter of Christ* that we looked at in Chapter 7 (cf. Mirk 172).[7] The strong form of the theory, on the other hand — despite wide acceptance among the Greek fathers, together with the qualified support of Gregory the Great and even Augustine (Aulen 47–55) — was forced to lead a rather more shadowy existence after the publication of *Cur Deus Homo*.

Though Anselm's views, which were broadly shared by influential textbooks like *The Sentences* of Peter Lombard (see Marx 1995, 7–27), were to make the image of the trickster-Christ unappealing to most later schoolmen, its appearance in the popular *Gospel of Nicodemus* nonetheless ensured its survival outside academic circles (99). In the demonic debate that precedes the harrowing of hell, Inferus makes it quite clear that Christ's victory is an inevitable consequence of Satan's having overstepped his rights: "Et in quo nullam culpam cognouisti quare sine ratione iniuste eum crucifigere ausus fuisti et ad nostram regionem innocentem et iustum perduxisti?" [why have you dared to crucify unjustly and without cause him in whom you found no fault, and brought an innocent and just man into our realm?] (23.1:32–35; 44). The redemption is brought about by a combination of Satan's folly — "Ignorasti ut insipiens quod egisti" [Like a fool you are blind to what you've done], says Inferus (23.1:6–7; 43) — and Christ's cunning. When Satan argues that Christ cannot have been divine because he expressed a human fear of death, Inferus replies, "Et si dicit se mortem timere, capere te uult et ue tibi erit in sempiterna secula [and if he says he fears death, he wishes to deceive you, and you shall suffer everlasting woe]" (20.2:9–10; 39). Thus, for all that it may have aroused scholastic distaste, the image of the trickster-Christ received powerful endorsement from this well-known apocryphal gospel.

Not surprisingly, then, the theory of the devil's rights is often prominent in vernacular treatments of the harrowing of hell. The Auchinleck version of a thirteenth-century dramatization, for instance, has Satan claim,

Par ma fay! ich hald mine
al þat ben hereinne;
wiþ resoun wil y telle þe
þat þer ogain may þou nouȝt be,
þat me bihoueþ haue & hald
& wiþouten ende wald;
for whoso biggeþ aniþing,
It owe to ben his wiþouten lesing;
adam hungri come me to,
manred y made him me to do;
for an appel þat y ȝaf him
he is min & al his kin.
(85–96; *Middle-English Harrowing* 9)

Christ responds to Satan's picturesque claim that the trothplight binding Adam to his service had been sealed with a token apple, by pointing out that this apple had not in fact belonged to Satan and thus that the contract made with it was invalid. Their exchange represents a rather unusual variation on what I have called the weak form of the theory of the devil's rights, but in the Towneley and York "Deliverance" we encounter its strong version in the person of Christ the trickster.[8] Responding to Satan's refusal to recognize his divinity—"Thy fader knew I well by syght, / he was a wright, his meett to wyn" (*Towneley* 25:245–46)—Jesus confesses:

My godhed here I hyd
In mary, moder myne,
where it shall neuer be kyd
to the ne none of thyne.
(263–66)

Later, the Towneley version offers one of the more striking instances of a supernatural contract when Satan responds to Christ's promise that henceforth those who refuse to believe in the incarnation shall be doomed eternally to hell by offering to strike hands on what seems to him an admirable bargain (25:343).

In addition to these treatments of the harrowing of hell and an occasional appearance of the theme in Old English verse,[9] there is a most interesting literary exposition of the thesis of the devil's rights in Robert Grosseteste's *Château d'amour*, an Anglo-Norman poem written in the first half of the thirteenth century and first translated into Middle-English early in the fourteenth. Probably best known as a source for Langland's crucifixion passus (to which we shall return), the *Château d'amour* is a remarkable piece to have come from the hands of a trained theologian, particularly one who evidently intended his poem "to provide an audience without theological training with an outline of Christian theology" (Southern 1986, 225). It falls into two sections—the first, a sketch of the old law culminating in an allegory of the four daughters of God and prophecies of the incarnation, the second, and longer, an allegorical representation of the Virgin as a castle, followed by an extended commentary on Isa. 9:6 ("Wonderful, Counselor, God the Mighty, the Father of the world to come, the Prince of Peace").

The devil's rights provide the main focus for the long section in which God's role as counselor (i.e., advocate or lawyer) is described (945–1220), though they occasionally surface elsewhere in the poem (e.g., 197–274).[10] Grosseteste portrays Christ as our champion always ready to defend our rights:

> And ich þe rede þou suwe me:
> Ichulle þe batayle nyme for þe.
> To ple ichulle þis princes hauen
> And þi rihte ichulle crauen,
> For icham of þi lynage,
> I may crauen þin heritage;
> And icham of freo nacion,
> Me ou[ȝ]te ihere my reson;
> And ichabbe iwust wiþ wynne
> Þe þreo lawen wiþouten synne.
> For þe ichulle to batayle wende,
> [And] siker beo þou of ful good ende,
> For ichulle an ende ouurcome þat fiht
> And to-dreynen [Fr. *dereignerai*] al þi riht.
> (963–976)

In this passage, as in several others (Alford 1977, 943–44; Southern 1986, 226 n.33), Grosseteste shows an intimate knowledge of common-law procedure. Heaven ("þis princes hauen") is ours by right, and Christ, as an important kinsman and an expert in the law, has the legal standing to defend us in court. Since this is a property dispute, imagined as a writ of right case, he will wager battle for us, and we can have confidence that with him as our champion our claim will be fully vindicated (deraigned). Earlier in the poem Grosseteste had shown how Adam, by becoming the devil's serf, had not only forfeited his seisin but also—just as under the king's law (239–40)—his right to plead his own case in court:

> And þeuwe and þral may not craue
> Þorw riht non heritage to haue:
> As sone as he is þral bicome,
> His heritage is him binome.
> In court ne in none londe
> Me ne ouȝte onswere him ne vnderstonde.
> (249–54)

The allegory in this section is imperfectly conceived, since, with Christ taking on the role of demandant for a human race without legal standing, the forensic logic of writ of right procedure must cast the devil as tenant, in present possession of the property at issue; this can hardly be the case if the disputed property is heaven. However, when Grosseteste turns to the question of how Adam's descendants, deprived of their legal rights at the Fall, come to recover their law-worthy status, the allegory enters more familiar territory.

All three versions of the devil's rights theory are interwoven in Grosseteste's description of Christ's great redemptive battle with Satan at the crucifixion. Christ makes the claim that the devil forfeited his right to the human race when he broke his "foreward" with God by misleading Adam in the Garden of Eden (1066–78);[11] this is the weak form of the theory in which the devil technically has no rights. The poem, however, still proceeds as if he does, for Christ, in a second form of the theory, offers to ransom humanity with his own body (1109–26). Finally, and most dramatically, Christ assumes the role of the trickster at his incarnation, a role that implies the theory in its strongest form:

> Þo Jhesu, Godes sone, in þe world was ibore,
> So stille and derne he was þe fend fore
> Þat he of his come riht nouȝt nuste,
> [Ac] to beo lord and syre he truste,

As he hedde ben, ac his miht was binome
Þo þat Jhesu was ibore and into the world icome.
Wel þe fend him seiȝ in monnes weeden,
Ac he nust what he was ne wȝuch weren his deden.
He [seiȝ him] wel mon and icomen on monkunne,
Ac euere in þe world he liuede wiþoute sinne.
(1031–40)

Grosseteste even employs an image that derives ultimately from Gregory of Nyssa (Aulen 52) of Christ as a fishhook baited with human flesh in order to take the devil:

Þo was þe fend siker and wende wel eþe
Forte haue biȝeten þorw his deþe,
Ac he was cauȝt and ouercomen,
As fisch þat is wiþ hok inomen,
Þat whon þe worm he swoleweþ alast,
He is bi þe hok itiȝed fast.[12]
(1127–32)

That Grosseteste should move so easily between these different accounts of the devil's rights confirms the view that what we are dealing with here is no coherent theological dogma, but a series of imperfectly harmonized attempts to represent the redemption as a legal process for a society whose jural horizons were still dominated by oral trothplight. In the long run their internal contradictions must make all such attempts vulnerable to the "glacial legalism" that Richard Southern detects in Anselm (1963, 103) and to the textual consciousness that had fostered it (Stock 360–61), but their stubborn survival down to Grosseteste and beyond suggests an enduring appeal for the traditional imagination.[13]

Anselm had been able to offer an effective rebuttal to each of the three versions of the devil's rights theory. He had refuted its strong form (the trickster-Christ) by showing how the suggestion that God would stoop to deceit misrepresents his divine nature: "Though truth does not reveal itself to everyone, it denies itself to no one. Therefore, O Lord, you acted thus neither to deceive nor induce deception in others. But that you might do what had to be done in a particular manner, you stood firm in the truth at all times" (*Meditatio Redemptionis* 42–45; *Opera* 2.3:85). The weak version of the theory (Satan's flawed claim) he had countered by arguing that any implication that God must recognize some law other than his own will places unjustifiable limits on his power: "Did some necessity force the Most High thus to debase himself or the Most Powerful to struggle so hard to accomplish some end? Is not all necessity and impossibility subject to his will? Surely, what he wishes must happen, and what he does not wish is impossible. Therefore, it was by his will alone. . . . for there was no compulsion for God to save the human race in this manner" (*Meditatio Redemptionis* 59–64; *Opera* 2.3:86). Finally, he had dismissed the intermediate position (the payment of man's debt) by pointing out the dangerous dualism implicit in a world where God and the devil bargain with one another: "However, since the devil, or man, can only be God's creatures, and neither may exist outside the power of God, how should God engage in a lawsuit on behalf of one of his own, concerning one of his own, and against one of his own?" (*Cur Deus Homo* 1.7; *Opera* 1.2:56–57). It is easy to see why Southern should suggest that "Anselm's elimination of the Devil from the process of Redemption satisfies every rational instinct" (1990, 209), and he is surely right to argue for the pivotal importance of Anselm's thought for later generations: "in the company of Saint Anselm we are at the source of many experiences which had a transforming influence on the spiritual world" (1953, 254). It is to the Anselmian theory of atonement, after all, that Dante turns for his account of the redemption in canto 7 of the *Paradiso*. Nevertheless, we should recognize that this optimistic portrait has its darker side.

No doubt Anselm's efforts to transform God from victorious warrior into suffering man contributed much to the great twelfth-century shift from epic to romance so well described by Southern : (1953, 234–37), but it can be seen as effect as well as cause, as itself the product of a growing authoritarianism in both church and state. *Christus victor* had done sterling service in the battle for the souls of Clovis and Edwin, but by the end of the eleventh century the church was no longer looking over its shoulder at serious pagan rivals, and a Christ incarnated as *Homo patiens* offered a rather more salutary model for anyone who might be tempted to question ecclesiastical authority. Similarly, while a cosmic dualism may have seemed natural enough to those living under a bicentric system of folklaw arbitration, kings who were beginning to see themselves as lawmakers rather than mere lawfinders must have found the image of a God subject to nothing but his own will particularly attractive.

Where I find Southern less convincing, however, is not in the argument that the Anselmian revolution "opened the door to a new phase of religious history," but in his claim that this meant "an easier future for believers" (1990, 215). When he writes that "the old view of the warrior Redeemer was associated with a harshly limited prospect of salvation for the few," he seems to me to be seriously underestimating the appeal of the covenantal model for the traditional consciousness. A god who respects his covenant even with the devil, a god driven to legalistic subterfuge in order to outwit an opponent with an ostensibly impregnable case, is also a god who can be depended upon to keep his word. When Christ dissolves his bargain with the devil, he strikes another with the human race, and his human dependents have every reason to expect that the same punctilious legalism will be exercised in defense of their own rights. Thus, far from emphasizing the difficulty of attaining salvation, the theory of the devil's rights can just as well promote an optimistic confidence in the efficacy of the new covenant. As Grosseteste writes in the *Château d'amour*:

> Baldeliche we mouwe þorw him craue
> Vre rihtes in heuene to haue,
> For he haþ alle þe lawen iwust,
> Of o poynt ne haþ he mist.
>
> (1473–76)

Such sentiments continue to be heard throughout the Middle Ages, and, though the trail grows fainter from the twelfth century onward, their very survival in written record after the Anselmian revolution is significant. They are there unsurprisingly in Cynewulf's *Christ*:

> Sib sceal gemæne
> englum ond ældum a forð heonan
> wesan wideferh. Wær is ætsomne
> godes ond monna, gasthalig treow,
> lufu, lifes hyht, ond ealles leohtes gefea.
>
> (581–85; K&D 3:19)

[There shall be a mutual peace between men and angels henceforth for ever. A compact is established between God and the human race, a spiritual covenant, love, the pleasure of life, and the joy of all light.]

But they can still be heard, much muted, in Christ's promise in the Towneley "Deliverance," over six hundred years later: "And thay that lyst to lere my law, and lyf therby, / Shall neuer haue harmes here, bot welth as is worthy" (*Towneley* 25:341–42). Even in Ricardian England, John Mirk's is not the only voice to proclaim firm faith in God's covenant. The same confident note is struck in the first of the Vernon lyrics on *Deo gratias*:

> 3if we þis word in herte wol haue,
> And ay in loue and leute leende,

Of crist bi couenaunt we mow craue
Þat Ioye þat schal neuer haue ende,
Out of þis world whon we schul wende,
In-to his paleys for to paas.
(*RL14C* 134)

Predictably, perhaps, the second of the Vernon *Deo gratias* lyrics (138–39) is far less confident.

One thing all such passages have in common is a strong sense of the reciprocity of the covenant between God and humanity, but it is precisely such reciprocity that Anselm denies. "God," he writes, "owes nothing to anyone; rather, all creatures are in his debt. Thus it is not fitting for human beings to act toward God as if with an equal" (*Cur Deus Homo* 1.19; *Opera* 1.2:86). If the devil has no rights in this redemptive economy, it follows that neither do we. Though God, Anselm implies, would never do anything so dishonorable as to break his word (*Cur Deus Homo* 2.5; *Opera* 1.2:100), he clearly regards divine promises as *nuda pacta*, conferring only a debt of gratitude, never rights, on those they benefit. This is evidently how we must understand his similitude of the king who, for the sake of one good citizen, sends a pardon to all the others (*Cur Deus Homo* 2.16; *Opera* 1.2:118–19). It is a nice question whether, by opening the way "for a fresh appreciation of the human sufferings of the Redeemer" (Southern 1953, 236), Anselm really made Christ more accessible to the medieval imagination. Might we not reasonably expect people to have derived greater comfort from knowing that Christ was willing to act as their advocate in a cosmic lawsuit against the devil, than from hearing that he would stand to one side while they matched wits with an *improbus placitator* in the private courtroom of their own hearts ("locus autem placiti huius est cor hominis ipsius") (*Memorials* 65)? In nice questions of eschatological law it might seem safer to have the tricky lawyer on one's own side. Even Southern's claim that Anselm gave "mankind a new kind of dignity" (1990, 209) may stand in need of qualification. Is it altogether surprising that the creature Anselm imagines as owed nothing by God and whom he urges to meditate on the immensity of his own debts to the Savior should be described as a *homuncio* or 'manikin' (*Meditatio Redemptionis* 149; *Opera* 2.3:89)?

Anselm seems to have taken a rather stern line on personal salvation: several times in his letters he quotes Matt. 22:14, "many are called but few chosen" (Southern 1990, 215), usually with the additional admonition that his correspondents should not be too quick to assume that they are among the few. Southern attributes this to the austerity of Anselm's personal religious outlook, not to the inherent logic of his soteriology, but it might equally well be seen as a consequence of his rejection of covenantal theology. *Cur Deus Homo* may well have offered an easier future for those believers who were trained theologians and scholastics, but for the people at large its god must have appeared remote and unresponsive and the salvation he offered doubtful at best.

There are clear signs that traditional consciousness sought to fill the vacuum left by the success of Anselm's assault on covenantal theology by turning to the Virgin and the saints. Indeed the church itself may have encouraged such transference, and ironically even Anselm may have played a part in shaping the new cult of Mary that was to help bridge the widening gap between God and his human servants. The first use of the epithet *mediatrix* was traditionally ascribed to him (G. H. Williams 37), and Southern has convincingly demonstrated a link between the very earliest collection of miracles of the Virgin and a circle which centered on Anselm's nephew, the abbot of Bury St. Edmunds. Though Southern has described these miracles as "disinterested" and "indifferent to ordinary morality" (1953, 249–50), it is noteworthy that even the most disreputable recipients of the Virgin's bounty, such as the sacristan drowned on the way to visiting his mistress or Ebbo the thief, had previously singled her out for their particular devotion (*Liber de Miraculis* 4–5 and 8). Mirk's tale of the Virgin's soothing the sore throat of one of her worshipers with her own milk is a variant of a story which, if not part of the very first collection (Southern 1958, 187), was added to it at an early stage. Like its companions, it suggests that a theology of reciprocal obligation was being refocused on Mary in the wake of the Anselmian revolution. Interestingly enough, Grosseteste, one of the few later scholarly proponents of the devil's right's theory, offers us in the *Château d'amour* a Mary very different from "the *mater misericordiae*, the worker of miracles of pity and mercy of contemporary legends" (Southern 1986, 227).

Not only the cult of the Virgin, but saints' cults in general flourished in the wake of declining official support for covenantal theology. Gurevich suggests that a "distant and incomprehensible deity was overshadowed by intimate and accessible saints, endowed with human features and active among the people" (1988, 73), and quotes in support Jacob de Voragine's observation that "we see that some shewe more gretter affection to a saynt/ than they doe to god" (*STC* 24873, fols. 22^{b}–23). Gurevich seeks to illustrate this kind of mentality with two modern anecdotes from Axel Munthe. Munthe reports meeting a mason on Capri who felt no compunction about working on Good Friday, arguing that Christ was "not so great [a saint] as Sant'Antonio, who has done more than one hundred miracles. How many miracles has Gesù Cristo done?" Even more striking was Munthe's conversation with an old

Neapolitan friar who "made no secret of his private opinion that Christ owed his reputation solely to His having the Madonna for His Mother. As far as he knew Christ had never saved anybody from cholera. His Blessed Mother had cried her eyes out for Him. What had He done for Her in return?" (1988, 216–17). Those, like Gurevich, who hear in such scraps distant echoes of the unrecorded customary theology of the Middle Ages, may find themselves uneasy about Southern's conviction that Anselm was harbinger of a newly humanized Christ.

Before returning to the Ricardian poets, we might notice one final aspect of Anselm's soteriology that has implications for understanding later medieval attitudes to God's covenants. As George Huntston Williams has pointed out, the dominant sacrament of the early church was baptism and this sacrament was originally administered only at Eastertide and only to adults, who would then proceed directly to their first communion. Under these circumstances baptism became intimately associated with ideas of redemption: "The primary sacramental means for the appropriation . . . of the work of Christ . . . was the sacramental ablution, death, and regeneration of Baptism" (17). By the end of the eleventh century, however, infant baptism (which might be administered at any time of year) was gaining in popularity and was increasingly being seen as merely a prelude to the all-important sacrament of the Eucharist, which was prepared for by penance. For Williams, Anselm stands at the critical point in an important shift "from the once-for-all Baptismal-Eucharist experience of patristic Christianity with its stress on the liberation from demons and the sacral enrollment of each Christian recruit under *Christus victor* to the scholastic interest in the penitential-Eucharistic experience of the repetitive restoration of justice and of progressive incorporation in the *Homo patiens* slain on the altar for the sins of the whole world" (64). Though Williams does not stress the covenantal implications of this shift, it seems evident that those who conceive of their relationship with God primarily in terms of a contract will found their Christianity on the baptismal pledge with its guarantee of salvation for all who keep faith, whereas those who fear that their God owes them nothing will need continual access to divine grace through the eucharistic presence.

One of the commonest figures of baptism for the early church was the passage through the Red Sea, and so strong was the association between baptism and Easter for the poet of the Old English *Exodus* that when he set out to dramatize this story for his audience, he naturally turned for his theological underpinning to the liturgical readings prescribed for Holy Saturday (Bright). The resulting interweaving of "the themes of . . . covenant and fulfillment, judgment and salvation, baptism and Easter" (Earl 570) offers a particularly fine testimonial to the imaginative power of the older ethos; certainly, there is little in the religious poetry of the later Middle Ages to match its heroic, confident, and above all unblushingly covenantal view of human history,

> wile nu gelæstan þæt he lange gehet
> mid aðsware, engla drihten,
> in fyrndagum fæderyncynne,
> gif ge gehealdað halige lare,
> þæt ge feonda gehwone forð ofergangað.
> (558–62; K&D 1:106–07)

[The Lord of angels will now perform what he has on oath long promised our ancestors in former times that you shall in future overcome every enemy if you observe his sacred teaching.] After Anselm, mainstream theology would no longer, in Williams's words, be concerned "with the renunciation of the demons of one's preconversion life, but with the fulfillment of penance for one's post-Baptismal sins" (13). Henceforward, only in theological backwaters will we find preachers like John Mirk willing to compare the faithful Christian to a steady worker whose future is assured: "for a good seruand þat hath a good maystyr, he maketh but onys cownant wyth hym" (44). For Mirk the single ritual of the servant's engagement, not a perpetual ritualized forestalling of his dismissal, is what is important: "right soo Goddys seruandys maketh couenant wyth hym, onys at þe fonte whan þay ben jcrystenet. And soo holden forth hor couenantys, hauyng full tryst yn hor God þat he woll at hor endyng . . . ȝeuen hom auauncement in his court of Heuen" (45). For Anselm, by contrast, humanity is a backsliding servant only able to avoid well-deserved dismissal by virtue of a license entitling him to the repeated forgiveness of his master—"unde se potest, ut antea, reconciliare" (*Memorials* 64). This kind of eucharistic thinking was to dominate the soteriology that Anselm bequeathed to the later Middle Ages.

In such a world, then, attitudes toward covenantal theology must become inextricably involved with questions of sacramental causality. Bernard of Clairvaux seems to have been unusual among twelfth-century theologians in arguing that the sacraments function like the tokens used in trothplight (he gives the example of a ring used to invest someone with the title to an estate), and consequently that "grace does not seem to be communicated directly in and through the sacraments" (Courtenay 1973, 114). This view, known to later theologians as *sine qua non* causality, clearly reflects an underlying belief that God's grace "operates according to a pact or covenant" (117), so that Bernard is, for instance, prepared to claim that "God is not free to reject those who have been baptized and who desire salvation" (116). The majority of twelfth-

and thirteenth-century schoolmen, however, agreed with Anselm that God was under no obligation to humanity; accordingly, they were reluctant to accept Bernard's view of the sacraments as the symbolic clothing of a spiritual pact. The orthodox position, articulated by Aquinas and later accepted by the Council of Trent, was that the sacraments possessed an inherent virtue to confer grace *ex opere operato* on those who were spiritually prepared to receive it; in Aquinas's succinct phrase, "the sacraments of the New Law not merely signify but actually cause grace" (3a.62.1; 56:52–53). This view, generally referred to as instrumental causality, minimized the covenantal implications of the sacraments in the interests of promoting divine, or (the skeptic might suggest) ecclesiastical, authority. Nonetheless, covenantal theology was to enjoy a significant revival in the fourteenth century, when the *moderni* discovered in the doctrine of God's two powers a way of solving the old problem of how of an omnipotent creator might be placed under an obligation to his own creation.

By the later Middle Ages the distinction between the two aspects of God's *potentia*, his absolute and his ordained power (*potentia absoluta* and *potentia ordinata*), had become a scholastic commonplace. Though the germ of this distinction can be detected as early as Anselm (Courtenay 1975, 60–61), it only reached maturity with Albertus Magnus and his pupil Thomas Aquinas in the middle of the thirteenth century (Oakley 48–49). Originally a dialectic tool fashioned to deal with such classic scholastic conundrums as "whether God's attribute of omnipotence requires us to believe that he has the power to do otherwise or better than he has in fact willed to do" (47), it was reshaped by the *moderni* to serve the cause of a revived covenantalism, allowing them to argue that while an omnipotent God owes us nothing *de potentia absoluta*, we may still have complete faith in his commitment to honor his promises *de potentia ordinata*. The most significant of these promises was the guarantee of salvation to those who "freely do the best they can (*faciunt quod in se est*)" (62), a view which led them to downplay the instrumental power of the sacraments and inevitably brought upon them a charge of semi-Pelagianism.[14]

The fundamental importance of covenantal theology for this school has been stressed by both Alister McGrath and William Courtenay. For McGrath the idea of a 'covenant' or 'contract' between God and man is the "fulcrum about which 'nominalist' doctrines of justification turn" (1981, 114), while for Courtenay what distinguished the movement is "a conception of the centrality, efficacy, and dependability of verbal, contractual agreements for all aspects of the relationship between God and man" (1974, 51). Courtenay goes on to point out that none of the elements we have touched on here (*sine qua non* causality, God's two powers, semi-Pelagian soteriology) was particularly novel in itself: "The unique feature of Ockhamist thought was that these ideas were all present and grounded in the idea of a pact or covenant—willed verbal agreements that are no less dependable and certain because they are in origin voluntary" (51).[15] Strictly speaking, of course, such agreements could never be truly reciprocal (unlike Uhtred of Ulchel's bargains with Becket and Godric, for instance), for when the *moderni* spoke of a *pactum* between God and man they were clearly thinking of a covenant "established unilaterally by God" (McGrath 1987, 81); nonetheless, "the Nominalists often interpreted the covenant of salvation in the sense that God was a debtor, committed to reward with grace, and, eventually, with eternal life the man who did what was in him" (Courtenay 1971, 118). It is in this sense that Francis Oakley can talk of the God of the *moderni* as having "chosen to accept men as partners in the work of their salvation" (62), a strikingly different soteriological economy from the one Anselm had bequeathed to the High Middle Ages, and consonant with what McGrath represents as "a general transition from a concept of *ontological* to *covenantal* causality" (1987, 82).

Such ideas were hotly debated in Oxford in the second quarter of the fourteenth century and roundly condemned by the Merton scholar Thomas Bradwardine in his *De causa Dei*, completed by 1344 (Leff 265–66). Heiko Oberman's characterization of the differences between Bradwardine and the Dominican Robert Holcot, one of his most prominent opponents, nicely epitomizes the movement's radical break with the Anselmian tradition: "Whereas Bradwardine had regarded man as the *instrument* of God who was the first to move (in creation) and the first to choose (in redemption), Holcot saw man as the *partner* of God in a covenantal relationship to which God had freely committed himself. Within this covenantal relationship, immutable because of God's fidelity and inner consistency, man had to determine the course of his own life and shoulder the responsibility for his eternal lot; God would support his serious efforts" (136). For our purposes this debate is significant because Chaucer's allusion to it later in the century ("Nun's Priest's Tale" 3234–50) shows that its issues were not quarantined within college cloisters and lecture halls; indeed, at the very time he was completing the *De causa Dei* Bradwardine was employed as chaplain and confessor to Edward III, later accompanying the young king on his Crécy campaign (Leff 2–3), so that some of Chaucer's senior colleagues at court may well have been able to remember him. Regardless of whether Ricardian writers wrestled with the issues of covenantal theology under the direct influence of such debates, however, it seems likely that both poets and theologians were responding to deeper forces at work in society. That a sophisticated schoolman like Holcot and a provincial pastor like Mirk should both have been led to think of salvation in terms of a covenant offers a suggestive context in which to consider the theological implications of the Ricardian crisis of truth.

Covenantal Theology in Langland and the Cotton-Nero Poet

At the height of the storm in *Patience* Jonah's pagan crew make vows to their gods in the hope of deliverance:

Summe to Vernagu þer vouched a-vowes solemne,
Summe to Diana deuout and derf Neptune,
To Mahoun and to Mergot, þe mone and þe sunne,
And vche lede as he loued and layde had his hert.
(165–68)

Vows such as these seem to have been common in the Middle Ages: there is no reason to suppose Thomas Cantilupe a particularly nautical saint, yet when papal commissioners visited his shrine in Hereford on Tuesday, August 29, 1307, as part of the process of his canonization, they found among the votive offerings left at his tomb 170 silver ships, 41 ships made of wax, and a number of ships' anchors (Finucane 98).[16] Evidently, making vows to honor saints who procured them a safe landfall was a regular practice among storm-tossed sailors in the Middle Ages.[17] In *Patience*, of course, it takes not only a vow to Jonah's God, but the ditching of the prophet himself, to calm the waves, but the grateful sailors are prompt to honor their benefactor as soon as they reach shore:

Þer watȝ louyng on lofte, whan þay þe londe wonnen,
To oure mercyable God, on Moyses wyse,
With sacrafyse vp-set and solemne vowes,
And graunted hym on to be God and graythly non oþer.
(237–40)

The simple faith which leads to the conversion of these pagan sailors is contrasted in the poem with Jonah's faithlessness.

Jonah, too, makes a vow in extremis, but the subsequent history of his relationship with his deliverer is very much more complex. From the belly of the whale, he swears:

Bot I dewoutly avowe, þat verray betȝ halden,
Soberly to do þe sacrafyse when I schal saue worþe,
And offer þe for my hele a ful hol gyfte,
And halde goud þat þou me hetes, haf here my trauthe.
(333–36)

Back on dry land, Jonah sets about fulfilling this vow by preaching in Nineva and warning the citizens of their approaching destruction, but so successful is he that the city throws itself into an elaborate display of penitence and thus averts the predicted catastrophe. Jonah now feels that God, by sparing the city, "Þaȝ he oþer bihyȝt" (408), has broken his word, and made his prophet look a fool. More dramatically, he even appears to accuse his God of lying: "For me were swetter to swelt as swyþe, as me þynk, / Þen lede lenger þi lore þat þus me les makeȝ" (427–28).[18] It is no surprise, after this, that Jonah should be taught a swift lesson in humility. The seemingly wanton destruction of the woodbine shading the "lefsel of lof" (448) to which Jonah has retreated soon has him remonstrating with God in terms which suggest an aggrieved servant complaining about his master's unfair treatment: "A, þou maker of man, what maystery þe þynkeȝ / Þus þy freke to forfare forbi alle oþer?" (482–83).[19] God's observation that his prophet is making a great deal of fuss "for so lyttel" (492), provokes a faintly ludicrous expression of self-righteous indignation—" 'Hit is not lyttel,' quoþ þe lede, 'bot lykker to ryȝt' " (493)—but God is quick to show that his freedom to deal with his own in whatever way he wishes puts him beyond any human concept of rights and obligations. We are left with the completely orthodox lesson that while we owe him absolute obedience, God owes us nothing in return; like the narrator of the opening lines who has learned that there is no point in *grychchyng* when his master sends him on an errand to Rome (49–53), we are expected to find in the virtue of patience the strength to endure the whims of a God accountable to no one but himself.[20]

While Jonah is *loltrande* in his bower happily contemplating his woodbine he takes no thought for his physical survival: "Þat of no diete þat day—þe deuel haf—he roȝt" (460). The Cotton-Nero poet evidently thinks of this as culpable negligence, yet, ironically, it can be made to seem very like the kind of life that Langland's Patience actually recommends:

> Thouȝ neuere greyn growed, ne grape vpon vyne,
> Alle þat lyueþ and lokeþ liflode wolde I fynde
> And þat ynogh; shal noon faille of þyng þat hem nedeþ:
> [We sholde noȝt be to bisy abouten oure liflode.]
> *Ne soliciti sitis &c.*[21]
>
> (*PPl* B.14:31 ff.)

The contrast between the two writers on the subject of patient poverty is very marked and at root it springs from their quite different attitudes to God's covenant. For the Cotton-Nero poet patience is a practical, worldly virtue: a kind of emotional self-control (*Patience* 27) that helps reconcile him to misfortunes—such as his own poverty (46)—that cannot be avoided and teaches him not to put too much trust in worldly pleasure. At times it comes close to resembling equanimity, or even discretion: "Be preue and be pacient in payne and in joye" (525). This patience teaches stoical endurance in a world ruled by an unpredictable deity. For Langland, on the other hand, patient poverty is a positive theological virtue that reflects the poet's eagerness to believe that God is obliged to reward those who practice it with a place in heaven.

Ironically, one of Langland's strongest statements of this belief alludes to those very beatitudes with which *Patience* begins:

> And patriarkes and prophetes and poetes boþe
> Writen to wissen vs to wilne no richesse,
> And preiseden pouerte with pacience; þe Apostles bereþ witnesse
> That þei han Eritage in heuene, and by trewe riȝte,
> Ther riche men no riȝt may cleyme but of ruþe and grace.
> (B.10:344–48)

But when Will objects to this with a schoolman's "contra," he does so not on the orthodox grounds that no one, not even the poor, can claim ***a true right*** to heaven, but with the much less conventional argument that all Christians, even the wealthy, enjoy such a right: "That is baptiȝed beþ saaf, be he riche or pouere" (B.10:351). Will is to learn the naïveté of this position in passus 14 when Patience lectures Hawkyn on the virtues of poverty, but its essential covenantalism is still not wholly abandoned: "[al] poore þat pacient is [of pure riȝt] may cleymen, / After hir endynge here, heueneriche blisse" (B.14: 260–61). When Judson Allen spoke of Langland's "theology of entitlement" (Adams 1988b, 231), it was no doubt passages such as this that he had in mind.

Langland's sympathy with the covenantalist position manifests itself in his espousal of a pre-Anselmian soteriology, most marked in Will's sixth vision (the crucifixion and harrowing of hell), where, as R. A. Waldron has shown (78–80), the influence of Grosseteste's *Château d'amour* is particularly strong. Both Langland and Grosseteste conceive of the redemption as a legal process (a judicial battle between Christ and the devil fought on behalf of the human race), which makes Langland no less vulnerable than Grosseteste had been to Anselm's refutation of the devil's rights theory. No doubt Alford is right to claim that Langland's solution to the problems of the atonement is inherently more poetic than Anselm's (1977, 944), but this should not be taken to imply that the theologian in Langland is simply capitulating to the poet. On the other hand, despite his evident familiarity with scholastic debate (see M. Bloomfield 161–69), Langland can hardly be expected to make the traditional theology he is here concerned with conform to the rigorous *sic et non* of the schools, and James Simpson's recent suggestion that he "is not himself promoting the 'Devil's rights' theory, since Christ proves that Lucifer does not have legal possession of mankind," (215), fails to appreciate that such inconsistencies typify this theology even in the hands of scholars far more subtle than Langland. We have seen how Grosseteste conflated weak and strong forms of the theory without embarrassment, so when Langland makes Christ pay a ransom he does not owe, or trick his opponent out of a title that does not exist, he is putting himself in distinguished company.

From the first introduction of the metaphor of Christ as champion early in the Dobet section of the poem to the explication of Christ's name at the beginning of Dobest, Langland consistently presents Christ engaged in a legal battle with the devil for the possession of the human race: "þanne sholde Iesus Iuste þerfore, bi Iuggement of armes / Wheiþer sholde fonge þe fruyt, þe fend or hymselue" (B.16:95–96). And in his final triumph Jesus appears unambiguously as the old *Christus victor* against whom Anselm had argued so effectively:

> [Who was hardiere þan he? his herte blood he shadde
> To maken alle folk free þat folwen his lawe.]
> And siþ [alle hise lele liges largely he yeueþ]
> Places in Paradis at hir partynge hennes
> He may [be wel] called conquerour, and þat is crist to mene.
> (B.19:58–62)

Unlike Simpson, I find no traces of the Anselmian satisfaction theory in this sixth vision, and the particular passage he quotes to support his view — Christ's address to Satan: "lo! here my soule to amendes . . ." (B.18:327 ff.) — seems to me clearly to conform to the older soteriological model: unlike Anselm's God-man who must render satisfaction to God himself, Langland's Christ is here making amends directly to the devil. This is quite different from the Anselmian scheme, in which the devil is relegated to a merely supporting role.

The detailed working out of the legal motif, however, is no more consistent in Langland than it had been in Grosseteste. Humanity, for instance, cannot, strictly speaking, be both the demandant whose right is championed by Christ and at the same time the fee which is in demand, at once a party to the dispute and the object of it; the battle, in other words, cannot logically be fought by a champion wearing "Piers paltok þe Plowman" (B.18:25) in order to "fecche . . . Piers fruyt þe Plowman" (B.18:20) from the devil. Moreover, though the trial is broadly represented as a civil battle fought in accordance with writ of right procedure (this would have been the only kind of legal duel in Langland's day to permit the use of champions), it contains a number of procedural solecisms, most of which arise from his conflating the legal duel with a chivalric joust (see Clifton). Langland's battle, unlike Grosseteste's, is clearly fought to establish ownership, not of real estate, as the actual process would have required, but of movable property (the fruit of the tree of charity).[22] Though the battle itself is correctly concluded with Longinus (Death's champion) yielding himself recreant (B.18:100), the oath and counter-oath which initiate it should properly have been put in the mouths of the champions themselves not their principals:

> Deeþ seiþ he shal fordo and adoun brynge
> Al þat lyueth [or] loketh in londe [or] in watre.
> Lif seiþ þat he lieþ, and leiþ his lif to wedde.[23]
> (B.18:29–31)

Similarly, though Jesus is accurately represented as arriving barefoot for the combat (B.18:11), he is later incorrectly described as wearing a helmet and habergeon (B.18:23), and his opponent, Longinus, as armed with a spear (B.18:78).[24]

To make matters worse, at least two other kinds of lawsuit are interwoven with this principal one. In the first, humanity is a chattel which has been "attached" by the devil and held like a distrained animal in his pinfold until its owner can redeem it (B.16:261–66); this action, analogous to common law replevin (see Plucknett 1956, 367–69), is concluded by Christ's making amends to the devil by his death and duly recovering his rightful property: "So leue [it] noȝt, lucifer, ayein þe lawe I fecche hem, / But by right and by reson raunsone here my liges" (B.18:348–49). In the second, Christ as king proceeds against Lucifer as a felon (B.18:351) for stealing humankind (B.18:339) in what is clearly a criminal not a private action; since Lucifer cannot defend it, we must presume that he loses this case by default (B.18:404–6).

As in Grosseteste, weak forms of the devil's rights theory, in which Lucifer's title to humanity is shown to be unfounded (B.18:286–92), stand alongside strong forms, in which Christ is reduced to trickery in order to outwit his opponent. The ancient motif of the trickster-Christ disguising himself in human form in order to deceive the devil makes its appearance when Christ jousts in Piers's arms "that [he] be not [y]knowe here" (B.18:24) and later in his confrontation with Lucifer:

> And I in liknesse of a leode, þat lord am of heuene,
> Graciousliche þi gile haue quyt: go gile ayein gile!
> And as Adam and alle þoruȝ a tree deyden,
> Adam and alle þoruȝ a tree shul turne to lyue,
> And gile is bigiled and in his gile fallen.
> (B.18:356–60)

It is no surprise that such an account of the atonement should lead to a firm promise of salvation for those who enter the new covenant with God, in what G. H. Williams would regard as a baptismal economy rather than a eucharistic one, but Langland goes even further:

> A[c] to be merciable to man þanne my kynde [it] askeþ,
> For we beþ breþeren of blood, [ac] noȝt in baptisme alle.
> Ac alle þat beþ myne hole breþeren, in blood and in baptisme,
> Shul noȝt be dampned to þe deeþ þat [dureþ] wiþouten ende.
> (B.18:375–78)

Robert Worth Frank comments on this remarkable passage that Langland "almost says that all men will be pardoned" (94); Thomas D. Hill actually sees a clear endorsement of universal salvation at this point (1991); and Nicholas Watson regards such explicit universalism as "a vital pole of Langland's thought" (160), reflecting a kind of vernacular theology that is "a horizontal, not a top-down, affair" (171).

As we have seen, covenantal theology will tend to describe baptism as a conditional contract between the Christian and God—those who enter this contract being guaranteed salvation so long as they follow the new law.[25] While Calvin's example proves that a tendency to Pelagianism is not an inevitable consequence of covenantalism, nevertheless, as McGrath points out, "any covenant theology runs the risk of diminishing God's spontaneous graciousness and of making God appear under an obligation to man" (1981, 117); certainly such a tendency seems generally to have characterized the pastoral theology of preachers like Mirk and even to have infiltrated the scholastic theology of the *moderni*. From what has been said, it should be clear that I am in broad sympathy with those who regard Langland as a semi-Pelagian (Adams 1988a, 95–96), but seen in covenantal terms his position is nonetheless far from straightforward. For much of the central part of the poem (from the tearing of the pardon through to the harrowing of hell) the dreamer is obsessed by a paradox he finds at the very heart of the baptismal contract. Dowel, the argument runs, is either possible for sinful humanity or it is not. If it is not, how can God justly enter into a contract whose fulfillment is impossible? If it is, how can God justly deny salvation to the virtuous unbaptized, since those who respect a contract that is not even formally binding on them might be argued to be more virtuous than those who are legally obliged to respect its terms? The first horn of this covenantal dilemma threatens to undermine the importance of good works, the second the sacrament of baptism. From this perspective, the poem's pilgrimage to truth can be seen, at least in part, as an investigation into the ambiguous nature of God's troth.

Though there are some hints of it in Conscience's distinction between the two kinds of meed (B.3:231 ff.), the investigation begins in earnest with the enigmatic conclusion to the second vision where Truth sends Piers and his heirs a pardon which turns out to be no pardon at all but a simple exhortation to do well and which Piers angrily tears in two. Whatever the precise meaning of Piers's anger here (and I think it might be argued that he sees instantly, what Will must discover at painful length, the ambiguous nature of the pardon), Truth's unequivocal promise, "qui bona egerunt ibunt in vitam eternam," leads Piers to renounce his life of virtuous labor:

> "I shal cessen of my sowyng," quod Piers, "& swynke no3t so harde,
> Ne aboute my [bilyue] so bisy be no moore;
> Of preieres and penaunce my plou3 shal ben herafter,
> And wepen whan I sholde [werche] þou3 whete breed me faille.
> . . . .
> That loueþ god lelly his liflode is ful esy."
>
> (B.7:122–27)

The full meaning of this gesture, as Malcolm Godden suggests (149–50,) will not really be made clear until after we meet Haukyn the Active Man. Haukyn, who associates himself with Piers in his very first speech (B.13:237), and whom the C-text actually calls "Peres prentys" (15:195), explains to Conscience the difficulty he has in keeping clean his baptismal "cote of Cristendom" (B.13:273):

> And kouþe I neuere, by crist! kepen it clene an houre
> That I ne soiled it wiþ si3te or som ydel speche,
> Or þoru3 werk or þoru3 word or wille of myn herte
> That I ne flobre it foule fro morwe til euen.
>
> (B.14:12–15)

And in a speech strongly reminiscent of Piers's earlier one, Patience suggests that, if he will only renounce his life of labor, God will provide:

> "And I shal purueie þee paast," quod Patience, "þou3 no plou3 erye,
> And flour to fede folk wiþ as best be for þe soule;
> Thou3 neuere greyn growed, ne grape vpon vyne,
> All þat lyueþ and lokeþ liflode wolde I fynde
> And þat ynogh; shal noon faille of þyng þat hem nedeþ:
> *Ne soliciti sitis &c.*"
>
> (B.14:29–33)

As we have seen, Patience's exposition of the virtues of poverty contains one of the poem's strongest assertions of faith in God's covenant (B.14:260–61), but so hard is the fulfillment of its condition that Haukyn is led to bewail the burden of having to live in a world where sin is unavoidable:

> "Allas," quod Haukyn þe Actif man þo, "þat after my cristendom
> I ne hadde be deed and doluen for dowelis sake!
> So harde it is," quod Haukyn, "to lyue and to do synne."
>
> (B.14:323–25)

At this point in the poem a baptismal contract conditional on doing well (or rather, on not doing evil) seems to offer but a slim hope of salvation. However, as we shall see, a counter-movement which holds out a genuine promise of reward for virtue has already been set on foot.

Haukyn's soiled halter (B.14:1–15), as Langland implies when he links it with a quotation from Luke 14:20, is intended to recall the parable of the wedding guest whose lack of an appropriate garment condemns him to outer darkness (Matt. 22:13). In neither Luke nor Matthew is it specifically stated that this guest is dressed in foul clothes but Langland was not alone in making this assumption. The opening section of *Cleanness* expounds the parable at some length, and its description of the wedding guest's appearance reminds one immediately of Haukyn:

> A þral þryȝt in þe þrong unþryvandely cloþed,
> Ne no festival frok, bot fyled with werkkes;
> Þe gome watz ungarnyst wyth god men to dele.
> And gremed þerwyth þe grete lord, and greve hym he þoȝt.
> "Say me, frende," quod þe freke with a felle chere,
> "Hou wan þou into þis won in wedez so fowle?
> . . . .
> How watz þou hardy þis hous for þyn unhap [to] neȝe,
> In on so ratted a robe and rent at þe sydez?"
>
> (135–44)

Like Langland, the Cotton-Nero poet makes the coat emblematic of its wearer's spiritual state (169–72) and, though in much shorter compass, lists the sins whose stains will bar his entry to the heavenly feast (177–92). As was the case with *Patience*, however, the contrasts with Langland here prove far more instructive than the parallels.

Cleanness's consistently authoritarian perspective—arising from what Charles Muscatine has called its poet's "allegiance to high-medieval feudalism"

(40)—allows little room for the kind of sympathy for the poor and the afflicted demonstrated in *Piers Plowman*. On Langland's eschatological balance sheet, the "muche murþe" taken by the rich "in mete and cloþyng" (B.14:157) is due for repayment after death, while the poor may feel confident of their share of heavenly mirth as compensation for a life of "langour and defaute" here on earth (B.14:118); for the Cotton-Nero poet, by contrast, the association between vice and shabby clothing makes virtue appear an almost exclusively aristocratic attribute:

For what urþly haþel þat hyȝ honor haldez
Wold lyke if a ladde com lyþerly attyred,
When he were sette solempnely in a sete ryche?
(*Cleanness* 35–37)

Where the master in Luke's version of the parable sends his servant to search out replacements for his recalcitrant guests among the poor, the maimed, the halt, and the blind (14:21), the Cotton-Nero poet carefully respects the rules of precedence by filling his hall with bachelors and squires (86–87), before turning as a last resort to "blynde and balterande cruppelez" (103).

Like Langland (though with little of his passionate self-engagement), the Cotton-Nero poet asks how salvation is possible in a world where sin is unavoidable:

Þus is he kyryous and clene þat þou his cort askes;
Hou schulde þou com to his kyth bot if þou clene were?
Nou ar we sore and synful and souly uch one,
Hou schulde we se, þen may we say, þat Syre upon throne?
(1109–12)

He answers, with a confidence quite alien to Haukyn, that it is to be attained through sacramental grace:

Ȝis, þat Mayster is mercyable, þaȝ þou be man fenny
And al tomarred in myre, whyl þou on molde lyvyes;
Þou may schyne þurȝ schryfte, þaȝ þou haf schome served,
And pure þe with penaunce tyl þou a perle worþe.
(1113–16)

Just as the pearl shines more brightly when it is washed in wine (1127), the sinful soul may "polyce hym at þe prest" (1131) in preparation for its heavenly reward. This is the answer of a poet who understands theological truth quite differently from Langland.

Trawþe is, indeed, an important term in *Cleanness*, but its primary denotation is that of 'faith', a sense, I have suggested, that was mainly current in the north at this time. Adam's disobedience is described as a failure "in trawþe" (236), the temple is destroyed because the Jews "in her fayth watz founden untrwe" (1161), and Nebuchadnezzar, after his return to sanity, is said to have "l[o]ved þat Lorde and leved in trawþe" (1703). God's covenant here retains little of the old sense of reciprocity; as soon as we try to think of it as a contract between God and humanity, we see at once how very one-sided it is. As Michael W. Twomey puts it, *Cleanness* "is a poem of divine justice in which sinners are judged according to the requirements of the covenant of faith and obedience — *trawþe* — and then destroyed by a Deity whose demand for purity is absolute and inflexible" (117). True, the poet's tone is harsher because his examples of broken faith are taken from the Old Testament, but even his paraphrase of the sixth beatitude, which serves as the text for this verse sermon (Brzezinski 167–68), effectively weakens its covenantal force:

Þe haþel clene of his hert hapenez ful fayre,
For he schal loke on oure Lorde wyth a bone chere;
As so saytz, to þat syȝt seche schal he never
þat any unclannesse hatz on, auwhere abowte.
(27–30)

In other words, an unequivocal commitment to reward the clean in heart with the sight of God ("beati mundo corde quoniam ipsi Deum videbunt") is restated as a threat that those who retain any vestige of uncleanness will be denied such a sight. On at least two occasions later in the poem (549–52; 573–76) a similar construction is put on this beatitude.

Langland, too, had seen penitence as a way of cleansing the soul's sin-stained garments (B.14:16–24). Indeed, compared with the Cotton-Nero poet's harsh view of the consequences of backsliding (*Cleanness* 1133–48), he seems prepared to allow it even greater efficacy: "Confession and knowlichynge [and] crauynge þi mercy / Shulde amenden vs as manye siþes as man wolde desire" (B.14:187–88). However, Haukyn, as we have seen, is not reassured — no doubt because, as he has already told us, an hour after the priest has shriven him his coat is as soiled as before (B.14:12). Of course, Haukyn's tears, which bring to an end the fourth vision, can be taken as a positive sign — a manifestation of the *cordis contricio* without which sacramental penance, as Patience makes clear (B.14:196–98), is an empty gesture. Nevertheless, the central problem is still unresolved: Haukyn weeps, not merely for his past sins, but for the inevitability of his future ones, and thus puts himself in danger of *wanhope* (cf. B.13:406–8). The passus that follows (passus 15), a stepping stone from Dowel to Dobet, is one of the longest and most difficult in the poem, but by the time Will blesses Anima "for Haukyns loue þe Actif man" at the opening of passus 16 we feel that an answer has begun to emerge. In order to understand its significance, however, we must return to an earlier stage of the debate.

In the inner dream of the third vision, which occupies most of passus 11, Scripture had been shown preaching a sermon on the parable of the wedding guest with particular emphasis on the harsh lesson with which Matthew concludes it (22:14):

> *Multi* to a mangerie and to þe mete were sompned,
> And whan þe peple was plener comen þe porter vnpynned þe yate
> And plukked in *Pauci* pryueliche and leet þe remenaunt go rome.
> (B.11:112–14)

Langland does not give us the substance of Scripture's sermon, but he may well have had in mind the kind of austere theology the Cotton-Nero poet offers us when he suggests that it would have done little to strengthen the faith of "lewed men" (B.11:108–10). Certainly, Scripture's earlier strictures, by leading Will to question whether we can truly learn anything of our prospects for salvation, had precipitated the heedless concupiscence with which this inner dream had begun. Once again, her effect on Will is to plunge him into doubt over the certainty of salvation, and more specifically over the efficacy of his own baptismal compact with God:

> Al for tene of hir text trembled myn herte,
> And in a weer gan I wexe, and wiþ myself to dispute
> Wheiþer I were chosen or noȝt chosen; on holi chirche I þouȝte
> That vnderfonged me atte font for oon of goddes chosene.
> (B.11:115–18)

He has no sooner managed to reassert his faith in this pact and the rights that it confers — "'Thanne may alle cristene come,' quod I, 'and cleyme þere entree / By þe blood þat he bouȝte vs wiþ, and þoruȝ bapteme after'" (B.11:123–24) — than he is confronted with the disturbing example of one who has escaped from hell without having entered into any covenant with God whatsoever.

Trajan's first words, "Ye? baw for bokes!" (B.11:140), by associating him with the *lewed* rather than the *lered*, immediately places him in the context of the debate between Will and Scripture on the importance of learning (*clergie*) to salvation which frames the inner dream. This debate, first sparked by Will's naive faith in the baptismal covenant (B.10:349–51), had led to his celebration of the life of simple faith at the end of passus 10:

> Arn none raþer yrauisshed fro þe riȝte bileue
> Than are þise [kete] clerkes þat konne manye bokes,
> Ne none sonner saued, ne sadder of bileue,
> Than Plowmen and pastours and [pouere] commune laborers,
> Souteres and shepheres; [swiche] lewed Iuttes
> Percen with a Paternoster þe paleys of heuene
> And passen Purgatorie penauncelees at hir hennes partyng
> Into þe [parfit] blisse of Paradis for hir pure bileue,
> That inparfitly here knewe and eke lyuede.
>
> (10:463–71)

Yet Trajan's abrupt intrusion poses an immediate threat to this pious idyll. Langland goes out of his way to emphasize the fact that Trajan was never baptized. Twice the emperor describes himself as "an vncristene creature" (B.11:143 and 155); Ymaginatif is even more explicit: "Troianus was a trewe knyght and took neuere cristendom" (B.12:283). Clearly, then, he can have had no share in the "pure bileue" that had given Will's idealized common laborers a safe-conduct to heaven despite their imperfections. On the contrary, Langland leaves little doubt that his salvation is owed solely to his good works and to his unwavering devotion to ethical truth, certainly not to some kind of sacramental intervention on his behalf: "Nouȝt þoruȝ preiere of a pope but for his pure truþe / Was þat Sarsen saued" (B.11:156–57).[26] Ironically, then, Will's assumption that "[a] barn wiþouten bapteme may noȝt be saued" (B.11:82) is first tested, not by the "lettred men" whom he truculently challenges, but by this scorner of books.

Judged by all but the most liberal theological standards of his day, Langland's account of Trajan's salvation here is heterodox. Some, including Aquinas, were prepared to allow that salvation might be possible for the righteous heathen who had never had the chance to learn of the Christian faith, but Trajan certainly does not fall into that category. Nor, at least not in Langland's account, did he enjoy the benefits of a posthumous baptism like that performed by Saint Erkenwald. *St. Erkenwald* makes clear that its central figure (like Trajan, that rarest of medieval creatures, an honest judge) had lived long before the Christian era—"a paynym vnpreste þat neuer thi plite knewe" (285)—yet had still had to wait for his uncorrupted body to be baptized with a bishop's tears—"þe bryȝt bourne of þin eghen—my bapteme is worthyn" (330)—before he could enter heaven. Gordon Whately indeed argues that *St.*

Erkenwald "presents the story in such a way as to magnify the role and prestige of the bishop and the visible sacramental church" (342) in order to counter just such "radical antiecclesiastical interpretations of the Gregory/Trajan story" (353) as *Piers Plowman*'s. Langland's position here does not seem to have been a totally idiosyncratic one, however, for Walter Hilton implies that it was a common error: "þese men gretly and greuously erre þat saien þat Iewes and Sareȝeins, bi keping of þeir own law, moun be mad saf þawȝ þei trowe not in Ihesu Crist als haly kirke trowes, in als mikel as þei wene þat þeir owne trowþ is good and siker and suffisaunt to þair saluacioun, and in þat trouþ þei doo, as it semes, many gode dedes of riȝtwisnes, and perauenture if þei knewe þat cristen feiþ ware better þen þaires is þei wold leue þeire own and take it þat þei þerfore schuld be saf. Nai, it is not inowȝ so" (quoted by N. Watson 175 n. 8). Whether Hilton is thinking of ill-considered popular opinions or the dangerous semi-Pelagianism of the *moderni* in this passage is unclear, but a story in Mechtild of Hackeborn's *Booke of Gostlye Grace* confirms that such questions were being widely debated: when Mechtild, prompted by a friar, asks God about the fate of Trajan, he refuses to tell her, arguing that it is better to leave people in ignorance "þat the fayth of holy cherch þorowe þat be þe more enhausede and worscheppede" (570).

Although Trajan aligns himself with the *lewed* in the inner dream of passus 11, the return to the outer vision in passus 12 sees his cause taken up by one of the poem's most stalwart defenders of *clergie*, Ymaginatif. Ymaginatif's prediction of salvation for those who do what is in them to do (B.12:32–39) and his confidence that the just are to be saved, however narrowly (B.12:281–82), mark him as precisely the kind of theologian who would have roused Bradwardine's ire, and I suspect Janet Coleman is right to see in him a representative of the semi-Pelagian *moderni*. Langland may be temperamentally attracted to such a position, but he is clearly aware of its difficulties. When Ymaginatif defends Trajan with arguments which are strikingly similar to the ones Hilton dismisses, we are meant, I fancy, to be conscious of their dangerous radicalism:

> Ac truþe þat trespased neuere ne trauersed ayeins his lawe,
> But lyueþ as his lawe techeþ and leueþ þer be no bettre,
> And if þer were he wolde amende, and in swich wille deieþ—
> Ne wolde neuere trewe god but [trewe] truþe were allowed.
> (B.12:287–90)

If Haukyn represents one horn of the dilemma that sets the need for a baptismal covenant against the necessity of living well, Ymaginatif represents the other, and like Haukyn his function is primarily heuristic.

Langland's purpose in this part of the poem may well have been misunderstood by his contemporaries for many of the revisions in the C-text seem designed to allay suspicions that its author might himself be harboring radical sympathies. The removal of Will's debate with Scripture about the baptismal covenant, the refashioning of Rechelesnesse into what Janet Coleman regards as a "poetic counterpart" of Thomas Bradwardine (145), and the heavy reduction of Haukyn's role (including cutting his reaction to Patience's sermon) certainly move the C-text "away from the more radical *modern* ethic of Ockham and Holcot, with its emphasis on salvation through good works performed naturally" (J. Coleman 145), but they are also part of a wider reconsideration of covenantalism in the poem and its theology of entitlement. From this perspective the revisions in these Dowel passus are of a piece with such earlier rewriting as the introduction of the distinction between *mede* and *mercede* (C.3) or the suppression of the tearing of the pardon (C.9). To take only one example: Ymaginatif in the B-text ends his discussion of Trajan with a covenantal acrostic on the word *deus* ("*d*ans *e*ternam *u*itam *s*uis") which he calls "a greet mede to truþe" (B.12:294), but the C-text replaces this acrostic with a quotation from the parable of the talents, "quia super pauca fuisti fideles" (Matt.25:23), and a gloss to the effect that our salvation must always depend on God's generosity not his good faith:

> And þat is loue and large huyre, yf þe lord be trewe,
> And a cortesye more þen couenant was, what so clerkes carpe,
> For al worth as god wol.
>
> (C.14:215–17)

I suspect that, where the B-text generally reflects Langland's sympathy for a theology of entitlement that was omnipresent in traditional culture, the C-text attempts, not always successfully or consistently, to modify views he feared might be taken as support for scholastic opinions whose orthodoxy was seriously in question.

Trajan's is not the only irregular salvation to be considered in the central passus of *Piers Plowman*, and his antitype is provided by the thief crucified with Jesus (B.10:420–27), who is clearly saved not by merit but by faith. Ymaginatif, Langland's most prominent spokesman for a theology of entitlement, refers to the doctrine of heavenly degree, when he considers the status of this thief:

> Ac þou3 þat þeef hadde heuene he hadde noon hei3 blisse,
> As seint Iohan and oþere Seintes þat deserued hadde bettre.
> Ri3t as som man yeue me mete and [sette me amydde þe floor];
> [I] hadde mete moore þan ynou3, ac no3t so muche worshipe

As þo þat seten at þe syde table or wiþ þe soucreynes of þe halle,
But as a beggere bordlees by myself on þe grounde.
(B.12:196–201)

Such a view would no doubt have seemed perfectly reasonable to the dreamer in *Pearl*—"quen mad on þe fyrst day!" (486)—but, despite its unexceptionable orthodoxy, it had been strongly rejected by the Pearl-maiden herself:

The court of þe kyndom of God alyue
Hatȝ a property in hytself beyng:
Alle þat may þerinne aryue
Of all þe reme is quen oþer kyng.[27]
(445–48)

Once again, such comparison between Langland and the Cotton-Nero poet sheds some interesting light on their opposing attitudes to the nature of God's covenant.

Of the four poems in the Cotton Nero A.10 manuscript, *Pearl* confronts the problems of a theology of entitlement most directly. At its heart lies Matthew's perplexing parable of the workers in the vineyard, retold in great detail by the Pearl-maiden in order to convince the skeptical dreamer that her heavenly status is no anomaly (501–72). This parable, by portraying God's relationship with humanity in terms of a contractual agreement between the owner of an estate and his day laborers creates obvious difficulties for the anticovenantalist: if the penny wage offered by the master and accepted by his workers represents heaven, then those who have toiled through the heat of the day are undeniably entitled to their reward, regardless of what they believe is owed to others who have worked a shorter shift:

Frende, no waning I wyl þe ȝete;
Take þat is þyn owne, and go.
And I hyred þe for a peny agrete,
Quy byggyneȝ þou nou to þrete?
Watȝ not a pené þy couenaunt þore?
Fyrre þen couenaunde is noȝt to plete.
(558–63)

On the other hand, the covenantalist can take little comfort from the householder's refusal to tailor reward to merit, nor from the grim moral which this parable shares with that of the ill-dressed wedding guest, that "mony ben called, þaȝ fewe be mykeȝ" (572). Can this mean that their last-minute grumbling costs the first-hired the reward their day-long toil had earned them? This is certainly the way the Harley lyricist interprets the ending:

> Þis mon þat Matheu ȝef
> a peny þat was so bref
> þis frely folk vnfete,
> ȝet he ȝyrnden more,
> ant saide he come wel ȝore,
> ant gonne is loue forlete.
> (*Harley Lyrics* 10:55–60)

Other commentators find the possibility of such an interpretation so repugnant to their sense of justice that they prefer to cavil at Matthew's word *murmurabant*: for Ælfric it had expressed the laborers' sadness (*heora gnornung*) at having been kept so long from the heavenly kingdom (*Catholic Homilies* 46:156–60), while the author of the *English Wycliffite Sermons* even goes so far as to interpret it as "wondryng in sowle and þankyng of Godis grace" (1:382). Only by means of such forced readings as these is the medieval preacher able to reassure his flock that "God doþ no wrong to hem" in this parable.

For all the difficulties of this central text, the Cotton-Nero poet shows no more sympathy with a theology of entitlement in *Pearl* than he had in *Patience* or *Cleanness*. The Pearl-maiden follows her retelling of the parable of the vineyard with the unequivocal declaration that she has more joy in her heavenly reward "Þen alle þe wyȝeȝ in þe worlde myȝt wynne / By þe way of ryȝt to aske dome" (579–80). When the dreamer complains that God seems to be acting unjustly, she quotes him Psalm 142:2, "in thy sight no living man shall be justified," and issues a dire warning against regarding salvation as a matter of legal right:

> Forþy to corte quen þou schal com
> Þer alle oure causeȝ schal be tryed,
> Alegge þe ryȝt, þou may be innome,
> By þys ilke spech I haue asspyed.
> (701–04)

The heavy use of legal terminology in this passage has been noted by Dorothy Everett and Naomi Hurnard, whose gloss is surely correct: "Therefore, when you shall come to court where all our cases shall be tried, if you plead [legal] right, . . . you may be . . . refuted in argument by this [verse from Psalm 142] that I have seen" (11). Though the Pearl-maiden had sketched two paths to salvation—"Þe ryȝtwys man schal se hys face, / Þe harmleȝ haþel schal com hym tylle" (675–76)—righteousness appears almost as insubstantial a state for the Cotton-Nero poet here as it had been for Haukyn, while the only kind of entitlement the poet truly recognizes seems to be that conferred by the postbaptismal innocence of the Pearl-maiden herself. When she prays that the dreamer may be saved "by innocens and not by ryȝte" (708) she is clearly alluding to salvation by grace not merit, for, as the poem's final lines make clear, the best sinful humanity can hope for is the sacramental innocence offered by Christ through his Eucharist:

Þat in þe forme of bred and wyn
Þe preste vus scheweȝ vch a daye.
He gef vus to be his homly hyne
Ande precious perleȝ vnto his pay.
(1209–12)

A God to whom everything is owed and from whom nothing is due is fittingly epitomized in this final line with its echoes, as Howard Schless has shown, of the old absolutist maxim *quod principi placet, habet legis vigorem*.

Langland's version of the choice between the paths to heaven taken by the "ryȝtwys man" and the "harmleȝ haþel" is framed as a choice between Trajan and Haukyn, neither of whom, as we have seen, appears a very safe guide. Haukyn's example had taught the hard lesson that the sacramental innocence Conscience offers (B.14:16–28) can only guarantee salvation when fortified by a life of penitential austerity such as Patience recommends (B.14:276–322)—a life enviably accessible to the "pouere commune laborer" perhaps, but permanently closed to Will's lettered introspection. His pilgrimage to truth had thus been sidetracked into a fruitless quest for sinlessness (from "do well" to "do no evil"), and Anima in passus 15 must return Will to the more optimistic search for positive virtue. The path toward which Trajan had gestured is now reopened in the context of the Christian covenant.

For the modern reader, Anima's long discourse on the conversion of the heathen (B.15:387–613) is not one of *Piers Plowman*'s most rewarding passages, but it allows Langland to return to an aspect of the divine covenant raised by Scripture when Will had first expressed his naive faith in baptism as a guarantee of salvation. The promise that "That is baptiȝed beþ saaf," she had explained, refers only to those heathens baptized *in extremis* (B:10:351–53),[28] but Christians have more stringent conditions to fulfill: "For euery cristene creature sholde be kynde til ooþer, / And siþen heþen to helpe in hope of amendement" (B.10:368–69). That performing works of charity should be regarded as a condition of God's covenant is unsurprising in itself but that Langland should choose to concentrate on this specific work is significant. By singling out the conversion of the heathen, Anima makes it clear that Ymaginatif's view of extracovenantal salvation is dangerously extreme:

> so it fareþ by a barn þat born is of wombe;
> Til it be cristned in cristes name and confermed of þe bisshop,
> It is heþene as to heueneward and helplees to þe soule.
> (B.15:456–58)

Furthermore, he portrays proselytizing as a charitable task that is particularly suited to the *lered* and one quite as likely to provide them with opportunities for patient suffering as a life of *lewed* poverty (B.15:269–306). Langland in fact reads the eschatological parables that are so important to *Pearl* and *Cleanness* as specific lessons for the priesthood. Laboring in the vineyard is interpreted as preaching the word of God: "For cristene and vncristene crist seide to prechours / *Ite vos in vineam meam &c.*" (B.15:499–500);[29] and those who refuse the invitation to the wedding feast are pointedly said to be the indolent prelates "þat han hir wil here" (B.15:486–88). Finally, by making conversion of the heathen his example of Dowel Langland can look back to that heroic age when "Elleuene holy men al þe world tornede" (B.15:438), when Augustine of Canterbury first taught the English the "cros to honoure" (B.15:447), and when even kings (like Edmund and Edward) might become patterns of charity (B.15:223–24). There is clear nostalgia here for the theological economy founded on the "sacral enrollment of each Christian recruit under *Christus victor*" (G. H. Williams 64) that had been dealt a mortal blow by Anselm. Thus, passus 15 not only revives the question of Trajan's conversion in the Dowel section of the poem, but anticipates Christ's crucifixion in passus 18 (Dobet's supreme example of charity), and Dobest's building of the barn of Unity in passus 19. It is no accident that the great motif of Christ the champion first makes its appearance in this passus (B.15:216).

By making honest marriage his first example of Dowel in passus 12, Ymaginatif had revealed his faith in salvation for those who, as the *moderni* would say, do what is in them to do:

> For he dooþ wel, wiþouten doute, þat dooþ as lewte techeþ.
> That is, if þow be man maryed þi make þow louye
> And lyue forþ as lawe wole while ye lyuen boþe.
> (B.12:32–34)

For Haukyn, on the other hand, the first stains to spoil the garment in which he will be called to the heavenly wedding feast are the direct result of his own married state:

"I haue but oon hool halter," quod haukyn, "I am þe lasse to blame
Thouȝ it be soiled and selde clene: I slepe þerInne o nyȝtes;
And also I haue an houswif, hewen and children—
Vxorem duxi ideo non possum venire—
That wollen bymolen it many tyme maugree my chekes."
(B.14:1–4)

Like Haukyn, Will is married, but when his wife and daughter are introduced at the end of the sixth vision, it is, significantly, to affirm a renewed faith in the power of God's covenant:

men rongen to þe resurexion, and riȝt wiþ þat I wakede
And called kytte my wif and Calote my doghter:
"[Ariseþ] and reuerence[þ] goddes resurexion,
And crepe[þ] to þe cros on knees and kisse[þ] it for a Iuwel
For goddes blissede body it bar for oure boote;
And it afereþ þe fend, for swich is þe myȝte
May no grisly goost glide þere it [shadweþ]."
(B.18:425–31)

If there is any truth in my claim that the contrast between Haukyn and Ymaginatif provides Langland with a framework for exploring the difficult question of God's troth, there can be no better illustration of his own deep sympathy with the traditional position than this powerful rejection of Haukyn's pessimism at the end of passus 18.

Langland's covenantalism certainly aligns him more closely with Holcot than with Bradwardine, and its articulation may indeed owe something to the teaching of the *moderni*,[30] but its roots run far deeper than the Oxford schools of his youth. Will draws Kytte and Calote to his side beneath the comforting shelter of the cross after witnessing Christ's triumphant battle to restore rights that were ancient even when Anselm was writing. It is a moving gesture of communal faith in the protective power of God's covenant, but, like the neighborly piety of Mirk's sermons, it belongs to a world already under threat. Divine trothplight, despite the brief respectability accorded it by the *moderni*,[31] had in the end to succumb to Ricardian *truth* as surely as its human counterpart would do. Standing on the other side of the cultural shift this book has sought to chronicle, we can barely still trace our lineage back to Will's shadowy family; our true genealogy can only begin with the lonely father of *Pearl*.

Epilogue

In the first story of the *Decameron* we are introduced to a crooked lawyer, Ser Ceperello of Prato, who makes so hypocritical a death-bed confession while on a visit to Burgundy that the local populace is led to venerate him as a saint after his death. At one period of his life, Boccaccio tells us, this unprincipled man had made a handsome living for himself in Paris, for "in France at that time the very greatest confidence was placed in oaths, so, having no worries about perjuring himself, he would dishonestly win any lawsuit that depended upon his being called upon to swear on his faith to speak the truth" (*Opere* 4:34). Since the date of Ser Ceperello's fictional death can be fixed from historical references within the tale to the very beginning of the fourteenth century (his journey to Burgundy is prompted by Charles Sans Terre's invasion of Italy in 1301), and since we know that Boccaccio himself was writing the *Decameron* some fifty years later, it is very tempting to see this story as offering firm evidence for dating a crucial period in the breakdown of ethical and legal truth in France to the first half of the fourteenth century, and to assume that, just as the English were to become aware of the same kind of breakdown over the following half century, so Italians must have experienced something similar fifty years earlier. However superficially attractive so neat a time scheme might appear, it must be taken with a generous pinch of salt, for as we have seen the crisis of truth in England (and, by inference, in other of European countries) was very much more protracted, uneven, and sporadic than Boccaccio's deceptively simple account might suggest. Nonetheless, the north/south axis to which he draws attention in this tale is an intriguing one, if only because it offers me an opportunity to broaden the primary focus of my study.

Clanchy cites a notary called Giovanni di Bologna, who, while in the service of John Pecham, archbishop of Canterbury, in the 1280s, drew the following distinction between the legal practices of the English and those of his compatriots: "Italians, like cautious men, want to have a public instrument for practically every contract they enter into," he wrote, "but the English are just the opposite, and an instrument is very rarely asked for unless it is essential" (1993, 52). Whether or not, as Clanchy claims, Giovanni underestimates the importance of written records to the English at this period, his testimony as to their *comparative* importance (or rather unimportance) remains compelling.

There is every reason to believe that "trust in the authority of written word developed more rapidly on the European continent than in England, where oral procedure was preserved in the legal procedures of the common law" (Bäuml 1984, 45). It is very difficult to imagine a lawyer in Ricardian England speaking of the unwritten customary law of his own country with the venom of the Neapolitan jurist Lucas de Penna (d. ca. 1390): "Langobardae non merentur leges dici, sed foeces" [they better deserve the name Lombard turds than Lombard laws] (quoted by W. Ullmann 1969, 73).[1] Neither can one imagine an English merchant in Chaucer's London writing in his notebook, as did the Florentine Giovanni di Pagolo Morelli (ca. 1400): "Never trust anyone; make things clear—more so with a relative or friend than with outsiders, but with everybody; use notarial forms, with bonds released through a guild; do not trust a document copied into books, except by a third party" (quoted by Klapisch-Zuber 78 n. 50).[2] The surviving account book of Gilbert Mawfield does not begin to approach Morelli's exacting standards; some loans are secured with bonds, some by warrantors, some with sealed indentures, some with objects in pawn, and some—including one to Geoffrey Chaucer (*CLR* 500)—with no recorded security at all (Rickert 114–15). Like many later travelers to Italy, Chaucer must surely have noticed they did things differently there.[3]

I draw attention to the Italian experience because it has an important bearing on the later social history of truth in England. As *truth* made further inroads into the semantic territory formerly occupied by *sooth*, it left a sizable gap in the ethical vocabulary of the language; when one could no longer refer to the 'trouthe' of a trustworthy person without fear of being misunderstood what other terms were available? One word, above all, came to fill this gap, *honesty*. It is something of a surprise to learn that the *OED*'s first recorded instance of the prevailing modern sense of this word ('uprightness of disposition and conduct; integrity, truthfulness, straightforwardness: the quality opposed to lying, cheating or stealing' [s.v. *honesty* 3d.]) is as late as 1579—though we should note that this sense had been anticipated by the adjectival form a generation or so earlier (Empson 186–87). William Empson's lively essays have made abundantly clear how rich a source of irony and ambiguity the word *honest* was in the period between Queen Elizabeth and Queen Anne (185–249), but he shows little interest in the earliest history of the word, nor is he concerned with discovering "why it is only in English that this romance word has come to mean telling truth" (185). This is certainly not the place to remedy his omission, but I want to make one rather obvious etymological point: Latin *honestas* is cognate with *honor* and originally denoted a social rather than a moral or legal attribute (Andreas Capellanus's *Liber de arte honeste amandi* is a disquisition on aristocratic, noble, or courtly love, certainly not love that is either moral or licit). The semantic extension of the English word *honesty*, then, might properly be seen as symptomatic of that new cultural vocabulary that Marvin Becker associates with the onset of a civil society in Italy in the late thirteenth century (and in northern Europe two centuries later), and which he regards as marking a tilt away from "an overdetermined world of archaic obligation, feudal solidarity, and communal restriction" (83).

Becker is stronger on symptoms than diagnoses but he leaves the impression that he believes the steady northward migration of the civil society in the late Middle Ages and early Renaissance to have been primarily a matter of Italian cultural prestige. Though there were certainly those in Tudor England who would have agreed with him, English attitudes to Italy in the sixteenth century were often ambiguous and might even be described as schizophrenic (K. Bartlett 46): if for some Italy was "the graduate school of humanism and the *vita civile*" (49), for many others it was an "arena of murder, treachery, licentiousness, and atheism" (46). As Bartlett points out, there was a tendency for the first view to be promulgated by courtiers, and the second by "teachers, scholars, publicists and patriots" (59), but perhaps the most striking thing about the two attitudes is that they cannot simply be put down to religious partiality; the *italianati* prove quite as liable to have been stern Puritans as High Anglicans (47). While it should be evident from everything that has gone before that I am unlikely to waste much time scraping about in the thin topsoil of Italian humanism for the roots of whatever general "tilt away from an archaic society" Tudor England experienced (see Becker 140), it is, nonetheless, in my view entirely understandable that the old concept of trouthe dislodged by this tilt should have found its main replacement in the idiom of the *vita civile*.

During the late Middle Ages, as we have seen, it was becoming increasingly difficult to maintain the fiction that law and morality were indivisible, and by the sixteenth century the fissure that had opened up between the two could no longer be ignored, even in England. Thomas Wilson's *Discourse on Usury* (1572), which agues that the regulation of this commercial reality should be transferred from the preacher to the lawyer, has been cited as a symptom of the new attitude (Alford 1977, 948), yet in actuality even religion was hardly any longer much of a counterweight to law in the new Tudor regime of truth; in so far as honesty was grounded anywhere, it was in the vocabulary of gentility.[4] That is why a seductive Italy that had already passed through its transition to a civil society posed such a threat for Tudor reactionaries like Sir John Cheke, Roger Ascham, and William Harrison; here, for instance, is how Harrison (1577) represents the typical attitudes of young English gentlemen newly returned from Italy: "Faith and truth is to be kept where no loss or hindrance of a further purpose is sustained by holding of the same . . . ; He is a fool that maketh account of any religion, but more fool that will lose any part of his wealth or will come in trouble for constant leaning to any . . . ; I care not what you talk to me of God, so as I may have the prince and the laws of the realm on my side" (114–15). But while moralists like Harrison were concerned lest Italy should be turning English gentlemen into lawyers, the humanist Thomas Starkey, was arguing that the real answer lay in turning English lawyers into gentlemen: "for though thes lawys wych I have so praysyd be commyn among them, yet bycause the nobylyte ther commynly dothe not exercyse them in the studys therof, they be al applyd to lucur & gayne, bycause the popular men wych are borne in poverty only doth exercyse them for the moste parte wych ys a grete ruyne of al gud ordur & cyvylyte" (129–30).

As I have been at some pains to stress, throughout the late Middle Ages one of the main combat zones between the forces of ethical and intellectual truth had been the law,[5] but with the Renaissance a major new front was opened up (a front that still sees its share of action even in the late twentieth century): the world of experimental science. Standing with a foot in either camp, Francis Bacon saw with particular clarity that there was a distinction to be drawn between "theological and philosophical truth," on the one hand, and "the truth of civil business," on the other (342). Arguably, the objective truth investigated in seventeenth-century laboratories was hardly less permeated by ethical truth than that debated in fourteenth- and fifteenth-century courtrooms, but, as Steven Shapin has so brilliantly taught us, it was not in the court of conscience that truth was now to be adjudicated, but in the academy of gentility: "The Royal Society's 'modern' rejection of authority in scientific matters quite specifically mobilized codes of presumed equality operative in early modern gentle society. . . . While the society of schools might put one man in fear of another, conjoining institutional standing and epistemic authority, the Royal Society insisted upon egalitarian codes operative in gentlemanly conversation. Conversation was, thus, not only a mark of epistemic efficiency, it was also a civil end in itself. No conception of truth could be legitimate if pursuing and maintaining it put civil conversation at risk" (123). Such truth may have been a pale reflection of the quality that had once defined the fundamental cultural identity of Ricardian England, but by the seventeenth century its ethical and intellectual constituents had been so long disarticulated by written record that not even that "deified Mortal" Robert Boyle (Shapin 188) could put them back together again.

Appendix

Law in the Nigerian Novel: Some Ricardian Connections

> The world of the written word was opened to the Native of Africa at the time when I lived out there. I had then, if I wanted to, an opportunity of catching the past by its tail and of living through a bit of our own history: the period when the large plain population of Europe had in the same way had the letter revealed to them.
>
> Karen Blixen, *Out of Africa*

ON JANUARY 20, 1896, A DETACHMENT of British troops stormed the palace of the Ashanti king Prempeh in Kumasi, in what is now Ghana. Inside, according to one of the commanders of the expedition, Robert Baden-Powell (the future founder of the Boy Scouts), they found "piles of the tawdriest and commonest stuff mixed indiscriminately with quaint, old, and valuable articles, a few good brass dishes, large metal ewers, Ashanti stools, old arms, etc." (Bailey 390 n. 6). Predictably the palace was looted, and Major Charles Barter, a fellow officer of Baden-Powell's, took one of the large metal ewers back with him to England, where he sold it to the British Museum for fifty pounds; C. H. Read, keeper of British and Medieval Antiquities at the time, must have been surprised to discover that his department had thereby acquired a late-fourteenth-century English water jug, evidently made for use in the court of King Richard II (see frontispiece). Not the least of its interesting features is an inscription recording two middle English proverbs, one of which reads, "DEME THE BEST IN EVERY DOUT / TIL THE TROWTHE BE TRYID OWTE" (cf. Whiting B268). How this ewer made the journey from the court of a late-fourteenth-century English king to that of a late-nineteenth-century Ashanti one must always remain a mystery,[1] but however exotic the wanderings of the actual vessel itself, the cultural distance traveled by the proverbial trouthe of its inscription was arguably, as I have implied elsewhere in this book, somewhat less dramatic. I have remarked on the striking similarities between the premises underlying medieval folklaw and the traditional legal order revealed in twentieth-century West African fiction, and I shall here attempt to articulate these parallels in a more systematic way; at the very least, this appendix may serve as a useful introduction to one aspect of the literature of Nigeria for those readers who have as yet had no opportunity to explore this remarkably rich and suggestive body of work.

To make comparative claims about the effects of oppression is always to risk betraying an outsider's insensitivity, yet there is one sense, I believe, in which the hand of colonialism rested more lightly on the interior of southern Nigeria than on many other regions of Africa. The sacking of King Prempeh's palace in Ghana took place towards the end of the period of Victorian expansion into Africa, yet even so the equivalent assault upon the Igbo of Nigeria was still five years away: only in 1901 did Lt. Col. L. H. Montenaro march his troops into the heart of Igboland where, after committing similar atrocities at the shrine of Aro-Chukwu near the Cross River, he raised the union jack in the name of King Edward VII.[2] By 1901 this kind of Maxim-gun adventurism had already begun to fall out of favor and a mere fifty years later Macmillan's winds of change were starting to blow through Africa. Many of the older Nigerians who watched their country's national flag replace the union jack at the independence celebrations in 1960 must have still been able to remember the first arrival of the British less than sixty years earlier. Moreover, since the climate of southern Nigeria proved inhospitable to Western farming methods, the country never attracted the kind of European settlers whose colonization of eastern and southern Africa turned the quest for independence in Kenya, Zimbabwe, and South Africa into a protracted and bloody struggle. Though southern Nigeria certainly had its fair share of missionaries and traders (those inevitable camp-followers of the colonial enterprise), and though it too suffered under the administrative clumsiness of district commissioners and their paramount chiefs, colonialism never rooted itself deep in the very soil of the country.[3] Indigenous law, in particular, seems to have survived the colonial experience relatively unscathed. Though the British established a system of local courts — first called Native (later, Customary) Courts — to enforce a hybrid mixture of imported and aboriginal law (Obilade 17–33), traditional modes of adjudication were never wholly eliminated in the south; indeed, they appear to have received a new lease on life since independence (Nzimiro 118–128).

In another sense, however, the effects of colonialism on southern Nigeria have been dramatic. Literacy has been accepted by the Igbo and Yoruba people with a rapidity and enthusiasm that is truly astonishing, and the same sixty years that have seen British colonialism come and go have witnessed a literate revolution for which it is difficult to think of a parallel.[4] That a country which still preserves its ancient oral poetry should at the same time foster a winner of the Nobel Prize for literature is quite remarkable: at the risk of sounding like a crude progressivist, which is far from my intention, to think of Wole Soyinka's being able to listen to O̱kabo Ojobolo reciting the *Ozidi* epic is a little like imagining William Golding's being able to attend an authentic performance by the *Beowulf* poet. For twentieth-century Nigerian novelists, the combination of a comparatively brief experience of colonial oppression with a extraordinarily rapid acceptance of literacy has meant that the rivalry between traditional and progressive cultures in the recent history of their country has been thrown into particularly sharp focus, and this rivalry has come to play a dominant role in much of their writing. Where authors in other African countries have been understandably drawn to focus on the struggle of their people for political independence, Nigerians, particularly those who have written so-called village novels, have been free to explore the dislocation of their traditional culture caused in large part by the introduction of literacy. As a character in Achebe's *Anthills of the Savannah* remarks, "So, two whole generations before the likes of me could take a first class degree in English, there were already barely literate carpenters and artisans of British rule hacking away in the archetypal jungle and subverting the very sounds and legends of daybreak to make straight my way" (109). For the medievalist this gives their work a particular fascination and significance.

Just like the folklaw of medieval Europe, the indigenous legal order of southern Nigeria seems to have been built squarely upon the institution of the judicial oath. Earlier in this book, I discussed accounts of the trial of Queen Isolt for adultery and the central importance in them of her oath of exculpation. Here, by way of comparison, is how the main character of Flora Nwapa's novel *Efuru* describes her exoneration from a similar charge: "I called my age-group and told them formally what I was accused of. According to the custom of our people, selected members of my age-group followed me to the shrine of our goddess — Utuosu. There I swore by the name of Utuosu, she should kill me if I committed adultery. She should kill me if since I married Eneberi any man in our town, in Onicha, Ndoni, Akiri, or anywhere I had been, had seen my thighs. I remained for seven Nkwos and now I am absolved. Utuosu did not kill me. I am still alive. That means I am not an adulterous woman" (220). It is difficult to resist the temptation of pointing out the striking verbal coincidence of "[no] man in our town . . . had seen my thighs" with Béroul's "entre mes cuisses n'entra home," but of course the differences are almost as marked. Quite apart from the simple fact that Efuru, unlike Iseut, is innocent and thus has no need to employ equivocation or a tricked oath to clear herself, there is the obvious gender differentiation here: Efuru is not required to appear before a male tribunal in order to clear her name. There is also the interesting time limit (seven Nkwos) set on the goddess's retribution; this feature appears in other novels—for instance, with Olumba's oath in Amadi's *Great Ponds* (86)—and is clearly no inconsequential detail.[5] I know of no similar form in European folklaw (it would no doubt have exacerbated the church's sense of discomfort over the way the judicial oath might seem to be tempting God), but nonetheless there can be little doubt that Efuru's oath and Iseut's are at root performing an identical juridical function.

In many ways, Nigerian novelists portray a society even more willing to put its trust in the sanctity of oath-taking than that of the Anglo-Saxons. Elechi Amadi, writing of the great prestige enjoyed by the god Amadioha, insists that "no man was intrepid enough to swear by him when he was guilty" (*The Concubine* 15), and the strength of such convictions explains why Nigerian procedure, unlike that of the European folklaw, might be prepared to accept an unsupported judicial oath even in the face of potential witness proof: "even if one party was able to produce an ovewhelming number of witnesses, the other party still had the right to demand trial by swearing" (Amadi 1982, 84; cf. Meek 238–42). A number of Nigerian writers have asserted the superiority of their traditional system to Western legal process: "Modern courts of law may err at times in the dispensation of justice," writes the Igbo folklorist Rems Nna Umeasiegbu, "but cases and disputes settled with oaths are impartial" (19). We have seen that under the European folklaw the imposition of a judicial oath might be merely an incitement to further feuding, but Umeasiegbu denies the very possibility of such refractoriness among the Igbo: "No person has ever been known to have told lies to a god. The penalty for taking a false oath is instant death. The defendant and plaintiff shake hands and walk away as friends" (20). No doubt, there is a degree of wishful thinking here, but the fact remains that southern Nigerians seem to have felt far less need than medieval Europeans to resort to ancillary procedures such as combat as a way of reinforcing the operation of the judicial oath: in Amechi Akwanya's *Orimili* an aggrieved litigant in a land dispute asks rhetorically, "would you not rather do as our fathers used to do when they were beset by a greedy neighbour? Would you not sharpen your broadsword, and send word to your opponent to sharpen his and meet you at the site?" (128–29), but his companion's shocked reaction clearly indicates that such violent self-help is viewed as an entirely extralegal expedient.

Though we find occasional hints of something resembling compurgation or witness proof,[6] the main mechanism for authenticating dubious judicial oaths in Nigerian folklaw was evidently the ordeal, a process that appears to have been particularly useful in cases of suspected sorcery or witchcraft. In Achebe's *Arrow of God*, for instance, a disreputable medicine man is described as having had "more than twice . . . to take kolanut from the palm of a dead man to swear he had no hand in the death" (196), and in *The Healers*, by the Ghanaian novelist Ayi Kwei Armah, the hero, a suspect in a case of ritual murder, is confronted with having to swallow a "fatal drink of truth" in order to clear himself (118–23); this seems to be a version of the ordeal by sasswood bark (Meek 227; Amadi 1982, 86) in which the accused is required to drink a potentially lethal toxin—though in this particular case, suspecting that the ordeal has been rigged, the hero manages to escape before swallowing it. The Yoruba chief Anthony Enahoro has left us a remarkable account of an incident from his youth (in the 1930s) when an ordeal by red-hot iron was used to establish the paternity of the child of one of his mother's housemaids. He recalls handling the red-hot ax-head himself and finding it quite cool, then watching as it passed to the main suspect: "He stared at the ominous implement for some moments, gritted his teeth and put his hand to it. With a yell he let go, and his hand came away with nasty burns. Paternity was established and the maid was vindicated" (41).

Amadi suggests that ordeal was resorted to only "when doubts could not be resolved" (1982, 86), and it seems that Nigerian folklaw, no less than Anglo-Saxon, preferred its evidence to be manifest and unequivocal. Students of Old English who cut their teeth on Ælfric's *Life of Saint Edmund* will recall his story of the thieves who try to break into the saint's shrine at night, one striking on the door hasps with a hammer, another climbing to a window with a ladder, another trying to dig under the door with a spade, whilst yet one more, rather charmingly, "with a file filed about"; but they labored in vain, says Ælfric, for "the saintly man miraculously bound them, each one as he stood, working away with his tool . . . and so they remained until morning" (*Lives* 2:328–30). Though I suppose there is a possibility of its contamination from a European source, I prefer to believe that the following story from Echewa's *I Saw the Sky Catch Fire* provides independent evidence of a similar cultural need in Nigerian folklaw for evidence to be public, tangible, and incontrovertible: "Among the wonders that made Koon-Tiri legend, thieves who went to his house one night—they came from a distant town and apparently did not know whose house they were robbing—fell under a spell and were found warming themselves by a log fire the next morning, unable to leave until he lifted the spell more than a week later" (128). It is perhaps a reflection on the differing attitudes to legal authority in the two societies that the would-be robbers of Saint Edmund's tomb are hanged (on the orders of a bishop, no less), while Koon-Tiri merely exacts a week of free labor from his thieves before letting them go.

One of most common medieval institutions by which a public demonstration of manifest guilt might be secured, the hue and cry, has its close counterpart in twentieth-century West Africa. Readers of the *Canterbury Tales* will recall the boisterous rabble that chases Daun Russell to the woods in "The Nun's Priest's Tale," but the legal expedient Chaucer is there burlesquing appears in a quite different guise in Wole Soyinka's novel *The Interpreters*: "It began just behind Oyingbo market where vocational idlers sheltered briefly from the rain, emerged to filter through incautious wares, picking off a bare existence. The hunt picked them up on its way. Then the touts joined in. And the watch peddlers rammed suspect 17-jewel instruments down deep pouches and swelled the running ranks . . . Sagoe leapt off the bus and joined the throng—Run, Barabas, run, all underdog sympathetic. Run, you little thief or the bigger thieves will pass a law against your existence as a menace to society" (113–14). No doubt the translation of this particular hue and cry from village market square to downtown Lagos (together with the narrator's literate detachment, his sense of being an outsider in his own society) helps explain the sympathy for the underdog here, but in the eyes of a Western historian like Rebecca Colman, who had witnessed similar spectacles in East Africa, our own "loss of that spontaneous sense of communal responsibility" to which they attest is a matter of some regret (575). As in medieval Europe, such expressions of collective authority could certainly be cruel or misdirected, but in a local setting, at least, they might also reflect the profound sense communal integrity that is celebrated at the end of Achebe's *Arrow of God*: "No man however great was greater than his people . . . no one ever won judgement against his clan" (230).

If both West African and European folklaw prefer their evidence and proof to be public and tangible, the same is true of a common form of punishment that both share, ritual shaming. I have had occasion earlier to refer to such sanctions as the stocks, the pillory, the tumbrel, and the charivari, and, just like the lecherous priest whom John Stow recalls seeing in his youth "on three Market dayes conueyed through the high streete and Markets of the Citie with a Paper on his head, wherein was written his trespasse . . . and euery day rung with Basons" (1:190), Nigerian malefactors, too, might expect to be exposed to ritual humiliation. I. N. C. Aniebo in *Of Wives, Talismans, and the Dead*, for instance, describes a case of incest which provoked a village masquerade to sing ribald songs outside the couple's dwelling (97), and Wole Soyinka in his autobiography *Aké* recalls witnessing a regular spectacle in his hometown: "Whatever form it took, its principal feature was this: a youthful culprit with evidence of his or her transgression tied to the neck or carried on the head. Next came the guardian or parent, wielding the corrective whip from time to time. As they went through the streets layabouts and urchins were encouraged to swell the numbers, jeering and singing at the top of their voice. They picked up tins and boxes along the way and added an assortment of rhythm to which the culprit was expected to dance" (87). Among the Igbo the "custom of parading a thief through the village, with what he had stolen tied round his neck" is called *mbembe* and in *The Crippled Dancer* Echewa suggests that it is now falling out of use: "That thief! The only reason he has not been carried in *mbembe* is that this village is no longer what it used to be" (47).

There is probably a wider variation in their punitive practices than in any other aspect of the two folklaws, but in general there seems to have been rather less interest in harsh exemplary punishment in southern Nigeria than in early medieval Europe. No doubt this is in part due to a comparatively greater emphasis on compromise and reconciliation in Nigeria than in Europe: "My father told me that he had been told that in the past a man who broke the peace was dragged on the ground through the village until he died," says a village elder in Achebe's *Things Fall Apart*; "but after a while this custom was stopped because it spoilt the peace which it was meant to preserve" (22–23). In medieval Europe, as we have seen, the kind of extralegal dispute settlement embodied in the maxim *pactum legem vincit* was gradually undermined by the encroachment of centralized justice,[7] but an equivalent ethos seems to have maintained its cultural prestige in traditional Nigerian courts until very recently: "our duty is not to blame this man or to praise that," as the spokesman for a village tribunal in Achebe's *Things Fall Apart* says, "but to settle the dispute" (66). Amechi Akwanya's novel *Orimili* provides a detailed description of a prolonged land dispute which has been submitted to mediators and suggests something of the kind of social dynamic that must once have informed the corresponding institution in medieval Europe: "One had to assume that, as a titled man, Ogbuefi Ikedi would not lie; and that was a good enough reason for the arbitrators to take it that both Nwalioba and Ikedi were speaking the truth. . . . Wherever they said was the boundary between their two properties, then that was the boundary. For both were titled men, and could not lie. Therefore, if their claims failed to coincide, it must be owing to a genuine confusion. All that one had to do was to find the half-way point between Nwalioba's boundary and Ikedi's, and make it the common boundary for the two worthies!" (17). Unfortunately, such a compromise proves unacceptable to the parties and the mediators are forced to bring greater pressure to bear on them: "Uderika Nwanne, the chief speaker among the middlemen, [explained] what they were going to do if Nwalioba and Ikedi failed to come to terms. They would take over the entire property, not just the part under dispute, and they would hand it over to the town to use as a market-place" (127). It is quite clear that traditional Igbo society invested considerable authority in such arbitration methods and took a correspondingly stern view of the contumelious and the intransigent.

One final aspect of the European folklaw that I have discussed earlier in this book—its curious ability to combine an exaggerated respect for formal rules with a very practical readiness to bend them to accommodate local contingencies—is clearly present in Nigerian folklaw as well. One could hardly ask for a better illustration of this flexibility than the story told in Chinua Achebe's poem "Those Gods Are Children" of a man, convicted of killing his brother, whose punishment is deferred because he has a young family dependant upon him:

> The land and all its deities
> screamed revenge: a head for a head
> and poised their spear
> to smite the town should it
> withhold the due. The man
> was ready. The elders' council
> looked at him and turned
> from him to all the orphans doubly
> doomed and shook their heads:
> the gods are right and just! This man
> shall hang but first may he
> retrieve the sagging house
> of his fathers.
>
> (*Beware Soul Brother* 47)

Many years later, after his children have reached adulthood, as the man lies dying of a fever:

> Patient
> elders peering through the hut's dim
> light darkened more by smoke
> of smouldering fire under his bed
> steady-eyed at a guilt they had stalked
> across scrublands and seven rivers, a long-prepared
> hangman's loop in their hand
> quickly circled his neck
> as he died
>
> and the gods
> and ancestors
> were satisfied
>
> (48)

Such bending of the brittle twig of justice cannot long survive the introduction of letters, and while the optimistic young hero in Echewa's *Crippled Dancer* may eagerly await a future in which justice will have become "truly brittle and unbendable," and truth, "less kinky and knotted and more streamlined" (107), the novel itself depicts the process of transition as far from painless or uniformly benign. Faced with a similar literate calcification of legal procedure, people in the Middle Ages must often have been troubled by the way the growing prestige of written law was robbing them of their freedom to adapt narrow forms to the larger needs of social justice.

I have already suggested that one of the most intriguing aspects of recent Nigerian history is the rapid spread of literacy and the transforming effect this has had on its traditional institutions. Once again, signs of such transformation are easy to find in the work of the novelists. At root, of course, is the way written evidence threatens to compromise honor through its inability to make any allowance for honest mistake. T. M. Aluko's *One Man, One Wife*, for instance, describes a case in which an old man called Salawu sues to recover money spent on his ex-wife in the course of their brief marriage; the proceedings are adjourned for a week, and when they resume the plaintiff, asked for the second time to state the sum he is seeking to recover, gives the amount as thirty-seven pounds and eight shillings (or almost one hundred and fifty standard "sacs" of money):

> "I know nothing of his hundred and fifty sacs—let me say that at once," the young woman cried. "If that is what the court clerk wrote down in his book, he had better rewrite his book. I know nothing about it."
>
> "Thirty-five pounds and six shillings." The court clerk read out what he had down in his book.
>
> "You said thirty-five pounds and six shillings last week, Salawu," Chief Eketa addressed the man. "Now you have come here with another figure today. How is that? It is the truth we want in this court. It is the truth that the White Man wants." (41)

This scene graphically illustrates the way written record can threaten ethical truth in an oral society: measured against the objective truth of the white man's book—the book that "never lies" (45)—Salawu's human truth is inevitably found wanting. Ironically, this case, after dragging on for four more months, is finally settled in the young woman's favor, because Salawu's chief witness had died of tetanus in the meantime, "a sure sign of punishment from the gods for his bearing false witness" (45).

In southern Nigeria, as in Angevin and Plantagenet England, the disruptive effects of literacy seem to have been greatly exacerbated by the presence of an efficient bureaucracy deployed to validate a centralized and authoritarian government. Before the arrival of the British, the Igbo (if not the Yoruba) appear to have had very little in the way of a central organization, the people owing their primary loyalty to villages loosely organized into confederations rather than to anything resembling a hierarchical state. They seem indeed to have regarded any suggestion of political hierarchy with profound suspicion: "Long, long ago there had been a fifth title in Umuaro—the title of king," writes Achebe in *Arrow of God*, "but the conditions for its attainment had been so severe that no man had ever taken it" (209). The British viewed such domestic republicanism as incompatible with efficient colonial government and sought to put a stop to it by promoting local dignitaries to positions of genuine authority: "Our people, the White man said, were 'ungovernable.' They had no natural rulers. So he appointed chiefs to represent the people to him and him to the people. Thereafter, he could say: 'Your chiefs agreed to sell half the land you own for nothing. Your chiefs have agreed that should pay a new tax. Your chiefs have agreed that the women and the goats and the sheep should all be counted, so everything in the district will be counted. See here? Here are their thumbprints. That's how they signed the agreement'" (Echewa, *I Saw the Sky Catch Fire* 35). Evidently, what underpinned the authority of the new system was as much the civil servant's pen as the mercenary's sword: "he had power; he could shout in my face; he could do what he liked," says the hero of Achebe's *Arrow of God* of a young white official he had seen; "Why? Because he could write with his left hand" (189). As a result, in traditional Nigerian society, as in fourteenth-century England, lawyers seem to have been particularly detested: "'Law-yer! Law-yer!' Grandma Gbemi cried in distress. 'Shonponna my god forbid that I should ever have anything to do with lawyers. They turn innocent people's cases round and send them to gaol'" (Aluko, *One Man, One Wife* 154). It is unsurprising, then, to learn that the Igbo women who led the great rebellion of 1929 vented their anger on the literate machinery of the law as unerringly as the English peasants of 1381 had done: "the women occupied the courthouse, smashed the dock and the chairs, set fire to the records. . . . They sang. They danced. They stomped. They held mock trials" (Echewa, *I Saw the Sky Catch Fire* 174–75).[8]

As in Ricardian England, much of the power of the ruling class was evidently derived from its ability to manipulate written documents in a society still deeply committed to a system of oral trothplight: "You have no redress in law, you know that," says a corrupt politician to a gullible nonliterate in Soyinka's *Season of Anomy*; "an agreement is an agreement. There is nothing in this world so powerful as a piece of paper to which a man has put his fingerprint in front of witnesses. Nothing can wash the fingerprint away" (127). A graphic illustration of the way the new regimen weakened the old loyalties by compromising ancient reliance on the sanctity of oath-taking is offered by one of Achebe's short stories, "Vengeful Creditor," in which a servant tells his master how he is going to falsify his age in order to get the free education the government is offering to those under fifteen: " 'I no go fail, oga,' said the gardener. 'One man for our village wey old pass my fader sef done register everyting finish. He just go for Magistrate Court and pay dem five shilling and dey swear-am for Court juju way no de kill porson; e no fit kill rat sef' " ["I shall not fail, sir," said the gardener. "An old man from our village, even older than my father, was registered successfully. He just went to the magistrate's court, paid five shillings and swore an oath, for the court juju is no threat to anyone; he couldn't even kill a rat"] (*Girls at War* 53). When the hero of Soyinka's play *Death and the King's Horseman* is asked for his word of honor by a British administrator, he responds witheringly: "You have my honour already. It is locked up in that desk in which you will put away your report of this night's events. Even the honour of my people you have taken already; it is tied together with those papers of treachery which make you masters in this land" (67).

That those who have lived through the profound cultural dislocation caused by the introduction of literacy should experience a strong sense of Saturnian malaise is hardly surprising. Just as in Ricardian England, writers in twentieth-century Nigeria frequently make us aware of widespread disenchantment with a world turned upside down: "the soil is no longer fertile, for the earth, outraged, has withheld her kindness from man. People cheat these days—they cheat even their own brothers. Women bully their husbands and produce children that resemble neither father nor mother" (Munonye, *Obi* 23).[9] Where, for the purposes of the cultural historian at least, the Nigerian novelists score over the Ricardian poets, however, is in their comparatively more clear-sighted analysis of cause and effect. I have argued at length that an ambivalent attitude to the technology of writing (a half-awareness of how it had compromised and weakened ancient values) is implicit in much of the literature of Ricardian England, but in many Nigerian novels the association is made quite explicitly. "You are very young, a child of yesterday," says an elder to the English-educated hero of Achebe's *No Longer at Ease*; "you know book. But book stands by itself and experience stands by itself" (74). And the hero's grandfather in Echewa's *Crippled Dancer* similarly associates those who have learned to make the white man's "fowl-scratch on paper" with spiritual shallowness: "it seems you have been turned into perpetual children, with no depth of understanding of how things truly are" (94).

The law and legal themes are as omnipresent in the work of twentieth-century Nigerian writers as they are in the literature of medieval Europe. In this appendix I have inevitably concentrated on the representation of traditional law, but one should not forget those other Nigerian novels that deal with the problems created by the imported jurisprudence of British colonialism. T. M. Aluko's *Wrong Ones in the Dock*, to pick one of the most dramatic, chronicles a murder trial in postindependence Nigeria, concluding with a bitter indictment of the legacy of the common law: "what the judge handed down was judgment without justice. It was unfortunately all that he was competent to give in the circumstances of the cumbersome judicial system which he operated. . . . Real justice was impossible under a truth-inhibiting judicial system which had been imported from a foreign clime and which . . . has yet . . . to grow roots that will reach down to the ground water of true justice" (185). Of all the Nigerian novels dealing with legal themes, however, perhaps the richest and most suggestive is T. Obinkaram Echewa's *Crippled Dancer*. It recounts an old man's legal battle with a despotic local chief from the point of view of his educated grandson, and though the grandfather's heroic refusal to abandon a faith "deeply rooted in Ultimate Equity" (188) in the face of his opponent's blatant legal chicanery casts Nigerian folklaw in a particularly rosy light, Echewa never falls into the trap of sentimentalizing traditional justice: "it is true that the old days had their virtues and their valour, but then they were also full of vice and folly, which have merely been washed clean by memory" (39). The strength of his analysis, in fact, lies in its clear-eyed recognition of the destructive consequences of cultural hybridization—"perhaps the new evil has impregnated the old kind, and their bastard offspring is now what terrorises us" (41) The question with which his novel ends is one that those who suffered through a comparable crisis in Ricardian England must also have often asked themselves: "to say that the truth was in the past with the spirit of the dead ancestors was no safer than to say that it was in the present with the consensus of the living. Where, indeed, was the truth?" (227).

God be with trewþe, qwer he be.
I wolde he were in þis cuntre!
(*HP* 59)

Notes

Preface

1. The adherents of two historical schools in particular have felt that the word *crisis* appropriately reflects aspects of fourteenth-century experience: economic historians have used it of the sharp economic decline that occurred in the first half of the century, succeeding a long period of steady growth (see Perroy, B. Campbell), and Marxist historians of the violent social unrest that erupted in the second half of the century (Dobb 42–50; Anderson 197–209; Hilton 1990, 166–72). For an airing of the differences between these two schools see Aston and Philpin.

2. Cf. Ian Watt's discussion of the formal realism of early novelists "in terms of the procedures of another group of specialists in epistemology, the jury in a court of law" (32).

Chapter 1. From Troth to Truth

1. Ruth Bird remarks on the curious fact "that the burning of the 'Jubilee Book', which is one of the main complaints of the crafts against Exton, did not take place, according to Letter-Book H, until 1387, the year after the petitions" (94 n. 4).

2. The closest parallel I have found, however, comes from a description of the papal curia in *The Simonie*: "Ȝif Trewþ come amonge hem, iwys, he shal be ded. / Þer ne dare he noȝt com, for doute to be slayn" (c.20–21).

3. This seems to be an elaboration of Augustine's commentary on Psalm 61: "occultari potest ad tempus veritas; vinci non potest" [truth may be hidden for a while, but not conquered] (*PL* 36:740).

4. As Kail remarks, the Digby poems as a whole "contain many a line in defence of truth, and to the suppression of falsehood" (viii).

5. The fissioning of the forms *troth* and *truth* which enables us to separate these legal senses from all the others is, of course, a postmedieval phenomenon.

6. The *Old English Version of the Heptateuch*, for instance, translates "sanguis foederis" ["the blood of the covenant"] as "ðære treowðe blod" (Exod. 24:8) and "si . . . custodieritis pactum meum" ["if you will . . . keep my covenant"] as "Gyf ge . . . mine treowða gehealdað" (Exod. 19:5). Cf. D. Green 118.

7. *Wed* is, in fact, the term most frequently used to translate both *foedus* and *pactum* in the OE Heptateuch (A. B. Smith 71 & 137), and the semantic overlap between *treow* and *wed* is suggested by the OE rendering of "constituam pactum meum illi in foedus sempiternum" ["I will establish my covenant with him for a perpetual covenant"]: "ic sette min wedd to him in ecne truwan" (Gen. 17:19).

8. Cf. Arcite's list of Palamon's ideal qualities, "trouthe, honour, knyghthede" ("Knight's Tale" 2789), or the description of "Charles Olyver, that took ay heede / Of trouthe and honour" ("Monk's Tale" 2387–88).

9. The *Promptorium Parvulorum* distinguishes the adjective "ryght of trewth" from simple "ryght" (*rectus*), and glosses it as *iustus* or *equus* (374).

10. In Chinua Achebe's story "Girls at War," a Red Cross official who launches into drunken tirade against the decadence of wartime Biafra is described as "a man of truth" by the main character in the story (119). It is possible that this means simply 'a speaker of the truth', but if Achebe is using the word in its ethical sense, he is employing an interesting archaism. Ezeulu, the hero of Achebe's *Arrow of God*, is similarly described: "After all, he reminded himself, it was Wintabota who a few years ago proclaimed him a man of truth from all the witnesses of Okperi and Umuaro" (175).

11. Thus Latin *credentia* might be either "la confiance qu'on inspire ou qu'on accorde" (Timbal 16); for an analogous development with *fides* see Benveniste 1966, 116–18.

12. See also the examples given by Arthur 87–89.

13. That this is not some Lollard eccentricity is proved by the fragmentary *Fourteenth Century English Biblical Version*, apparently made for nuns and entirely orthodox, which translates *veritas* in the same way (e.g., at 1 Cor. 5:8 and 1 Tim. 4:3).

14. It may be that the phrase *verray trouthe* in Chaucerian usage is intended to underscore a theological sense: the Parson, for instance, says that "Crist is verray trouthe" ("Parson's Tale" 593), and Chaucer's fellow-courtier, Sir John Clanvowe, writes of worldly rewards, "we mowne bee riȝt siker þat bifore God, þat is verrey treuth, þei been neither richesses ne worsshipes" (69). Thus, when the narrator in Thomas Usk's *Testament of Love* claims that his soul has been brought into "parfit blisse" by a new understanding of the relationship between will and reason, his guide, Love (later identified with Holy Church), comments, "very trouth . . . hast thou now conceyved of these thinges in thyne herte" (132); Usk seems here to be associating *trouth* with divine revelation.

15. The *Promptorium Parvulorum* offers "trowth and levte" as the equivalent of *fidelitas* (492). Kean defines Langland's *lewte* as "the Aristotelian virtue of Justice . . . 'complete virtue, but not absolutely, but in relation to our neighbour'" (256), a definition that would certainly imply considerable semantic overlap between *lewte* and *trouthe*.

16. This distinction is discussed at length in the OE version of Augustine's *Soliloquies*. When Reason asks Augustine, "hweðer þe þince þæt hyt æll an si, soð and soðfesnesse" [do *soþ* and *soþfastness* seem to you the same thing?], he replies that they are distinct, just as wisdom or purity are distinct from whatever is wise or pure; *soþfastness*, he continues, is the higher quality: "Forðam æall þætte soð byd, byd of soðfestnesse soð" [for all that is true, is true by virtue of the Truth] (81.12–19).

17. The choice between *trouthe* and *sooth* in this context was a fine one: the scribe of MS F of *Piers Plowman*, for instance, changes *truþe* in "[Ac] for drede of þe deeþ I dar noȝt telle truþe" (B.15:414) to *þe soþe*. A case might even be made, I think, that the character of Sothnesse who leads a phantom existence in the various versions of the "Visio" (see *Z Version* 16) represents an unsatisfactory attempt to articulate this quality of dangerous plain-speaking, a sense which seems to lie somewhere between what I have called the ethical and intellectual senses of *truth*. This sense is certainly rendered by

sooth in other Ricardian texts, as in the Vernon lyric "hos seiþ þe soþe, he schal be schent" (*RL14C* 152–54), or Usk's "also, to say tr[o]uthe rightfulliche (but in jugement) otherwhile is forboden, by that al sothes be nat to sayne" (32).

18. Kane (24 n. 19) points out that though the *OED* credits Langland with the earliest example of *truth* meaning 'that which is in accordance with the fact', its citation is erroneous. Of Kane's own "more satisfactory" examples only B.4:1576 and B.15:414 seem to me any better, and even they are not incontestable.

19. E.g., B.2:122, 5:596, 6:130, 9:101, 18:147; this half-line is also picked up by the author of *Mum and the Sothsegger* (M487). I am not persuaded by Alford's suggestion that this is an example of Langland's punning (1988a, 159).

20. The considerable confusion of the MSS over this line might lend support to such a suggestion (Manly and Rickert 5:500); for instance: "Depper in this and trewly for to lere" (Ha[1]); "Depper in this matere trouthe to lere" (Hk); "Depper in this caas he troweþ for to lere" (La); "Depper in this the trouthe for to here" (Bo[2]); and "Depper in this caas a trouthe to bere" (Ry[1]).

21. The only pre-fourteenth-century citation of the sense 'consistent with fact' in the *OED* (s.v. *true* a. 3) is certainly erroneous. In Laȝamon's lines "Belin ihærde sugge, þurh summe sæg treowe. / of his broðer wifðinge" (2217–18), *sæg treowe* is not, as the editors presumably imagined, 'a true saying' but 'a true [i.e., reliable] man'; *sæg* > OE *secg* [*MED* s.v. *segg* n.(2)]. *MED* (s.v. *treu(e* adj. 11a) gives no examples of this sense before the fourteenth century.

22. For a somewhat different approach to this problem which would characterize the two extremes in terms of "contextualization" and "differentiation," see Denny.

23. Boyer (47–48) categorizes three kinds of hypothesis that have typically been advanced to explain such inconsistencies: (1) that "the people concerned are simply illogical" (the now generally discredited position of Lévy-Bruhl); (2) that "there is a linguistic misunderstanding" (cf. Gellner 42); (3) that "people have a special way . . . of relating belief and experience" (the explanation Gellner favors). Clearly Lord's explanation here belongs to Boyer's second category; for another instance of this kind of rationalization, see Empson 375–90.

24. A good example of such ideological bias occurs in Gluckman's debate with Bohannan over the question of whether modern jurisprudential terminology can be applied to legal systems of a quite different order. For Gluckman what we mean by law is Western law and terms and concepts which have no equivalent in our jurisprudence must therefore be ipso facto extralegal (the logical extension of this position is Diamond's, "peoples like the Tiv . . . have no law") (320). Gluckman accuses Bohannan of cultural solipsism for insisting on the untranslatability of such terms as *mimi* and *vough*, generally preferring instead to regard them as rough equivalents of familiar legal terms, their imprecision deriving from the unsophisticated nature of the systems they articulate. In this instance, he suggests, *mimi* is merely the 'white lie' which British or American judges would be almost as likely as Tiv ones to hear in their courts (1974, 307–08), but this ignores Bohannan's point that *mimi* is a central concept in Tiv justice in a way that 'white lie' can never be in ours. If Bohannan's observations are correct, then the premises of Tiv justice are not merely imprecisely articulated versions of our own, they are radically different. On the general context of the Bohannan-Gluckman debate, see Roberts 198–206.

25. The only instances of the word earlier than the Ricardian period given by the

OED come from *Cursor Mundi* (ca. 1300) at lines 2295 and 4518. Neither of these instances, however, occurs in BL MS Cotton Vespasian A. III—the copy generally thought to be closest to the original text. The earliest manuscript in which they appear is Göttingen University MS Theol. 107, which dates from the second half of the fourteenth century.

26. Gellner and Ong disagree fundamentally about the nature and causes of their respective conceptual divides, however. For Gellner literacy is a necessary but far from sufficient cause of the shift from multistranded to single-stranded thinking; Ong, on the other hand, though he dissociates himself from Lévy-Bruhl, sees a shift from prelogical to logical thought as the natural consequence of the spread of alphabetic literacy (49–57). The relationship between literacy and cognition has been the subject of much recent debate in the social sciences. Advocates of what Jack Goody calls "single-factor determinism" (xv) in its most extreme form would see the capacity for abstract thought and even logic itself as the direct product of literacy—"the chirographic base of logic," as Ong calls it (53). However, Goody, who is sometimes accused of promoting this view (see Street 44–65), denies suggesting that the introduction of writing "immediately or necessarily" caused such changes: "while writing helped to develop new types of formal logical operation, it did so initially by making explicit what was implicit in oral cultures, which were neither pre-logical nor yet alogical except in a very narrow sense of those words" (Goody 182). Hutchins has convincingly shown that quite complex syllogistic arguments are well within the capacity of the members of an oral society, and Gluckman gives an excellent example of the application of legal logic among the Zulus (1974, 311–12). Alexander Luria, who is sometimes cited in this context (Ong 52–53; Havelock 1986, 38–40), did not report an absolute division between his literate and nonliterate subjects in tests designed to measure their capacity for abstract thinking and logical deduction (116, 134), and even the way he interprets those data most favorable to his theory is open to serious question (see Fernández-Armesto 91–94). One might notice that a somewhat different categorization of cognitive development, derived from Piaget, is sometimes applied to the Middle Ages (Radding 1978; LePan). "The natives are children," as Forster and Soyinka recognize, is as common a canard as "the natives are liars"; it evidently takes time, even in the West, to wean children from an inclination to multistranded thought (cf. Fernández-Armesto 17–21).

Chapter 2. Trothplight

1. In his campaign to direct energy away "from functionalist accounts of the devices on which societies rest towards interpretive ones of the kinds of lives societies support" (93), Clifford Geertz has urged that we concern ourselves with meaning rather than machinery (232), but in practice the distinction is rarely as neat as this formulation suggests. As Spiegel dryly remarks of Geertz's celebrated interpretation of a Balinese cockfight, "those who bet on the cocks are not only expressing their peculiar understanding of the nature of Balinese social culture . . . but hoping to profit materially from the animal violence that ensues" (85).

2. I use the term *folklaw*, a calque on OE *folcriht*, to refer to the customary law of not only the Anglo-Saxon and other Germanic peoples but of small-scale, traditional

societies in general. In contrasting it later with the king's law I do not mean to imply uncritical acceptance of Heinrich Brunner's categorization of the difference between *Volksrecht* and *Königsrecht* (1:405–12), nor to deny the force of Susan Reynolds's objection that any distinction between the two belongs to historians and not to the Middle Ages (1984, 20). Nevertheless, the term *folklaw* remains useful in discussing the "legal order" (Berman 1983, 80) of an earlier period, as well as those elements of that order that survive down to more recent times: it avoids having to resort to such ideologically loaded terms as *archaic* or *primitive*, allowing us to emphasize those features that distinguish this order from later law without denying its judicial function altogether. Cf. Hoebel's use of the term *law-ways*.

3. Though early Roman law had had its own equivalent of the ceremonial contract, known as the *nexum* (Maine 1864, 304–8), such clothing should be distinguished from the classical Roman use, where even formless contracts, such as sale or partnership, could be described as "clothed" since a *nudum pactum* meant simply an unenforceable agreement: "a contract was a Pact (or Convention) *plus* an Obligation. So long as the Pact remained unclothed with the Obligation, it was called *nude* or *naked*" (313). Bracton, however, perhaps reacting against the canonists (P&M 2:196), regards the physical handing-over as itself a kind of clothing: "It is also necessary that livery (*traditio*) of the thing follow the gift . . . otherwise it will be regarded as a nude promise (*nuda promissio*) rather than a gift" (2:64). For a similar domestication of Roman terminology in the formulation of the doctrine of consideration, see Baker 1981, 352–54.

4. Though Wallace-Hadrill claims that "the barbarian law of possession or seisin can now be shown to derive from the Vulgar Roman law of *possessio*" (8), Ernst Levy is far less dogmatic: "the reception of forms does not have to be one of institutions. Frequently it intimates solely that the way of thought as expressed in the borrowed phraseology appealed to the minds of the borrowing people because they had similar, if unformulated, notions of their own" (99). In particular, Levy suggests that, since similar attitudes to possession are also found in Greek (69) and archaic Roman law (71), the idea of *possessio* may simply reflect "a natural approach for men not trained in a refined system of logically arranged concepts" (99). One should add that it might equally easily occur to people who relied primarily on memory rather than written record. For the vexed problem of Germanic and Roman influences in general, see Ian Wood (7–22); Wood concludes that "the dichotomy between a supposed law of the Germanic forests and that of the Roman forum" has been "a hindrance to the understanding of post-Roman dispute settlement." See also Susan Reynolds (1984, 15).

5. For the distinction between rights *in personam* and rights *in rem* (often clearer in principle than in practice), see Hohfeld 65–114.

6. Even in 1334, we find a lawyer pointing out that, "not long ago, it was not known what an advowson was, but, when the intention was to give an advowson to another, it would be expressed in the charter that the alienor gave the church" (quoted by Holdsworth 3:98); Holdsworth sees this as a sign that the common law only began "to appreciate the distinction between a corporeal and an incorporeal thing" as late as the fourteenth century.

7. Though it is customary to refer to the author of Pollock and Maitland's *History of English Law* as Maitland, the more active partner need not be held responsible for this view: "Sir Frederick Pollock's contribution — a chapter on the Anglo-Saxons — is reli-

ably reported to have caused Maitland to speed up his writing of the remainder, in order to prevent any more pieces coming from his collaborator" (Elton 5); for a more charitable account, see Wormald 1996, 2–4.

8. In the late twelfth century, Glanvill, for instance, classifies debt as property (see Seipp 1994, 35); cf. the early association of the action of detinue (an action for the recovery of specific chattels) with the action of debt (see P&M 2:174).

9. A medieval exemplum tells of a poor widow who asks the emperor Trajan for justice; when he promises to look into her case as soon as he returns from the wars, she points out that should he be killed in battle he will die with his debt to her undischarged (Higden 5:4–6). Robert Service's line "Now a promise made is a debt unpaid" (from "The Cremation of Sam McGee") proves the longevity of such ideas in the popular, if not the legal, imagination.

10. The confusion between tort and contract in general is widespread and of long standing: "The law of Edward I's reign draws no clear line between tort and contract" (Holdsworth 2:369), and in the fifteenth century the action of *assumpsit* treats certain kinds of contractual disputes as if they were tortious. Some twentieth-century commentators (e.g., Gilmore) have argued that contract is once again in danger of being swallowed by tort, and it would be intriguing to speculate on this tendency as symptomatic of Ong's "secondary orality"; Stevens (esp. 151–200) might offer a good starting point for such speculation.

11. No solution, of course, can ever be entirely satisfactory; for instance, Bohannan himself must have decided that our concept of debt could be applied to certain Tiv cases with comparatively less distortion than that of contract. Ironically, U. U. Uche suggests that the Tiv word *injô*, which Bohannan renders as 'debt', can also mean 'liability' (13).

12. However, it might be objected that there is at least some degree of historical continuity between Roman law and that of modern Western societies, whereas the claim that Tiv law is 'primitive' is an ideological assumption. When Gluckman calls Bohannan a cultural solipsist, "unable to compare and generalize" (1965, 183), he really means that Bohannan is reluctant to employ comparative methods in support of an evolutionary theory of Western law. The circularity of claiming that "the Tiv are not unique" (212) after sweeping what is most distinctive about their judicial system under the carpet of familiar terminology is obvious. On the Gluckman-Bohannan dispute, see Moore 135–48.

13. This Roman domestication of customary law can usefully be considered in terms of the way in which recent colonial administrations have sought to domesticate traditional African law. When Roberts describes a set of documents as consisting largely "of inventories of rules purporting to constitute the 'customary law' of each society," though lacking explanation of how these rules are selected, or "how they actually work in the society concerned" (195), he might easily be referring to the laws of the Visigoths or the Burgundians rather than the reports of the British Restatement of African Law Project; mutatis mutandis, his complaint that "the reader is left with the impression . . . that [these rules] operate in the same way as rules of English law are conventionally seen to operate," might equally be made of almost any Germanic code. For further discussion, see Gilissen (esp. 197–274).

14. This does not mean, however, that such legal forms are determined simply by the conditions of material existence, as Diamond seems to think. I believe it is quite

wrong to draw cross-cultural inferences on such grounds and to argue, for instance, that because pre-Christian Germanic tribes had attained an economic level roughly equivalent to that of the Nguni, who do not use oaths, the oath must therefore have been introduced into Germanic procedure at a later stage (297–300).

15. For the *wandilanc*, which remains mysterious, see Du Cange, s.v. *Andelangus*; perhaps the most probable of the solutions offered there is 'handshake' (from *hand* [or **want* 'glove'] and *lagen*, *legen*, or *langen*).

16. No doubt, the last of these was intended to represent the hunting of vermin, the driving out of wolves, or some similar duty for which feudal tenure had been granted (see Cherry 112).

17. The pennies symbolize Baldonet's acknowledgment of his liability for the annual tax, the *chevage* or *census de capite*, which was paid by all serfs, and which Marc Bloch calls "le signe, par excellence, de la servitude" (1933, 291).

18. In an early-tenth-century dispute between Helmstan and Æthelhelm over ownership of lands at Fonthill, the court viewed Helmstan's possession of a deed, even though it was not a deed made in his favor (it recorded a grant of the lands in question from Æðeldryð to Osulf) as justifying his being put to the oath rather than his opponent: "ða ðuhte us eallan ðe æt ðære some wæran, ðæt Helmstan wære aðe ðæs ðe near" [then it seemed to all of us who were present in court that Helmstan was therefore the nearer to the oath], a decision King Alfred later upholds (Harmer 31). This principle also appears in a late tenth-century case from Ely: "propior erat ille, ut terram haberet, qui cyrographum habebat quam qui non habebat" [he who had the charter was nearer (to the oath) that he should have the land, than he who did not] (*Liber Eliensis* 99).

19. As late as the early fifteenth century we hear of a sheet of paper being handed over "par figure" in the course of a ceremonial restitution of legal rights in Dijon (Ligeron and Petitjean 290).

20. The terms generally used by English legal historians to describe these symbolic objects are *gage* and *wed*. Maitland seems to favor the first (P&M 2:117–18, 185–88), and Holdsworth the second (2:83–89). I use a third term, *token*, not because it is more frequently found in specifically legal contexts, but because it has the obvious advantage of having preserved something of its original sense to modern times. It is, moreover, more precise than *wed*, which in Old English had also the generalized sense of 'agreement' (a synonym, as we have seen, of *treowþ*): in the OE Heptateuch God describes the rainbow by which he establishes his covenant with Noah (surely, the most spectacular of all such mnemonic displays) as a "tacn mines weddes [signum foederis]" (Gen. 9:12).

21. This is not to imply that more familiar forms did not exist. Glanvill shows us something very like a pawn (*vadium* or 'gage') being used to secure a loan (10.6), and something very like a down payment (*arra* or 'earnest-money') to secure a bargain (10.15); there is no reason to imagine that such forms (despite some clear Roman precedents) are a rediscovery of the twelfth century.

22. Cf. the old beggar's asseveration in Hoccleve's *Regement of Princes* when he promises the poet that Prince Henry will prove sympathetic to his plight: "And but he qwenche þi grete heuynesse, / My tonge take, and slitte in peeces tweyne" (1851–52).

23. Maitland points out that "a man who has lost an ear in honorable warfare will sometimes obtain an explanatory charter from the king, for it is dangerous as well as shameful to go about earless" (P&M 2:498). Esther Cohen cites an early-fifteenth-

century letter of remission from France in which a killer seeks to excuse his act by pointing out that his victim had had an ear lopped off and must therefore have been a dangerous person (166).

24. See, for instance, Gregory of Tours's account (10.18; 2:372–74) of the treatment of the would-be assassins of Childebert II, and the "lurid passage" on mutilation in Wulfstan's *Narratio Metrica de Sancto Swithuno* (quoted by Whitelock 1968, 83–87). In cases of treason throughout the Middle Ages, mutilation was often a degrading preliminary to capital punishment.

25. The fifteenth-century poem "Instructions for Purchasing Land" (*SL* 70–71) clearly views the charter as a standard element in acquiring land: "And if þou maye in any wysse, / mak þi charter with warrantyse / To thyne heyres & assygners also, / thus shall a wysse pvrchaser doo" (lines 17–20).

26. The *blæshorn* may well refer to the horn which travelers off the beaten track were required to sound to prove their honest intent (*Laws of Wihtræd*, 28; Liebermann 1:14). As such, like the ox's bell and the dog's collar, it would be an identification symbol ("ælc is melda geteald"), and the shilling tariff could be then construed as the penalty for failure to employ it.

27. Anyone tempted to regard this analogy as far-fetched might care to consult Homans' description of betrothal and wedding customs in the thirteenth-century English village (160–176).

28. Cf. Steiner's description of the use of the dracaena leaf to initiate legal proceedings among the Chagga of Southeast Africa (367).

29. Paul Hyams has recently likened the medieval handslap to the high (or low) five of African-Americans (1996, 240–41); its earlier currency is reflected in the etymology of the verb *to swap* and in the expression *to strike a bargain* (see Lucke).

30. For a quite different explanation of the Strasbourg oaths, see Stock 24, and Illich and Sanders 64. One might compare, however, the English coronation oath, which, while often recorded in Latin, was almost certainly actually sworn in the vernacular (Richardson 1949, 46), or the vernacular forms of the marriage vows that are frequently inserted into the Latin service books in the Middle Ages.

31. Wormald has argued that this refers to an oath of allegiance, modeled on those known to have been exacted by Charlemagne from his subjects (1977, 114), but though such oaths do seem to have been employed by later Anglo-Saxon kings (J. Campbell 45–47), the article that follows this one in Alfred's code looks as if it is meant to qualify a general exhortation to keep faith: "Anyone wrongfully compelled [by his oath] either to betray his lord or to assist in a crime would do better to be forsworn than to comply" (1.1; Liebermann 1:46).

32. Cf. 2 Cnut (ca. 1030), 22.1 and 36.1 (Liebermann, 1:324 and 338).

33. In a list of fines for various slanders in the *Pactus Legis Salicae* (118–20), to call someone a *delator* or *falsator* cost fifteen shillings (30.7) — five times the assessment for accusing someone of cowardice (30.6), and only exceeded by the penalty for calling an innocent woman a whore (30.3).

34. Cf. the proclamation of Khama the Great (1875–1923), founder of modern Botswana: "I also said that you were only entitled to sell your livestock in the well-known towns where you are known and cannot be suspected of having stolen the property" (cited by Head 39).

35. A very dim echo of this procedure might be detected in the English legal

fiction known as "feoffment to use," which was widely employed in the fourteenth and fifteenth centuries (cf. Bean 1968, 128–29).

36. "The *denier à Dieu* . . . was however certainly not set against the price; it was a supplementary sum provided by one of the parties and normally put to pious uses" (Esmein 24).

37. With the later triumph of authoritarian law, such borrows were to become indistinguishable from modern sureties: Gawain and Percival, Launfal's "borwes . . . tyll a certayn day," are clearly there to ensure that he keeps his day in court (Chestre 811–16), and, as in the story in *The Seven Sages of Rome* where a callous thief leaves the cousin who had offered "to be hys borowe tyll a certen day" (1433) to be hanged in his place, they are assuming personal liability for him. Their role seems virtually identical to that of the mainpernor (cf. *Gamelyn* 743–46).

38. Such an attitude to judicial decision making can be detected in the English common law right down to the end of the Middle Ages (Baker 1985, 57).

39. Similar provisions for challenging the judge still survive in late medieval French custumals (see Esther Cohen 63).

40. The earlier of the Alemannic codes (early seventh century) is also called a *pactus*, but since it has only survived in fragmentary form we cannot be certain how this term was intended; its editor, Karl Lehmann, however, offers as one possible meaning: "pactus significat conventionem populi cum principe" (*Leges Alamannorum* 6).

41. Cf. Ewers's description of a successful raid by Blackfeet warriors in nineteenth-century America: "Next morning they divided the captured horses. Unless the party had decided upon an equal distribution of the animals taken, each man could claim the horses he had led out of camp or the range stock he had run off. Bitter arguments over the ownership of range stock jointly run off by several Indians sometimes followed. It was the leader's duty to settle these disputes as equitably as possible. Some leaders gave fine horses they themselves had taken to members of their parties who could claim none. A leader's generosity helped him to maintain a reputation as a popular leader who would not want for followers in the future" (134).

42. Keynes (1992), arguing that the writer is not a principal in the lawsuit but merely a witness (56), fails to appreciate that as the former owner of the Fonthill estate he would have been liable to compensate its present owner should it have been proved that he had had no right to sell it.

43. Not only had Charlemagne replaced the old *raginburgii* by permanent judges known as *scabini* (Estey), but he had insisted that their decisions should be based on written law not their own judgment [secundam scriptam legem . . . non secundum arbitrium suum] (Ganshof 63 & n.95). According to Asser (93–94), Alfred attempted to shame his aldermen and reeves into learning to read and his son decreed that reeves should decide cases by the book: "swa . . . hit on ðære dombec stande" (1 Edw. Pr.; Liebermann 1:138), but even these acts need not have been intended as first steps towards establishing a professional judicature; they may simply have been part of a campaign to forestall unwelcome appeals.

44. Wormald, who believes that the Anglo-Saxon monarchy was a far more active presence in legal disputes than such passages seem to suggest, interprets them to mean "no more than that English kings disliked being pestered" (1986, 162). It might be nearer the truth to say that they were reluctant to become involved, preferring to leave the responsibility in the hands of local officials.

45. Pollock's conclusion that genuine contracts did not exist in Anglo-Saxon England is based on his failure to find "evidence of any regular process of enforcing contracts" (P&M 1:57). From the perspective of the modern lawyer an unenforceable contract (that is to say, unenforceable by the state) is a contradiction in terms; as Holdsworth puts it, "to say that agreements and promises have existed in a remote antiquity is one thing; to say that such agreements were enforceable at law—were contracts—is quite another" (2:82). When we must wait till Bracton's day for the king's courts to begin "as a special favour to think of enforcing by action of covenant 'privatae conventiones'" (Holdsworth 3:416), it seemed natural to suppose that there was no true law of contract before his time.

46. For other examples, see *LHP* ch. 7.3a (p. 100) and ch. 57.1a (p. 176). Even more striking is the suggestion that private agreement can override an established legal procedure, such as the rules governing what would later be called *essoins* (reasons for nonappearance in court), ch. 59.2c (p. 182).

47. For an interesting discussion of the maxim "convenance loi vainc" in thirteenth-century French custumals and the construction put upon it by later commentators, see Esmein (28–30).

48. See, for example, Radding's account of the passing of the medieval ordeal (1979).

Chapter 3. The Folklaw

1. The use of staves and shields (*cum fustibus et scutis*) in such contests goes back at least to the Carolingian period (R. Bartlett 110), but though the horned staff, recorded on both sides of the Channel, is doubtless very ancient, its precise form remains somewhat obscure (P&M 2:633–34). There are two problems: whether the term *baculus cornutus* refers to the shape of the tip (i.e., curved like a ram's horn) or the material it was made of, and whether the better documented and illustrated criminal cases (see, e.g., H. Davis) provide a reliable guide for civil proceedings like this one. There is a useful, if inconclusive, review of the evidence in M. Russell 1983a, 432–36. In the various reports of the Northampton case, the tip is described both as a *corn* (*Eyre of Northamptonshire* 2:556) and as a *crok* (2:550), and the latter word seems to refer to its curved shape. Conflicting measurements are given for the length of the staff in the reports: one gives five quarters of an ell (2:548) and the other speaks simply of *bastons de .v. quarters* (2:556). Five quarters of an ell would give a staff nearly six feet long (considerably longer than in other records), and the English ell (45 inches), which is itself five quarters of a yard, seems a more probable length. (It is tempting to suppose that *quarterstaff*, a word whose etymology the *OED* regards as obscure, is simply a clipped form of *five-quarter-staff*.) The reports agree that the shields measured one ell by three-quarters (of a yard [?]), which would yield dimensions of 45 by 27 inches.

2. See Stones 1954, 2–3 n. 10 and 7 n. 1. In 1386 Chaucer was to testify on behalf of Sir Geoffrey's nephew Richard in the celbrated Scrope-Grosvenor trial (*CLR* 370–74).

3. Earlier authorities, convinced of the essential barbarism of the folklaw, have generally painted battle with shield and club in the bloodiest colors, but Blackstone may have been closer the mark when he described it as "bearing a near resemblance to certain rural athletic diversions" (quoted by Holdsworth 1:678–79).

4. This is not to imply that such combats were frequent; the space that the chronicler Thomas Walsingham gives to the battle between Sir John Annesley and Thomas Katrington, fought at Westminster in 1380 (*Historia* 1:430–34), suggests that he saw it as a dramatic and unusual event; indeed, at one point he calls their combat a "new thing" (1:430). For the legal and political context of this event, see Bellamy 1966.

5. See Hamil, and Clanchy 1978, 29–32. Richard Brierley, who robbed Chaucer of 10 pounds in September 1390, was hanged after losing a battle of this kind (*CLR* 482–83). There is a particularly vivid account of a criminal combat between "ij poore wrecchys" in *Gregory's Chronicle* for 1455/56 (199–202).

6. In Montenegro, where feuding was endemic until very recently, people seem to have evolved elaborate mechanisms for resolving even the most deeply entrenched feuds (Boehm 121–42). But see Miller's concerns about a romantic tendency to exaggerate the effectiveness of nonadjudicatory modes of dispute resolution in traditional societies (1990, 299).

7. This peremptory tone is also noticeable in legislation. Where Anglo-Saxon kings merely seek to have their wishes be made public (*cyþan*), Norman kings demand (*mando et precipio*) that their wishes be respected (Goebel 416 and n. 277).

8. In the preface to the tenth edition of his *Ancient Law* (1884), Maine remarked that in the twenty-three years since its first publication, "the observation of savage or extremely barbarous races [had] brought to light forms of social organization extremely unlike that to which [the author] has referred the beginnings of law." It is intriguing to speculate on what he might have made of the vast mass of ethnological material now available to historians.

9. A similar point could be made about the ordeal, which, as Miller puts it, "was there to be used in a pinch" (1988, 196).

10. These fictional oaths might be compared with the actual ones given by Esther Cohen 57–59.

11. *Averment* (from L. *ad* + *verificare*) is now thought of as an alternative to oath-swearing, but this was not necessarily the case earlier. Thus, in a case of debt from 1313, the defendant declares himself "ready to aver by his law . . . that [he] owes him naught" (*YB 6&7 Edw. 2 (pt. 2)* , 54), an averment that would certainly have necessitated his swearing an oath. However, averment "per simplex dictum suum" [by one's word alone] or "in fide qua tenentur domino regis" [by the faith owed to the king] seems to have arisen in the thirteenth century as an alternative to swearing a full formal oath (*BC* 2:56–58), and the later usage presumably derives from this.

12. In Akwanya's *Orimili*, a father's premature death leaves his family in a quandary: "They knew the boundaries of their lands only because they had been farming them. But if a case similar to that between Nwalioba and Ikedi were to arise, they would not have been able, for the most part, to swear on their father's authority where the boundary was" (64).

13. For an even later case from Germany (1796), in which an investigating magistrate is driven by the conflicting testimony of villagers to try and settle matters with a judicial oath, see Sabean 187–88.

14. As Charles-Edwards has written, "the distinction between rules, written law and the whole process of which they form a part creates a difficulty for anyone who would understand medieval law" (4); he offers as illustration a story from the *Mabinogion* in which Manawydan, having caught one of his enemies stealing grain, chooses

not to impose the "law of the thief" (hanging), preferring rather to regard this law as a "trump card which could be used to bring the other side to agree a just peace" (3). Lloyd Bonfield has argued that this kind of legal order survived in manorial courts throughout the Middle Ages.

15. In Amadi's *Great Ponds*, we might remember, each side is eager to pass the burden of proof over to the other: "each village insisted that the other should do the swearing" (84).

16. Even in the king's courts, if the defendant took an affirmative position (e.g., "the debt has been paid"), proof might sometimes be awarded to the plaintiff (*Bracton's Note Book* 3:455–56, pl.1574), and the plaintiff's offer of *suit and good deraignment*, "il en ad sute et derreyne bone"—a frozen formula which survives in certain actions down to the yearbook period (e.g., *YB 12 Edw. 2 (pt. 2)*, 118)—implies that suitors had at one time been ready to act as oath-helpers whenever the burden of proof might be shifted back to their side. Cf. a 1223 borough ordinance from Carlow: "it shall be lawful for the said burgesses to deraign and prove their debts by a suit of law-worthy men" [debita sua per sectam legalium virorum derationare et probare] (Ballard and Tait 187).

17. Downer's explanation of the *iuramentum planum* as an oath which in order to be valid does not need to be sworn "in exact terms and form" (*LHP* 321 n. 9.6) is unconvincing; the equivalent OE term is *unfored að* 'unbroken oath', which seems to imply an oath sworn as a whole not broken into clauses.

18. In the case of judicial combat, which, as Maitland points out, functioned in effect as a "bilateral ordeal" (P&M 2:600), both parties went to the proof, but even here there was asymmetry since appellants had to win the battle outright in order to prove their oath, whereas appellees had merely to avoid defeat, usually until the stars came out (Bracton 2:400).

19. Even this generalization might be challenged: J. S. Furley writes of the city court of late medieval Winchester: "the number of compurgators varied: it is never more than nine, rarely less than two; I have only found one case in which only one was required, and once for a trifling debt of sixpence the defendant is said to have 'made his law' as though his own word sufficed" (1923, 139). Speaking of manorial courts, Beckerman writes that "third- and sixth-handed [oaths] were the most common number; a twelfth-handed oath usually signified a more serious offense" (206 n. 44).

20. Such views were not universal, however: "compurgators . . . were usually men who either knew the facts of discharge or honestly believed that the defendant who offered to wage his law was telling the truth. Unless such was the state of affairs, no procedure could work justly" (Henry 88).

21. As A. W. B. Simpson points out, if compurgators were corruptible, jurymen were no less so (1987, 140).

22. Riedel notes only one allusion to it (in *Guillaume de Dole*) among the French romances he chooses to discuss (77); pace Boone (5–6), I know of no indisputable example from English romance.

23. There is a convenient collation of Idley's text with that of Mannyng in D'Evelyn's introduction to her edition of Idley (54–55).

24. A common preamble to the form of ordeal by cold water on the continent, for instance, says that it was instituted by Louis the Pious and Pope Eugenius II (824–27) to provide an alternative to people perjuring themselves upon the relics of the saints (*Formulae* 617). The official silence is sometimes broken, however, and we find such

rubrics as "then let him make the oath and carry the iron to the place assigned" (616), or "then, as the custom is, let him swear and carry the iron a specific distance" (662), or "then, the oath having been given, let him be immersed" (676).

25. Hexter has noted medieval examples of such "tricked" (as opposed to "equivocal") oath proving (2).

26. It should be noted that some ordeals, such as the Icelandic turf ordeal (Miller 1988, 200–2), are undignified or humiliating rather than painful or dangerous.

27. Early Irish law offers an interesting parallel in its use of fasting (*troscud*) as a way in which a plaintiff might press a case against a social superior (F. N. Robinson); those prepared to starve themselves in order to right a wrong done them must, the logic runs, be acting in good faith. Judicial fasting is recorded in Hindu as well as Irish law (F. Kelly 182–83 n. 29), but the principle underlying it seems widespread. In a novel by the Nigerian writer Flora Nwapa, a creditor ensconses herself on the doorstep of her debtor (who is incidentally of a higher social status) and refuses to leave until she is paid (*Efuru* 47), and Karen Blixen describes an incident where an elderly Kikuyu couple who believe that they have a legal claim against her camp outside her house (102–3). The hunger strike is, of course, an extralegal modern manifestation.

28. The *Tristran* of Thomas of Britain, composed in England, or at least for the Angevin court, in Anglo-Norman in the second half of the twelfth century, survives only in fragments, but what appears to be a fairly literal translation of it was made in Norway in the next century. This is the form in which the earliest account of the trial of Isolt for betraying her husband, King Mark, with his nephew Tristran has come down to us.

29. Cf. the variant forms of Amiloun's oath in the three MSS of *Amis and Amiloun*: "sir Amiloun swore & gan to say / As wis as he neuer *kist* [var; *neyghed*; *had*] þat may, / Our leuedi schuld him spede" (1294–96).

30. Cf. "The Wife Wrapt in Wether's Skin" (Child 5:104–07), where a husband makes provision against a possible future charge of wife-beating.

31. In Béroul's version, where Iseut's simple oath is sufficient to clear her, the verbal equivocation is even cleverer. Béroul's Iseut too has been carried (this time across a marsh) by Tristran (this time disguised as a leper), and the poet is careful to specify that she rides astride him—"janbe deça, janbe dela" (3940)—so that she can later swear that no man has entered between her thighs but the beggar who has just carried her—and King Mark, her lawful husband: "Q'entre mes cuises n'entra home / Fors le ladre qui fist soi some, / Qui me porta outre les guez, / Et li rois Marc mes esposez" (4205–8). For a later example of a similar equivocal oath, see the *Quinze joyes de mariage* (51).

32. The equivocation depends on an unusual word order, *at þar* for *þar at* 'thereat'; since *at* can be both a preposition and a postpositive negative, *ek var-at þar*, which appears to mean 'I was not there', might also be construed as *ek var at-þar*, meaning 'I was thereat' or 'I was about it' (Magoun). Interestingly, this particular equivocation, like the message "Edwardum occidere nolite timere bonum est" in Marlowe's *Edward II* (sc. 21), works better in writing than it could ever have done orally.

33. Cf. Gudrun's quibble in the *Laxdœla Saga* that of all the men in the land she will marry only Thorgils—a promise which of course leaves her free to marry someone outside the land (ch. 65; 195). She frames the ambiguous language ("með undirmálum") of this oath in consultation with Snorri the Priest, who advises her to make

the promise before few witnesses and those few not of the most astute (ch. 59; 178); in the event, Thorgils completely fails to see through it ("sér hann ekki í þetta") (ch. 60; 181).

34. A very similar story is told of the bailiff of Shrewsbury, a little further along Richmond's march ("Life" 217 n. 28), but such ruses go back a long way: Joinville tells of a marshal of the Templars who informs Saint Louis that he cannot advance the king money from the knights' treasury because it is against his oath, but then connives in a fiction whereby he meets the king's envoy (Joinville himself, weak with illness) at the treasury door, observes him feebly wave an ax about, and exclaims, "since you evidently intend to use force against us, we will let you have the keys" (quoted by Blakey 22).

35. But see Besnier: "for the fact that the trial process is directed to the fundamental end of clarifying the formal question to be submitted to proof, one could hardly adduce better evidence than Yseult's ordeal" (135 n. 1).

36. Cf. the account of a horse-stealing case from 1220 in which Philip, the defendant, had apparently tried to claim that the horse in question had been originally owned by one Elias Piggun (a man who seems to have been little better than a hired champion), and then sought to vouch him to warranty (i.e., pass the role of defendant over to him) in the hope that the plaintiff, fearing the possibility of trial by battle against a formidable opponent, would then drop the charge. Despite Piggun's far from savory reputation, he still apparently felt the need to have had technical possession of the disputed horse before he could swear that it had been his own proper chattel ("de proprio catallo suo"), for a local jury found that "after this action had begun in the court of Cheshunt, Philip handed over the horse to Elias Piggun, the would-be warrantor, in order to enable him to swear safely" [et sic posset secure jurare] (*SPC* 1:126).

37. For an analagous example of sanctioned equivocation from modern Crete, see Herzfeld 312.

38. Isidore's maxim turns up in Ivo of Chartres's *Panormia* (*PL* 161:1332) and Peter Lombard's *Sentences* (*PL* 192:838). It even makes an appearance in the *Leges Henrici Primi* (ch. 5.29a; 94).

39. Thus Aquinas reformulates Isidore's maxim entirely in terms of the swearer's intention (*Summa* 2a2æ.89.7; 39:224–52). So far had this kind of thinking developed by the late sixteenth century that in Martin Azpilcueta's treatise on equivocation (1584), "the hearer becomes a supernumerary figure, a person who is not really there" (Malloch 1978, 134).

40. It also turns up in actual ecclesiastical cases as well: in an early-fifteenth-century breach of promise case from Troyes, for instance, the defendant claims that when she had offered the plaintiff the drink that was to mark their espousal, instead of saying, "je vous donne ce gobelet en nom de marriage," she had actually used the words, "en nom de mal rage" [in the name of rabies] (*Inventaire* 344).

Chapter 4. The King's Law

1. I have augmented the depositions printed by Barbour with the others from the same file (PRO C 1/19/354). Punctuation is editorial.

2. This ancient ritual seems to have placed the burden of providing the drink on the buyer: at the Fair Court of St. Ives in 1275 a plaintiff called Thomas claimed that he

had bought a coffer from a certain Adam for sixpence, "whereof he gave to the said Adam twopence and a drink [*duos den. et beverech*] in advance" (*SPM* 138–39). The court recognized this as binding and fined Adam for failing to deliver the coffer.

3. Cf. Lentz's revisionary study of ancient Greek literacy which "supports a conception of gradual increase in the influence of writing throughout the Hellenic period, not an immediate, or even an eventual, triumph over the older oral culture" (176).

4. For a skeptical account of such progression by successive stages, see Joyce Coleman 19.

5. Cf. Goebel's claim that "the Conqueror's ordinance on proof is remarkable because it is a departure from the principle that law is personal" (416).

6. However, the common methods of execution under the folklaw (drowning by the tide, throwing from cliffs, burial alive) suggest an attitude to capital punishment quite different from the public hanging of the king's law. All represent a kind of symbolic expulsion of the culprit from the community and tend to take place at the edge of town—cf. Juliana's execution "londmearce neah" (365; K&D 3:131)—whereas hanging on the common gallows is a public assertion of authority, primarily intended as a warning to others. A late-fifteenth-century ordinance from Hastings mentions that condemned felons "of olde tyme" were thrown from a cliff, but now "of a newe and speciall grace and graunte of our lorde the kynge," they are to be hanged "accordyng to the commune lawe of Inglonde" (*BC* 1:76). There is at least one case from fifteenth-century Folkestone of the townspeople threatening to throw someone from a cliff (cited by Avery 138).

7. This principle survived in borough courts to the very end of the Middle Ages and a late fifteenth-century ordinance from Romney requires the appellant who is unable to find an executioner and unwilling to take on the task himself to "dwelle in prison with the felon unto the time that he wyll do that office or else find an hangman" (*BC* 1:74); for other examples see *BC* 1:55, 73–76.

8. There is a literary analogue to this trick in the question Arthur puts to the elder sister at the end of Chrétien de Troyes's *Yvain*: "'Ou est', fet il, 'la dameisele, / Qui sa seror a fors botee / De sa terre et deseritee / Par force et par male merci?' / 'Sire!', fet ele, 'je sui ci.'" (6384–88) ["Where," he said, "is the lady who has driven her sister from her land and deprived her of her inheritance with pitiless violence?" "Sir," she said, "here I am."] The lady realizes her mistake too late, and though she complains that, if she has spoken carelessly ("se j'ai dite / Une response nice et fole" [6396–97]), she should not be taken at her word ("Ne me devez prandre a parole" [6398]), Arthur remains unsympathetic.

9. Cf. this typical verdict in a fourteenth-century case: "The jurors declared that Robert, wishing to kill Walter, assaulted him with a knife and pursued him from place to place and to a certain lane blocked by a cart. Walter could not flee any further and in self-defence and to escape death with a knife attacked Robert, who died. The jurors declared that Robert had been wounded in the front and that Walter could not have escaped" (*1341 Royal Inquest* 130.1211). A similar verdict from 1389 on one Alexander Broadbred is given in *CLR* 357 (case 3).

10. See, for instance, Teeven's bald claim, based on three fourteenth-century statutes against the "perjury which horribly continues and daily increases in the common jurors of the kingdom" (n. 32), that "perjury was rife . . . in trial by jury" (54).

11. Stephen reports a case from 1328 in which the charge, "felonice abduxit unum equum rubrum price de tant," enabled the accused to escape because "it did not say whether he had taken the horse feloniously or whether he had led it away feloniously after it had been delivered to him lawfully" (3:136). On such "nice and tender exceptions" in general, see Holdsworth 3:617–18 (an account based mainly on Hale's *Historia Placitorum Coronae*), where most of the examples are from the sixteenth and seventeenth centuries; for various earlier examples, see *SCKB* 2:xxxvi–xxxvii; 3:8 (1294); 4:6 (1308); 5:30 (1328); 6:23 (1343) and 133 (1366); 7:5 (1378).

12. As a rough guide, the *Statutes of the Realm* devotes 4 pages to the twelfth century (Henry I to Richard I), 192 pages to the thirteenth (John to Edward I), and 355 pages to the fourteenth (Edward II to Richard II). Judging by the repetitive nature of many of the fourteenth-century statutes, they cannot have been very effectively enforced.

13. If, for example, a servant were to leave before his appointed term he could be sued under the Statute of Labourers, but if an apprentice did so, his master was forced to swear out a writ alleging abduction *vi et armis* because the statute, apparently by oversight, had failed to mention apprentices (Milsom 1981, 292). The high point in such formalistic interpretation of statutes was reached with a Tudor act which had to be redrafted because its prohibition against stealing horses, mares, and geldings (in the plural) was construed as condoning the theft of single animals (Bellamy 1984, 149).

14. For a particularly ludicrous instance in which "Heselhawe" was allowed as an alternative for "Haselhawe" in one case, but "Uaghan" was not accepted as an alternative for "Waghan" in a case three years later, see Plucknett 1922, 88.

15. J. S. Furley writes of the city court of thirteenth-century Winchester: "I have counted eighteen separate meetings of the Court at which one Thomas Stapilton, a weaver, is summoned for debt, distrained, distrained again, distrained 'as already many times' (so adds the wearied clerk), and the year's roll ends without our ever knowing whether the creditor ever succeeded in getting his elusive debtor into Court" (1923, 137).

16. As in the ingenious tactic, employed where more than one party was being sued, known as *fourching*. This involved the defendants taking turns to default: since the court could hardly penalize the fourcher who actually appeared, and was barred from penalizing the defaulting fourcher for merely a single nonappearance, it was forced constantly to reset the trial date. In 1345, when a plaintiff tried to put a stop to a seven-year delay on a writ of debt, the court could find no way out and the defendants were "left fourching still *in infinitum*" (*YB 19 Edw. 3*, xxvi).

17. In land disputes, particularly, the winning of a case in one form might merely lead to its resurrection in another. A plaintiff might recover his family's manor by *writ of novel disseisin*, his son might lose it on a *writ of entry*, and his grandson win it back again with a *writ of right*. For a series of such moves in a dispute lasting from 1264 to 1380, see R. Palmer 1984.

18. A royal statute of 1284 excepts from the conditions of oral pleading the "dura consuetudo": "qui cadit a syllaba cadit a tota causa" [who fails in one syllable loses the whole case] (Holdsworth 1:301), but this laudable objective was evidently not achieved. Local courts seem to have been more flexible in their attitude to such verbal slips; see, for instance, the restrictions on "miskenning" repeated in several borough ordinances (*BC* 2:1–4).

19. The principles upon which judges might accept or reject such quibbles are not always clear. In one case where the abbreviation for *tenamentum* appears in the writ as *tem*, rather than in the accepted form *ten*, the judge allows *tem* to stand on the curious grounds that there are two *ms* later in the word (*YB 13/14 Edw. 3*,212–13).

20. In other cases, the selfsame witness was quite happy to recall two quite separate dates as being the exact day on which one of his relatives had been born, married, or died. In 1328, for instance, Robert de Milneburn of Newcastle-upon-Tyne testified that his father had died on March 24, 1307, the day Robert Bertram was baptized, and two years later that his father's death had coincided with David de Strabolgi's baptism on February 1, 1308 (M. Martin 526–27). The attitude of literate authority to this kind of creative memorialization was predictably hostile: a fourteenth-century religious exemplum against perjury, for instance, tells of a group of witnesses who, because they "invent accidents to themselves and their families to explain their memory of the day [on which a pretended contract was drawn up], are punished by those very accidents befalling them" (J. A. Herbert 633).

21. See also *YB 18 Edw. 3*, 436–37. St. German's student remarks that a special treatise [*tractatus specialis*] would be needed to deal with all such cases, "where the intent of the parties will be frustrated because it is not in accordance with the law" (143).

22. The opposite situation, where a plaintiff tries to break down a single large debt into two sums of thirty-nine shillings elevenpence and a farthing in order to keep his case in a local court (*YB 20 Edw. 3 [pt. 2]*, 147), should serve to remind us that not all litigants saw the king's courts as a source of superior justice.

23. For the argument that the allegation of trespass *vi et armis* constituted a "low-threshold test" (i.e., "it demanded some application of force"), rather than a legal fiction, see R. Palmer (1993, 152–66); however, the cases he discusses require us to interpret "force" in so general and imprecise a fashion that it might as well be termed a fiction. See also *YB 8–10 Rich. 2*, 146.

24. Knights of the Post are first mentioned around 1516, but the institution is possibly much earlier (*Reports* 2:115–16).

25. The yearbooks occasionally show signs, in Plucknett's words, of a "break with the older idea of seisin and of the paramount importance of what passed at the ceremonial livery, and a tendency towards the modern respect for the written instrument" (*YB 13 Rich. 2*, xlix), though one early commentator on the 1389 case which prompted Plucknett to make this remark wrote in the margin "vide mirabile judicium."

26. For a more detailed chronology, see Ibbetson 1986, esp. pp. 86–94; Ibbetson concludes that "the requirement . . . was not introduced by a single bold stroke, but rather in the stumbling, crab-like manner beloved of the Common Law" (93).

27. Even earlier (1292), the London Letter Books record what looks like a professional compurgator "being convicted of taking bribes for making false law in the Sheriffs' Courts and other Courts and Sokes in the City of London" (Riley 29).

28. For a dissenting view of this case, see R. Palmer (1993, 171–80).

29. For the distinction between the two, see F. Stenton 152–64.

30. This is not to suggest, of course, that the actual performance of homage might not be recorded in an official register (see Strohm 1989, 16); no doubt such registers served the tenant's interests quite as much as the landlord's. For an early-fifteenth-century certificate of homage and fealty from Lancashire, see Myers, *EHD* 1117–18.

31. See Strohm (1989, 13–21) for an interesting categorization of this phenomenon as the replacement of sacralized vertical relationships with contractual horizontal ones. It will be evident that Strohm and I disagree on a number of points of detail and emphasis.

32. Like Strohm (1989, 20), however, I believe Carpenter overstates the case when she writes that "the written contract itself no more implied a commercial attitude than did the spoken pledge of the less literate feudal age" (1980, 529–30).

33. Cf. the following sealing clause in a land grant to Oseney Abbey (made about 1190 but translated in the mid-fifteenth century): "And þis yifte graunte and warantiȝyng truly to be holde I adam porter for me and my heyres haue I-pliȝght my trowth and with my seele puttyng to haue i-strenghthe hit" (*English Register* 55).

34. The price of litigation in the late Middle Ages was substantial: one fifteenth-century litigant, for instance, paid over fifty shillings for a single charter (G. Fowler), and his protracted lawsuit with John Aynesworth at the end of the century cost Robert Pylkington more than a hundred pounds in legal costs (*Report* 43 and 56).

35. Though not noticed by Whiting, this line is evidently a variation on the proverb "The weaker has the worse" (Whiting W129). The meaning appears to be that the weaker will always fare worse in a battle of writs; cf. the variant printed in Whiting from Heywood's *Epigrammes* (1555): "The weaker hath the woorse, in wrestlyng alway."

36. For other printed examples of such maintenance contracts, see Raftis 1964, 42–46, and Clark 317–19.

37. Though there were rumblings as early as Cnut, it was the Normans who had first "sharpened [outlawry] into an edged weapon" (Goebel 419) and eradicated its regional character (423).

Chapter 5. Folvilles' Law

1. That the story is apocryphal is suggested by Walsingham's report that Richard II dismissed the Essex rebels in 1381 with virtually the same words: "Rustici quidem fuistis et estis" (*Historia* 2:18).

2. The *Ledger-Book* preserves a writ from Edward I to the justiciar of Chester instructing him to hold an inquisition, "by the oath of honest and lawful men of your bailiwick," into the customs and services owed the abbot by the men of Darnhall (48–49). For the complexities of common law proof of villein status and villein tenure, see Hyams 1980, esp. 163–219.

3. Langland's Sloth confesses to knowing "rymes of . . . Randolf Erl of Chestre" as well as of the celebrated folk hero Robin Hood (*PPl* B.5:395). On the possible identity of the real Randolf, see Alexander.

4. Such faith seems to reflect values of great antiquity (cf. Davies and Fouracre 239).

5. Cf. also the actions of the discontented tenants of a neighboring Cheshire abbey, St. Werburg's, in the Peasants' Revolt (Clarke 59).

6. Even as late as the sixteenth century we find enclosure riots arising from alliances between the gentry and the peasantry (Manning 31–81).

7. Royal purveyors were widely unpopular. For an extended attack on the system they administered, described at one point as "illo prerogativo diabolico" (quoted by

Boyle 333), see the *De Speculo Regis Edwardi III*, written by William of Pagula, probably in 1332.

8. E.g., *Wiltshire Gaol Delivery* 130.849, and *Trailbaston* 2:35.50; 50.66; 67.97.

9. To the references given by Heffernan ("Lovedays," nn. 18 and 27–31) may be added *Mum* lines 1141–48 and *Friar Daw's Reply* lines 140–41 (Heyworth 77).

10. For examples of such documents in English, see *Paston Letters* 1:8–12 (1426/7), and Morsbach 19–24 (1439) & 50–52 (1459).

11. The approvement of William Rose, 1389, gives a vivid picture of the modus operandi of "a common horse-thief and highwayman" of this period (J. Post 100).

12. To these might be added a number of cases heard by Shareshull of men accused of disturbing the sessions of other justices; they include the imprisonment of a justice of the peace in Eynsham Abbey by a crowd acting "like madmen and men possessed" (Putnam 1950, 147), a brawl in court, an armed assault on a judge, and a charge of bringing a concealed weapon into the courtroom (130).

13. This incident is included in a list of crimes for which the knight, Sir Robert Darcy, later received a royal pardon; it is a list of which even Eustace Folville might have felt proud (*CPR* 1358–61, 463–64).

14. It is impossible in translation to bring out the legal wit of the poem's language. Thus *delay* (20) can refer to a legal postponement; *ploy* (54) means not only 'order' (as in 'the natural order') but also 'an action at law'; *chanter* (20 and 98) can mean 'to pronounce on [in court]' as well as 'to sing'; and *eyrer* (98) can be used of a traveling royal assize (the eyre) in addition to its the more general sense, 'to wander' (L. *errare*). The reference to the the jay's flight (19) may be intended as an ironic allusion to summary imprisonment, since jays were commonly kept as cage birds in the Middle Ages.

15. The *vert* was the technical term for the greenwood, used in the forest laws (see D. Stenton 1965b, 110).

16. In addition to the articles by Bellamy (1964, 1964/65) and Stones (1957), see Saul (1981), 174–83, and Hilton (1966), 248–61. A number of similar gangs can be found in Hanawalt (1975), though her general attitude to them is strongly authoritarian; see also Hanawalt (1979), 201–13.

17. "Que ore vueille vivre come pork merra sa vie" means literally 'if he wants to live, he shall lead the life of a swine'; medieval pigs were often turned loose to feed in the forest (see D. Stenton 1965b, 110).

18. I have given the version printed in *SCKB* 7:84–85, but added my own punctuation and capitalization and two emendations taken from a different version printed in Dobson 383–84 (see Chambers and Daunt 276). The translation offered in the Selden Society volume is not entirely trustworthy.

19. It is used of the incarnation in some fourteenth-century sermon verses: "He yaf himself as good felawe" (*Reliquiae* 2:121).

20. Sir John Clanvowe's *Two Ways* contains a tirade against those who "now . . . been cleped of þe world 'goode felawes' . . . and goon to þe tauerne and to þe bordel" (71–72), and the English phrases "kyng of felawys" and "cro[u]ny[d](?) felawe" are used in a Latin sermon in much the same context (cited by Wenzel 1986, 190).

21. Cf. the story of the Nottinghamshire man, John Shirle, who was hanged a month after the Peasants' Revolt, for criticising royal officials "in a tavern in Briggestrete in Cambridge, where many were assembled to listen to his news and worthless talk" (ed. Dobson xxviii).

22. This punishment was quite standard (*Munimenta Gildhallae* 1:601), and there are several earlier examples in the London Letter Books (e.g., Riley 315–16 [1364]). See also Greene *Early English Carols* 289 and 504 (no. 471 and n.). Chambers and Daunt suggest that the whetstone was used "in token of a tongue too sharp for its owner's safety" (250), but the figure of the liar's tongue as a sharp weapon was commonplace (Sheneman), and D. W. Robertson relates it to the "deceitful 'sharp razor'" of Psalm 51 (20). The whetstone may have carried the veiled threat that further offenses would be punished by mutilation; cf. Owst 1961, 298–99.

23. These verses were widely known in the late Middle Ages and a version was printed in Caxton's *Chaucer* (see Skeat lxxxi–lxxxii and 450); Skeat suggests that there is an echo of them in *Lear* 3.2.95. See also *HP* 145–46 (no. 58).

24. To judge from the proverbial catchphrase *si dedero* in the pseudonymous letter of "Jak Trewman," John Ball too was hostile to the legal establishment (see R. Green 1992, 184).

25. Three explanations have been proposed: (1) that the peasants were seeking a restoration of the right to bear arms that had been guaranteed by Edward I's Statute of Winchester (1285); (2) that they were appealing to the prestige of Doomsday (sometimes called the Book of Winchester) as a protection for their ancient privileges; (3) that they were referring to the particularly lenient treatment of felons under Winchester borough customs (Hilton 1973, 226). A fourth possibility is that "the law of Winchester" was a proverbial way of referring to a kind of borough jurisdiction that was relatively independent of the common law: "Winchester custom gave its citizens the right of having cases [of land title] tried in their own Court and not at Westminster, and 'grant asise' is specially mentioned in the *Usages* as one of the cases where common law did not apply in the City" (Furley 1927, 22). Evidence for this situation's being proverbial is provided by a Scottish ordinance of uncertain date (but attributed to William the Lyon who died in 1214): "alsua he has grantit to þame þat nane of thame do batale bot of þe mutis þat fallis to þe kingis croune And ȝit at þai be derenȝeit be þe law of wynchester þat is þrou þe acquittance of xij lele men þat ar burgess" (*Acts* 356). This solitary instance may seem slight evidence for the currency of a proverbial expression, but, then, if it were not for a single line in *Richard the Redeless* (3:145), we should not know that "þe lawe of Lydfford" was a proverbial way of referring to the summary excecution of criminals in the late fourteenth century (*Mum* p. 16).

26. Although its roots reach back to the thirteenth century (Hanawalt 1986a, 33), this practice had become so common by 1377 as to provoke a parliamentary petition (*RP* 3:21–22; Dobson 76–78) and the provision of special commissions of oyer and terminer in order to discourage such dangerous presumption on the part of the peasantry (Tillotson).

27. Paul Strohm's fascinating discussion of the carnival element in the Peasants' Revolt (1992, 33–56) seems to me to lay too great an emphasis on the carnival as as "inherently evanescent antistructure" (54).

Chapter 6. Truth and Treason

1. For the Anglo-Saxon term *hlafordswican*, see Wulfstan (71–80), and Whitelock's note 73.

2. Cf. the oath sworn by the mayor of London to Henry III after his defeat at the battle of Lewes (1264): "Lord, as long as you are willing to be a good king and lord to us, we shall be faithful and devoted to you" (quoted by Kern 130).

3. The older doublet survives at least as late as *Havelok*: "And siþen shal Ich understonde / Of you, after lawe of londe, / Manrede and holde-oþes boþe" (2815–17; cf. 2779–82).

4. In vernacular contexts such as this, however, we should be careful not to misapply Latin legal terms, which, if Susan Reynolds is right (1994, 22–34), are in any case apt to be seriously misunderstood by modern historians; Kay, the poem's most recent editor translates *vassal* here simply as 'knight.'

5. Cf. Bracton: "if he dissembles for a time and keeps silent as though consenting and assenting, he will be a manifest betrayer of the lord king, whether the accused is his own man or another's" (2:335). Pollock, on the other hand, seeks to explain William's "act of gross iniquity" in discriminating between the punishments of the two earls by reference to the principle of the personality of law (P&M 1:91).

6. Nonetheless, the first recorded example of unfurled banners being adduced as proof of treason in an English trial is as late as 1305 (Bellamy 1970, 37), and Maitland suggested that levying war against the king was "the newest item in the catalogue" of treasons made by the 1352 statute (P&M 2:505). Even in France, levying war was not regularly treasonable before the second decade of the fourteenth century (Cuttler 31).

7. An *armiger* and two *valetti* are named as Gerberge's associates in the first exploit, and two *valetti* and two *garciones* in the second. Only one of the valets was present on both occasions. PRO, MS KB 27/349 Rex m.6.

8. In defense of their use of this terminology, commentators have sometimes cited the earlier authority of *Britton*'s remark that "poet estre treysoun graunt et petit." But *Britton* seems to mean something quite different by this distinction: 'great' treason is plainly not restricted to crimes against the king, since an example of it is "those who poison their lords, or others," and 'petty' treason appears to refer not so much to a separate class of offenses as to those cases that have less serious consequences. "Let them be judged to the judgement of the pillory or to loss of an ear if the crime be minor [*si le fet soit simple*] and if the crime be great and dreadful [*si le fet soit graund et led*], so as to cause loss of inheritance or permanent harm, let them be judged to death" (*Britton* bk. 1, ch. 9.4; 1:41).

9. Maitland believed that the principle of forfeiture to the lord was what led to all these crimes being grouped under the heading of *felony* (P&M 1:304), but it may rather have been due to a more fundamental association (quite explicit in Beaumanoir) between betrayal and any kind of secret or covert act.

10. In dealing with the exceptions that may be taken against appeals of treason, *The Mirror of Justices* offers a particularly telling example: "as to an agreement by oath of fealty, [the defendant] may say that the appellant revoked the compact with him [qe cele alliaunce defist lactour ver li] at this or that point" (101). This is not Beaumanoir's situation where it is the defier who has sought to protect himself against a future charge of treason by making an open defiance, for here it is the one defied who is being advised to cite the defiance in his own defense; this can only mean one of two things: either (where the tenant is defendant) that the lord is imagined as having defied his own tenant, or else (where the lord is defendant) that the tenant is envisaged as having appealed his own lord of treason.

11. Steven Justice has offered a very different (and in my view somewhat strained) explanation of similar accusations of treason made against Chancellor Sudbury in 1381: "underlying this assertion . . . [is] the rebels' claim that the regnal person of the king resided in themselves" (100).

12. Bracton gives this oath as follows: "Each will swear . . . that in the counties into which they are to travel they will do right justice to the best of their ability to rich and poor alike, and that they will observe the assize according to the articles set out . . . and that they will execute all that is right and just in matters pertaining to the crown of the lord king" (2:309). This is probably a précis of a much fuller oath, however; one appended to a statute of 20 Edw. 3 (1346) is approximately six times the length of Bracton's (*SR* 1:305–6). For the text of the oath sworn by serjeants at law, see Baker (1984, 88).

13. Probably the most notorious instance occurred in 1394 when the king reportedly struck Arundel a violent blow with a staff grabbed from an usher in Westminster Abbey, apparently because he had arrived too late to join in the funeral procession for Queen Anne (Walsingham, *Annales* 424; see also, G. B. Stow 90–91).

14. Walsingham's *Annales Ricardi Secundi* describes these second-generation appellants throwing down their gloves before the earl "with physical gestures and grotesque cavortings ("indecoris saltationibus"), behaving more like stage torturers ("tortores theatrales") than knights and sober men" (215), actions possibly intended to remind onlookers of how gloves has flown about the place like snowflakes ("tanquam nix, undique in loco volabant cirothece") in the earlier parliament (Favent 16). Other parallels that look intentional include the fact that both sets of appellants appeared in matching robes (Favent 14; Adam of Usk 12), that the same judge, Walter Clopton, acted as legal adviser on both occasions (in 1388 he had done so within days of his appointment), and that Arundel was sentenced to be beheaded on Tower Hill, "where Simon Burley was beheaded" (*Eulogium* 3:375). The first appellants, by denying their victims the option of battle (the normal response to an appeal) on the grounds that this was inappropriate where there were credible witnesses, had left them very little room for maneuver (*Westminster Chronicle* 309–11), so that when, not only the king, but a former collaborator, the earl of Derby, appeared in court to testify against him, Arundel found himself truly hoist with his own petard. The duke of Lancaster, who, as High Steward, supervised the proceedings, made precisely this point: "since parliament is accusing you, you have deserved, according to your own law [secundum legem tuam], to be sentenced unheard" (*Eulogium* 3:374).

15. This is probably Adam of Usk's rather dramatic rendering of one of Arundel's rebuttals which is given in the *Eulogium Historiarum* as follows: "it is the king's greatest prerogative to be able to grant pardon for any kind of crime, and if you have been saying that he either cannot or should not grant a pardon, you have done more damage to his prerogative than I have" (3:375). Arundel may even have been anticipating the kind of complaint made by the Kentish rebels in 1450, that it is "the higheste poynt of tresone that anny subgecte may do azenst his prynse for to make hym reygne in perjurie" ("Declaration" 266–67). On the other hand, the charge may refer to some aspect of the duke's activities during the northern rebellion of 1393, when the two found themselves on opposite sides (see Bellamy 1964/65, 265–66).

16. Richard may even have contemplated trying to foist a forged document on Parliament. Tait regards an apocryphal confession, which represents Gloucester as freely acknowledging that he plotted and committed "faussete et traison" against the

king and others, as a French fabrication made after Richard's death in order to clear his name (216), but Richard himself had a far stronger motive for forgery in 1397.

17. An elaborate account of a new conspiracy in 1397 in the *Chronicque de la Traison et Mort de Richart II* has been shown to be "sheer fantasy" (J. Palmer 401–5); but cf. Bellamy 1964/65, 274.

18. E.g., Walsingham, *Historia* 2:224–25, and *Annales* 215; *Eulogium* 3:375. The *Annales* clarify a point which is less obvious in the passage from Adam of Usk quoted above, that Arundel took his stand on two distinct royal pardons, the first, a general one granted at the time of the Merciless Parliament, and the second, a specific pardon granted to him in 1394 (see *CPR* 1391–96, 406). Both these pardons had apparently been revoked before the trial (Adam of Usk 10); both are mentioned in the parliamentary report of the proceedings (*RP* 3:377), and in the articles of Richard's deposition (ch. 21; *RP* 3:418).

19. The word *prodicione* here is editorial. The orginal manuscript reading, *perdonacione*, makes little sense, but it is not difficult to see how a scribe, unable to believe that his exemplar was implying that the king's action was treasonable, made this slip.

20. For the circumstances surrounding this incident and the possibility that Richard was actually deposed for a short while at the end of December 1387, see Clarke 91–95.

21. There was of course an enormous amount of scholastic debate on this general topic, much of it conveniently summarized in an appendix to Kingsford's edition of *The Song of Lewes* (pp. 123–46). At the time of the Investiture Conflict many defenders of Gregory VII had been moved to attack the idea of royal prerogative, and one in particular, Manegold, may well have been reflecting traditional Germanic thinking when he wrote that "no one can make himself emperor or king; the people exalts one man that he may govern and rule them justly. If he breaks the contract (*pactum*) under which he was chosen, the people are free from the duty of subjection, since he has first failed to keep faith" (p. 130). See further I. Robinson (128–31). With the notable exception of John of Salisbury, however, few later schoolmen were willing to give unqualified endorsement to the subject's duty to resist, if necessary with violence, an unjust or tyrannical ruler.

22. Though this passage, the so-called *addicio de cartis*, does not appear in the oldest manuscripts, it was certainly added to the text at a very early stage; whether it is regarded as a forgery or an authentic afterthought comes down largely to a question of style—Schulz (173–75) arguing for the former position and Richardson (1965, 31–35) for the latter. Tierney's conclusion is probably the safest: "it might indeed seem that the *addicio de cartis*, if it was not written by Bracton, was a deliberate pastiche" (311).

23. The only set of articles for Edward II's deposition to have come down to us was printed in Adam Clarke's reissue of Rymer's *Foedera* from chronicle, rather than official, sources (Hardy 2:xlv), but it may well represent some more authoritative document now lost (perhaps destroyed on Richard's own orders). The articles themselves seem to have originated with John Stratford, bishop of Winchester, acting head of the Exchequer at the time (Wilkinson 2:158).

24. On the legal status of this parliament, see Strohm (1992, 81).

25. Though the editor of this letter, Ralph Griffiths, suggests that "its general orthography would not be out of place in the fifteenth century" (n. 22), both its vocabulary (i.e., *initiate*, *reluctancy*, *repine*) and style are plainly post medieval.

26. The account of the development of the English coronation oath given here is

essentially that of Richardson (1960), though we should certainly not ignore Hoyt's caveat about the unsatisfactory nature of our evidence for the wording of coronations oaths before the fourteenth century and the dangers of making extravagant claims for novelty in 1308.

27. Richardson has argued that this promise incorporates the older pledge to maintain the rights of the crown unimpaired (1949, 61–63); certainly, Edward himself and at least one of his subjects believed that he had bound himself to such a course (Kantorowicz 1957, 357 and n. 152).

28. The significance of this tense (Fr. *aura eslu*; L. *elegerit*) has generated much discussion from the seventeenth century onward: "do these words refer to the laws to be made in the future or to those already made?" (Richardson & Sayles 1935/36, 141).

29. The articles of deposition are printed in the *Rotuli parliamentorum* (3:417–22) but their numbering there continues the chapter numbering from the beginning of the session so that the first of the articles is chapter 18 of the record. To convert the numbering used here to the numbering of the printed text one must add 17; thus the ten articles that specifically mention Richard's perjury (3, 11, 12, 13, 18, 22, 27, 29, 32, 33) appear in the printed text as chapters 20, 28, 29, 30, 35, 39, 44, 46, 49, and 50.

30. Richardson and Sayles suggest that "this clause had ceased to be regarded as part of the oath at all, and had become merely a preliminary interrogation" (1935/36, 144).

31. I am, however, less convinced by Donaldson's argument that the word *communes* contains no specific reference to Parliament here. Both *Richard the Redeless* and the political poems in MS Digby 102 (ed. Kail) use the word in this sense, and this seems especially appropriate in an allusion to a coronation ceremony; the C-text reading "Myght of tho men" (i.e., the knights) appears to support this point (C.Pro.:140). Donaldson seems to have been led to this argument by the conviction that any claim that Langland would have supported Parliament's right to direct the king makes the poet appear uncharacteristically radical, but Langland comes close to supporting such a position elsewhere (e.g., B.19:302–4), and in any event a good case might be made for regarding this as a conservative rather than radical position in the late-fourteenth-century English context.

32. In one copy of "O deus immense," a manuscript apparently prepared under Gower's own supervision, the scribe has written *nota* opposite these particular lines (Coffman 961).

33. Ulpian did not apparently mean by *placuit* what English commentators in the thirteenth and fourteenth centuries took him to mean: "The *princeps* is not entitled to do what he likes, as a non-professional reader might assume, but he has the legal power to make law. This usage of the word *placere* is well known to every reader of the *Digest*" (Schulz 154).

34. See Rosenthal's excellent study of the role of the "wicked adviser" in late medieval political thought—though my own reading makes this figure rather less of a legal fiction than his.

35. Norman Doe has recently discussed the emergence in the fourteenth and fifteenth centuries of "the first signs of a substantive law which treats harmful conduct directly" (3), but unfortunately he has little to say about the law of treason.

36. See Putnam's argument that the act of 1352 was primarily drafted by Chief Justice Shareshull (1943/44, 265–67).

37. When Charles d'Orléans was released in 1440, an official copy of "þe ooth þt þe Duc of Orleance hath maad, þe whiche is writen in parchement and in þe which þe said Duc wt his owne hand hath writen his name" was handed over to the keeper of the privy seal for safe keeping (*Proceedings and Ordinances* 5:175–76) despite the duke's having sworn it on the Gospels under threat of perpetual damnation (*Foedera*, 3rd ed., 5 (1):102); and after the failure of Richard of York's first insurrection in 1452, Henry VI's advisers were careful to make sure that his renewed oath of allegiance was given a similarly tangible form: this "small strip of parchment, signed in a bold firm hand 'R. York,' and bearing some fragments of the duke's seal," is still to be seen in the Public Records Office today (Scofield 1:17).

Chapter 7. Charter and Wed

1. For an early fourteenth-century case in which a local jury similarly refused to be overawed by written evidence, see *The Chronicle of Jocelin of Brakelond* 123–24.

2. Cf. "I have known them [the Digger Indians of California] to swim rivers when the waters were high and dangerous in order to carry a letter to its destination. They are exceedingly faithful in this business, having a superstitious dread of that mysterious power which makes *a paper talk without a mouth*" (Ridge 130).

3. Such cases were certainly not restricted to England; see, for example, *Inventaire* 282.

4. Langland seems to be alluding to such practices when he makes *Spes* boast of his *patente*: "'Whoso wercheþ after þis writ, I wol vndertaken, / Shal neuere deuel hym dere ne deeþ in soule greue; / For, þouȝ I seye it myself, I haue saued with þis charme / Of men and wommen many score þousand'" (*PPl* B.17:18–21; cf. C.19:17–20).

5. Legends of Saint Margaret were also felt to be particularly valuable as talismans for women in childbirth: for a detailed discussion of books and scrolls used in this context, see Wogan-Browne 46–50. Rabelais alludes to the reading of Saint Margaret's legend to women in labor, both in his account of Gargantua's birth (in ch. 6 of the first edition; *Oeuvres* 1:29 n. 3), and in the preface to *Pantagruel* (1:217).

6. In rural areas such practices long outlasted the Middle Ages. Keith Thomas gives an example of a written talisman being used to cure a toothache as late as 1804 (329), and the Lancashire antiquarian Ammon Wrigley recalls a farmer's wife in the 1870s tying "a written verse from the Bible round one horn of each cow" to protect it from witchcraft, adding that "in some shippons [barns] a verse was nailed at the head of each stall" (47).

7. This practice was still current in the lifetime of the Protestant divine Joseph Hall (d. 1656): the bishop remarks that the Gospel of John, "printed in a small roundel" was sold to "credulous ignorants with this fond warrant, that whosoever carries it about with him shall be free from the dangers of the day's mishaps" (quoted by Thomas 34).

8. Cf. William Thorpe: "I vndirstonde a book is no þing ellis, no but a þing compilid togidere of diuerse creaturis . . . and to swere bi ony creature boþe Goddis lawe and mannes lawe is þeraȝen" (*Two Wycliffite Texts* 34).

9. Some charming stage business in the Chester play of *The Purification* offers a nice illustration: Simeon, incapable of believing the literal truth of Isaiah's prophesy "a

virgin shall conceive" (7:14), erases the word *virgin* from his Bible and writes *a good woman* in its place, only to have an angel secretly change it back again. Unable to believe his eyes the first time, he repeats the experiment and invites Saint Anne to witness the results: "My faye, yet eft will I see / whether my letters changed be. / A, hye God in Trinitee, / honored be thou aye. / For goulden letters, by my lewtye, / are written through Godes postie / syth I layd my booke from mee" (*Chester Mystery Cycle* 1:207). The story also appears in the *Stanzaic Life of Christ* 2737–2804.

10. There are similar passages in Robert Mannyng of Brunne's *Handlyng Synne* (2737–60), and in a poem on the Ten Commandments from Bodleian MS Laud 463 (*Kildare-Gedichte* 200–201).

11. The figure of the edible book, tasting of honey, is to be found in Ezek. 3:1–3 and Rev. 10:10.

12. It may, however, owe something to abstruse theological discussion of the reference to Christ as the *verbum breviatum* in Rom. 9:28 (see Spencer 140). For the scholastic tradition of the *verbum breviatum*, see Lubac 2:181–97.

13. In a variant form of the figure, Christ's crucified body is compared to a skin stretched out by the parchment-maker. One late-fourteenth-century translation of the immensely popular Pseudo-Bonaventuran *Meditations on the Life and Passion of Christ*, for example, describes his body "sprede o-brode one þe crosse more straite þan any parchemyne-skyne es sprede one þe harowe," a detail not found in the original (Horstman 1:206); a meditation on the five wounds from the same period is even more graphic: "ȝet oure blessed fadir of heuene spared not his owen sone but suffrede hym to be streyned on the harde cros, moore dispitously & greuously þan euer was schepys skyn streyned on the wal or vp-on þe parchemyn-makeris harowe aȝens þe sonne to drye" (Horstman 2:440).

14. About 1275, in the Anglo-Norman *Manuel des Pechiez* (quoted by Arnould 240–41), and a little later in an English hymn of Friar William Herebert (d. 1333): "Vor loue þe chartre wrot, / Þe enke orn of hys wounde" (*RL14C* 19). One of the most daring adaptations of this figure to a Marian context is Pierre Bersuire's: "Christ is a sort of book written into the skin of the virgin" (quoted by Gellrich 1985, 17).

15. There is no direct counterpart of lines 1527–28 in the original Latin text, the *Philomena* by John of Howden (cf. sts. 558–61).

16. There are further examples of this figure in chapter 53 of the Monk of Farne's *Meditacio ad crucifixum* (191–92); in the ME translation of Henry Suso's *Orologium Sapientiae* (cited in *Meditations on the Life and Passion of Christ* xxviii n. 2); and in a versified *Hundred Meditations* (Brown and Robbins 1035), a popular supplement to the *Orologium* (cited in *Late Medieval Religious Plays* xciv; cf. lxxx).

17. It is found in a letter to a nun by Jordan of Saxony (quoted by Smalley 283 n. 3); in Caesarius of Heisterbach's collection of exempla, the *Dialogus Miraculorum* (quoted by Wattenbach 209–10); and in a sermon written by the Cistercian fabulist Odo of Cheriton (quoted by Curtius 319).

18. Cf. John Mirk's late-fourteenth-century collection, *The Festial* (172; cf. 126), and an early-fifteenth-century Lollard homily (*Lollard Sermons* 113).

19. The slightly earlier "Chartre of Heuene," one of the originally independent tracts collected by the author of *Pore Caitiff* to "teche symple men and wymmen of good will the right weie to heuene" (quoted by Brady 529), might be taken to represent the older style of homily on the crucified charter. After an opening description of the actual

charter, which serves it for a theme, the tract goes on to urge the Christian "to keep the Charter in mind, and to live logically according to his faith . . . to think of the last day and the fates that await the good and the evil . . . [to] live properly now, doing penance, seeking the company of the good, performing his actions to please God" (Brady 540); all this smacks far more of the homily than of private meditation. *Pore Caitiff* remains unedited, but Spalding prints the first part of this particular tract as an appendix to her edition of *The Middle English Charters of Christ* (100–102), and the whole piece was printed by Richard Lant, ca. 1542 (*STC* 19187).

20. In such sermons the popular preacher was drawing upon a stock of familiar metaphors that were equally available to the moralizing poet: cf., for instance, the verse "ABC" on the Passion (lines 1–17; in Furnivall 244); the "Disputation between Mary and the Cross" found among the Vernon poems (*Minor Poems* 2:617); and one of the poems in the Digby MS (Kail 78).

21. Interestingly, one copy is found in the Vernon Manuscript, a volume possibly written at Bordesley Abbey (Breeze 1987, 114 n. 9; Pearsall 1977, 140), the house where John Northwood copied "The Letter of Charlemagne" into his commonplace book.

22. The more common figure is 5,475, arrived at by multiplying the number of days in the year by fifteen: "if þou sai ilk dai of þe ȝere fiftene: þou sal sai als many pater nostres in the hale ȝere" (Horstman 1:121; cf. Duffy 254–55), but other figures, including the 4,560 given here, are also found (see Breeze 1985).

23. In *Eger and Grime* a similar sword (though this one is unbroken) is kept by a widowed mother "Till her owne sonne be att age and land, / And able to welde his fathers brande" (lines 575–76); interestingly, when Grime borrows this weapon for his brother-in-arms, Sir Eger, to use in a crucial battle, its keeper requires "the deeds of both their lands" (lines 592) as security for its return.

24. Other objects, such as coins and rings, might also be divided in this way. Gregory of Tours tells us that the exiled Frankish king Childeric broke a gold coin into two pieces and left one half with a friend as a token to be sent to let him know when it was safe to return (2.12; 1:94), and the "broken-token" survives to this day as a ballad motif: "She's broken a ring from her finger, / And to Beichan half of it gave she: / 'Keep it to mind you of that love / The lady bore that set you free.'" (Child 1:470).

25. Cf. the *Sachsenspiegel*'s directions to the widow as to the disposal of her husband's war-gear (*herwede*): "where two or three [brothers] are born to the same war-gear, the eldest first takes the sword, then she divides up the rest [e.g., war-horse, armor] among them. If the sons are not yet of age, the eldest relative of equal rank on the father's side shall take sole possession of it and act as guardian of it for the children" (1.22.5 and 23.1; 89–90).

26. Not that sexual symbolism in such a context is the discovery of late-nineteenth-century Vienna; see, for example, the traditional ballads "Leesome Brand" (Child 1:177–84) and "Sheath and Knife" (Child 1:185–87).

27. It is tempting to compare it with the "sticke of holly" carried by the Gaveller in the Forest of Dean, apparently as a staff of office (*Book of Dennis* 74).

28. See Keen (1965a): "A banner or a pennon was a man's personal emblem; therefore when it was displayed he was committed on his honour to battle" (107–8).

29. Cf. a trespass case from 1387, where the lawyer defending two men accused of stealing charters argued that the muniments "pertain [*touchent*] to their inheritance and so the deeds belong to them [*atteignent les faits a eux*]" (*YB 11 Rich. 2*, 25).

30. When charters are mentioned in Anglo-Saxon lawsuits, the issue, as we have seen, often turns on the physical possession of the documents in question—see, for example, Birch nos. 291, 591, and 1064. In the first of these cases, the mere fact that the West Saxon king Cynewulf was in possession of title deeds from the monastery of Cookham (even though they took the form of a grant from the Mercian king Æthelbald to Christchurch, Canterbury) seems to have offered him, in his own mind at least, grounds for appropriating the monastic estate; he appears, in other words, to have thought of these deeds as somehow "savouring of" the realty he was claiming.

31. In some texts the identification seems to have extended to the material form in which the poem was recorded: three late-sixteenth-century copies of the charter (Spalding's A, B, and C), apparently made for antiquarian purposes, depict it as a physical document, with crude drawings of the seals dangling from it (Spalding xix–xxiii), and in a copy from the first half of the fifteenth century (E), "the Deed is represented as inscribed upon an immense sheet, held in the two hands of Christ on the Cross. . . . To the middle of the lower edge of the Charter is attached a pointed seal, drawn as though fastened by thongs" (Spalding xxiv; see Gray 1972, fig. 5). From such copies Spalding concludes that the original text of the short *Charter* must have been "written in imitation of a legal document" with "either an actual seal, or a representation of one" (lxiv). Indeed, one copy of the standard short *Charter* (C) is written on a single sheet like an actual charter, while a textually independent *Carta Dei* (printed by Spalding 97–98) was copied out on the back of an actual deed granting an estate in Kent in 1395 (xiv), and a partial copy of the A-text of the long *Charter* on the back of a legal deposition of 1412 from Oxford (xxxii–xxxiii).

32. Cf. Langland: "A[c] if þe [pouke] wolde plede herayein, and punysshe vs in conscience, / [We] sholde take þe Acquitaunce as quyk and to þe queed shewen it: / *Pateat &c.: Per passionem domini*, / And putten of so þe pouke, and preuen vs under borwe" (*PPl* B.14:189–91).

33. Cf. Criseyde's gifts of a glove (*Troilus* 5:1013), a bay steed (5:1038), and a sleeve (5:1043) to Diomede, none of which is in Boccaccio (Chaucer has added them from Benoît de Sainte-Maure).

34. His point seems to be that though the consecrated bread and wine function *like* signs, their consecration makes them far *more* than mere signs (see *De Apostasia* 223); in the *Trialogus* he says that what, in its own nature, is truly bread is *sacramentally* (not simply figuratively) the body of Christ (258).

35. Cf. the truculent response of the Lollard Richard Wyche (in 1402) to his interrogator's assertion that Christ's body is present in the Eucharist *in specie*, not *in forma*: "Tunc totus populus est extra fidem" ("Trial," 532).

36. This is paraphrase of a sentence from Wyclif's *De Blasphemia*: "Sicut enim intrans domum et videns ymaginem, non suspendit consideracionem suam quo ad naturam ymaginis, utrum sit de quercu, buxo vel salice, sed totam intencionem et devocionem suam suspendit in signato; consimiliter est de Eukaristie sacramento" (24).

37. This ambiguous formula, warranted by Wyclif's own Latin writings (e.g., *Trialogus* 249), appears as early as the second of the *Confessions* (*Selections* 17) and the Sunday Epistle cycle of the *English Wycliffite Sermons* (1:675). It had often been used in the fourteenth century with no particular heretical overtones (cf. *Harley Lyrics* 15:59, *Minor Poems of the Vernon MS* 24:1, 25:2, 495:70, and *Pearl* 1209), and even appears in perfectly orthodox works of pastoral instruction (eg., Mirk 173 and *Lay Folks Mass Book*

40 [C.237], 41 [F.213]). Wyclif's followers apparently found it particularly useful when dealing with awkward questioning by the authorities (*Two Wycliffite Texts* 53 [Thorpe], *Fasciculus Zizaniorum* 438 [Oldcastle], and "Trial" 532 [Wyche]).

38. For Garnet's authorship of the *Treatise of Equivocation* (ca. 1600), see Malloch (1966).

39. Evidently Herefordshire (see *Fasciculus Zizaniorum* 501).

40. There exist two mutually incompatible versions of this escape. A recantation (*Fasciculus Zizaniorum* 501–5)—ostensibly made in Durham before Bishop Walter (see Snape 359 n. 24) and implying that Wyche was released after abjuring his heresy—seems to be contradicted by Wyche's own account, given before the archiepiscopal court in Canterbury in 1419 (*Register* 3:57). Wyche suggests that he was first transferred to the jurisdiction of the archbishop of York, and later released by the court of chancery, to which his case had been removed by a writ of *corpus cum causa*; such writs were commonly employed to redress cases of wrongful imprisonment (Baker 1990, 168; cf. *SCC* 8–10, 80–81, 121), and it seems at least possible that Chancery upheld Wyche's claim that there had been procedural irregularities in the Durham inquest (see "Trial" 537). Interestingly, the Canterbury inquisition seems to have been undecided about the question of an earlier abjuration (*Register* 1:cxxxiv).

Chapter 8. Rash Promises

1. The combination of these three qualities (which derives from Jer.4.2) is a commonplace; cf. Chaucer "Parson's Tale" 592, and Usk, *Testament* 32.

2. "The decretists developed the principle that an act was voluntary if there had been even the slightest expression of free-will: 'Voluntas coacta voluntas est'" (Vodola 87).

3. Even on questions of law, church courts were apparently not completely impervious to local custom, nor did practicing canon lawyers feel bound to take the *corpus iuris canonici* as their sole point of legal reference (Donahue 674–78).

4. It is no doubt dangerous to generalize from the amount of evidence so far available, but there does appear to have been a steady increase in the number of contract cases heard by church courts in the course of the fifteenth century: Donahue reckons that *fidei laesio* cases from York ran at about five percent of the total in the fourteenth century (658), whereas Helmholz suggests that in every diocese for which figures are available "fidei laesio reached (or retained) a high level of use in the late fifteenth century" (1975, 427; also n. 87). Helmholz had earlier noted that while eighty-four breach of faith cases were heard in Canterbury in 1416, by the end of the century "hundreds . . . were being heard every year" (407).

5. Treitel comments on Williston's claim that "the common law does not require any positive intention to create a legal obligation as an element of contract": "[such a view] is hard to apply where words are spoken in jest or anger. Williston admits that there is no contract in such cases. This can only be reconciled with the objective test by saying that jest and anger are circumstances which a reasonable man can take into account; but if so the test ceases to be purely objective" (132).

6. This principle is not restricted to Africa. Alessandro Duranti, for example, has recently concluded from a study of village assemblies in Samoa that "a speaker must

usually deal directly with the circumstances created by his words and cannot hide behind his alleged original intentions" (33); Samoans, he claims, do not share our view that "speakers/actors have control over their actions/words *independently* of other people's recognition of those actions/words" (42), and as a result, "Samoan social actors seem more eager to act upon conventions, consequences, actions, public image, rather than upon individual intentions" (44).

7. Neither of Williams's two main arguments seems to me compelling. In the first place, his demonstration that Homeric Greeks possessed a concept of intention not dissimilar to our own (50–52) is beside the point, for what is at issue is not the concept of intention in itself but the weight assigned to it in law; archaic Greek law, like medieval folklaw, exhibits a principled objection to considering intention as a factor in assessing guilt in a way that is quite alien, not only to modern law but to modern notions of justice in general. Second, his suggestion that modern law, too, may sometimes hold people responsible for things done inadvertently and that we have been led to exaggerate the difference between Homeric Greeks and ourselves by "forgetting the law of torts" (63) contains some special pleading: strict liability is rare in modern tort law (it is restricted, in practice, to responsibility for the escape from effective containment of something known to be dangerous, such as a wild animal, dammed up water, or radioactive material), and absolute liability is even rarer. The law of torts, moreover, is permeated by the concept of negligence — a concept which plainly serves as a bridge between intention and liability (even if we cannot be shown to have intended a tortious act, we may still be held liable if we fail to show that we intended to prevent it).

8. Such stories are not restricted to romance: Frederick II is reported to have had one of his falcons judicially condemned for killing a young eagle (Kantorowicz 1931, 347).

9. The two cases recorded in England and the one in Scotland are all post-medieval; in fact, the earliest records of common-law animal trials are from New England. There is a strong likelihood, however, that this paucity of evidence is due to the nature of the records rather than the absence of the practice (see Jamieson 45).

10. This is not to imply that all deodands were necessarily inanimate: trampling horses and goring oxen might also become deodands (see Finkelstein).

11. Peter Abelard, one of the first theologians to stress the importance of intention in the assessment of sin, was certainly writing within a penitential tradition and has been argued to have been reacting against "the crudities" of the "existing penitential system" (xxxii and n. 3); he was evidently reacting against the crudities of secular justice also: "we, however, who are not capable of discussing this [the role of intention], direct our judgement particularly to deeds, and we punish not so much faults as deeds" [nec tam culpas quam opera punimus] (42–43). Cf. Chenu 17–32.

12. The doctrine of consideration itself dates only from the middle of the sixteenth century (see Baker 1981).

13. Drawing a distinction between oaths about past or present events and oaths concerning future ones, Aquinas says that in the former case, "the obligation rests upon the act of swearing, that is, one must swear what in fact is or was true. But in oaths concerning things to be done, the obligation falls upon the deed which one confirms by the oath; for one is bound to make what one swore true or else there is no truth in the oath" [tenetur enim aliquis ut faciat verum esse id quod juravit, alioquin deest veritas juramento] (2a2æ.89.7; 39:221). From such a perspective, breach of promise was, as A. W. B. Simpson puts it, "a sort of retrospective act of falsification" (1987, 386).

14. Cf. Balfour's *Practicks* (1579): "ane hecht or simple promise, utherwayis callit *pollicitatio*, quhilk is ane promise of ane man allanerlie to ane uther" (1:189).

15. For an interesting challenge, mounted by an anthropologist, to the assumption that the premises of speech act theory (including intentionality) are universal, see Rosaldo.

16. The practice of infant baptism, where there could be no question of an act of the will, was treated by canonists as a special case: "Laurentinus admitted that the baptismal obligation could never be fully justified in juristic terms, and that this form of contracting an obligation was unique to baptism" (Vodola 92; cf. Aquinas 3a.68.9; 57:106–10).

17. Elizabeth Fowler has cited a case from 1478 to prove that in the law's view "a wife's will is void during the marriage" (772), but this quotation is somewhat misleading since counsel is here referring to a will in the sense of a testament, and is, in fact, making an argument in defense of the wife's rights: "If this will were good a wife's inheritance would not be safe from her husband's alienation during the marriage" (Baker and Milsom 100). The case is further complicated in that it derives from an original decision in chancery concerning land, not chattels.

18. But cf. Maitland: "We can not, even within the sphere of property law, explain the marital relationship as being simply the subjection of the wife to the husband's will" (P&M 2:407).

19. In the strange back-to-front way in which so much medieval common law demands to be read, such arguments might actually be taken to imply that there was in fact widespread popular acceptance of the married woman's contractual capacity, the doctrine simply offering an ingenious (and potentially collusive) line of defense for husbands seeking to avoid liability for their wives' debts—functioning, in other words, as a shield rather than a sword. Consider, for instance, the analogous argument in *Selby v. Palfrayman* (1389), where a man impleaded to account for the price of nine tuns of wine, defended himself by claiming that "our wife dwells at B which is a merchant town where she is a common taverner and wine-seller, and we say that the plaintiff without our assent, accord, or agreement bailed the tuns to her to sell"; interestingly, the plaintiff does not dare challenge this point (*YB 13 Rich. 2*, 80). Though this case refers in the first instance to borough rather than common law, "any picture of the juridical position of the bulk of the population," as T. F. T. Plucknett, its editor, points out, "must be taken subject to the important reservation that the extent of local custom may be larger than at present suspected" (xlvii). Cf. *BC* 1:222–28, and Carruthers 219 n. 11.

20. It seems worth pointing out that married women were not the only legal persons to be subject to such circumscription of the will: A. W. B. Simpson suggests that a similar position was taken on the contractual capacity of members of monastic and educational institutions (1987, 539–40), and in a 1385 case the question of the joint liability husband and wife is compared to that of abbot and monk (*YB 8–10 Rich. 2*, 208–9). In fact, since almost everyone in medieval society found himself subject to a higher authority of some kind, in practice hardly anyone (speaking in juridical, rather than theological, terms) might be said to have possessed truly free will. Thus in Chaucer's "Clerk's Tale," Griselde's father tells the marquis, in a line unmistakably reminiscent of Christ's prayer in the garden of Gethsemane (Matt. 26:39), "'Lord,' quod he, 'my willynge / Is as ye wole, ne ayeynes youre likynge / I wol no thyng, ye be my lorde so deere'" (319–21).

21. Even in the late medieval schools such a view, though perhaps not framed in

quite these terms, might have found its defenders. The debate between the rationalists, such as Aquinas, for whom the will was subject to the intellect, and the voluntarists, such as Duns Scotus and William of Ockham, for whom the will was preeminent, raged throughout the fourteenth century (see J. Bowers 41–60).

22. Cf. McBryde's speculation that "the restrictive Scottish rules on the constitution and proof of obligations were a method of protection of the rash, inexperienced or careless from the consequences of a chance expression" (277).

23. Wagering and gaming forms an odd branch of contract law (see Treitel 389–408); despite their long-standing validity at English common law, by the early nineteenth century wagers were becoming increasingly difficult to enforce, and after the Gaming Act of 1845 enforcement became almost impossible; some wagers, however, particularly where what is at stake is the performance of a service rather than the payment of money, are still theoretically enforceable even today.

24. *Sir Amadace* offers another example: "Butte a forwart make I with the or that thou goe / That evyn to part betwene us toe / The godus thou hase wonun and spedde" (490–92).

25. Interestingly, the one situation which clearly justified a contract's being voided for fraud was where a party who was illiterate affixed his seal to a bond which had been incorrectly read aloud to him (A. W. B. Simpson 1987, 98–99; cf. P&M 2:535–36). For a case from the Ricardian period, see *SCT* 2:155.

26. In *The Tale of Beryn* the hero finds himself in court because, as a result of wagering on a chess game, he is held to have bound himself to hand over his five merchant ships to his opponent unless he can drink up all the salt water in the sea (1759–69 and 3083–100).

27. Bereford may have had Bracton in mind in his discussion of impossibility for he appears to have got the maxim *volenti non fit iniuria* from him (2:149 and elsewhere). Bracton in his turn seems to have got it from the *Summa Aurea* of the thirteenth-century Oxford canonist William of Drogheda (d. 1245).

28. Simpson's slip in giving the date as 1355 (1987, 31) obscures the fact that Arnold (1987, 511–12) is concerned with the same case.

29. The form of words used by Dorigen, "by heighe God above" ("Franklin's Tale" 989)—confirmed in her subsequent account, "Thus have I seyd . . . thus have I sworn" (1464)—indicates that her promise was made under oath, while the formulaic "Have heer my trouthe" (998)—confirmed by Aurelius's later statement, "And in myn hand youre trouthe plighten ye" (1328)—shows that it is formally confirmed with a ritual handshake. These two elements, the oath and the handclasp, constitute the minimum formal requirements of the "procedural contract" and would probably have made Dorigen's offer actionable, at least formally, in a borough or franchisal court (*BC* 2:lxxx), as also under canon or civil law (P&M 2:202)—though not of course in the court of Common Pleas.

30. The doctrine of *animus*, as it appears in Justinian, seems to have been grafted onto classical Roman law by jurists of the Eastern Roman Empire: "the Byzantines were the first to attribute to the parties an intention directed towards the attainment of a specific legal consequence, to make the intention supreme even where it is unexpressed and undemonstrable. It is intention in this form, and in this form alone that we designate by the mainly post-Classical word *animus*" (Pringsheim 48).

31. Of the Roman *obligationes de consensu* (buying and selling, letting for hire,

partnership, and trusteeship), Zimmermann writes, "As far as the old liability transactions of pre-classical law were concerned, it did indeed matter only that the actual form had been complied with. The actual intention of the parties was irrelevant. Already in classical law, however, this situation had changed very considerably. No formal act was needed for the conclusion of consensual contracts; they were based merely on the consent of the parties and they formed the nucleus around which the modern law of contract was to develop" (564).

32. Cf. Gilbert of the Haye's version of the same passage: "we hald in haly wrytt that all ath or obligacioun suld be tane in the fassoun and entencioun that he that ressavis it understandis it, that is to say, he that it is maid to" (1:178).

33. The author of *The Mirror of Justices*, for instance, defines law as "nothing else but the rules laid down by our holy predecessors in Holy Writ for the salvation of souls from everlasting damnation" (2), and in his subsequent discussion of the minutiae of common-law procedure he repeatedly uses the word *sin* where we would normally expect terms like *crime* or *offense*: "it is an abuse to amerce a man on the warrant of a presentment of a personal trespass, since no one is amerciable save for sin [*pecchie*] in a real or mixed action" (159).

34. E.g., the Harley lyric *Advice to Women*: "when trichour haþ is trouþe yplyht, / byswyken he haþ þat suete wyht, / þah he hire oþes swere" (12:22–24); cf. the passage from Robert Mannyng of Brunne quoted by Homans (167), or *Piers Plowman* B. 20:114–20. See also Franklin.

35. This is implied by the frequency with which matrimonial litigation turns on the actual words sworn at betrothals and espousals (Helmholz 1974, 36–40; Sheehan 1971, 245–47).

36. It seems quite clear that the oath became progressively more elaborate with the passage of time (a phenomenon that can also be observed in the French marriage rites printed by Molin and Mutembe [283–318]). Thus, the earliest recorded formula (ca. 1217), though said to possess great power ("in hiis enim verbis consistit vis magna"), is not formally an oath at all: "I take you *N.* for mine" [Ego accipio te .N. in meam] (*Councils and Synods* 2.i:87). By contrast a rubric in the late thirteenth-century Crawford MS of the Sarum rite has "the man shall take her in God's faith and his own to keep in sickness and in health," to which the early-fourteenth-century Paris Arsenal MS adds "as long as she shall live" (*Sarum Missal* 413). By the early fifteenth century, however, such oaths have become considerably fuller: a version of the York rite from 1403 has "Here I take þe N. to my wedded wyfe, to hald and to haue at bed and at borde, for fayrer for layther, for better for wers, in sekeness and in hele, till ded us depart, and þare to I plyght my trowth" (*Manuale . . . Eboracensis* xvi). This formula, with only slight modifications, appears in the early printed versions of the Sarum, York, and Hereford rites, and probably originates with the revision of the Sarum rite that took place in the late fourteenth century (*Manuale . . . Sarisburiensis* xiii–xix).

37. It is tempting to suppose that marriage oaths were made at the church door for the same reason that Robert the Pious had provided a splendid, but empty, reliquary for his subjects to swear on—as a "pious fraud" to prevent them compounding their inevitable perjuries (Helgaud 76–77). Gratian, after citing several similar pious frauds (as when the Roman consuls made their citizens take an oath of loyalty upon a roll containing some such promise as not to turn the Po into the Nile, "lest, having renounced their obedience, they should be ensnared by the guilt of perjury"), denies

that these can really mitigate the offense (pt. 2, ca. 22, qu. 5, ch. 11; 885–86). Nevertheless, popular opinion may well have continued to regard such formal safeguards as efficacious.

38. One ecclesiastical remedy for unlicensed cohabitation was to make the couple contract with words of future consent ("I take you as mine from now, if afterwards I know you carnally"), which would make them legally married should they later return to their old ways, and a mid-thirteenth-century edict, apparently recognizing that such contracts were likely to be ignored, specifies that they should be made without an oath (*absque iuramento*); interestingly, however, it does suggest that they should be recorded in writing (*Councils and Synods* 2.ii:598).

39. Hostiensis says that "any condition not reproved by the canons can be used in marriage" (Helmholz 1974, 56 n. 108).

Chapter 9. Bargains with God

1. As Douglas Gray has written of late medieval religious literature, "it is very difficult to draw firm dividing lines between 'low' and 'high' culture. There is constant overlap and interaction" (1990, 2). Cf. Peter Brown's reservations about the usefulness of a "two-tiered" model of culture for late antiquity (1981, 17–22), and Gurevich's analysis of the "complex and contradictory synthesis" (1988, xx) of official and popular forms in the early and High Middle Ages. Eamon Duffy has recently argued against the view that there was "a wide gulf between 'popular' and 'élite' religion" in the late Middle Ages (2), though he goes somewhat further than I would choose to do: while the gulf between lord and peasant in this respect may well have been smaller than is sometimes supposed, I find it more difficult to believe that learned and vernacular theological traditions were entirely homogeneous.

2. This story derives from Gregory the Great (Gurevich 1988, 188).

3. These all appear on a contemporary list of votive objects left at the tomb of Bishop Thomas Cantilupe in the twenty-five years following his death and submitted as part of the process of his canonization in 1307 (Finucane 98). That the human figures probably represented the votaries rather than the actual saint is suggested by the fact that a female figurine in wax was found at the shrine of Edmund Lacy in Exeter Cathedral in 1943 (Radford).

4. The precise location of this priory is something of a mystery. None of the locations so far proposed for Bokenham's birth (Reigate in Surrey, Markby in Lincolnshire, and Old Bokenham in Norfolk) satisfies the dual requirement of being in Suffolk (Bokenham says that he writes in the English of Suffolk) and being near an Augustinian priory known to have contained a relic of Saint Margaret. My own guess is that he may have been born near Easton Bavent, which was once on the Suffolk coast and has now disappeared into the sea. This parish contained "a chapel dedicated to Saint Margaret [which] seems to have possessed a great deal of sanctity for pilgrimages were frequently made to St. Margaret Easton" (Suckling 2:312). However, I have found no evidence that the chapel possessed a relic of Saint Margaret's foot, nor that it was owned by an Augustinian priory, though the important priory of Blythburgh was no great distance away.

5. Cf. this versified deathbed prayer: "Than see I right wele ther is no way butt

oone, / Now helpe me, deere lady, Kateryn, and John, / Cristofer & George, myne avowries, echone!" (*RL15C* 255).

6. Alford seems to regard this weak form as a post-Anselmian compromise—an attempt to retain the drama of a cosmic battle between good and evil without conceding any actual rights to the devil (1977, 944)—but similar views were propounded by the Greek fathers (see Aulen 48).

7. For a selection of citations from the Fathers, including Augustine, in support of this position, see Schmitt's note on Anselm's discussion of the *chirograhum decreti* of Col. 2:14 (*Opera* 1.2:58.1–6); Anselm, of course, dissociates himself from their opinion.

8. The role of the devil's rights in the English drama has been the subject of some debate: Fry's argument that they provide the organizing principle of the N-Town cycle has been questioned by several scholars, most notably C. W. Marx (1985). Here, and in his recent book (1995), Marx seeks to dissociate what I have been calling the trickster-Christ from the "abuse-of-power theory." The point that the dramatists appear to have been trying to play down this theory is well taken and may indeed reflect contemporary theological orthodoxy; it is also hard to quarrel with Marx's conclusion that "in the plays the presentations of the Redemption show an eclectic character" (29). For our purposes, however, it is enough to show that unmistakable traces of an older covenantal view continue to surface in such contexts.

9. For example, *Elene*, 900 ff. (K&D 2:91). For an analysis of *The Dream of the Rood* in terms of the devil's rights, see Woolf.

10. I quote from the early-fourteenth-century English translation, which, since it tends to emphasize and expand those passages where the devil's rights are discussed in the original (see Sajavaara's introduction 235–36), is particularly suitable for my purposes.

11. The source of this "foreward" is evidently Col. 2:14; the English translator seems to have had trouble with the lines, "le covenant est fermez, / En la curt Deu cirographez" (1031–32), rendering *cirographez* by the nonce word *congraffet* (1058).

12. Cf. Jacob de Voragine: "Jesu Cryst hath hydd the hoke of hys dyuynyte vnder the mete of our humanyte / and the fend wold take the mete of the flesshe / and was taken wyth the hooke of the godhede" (*STC* 24873, fol. xvi[b]).

13. This appeal is reflected in the scholastic tradition also. Works like the *Conflictus inter Deum et Diabolum* (Marx 1990), which were evidently written for "a learned, clerical and university audience" (17), though they set out to demonstrate that the devil has no rights over the human race, still do so in the setting of a courtroom confrontation between Christ and Satan. Such a setting, however humorously employed, implicitly recognizes a law that governs both disputants, and hence covertly endorses what I have been calling the weak form of the devil's rights theory. One might note, however, that even this text begins by reminding us how "Christ's pious fraud disarmed the malevolent fraud of the Devil," and how "with the antidote of his divine mercy he destroyed the poison which flooded the world through our first parents in the mousetrap of the cross" (lines 3–5).

14. This charge was made against Ockham as early as 1326 (McGrath 1981, 112), and against Ockham's followers by Thomas Bradwardine in his *De causa Dei contra Pelagium* (ca. 1344); whether it was justified or not is of course a quite different question. McGrath has argued that "the charge of Pelagianism is deflected by pointing

to the utterly gratuitous character of the underlying covenant itself" (115), yet even he concedes that Holcot and d'Ailly adopt a theology that "approaches (although it cannot actually be said to constitute) some form of Pelagianism" (1987, 73).

15. Even the well-known requirement that we do what is in us to do as a condition of our salvation seems to arise from coventantal thinking, reminding one, for instance, of Aquinas's discussion of supervening impossibility in contracts: "Suppose someone swears that he will pay some money, which he later loses through force or theft, then he would seem to be excused from performing his oath, though he is still bound to do whatever he is able to do" [licet teneatur facere quod in se est] (2a.2æ.87.7; 220–22).

16. Similar votive objects, some offered very recently, are still to be seen in the monastery of the Archangel Michael at Panormitis on the Greek island of Simi.

17. See Mirk 17; *Beryn* (lines 3483–91) offers another literary instance.

18. It is evidently an accusation that the poem's editor, J. J. Anderson, finds hard to stomach; by glossing *les* as an adjective 'false, untruthful' he shifts the burden of mendacity onto Jonah ("you have made a liar of me"). However, the idiom to *maken lie(s)* 'to tell lies' is well attested in Middle English—*MED* s.v. *li(e* n. (1) (a)—and is even used in a similar context in *Pearl*: "I halde þat iueler lyttel to prayse . . . Þat leueȝ oure Lorde wolde make a lyȝe" (301–4); even if *les* is here interpreted as the reflex of OE *leas* rather than OE *lyge*, it may still be taken as a noun 'falsehood' since the *MED* also records an idiom *maken les(e)*—s.v. *les(e* n. (2) 1.(a). For the medieval idea of breach of promise as "a sort of retrospective act of falsification" see A. W. B. Simpson (1987, 386).

19. As in Chaucer's pun "whil this maister hadde of hym maistrye" ("Monk's Tale" 2499), there seems to be a play here on the etymological link between *mastery* and *master*.

20. A very similar situation is created by Griselde's covenant with Walter in "The Clerk's Tale" (351–64) which binds her to certain duties but apparently invests her with no rights.

21. Kane and Donaldson regard the line following line 33, which is well attested in the MS tradition, as spurious.

22. Lucifer's later claim to have been "seised seuene [þousand] wynter" (B.18: 284) does not alter this; though the term *seisin* is generally applied to real property, one might also be seised of chattels or even, as here, of persons. Cf. disputes over villein status, particularly those which, at least before 1350, were fought on a writ *de libertate probanda* (Holdsworth 3:497); such disputes were never settled by battle, however.

23. I can see no real justification for Anna Baldwin's view that Life and Death are the champions here (66–72), nor am I convinced by her claim that the later confrontation between Christ and Lucifer in hell is portrayed as a duel of chivalry, fought to prove a charge of treason (72–76).

24. In practice, knights would rarely if ever have acted as champions in civil cases, but, since there seems to have been some feeling that the traditional weapons of shield and staff were uncourtly, when the romances portray knights as civil champions (in *Ywain and Gawain* or *The Anturs of Arthur*, for instance), they generally fight, as here, with knightly weapons. The author of *The Mirror of Justices* calls it an abuse that "a knight should have arms different from those which another man has" (173), but he is probably thinking of battle in felony or, possibly, treason cases.

25. A similar tendency can be detected among the canon lawyers, for whom the

contractual aspect of baptism was paramount: "the implication [of the *Glossa Palatina*] was that the grace of baptism shifted the individual to a different plane from that of his natural birth and entitled him to expect salvation" (Vodola 96).

26. For an ingenious defense of an opposing position, see Minnis, esp. 163–69.

27. Critics have been unwilling to acknowledge *Pearl*'s heterodoxy on this point (see Gordon's ed. pp. xxiv–xxv), and several, such as Sledd (381) and Hillman, seem more concerned with saving doctrinal appearances for the poet than accepting his text at face value. I have been arguing that the Cotton-Nero poet is theologically far more conventional than Langland, but in this instance I suspect he was quite prepared commit a minor doctrinal solecism in defense of what he saw as a larger orthodoxy (anti-Pelagianism).

28. It seems simpler to read C's lines "For Sarrasynes may be saued so yf they so byleued / In þe letynge of here lyf" (17:123–24) as merely a restatement of this point, rather than, as George Russell would have it, as a cryptic allusion to the heretical views of Uhtred of Bolton.

29. Cf. *PPl* B.10:478–82. Such concentration on the first estate here may well be eccentric. Wimbledon, for instance, sees the various labors performed in the vineyard as representative of the tasks appropriate to each of the three orders of society: "Ryȝt so in þe chirche beeþ nedeful þes þre offices: presthod, knyȝthod, and laboreris. To prestis it falliþ to kutte awey þe voide braunchis of synnis wiþ þe swerd of here tonge. To knyȝtis it falliþ to lette wrongis . . . And to laboreris it falleþ to trauayle bodily . . ." (63).

30. See, for example, the telling phrase added by Anima to the quotation from Saint Bernard: "'*Beatus est*,' seiþ Seint Bernard, '*qui scripturas legit / Et verba vertit in opera* fulliche to his power'" (B.15:60–61). There is no equivalent of "fulliche to his power" in Bernard's original, which comes from his *Tractatus de Ordine Vitae*, ch. 2 (*PL* 184:566b).

31. It was to be revived once more by Protestant divines like Tyndale in the early sixteenth century (see Møller 50–54, and McGiffert), and, with a particularly Calvinist cast, by the later Puritans (Møller).

Epilogue

1. For a wonderfully garbled account of English legal process (ca. 1500) by an Italian traveler who evidently found it completely baffling, see *Relation* 32–34.

2. How many Londoners in 1376, one wonders, would have reacted like the Genoan merchant Lodowic Gentyl to having a bag stolen on Westminster Bridge: he rushed straight to the mayor "to register the loss so that all deeds sealed with his seal from that day should be void" (Childs 71–72)?

3. I do not mean to imply by this that Chaucer reacted to Italy with "open-mouthed stupor"—David Wallace's caricature of traditional scholarly accounts of his Italian journeys (9). Wallace's brilliant exposition of the way Chaucer explored the cultural continuities between the two countries (9–64) should not blind us to the important disjunctions that also existed.

4. Cf. Pocock's discussion of the role of manners in the formation of a new humanist jurisprudence (37–50).

5. This is not to imply that by the early modern period the lawyers had largely

solved their problems: "The evidentiary regime of the eighteenth-century English courtroom," writes James Oldham, "as far as truth-telling was concerned, was incoherent" (96).

Appendix: Law in the Nigerian Novel

1. Bailey suggests they may have been a gift from English traders along the Gold Coast in the sixteenth century (389–90); other possible routes might be deduced from Bovill, esp. 98–131.

2. The coastal areas had, of course, long been in contact with Europeans, and from the mid-nineteenth century the Niger River had afforded some access to the interior of the country for missionaries and traders; Onitsha, in particular, became a center for their activities after 1856.

3. That the direct political legacy of colonialism includes the appalling war in Biafra and the atrocities of the current military dictatorship need not vitiate this claim for the continued integrity of the underlying structures of Igbo and Yoruba culture.

4. This is, of course, inevitably something of an oversimplification: several centuries before European colonization, West Africa had evolved a number of indigenous ideographic scripts, and Arabic craft-literacy had long been established in northern Nigeria (Obiechina 1–8); even European alphabetic literacy has a longer history in Nigeria than is sometimes recognized (8), and missionary activity was to extend it from coastal areas into the Niger delta and along the Niger River as early as the 1840s (see Emenyonu 19–32). Nonetheless, it seems quite clear the great mass of people living in the interior of southern Nigeria were not exposed to alphabetic literacy much before the beginning of the twentieth century.

5. The fact that Nwapa is Igbo and Amadi is Ikwerri suggests that the procedure is not a localized one.

6. In C. K. Meek's account of a trial (ca. 1912) for the theft of yams the plaintiff says, "I was not the only one who saw you—there are others. If I am asked to swear, these others will forbid me to do so, for they are prepared to swear themselves" (239). Cf. Nzimiro: "where the evidence is in doubt, the court may order one or other of the parties or their witnesses to swear to its truth, that is, to invoke a local deity to prove the truth of his assertion by killing or harming him or his relatives if he has given false evidence" (122); from the context this appears to be a judicial rather than an evidentiary oath.

7. There are signs of a similar development in Nigeria in recent years (see Igbokwe).

8. Echewa's fictional account is based on actual events: "The rioters were women—not a few enthusiasts, but women *en masse*—who formed themselves into mobs, armed themselves with cudgels, and marched up and down the country, holding up the roads, howling down the Government, setting fire to the Native Court buildings, assaulting their chiefs, and working themselves generally into such a state of frenzy that on several occasions they did not hesitate to challenge the troops sent to restore order. . . . The manner in which the riots had been conducted had made it evident that there were other predisposing causes of discontent [than the fear of new taxes], and chief among these was the widespread hatred of the system of Native Administration conducted through

the artificial channel of Native Courts, the members of which, under the name of 'Warrant Chiefs', had come to be regarded as corrupt henchmen of the Government, rather than as spokesmen and protectors of the people" (Meek ix).

9. Cf. "What are we going to do about thieves in this town? The world is bad. In my youth, there was no stealing" (Nwapa, *Efuru* 176); "Orimili, we have seen nothing yet in this disordered age; nothing, I tell you. How do you know that by next year we won't be hearing of children auctioning off their parents for money?" (Akwanya, *Orimili* 125); "I thought to myself: you do not belong to this age, old man. Men of worth nowadays simply forget what they said yesterday" (Achebe, *A Man of the People* 135).

Bibliography

Primary Sources

Abelard, Peter. *Ethics*. Ed. and trans. David Luscombe. Oxford: Clarendon Press, 1971.

[*Abridgements*]. *Les Reports des Cases en Ley [Edward II-Henry VIII]*. Abridged by John Maynard, Robert Brook, Anthony Fitzherbert, and Nicholas Statham. London: George Sawbridge, 1678–80. Reprint Abingdon: Professional Books, 1979–81.

Achebe, Chinua. *Things Fall Apart*. AWS 1. 1958. London: Heinemann, 1985.

——. *No Longer at Ease*. AWS 3. 1960. London: Heinemann, 1987.

——. *Arrow of God*. AWS 16. 1964. 2nd ed. London: Heinemann, 1974.

——. *A Man of the People*. AWS 31. 1966. London: Heinemann, 1988.

——. *Beware, Soul Brother*. AWS 120. 1971. London: Heinemann, 1972.

——. *Girls at War and Other Stories*. AWS 100. 2nd ed. London: Heinemann, 1977.

——. *Anthills of the Savannah*. AWS. 1987. Oxford: Heinemann, 1988.

The Acts of the Parliament of Scotland, I (1124–1423). Edinburgh, 1844.

"Adam Bell, Clym of the Clough, and William of Cloudesly." In *The English and Scottish Popular Ballads*, ed. F. J. Child. Boston: Houghton Mifflin, 1882–98. 3:14–39.

[Adam of Usk]. *Chronicon Adæ de Usk, A.D. 1377–1404*. Ed. and trans. Edward M. Thompson. London: Murray, 1876.

[Ælfric]. *Ælfric's Lives of Saints*. Ed. W. W. Skeat. 2 vols. in 4 parts. EETS (o.s.) 76, 82, 94, 114. London, 1881–1900.

——. *Ælfric's Catholic Homilies. The Second Series: Text*. Ed. Malcolm Godden. EETS (s.s.) 5. London, 1979.

Akwanya, Amechi Nicholas. *Orimili*. AWS. Oxford: Heinemann, 1991.

Aluko, T. M. *One Man, One Wife*. AWS 30. London: Heinemann, 1967.

——. *Wrong Ones in the Dock*. AWS 242. London: Heinemann, 1982.

Amadi, Elechi. *The Concubine*. AWS 25. London: Heinemann, 1966.

——. *The Great Ponds*. AWS 44. 1969. London: Heinemann, 1975.

——. *The Slave*. AWS 210. London: Heinemann, 1978.

Amis and Amiloun. Ed. MacEdward Leach. EETS (o.s.) 203. London, 1937.

Ancrene Wisse: The English Text of the Ancrene Riwle, Edited from MS Corpus Christi College Cambridge 402. Ed. J. R. R. Tolkien. EETS (o.s.) 249. London, 1962.

Aniebo, I. N. C. *Of Wives, Talismans and the Dead*. AWS 253. London: Heinemann, 1983.

The Anonimalle Chronicle, 1333–1381. Ed. V. H. Galbraith. Manchester: Manchester University Press, 1970.

[Anselm]. *Memorials of St. Anselm*. Ed. R. W. Southern and F. S. Schmitt. London: British Academy, 1969.

——. *S. Anselmi Cantuariensis Archiepiscopi Opera Omnia*. Ed. F. S. Schmitt. 2 vols. Stuttgart: Frommann, 1968.

Anthology of Chancery English. Ed. John H. Fisher, Malcolm Richardson, and Jane L. Fisher. Knoxville: University of Tennessee Press, 1984.

Antiquarian Repertory. Ed. Francis Grose and Thomas Astle. 4 vols. 1775. New ed. London, 1807–9.

An Apology for Lollard Doctrines, attributed to Wicliffe. Ed. James H. Todd. CS. 1st ser. 20. London, 1842.

Aquinas, St. Thomas. *Summa theologiae*. Gen. ed. Thomas Gilby and T. C. O'Brien. 60 vols. London: Eyre & Spottiswoode; New York: McGraw-Hill, 1964–76.

Arber, Edward, ed. *The First Three English Books on America*. Birmingham, 1885.

Armah, Ayi Kwei. *The Healers*. AWS 194. Oxford: Heinemann, 1979.

Arnold, Thomas, ed. *Select English Works of John Wyclif*. 3 vols. Oxford: Clarendon Press, 1869–71.

Aspin, Isabel S. T., ed. *Anglo-Norman Political Songs*. ANTS 11. Oxford, 1953.

[Asser]. *Asser's Life of King Alfred*. Ed. William H. Stevenson. Oxford: Clarendon Press, 1904.

Assises de Jérusalem. Ed. Le Comte Beugnot. 2 vols. Paris: Imprimerie royale, 1841–43.

Athelston. In *Middle English Metrical Romances*, ed. W. H. French and C. B. Hale. New York: Russell & Russell, 1964. 179–205.

Augustine. *Soliloquies*. See *King Alfred's Version of St. Augustine's* Soliloquies.

Awntyrs off Arthur at the Terne Wathelyne. Ed. Robert J. Gates. Philadelphia: University of Pennsylvania Press, 1969.

Baker, J. H., and S. F. C. Milsom, eds. *Sources of English Legal History: Private Law to 1750*. London: Butterworths, 1986.

Bacon, Francis. [*Selections*]. Ed. Brian Vickers. Oxford Authors. Oxford: Oxford University Press, 1996.

Balfour, Sir James. *The Practicks*. Ed. Peter G. B. McNeill. 2 vols. Edinburgh: Stair Society, 1962–63.

Ballard, Adolphus, and James Tait, eds. *British Borough Charters, 1216–1307*. Cambridge: Cambridge University Press, 1923.

Barbour, John. *The Bruce*. Ed. W. W. Skeat. 4 vols. EETS (e.s.) 11, 21, 29, 55. London, 1870–77.

Bartholomew of Exeter. *The Penitential*. In Adrian Morey, *Bartholomew of Exeter, Bishop and Canonist*. Cambridge: Cambridge University Press, 1937. 161–300.

Beaumanoir, Philippe de. *Coutumes de Beauvaisis*. Ed. Am. Salmon. 2 vols. 1899–1900. Paris: Picard, 1970.

[Bede]. *Bede's Ecclesiastical History of the English People*. Ed. and trans. Bertram Colgrave and R. A. B. Mynors. Oxford: Clarendon Press, 1969.

Beowulf. Ed. F. Klaeber. 3rd ed. Boston: Heath, 1950.

Béroul. *The Romance of Tristran: A Poem of the Twelfth Century*. Ed. A. Ewert. Oxford: Blackwell, 1963.

Birch, Walter de Gray, ed. *Cartularium Saxonicum: A Collection of Charters Relating to Anglo-Saxon History*. 3 vols. and index. London: Whiting, 1885–99.

[Blixen, Karen]. Dinesen, Isak, *Out of Africa*. New York: Random House, 1938.

Boccaccio, Giovanni. *Tutte le opere*. Ed. Vittore Branca. 12 vols. Verona: Mondadori, 1964– .

Bokenham, Osbern. *Legendys of Hooly Wummen*. Ed. Mary S. Serjeantson. EETS (o.s.) 206. London, 1938.

Le Bone Florence of Rome. Ed. Carol F. Heffernan. Manchester: Manchester University Press, 1976.

Book of Dennis. In H. G. Nicholls, *Iron Making in the Olden Times*. London: Bartlett, 1866. 71–82.

The Book of the Knight of La Tour-Landry. Ed. Thomas Wright. Rev. ed. EETS (o.s.) 33. London, 1906.

Borough Customs. Ed. Mary Bateson. 2 vols. SS 18 and 21. London, 1904–1906.

Bracton, Henry. *De legibus et consuetudinibus Angliae*. Ed. George Woodbine and trans. S. E. Thorne. 4 vols. Cambridge: Harvard University Press, 1968–77.

Bracton's Note Book. Ed. F. W. Maitland. 3 vols. London: Clay, 1887.

Brevia Placitata. Ed. G. J. Turner. SS 66. London, 1951.

[Brinton, Thomas]. *The Sermons of Thomas Brinton, Bishop of Rochester (1373–1389)*. Ed. Mary A. Devlin. 2 vols. CS 3rd ser., 85 and 86. London, 1954.

Britton. Ed. and trans. F. M. Nichols. 2 vols. Oxford: Clarendon Press, 1865.

Brown, Carleton, ed. *Religious Lyrics of the Fifteenth Century*. Oxford: Clarendon Press, 1939.

——. *Religious Lyrics of the Fourteenth Century*. 2nd rev. ed. Oxford: Clarendon Press, 1952.

Brunner, Karl, ed. "Mittelenglische Todesgedichte." *Archiv für das Studium der neueren Sprachen und Literaturen* 167 (1935): 20–35.

Calendar of London Trailbaston Trials under Commissions of 1305 and 1306. Ed. Ralph B. Pugh. London: HMSO, 1975.

Calendar of the Patent Rolls Preserved in the PRO. (1232–1509). 52 vols. London: HMSO, 1891–1916.

Calendar of Select Pleas and Memoranda of the City of London, 1381–1412. Ed. A. H. Thomas. Cambridge: Cambridge University Press, 1932.

Calendars of Proceedings in Chancery in the Reign of Queen Elizabeth. 3 vols. London: Record Commission, 1827–32.

Capgrave, John. *The Life of St. Katharine of Alexandria*. Ed. Carl Horstmann. EETS (o.s.) 100. London, 1893.

Capitularia regum Francorum. Ed. Alfred Boretius. MGH. *Leges*: 2nd section, 1. Hanover, 1883.

Chambers, R. W., and Marjorie Daunt, eds. *A Book of London English, 1384–1425*. Oxford: Clarendon Press, 1931.

La Chanson de Roland. Ed. William Calin. New York: Appleton-Century-Crofts, 1968.

Chaucer, Geoffrey. *The Riverside Chaucer*. Ed. Larry D. Benson. 3rd ed. Boston: Houghton Mifflin, 1987.

Chaucer Life-Records. Ed. Martin M. Crow and Clair C. Olson. Oxford: Clarendon Press, 1966.

The Chester Mystery Cycle. Ed. R. M. Lumiansky and David Mills. 2 vols. EETS (s.s.) 3, 9. London, 1974–86.

Chestre, Thomas. *Sir Launfal*. Ed. A. J. Bliss. London and Edinburgh: Nelson, 1960.

Li Chevaliers as devs espees: Altfranzösischer Abenteuerroman. Ed. Wendelin Foerster. Halle: Niemeyer, 1877.

Child, F. J., ed. *The English and Scottish Popular Ballads*. 5 vols. Boston: Houghton Mifflin, 1882–98.

Child Marriages, Divorces, and Ratifications, &c. In the Diocese of Chester, A.D. 1561–66. Ed. F. J. Furnivall. EETS (o.s.) 108. London, 1897.

Chrétien de Troyes. *Yvain*. Ed. T. B. W. Reid. Manchester: Manchester University Press, 1942.

——. *Le Chevalier de la charette*. Ed. Mario Roques. CFMA. Paris: Champion, 1958.

The Chronicle of Jocelin of Brakelond. Ed. and trans. H. E. Butler. London: Thomas Nelson, 1949.

Clanvowe, Sir John. *The Works of Sir John Clanvowe*. Ed. V. J. Scattergood. Cambridge: Brewer, 1975.

[*Cleanness*]. *Purity*. Ed. Robert J. Menner. New Haven: Yale University Press, 1920.

Cook, Albert S., ed. *Biblical Quotations in Old English Prose Writers*. London: Macmillan, 1898.

Councils and Synods with Other Documents Relating to the English Church. Vol. 2, pts. 1 and 2. Ed. F. M. Powicke and C. R. Cheyney. Oxford: Clarendon Press, 1981.

The Court Baron. Ed. F. W. Maitland and W. P. Baildon. SS 4. London, 1891.

Coutumiers de Normandie. Ed. Ernest-Joseph Tardif. 2 vols. Rouen and Paris, 1881–96.

Cursor Mundi. Ed. R. Morris. 7 vols. EETS (o.s.) 57, 62, 66, 68, 99, 101. London, 1874–93.

"Declaration . . . of the grounds of the insurrection which took place in Kent in 1450." HMC. *Eighth Report (Appendix, Pt. 1)*. London: Spottiswoode, 1881.

De Speculo Regis Edwardi III. Ed. J. Moisant. Paris: Picard, 1891.

"De Veritate & Conscientia." In George Kane, "Middle English Verse in MS Welcome 1493." *London Mediæval Studies* 2 (1951): 61–65.

Dives and Pauper. Ed. Priscilla H. Barnum. EETS (o.s.) 275 and 280. London, 1976–80.

Dobson, R. B., ed. *The Peasants' Revolt of 1381*. 2nd ed. London: Macmillan, 1983.

Dunbar, William. *Poems*. Ed. James Kinsley. Oxford: Clarendon Press, 1979.

Earl of Toulouse. In *Middle English Metrical Romances*, ed. W. H. French and C. B. Hale. New York: Russell & Russell, 1964. 383–419.

The Early South English Legendary or Lives of Saints. Ed. Carl Horstmann. EETS (o.s.) 87. London, 1887.

"Early Trailbaston Proceedings from the Lincolnshire Roll of 1305." Ed. Alan Harding. In *Medieval Legal Records*, ed. R. F. Hunnisett and J. B. Post. London, HMSO, 1978. 143–68.

Echewa, T. Obinkaram. *The Land's Lord*. AWS 168. London: Heinemann, 1976.

——. *The Crippled Dancer*. AWS. London: Heinemann, 1986.

——. *I Saw the Sky Catch Fire*. New York: Plume, 1993.

Eger and Grime. In *Middle English Metrical Romances*, ed. W. H. French and C. B. Hale. New York: Russell & Russell, 1964. 671–717.

Emaré. In *Middle English Metrical Romances*, ed. W. H. French and C. B. Hale. New York: Russell & Russell, 1964. 423–55.

Enahoro, Anthony. *Fugitive Offender: The Story of a Political Prisoner*. London: Cassell, 1965.

English Lawsuits from William I to Richard I. Ed. R. C. Van Caenegem. 2 vols. SS 106 and 107. London, 1990–91.

The English Register of Oseney Abbey, by Oxford. Ed. Andrew Clark. EETS (o.s.) 133 and 144. London, 1907 and 1913.

English Wycliffite Sermons. Ed. Anne Hudson and Pamela Gradon. 4 vols. Oxford: Clarendon Press, 1983– .

Erasmus. *Enchiridion militis christiani*. Ed. Anne M. O'Donnell. EETS (o.s.) 282. Oxford, 1981.

Eulogium Historiarum. Ed. F. S. Haydon. 3 vols. RS. London, 1858–63.

The Eyre of Kent, 6 & 7 Edward 2. Ed. F. W. Maitland, L. W. V. Harcourt, and W. C. Bolland. SS 24. London, 1910.

The Eyre of London, 1321. Ed. H. M. Cam. 2 vols. SS 85 and 86. London, 1968–69.

The Eyre of Northamptonshire, 3 & 4 Edward 3. Ed. Donald W. Sutherland. 2 vols. SS 97 and 98. London, 1983.

Fasciculus Morum: A Fourteenth-Century Preacher's Handbook. Ed. and trans. Siegfried Wenzel. University Park: Pennsylvania State University Press, 1989.

Fasciculus Zizaniorum. Ed. Walter W. Shirley. RS. London, 1858.

Favent, Thomas. *Historia siue narracio de modo et forma mirabilis parliamenti*. Ed. M. McKisack. Camden Miscellany 14, CS 3rd ser., 37. London, 1926.

Flasdieck, Hermann M., ed. *Mittelenglische Originalurkunden, 1405–1430*. Alt- und Mittelenglische Texte 11. Heidelberg, 1926.

Floris and Blancheflour. In *Middle English Metrical Romances*, ed. W. H. French and C. B. Hale. New York: Russell & Russell, 1964. 824–55.

Foedera, coventiones, litterae et cujuscunque generis acta publica &c. (1) Ed. Thomas Rymer and George Holmes. 3rd ed. 10 vols. The Hague: Neaulme, 1739–45. (2) Ed. Thomas Rymer, Adam Clarke, Frederic Holbrooke, and John Caley. New ed. 4 vols. London: Record Commission, 1816–69.

Formulae Merowingici et Karolini Aevi. Ed. Karl Zeumer. MGH. *Leges*: 5th section (*Formulae*). Hanover, 1886.

Forster, E. M. *A Passage to India*. 1924. Harmondsworth: Penguin Books, 1961.

Fortescue, Sir John. *De laudibus legum Anglie*. Ed. and trans. S. B. Chrimes. Cambridge: Cambridge University Press, 1942.

——— *The Governance of England: Otherwise Called The Difference between an Absolute and a Limited Monarchy*. Ed. Charles Plummer. Oxford: Clarendon Press, 1885.

Fouke le Fitz Waryn. Ed. E. J. Hathaway, P. T. Ricketts, C. A. Robson, and A. D. Wilshere. Oxford: ANTS, 1975.

A Fourteenth Century English Biblical Version. Ed. A. C. Paues. Cambridge: Cambridge University Press, 1904.

French, W. H., and C. B. Hale, eds. *Middle English Metrical Romances*. 1930. New York: Russell & Russell, 1964.

Frithegodi Monachi Breuiloquium Vitae Beati Wilfredi, et Wulfstani Cantoris Narratio Metrica de Sancto Swithuno. Ed. Alistair Campbell. Zurich: Thesaurus Mundi, 1950.

Froissart, Jean. *Chroniques (le manuscrit d'Amiens)*. Ed. George T. Diller. Vols. 1– Geneva: Droz, 1991– .

Furnivall F. J., ed. *Political, Religious, and Love Poems*. EETS (o.s.) 15. London, 1866.

Gamelyn. In *Middle English Metrical Romances*, ed. W. H. French and C. B. Hale. New York: Russell & Russell, 1964. 209–35.

[Garnet, Henry]. *A Treatise of Equivocation*. Ed. David Jardine. London: Longman, 1851.

"A Gest of Robyn Hode." In *The English and Scottish Popular Ballads*, ed. F. J. Child, Boston: Houghton Mifflin, 1882–98. 3:39–89.

Gesta Romanorum. Ed. Hermann Oesterley. 1872. Hildesheim: Georg Olms, 1963.
[Gilbert of the Haye]. *Gilbert of the Haye's Prose Manuscript (A.D. 1456)*. Ed. J. H. Stevenson. 2 Vols. STS. Edinburgh, 1901 and 1914.
[Glanvill]. *Tractatus de legibus et consuetudinibus regni Anglie qui Glanvilla Vocatur*. Ed. and trans. G. D. G. Hall. London: Nelson, 1965.
Gordon, E. V., ed. *Introduction to Old Norse*. 2nd ed., rev. A. R. Taylor. Oxford: Clarendon Press, 1958.
The Gospel of Nicodemus. Ed. H. C. Kim. Toronto: Pontifical Institute of Mediaeval Studies, 1973.
Gottfried von Strassburg. *Tristan und Isolde*. Ed. F. Ranke. Dublin and Zurich: Weidmann, 1967. (Trans. A. T. Hatto. Harmondsworth: Penguin Books, 1960.)
[Gower, John]. *The English Works of John Gower*. Ed. G. C. Macaulay. 2 vols. EETS (e.s.) 81 and 82. London, 1900–1901.
———. *Complete Works: The French Works*. Ed. G. C. Macaulay. Oxford: Clarendon Press, 1899.
———. *Complete Works: The Latin Works*. Ed. G. C. Macaulay. Oxford: Clarendon Press, 1920.
Gratian. *Decretum Magistri Gratiani*. Ed. Emil Friedberg. *Corpus Iuris Canonici* 1. Leipzig: Tauschnitz, 1879.
Greene, Richard L., ed. *The Early English Carols*. 2nd ed. Oxford: Clarendon Press, 1977.
[Gregory of Tours]. *Gregorii Episcopi Turonensis Historiarum Libri Decem*. Ed. Rudolf Buchner. 2 vols. Darmstadt: Wissenschaftliche Buchgesellschaft, 1955–56.
Gregory's Chronicle. Ed. James Gairdner. CS n.s. 17. London, 1876.
[Grimestone]. Wilson, Edward. *A Descriptive Index of the English Lyrics in John of Grimestone's Preaching Book*. Medium Ævum Monographs, n.s. 2. Oxford: Society for the Study of Medieval Languages and Literatures, 1973.
[Grosseteste, Robert]. *Le Château d'amour de Robert Grosseteste, évêque de Lincoln*. Ed. J. Murray. Paris: Champion, 1918.
———. *The Middle English Translations of Robert Grosseteste's* Château d'amour. Ed. Kari Sajavaara. Helsinki: Société Néophilologique, 1967.
The Harley Lyrics: The Middle English Lyrics of MS. Harley 2253. Ed. G. L. Brook. 3rd. ed. Manchester: Manchester University Press, 1964.
Harmer, F. E., ed. and trans. *Select English Historical Documents of the Ninth and Tenth Centuries*. Cambridge: Cambridge University Press, 1914.
Harrison, William. *The Description of England*. Ed. Georges Edelen. Ithaca, N.Y.: Cornell University Press, 1968.
Havelok. Ed. G. V. Smithers. Oxford: Clarendon Press, 1987.
Head, Bessie. *Serowe: Village of the Rain Wind*. AWS 220. London: Heinemann, 1981.
Helgaud de Fleury. *Vie de Robert le Pieux: Epitoma vitae regis Roberti pii*. Ed. Robert-Henri Bautier and G. Labory. Paris: Centre national de la recherche scientifique, 1965.
[Henryson, Robert]. *The Poems of Robert Henryson*. Ed. Denton Fox. Oxford: Clarendon Press, 1981.
Heyworth, P. L., ed. *Jack Upland, Friar Daw's Reply, and Upland's Rejoinder*. London: Oxford University Press, 1968.
[Higden, Ranulf]. *Polychronicon Randulphi Higden monachi Cestrensis.* Ed. Joseph R. Lumby. 9 vols. RS. London: HMSO, 1865–86.

Hoccleve, Thomas. *Works: The Regement of Princes and Fourteen Minor Poems*. Ed. F. J. Furnivall. EETS (e.s.) 73. London, 1898.

Holland, Sir Richard. *The Buke of the Howlat*. In *Scottish Alliterative Poems*, ed. F. J. Amours, STS, 1st ser. 27 and 28, Edinburgh, 1892–97. 47–81.

Horstman, C., ed. *Yorkshire Writers: Richard Rolle of Hampole . . . and His Followers*. 2 vols. London: Sonnenschein, 1895–86.

[Howden, John of]. *John Hovedens Nachtigallenlied*. Ed. Clemens Blume. Analectica Hymnica 4. Leipzig, 1930.

Hunnisett, R. F. and J. B. Post, eds. *Medieval Legal Records*. London: HMSO, 1978.

[Idley]. *Peter Idley's Instructions to His Son*. Ed. Charlotte D'Evelyn. Boston: Modern Language Association of America, 1935.

Inventaire sommaire des archives départementales antérieures à 1790. Aube: Archives Ecclésiastiques. Ser. G. Vol. 2. Ed. H. d'Arbois de Jubainville and F. André. Paris: Picard, 1896.

James, M. R., ed. "Twelve Medieval Ghost-Stories." *English Historical Review* 37 (1922): 413–22.

Joinville, Jehan, Seigneur de. *La Vie de Saint Louis*. Ed. Noel L. Corbett. Sherbrooke: Naaman, 1977.

Jones, Michael, and Simon Walker, eds. *Private Indentures in Peace and War, 1278–1476*. Camden Miscellany 32. CS 5th ser. 3, London, 1994. 1–190.

Jumbam, Kenjo. *The White Man of God*. AWS 231. London: Heinemann, 1980.

Kail, J., ed. *Twenty-Six Political and Other Poems*. EETS (o.s.) 124. London, 1904.

Die Kildare-Gedichte. Ed. W. Heuser. Bonner Beiträge zur Anglistik 14. Bonn, 1904.

King Alfred's Version of St. Augustine's Soliloquies. Ed. Thomas A. Carnicelli. Cambridge, Mass.: Harvard University Press, 1969.

King Horn. In *Middle English Metrical Romances*, ed. W. H. French and C. B. Hale. New York: Russell & Russell, 1964. 25–79.

Knighton, Henry. *Chronicon*. Ed. Joseph R. Lumby. 2 vols. RS. London: HMSO, 1889–95.

———. *Knighton's Chronicle, 1337–1396*. Ed. G. H. Martin. Oxford Medieval Texts. Oxford: Clarendon Press, 1995.

Krapp, George Philip, and Elliott Van Kirk Dobbie, eds. *The Anglo-Saxon Poetic Records: A Collective Edition*. 6 vols. New York: Columbia University Press, 1931–42.

[Laȝamon]. *Laȝamon's Brut*. Ed. G. L. Brook and R. F. Leslie. 2 vols. EETS (o.s.) 250 and 277. London. 1963–78.

Lancelot: Roman en prose du treizième siècle. Ed. Alexandre Micha. 9 vols. Geneva: Droz, 1978–83.

Langland, William. *Piers Plowman: The A Version*. Ed. George Kane. London: Athlone Press, 1960.

———. *Piers Plowman: The B Version*. Ed. George Kane and E. Talbot Donaldson. London: Athlone Press, 1975.

———. *Piers Plowman: An Edition of the C-text*. Ed. Derek Pearsall. London: Arnold, 1978.

———. *Piers Plowman: The Z Version*. Ed. A. G. Rigg and Charlotte Brewer. Toronto: Pontifical Institute of Mediaeval Studies, 1983.

Las Casas, Bartolomé de. *History of the Indies*. Trans. Andrée Collard. New York: Harper & Row, 1971.

The Late Medieval Religious Plays of Bodleian MSS Digby 133 and E Museo 160. Ed. Donald C. Baker, John L. Murphy, and Louis B. Hall. EETS (o.s.) 283. Oxford, 1982.

Laxdœla Saga. Ed. Einar Sveinsson. Íslenzk fornrit, 5. Reykjavik, 1934.

The Lay Folks Mass Book. Ed. Thomas F. Simmons. EETS (o.s.) 71. London, 1879.

The Ledger-Book of Vale Royal Abbey. Ed. J. Brownbill. Lancashire and Cheshire Record Society Publications, 68. Manchester, 1914.

Leges Alamannorum. Ed. Karl Lehmann. MGH. *Leges*: 1st section, 5 (pt. 1). Hanover, 1966.

Leges Burgundionum. Ed. L. R. de Salis. MGH. *Leges*: 1st section, 2 (pt. 1). Hanover, 1892.

Leges Henrici Primi. Ed. and trans. L. J. Downer. Oxford: Clarendon Press, 1972.

Leges Langobardorum. Ed. F. Bluhme and A. Boretius. MGH. *Leges*: 4. Hanover, 1868.

Libellus de Vita et Miraculis S. Godrici, Heremitae de Finchale. Ed. Joseph Stevenson. Surtees Society 20. London: Nichols, 1847.

Liber de Miraculis Sanctae Dei Genetricis Mariae. Ed. Thomas F. Crane. Ithaca, N.Y.: Cornell University Press, 1925.

Liber Eliensis. Ed. E. O. Blake. CS 3rd ser., 92. London, 1962.

Liebermann, F., ed. *Die Gesetze der Angelsachsen*. 3 vols. 1903–16. Sindelfingen: Scientia Aalen, 1960.

"The Life of Sir Rhys ap Thomas." In Ralph A. Griffiths, *Sir Rhys ap Thomas and his Family: A Study of the Wars of the Roses and Early Tudor Politics*. Cardiff: University of Wales Press, 1993. 133–270.

Little, A. G., ed. *Franciscan Papers, Lists, and Documents*. Manchester: Manchester University Press, 1943.

Le Livre des serfs de Marmoutiers. Ed. André Salmon. Tours: Société archéologique de Touraine, 1864.

Le Livre des usaiges de la conté de Guysnes. Ed. Louis Carolus-Barré. In *Le Droit économique et social d'une petite ville Artésienne à la fin du moyen-âge*, ed. Georges Espinas. Lille and Paris: Bibliothèque de la société du droit des pays Flamands, Picards et Wallons, 1949. 1–177.

Lollard Sermons. Ed. Gloria Cigman. EETS (o.s.) 294. Oxford, 1989.

["Lovedays"]. "A Middle English Poem on Lovedays." Ed. Thomas J. Heffernan. *Chaucer Review* 10 (1975/76): 172–85.

Lydgate, John. *Lydgate's Troy Book*. Ed. Henry Bergen. 4 vols. EETS (e.s.) 97, 103, 106, 126. London, 1906–35.

———. *The Siege of Thebes*. Ed. Axel Erdmann. EETS (e.s.) 108. London, 1911.

[Malory, Sir Thomas]. *Caxton's Malory: A New Edition of Sir Thomas Malory's Le Morte Darthur*. Ed. J. W. Spisak and W. Matthews. 2 vols. Berkeley and Los Angeles: University of California Press, 1983.

Mannyng, Robert, of Brunne. *Handlyng Synne*. Ed. Idelle Sullens. Medieval and Renaissance Texts and Studies 14. Binghamton, N.Y., 1983.

Manuale ad usum Sarisburiensis. Ed. A. Jefferies Collins. Henry Bradshaw 5 Soc. 91. London, 1960.

Manuale et Processionale ad Usum Insignis Ecclesiae Eboracensis. Ed. W. G. Henderson. Surtees Soc. 63. Durham, 1875.

Marlowe, Christopher. *The Complete Works, Vol. 3: Edward II*. Ed. Richard Rowland. Oxford: Clarendon Press, 1994.

[Mechtild of Hackeborn]. *The Booke of Gostlye Grace of Mechtild of Hackeborn*. Ed. Theresa A. Halligan. Toronto: Pontifical Institute of Medieval Studies, 1979.

Meditations on the Life and Passion of Christ. Ed. Charlotte D'Evelyn. EETS (o.s.) 158. London, 1921.

Memorials of St. Anselm. Ed. R. W. Southern and F. S. Schmitt. London: Oxford University Press, 1969.

The Middle-English Harrowing of Hell and Gospel of Nicodemus. Ed. William Henry Hulme. EETS (e.s.) 100. London, 1907.

Mills, Maldwyn, ed. *Six Middle English Romances*. London: Dent, 1973.

The Minor Poems of the Vernon MS. Ed. Carl Horstmann and F. J. Furnivall. 2 vols. EETS (o.s.) 98 and 117. london, 1892 and 1901.

[Mirk, John]. *Mirk's Festial: A Collection of Homilies by Johannes Mirkus*. Ed. Theodor Erbe. EETS (e.s.) 96. London, 1905.

The Mirror of Justices. Ed. William J. Whittaker. SS 7. London, 1895.

[The Monk of Farne]. *The Meditations of the Monk of Farne*. Ed. Dom. Hugh Farmer. *Analecta Monastica* 4 (1957): 141–245.

Monumenta Juridica: The Black Book of the Admiralty. Ed. Travers Twiss. 4 vols. RS. London, 1871–76.

Morsbach, Lorenz, ed. *Mittelenglische Originalurkunden von der Chaucer-Zeit bis zur Mitte des XV. Jahrhunderts*. Alt- und Mittelenglische Texte 10. Heidelberg, 1923.

Mum and the Sothsegger. Ed. Mabel Day and R. Steele. EETS (o.s.) 199. London: 1936.

Munimenta Gildhallae Londoniensis. Ed. H. T. Riley. 4 vols. RS. London: 1859–62.

Munonye, John. *The Only Son*. AWS 21. London: Heinemann, 1966.

——. *Obi*. AWS 45. London: Heinemann, 1969.

Myers, A. R., ed. *English Historical Documents, 1327–1486*. Lodon: Eyre and Spottiswoode, 1969.

[Ngũgĩ Wa Thiong'o]. James Ngugi. *A Grain of Wheat*. AWS 36. London: Heinemann, 1968.

[Niger, Ralph]. *Radulfi Nigri Chronica*. Ed. Robert Anstruther. London: Caxton Society, 1851.

Novae Narrationes. Ed. Elsie Shanks. SS 80. London, 1963.

Nwapa, Flora. *Efuru*. AWS 26. London: Heinemann, 1966.

"Oldcotes v. d'Arcy." Ed. P. A. Brand. In *Medieval Legal Records*, ed. R. F. Hunnisett and J. B. Post. London, HMSO, 1978. 64–113.

Old English Glosses, Chiefly Unpublished. Ed. Arthur S. Napier. Anecdota Oxoniensia, 4:11. Oxford: Clarendon Press, 1900.

Old English Glosses in the Épinal-Erfurt Glossary. Ed. J. D. Pheifer. Oxford: Clarendon Press, 1974.

The Old English Version of the Gospels. Ed. R. M. Liuzza. EETS (o.s.) 304. Oxford, 1994.

The Old English Version of the Heptateuch, Ed. S. J. Crawford, rev. N. R. Ker. EETS (o.s.) 160. London, 1969.

The Ormulum. Ed. Robert Holt. 2 vols. 2nd ed., rev. R. M. White. Oxford: Clarendon Press, 1878.

"The Outlaw's Song of Trailbaston." In *Anglo-Norman Political Songs*, ed. Isabel S. T. Aspin, ANTS 11, Oxford, 1953. 67–78.

The Ozidi Saga: Collected and Translated from the Ijo of Okabou Ojobolo. J. P. Clark. Ibadan: Ibadan University Press and Oxford University Press, 1977.

Pactus Legis Salicae. Ed. Karl A. Eckhardt. MGH. *Leges*: 1st section, 4 (pt. 1). Hanover, 1962.

Paston Letters and Papers of the Fifteenth Century. Ed. Norman Davis. 2 vols. Oxford: Clarendon Press, 1971–76.

Patience. Ed. J. J. Anderson. Manchester: Manchester University Press, 1969.

Pearl. Ed. E. V. Gordon. Oxford: Clarendon Press, 1953.

Pecock, Reginald. *The Repressor of Over Much Blaming of the Clergy*. Ed. Churchill Babington. 2 vols. RS. London: HMSO, 1860.

———. *The Donet by Reginald Pecock*. Ed. Elsie Vaughan Hitchcock. EETS (o.s.) 156. London, 1921.

Perry, George G., ed. *Religious Pieces in Prose and Verse Edited from Robert Thornton's Manuscript*. EETS (o.s.) 26. London, 1867.

The Peterborough Chronicle, 1070–1154. Ed. Cecily Clark. 2nd ed. Oxford: Clarendon Press, 1970.

[Peter of Blois]. *The Later Letters of Peter of Blois*. Ed. Elizabeth Revell. Auctores Britannici Medii Aevi 13. Oxford: British Academy, 1993.

Pierce the Ploughmans Crede. Ed. W. W. Skeat. EETS (o.s.) 30. London, 1906.

Pisan, Christine de. *The Book of Fayttes of Armes and of Chyualrye*. Tr., William Caxton. Ed. A. T. P. Byles. EETS (o.s.) 189. London, 1932.

Placita corone, or La corone pledee devant justices. Ed. J. M. Kaye. SS (s.s.) 4. London, 1966.

The Plowman's Tale. In *Chaucerian and Other Pieces: A Supplement to the Complete Works of Geoffrey Chaucer*, ed. Walter W. Skeat. London: Clarendon Press, 1897. 147–90.

Proceedings and Ordinances of the Privy Council of England. Ed. N. Harris Nicolas. 7 vols. Record Commission. London, 1834–37.

Proceedings before the Justices of the Peace in the Fourteenth and Fifteenth Centuries: Edward III to Richard III. Ed. Bertha H. Putnam. Cambridge, Mass.: Ames Foundation, 1938.

Promptorium Parvulorum: The First English-Latin Dictionary. Ed. A. L. Mayhew. EETS (e.s.) 102. London, 1908.

Purity: A Middle English Poem. Ed. Robert J. Menner. Yale Studies in English 61. New Haven: Yale University Press, 1920.

Les Quinze joyes de mariage. Ed. Joan Crow. Oxford: Blackwell, 1969.

[Quixley]. MacCracken, Henry N. "Quixley's Ballades Royal (?1402)." *Yorkshire Archaeological Journal* 20 (1909): 33–50.

Rabelais, François. *Oeuvres complètes*. Ed. Pierre Jourda. 2 vols. New ed. Paris: Classiques Garnier, 1991.

Raoul de Cambrai. Ed. and trans. Sarah Kay. Oxford: Clarendon Press, 1992.

Recusant Documents from the Ellesmere Manuscripts. Ed. Anthony G. Petti. Records Ser., 60. London: Catholic Record Society, 1968.

The Reformation of the Ecclesiastical Laws. Ed. Edward Cardwell. Oxford: Oxford University Press, 1850.

Regiam Majestatem. Ed. Lord Cooper. Edinburgh: Stair Society, 1947.

Reginaldi Monachi Dunelmensis Libellus de Admirandis Beati Cuthberti Virtutibus. Ed. James Raine. Surtees Society 1. London: Nichols, 1835.

The Register of Henry Chichele, Archbishop of Canterbury, 1414–1443. Ed. E. F. Jacob, with H. C. Johnson. 4 vols. Canterbury and York Soc., 42, 45, 46, 47. Oxford: Clarendon Press, 1938–47.

A Relation or Rather a True Account of the Island of England. Ed. and trans. Charlotte A. Sneyd. CS 37. London, 1847.

Reliquiae Antiquae. Ed. Thomas Wright and J. O. Halliwell. 2 vols. London, 1841–43.

Report on Manuscripts in Various Collections, II. HMC. London: HMSO, 1903.

The Reports of Sir John Spelman. Ed. J. H. Baker. 2 vols. SS 93 and 94. London, 1976–78.

Ridge, John Rollin. *The Life and Adventures of Joaquín Murieta, the Celebrated California Bandit*. 1857. Norman: University of Oklahoma Press, 1955.

Riley, Henry Thomas, ed. and trans. *Memorials of London and London Life in the Thirteenth, Fourteenth, and Fifteenth Centuries*. London: Longmans, 1868.

Robbins, Rossell Hope, ed. *Historical Poems of the Fourteenth and Fifteenth Centuries*. New York: Columbia University Press, 1959.

[Robert of Avesbury]. *Adæ Merimuth Continuatio Chronicarum. Robertus de Avesbury de Gestis Mirabilibus Regis Edwardi Tertii*. Ed. E. M. Thompson. RS. London: HMSO, 1889.

[Robert of Blois]. *Beaudous: Ein altfranzösischer Abenteuerroman des dreizehnten Jahrhunderts*. Ed. Jacob Ulrich. Berlin: Mayer and Müller, 1889.

Robertson, A. J., ed. *Anglo-Saxon Charters*. 2nd ed. Cambridge: Cambridge University Press, 1956.

Rolle, Richard. *Richard Rolle: Prose and Verse*. Ed. S. J. Ogilvie-Thomson. EETS (o.s.) 293. Oxford, 1988.

Rolls of the Justices in Eyre: Lincolnshire 1218–1219 and Worcestershire 1221. Ed. Doris M. Stenton. SS 34. London, 1934.

Rothwell, Harry, ed. *English Historical Documents, 1189–1327*. London: Eyre and Spottiswoode, 1975.

Rotuli parliamentorum Anglie hactenus inediti [1279–1373]. Ed. H. G. Richardson and George Sayles. CS 3rd ser., 51. London, 1935.

Rotuli Parliamentorum ut et petitiones et placita in parliamento [1278–1503]. 6 vols. n.p., n.d. Index, 1832.

Sachsenspiegel: Landrecht. Ed. Karl A. Eckhardt. MGH. *Fontes Iuris*: n.s. 1 (pt. 1). 2nd ed. Gottingen: Musterschmidt, 1955.

The Saga of the Volsungs, with the Saga of Ragnar Lodbrok, Together with the Lay of Kraka. Tr. Margaret Schlauch. New York: Norton, 1930.

The Sarum Missal. Ed. J. Wickham Legg. Oxford: Clarendon Press, 1916.

Secretum Secretorum. Ed. M. A. Manzalaoui. EETS (o.s.) 276. London, 1977.

Secular Lyrics of the Fourteenth and Fifteenth Centuries. Ed. R. H. Robbins. 2nd ed. Oxford: Clarendon Press, 1955.

The Sege of Melayne. In *Six Middle English Romances*, ed. Maldwyn Mills. London: Dent, 1973. 1–45.

Seinte Marherete þe Meiden ant Martyr. Ed. Francis M. Mack. EETS (o.s.) 193. London, 1934.

Select Cases before the King's Council, 1243–1482. Ed. I. S. Leadham and J. F. Baldwin. SS 35. Cambridge, Mass., 1918.

Select Cases in Chancery, A.D. 1364–1471. Ed. William P. Baildon. SS 10. London, 1896.

Select Cases in the Court of King's Bench, 1–7. Ed. G. O. Sayles. SS 55, 57, 58, 74, 76. 82, 88. London, 1936–71.

Select Cases of Trespass from the King's Courts, 1307–1399. 2 vols. Ed. Morris S. Arnold. SS, 100 and 103. London, 1985–87.

Select Cases on Defamation to 1600. Ed. R. H. Helmholz. SS 101. London, 1985.

Select Pleas in Manorial and Other Seignorial Courts. Ed. F. W. Maitland. SS 2. London, 1889.

Select Pleas of the Crown, 1: A.D. 1200–1225. Ed. F. W. Maitland. SS 1. London, 1888.

Selections from English Wycliffite Writings. Ed. Anne Hudson. Cambridge: Cambridge University Press, 1978.

The Seven Sages of Rome (Southern Version). Ed. K. Brunner. EETS (o.s.) 191. London, 1933.

A Short-Title Catalogue of Books Printed in England, Scotland, and Ireland, 1475–1640. Compiled A. W. Pollard and G. R. Redgrave. 2nd rev. ed. 3 vols. London: Bibliographical Society, 1986–91.

The Simonie: A Parallel Text Edition. Ed. Dan Embree and Elizabeth Urquhart. Middle English Texts 24. Heidelberg: Carl Winter, 1991.

Sir Amadace. In *Six Middle English Romances*, ed. Maldwyn Mills. London: Dent, 1973. 169–92.

[Sir Beues]. The Romance of Sir Beues of Hamtoun. Ed. Eugen Kölbing. 3 vols. EETS (e.s.) 46, 48, 65. London, 1885–94.

Sir Degaré. In *Middle English Metrical Romances*, ed. W. H. French and C. B. Hale. New York: Russell & Russell, 1964. 287–320.

Sir Gawain and the Green Knight. Ed. J. R. R. Tolkien and E. V. Gordon. 2nd ed., rev. Norman Davis. Oxford: Clarendon Press, 1967.

Sir Gowther. In *Six Middle English Romances*, ed. Maldwyn Mills. London: Dent, 1973. 169–92.

Sir Orfeo. Ed. A. J. Bliss. 2nd ed. Oxford: Clarendon Press, 1966.

Sir Tristrem. Ed. George P. McNeill. STS, 1st ser., 8. Edinburgh, 1886.

Sisam, Kenneth, ed. *Fourteenth Century Verse and Prose*. Corrected ed. Oxford: Clarendon Press, 1970.

Skeat, Walter W., ed. *Chaucerian and Other Pieces: A Supplement to the Complete Works of Geoffrey Chaucer*. London: Clarendon Press, 1897.

The Song of Lewes. Ed. C. L. Kingsford. Oxford: Clarendon Press, 1890.

A Source Book of English Law. Ed. A. K. R. Kiralfy. London: Sweet & Maxwell, 1957.

Soyinka, Wole. *The Interpreters*. AWS 76. 1965. London: Heinemann, 1970.

———. *Season of Anomy*. 1973. London: Arena, 1988.

———. *Death and the King's Horseman*. London: Eyre Methuen, 1975.

———. *Aké: The Years of Childhood*. 1981. New York: Vintage, 1983.

Spalding, Mary C., ed. *The Middle English Charters of Christ*. Bryn Mawr Monographs 15. Bryn Mawr, Pa.: Bryn Mawr College, 1914.

A Stanzaic Life of Christ. Ed. Francis A. Foster. EETS (o.s.) 166. London, 1926.

Starkey, Thomas. *A Dialogue between Pole and Lupset*. Ed. T. F. Mayer. CS 4th ser., 37. London, 1989.

Statutes of the Realm (1101–1713). 11 vols. London: Record Commission, 1810–28.

St. Erkenwald. Ed. Ruth Morse. Cambridge: Brewer, 1975.

St. German, Christopher. *Doctor and Student*. Ed. T. F. T. Plucknett and J. L. Barton. SS 91. London, 1974.

Stow, John. *A Survey of London*. Ed. C. L. Kingsford. 2 vols. Oxford: Clarendon Press, 1908.

Studer, Paul, and Waters, E. G. R., eds. *Historical French Reader: Medieval Period*. Oxford: Clarendon Press, 1924.

The Tale of Beryn. Ed. F. J. Furnivall. EETS (e.s.) 105. London, 1909.

The 1341 Royal Inquest in Lincolnshire. Ed. B. W. McLane. Publications of the Lincoln Record Society, 78. Woodbridge: Brewer, 1988.

The Towneley Plays. Ed. Alfred W. Pollard. EETS (e.s.) 71. London, 1897.

Trailbaston. Derbyshire. Ed. Cecil E. Lugard. 3 vols. Private edition. Ashover, Derbyshire, 1933–35.

Treharne, R. E., and I. J. Sanders, eds. *Documents of the Baronial Movement of Reform and Rebellion, 1258–1267*. Oxford: Clarendon Press, 1973.

"The Trial of Richard Wyche." Ed. F. D. Matthew. *English Historical Review* 5 (1890): 530–44.

Tristrams Saga ok Ísondar. Ed. E. Kölbing. Heilbronn: Henninger, 1878. Trans. Paul Schach. Lincoln: University of Nebraska Press, 1973.

Turville-Petre, Thorlac, ed. *Alliterative Poetry of the Later Middle Ages*. Washington, D.C.: Catholic University of America Press, 1989.

Two Wycliffite Texts. Ed. Anne Hudson. EETS (o.s.) 301. Oxford, 1993.

Usk, Thomas. *The Testament of Love*. In *Chaucerian and Other Pieces: A Supplement to the Complete Works of Geoffrey Chaucer*, ed. Walter W. Skeat. London: Clarendon Press, 1897. 1–145.

"Versus Compositi de Roger Belers." Ed. R. H. Bowers. *Journal of English and Germanic Philology* 56 (1957): 440–42.

Víga-Glúms Saga. Ed. G. Turville-Petre. 2nd ed. Oxford: Clarendon Press, 1960. Trans. Lee M. Hollander. New York: Twayne, 1972.

Walsingham, Thomas. *Historia Anglicana*. Ed. H. T. Riley. 2 vols. RS. London, 1863–64.

——. *Gesta Abbatum Monasterii S. Albani*. Ed. H. T. Riley. 3 vols. RS. London, 1867–69.

——. *Annales Ricardi Secundi*, in *Chronica monasterii S. Albani Johannis de Trokelowe et Henrici de Blaneforde . . . necnon quorundam anonymorum chronica et annales*, ed. H. T. Riley. RS. London, 1866.

The Westminster Chronicle, 1381–1394. Ed. and trans. L. C. Hector and Barbara F. Harvey. Oxford: Clarendon Press, 1982.

Whitelock, Dorothy, ed. *English Historical Documents, c.500–1042*. London: Eyre & Spottiswoode, 1955.

Wilkins, David, ed. *Concilia Magnae Britanniae et Hiberniae*. 4 vols. London, 1737.

[William of Shoreham]. *The Poems of William of Shoreham*. Ed. M. Konrath. EETS (e.s.) 86. London, 1902.

Williams, John. *A Narrative of Missionary Enterprises in the South Sea Islands*. London: John Snow, 1838.

Wiltshire Gaol Delivery and Trailbaston Trials, 1275–1306. Ed. Ralph B. Pugh. Wiltshire Record Society 33. Devizes, 1978.

[Wimbledon, Thomas]. *Wimbledon's Sermon: "Redde Rationem Villicationis Tue": A Middle English Sermon of the Fourteenth Century*. Ed. Ione Kemp Knight. Pittsburgh: Duquesne University Press, 1967.

The Winchester Anthology: A Facsimile of British Library Additional Manuscript 60577. Intro. Edward Wilson. Cambridge: Brewer, 1981.

A Worcestershire Miscellany Compiled by John Northwood, c. 1400. Ed. Nita Scudder Baugh. Philadelphia: [Bryn Mawr], 1956.

Wright, Thomas, ed. *Political Songs of England*. New ed. by Peter Coss. 1839. Cambridge: Cambridge University Press, 1996.

——. *Political Poems and Songs Relating to English History*. 2 vols. RS. London: HMSO, 1859–61.

Wulfstan. *Sermo Lupi ad Anglos*. Ed. D. Whitelock. 2nd ed. London: Methuen, 1952.

[Wycliffite Bible]. *The Holy Bible . . . made from the Latin Vulgate by John Wycliffe and his Followers*. Ed. Josiah Forshall and Frederick Madden. 4 vols. Oxford: Oxford University Press, 1850.

[Wyclif, John]. *Trialogus cum supplemento trialogi*. Ed. Gotthardus Lechler. Oxford: Clarendon Press, 1869.

——. *The English Works of John Wyclif*. Ed. F. D. Matthew. EETS (o.s.) 74. London, 1880.

——. *Tractatus de apostasia*. Ed. Michael H. Dziewicki. London: Wyclif Society, 1889.

——. *De eucharistia tractatus maior*. Ed. Iohann Loserth. London: Wyclif Society, 1892.

——. *Tractatus de blasphemia*. Ed. Michael H. Dziewicki. London: Wyclif Society, 1893.

Wynnere and Wastoure. Ed. Stephanie Trigg. EETS (o.s.) 297. Oxford: 1990.

Year Books of the Reign of King Edward the First. Michaelmas Term Year 33 and Years 34 and 35. Ed. Alfred J. Harwood. RS. London: HMSO, 1879.

Year Books of Edward II. 2 and 3 Edward II. Ed. F. W. Maitland. SS 19. London, 1904.

——. *3 and 4 Edw. 2*. Ed. F. W. Maitland and G. J. Turner. SS 22. London, 1907.

——. *5 Edw. 2 (1311)*. Ed. G. J. Turner and T. F. T. Plucknett. SS 63. London, 1947.

——. *5 Edw. 2 (1312)*. Ed. W. C. Bolland. SS 33. London, 1916.

——. *6 & 7 Edw. 2 (pt. 2)*. Ed. W. C. Bolland, F. W. Maitland, and L. W. V. Harcourt. SS 27. London, 1912.

——. *12 Edw. 2 (pt. 1)*. Ed. J. P. Collas and T. F. T. Plucknett. SS 70. London, 1953.

——. *12 Edw. 2 (pt. 2)*. Ed. J. P. Collas. SS 81. London, 1964.

Year Books of the Reign of King Edward the Third. Years Twelve and Thirteen. Ed. L. O. Pike. RS. London: HMSO, 1885.

—— *13 & 14 Edw. 3*. Ed. L. O. Pike. RS. London: HMSO, 1886.

——. *14 Edw. 3*. Ed. L. O. Pike. RS. London: HMSO, 1888.

——. *14 & 15 Edw. 3*. Ed L. O. Pike. RS. London: HMSO, 1889.

——. *16 Edw. 3 (pt. 1)*. Ed. L. O. Pike. RS. London: HMSO, 1896.

——. *17 Edw. 3*. Ed. L. O. Pike. RS. London: HMSO, 1901.

——. *17 & 18 Edw. 3*. Ed. L. O. Pike. RS. London: HMSO, 1903.

——. *18 Edw. 3*. Ed. L. O. Pike. RS. London: HMSO, 1904.

——. *18 & 19 Edw.3*. Ed. L. O. Pike. RS. London: HMSO, 1905.

——. *19 Edw. 3*. Ed. L. O. Pike. RS. London: HMSO, 1906.

——. *20 Edw. 3 (pt. 2)*. Ed. L. O. Pike. RS. London: HMSO, 1911.

Year Books of Richard II. 2 Richard II, 1378–1379. Ed. Morris S. Arnold. Ames Foundation. Cambridge, Mass., 1975.

——. *7 Rich. 2*. Ed. Maurice J. Holland. Ames Foundation. Cambridge, Mass., 1989.

——. *8–10 Rich. 2*. Ed. L. C. Hector and Michael J. Hager. Ames Foundation. Cambridge, Mass., 1987.

——. *11 Rich. 2*. Ed. Isobel D. Thornley. Ames Foundation. London, 1937.

——. *12 Rich. 2*. Ed. G. F. Deiser. Ames Foundation. Cambridge, Mass., 1914.

——. *13 Rich. 2*. Ed. Theodore F. T. Plucknett. Ames Foundation. London, 1929.

Year Books of Henry VI. 1 Henry VI, A.D. 1422. Ed. C. H. Williams. SS 50. London, 1933.

Year Books of Edward IV. 10 Edward IV and 49 Henry VI, A.D. 1470. Ed. N. Neilson. SS 47. London, 1931.

Ywain and Gawain. Ed. Albert B. Friedman and N. T. Harrington. EETS (o.s.) 254, London, 1964.

Secondary Sources

Adams, Robert. "Langland's Theology." *A Companion to Piers Plowman*, ed. John A. Alford. Berkeley: University of California Press, 1988a. 87–114.

——. "Mede and Mercede: the Evolution of the Economics of Grace in the *Piers Plowman* B and C Versions." In *Medieval English Studies Presented to George Kane*, ed. E. D. Kennedy. Cambridge: Brewer, 1988b. 217–32.

Aers, David. *Community, Gender, and Individual Identity: English Writing, 1360–1430*. London: Routledge, 1988.

Alexander, J. W. "Ranulf III of Chester: An Outlaw of Legend?" *Neuphilologische Mitteilungen* 83 (1982): 152–57.

Alford, John A. "Literature and Law in Medieval England." *Publications of the Modern Languages Association of America* 92 (1977): 941–51.

——. *Piers Plowman: A Glossary of Legal Diction*. Cambridge: Brewer, 1988a.

——, ed. *A Companion to Piers Plowman*. Berkeley: University of California Press, 1988b.

Amadi, Elechi. *Ethics in Nigerian Culture*. Ibadan: Heinemann Educational Books, 1982.

Anderson, Perry. *Passages from Antiquity to Feudalism*. 1974. London: Verso, 1978.

Andersson, Theodore M., and W. I. Miller. *Law and Literature in Medieval Iceland: Ljósvetninga Saga* and *Valla-Ljóts saga*. Stanford: Stanford University Press, 1989.

Archibald, Elizabeth. "Declarations of 'Entente' in *Troilus and Criseyde*." *Chaucer Review* 25 (1991): 190–213.

Arnold, Morris S. "Law and Fact in the Medieval Jury Trial: Out of Sight, Out of Mind." *American Journal of Legal History* 18 (l974): 267–80.

——. "Fourteenth-Century Promises." *Cambridge Law Journal* 35 (1976): 321–34.

——. "Accident, Mistake, and Rules of Liability in the Fourteenth-Century Law of Torts." *University of Pennsylvania Law Review* 128 (1979): 361–78.

——. "Towards an Ideology of the Early English Law of Obligations." *Law and History Review* 5 (1987): 505–21.

Arnold, Morris S., Thomas A. Green, Sally A. Scully, and Stephen D. White, eds. *On the Laws and Customs of England: Essays in Honor of Samuel E. Thorne*. Chapel Hill: University of North Carolina Press, 1981.

Arnould, E. J. *Le* Manuel des péchés: *Etude de littérature religieuse anglo-normande (treizième siècle)*. Paris: Droz, 1940.

Arthur, Ross G. *Medieval Sign Theory and* Sir Gawain and the Green Knight. Toronto: University of Toronto Press, 1987.

Aston, Margaret. *Lollards and Reformers: Images and Literacy in Late Medieval Religion*. London: Hambledon Press, 1984.

———. "Corpus Christi and the Corpus Regni: Heresy and the Peasants' Revolt." *Past and Present* 143 (1994): 3–47.

Aston, T. H. and C. H. E. Philpin, eds. *The Brenner Debate: Agrarian Class Structure and Economic Development in Pre-Industrial Europe*. Cambridge: Cambridge University Press, 1985.

Aulen, Gustaf. *Christus Victor*. Trans. A. G. Herbert. 1930. London: Macmillan, 1969.

Avery, Margaret E. "The History of Equitable Jurisdiction of Chancery before 1460." *Bulletin of the Institute of Historical Research* 42 (1969): 129–44.

Bailey, Martin. "Two Kings, Their Armies and Some Jugs: the Ashanti Ewer." *Apollo* (December 1993): 387–90.

Baker, John H. "New Light on Slade's Case, II." *Cambridge Law Journal* 29 (1971): 213–36. (Rprinted in Baker, *Legal Profession*, 393–432.)

———. "Origins of the Doctrine of Consideration, 1535–1585." In *On the Laws and Customs of England: Essays in Honor of Samuel E. Thorne*, ed. Morris S. Arnold et al. Chapel Hill: University of North Carolina Press, 1981. 336–58. Reprinted in Baker, *Legal Profession*, 369–91.

———. *The Order of Serjeants at Law*. SS (s.s.) 5. London, 1984.

———. "English law and the Renaissance" *Cambridge Law Journal* 46 (1985): 46–61. Reprinted in Baker, *Legal Profession*, 461–76.

———. *The Legal Profession and the Common Law: Historical Essays*. London: Hambledon Press, 1986.

———. *An Introduction to English Legal History*. 3rd ed. London: Butterworths, 1990.

Baldwin, Anna P. "The Double Duel in *Piers Plowman* B XVIII and C XXI." *Medium Ævum* 50 (1981): 64–78.

Baldwin, John W. "The Intellectual Preparation for the Canon of 1215 against Ordeals." *Speculum* 36 (1961): 613–36.

Barbour, W. T. *The History of Contract in Early English Equity*. Oxford Studies in Social and Legal History, 4, ed. Paul Vinogradoff. Oxford: Clarendon Press, 1914.

Barfield, Owen. "Poetic Fiction and Legal Diction." In *Essays presented to Charles Williams*. London: Oxford University Press, 1947. 106–27.

Barraclough, G. "Law and Legislation in Medieval England." *Law Quarterly Review* 56 (1940): 75–92.

Barron, C. M. "The Tyranny of Richard II." *Bulletin of the Institute of Historical Research* 41 (1968): 1–18.

———. "The Expansion of Education in Fifteenth-Century London." In *The Cloister and the World: Essays for Barbara Harvey*, ed. J. Blair and B. Goldring. Oxford: Clarendon Press, 1996. 219–45.

Barron, W. R. J. "The Penalties for Treason in Medieval Life and Literature." *Journal of Medieval History* 7 (1981): 187–202.

Bartlett, Kenneth R. "The Strangeness of Strangers: English Impressions of Italy in the Sixteenth Century." *Quaderni d'italianistica* 1 (1980): 46–63.

Bartlett, Robert. *Trial by Fire and Water: The Medieval Judicial Ordeal*. Oxford: Clarendon Press, 1986.

Bately, Janet M. "King Alfred and the Old English Translation of Orosius." *Anglia* 88 (1970): 433–60.

Bateson, Mary. "A London Municipal Collection of the Reign of King John." *English Historical Review* 17 (1902): 480–511, 707–30.

Bäuml, Franz H. "Varieties and Consequences of Medieval Literacy and Illiteracy." *Speculum* 55 (1980): 237–65.

———. "Medieval Texts and the Two Theories of Oral-Formulaic Composition: A Proposal for a Third Theory." *New Literary History* 16 (1984): 31–49.

Bean, J. M. W. *The Decline of English Feudalism, 1215–1540*. Manchester: Manchester University Press, 1968.

———. *From Lord to Patron: Lordship in Late Medieval England*. Manchester: Manchester University Press, 1989.

Becker, Marvin B. *Civility and Society in Western Europe, 1300–1600*. Bloomington: Indiana University Press, 1988.

Beckerman, John S. "Procedural Innovation and Institutional Change in Medieval English Manorial Courts." *Law and History Review* 10 (1992): 197–252.

Bellamy, John G. "The Coterel Gang: An Anatomy of a Band of Fourteenth-Century Criminals." *English Historical Review* 79 (1964): 698–717.

———. "The Northern Rebellions in the Later Years of Richard II." *Bulletin of the John Rylands Library* 47 (1964/65): 254–74.

———. "Sir John de Annesley and the Chandos Inheritance." *Nottingham Medieval Studies* 10 (1966): 94–105.

———. *The Law of Treason in England in the Later Middle Ages*. Cambridge: Cambridge University Press, 1970.

———. *Criminal Law and Society in Late Medieval and Tudor England*. Gloucester: Sutton. 1984.

Bennett, Michael J. "A County Community: Social Cohesion amongst the Cheshire Gentry, 1400–1425." *Northern History* 8 (1973): 24–44.

Benveniste, Émile. *Problèmes de linguistique générale*. Paris: Gallimard, 1966.

———. *Le Vocabulaire des institutions indo-européennes: 1. Économie, parenté, société*. Paris: Editions de minuit, 1969.

Berger, Raoul. "From Hostage to Contract." *Illinois Law Review*, 35 (1940): 154–74, 281–92.

Berman, Harold J. "The Background of the Western Legal Tradition in the Folklaw of the Peoples of Europe." *University of Chicago Law Review* 45 (1978): 553–97.

———. *Law and Revolution: The Formation of the Western Legal Tradition*. Cambridge, Mass.: Harvard University Press, 1983.

Besnier, Robert. "*Vadatio legis et leges*: Les Preuves de droit commun à l'époque des coutumiers normands." *Revue historique de droit français et étranger*, 4th ser., 19/20 (1940/41): 88–135.

Binchy, D. A. "Celtic Suretyship, a Fossilized Indo-European Institution." In *Indo-European and Indo-Europeans*, ed. George Cardona, H. M. Hoenigwald, and A. Senn. Philadelphia: University of Pennsylvania Press, 1970. 355–67.

Bird, Ruth. *The Turbulent London of Richard II*. London: Longmans, Green, 1949.

Blaess, Madeleine. "L'Abbaye de Bordesley et les livres de Guy de Beauchamp." *Romania* 78 (1957): 511–18.

Blakey, Brian. "Truth and Falsehood in the *Tristran* of Béroul." In *History and Structure of French: Essays in Honour of Professor T. B. W. Reid*, ed. F. J. Barnett. Totowa, N.J.: Rowman & Littlefield, 1972. 19–29.

Blamires, Alcuin. *The Canterbury Tales*. Atlantic Highlands, N.J.: Humanities Press, 1987.

Blanch, Robert J., and Julian N. Wasserman. "Medieval Contracts and Covenants: The Legal Coloring of *Sir Gawain and the Green Knight*." *Neophilologus* 68 (1984): 598–610.

Blatcher, M. "Touching the Writ of Latitat: An Act 'Of No Great Moment.'" In *Elizabethan Government and Society: Essays Presented to Sir John Neale*, ed. S. T. Bindoff. London: Athlone Press, 1961. 188–212.

Blenner-Hasset, Roland. "Autobiographical Aspects of Chaucer's Franklin." *Speculum* 28 (1953): 791–800.

Bloch, Marc. "Les formes de la rupture de l'hommage dans l'ancien droit féodal." 1912. Reprinted in *Mélanges historiques*. Paris: Ecole pratique des hautes études, 1963. 1:189–209.

———. "European Feudalism." 1931. Reprinted in *Mélanges historiques*. Paris: Ecole pratique des hautes études, 1963. 1:177–88.

———. "Liberté et servitude personelles au moyen âge, particulièrement en France." 1933. Reprinted in *Mélanges historiques*. Paris: Ecole pratique des hautes études, 1963. 1:286–355.

———. *Feudal Society.* 2 vols. Trans. L. A. Manyon. 1940. Chicago: University of Chicago Press, 1961.

Bloch, R. Howard. *Medieval French Literature and Law*. Berkeley: University of California Press, 1977.

Bloomfield, Leonard. *Language*. 1933. London: George Allen & Unwin, 1935.

Bloomfield, Morton W. *Piers Plowman as a Fourteenth-Century Apocalypse*. New Brunswick: Rutgers University Press, [1961].

Boehm, Christopher. *Blood Revenge: The Anthropology of Feuding in Montenegro and Other Tribal Societies*. Lawrence: University Press of Kansas, 1984.

Bohannan, Paul J. *Justice and Judgement Among the Tiv*. London: Oxford University Press, 1957.

———. "The Differing Realms of the Law." *American Anthropologist* 67.6, Pt. 2 (1965): 33–42.

Bolland, William Craddock. *The Year Books*. Cambridge: Cambridge University Press, 1921.

———. *A Manual of Year Book Studies*. Cambridge: Cambridge University Press, 1925

Bonfield, Lloyd. "The Nature of Customary Law in the Manor Courts of Medieval England." *Comparative Studies in Society and History* 31 (1989): 514–34.

Boone, Lalia Phipps. "Criminal Law and the Matter of England." *Boston University Studies in English* 2 (1956): 2–16.

Bowers, John M. *The Crisis of Will in* Piers Plowman. Washington D.C.: Catholic University of America Press, 1986.

Bovill. E. W. *The Golden Trade of the Moors*. 2nd ed. London: Oxford University Press, 1969.

Bowers, R. H. "'Foleuyles Lawes' ('Piers Plowman,' C.XXII.247)." *Notes and Queries* 206 (1961): 327–28.

Boyer, Pascal. *Tradition as Truth and Communication*. Cambridge: Cambridge University Press, 1990.

Boyle, L. E. "William of Pagula and the *Speculum Regis Edwardi III*." *Mediaeval Studies* 32 (1970): 329–36.

Brady, Mary Teresa. "The Pore Caitif: An Introductory Study." *Traditio* 10 (1954): 529–48.

Breeze, Andrew. "The Number of Christ's Wounds." *Bulletin of the Board of Celtic Studies* 32 (1985): 84–91.

———. "The Charter of Christ in Medieval English, Welsh and Irish." *Celtica* 19 (1987): 111–20.

Brewer, D. S. "Honour in Chaucer." *Essays and Studies* 26 (1973): 1–19.

Bright, James W. "The Relation of the Cædmonian *Exodus* to the Liturgy." *Modern Language Notes* 27 (1912): 97–103.

Brooks, Nicholas. "The Organization and Achievements of the Peasants of Kent and Essex in 1381." In *Studies in Medieval History Presented to R. H. C. Davis*, ed. Henry Mayr-Harting and R. I. Moore. London: Hambledon Press, 1985. 247–70.

Brown, Carleton, and Rossell Hope Robbins. *The Index of Middle English Verse*. New York: Columbia University Press, 1943.

Brown, Peter. "Society and the Supernatural: A Medieval Change." *Daedalus* (Spring 1975): 133–51.

———. *The Cult of the Saints: Its Rise and Function in Latin Christianity*. Chicago: University of Chicago Press, 1981.

Brown, Peter, and Andrew Butcher. *The Age of Saturn: Literature and History in* The Canterbury Tales. Oxford: Blackwell, 1991.

Brunner, Heinrich. *Deutsche Rechtsgeschichte*. Rev. ed. 2 vols. 1906 and 1927. Berlin: Duncker & Humblot, 1958 and 1961.

Bryan, W. F., and Germaine Dempster, eds. *Sources and Analogues of Chaucer's* Canterbury Tales. 1941. New York: Humanities Press, 1958.

Brzezinski, Monica. "Conscience and Covenant: The Sermon Structure of *Cleanness*." *Journal of English and Germanic Philology* 89 (1990): 166–80.

Bühler, Curt F. "Prayers and Charms in Certain Middle English Scrolls." *Speculum* 39 (1964): 270–78.

Burnley, J. D. *Chaucer's Language and the Philosophers' Tradition*. Cambridge: Brewer, 1979.

Burrow, John A. *A Reading of Sir Gawain and the Green Knight*. London: Routledge, 1965.

———. *Ricardian Poetry: Chaucer, Gower, Langland and the* Gawain *Poet*. London: Routledge & Kegan Paul, 1971.

Bynum, Caroline W. *Holy Feast and Holy Fast: The Religious Significance of Food to Medieval Women*. Berkeley: University of Californa Press, 1987.

Calin, William C. *The Old French Epic of Revolt: Raoul de Cambrai, Renaud de Montauban, Gormond et Isembard*. Geneva: Droz, 1962.

Cam, Helen M. "The General Eyres of 1329–30." *English Historical Review* 39 (1924): 241–52.

———. "The Decline and Fall of English Feudalism." *History* 25 (1940): 216–33.

Campbell, Bruce M. S., ed. *Before the Black Death: Studies in the 'Crisis' of the Early Fourteenth Century*. Manchester: Manchester University Press, 1991.

Campbell, James. "Observations on English Government from the Tenth to the Twelfth Century." *Transactions of the Royal Historical Society*, 5th ser., 25 (1975): 39–54.

Carpenter, Christine. "The Beauchamp Affinity: A Study of Bastard Feudalism at Work." *English Historical Review* 95 (1980): 514–32.

———. *Locality and Polity: A Study of Warwickshire Landed Society, 1401–1499*. Cambridge: Cambridge University Press, 1992.

Carruthers, Mary. "The Wife of Bath and the Painting of Lions." *Publications of the Modern Language Society of America* 94 (1979): 209–22.

Cashmere, John. "The Social Use of Violence in Ritual: *Charivari* or Religious Persecution." *European History Quarterly* 21 (1991): 291–319.

Chabaneau, C. "Le Romanz de Saint Fanuel." *Revue des langues romanes* 28 (1885): 118–23, 157–258; and 32 (1888): 360–409.

Charles-Edwards, T. M. *The Welsh Laws*. Cardiff: University of Wales Press, 1989.

Chenu, M.-D. *L'Éveil de la conscience dans la civilisation médiévale*. Montréal: Institute d'études médiévales, 1969.

Cherry, John. "Symbolism and Survival: Medieval Horns of Tenure." *The Antiquaries Journal* 69 (1989): 111–18.

Cheyette, Frederic L. "Suum Cuique Tribuere." *French Historical Studies* 6 (1970): 287–99.

Childs, Wendy. "Anglo-Italian Contacts in the Fourteenth Century." In *Chaucer and the Italian Trecento*, ed. Piero Boitani. Cambridge: Cambridge University Press, 1983. 65–87.

Chrimes, S. B. "Richard II's Questions to the Judges, 1387." *Law Quarterly Review* 72 (1956): 365–90.

Christianson, Paul. "Chaucer's Literacy." *Chaucer Review* 11 (1976): 112–27.

Clanchy, Michael T. "Law, Government, and Society in Medieval England." *History* 59 (1974): 73–78.

——. "A Medieval Realist: Interpreting the Rules of Barnwell Priory, Cambridge." *Perspectives in Jurisprudence*, ed. Elspeth Atwooll. Glasgow: University of Glasgow Press, 1977. 176–94.

——. "Highway Robbery and Trial by Battle in the Hampshire Eyre of 1249." In *Medieval Legal Records*, ed. R. F. Hunnisett and J. B. Post. London, HMSO, 1978. 26–61.

——. *England and Its Rulers, 1066–1272: Foreign Lordship and National Identity*. Oxford: Blackwell, 1983a.

——. "Law and Love in the Middle Ages." In *Disputes and Settlements: Law and Human Relations in the West*, ed. John Bossy. Cambridge: Cambridge University Press, 1983b. 47–67.

——. *From Memory to Written Record: England, 1066–1307*. 2nd ed. Oxford: Blackwell, 1993.

Clark, Elaine. "Some Aspects of Social Security in Medieval England." *Journal of Family History* 7 (1982): 307–20.

Clarke, Maude V. *Fourteenth-Century Studies*. Oxford: Clarendon Press, 1937.

Clementi, D. R. "Richard II's Ninth Question to the Judges." *English Historical Review* 86 (1971): 96–113.

Clifton, Nicole. "The Romance Convention of the Disguised Duel and the Climax of *Piers Plowman*." *Yearbook of Langland Studies* 7 (1993): 123–28.

Coffman, George R. "John Gower, Mentor for Royalty." *Publications of the Modern Language Association of America* 69 (1954): 953–64.

Cohen, Elizabeth S. "Between Oral and Written Culture: The Social Meaning of an Illustrated Love Letter." In *Culture and Identity in Early Modern Europe (1500–1800): Essays in Honor of Natalie Zemon Davis*, ed. Barbara B. Diefendorf and Carla Hesse. Ann Arbor: University of Michigan Press, 1993. 181–201.

Cohen, Esther. *The Crossroads of Justice: Law and Culture in Later Medieval France*. Leiden: Brill, 1993.

Coing, Helmut. "English Equity and the Denunciatio Evangelica of the Canon Law." *Law Quarterly Review* 71 (1955): 223–41.

Coleman, Janet. *Piers Plowman and the* Moderni. Rome: Edizioni di Storia e Letteratura, 1981.

Coleman, Joyce. *Public Reading and the Reading Public in Late Medieval England and France*. Cambridge: Cambridge University Press, 1996.

Colman, Rebecca V. "Reason and Unreason in Early Medieval Law." *Journal of Interdisciplinary History* 4 (1974): 571–91.

Constable, Giles. "Forgery and Plagiarism in the Middle Ages." *Archiv für Diplomatik* 29 (1983): 1–41.

Coulton, G. C. *The Medieval Village*. Cambridge: Cambridge University Press, 1925.

Courtenay, William J. "Covenant and Causality in Pierre d'Ailly." *Speculum* 46 (1971): 94–119.

———. "Sacrament, Symbol and Causality in Bernard of Clairvaux." In *Bernard of Clairvaux: Studies Presented to Dom Jean Leclercq*, ed. M. B. Pennington, Cistercian Studies 23. Washington D.C.: Cistercian Publications, 1973. 111–22.

———. "Nominalism and Late Medieval Religion." In *The Pursuit of Holiness*, ed. C. Trinkhaus and H. A. Oberman. Leiden: Brill, 1974. 26–59.

———. "Necessity and Freedom in Anselm's Conception of God." *Analecta Anselmiana* 4.2 (1975): 39–64.

Cramer, Peter. *Baptism and Change in the Early Middle Ages, c.200–c.1150*. Cambridge: Cambridge University Press, 1993.

Crane, Susan. "The Writing Lesson of 1381." In *Chaucer's England: Literature in Historical Context*, ed. Barbara A. Hanawalt. Minneapolis: University of Minnesota Press, 1992. 201–21.

Curtius, Ernst Robert. *European Literature and the Latin Middle Ages*. Trans. Willard R. Trask. 1948. New York: Harper & Row, 1963.

Cuttler, S. H. *The Law of Treason and Treason Trials in Later Medieval France*. Cambridge: Cambridge University Press, 1981.

Dane, Joseph A. "Double Truth in Chaucer's *Franklin's Tale*." *Studia Neophilologica* 63 (1991): 161–67.

David, Alfred. *The Strumpet Muse: Art and Morals in Chaucer's Poetry*. Bloomington: University of Indiana Press, 1976.

Davies, Wendy, and Paul Fouracre, eds. *The Settlement of Disputes in Early Medieval Europe*. Cambridge: Cambridge University Press, 1986.

Davis, H. W. C. "'Baculi Cornuti.'" *English Historical Review* 16 (1901): 730.

Davis, Natalie Zemon. "Printing and the People." In *Society and Culture in Early Modern France*, Stanford: Stanford University Press, 1975. 198–226.

———. *The Return of Martin Guerre*. Cambridge, Mass.: Harvard University Press, 1983.

———. "Charivari, Honor, and Community in Seventeenth-Century Lyon and Geneva." In *Rite, Drama, Festival, Spectacle*, ed. John J. MacAloon. Philadelphia: Institute for the Study of Human Issues, 1984. 42–57.

———. *Fiction in the Archives: Pardon Tales and their Tellers in Sixteenth-Century France*. Stanford: Stanford University Press, 1987.

Denholm-Young, N. *Seignorial Administration in England*. London: Oxford University Press, 1937.

Denny, J. Peter. "Rational Thought in Oral Culture and Literate Decontextalization." In *Literacy and Orality*, ed. David R. Olson and Nancy Torrance. Cambridge: Cambridge University Press, 1991. 66–89.

Derrida, Jacques. *De la grammatologie*. Paris: Éditions de minuit, 1967.

Dessau, Adalbert. "The Idea of Treason in the Middle Ages." In *Lordship and Community in Medieval Europe*, ed. Frederic L. Cheyette. Huntington, N.Y.: Krieger, 1975. 192–97.

D'Evelyn, Charlotte. "'Meditations on the Life and Passion of Christ': A Note on Its Literary Relationships." In *Essays and Studies in Honor of Carleton Brown*. New York: New York University Press, 1940. 79–90.

Dewindt, Edwin Brezette. *Land and People in Holywell-cum-Needingworth: Structures of Tenure and Patterns of Social Organization in an East Midlands Village, 1252–1457*. Toronto: Pontifical Institute of Mediaeval Studies, 1972.

Diamond, A. S. *Primitive Law Past and Present*. London: Methuen, 1971.

Dobb, Maurice. *Studies in the Development of Capitalism*. New York: International Publishers, 1947.

Dodds, E. R. *The Greeks and the Irrational*. Berkeley and Los Angeles: University of California Press, 1966.

Doe, Norman. *Fundamental Authority in Late Medieval English Law*. Cambridge: Cambridge University Press, 1990.

Donahue, Charles, Jr. "Roman Canon Law in the Medieval English Church: Stubbs vs. Maitland Re-examined after Seventy-Five Years in the Light of Some Records from the Church Courts." *Michigan Law Review* 72 (1974): 647–716.

Donaldson, E. Talbot. *Piers Plowman: The C-Text and Its Poet*. New Haven: Yale University Press, 1949.

Du Cange, Charles, ed. *Glossarium Mediae et Infimae Latinitatis*. Rev. Léopold Favre. 9 vols. Niort: Favre, 1883–87.

Duffy, Eamon. *The Stripping of the Altars: Traditional Religion in England, c. 1400–c. 1580*. New Haven: Yale University Press, 1992.

Dunning, T. P. Piers Plowman: *An Interpretation of the A Text*. Oxford: Clarendon Press, 1980.

Duranti, Alessandro. "Intentions, Self, and Responsibility: An Essay in Samoan Ethnopragmatics." In *Responsibility and Evidence in Oral Discourse*, ed. Jane H. Hill and J. T. Irvine. Cambridge: Cambridge University Press, 1992. 24–47.

Earl, James W. "Christian Traditions in the Old English *Exodus*." *Neuphilologische Mitteilungen* 71 (1970): 541–70.

Eisenstein, Elizabeth. *The Printing Press as an Agent of Change: Communications and Cultural Transformations in Early Modern Europe*. 2 vols. Cambridge: Cambridge University Press, 1979.

Elphinstone, H. W. "Notes on the Alienation of Estates Tail." *Law Quarterly Review*, 23 (l890): 280–88.

Elton, G. R. *F. W. Maitland*. London: Weidenfeld & Nicolson, 1985.

Emenyonu, Ernest N. *The Rise of the Igbo Novel*. Ibadan: Oxford University Press, 1978.

Empson, William. *The Structure of Complex Words*. 1951. Cambridge, Mass.: Harvard University Press, 1989.

Erb, Peter C. "Vernacular Material for Preaching in MS Cambridge University Library Ii. III. 8." *Mediaeval Studies* 33 (1971): 63–84.

Esmein, A. *Études sur les contrats dans le très-ancien droit français*. Paris: Larose & Forcel, 1883.

Estey, Francis N. "The *Scabini* and the Local Courts." *Speculum* 26 (1951): 119–29.

Everett, Dorothy, and N. D. Hurnard. "Legal Phraseology in a Passage in *Pearl*." *Medium Ævum* 16 (1945): 9–15.

Ewers, John C. *The Blackfeet: Raiders on the Northwestern Plains*. Norman: University of Oklahoma Press, 1958.

Faith, Rosamond. "The 'Great Rumour' of 1377 and Peasant Ideology." In *The English Rising of 1381*, ed. Rodney H. Hilton and T. H. Aston. Cambridge: Cambridge University Press, 1984. 43–73.

Fernández-Armesto, Felipe. *Truth: A History*. London: Bantam Press, 1997.

Finkelstein, Jacob J. "The Goring Ox: Some Historical Perspectives on Deodands, Forfeitures, Wrongful Death and the Western Notion of Sovereignty." *Temple Law Quarterly* 46 (1973): 169–290.

Finlayson, John. "*The Simonie*: Two Authors?" *Archiv für das Studium der neueren Sprachen und Literaturen* 226 (1989): 39–51.

Finnegan, Ruth. *Literacy and Orality: Studies in the Technology of Communication*. Oxford: Blackwell, 1988.

Finucane, Ronald C. *Miracles and Pilgrims: Popular Beliefs in Medieval England*. London: Dent, 1977.

Flandrin, Jean-Louis. *Sex in the Western World: The Development of Attitudes and Behaviour*. Trans. Sue Collins. Chur, Switzerland: Harwood, 1991.

Fletcher, Alan J. "John Mirk and the Lollards." *Medium Ævum* 56 (1987): 216–24.

Förster, Max. "Ein mittelenglischer Himmels-Schutzbrief (ca. 1470)." *Anglia* 42 (1918): 217–19.

Fowler, Elizabeth. "Civil death and the Maiden: Agency and Conditions of Contract in *Piers Plowman*." *Speculum* 70 (1995): 760–92.

Fowler, G. Herbert. "The Cost of a Charter, c.1439." *Bulletin of the Institute of Historical Research* 17 (1939): 30–31.

Fowler, R. C. "Legal Proofs of Age." *English Historical Review* 22 (1907): 101–3.

Frank, Jerome. "The 'Fight' Theory versus the 'Truth' Theory." In *Courts on Trial*, Princeton: Princeton University Press, 1950. 80–102.

Frank, Robert Worth. *Piers Plowman and the Scheme of Salvation*. New Haven: Yale University Press, 1957.

Franklin, Michael J. "'Fingres heo haþ feir to folde': Trothplight in Some of the Love Lyrics of MS Harley 2253." *Medium Ævum* 55 (1986): 176–87.

Friedrich, Paul. "Proto-Indo-European Trees." In *Indo-European and Indo-Europeans*, ed. George Cardona, H. M. Hoenigwald, and A. Senn. Philadelphia: University of Pennsylvania Press, 1970. 11–34.

Fry, Timothy. "The Unity of the *Ludus Coventriae*." *Studies in Philology* 48 (1951): 527–70.

Furley, J. S. *City Government of Winchester from the Records of the Fourteenth and Fifteenth Centuries*. Oxford: Clarendon Press, 1923.

———. *The Ancient Usages of the City of Winchester*. Oxford: Clarendon Press, 1927.

Galbraith, V. H. "A New Life of Richard II." *History* 26 (1942): 223–39.

———. "The Death of a Champion." In *Studies in Medieval History Presented to Frederick Maurice Powicke*, ed. R. W. Hunt, W. A. Pantin, and R. W. Southern. Oxford: Clarendon Press, 1948. 283–95.

Ganshof, F. L. *The Carolingians and the Frankish Monarchy: Studies in Carolingian History*. Trans. Janet Sondheimer. Ithaca, N.Y.: Cornell University Press, 1971.

Gaylord, Alan T. "The Promises in *The Franklin's Tale*." *ELH* 31 (1964): 331–65.

Geertz, Clifford. *Local Knowledge: Further Essays in Interpretive Anthropology*. New York: Basic Books, 1983.

Gellner, Ernest. *Plough, Sword and Book: The Structure of Human History*. London: Collins Harvill, 1988.

Gellrich, Jesse M. *The Idea of the Book in the Middle Ages: Language Theory, Mythology, and Fiction*. Ithaca, N.Y.: Cornell University Press, 1985.

———. "Orality, Literacy, and Crisis in the Later Middle Ages." *Philological Quarterly* 67 (1988): 461–73.

———. *Discourse and Dominion in the Fourteenth Century: Oral Contexts of Writing in Philosophy, Politics, and Poetry*. Princeton: Princeton University Press, 1995.

Gilissen, John, ed. *La Rédaction des coutumes dans le passé et dans le présent*. Bruxelles: Université Libre de Bruxelles, 1962.

Gilmore, Grant. *The Death of Contract*. Columbus: Ohio State University Press, 1974.

Ginzberg, Carlo. *The Cheese and the Worms: The Cosmos of a Sixteenth-Century Miller.* Trans. John and Anne Tedeschi. 1980. Harmondsworth: Penguin Books, 1982.

Gluckman, Max. "The Peace in the Feud." *Past and Present* 8 (1955): 1–14.

———. *Politics, Law and Ritual in Tribal Society*. Oxford: Blackwell, 1965.

———. "African Traditional Law in Historical Perspective." *Proceedings of the British Academy* 60 (1974): 295–337.

Godden, M. "Plowmen and Hermits in Langland's *Piers Plowman*." *Review of English Studies* n.s. 35 (1984): 129–63.

Goebel, Julius. *Felony and Misdemeanor: A Study in the History of the Criminal Law*. 1937. Philadelphia: University of Pennsylvania Press, 1976.

Goodman, Anthony. *The Loyal Conspiracy: The Lords Appellant under Richard II*. London: Routledge & Kegan Paul, 1971.

Goody, Jack. *The Logic of Writing and the Organization of Society*. Cambridge: Cambridge University Press, 1986.

Gordley, James. *The Philosophical Origins of Modern Contract Doctrine*. Oxford: Clarendon Press, 1991).

Gray, Douglas. *Themes and Images in the Medieval English Religious Lyric*. London: Routledge & Kegan Paul, 1972.

———. "Notes on Some Middle English Charms." In *Chaucer and Middle English Studies in Honour of Rossell Hope Robbins*, ed. Beryl Rowland. Kent, Ohio: Kent State University Press, 1974. 56–71.

———. "The Robin Hood Poems." *Poetica* 18 (1984): 1–39.

———. "Popular Religion and Late Medieval English Literature." In *Religion in the Poetry and Drama of the Late Middle Ages in England*, ed. Piero Boitani and Anna Torti. Cambridge: Brewer, 1990. 1–28.

Green, D. H. *The Carolingian Lord: Semantic Studies on Four Old High German Words*. Cambridge: Cambridge University Press, 1965.

Green, R. F. "Hearts, Minds, and Some English Poems of Charles d'Orléans." *English Studies in Canada* 9 (1983): 136–50.

———. "Chaucer's Victimized Women." *Studies in the Age of Chaucer* 10 (1988): 3–21.

———. "John Ball's Letters: Literary History and Historical Literature." In *Chaucer's England: Literature in Historical Context*, ed. Barbara A. Hanawalt. Minneapolis: University of Minnesota Press, 1992. 176–200.

Green, Thomas A. *Verdict According to Conscience*. Chicago: University of Chicago Press, 1985.

Green, V. H. H. *Bishop Reginald Pecock: A Study in Ecclesiastical History and Thought*. Cambridge: Cambridge University Press, 1945.

Grieve, Hilda. *The Sleepers and the Shadows: Chelmsford, a Town, Its People and Its Past, I*. Chelmsford: Essex Record Office, 1988.

Guenée, Bernard. *States and Rulers in Later Medieval Europe*. Trans. Juliet Vale. Oxford: Blackwell, 1985.

Gurevich, Aron J. *Categories of Medieval Culture*. Trans. G. L. Campbell. London: Routledge & Kegan Paul, 1985.

———. *Medieval Popular Culture: Problems of Belief and Perception*. Trans. Janos M. Bak and P. A. Hollingsworth. Cambridge: Cambridge University Press, 1988.

Hahn, Thomas, and R. W. Kaeuper. "Text and Context: Chaucer's *Friar's Tale*." *Studies in the Age of Chaucer* 5 (1983): 67–101.

Halphen, Louis. *Les Barbares des grandes invasions aux conquêtes turques du onzième siècle*. 5th ed. Paris: Presses Universitaires de France, 1948.

———. "La Justice en France au XIe siècle: Région angevine." *À Travers l'histoire du moyen âge* (Paris, 1950): 175–202.

Hamburger, Philip. "The Conveyancing Purposes of the Statute of Frauds." *American Journal of Legal History* 27 (1983): 354–85.

Hamil, Frederick C. "The King's Approvers: A Chapter in the History of English Criminal Law." *Speculum* 11 (1936): 238–58.

Hamilton, Walton H. "The Ancient Maxim of *Caveat Emptor*." *Yale Law Journal* 40 (1931): 1133–87.

Hanawalt, Barbara A. "Fur-Collar Crime: The Pattern of Crime among the Fourteenth-Century English Nobility." *Journal of Social History* 8.4 (1975): 1–17.

———. *Crime and Conflict in English Communities, 1300–1348*. Cambridge, Mass.: Harvard University Press, 1979.

———. *The Ties that Bound: Peasant Families in Medieval England*. Oxford: Oxford University Press, 1986a.

———. "Peasant Resistance to Royal and Seigniorial Impositions." In *Social Unrest in the Late Middle Ages*, ed. F. X. Newman. Binghamton, N.Y.: Medieval and Renaissance Texts and Studies, 1986b. 23–47.

Harding, Alan. *A Social History of English Law*. 1966. Gloucester, Mass.: Peter Smith, 1973.

———. *The Law Courts of Medieval England*. London: Allen & Unwin, 1973.

———. "Plaints and Bills in the History of English Law, Mainly in the Period 1250–1350." In *Legal History Studies, 1972*, ed. D. Jenkins. Cardiff: University of Wales Press, 1975. 65–86.

———. "The Revolt against the Justices." In *The English Rising of 1381*, ed. Rodney H. Hilton and T. H. Aston. Cambridge: Cambridge University Press, 1984. 165–93.

Hardy, Thomas Duffus. *Syllabus (in English) of the Documents . . . Contained in the Collection known as "Rymer's Foedera."* 3 vols. London: Longmans, Green, 1869–85.

Hart, H. L. A. *Essays in Jurisprudence and Philosophy*. Oxford: Clarendon Press, 1983.

Harwood, Britton. "Dame Study and the Place of Orality in *Piers Plowman*." *ELH* 57 (1990): 1–17.

Havelock, Erik A. *The Greek Concept of Justice from Its Shadow in Homer to Its Substance in Plato*. Cambridge: Harvard University Press, 1978.

———. *The Muse Learns to Write*. New Haven: Yale University Press, 1986.

Hazeltine, H. D. "The Formal Contract of Early English Law." *Columbia Law Review* 10 (1910): 608–17.

Hector, L. C. *Palaeography and Forgery*. London and York: St Anthony's Press, 1959.

Helmholz, R. H. *Marriage Litigation in Medieval England*. Cambridge: Cambridge University Press, 1974.

———. "Assumpsit and *Fidei Laesio*." *Law Quarterly Review* 91 (1975): 406–32.

———. "Crime, Compurgation and the Courts of the Medieval Church." *Law and History Review* 1 (1983): 1–26.

Henry, Robert L. *Contract in the Local Courts of Medieval England*. London: Longmans, Green, 1926.

Héraucourt, Will. "What is trouthe or soothfastnesse?" In *Englische Kultur in sprachwissenschaftlicher Deutung*, ed. Wolfgang Schmidt. Leipzig: Quelle & Meyer, 1936. 74–84.

Herbert, J. A. *Catalogue of Romances in the Department of Manuscripts in the British Museum, 3*. London: British Museum, 1910.

Herzfeld, Michael. "Pride and Perjury: Time and the Oath in the Mountain Villages of Crete." *Man* n.s. 25 (1990): 305–22.

Hewitt, H. J. *Cheshire under the Three Edwards*. Chester: Cheshire Community Council, 1967.

Hexter, Ralph J. *Equivocal Oaths and Ordeals in Medieval Literature*. Cambridge, Mass.: Harvard University Press, 1975.

Hill, Thomas D. "The Devil's Forms and the Pater Noster's Powers: 'The Prose Solomon and Saturn *Pater Noster* Dialogue and the Motif of the Transformation Combat." *Studies in Philology* 85 (1988): 164–76.

———. "Universal Salvation and Its Literary Context in *Piers Plowman* B.18." *Yearbook of Langland Studies* 5 (1991): 65–76.

Hillman, Mary V. " 'Inlyche' and 'Rewarde'." *Modern Language Notes* 56 (1941): 457–58.

Hilton, Rodney H. "A Thirteenth-Century Poem on Disputed Villein Services." *English Historical Review* 56 (1941): 90–97.

———. *A Medieval Society: The West Midlands at the End of the Thirteenth Century*. London: Weidenfeld & Nicholson, 1966.

———, ed. *Peasants, Knights and Heretics: Studies in Medieval English Social History*. Cambridge: Cambridge University Press, 1976.

———. *Bondmen Made Free: Medieval Peasant Movements and the English Rising of 1381*. 1973. London: Methuen, 1977.

———. "Was There a General Crisis of Feudalism?" In *Class Conflict and the Crisis of Feudalism*, 1985, London: Verso, 1990. 166–72.

Hilton, Rodney H., and T. H. Aston, eds. *The English Rising of 1381*. Cambridge: Cambridge University Press, 1984.

Hobsbawm, E. J. *Bandits*. Rev. ed. New York: Pantheon Books, 1981.

Hoebel, E. Adamson. *The Law of Primitive Man*. Cambridge, Mass: Harvard University Press, 1954.

Hohfeld, Wesley Newcomb. *Fundamental Legal Conceptions as Applied in Judicial Reasoning*. New Haven: Yale University Press, 1919.

Holdsworth, Sir William. *A History of English Law*. Vol. 1 (7th ed.); vol. 2 (4th ed.); vol. 3 (5th ed.). London: Methuen, 1956, 1936, 1942.

Holmes, Oliver Wendell. "The Path of the Law." *Harvard Law Review* 10 (1897): 457–78.

Holt, J. C. *Robin Hood*. London: Thames & Hudson, 1982.

Homans, George C. *English Villagers of the Thirteenth Century*. 1942. New York: Russell & Russell, 1960.

Horgan, A. D. "Gawain's *Pure Pentaungel* and the Virtue of Faith." *Medium Ævum* 56 (1987): 310–15.

Hoyt, Robert S. "The Coronation Oath of 1308: The Backround of 'Les Leys et Les Custumes.'" *Traditio* 11 (1955): 235–57.

Hudson, Anne. *Lollards and Their Books*. London: Hambledon Press, 1985.

———. *The Premature Reformation: Wycliffite Texts and Lollard History*. Oxford: Clarendon Press, 1988.

———. "'Laicus litteratus': The Paradox of Lollardy." In *Heresy and Literacy, 1000–1530*, ed. Peter Biller and Anne Hudson. Cambridge: Cambridge University Press, 1994. 222–36.

Hudson, John. *Land, Law, and Lordship in Anglo-Norman England*. Oxford: Clarendon Press, 1994.

Hughes, M. E. J. "'The feffement that Fals hath ymaked': A Study of the Image of the Document in 'Piers Plowman' and Some Literary Analogues." *Neuphilologische Mitteilungen* 93 (1992): 125–33.

Hurnard, Naomi D. *The King's Pardon for Homicide before A.D. 1307*. Oxford: Clarendon Press, 1969.

Hurstfield, Joel. "Political Corruption in Modern England: The Historian's Problem." *History* 52 (1967): 16–34.

Hutchins, Edwin. "Reasoning in Trobriand Discourse." *Quarterly Newsletter of the Laboratory of Comparative Human Cognition* 1.2 (1979): 13–17.

Hyams, Paul R. *Kings, Lords and Peasants in Medieval England: The Common Law of Villeinage in the Twelfth and Thirteenth Centuries*. Oxford: Clarendon Press, 1980.

———. "Trial by Ordeal: The Key to Proof in the Early Common Law." In *On the Laws and Customs of England: Essays in Honor of Samuel E. Thorne*, ed. Morris S. Arnold et al. Chapel Hill: University of North Carolina Press, 1981. 90–126.

———. "Warranty and Good Lordship in Twelfth Century England." *Law and History Review* 5 (1987): 437–503.

———. "Maitland and the Rest of Us." In *The History of English Law: Centenary Essays on 'Pollock and Maitland'*, ed. John Hudson, Proceedings of the British Academy, 89. Oxford: Oxford University Press, 1996. 215–41.

Ibbetson, David J. "Words and Deeds: The Action of Covenant in the Reign of Edward I." *Law and History Review* 4 (1986): 71–94.

———. "Sale of Goods in the Fourteenth Century." *Law Quarterly Review* 107 (1991): 480–99.

———. "From Property to Contract: The Transformation of Sale in the Middle Ages." *Journal of Legal History* 13 (1992): 1–22.

Illich, Ivan. *In the Vineyard of the Text: A Commentary to Hugh's Didascalion*. Chicago: University of Chicago Press, 1993.

Illich, Ivan, and Barry Sanders. *ABC: The Alphabetization of the Popular Mind*. San Francisco: North Point Press, 1988.

Igbokwe, Virtus Chitoo. "The Law and Practice of Customary Arbitration in Nigeria: *Age v. Ikewibe* and Applicable Law Issues Revisited." *Journal of African Law* 41 (1997): 201–14.

Ingram, Martin. "Ridings, Rough Music, and the 'Reform of Popular Culture' in Early Modern England." *Past and Present* 105 (1984): 79–113.

Ireland, R. W. "The Presumption of Guilt in the History of English Criminal Procedure." *Journal of Legal History* 7 (1986): 243–55.

Jamieson, Philip. "Animal Liability in Early Law." *Cambrian Law Review* 19 (1988): 45–68.

Jones, Michael. "An Indenture between Robert, Lord Mohaut, and Sir John de Bracebridge for Life Service in Peace and War." *Journal of the Society of Archivists* 4.5 (1972): 384–94.

Jones, W. R. "Keeping the Peace: English Society, Local Government, and the Commissions of 1341–44." *American Journal of Legal History* 18 (1974): 307–20.

Josipovici, Gabriel. *The World and the Book: A Study of Modern Fiction*. London: Macmillan, 1971.

Justice, Steven. *Writing and Rebellion: England in 1381*. Berkeley: University of California Press, 1994.

Kaeuper, Richard W. "Law and Order in Fourteenth-Century England: The Evidence of Special Commissions of Oyer and Terminer." *Speculum* 54 (1979): 734–84.

———. "An Historian's Reading of *The Tale of Gamelyn*." *Medium Ævum* 52 (1983): 51–62.

———. *War, Justice, and Public Order: England and France in the Later Middle Ages*. Oxford: Clarendon Press, 1988.

Kane, George. *The Liberating Truth: The Concept of Integrity in Chaucer's Writings*. The John Coffin Memorial Lecture, 1979. London: Athlone Press, 1980.

Kantorowicz, Ernst H. *Frederick the Second, 1194–1250*. Trans. E. O. Lorimer. London: Constable, 1931.

———. *The King's Two Bodies: A Study in Medieval Political Theology*. Princeton: Princeton University Press, 1957.

Kaye, J. M. "The Sacrabar." *English Historical Review* 83 (1968): 744–58.

Kean, P. M. "Love, Law, and *Lewte* in *Piers Plowman*." *Review of English Studies* n.s. 15 (1964): 241–61.

Keen, Maurice H. "Brotherhood in Arms." *History* 47 (1962): 1–17.

———. *The Laws of War in the Late Middle Ages*. London: Routledge & Kegan Paul, 1965a.

———. "The Political Thought of the Fourteenth-Century Civilians." In *Trends in Medieval Political Thought*, ed. Beryl Smalley. Oxford: Blackwell, 1965b. 105–26.

———. "Wyclif, the Bible, and Transubstantiation." In *Wyclif in His Times*, ed. Anthony Kenny. Oxford: Clarendon Press, 1986. 1–16.

———. *The Outlaws of Medieval Legend*. 2nd rev. ed. London: Routledge & Kegan Paul, 1987.

Kelly, Fergus. *A Guide to Early Irish Law*. Dublin: Dublin Institute for Advanced Studies, 1988.

Kelly, Susan. "Anglo-Saxon Lay Society and the Written Word." In *The Uses of Literacy in Early Mediaeval Europe*, ed. Rosamond McKitterick. Cambridge: Cambridge University Press, 1990. 36–62.

Kemp, Eric Waldram. *An Introduction to Canon Law in the Church of England*. London: Hodder & Stoughton, 1957.

Kern, Fritz. *Kingship and Law in the Middle Ages*. Trans. S. B. Chrimes. Oxford: Blackwell, 1956.

Keynes, Simon. "Royal Government and the Written Word in Late Anglo-Saxon England." In *The Uses of Literacy in Early Mediaeval Europe*, ed. Rosamond McKitterick. Cambridge: Cambridge University Press, 1990. 226–57.

———. "The Fonthill Letter." In *Words, Texts and Manuscripts: Studies in Anglo-Saxon Culture Presented to Helmut Gneuss*, ed. Michael Korhammer. Cambridge: Brewer, 1992. 53–97.

Klapisch-Zuber, Christiane. *Women, Family, and Ritual in Renaissance Italy*. Trans. Lydia Cochrane. Chicago: University of Chicago Press, 1986.

Lea, Henry Charles. *Superstition and Force*. 4th ed. Philadelphia: Lea, 1892.

Lear, Floyd S. *Treason in Roman and Germanic Law*. Austin: University of Texas Press, 1965.

Leclercq, Jean. "Aspects spirituels de la symbolique du livre au douzième siècle." In *L'Homme devant Dieu: Mélanges offerts au Père Henri de Lubac*, 3 vols. *Théologie* 56–58, Lyon-Fourvière: Aubier, 1963–64. 2:63–72.

Leff, Gordon. *Bradwardine and the Pelagians*. Cambridge: Cambridge University Press, 1957.

Le Goff, Jacques. *Time, Work, and Culture in the Middle Ages*. Trans. Arthur Goldhammer. Chicago: University of Chicago Press, 1980.

Lentz, Tony M. *Orality and Literacy in Hellenic Greece*. Carbondale: Southern Illinois University Press, 1989.

LePan, Don. *The Cognitive Revolution in Western Culture. Vol. 1: The Birth of Expectation*. Basingstoke: Macmillan, 1989.

Lévi-Strauss, Claude. *Tristes tropiques*. Paris: Librairie Plon, 1955.

Levy, Ernst. *West Roman Vulgar Law: The Law of Property*. Memoirs of the American Philosophical Society, 29. Philadelphia: American Philosophical Society, 1951.

Liestøl, Aslak. "Correspondence in Runes." *Mediaeval Scandinavia* 1 (1968): 17–27.

Ligeron, Louis, and Michel Petitjean. "La Coutume en rites: Quelques exemples de symbolisme juridique." *Mémoires de la société pour l'histoire du droit* 40 (1983): 283–93.

Lord, Albert B. *The Singer of Tales*. 1960. New York: Atheneum, 1965.

Lubac, Henri de. *Exégèse médiévale: Les quatre sens de l'écriture*. 2 vols. *Théologie* 41–42. Lyon-Fourvière: Aubier, 1959–1961.

Lucke, Horst K. "Striking a Bargain." *Adelaide Law Review* 1 (1962): 293–311.

Luria, A. R. *Cognitive Development: Its Cultural and Social Foundations*. Trans. M. Lopez-Morillas and L. Solotaroff. Cambridge, Mass: Harvard University Press, 1976.

MacCormack, Geoffrey. "Revenge and Compensation in Early Law." *American Journal of Comparative Law* 21 (1973): 69–85.

Macfarlane, Alan. *The Origins of English Individualism*. Oxford: Blackwell, 1978.

———. *Marriage and Love in England: Modes of Reproduction 1300–1840*. Oxford: Blackwell, 1986.

Maddicott, J. R. *Law and Lordship: Royal Justices as Retainers in Thirteenth- and Fourteenth-Century England*. Oxford: Past and Present Society, 1978.

———. "Magna Carta and the Local Community 1215–1259." *Past and Present* 102 (1984): 25–65.

Magennis, Hugh. "Treatments of Treachery and Betrayal in Anglo-Saxon Texts." *English Studies* 75 (1995): 1–19.

Magoun, Francis P. "Víga-Glumr's Equivocal Oath." *Neuphilologische Mitteilungen* 53 (1952): 401–408.

Maine, Henry Sumner. *Ancient Law: Its Connection with the Early History of Society and Its Relation to Modern Ideas*. 1st U.S. ed., 1864. Reprint, Tucson: University of Arizona Press, 1986.

———. *Dissertations on Early Law and Custom*. London: Murray, 1883.

Maitland, F. W. *The Forms of Action at Common Law*. 1909. Cambridge: Cambridge University Press, 1969.

Malinowski, Bronislaw. *Crime and Custom in Savage Society*. 1926. Totowa, N.J.: Rowman & Littlefield, 1985.

———. "The Problem of Meaning in Primitive Languages." In *The Meaning of Meaning*, ed. C. K. Ogden and I. A. Richards, 2nd ed. New York: Harcourt Brace, 1927. 296–336.

Malloch, A. E. "Some Notes on Equivocation." *Publications of the Modern Language Society of America* 81 (1966): 145–46.

———. "Equivocation: A Circuit of Reasons." In *Familiar Colloquy: Essays Presented to Arthur Barker*, ed. Patricia Bruckmann. Ottawa: Oberon Press, 1978. 132–43.

Manly, John M. and Edith Rickert. *The Text of the Canterbury Tales*. 8 vols. Chicago: University of Chicago Press, 1940.

Manning, Roger B. *Village Revolts: Social Protest and Popular Disturbances in England, 1509–1640*. Oxford: Clarendon Press, 1988.

Marchand, Louis. "L'Accroissement de prérogatives royales en matière monétaire dans les lettres de grace du trésor des chartes." In *La faute, la repression, et le pardon*, Actes du 107e congrès national des sociétés savantes, Brest, 1982. Paris: Comité des travaux historiques et scientifiques, 1984. 261–81.

Marsh, Deborah. "'I See by Sizt of Evidence': Information Gathering in Late Medieval Cheshire." In *Courts, Counties and the Capital in the Later Middle Ages*, ed. Diana E. S. Dunn. Stroud: Sutton Publishing, 1996. 71–92.

Martin, Henri-Jean. *The History and Power of Writing*. Trans. Lydia G. Cochrane. Chicago: University of Chicago Press, 1994.

Martin, M. T. "Legal Proofs of Age." *English Historical Review* 22 (1907): 526–27.

Marx, C. W. "The Problem of the Doctrine of the Redemption in the Mystery Plays and the *Cornish Ordinalia*." *Medium Ævum* 54 (1985): 20–32.

———. "An Edition and Study of the *Conflictus inter Deum et Diabolum*." *Medium Ævum* 59 (1990): 16–40.

———. *The Devil's Rights and the Redemption in the Literature of Medieval England*. Cambridge: Brewer, 1995.

Mathew, Gervase. *The Court of Richard II*. London: Murray, 1968.

McBryde, W. "The Intention to Create Legal Relations." *Juridical Review* (1992): 274–79.

McFarlane, K. B. "Bastard Feudalism." *Bulletin of the Institute of Historical Research* 20

(1943/45): 161–80. Reprinted in McFarlane, *England in the Fifteenth Century*, 23–43.

——. "A Business-Partnership in War and Administration 1421–1445." *English Historical Review* 78 (1963): 290–310. Reprinted in McFarlane *England in the Fifteenth Century*, 151–74.

——. *England in the Fifteenth Century: Collected Essays*. London: Hambledon Press, 1981.

McGiffert, Michael. "William Tyndale's Conception of Covenant." *Journal of Ecclesiasical History* 32 (1981): 167–84.

McGovern, William M., Jr. "Contract in Medieval England: Wager of Law and the Effect of Death." *Iowa Law Review* 54 (1968): 19–62.

——. "The Enforcement of Informal Contracts in the Later Middle Ages." *California Law Review* 59 (1971): 1145–93.

McGrath, Alister E. "The Anti-Pelagian Structure of 'Nominalist' Doctrines of Justification." *Ephemerides Theologicae Lovanienses* 57 (1981): 107–119.

——. *The Intellectual Origins of the European Reformation*. Oxford: Blackwell, 1987.

McIntosh, Marjorie K. "Immediate Royal Justice: The Marshalsea Court in Havering, 1358." *Speculum* 54 (1979): 727–33.

McKisack, May. *The Fourteenth Century, 1307–1399*. Oxford: Clarendon Press, 1959.

McKitterick, Rosamond. *The Carolingians and the Written Word*. Cambridge: Cambridge University Press, 1989.

——, ed. *The Uses of Literacy in Early Mediaeval Europe*. Cambridge: Cambridge University Press, 1990.

Meek, C. K. *Law and Authority in a Nigerian Tribe*. Oxford: Oxford University Press, 1937.

Mellinkoff, David. *The Language of the Law*. Boston: Little, Brown, 1963.

Mellinkoff, Ruth. "Riding Backwards: Theme of Humiliation and Symbol of Evil." *Viator* 4 (1973): 153–76.

Menner, Robert J. "The Man in the Moon and Hedging." *Journal of English and Germanic Philology* 48 (1949): 1–14.

Micha, A. "L'Épreuve de l'épée." *Romania* 70 (1948): 37–50.

Miller, William Ian. "Avoiding Legal Judgement: The Submission of Disputes to Arbitration in Medieval Iceland." *American Journal of Legal History* 28 (1984): 95–134.

——. "Ordeal in Iceland." *Scandinavian Studies* 60 (1988): 189–218.

——. *Bloodtaking and Peacemaking: Feud, Law, and Society in Saga Iceland*. Chicago: University of Chicago Press, 1990.

Milsom, S. F. C. "Not Doing Is No Trespass: a View of the Boundaries of Case." *Cambridge Law Journal* 13 (1954): 105–17. Reprinted in Milsom, *Studies*, 91–103.

——. "Sale of Goods in the Fifteenth Century." *Law Quarterly Review* 77 (1961): 257–84. Reprinted in Milsom, *Studies*, 105–32.

——. "Reason in the Development of the Common Law." *Law Quarterly Review* 81 (1965): 496–517. Reprinted in Milsom, *Studies*, 149–70.

——. "Law and Fact in Legal Development." *University of Toronto Law Journal* 17 (1967): 1–19. Reprinted in Milsom, *Studies*, 171–89.

——. *The Legal Framework of English Feudalism*. Cambridge: Cambridge University Press, 1976.

———. *Historical Foundations of the Common Law*. 2nd ed. London: Butterworths, 1981.

———. *Studies in the History of the Common Law*. London: Hambledon Press, 1985.

Minnis, A. J. "Looking for a Sign: The Quest for Nominalism in Chaucer and Langland." In *Essays on Ricardian Literature in Honour of J. A. Burrow*, ed. A. J. Minnis, Charlotte C. Morse, and Thorlac Turville-Petre. Oxford: Clarendon Press, 1997. 142–78.

Mitnick, John Marshall. "From Neighbor-Witness to Judge of Proofs: The Transformation of the English Civil Juror." *American Journal of Legal History* 32 (1988): 201–35.

Molin, Jean-Baptiste, and P. Mutembe. *Le Rituel du mariage en France du onzième au seizième siècle*. Théologie historique 26. Paris: Beauchesne, 1973.

Møller, Jens G. "The Beginnings of Puritan Covenant Theology." *Journal of Ecclesiastical History* 14 (1963): 46–67.

Moore, Sally Falk. *Law as Process: An Anthropological Approach*. London: Routledge & Kegan Paul, 1978.

Morgan, Gerald. "The Significance of the Pentangle Symbolism in *Sir Gawain and the Green Knight*." *Modern Language Review* 74 (1979): 769–90.

Morse, Ruth. *Truth and Convention in the Middle Ages: Rhetoric, Representation, and Reality*. Cambridge: Cambridge University Press, 1991.

Murtaugh, D. "Rhyming Justice in *The Friar's Tale*." *Neuphilologische Mitteilungen* 74 (1973): 107–12.

Muscatine, Charles. *Poetry and Crisis in the Age of Chaucer*. Notre Dame: University of Notre Dame Press, 1972.

Musson, Anthony. "Twelve Good Men and True? The Character of Early Fourteenth-Century Juries." *Law and History Review* 15 (1997): 115–44.

Neuss, Paula. "Images of Writing and the Book in Chaucer's Poetry." *Review of English Studies* 32 (1981): 385–97.

Nicholson, Peter. "The Analogues of Chaucer's *Friar's Tale*." *English Language Notes* 17 (1979): 93–98.

Nzimiro, Ikenna. *Studies in Ibo Political Systems*. London: Frank Cass, 1972.

Oakley, Francis. *Omnipotence, Covenant, and Order*. Ithaca, N.Y.: Cornell University Press, 1984.

Oberman, Heiko A. *Forerunners of the Reformation: The Shape of Late Medieval Thought*. New York: Holt, Rinehart & Winston, 1966.

Obiechina, Emmanuel N. *Language and Theme: Essays on African Literature*. Washington D.C.: Howard University Press, 1990.

Obilade, Akintunde Olusegun. *The Nigerian Legal System*. London: Sweet & Maxwell, 1979.

Odegaard, Charles E. "Legalis Homo." *Speculum* 15 (1940): 186–93.

Ogilvy, J. D. A. "Some Early Oath-Books." In *Studies in Language, Literature, and Culture of the Middle Ages and Later*, ed. E. Bagby Atwood and Archibald A. Hill. Austin: University of Texas Press, 1969. 179–81.

Okpewho, Isidore. *The Epic in Africa: Toward a Poetics of the Oral Performance*. New York: Columbia University Press, 1975.

Oldham, James. "Truth-Telling in the Eighteenth-Century English Courtroom." *Law and History Review* 12 (1994): 95–121.

Ong, Walter J. *Orality and Literacy: The Technologizing of the Word*. London: Methuen, 1982.

Osthoff, Hermann. *Etymologische Parerga*. Leipzig: S. Hirzel, 1901.
Owst, G. R. *Preaching in Medieval England*. Cambridge: Cambridge University Press, 1926.
——. *Literature and Pulpit in Medieval England*. 2nd ed. Oxford: Blackwell, 1961.
Page, R. I. "Anglo-Saxon Runes and Magic." *Journal of the British Archaeological Association*, 3rd ser., 27 (1964): 14–31.
Palmer, J. J. N. "The Authorship, Date, and Historical Value of the French Chronicles on the Lancastrian Revolution: II." *Bulletin of the John Rylands Library* 61 (1979): 398–421.
Palmer, Robert C. *The County Courts of Medieval England, 1150–1350*. Princeton: Princeton University Press, 1982.
——. *The Whilton Dispute, 1264–1380: A Socio-Legal Study of Dispute Settlement in Medieval England*. Princeton: Princeton University Press, 1984.
——. *English Law in the Age of the Black Death, 1348–1381: A Transformation of Governance and Law*. Chapel Hill: University of North Carolina Press, 1993.
Patterson, Lee. *Chaucer and the Subject of History*. London: Routledge, 1991.
Payling, Simon. "Law and Arbitration in Nottinghamshire, 1399–1461." *People, Politics, and Community in the later Middle Ages*, ed. Joel Rosenthal and Colin Richmond. Gloucester: Sutton, 1987. 140–160.
Pearsall, Derek, *Old and Middle English Poetry*. London: Routledge & Kegan Paul, 1977.
——. "Interpretative Models for the Peasants' Revolt." In *Hermeneutics and Medieval Culture*, ed. Patrick J. Gallagher and Helen Damico. Albany: State University of New York Press, 1989. 63–70.
Perroy, E. "À l'origine d'une économie contractée: Les Crises du quatorzième siècle." *Annales ESC*. 4 (1949): 167–82.
Petersen, Kate O. " Chaucer and Trivet." *PMLA* 18 (1903): 173–93.
Plucknett, Theodore F. T. *Statutes and Their Interpretation in the First Half of the Fourteenth Century*. Cambridge: Cambridge University Press, 1922.
——. "Impeachment and Attainder." *Transactions of the Royal Historical Society*, 5th ser., 3 (1953): 145–58.
——. *A Concise History of the Common Law*. 5th ed. London: Butterworths, 1956.
Pocock, J. G. A. *Virtue, Commerce, and History: Essays on Political Thought and History, Chiefly in the Eighteenth Century*. Cambridge: Cambridge University Press, 1985.
Pollock, Frederick, and Frederic William Maitland. *The History of English Law before the Time of Edward I*. 2nd ed., rev. S. F. C. Milsom. 2 vols. Cambridge: Cambridge University Press, 1968.
Posner, Richard A. *Law and Literature: A Misunderstood Relation*. Cambridge, Mass.: Harvard University Press, 1988.
Post, J. B. "The Evidential Value of Approvers' Appeals: The Case of William Rose, 1389." *Law and History Review* 3 (1985): 91–100.
Postles, David. "Pledge of Faith in Transactions in Land." *Journal of the Society of Archivists* 7 (1984): 295–98.
Powell, Edward. "Arbitration and the Law in England in the Late Middle Ages." *Transactions of the Royal Historical Society*, 5th ser., 33 (1983): 49–67.
——. "Settlement of Disputes by Arbitration on Fifteenth-Century England." *Law and History Review* 2 (1984): 21–43.
Prescott, Andrew. "London in the Peasants' Revolt: A Portrait Gallery." *The London Journal* 7 (1981): 125–43.

Pringsheim, Fritz. "*Animus* in Roman Law." *Law Quarterly Review* 49 (1933): 43–60, 379–412.

Putnam, Bertha H. "Chief Justice Shareshull and the Economic and Legal Codes of 135–1352." *University of Toronto Law Review* 5 (1943/44): 250–81.

——. *The Place in Legal History of Sir William Shareshull, Chief Justice of the King's Bench, 1350–1361*. Cambridge: Cambridge University Press, 1950.

Radding, Charles M. "Evolution of Medieval Mentalities: A Cognitive-Structural Approach." *American Historical Review* 83 (1978): 577–97.

——. "Superstition to Science: Nature, Fortune, and the Passing of the Medieval Ordeal." *American Historical Review* 84 (1979): 945–69.

Radford, U. M. "The Wax Images Found in Exeter Cathedral." *Antiquaries Journal* 29 (1949): 164–68.

Raftis, J. A. *Tenure and Mobility: Studies in the Social History of the Mediaeval English Village*. Pontifical Institute of Mediaeval Studies, Studies and Texts 8. Toronto: Pontifical Institute of Mediaeval Studies, 1964.

——. "Social Change Versus Revolution: New Interpretations of the Peasants' Revolt of 1381." In *Social Unrest in the Late Middle Ages*, ed. F. X. Newman. Binghamton, N.Y.: Medieval & Renaissance Texts & Studies, 1986. 3–22.

Rattray, R. S. *Ashanti Law and Constitution*. Oxford: Clarendon Press, 1929.

Redfield, Robert. "Primitive Law." *University of Cincinnati Law Review* 33 (1964): 1–22.

Reinsch, Robert. *Die Pseudo-Evangelien von Jesu und Maria's Kindheit*. Halle: Niemeyer, 1879.

Reynolds, Philip L. "The Dotal Charter as Theological Treatise." *Recherches de théologie ancienne et médiévale* 61 (1994): 54–68.

Reynolds, Susan. *Kingdoms and Communities in Western Europe, 900–1300*. Oxford: Clarendon Press, 1984.

——. *Fiefs and Vassals: The Medieval Evidence Reinterpreted*. Oxford: Clarendon Press, 1994.

Richardson, H. G. "Early Corontation Records: The Coronation of Edward II." *Bulletin of the Institute of Historical Research* 16 (1938): 1–11.

——. "The English Coronation Oath." *Speculum* 24 (1949): 44–75.

——. "The Coronation in Medieval England: The Evolution of the Office and the Oath." *Traditio* (1960): 111–202.

——. *Bracton: The Problem of His Text*. SS (s.s.) 2. London, 1965.

Richardson, H. G. and George Sayles. "The Early Statutes." *Law Quarterly Review* 50 (1934): 201–23 and 540–71.

——. "Early Coronation Records, I." *Bulletin of the Institute of Historical Research* 13 (1935/36): 129–45.

——. *The Governance of Medieval England from the Conquest to Magna Carta*. Edinburgh: Edinburgh University Press, 1963.

Rickert, Edith. "Extracts from a Fourteenth-Century Account Book." *Modern Philology* 24 (1927): 111–19, 249–56.

Riedel, F. Carl. *Crime and Punishment in the Old French Romances*. New York: Columbia University Press, 1938.

Riffaterre, Michael. "The Mind's Eye: Memory and Textuality." In *The New Medievalism*, ed. Marina S. Brownlee, Kevin Brownlee, and Stephen Nichols. Baltimore: Johns Hopkins University Press, 1991. 29–45.

Robbins, Rossell Hope. "Mirth in Manuscripts." *Essays and Studies* 21 (1968): 1–28.

———. "Dissent in Middle English Literature: The Spirit of (Thirteen) Seventy-Six." *Medievalia and Humanistica* n.s. 9 (1979): 25–51.

Roberts, Simon. *Order and Dispute: An Introduction to Legal Anthropology*. Harmondsworth: Penguin Books, 1979.

Robertson, D. W., Jr. "Simple Signs from Everyday Life in Chaucer." In *Signs and Symbols in Chaucer's Poetry*, ed. J. P. Hermann and J. P. Burke. University: University of Alabama Press, 1981. 12–26.

Robinson, F. N. "Notes on the Irish Practice of Fasting as a Means of Distraint." In *Putnam Anniversary Volume: Anthropological Essays Presented to Frederic Ward Putnam*. New York: Stechert, 1909. 567–83.

Robinson, I. S. *Authority and Resistance in the Investiture Contest: The Polemical Literature of the Late Eleventh Century*. Manchester: Manchester University Press, 1978.

Rosaldo, Michelle Z. "The Things We Do with Words: Ilongot Speech Acts and Speech Act Theory in Philosophy." *Language and Society* 11 (1982): 203–37.

Rosen, Lawrence. *The Anthropology of Justice: Law as Culture in Islamic Society*. Cambridge: Cambridge University Press, 1989.

Rosenthal, Joel T. "The King's 'Wicked Advisers' and Medieval Baronial Rebellions." *Political Science Quarterly* 82 (1967): 595–618.

Rowney, Ian. "Arbitration in Gentry Disputes of the Later Middle Ages." *History* 67 (1982): 367–76.

Rothwell, H. "Edward I and the Struggle for the Charters, 1297–1305." In *Studies in Medieval History Presented to Frederick Maurice Powicke*, ed. R. W. Hunt, W. A. Pantin, and R. W. Southern. Oxford: Clarendon Press, 1948. 319–32.

Rubin, Miri. *Corpus Christi: The Eucharist in Late Medieval Culture*. Cambridge: Cambridge University Press, 1991.

Russell, G. H. "The Salvation of the Heathen: The Exploration of a Theme in *Piers Plowman*." *Journal of the Warburg and Courtauld Institutes* 29 (1966): 101–116.

Russell, M. J. "Accoutrements of Battle." *Law Quarterly Review* 99 (1983a): 432–42.

———. "Trial by Battle Procedure in Writs of Right and Criminal Appeals." *Tijdschrift voor Rechtgeschiedenis* 53 (1983b): 123–34.

Sabean, David Warren. *The Power in the Blood: Popular Culture and Village Discourse in Early Modern Germany*. Cambridge: Cambridge University Press, 1984.

[Salter.] Elizabeth Zeeman. "Piers Plowman and the Pilgrimage to Truth." *Essays and Studies* n.s. 11 (1958): 1–16.

Saul, Nigel. *Knights and Esquires: The Gloucestershire Gentry in the Fourteenth Century*. Oxford: Clarendon Press, 1981.

———. "Conflict and Consensus in English Local Society." In *Politics and Crisis in Fourteenth Century England*, ed. John Taylor and Wendy Childs. Gloucester: Sutton, 1990. 38–58.

———. "Richard II and the Vocabulary of Kingship." *English Historical Review* 110 (1995): 854–77.

Scanlon, Larry. *Narrative, Authority, and Power: The Medieval Exemplum and the Chaucerian Tradition*. Cambridge: Cambridge University Press, 1994.

Scase, Wendy. "Writing and the Plowman: Langland and Literacy." *Yearbook of Langland Studies* 9 (1995): 121–31.

Schacht, Joseph. *An Introduction to Islamic Law*. Oxford: Clarendon Press, 1964.

Schless, Howard. "*Pearl*'s 'Princes Paye' and the Law." *Chaucer Review* 24 (1989): 183–85.

Schramm, Percy E. *A History of the English Coronation*. Trans. L. G. Wickham Legg. Oxford: Clarendon Press, 1937.

Schulz, Fritz. "Bracton on Kingship." *English Historical Review* 60 (1945): 136–76.

Scofield, Cora L. *The Life and Reign of Edward the Fourth*. 2 vols. London: Longmans, Green, 1923.

Scot, Forrest S. "Earl Wealtheof of Northumbria." *Archaeologia Aeliana*, 4th ser., 30 (1952): 149–213.

Searle, John R. *Speech Acts: An Essay in the Philosophy of Language*. Cambridge: Cambridge University Press, 1969.

Seipp, David J. "The Concept of Property in the Early Common Law." *Law and History Review* 12 (1994): 29–91.

———. "Crime in the Year Books." In *Law Reporting in Britain*, ed. Chantal Stebbings. London: Hambledon Press, 1995. 15–34.

Shannon, Edgar F. "Medieval Law in *The Tale of Gamelyn*." *Speculum* 26 (1951): 458–64.

Shapin, Steven. *A Social History of Truth: Civility and Society in Seventeenth-Century England*. Chicago: University of Chicago Press, 1994.

Sheehan, Michael M. "The Formation and Stability of Marriage in Fourteenth-Century England: Evidence of an Ely Register." *Mediaeval Studies* 33 (1971): 228–63.

———. "Choice of Marriage Partner in the Middle Ages: Development and Mode of Application of a Theory of Marriage." *Studies in Medieval and Renaissance History* 1 (1978a): 3–33.

———. "Marriage Theory and Practice in the Conciliar Legislation and Diocesan Statutes of Medieval England." *Mediaeval Studies* 40 (1978b): 408–460.

Sheneman, Paul. "The Tongue as a Sword: Psalms 56 and 63 and the Pardoner." *Chaucer Review* 27 (1993): 396–400.

Sherborne, James. "Perjury and the Lancastrian Revolution of 1399." *Welsh History Review* 14 (1988): 217–41.

Shinners, John R. "The Veneration of Saints at Norwich Cathedral in the Fourteenth Century." *Norfolk Archaeology* 40 (1988): 133–44.

Shoaf, R. A. *Dante, Chaucer, and the Currency of the Word: Money, Images, and Reference in Late Medieval Poetry*. Norman: Pilgrim Books, 1983.

Silving, Helen. "The Oath: 1." *Yale Law Journal* 68 (1959): 1329–90.

Simpson, A. W. B. "Contract: The Twitching Corpse." *Oxford Journal of Legal Studies* 1 (1981): 265–77.

———. *A History of the Common Law of Contract: The Rise of the Action of Assumpsit*. 2nd ed. Oxford: Clarendon Press, 1987.

Simpson, James. Piers Plowman*: An Introduction to the B-Text*. London: Longman, 1990.

Sledd, J. "Three Textual Notes on Fourteenth-Century Poetry." *Modern Language Notes* 55 (1940): 379–82.

Smalley, Beryl. *The Study of the Bible in the Middle Ages*. New York: Philosophical Library, 1952.

Smith, Andrea B. *The Anonymous Parts of the Old English Hexateuch: A Latin-Old English/Old English-Latin Glossary*. Cambridge: Brewer, 1985.

Smith, A. W. "Some Folklore Elements in Movements of Social Protest." *Folklore* 77 (1967): 241–52.

Smith, Wilfred Cantwell. "A Human View of Truth." *Studies in Religion* 1 (1971): 6–24.

Snape, M. G. "Some Evidence of Lollard Activity in the Diocese of Durham in the Early Fifteenth Century." *Archaeologia Aeliana,* 4th Ser., 39 (1961): 355–61.

Sommerville, Johann P. "The 'New Art of Lying': Equivocation, Mental Reservation, and Casuistry." In *Conscience and Casuistry in Early Modern Europe*, ed. Edmund Leites. Cambridge: Cambridge University Press, 1988. 159–84.

Southern, Richard W. "Lanfranc of Bec and Berengar of Tours." In *Studies in Medieval History Presented to Frederick Maurice Powicke*, ed. R. W. Hunt, W. A. Pantin, and R. W. Southern. Oxford: Clarendon Press, 1948. 27–48.

——. *The Making of the Middle Ages*. New Haven: Yale University Press, 1953.

——. "The English Origins of the 'Miracles of the Virgin.'" *Medieval and Renaissance Studies* 4 (1958): 176–216.

——. *Saint Anselm and His Biographer: A Study of Monastic Life and Thought, 1059–c. 1130*. Cambridge: Cambridge University Press, 1963.

——. *Robert Grosseteste: The Growth of an English Mind in Medieval Europe*. Oxford: Clarendon Press, 1986.

——. *Saint Anselm: A Portrait in a Landscape*. Cambridge: Cambridge University Press, 1990.

Speirs, John. *Medieval English Poetry: The Non-Chaucerian Tradition*. London: Faber & Faber, 1957.

Spencer, H. Leith. *English Preaching in the Late Middle Ages*. Oxford: Clarendon Press, 1993.

Spiegel, Gabrielle M. "History, Historicism, and the Social Logic of the Text in the Middle Ages." *Speculum* 65 (1990): 59–86.

Stacey, Robin Chapman. *The Road to Judgment: From Custom to Court in Medieval Ireland and Wales*. Philadelphia: University of Pennsylvania Press, 1994.

Starn, Randolph. "Historians and 'Crisis.'" *Past and Present* 52 (1971): 3–22.

Steele, Anthony. *Richard II*. Cambridge: Cambridge University Press, 1962.

Steiner, Franz B. "Chagga Truth: A Note on Gutmann's Account of the Chagga Concept of Truth in *Das Recht der Dschagge*." *Africa* 24 (1954): 364–69.

Stenton, Doris Mary. *English Justice between the Norman Conquest and the Great Charter*. London: Allen & Unwin, 1965a.

——. *English Society in the Early Middle Ages (1066–1307)*. Pelican History of England, 3. 4th ed. Harmondsworth: Penguin Books, 1965b.

Stenton, Sir Frank. *The First Century of English Feudalism, 1066–1166*. 2nd ed. Oxford: Clarendon Press, 1961.

Stephen, J. F. *A History of the Criminal Law of England*. 3 vols. London, 1883.

Stevens, Edward W., Jr. *Literacy, Law, and Social Order*. De Kalb: Northern Illinois University Press, 1988.

Stewart-Brown, R. "The Charter and Horn of the Master-Forester of Wirral." *Transactions of the Historic Society of Lancashire and Cheshire* 87 (1935): 97–112.

Stock, Brian. *The Implications of Literacy: Written Language and Models of Interpretation in the Eleventh and Twelfth Centuries*. Princeton: Princeton University Press, 1983.

Stones, E. L. G. "Sir Geoffrey le Scrope (c. 1285–1340), Chief Justice of the King's Bench." *English Historical Review* 69 (1954): 1–17.

——. "The Folvilles of Ashby-Folville, Leicestershire, and Their Associates in Crime, 1326–1347." *Transactions of the Royal Historical Society*, 5th ser., 7 (1957): 117–36.

Stow, George B. "Richard II in Thomas Walsingham's Chronicles." *Speculum* 59 (1984): 68–102.

Street, Brian V. *Literacy in Theory and Practice*. Cambridge: Cambridge University Press, 1984.

Strohm, Paul. *Social Chaucer*. Cambridge, Mass.: Harvard University Press, 1989.

——. *Hochon's Arrow: The Social Imagination of Fourteenth-Century Texts*. Princeton: Princeton University Press, 1992.

Suckling, Alfred. *The History and Antiquities of the County of Suffolk*. 2 vols. London: Weale, 1846.

Sutherland, D. W. "Legal Reasoning in the Fourteenth Century: The Invention of 'Color' in Pleading." In *On the Laws and Customs of England: Essays in Honor of Samuel E. Thorne*, ed. Morris S. Arnold et al. Chapel Hill: University of North Carolina Press, 1981. 182–94.

Tait, James. "Did Richard II Murder the Duke of Gloucester?" In *Historical Essays by Members of the Owens College, Manchester*, ed. T. F. Tout and J. Tait. London: Longmans, Green, 1902. 193–216.

Teeven, Kevin M. "Problems of Proof and Early English Contract Law." *Cambrian Law Review* 15 (1984): 52–72.

Thayer, James Bradley. *A Preliminary Treatise on Evidence at the Common Law*. Boston: Little, Brown, 1898.

Thomas, Keith. *Religion and the Decline of Magic: Studies in Popular Beliefs in Sixteenth and Seventeenth Century England*. 1971. Harmondsworth: Penguin Books, 1978.

Thompson, E. P. *The Making of the English Working Class*. London: Gollancz, 1963.

——. "'Rough Music': Le Charivari anglais." *Annales E. S. C.* 27 (1972): 285–312.

Thorne, S. E. "Livery of Seisin." *Law Quarterly Review* 52 (1936): 345–64. Reprinted in Thorne, *Essays*, 31–50.

——, ed. *A Discourse upon the Exposicion and Understandinge of Statutes*. San Marino: Huntington Library, 1942.

——. "The Early History of the Inns of Court with Special Reference to Gray's Inn." *Graya* 50 (1959): 79–96. Reprinted in Thorne, *Essays*, 137–54.

——. *Essays in English Legal History*. London: Hambledon Press, 1985.

Tierney, Brian. "Bracton on Government." *Speculum* 38 (1963): 295–317.

Tillotson, J. H. "Peasant Unrest in the England of Richard II: Some Evidence from Royal Records." *Historical Studies* 16 (1974): 1–16.

Tilsley, David. "Arbitration in Gentry Disputes: The Case of Bucklow Hundred in Cheshire, 1400–1465." In *Courts, Counties, and the Capital in the Later Middle Ages*, ed. Diana E. S. Dunn. Stroud: Sutton, 1996. 53–70.

Timbal, Pierre-Clément. *Les Obligations contractuelles dans le droit français des treizième et quatorzième siècles d'après la jurisprudence du parlement*. Paris: Centre national de la recherche scientifique, 1973.

Tooke, John Horne. *The Diversions of Purley*. New ed., rev. Richard Taylor. London: Thomas Tegg, 1840.

Treitel, G. H. *The Law of Contract*. 6th ed. London: Stevens, 1983.

Tuck, Anthony. *Richard II and the English Nobility*. London: Arnold, 1973.

Twomey, Michael W. "The Sin of *Untrawþe* in *Cleanness*." In *Text and Matter: New*

Critical Perspectives of the Pearl-*Poet*, ed. Robert J. Blanch et al. Troy, N.Y.: Whitston, 1991. 117–45.

Uche, U. U. *Contractual Obligations in Nigeria and Ghana*. London: Frank Cass, 1971.

Ullmann, Stephen. *Semantics: An Introduction to the Science of Meaning*. Oxford: Blackwell, 1962.

Ullmann, Walter. "Medieval Principles of Evidence." *Law Quarterly Review* 62 (1946): 77–87.

———. *The Individual and Society in the Middle Ages*. Baltimore: Johns Hopkins University Press, 1966.

———. *The Medieval Idea of Law as Represented by Lucas de Penna*. 1946. New York: Barnes and Noble, 1969.

———. *Principles of Government and Politics in the Middle Ages*. 4th ed London: Methuen, 1978.

Umeasiegbu, Rems Nna. *The Way We Lived*. AWS 61. London: Heinemann, 1969.

Underdown, David. *Revel, Riot and Rebellion: Popular Politics and Culture in England, 1603–1660*. Oxford: Oxford University Press, 1985.

Van Caenegem, R. C. *The Birth of the English Common Law*. 2nd ed. Cambridge: Cambridge University Press, 1988.

Veit-Brause, Irmline. "A Note on *Begriffsgeschichte*." *History and Theory* 20 (1981): 61–67.

Victoria History of the Counties of England: Chester, Vol. 3. Ed. B. E. Harris. London: Institute of Historical Research, 1980.

Victoria History of the Counties of England: Rutland, Vol. 2. Ed. William Page. London: St Catherine Press, 1935.

Victoria History of the Counties of England: Shropshire, Vol. 2. Ed. A. T. Graydon. London: Institute of Historical Research, 1973.

Vinaver, Eugene. "Arthur's Sword, or the Making of a Medieval Romance." *Bulletin of the John Rylands Library* 40 (1957/58): 513–26.

Vinogradoff, Paul. "Transfer of Land in Old English Law." In *Collected Papers of Paul Vinogradoff*, 2 vols. Oxford: Clarendon Press, 1928. 1:149–167.

Vodola, E. F. "*Fides et Culpa*: The Use of Roman Law in Ecclesiastical Ideology." In *Authority and Power: Studies on Medieval Law and Government Presented to Walter Ullmann*, ed. Brian Tierney and Peter Linehan. Cambridge: Cambridge University Press, 1980. 83–97.

Waldron, R. A. "Langland's Originality: The Christ-Knight and the Harrowing of Hell." In *Medieval English Religious and Ethical Literature, Essays in Honour of G. H. Russell*, ed. G. Kratzmann and J. Simpson. Cambridge: Brewer,1986. 66–81.

Walker, David M. *Principles of Scottish Private Law*. 4th ed. 4 vols. Oxford: Clarendon Press, 1989.

Wallace, David. *Chaucerian Polity: Absolutist Lineages and Associational Forms in England and Italy*. Stanford: Stanford University Press, 1997.

Wallace-Hadrill, J. M. *The Long-Haired Kings*. London: Methuen, 1962.

Watson, Alan. "The Evolution of Law: Continued." *Law and History Review* 5 (1987): 537–70.

Watson, Nicholas. "Visions of Inclusion: Universal Salvation and Vernacular Theology in Pre-Reformation England." *Journal of Medieval and Early Modern Studies* 27 (1997): 145–87.

Watt, Ian. *The Rise of the Novel: Studies in Defoe, Richardson, and Fielding*. 1957. Harmondsworth: Penguin Books, 1963.

Wattenbach, W. *Das Schriftwesen im Mittelalter*. 1896. Graz: Akademische Druck, 1958.

Waugh, Scott L. "Tenure to Contract: Lordship and Clientage in Thirteenth-Century England." *English Historical Review* 101 (1986): 811–39.

Weisberg, Richard, and Jean-Pierre Barricelli. "Literature and Law." In *Interrelations of Literature*, ed. Jean-Pierre Barricelli and Joseph Gibaldi. New York: Modern Language Association of America, 1982. 150–75.

Wenzel, Siegfried. *Verses in Sermons:* Fasciculus Morum *and Its Middle English Poems*. Cambridge, Mass.: Medieval Academy of America, 1978.

——. *Preachers, Poets, and the Early English Lyric*. Princeton: Princeton University Press, 1986.

Whately, Gordon. "Heathens and Saints: *St. Erkenwald* in Its Legendary Context." *Speculum* 61 (1986): 330–63.

White, Stephen D. "'*Pactum . . Legem Vincit et Amor Judicium*': The Settlement of Disputes by Compromise in Eleventh-Century Western France." *American Journal of Legal History* 22 (1978): 281–308.

Whitelock, Dorothy. "Wulfstan *Cantor* and Anglo-Saxon Law." In *Nordica et Anglica: Studies in Honor of Stefán Einarsson*, ed. Allan H. Orrick. The Hague: Mouton, 1968. 83–92.

Whiting, Bartlett Jere. *Proverbs, Sentences, and Proverbial Phrases*. Cambridge, Mass: Harvard University Press, 1968.

Wilkinson, B. *Constitutional History of Medieval England, 1216–1399*. 3 vols. London: Longmans, 1948–58.

Williams, Bernard. *Shame and Necessity*. Sather Classical Lectures 57. Berkeley and Los Angeles: University of California Press, 1993.

Williams, George Huntston. *Anselm: Communion and Atonement*. Saint Louis: Concordia, 1960.

Williams, Glanville L. *Liability for Animals*. Cambridge: Cambridge University Press, 1939.

Williams, Raymond. *Keywords: A Vocabulary of Culture and Society*. London: Fontana, 1976.

Williamson, Janet. "Dispute Settlements in the Manorial Court: Early Fourteenth-Century Lakenheath." In *East Anglian and Other Studies Presented to Barbara Dodwell*, ed. Malcolm Barber, Patricia McNulty, and Peter Noble. *Reading Medieval Studies* 11 (1985): 133–41.

Winfield, Percy H. *The History of Conspiracy and Abuse of Legal Procedure*. Cambridge: Cambridge University Press, 1921.

——. "The Myth of Absolute Liability." *Law Quarterly Review* 42 (1926): 37–51.

Wogan-Browne, Jocelyn. "The Apple's Message: Some Post-Conquest Hagiographic Accounts of Textual Transmission." In *Late Medieval Religious Texts and Their Transmission*, ed. A. J. Minnis. Cambridge: Brewer, 1994. 39–53.

Wood, Ian. "Disputes in Fifth- and Sixth-century Gaul: Some Problems." In *The Settlement of Disputes in Early Medieval Europe*, ed. Wendy Davies and Paul Fouracre. Cambridge: Cambridge University Press, 1986. 7–22.

Woodbine, George E. "The Language of English Law." *Speculum* 18 (1943): 395–436.

Woolf, Rosemary. "Doctrinal Influences on the *The Dream of the Rood*." *Medium Ævum* 27 (1958): 137–53.

Wormald, Patrick. "*Lex Scripta* and *Verbum Regis*: Legislation and Germanic Kingship from Euric to Cnut." *Early Medieval Kingship*, ed. P. H. Sawyer and I. N. Wood. Leeds: University of Leeds Press, 1977. 105–138.

———. "Charters, Law and the Settlement of Disputes in Anglo-Saxon England." In *The Settlement of Disputes in Early Medieval Europe*, ed. Wendy Davies and Paul Fouracre. Cambridge: Cambridge University Press, 1986. 149–68.

———. "Maitland and Anglo-Saxon Law: Beyond Doomsday Book." In *The History of English Law: Centenary Essays on 'Pollock and Maitland'*, ed. John Hudson, Proceedings of the British Academy, 89. Oxford: Oxford University Press, 1996. 1–20.

Wrigley, Ammon. *Annals of Saddleworth*. Enlarged ed. 1901. Oldham: Kelsall, 1979.

Wurtele, Douglas J. "Chaucer's Franklin and the Truth about 'Trouthe.'" *English Studies in Canada* 13 (1987): 359–74.

Yeager, Robert F. "*Pax Poetica*: On the Pacifism of Chaucer and Gower." *Studies in the Age of Chaucer* 9 (1987): 97–121.

Yunck, John A. "The Venal Tongue: Lawyers and the Medieval Satirists." *American Bar Association Journal* 46 (1960): 267–70.

———. *The Lineage of Lady Meed: The Development of Mediaeval Venality Satire*. Publications in Mediaeval Studies, 17. Notre Dame: University of Notre Dame Press, 1963.

Zajtay, Imre. "Le Registre de Varad: Un Monument judicaire du début du XIIIe siècle." *Revue historique du droit français et étranger*, 4th ser., 32 (1954): 527–62.

Zimmermann, Reinhard. *The Law of Obligations: Roman Foundations of the Civilian Tradition*. Cape Town: Juta, 1990.

Zumthor, Paul. *La Poésie et la voix dans la civilisation médiévale*. Paris: Presses Universitaires de France, 1984.

Acknowledgments

In writing this book I have incurred a great many debts, and without the encouragement and support of a number of my colleagues and students at The University of Western Ontario the task would have been very much more burdensome. I began writing it as junior colleague to C. B. Hieatt and A. K. Hieatt, and finished it with a new generation of medievalists, James Miller, Fiona Somerset, Jane Toswell, and Nicholas Watson, to cheer me on; to all these, but particularly to Nicholas Watson, I owe an immense debt of gratitude. Of colleagues outside the medieval period, and colleagues in other departments, Melitta Adamson, Peter Auxy, Robert Barsky, David Bentley, Angela Esterhammer, Minette Gaudet, Michael Groden, Richard Hillman, Leslie Murison, Ernie Redekop, Elizabeth Revell, Leon Surette, and Archie Young have all assisted in various ways, and Henri Boyi, Patrick Deane, Virginia Ola, Kathleen Morrison, and Tom Tausky, in particular, have helped by guiding my reading of African fiction. Two librarians, Roger Gardiner and David Murphy, have gone far beyond the call of duty to make straight my bibliographic meanderings, and a number of former and current graduate students — Brock Eayrs, Melanie Holmes, Jackie Jenkins, James Keddie, Patty Sunderland, and John Wooden — have given me much practical and intellectual support.

In the wider academic world, many colleagues have offered generous help and encouragement. Among senior scholars in my field I think with special gratitude of John Alford, John Burrow, Robert W. Frank, Douglas Gray, V. A. Kolve, Anne Middleton, Charles Muscatine, Derek Pearsall, Carter Revard, and George Rigg; Derek Pearsall, in particular, has given so unstintingly of his time and energy that I hope he will feel that this book is an adequate tribute to his scholarly generosity. Jim Rhodes and Caroline Barron both read early drafts of chapters about which I was having doubts and responded with kindness and good sense, and John Cherry, Rita Copeland, Bruce Holsinger, Paul Hyams, Richard Kaeuper, James Landman, Alastair Minnis, David Seipp, Ian Maclean, David Wallace, and Jocelyn Wogan-Browne have all assisted in various practical ways. With so rich a storehouse of learning to draw on, I can have no one but myself to blame for whatever failings still remain. Finally, my debts to Sharon Collingwood include, but go far beyond, the intellectual and the scholarly.

The Social Sciences and Humanities Research Council of Canada has supported this projects with two generous grants, a Leave Fellowship and a three-year Research Grant. At an early stage, when my confidence in the feasibility of the whole venture was sorely in need of a boost, it received the encouragement of a John Simon Guggenheim Memorial Foundation Fellowship; like all former Guggenheim Fellows, I will always feel a special debt of gratitude to that immensely civilized institution. At a much later stage, faced with another crisis of confidence, my spirits were revitalized by Jerry Singerman and his splendid staff at the University of Pennsylvania Press. Finally, I should like to thank Dean J. M. Good and the Smallman Fund of the Faculty of Arts at the University of Western Ontario for a generous subvention to help defray the costs of publishing a substantial manuscript.

The Ashanti Ewer is reproduced as a frontispiece by permission of the Trustees of the British Museum; the quotation from W. H. Auden's "The History of Truth" is reprinted by kind permission of Dr. Edward Mendelson; the quotation from Karen Blixen's *Out of Africa* is printed by permission of Clara Selborn, Literary Executor, The Rungstedlund Foundation; the quotation from A. P. Herbert's *More Uncommon Law* is reprinted by permission of A. P. Watt, Ltd., on behalf of Crystal Hale and Jocelyn Herbert; the quotation from Episode 18 of James Joyce's *Ulysses* (Oxford University Press Facsimile Reprint of the 1922 First Edition, page 922) is reprinted by permission of the Estate of James Joyce; the quotation from N. F. Simpson's *One Way Pendulum* is reprinted by kind permission of the author; and the quotation from Tennessee Williams's *Suddenly Last Summer* (© Tennessee Williams, 1958) is reprinted by permission of New Directions Pub. Corp.

Index